Mobile Application Development

An engineering manual for building mobile applications at scale

Sreejith K Rajendran

bpb

www.bpbonline.com

First Edition 2026

ISBN: 978-93-78548-772

LIMITS OF LIABILITY AND DISCLAIMER OF WARRANTY

Dedicated to

Ruanshi

Foreword

Ask yourself when you last made an important decision - a payment, a search, a conversation - without reaching for your phone. Mobile is no longer a channel; it is the primary surface through which people engage with the world. That shift was the product of decades of change: from the first handheld devices that could barely browse the web, through the app store revolution, to today's ecosystem of Super Apps and cross-platform frameworks. Understanding that history - where we came from, why certain ideas survived - is the foundation of good mobile engineering. Sreejith K Rajendran understands this deeply, and it shows on every page of this book.

I have had the privilege of working alongside Sreejith, and what has always impressed me is not just his technical depth but his instinct for what endures. Technologies come and go - the language of the moment gives way to the framework of the next cycle - but certain principles hold: write code that can be reasoned about, structure teams so quality compounds rather than decays, and never lose sight of the person on the other end of the screen. Sreejith has lived those principles across more than a decade of building scalable mobile applications, and this book is a faithful account of what he has learned.

One of the most persistent debates in our field is the choice between cross-platform and native development. Swift, Kotlin - including Kotlin Multiplatform - and Dart with Flutter each represent a serious answer, and the right choice depends heavily on context. Sreejith does not resolve the debate by fiat; he gives the reader a reasoning toolkit. This reflects the book's deeper conviction: the goal is not to master today's technology but to develop the judgment to navigate whatever comes next. Parts of this book will evolve as platforms do - but much of it, on what makes code maintainable, teams effective, and products genuinely reliable, will stand the test of time.

What distinguishes this book from a language tutorial is its insistence on craft in the fullest sense. Sreejith covers what good code looks like - how to structure it, scale a codebase as the team grows, and avoid the architectural obsessions that slow teams down. He attends equally to the dimensions that are too often treated as afterthoughts: user experience, app performance and responsiveness, binary size, reliability under constraint, and the auditability that serious applications demand. The chapters on team organization, quality strategy, and testing are written by someone who has had to build and scale engineering teams, not by someone theorizing from a distance.

This matters more than ever in an era of AI-assisted and AI-led software development. Tools like Claude Code and its peers can generate mobile code at remarkable speed - but speed without judgment compounds mistakes just as readily as it compounds progress. The developers who will stand out are not those who can prompt their way to a working screen, but those who know what good code looks like, can recognize when a cross-functional need has been missed, and understand how the pieces fit into a system that must be maintained and scaled by a team. The craft Sreejith writes about is precisely what makes the difference between someone who uses AI tools effectively and someone who is simply carried along by them.

Whether you are new to mobile development or a seasoned engineer looking to sharpen your thinking, this book has something for you. Sreejith writes not to impress but to illuminate - sharing what has worked, what has not, and why, with the generosity of someone who has genuinely benefited from the developer community and wants to give back to it.

Read it slowly, argue with it, and then go build something

Mujiruddin Shaikh (Mujir)

Bengaluru, 2026

About the Author

Sreejith K Rajendran is a passionate technology leader. Sreejith has experimented and taken risks, which have given him experience across diverse domains, platforms and organizations. Sreejith believes in sharing this knowledge with the community, which has motivated him to pursue the author journey. Sreejith has also taken up the role of Udemy instructor for one of the most challenging topics, Swift programming. Professionally, Sreejith's main contribution is to mobile development, and he has more than a decade of development expertise, along with exposure to working with multiple organizations and industry veterans. His experience gives him the advantage of sharing his point of view on things that have worked out and those that have failed. He has encountered all these while building scalable mobile applications for thriving business enterprises.

His expertise in engineering practices and thought leadership, along with the collated experiences from multiple projects and personal learning, has been pivotal in shaping his tech acumen in this diverse tech landscape.

Sreejith believes in continuous learning and aims to attain intellectual maturity in software engineering. Sreejith advocates for collaborative learning with fellow developers as a way to leverage machines to build something that lasts and adds value.

About the Reviewers

- **Amresh Kumar** is an engineering leader with deep expertise in mobile application development, microservices architecture, and cloud computing. He holds MTech from Indian Institute of Technology, Patna. Throughout his career, he has successfully guided engineering teams toward technical excellence.

  Amresh's professional journey reflects a passion for building robust native applications, fostering high-performing teams, and driving quality through collaboration with complex cross-functional product teams.

  He is currently working as engineering manager with REA Cyber City (a part of REA Group).

- **Vinisha Kolla** is an accomplished lead mobile developer with deep expertise in iOS and Flutter, and a track record of successful cross-platform development and app launches. She has extensive experience in understanding the entire mobile development ecosystem, from architecture design and UI/UX design principles to performance optimization and security best practices. Vinisha specializes in ensuring high-quality, scalable mobile solutions through rigorous code review, effective use of Agile methodologies, and a sharp focus on project execution and deliverables.

Acknowledgement

First and foremost, I want to express my gratitude to my father, Rajendran K R, who has always been a source of inspiration. I extend my heartfelt appreciation to my mother, Sujatha Rathnam P R, my better half, Greeshma, and her parents, Manoj D and Sheeba Manoj. Special mention goes to Dr. P R Sasi Kumar and P R Prakashan. The unwavering support throughout the journey of my life is a key motivation. To my beloved daughter, Ruanshi, you are my greatest inspiration.

The first program I ever wrote was under the guidance of my teacher, Gomathy G. With zero knowledge of computers or how they worked, it was she who strengthened the budding computer engineer in me. She is the primary reason behind the intellectual growth and sustenance in the software engineering industry.

Special thanks to Praseed Pai K T, who rekindled the idea of pursuing the publication of this book in one of our tech conversations and who has been a mentor, guiding my journey to satisfy intellectual curiosity beyond mobile development in software enginnering.

I consider myself fortunate to have had a group of individuals who challenged my ideas and pushed my limits. Recognizing and thanking them feels like the simplest but most meaningful gesture.

Special mention for Vinisha Kolla, Rajiv Rajan, Shebin Koshy, Kirti Agarwal, Ankur Sen, Anchal Kushwaha, Thomas Johnson, Sarath Soman, Amrithlal V S, Vaisakh V N, and Deepak Karthikeyan, who are individuals that I met in different walks of my professional journey.

Collaborating with exceptional leaders is a rare privilege, and I am truly grateful for the opportunity to work alongside Mujiruddin Shaikh, CTO of RBIH, and Sahil Kini, CEO of RBIH. Mujir, thank you for your belief in me — and thank you both for making me a part of your vision Building for Bharat. Publishing this book in association with you both stands as one of the most rewarding milestones of my professional life.

The curiosity of learning and bringing an idea to life got etched into my habits from some of the traits that I saw in two special individuals, Yasar P K and Chittesh V C. I thank you both.

Bringing a book to life and reaching a wider audience is only possible with a strong footprint in the publishing industry. I am immensely grateful to BPB Publications for their guidance and expertise in bringing this book to fruition. I thank BPB Publications and the team for believing in me and the vision of this book. Their support and assistance were invaluable, and I would not have imagined it any other way. This work stands stronger because of your invaluable contributions.

Lastly, I thank all readers for choosing to read this book. The contents of the book will provide insights to help in the mobile development journey. The book will help to increase the intellect around mobile development.

Preface

A handheld computing device brought the capability to create products, creating a massive shift in an individual's day-to-day activities. These products are in the form of software applications that can be installed on the computing device. In the current ecosystem, developing a mobile application is a key component in digital strategies to reach consumers. Developing a mobile application requires vision, focus, and expertise. Additionally, as with any software for mobile development, traits such as longevity, low maintenance, and effective change management at a viable cost can be achieved by investing in strategies to set up the right foundation. Reusing the available knowledge is a key catalyst for progress, and software as a domain has given freedom where the probability of different approaches will be available to solve the same problem. The right tools to optimize the decision-making process and the insights into avoiding anti-patterns are the ingredients to navigate such situations.

In this book, a diverse range of topics is covered. The reader will get the information from multiple dimensions. The information and experience garnered over a decade are condensed into the fourteen chapters divided into three horizons, namely gearing up, cross-cutting functions, and accelerators.

The book guides the readers, starting with the historical context of the mobile ecosystem. The perspective of how different players in the software industry see mobile development is then presented.

The narrative further moves the focus to planning a mobile application project, giving the reader entry to the world of program management. The book further looks at the different technology choices available for mobile development and their impact. The debate about cross-platform versus native is prevalent in the industry. The book presents enough details to the audience to make a decision when choosing between the technologies.

Further in the book, readers get to read about the means to set up a team and establish a quality strategy.

A mobile application is interactive in nature. The user interface developed is the heart of any mobile application, and thereby the code written should be clean and scalable. Managing the code related to the user interface has thus become critical. The team should ideally follow best practices to be effective in replicating interface design. Understanding techniques to collaborate with the user experience team and ensuring effectiveness in translating design deliverables are covered in the book. Scalability techniques to manage a codebase as the team grows form the theme that the reader gets to read further.

The day-to-day activity of the development team is to write the code for the mobile application. The program is powered by the language supported by the development framework. Practical exploration of three languages, Swift, Kotlin, and Dart, gives entry to the skills required for the day-to-day activity. A simple one-page application to understand the internal workings is explored as a code walkthrough for Flutter and Kotlin Multiplatform for Mobile.

A special class of application called Super App is one of a kind. Building a toy version on iOS will give the reader exposure to building a Super App.

The critical part of how to structure the code and architectural patterns and design is the second-to-last chapter, and the book concludes by exploring a few case studies.

The reader should not treat this book as a comprehensive guide with details and step-by-step instructions on technology. The book brings the knowledge that ensures the reader has enough ammunition to comprehend any topic on mobile with ease. The content of this book will make the reader intellectually strong and confident.

Every chapter in the book is independent of other chapters, with occasional cross-references. Therefore, a reader will be able to choose any chapter at random and get the insights for the relevant context presented in the chapter. After reading the book, one can play a key role as a strategic mobile development domain expert within an enterprise.

Chapter 1: Stepping into Mobile Development — The chapter introduces the mobile development world. This chapter intends to explore the nuances of mobile development and break some of the misconceptions prevailing around it. For a rookie in mobile development, the chapter will open a world of engineering involved in mobile development. If you are not a rookie mobile developer and have been enjoying developing applications, this chapter will present already known facts. The cultural alignment required for a team to succeed when approaching a mobile development program is the key takeaway in the chapter.

Chapter 2: Planning Your Mobile App Project — The success of a project can be attributed to proper planning to mitigate any risks and things that may go wrong. The chapter will provide the necessary elements for planning and empowering individuals involved in mobile development projects. The chapter concludes with a practical walkthrough of creating a project plan, from the start to defining the go-to-market strategy and examining the challenges encountered. The key takeaway will be the acumen and ammunition to create a robust plan for a project.

Chapter 3: Cross-platform Versus Native — A debate should be respectfully concluded to reach a progressive outcome. The decision makers, when presented with multiple options, will have to shed personal biases and put themselves in the shoes of different stakeholders while deciding to define the right strategy for the organization. The chapter presents the key ideas that one should have in the psyche to make an objective decision for technology choices, ensuring the grand scheme of things falls in place. The key takeaway will be the reasoning toolkit for the readers and an overview of a few technologies prevalent in the market.

Chapter 4: Organizing a Mobile Development Team — Getting insights into the proven strategies: those that have worked and those that have not worked, is important data when setting up a team. The chapter explores the foundational principles and considerations enabling the journey toward a leadership role in a mobile development team. An operationally stable team is essential to reduce chaos and ensure the quality of the software being written does not deteriorate. The key takeaway will be the best practices to be used and anti-patterns to be avoided in the journey of software development while setting up or being part of a team.

Chapter 5: Quality Assurance for Mobile Development — Quality assurance is an integral part of any software or product that one would want to circulate to users. In mobile development, this would be the key component that drives the success and brand retention to get the competitive edge. A separate book can be dedicated and written to cover the whole gamut of topics under quality assurance. However, in the context of this book, the chapter covers the key ideas relevant to pioneering in end-to-end mobile development. The key takeaway is the knowledge and ideas to define the QA strategy for a mobile application project.

Chapter 6: Balancing Design and Engineering — UI/UX design plays a crucial role alongside engineering requirements in ensuring that a mobile application aligns effectively with its platform. To encourage collaboration between teams designing UI/UX and the engineering team that translates the ideas into a seamless user experience, it's essential to find the right balance. This balance, where design and technical requirements may either compete or complement each other, is a common challenge faced by leaders in mobile development teams. This chapter explores creating a collaborative workflow that ensures operational efficiency and scalability for a team involved in mobile development. The key takeaway is the design thinking required for a mobile development team to balance design and engineering.

Chapter 7: Scalability in Mobile Development: Part 1 — Mobile application development is a continuously evolving journey. In order to gear up for the journey and to ensure a smooth experience in development, it is crucial to have the foundations laid out correctly. In the case where later in the journey, if the indicators emerge that the foundation needs to be corrected or modified, the recommendation is to act on them promptly without procrastinating to take action to do the course correction. This chapter explores techniques that, when leveraged, ensure operational efficiency and scalability for the team while developing a mobile application. The key takeaway is the process-related aspect essential for enabling the technology elements within a team to scale.

Chapter 8: Scalability in Mobile Development: Part 2 — The book has two chapters that focus on scalability; this chapter is the second part, which takes off from where the first part left off. The previous chapter focused on the process excellence required to scale. This chapter explores the capabilities required to be built and introduced to the team to enable the team to scale. The key takeaway is the powerhouse of knowledge that ensures the mobile codebase scales and sustains.

Chapter 9: Mobile Application Development and Cross-cutting Themes — For mobile applications, the accuracy, ease of use of the application, and presentation impact the end user. To achieve this, the development team can capitalize on techniques that complement the functionality of a mobile application. Such techniques are broadly categorized as non-functional requirements or common functional requirements. In the chapter, the key idea is to dive into the most important non-functional requirements around mobile application development. The key takeaway is the themes that often get ignored when prioritized against the functional requirements, termed as NFR or CFR for mobile applications.

Chapter 10: Introduction to Swift, Kotlin, and Dart — Fear often holds back individuals, making it harder to gain the confidence needed to become a polyglot in programming. The chapter explores what it really means to be a polyglot in mobile development. The narrative examines three popular programming languages and their ecosystems, comparing the similarities and differences. The second section of the chapter explores the Flutter framework for mobile development. The key takeaway is the understanding of the syntax of the three languages, along with the introduction to the Flutter framework.

Chapter 11: Kotlin Multiplatform for Mobile Development — Developing mobile applications on the Android platform is powered by the official language Kotlin. The Android **Software Development Kit (SDK)** is the API ecosystem that enables the development. The technology that takes the Android development kit to support multiple platforms beyond Android is the key theme explored in the chapter. The key takeaway of the chapter is the reasoning toolkit and familiarity with the Android ecosystem. The chapter, along with the Kotlin from the previous chapter, will give the reader exposure to playing around with the Android Software Development Kit, building a mobile application.

Chapter 12: Use Case of Developing a Super App — The theme explored in the chapter is centered around the challenges and the best practices that one should follow to build a class of mobile applications categorized as a Super App. One should be aware of a subtle difference while devising strategies to build a mobile app that scales to a monstrous codebase. The chapter will give a top-down overview of building such an application by exploring concepts and practicing by developing a Toy Super Application. The key takeaway is the familiarity and thought process to get started on building or being a part of a Super App ecosystem.

Chapter 13: Introduction to Mobile Architecture — The focus of the chapter is to create a logical map of a few architectures and patterns. The chapter carves out the common responsibility of components within the various architectures. The objective may not be to decide what is best, but to look at patterns that come along with the architecture. The chapter shares experiences for the use cases where the architecture has worked out well. At the end of the chapter, hopefully, the reader should be capable of watching out for an anti-pattern called architecture obsession. The anti-pattern can be avoided by keeping watch when the team is trying to force-fit a solution that may be an overkill for the context. The key takeaways are the ideas that help the reader to architect a mobile codebase.

Chapter 14: System Thinking in Mobile Development — The chapter contextualizes the topic discussed in the previous chapter and ties it to use cases under three major domains. Taking a use case is to give retrospective exposure that could become a baseline for the mobile application development that the reader undertakes. The larger goal of the chapter is to accelerate the reader's journey to think holistically, and the diverse domains discussed will give enough coverage for the same.

The chapters are followed by three appendices. The first two appendices give an introduction to the relevance of AI in the context of mobile development. Appendix A explores the mindset required for AI adoption and it covers the factor of trust in GenAI-generated software and organizational ownership when AI-assisted products fail. Appendix B presents three meta models for pragmatic GenAI adoption: the capability-vs-capacity lens, the skeptic-with-optimism mindset, and a knowledge hierarchy that maps how AI shifts the skills required of a developer. The AI as a subject warrants a dedicated book; however, these appendices equip the reader with a pragmatic mindset to apply AI-assisted engineering with confidence. The intent conveyed to the reader is to focus on fundamentals of software engineering enabling them to acquire the acumen to meaningfully contribute. The third appendix contains a collection of additional reading links, as well as the necessary citations and references to the original owners of the products, tools, and resources mentioned in this book.

The book will add tremendous value to any student or developer who is interested in software engineering. The major personas and the primary audience who will get the maximum out of this book are entry-level developers, senior mobile developers, and technology leads, architects, and consultants. A reader playing the role of junior/senior mobile developer aspiring to enter the leadership role or do advisory will have elevated top-down thinking in the mobile engineering space once the topics in mobile are imbibed. The technology lead/architect/consultant who works in techno-functional consulting space and is involved in setting up mobile practices will, with the information in the book, gain the ability to devise a better strategy for the organization.

The book shall have takeaways for secondary audiences, which include project managers, product owners, or business analysts. The key topics that would interest them would be organizational strategy to set up a mobile development team, planning/scoping a mobile development project, release management, and tech non-functional and cross-functional requirements that need to be considered in mobile app development projects.

A student pursuing mobile development will also be able to leverage the information in the book to get a strong foundation. The best-case scenario will be to have a mentor with whom the student can converse.

There is a high possibility that individuals follow different paths in their respective professional journeys. One path focuses on developing the practical, hands-on aspects of a skill or craft. The other emphasizes nourishing the intellectual curiosity about a subject and its broader context. The former sharpens the skill through consistent practice, improving speed and execution. The latter deepens knowledge by searching for knowledge that explores the origins, concepts, and connections surrounding the skill. A practitioner will be a better fit where fast execution is required, while an intellectually-driven individual will suit better for roles that demand long-term thinking and strategic insight.

This book is carefully crafted to hit the sweet spot to accomplish both: acquire skill and quench the intellectual curiosity. The book is laid out in a format where the concepts are ready to be used in the day-to-day activities and are extracted from the experiences of the industry. The book presents opinionated views and has been tested to sustain enterprise in developing mobile applications.

How to leverage the book?

The content of the book is very dense in nature, and reading this book should ideally be planned as a two-to-four-month journey. One may take a strategy by limiting the reading to five to ten pages per day. This should ideally be followed by the mental exercise to correlate the information read with real-life situations, either in retrospect from one's personal journey or from the community. The individual coming with no background in mobile should leverage the community to fast-track the learning. This strategy will also help such an individual become as effective as a seasoned mobile developer. With the advent of LLM chatbots, debating the key idea and contesting the real-life situation would also be a suggested approach to ground the information to the readers' advantage. Practicing the knowledge by building a mobile application or contributing to a team will help the knowledge to get ingrained into oneself.

There could be an alternative case where an existing developer is facing a kind of problem, for example, defining a QA strategy, building a Super App, trying to understand the technology choices, etc. In such a case, the individual can jump directly to the relevant chapter and tackle these one by one rather than following the chronological order laid out in the book. The book contains sections called thought experiments. These are areas where a reader should pause and try to do the activity suggested in the section. The idea of the thought experiments is to ground the concept discussed empirically. The section will be followed by an author's perspective as well, which can be used to compare with what the reader arrived at for the thought experiment.

Code Bundle and Coloured Images

Please follow the link to download the
Code Bundle and the *Coloured Images* of the book:

https://rebrand.ly/gv9m9gz

The code bundle for the book is also hosted on GitHub at
https://github.com/bpbpublications/Mobile-Application-Development.
In case there's an update to the code, it will be updated on the existing GitHub repository.

We have code bundles from our rich catalogue of books and videos available at https://github.com/bpbpublications. Check them out!

Errata

We take immense pride in our work at BPB Publications and follow best practices to ensure the accuracy of our content to provide an indulging reading experience to our subscribers. Our readers are our mirrors, and we use their inputs to reflect and improve upon human errors, if any, that may have occurred during the publishing processes involved. To let us maintain the quality and help us reach out to any readers who might be having difficulties due to any unforeseen errors, please write to us at: errata@bpbonline.com

Your support, suggestions and feedback are highly appreciated by the BPB Publications' Family.

Piracy

If you come across any illegal copies of our works in any form on the internet, we would be grateful if you would provide us with the location address or website name. Please contact us at business@bpbonline.com with a link to the material.

If you are interested in becoming an author

If there is a topic that you have expertise in, and you are interested in either writing or contributing to a book, please visit www.bpbonline.com. We have worked with thousands of developers and tech professionals, just like you, to help them share their insights with the global tech community. You can make a general application, apply for a specific hot topic that we are recruiting an author for, or submit your own idea.

Reviews

Please leave a review. Once you have read and used this book, why not leave a review on the site that you purchased it from? Potential readers can then see and use your unbiased opinion to make purchase decisions. We at BPB can understand what you think about our products, and our authors can see your feedback on their book. Thank you!

For more information about BPB, please visit www.bpbonline.com.

Join our Discord space

Join our Discord workspace for latest updates, offers, tech happenings around the world, new releases, and sessions with the authors:

https://discord.bpbonline.com

Table of Contents

CHAPTER 1
Stepping into Mobile Development

Introduction

Technological advancement over the recent years has brought the possibilities of computation at our fingertips, opening a wide range of business use cases. The internet boom has created a connected ecosystem, which has made technology move forward with its own nuances. There are different forms of compact handheld devices that operate for different use cases; for example, pocket calculators, digital thermometers, mobile phones, wearables, etc.

The technology and engineering behind these devices have their own learning curve. The topics discussed throughout the book are centered around the class of computing handheld devices called mobile phones and the application development on these.

Being a mobile developer is one such opportunity to impact an individual's life through these handheld, compact devices.

It is worth noting that the first reference to a conceptual handheld computing device, envisioned by *Alan Kay*, was the *Dynabook*, a portable computer concept that he first proposed in 1972. *Newton Message Pad*, released by *Apple* in 1993, is widely cited as one of the first mass-market **personal digital assistants** (**PDAs**) and an early landmark in commercial handheld computing.

Structure

This chapter covers the following topics:

- Mobile development industry
- Classification of roles in the mobile industry
- Mobile operating system
- Consumer segment classification of mobile application
- Mobile-first and non-mobile-first strategies
- Sharing experiences of aspiring mobile developers
- Challenges faced in mobile development
- Thought experiment

Objectives

This chapter introduces the mobile development world. The aim of this chapter is to explore the nuances of mobile development and dispel some of the misconceptions prevailing around it. For a rookie in mobile development, the chapter will open up a world of engineering involved in mobile development. If you are not a rookie mobile developer and have been enjoying developing applications, this chapter will present the facts, contextualized to mobile application development. On the contrary, if you are a mobile developer, the chapter will take you down memory lane, rekindling the mobile enthusiast inside you.

After reading the chapter, you will be able to feel a cultural alignment with the mobile development team. This will also help to develop a mindset to succeed when approaching a mobile development project. Taking a tour from the perspective of a person from a non-mobile background and seeing the mobile world with the intent to move toward mobile development would be the key ingredient that drives the narrative of this chapter. The reader will feel the transformation by acquiring the ontological expertise in the mobile application development domain. The chapter will bring a mindset shift required for sustaining and progressing with confidence in the world of mobile development.

Mobile development industry

Mobile application development is the process of creating software that can be deployed on a handheld computing device, otherwise known as a **mobile phone**. The mobile application developed interacts with the host mobile operating system to provide an experience to the end user for the respective use case. The mobile application can be standalone in nature or could form an entity within a connected ecosystem of distributed services provided to end users. The evolution of the mobile device from feature phone to supercharged computing device at fingertips has given the world remarkable capabilities. This capability is equivalent to what sophisticated processing machines could achieve in the earlier days of technology. This is a remarkable feat of technology that has driven the revolution. The organizations are now able to penetrate the market and create software that hooks the consumer to the handheld device. The terms consumers and customers are used interchangeably in the book, although there exists a subtle difference between these in the context of purchasing goods or services. A customer is a person who purchases, and a consumer is the one who uses it. A customer need not necessarily be a consumer.

Note: **Feature phones are the earlier version of mobile devices, where input was via a hardware keyboard; later versions of mobile phones are touch-enabled, where the input is via screens.**

A historical reflection of the era of mobile computing can be best done by looking at the time when the smartphone was considered a fantasy. If we hypothetically time-travel back to history and talk to individuals of that time regarding smartphones, it would seem to them the wildest possibility that can happen in a dream. It would have been unimaginable for an individual to comprehend the possibility of a computing device being pocket-sized.

As we fast forward, the major advancements came in when technology overcame the following problems:

- Computing devices were not pocket-sized.
- Connectivity was limited.
- A huge amount of time was required for information to travel as the distance increased.

As of today, there are many innovations and much progress in terms of technology and convenience. Individuals who lived in both eras would feel the comfort that the technology-powered mobile has brought to their lives. The way we communicate, conduct business, do shopping, capture photos and videos, track health information at our fingertips, and many other aspects of our lives have been influenced and supported by mobile phones. A perspective that everyone will unanimously agree on is that the world has adapted to the changes mobile phones have brought to our lives.

For most individuals, it would be tough to renounce these comforts that have come to life. The list of these comforts will keep growing as there are more innovations and improvements to the mobile.

All these indicate the rise of opportunities for hardware and software manufacturing industries to focus on mobile computing devices and the ecosystem around them. This has thus become part of the economic and technological growth.

Classification of roles in the mobile industry

Let us now investigate the broad dimensions of the functional role of mobile development. The purpose of this classification is to provide a sense of the different layers of influence that define the industry. The role may have overlapping responsibilities. The purpose that drives each of these organizations and the individuals in these roles may differ. Each role will thus leverage a computing device that translates an idea, enabling a mobile application to reach end consumers. The following list gives a few examples:

- **Mobile hardware manufacturers**: Apple (iPhone devices), Samsung, Oppo, Google
- **Mobile application developer**: Independent developer, Amazon, Facebook
- **Development tools/framework creators**: IntelliJ, Flutter community, React Native community, New Relic (application performance monitoring provider)
- **Support groups**: Figma, Invision, Project Management/Collaboration Tool Creators, Zeplin

One should recognize that the organizations mentioned in the examples may support multiple roles. *Apple Inc.* is an example of having all these roles in the ecosystem.

The intent that drives these roles can be imbibed from the following anecdotes:

- A mobile hardware manufacturing organization takes authority in defining the specifications of a manufactured device, developing the operating system, and providing a framework for other companies to build applications. The company Apple Inc. is an example of this category. Apple owns the hardware and the software tools that others can use to create the application. Any other organization building a mobile application for Apple devices has a dependency and necessity to follow the guidelines defined by Apple Inc. for the application to be available for public use. The mobile application developed goes through the review process from Apple Inc., which may get rejected when it fails to meet the guidelines.
- An organization with a significant focus on manufacturing hardware takes support from other organizations for the operating system/software. An example of this category is hardware manufacturers using the variations of Android OS. The Android OS is an open-source operating system commercially sponsored by *Google* and with contributions from various other organizations. Due to the open-source nature of the Android OS, hardware organizations will have access to and can customize the operating system's behavior.
- An organization/group is concentrating on developing applications deployed on different mobile devices in the market. The following are a few examples of such organizations:
    - Retail organizations expand business by providing online shopping experiences via mobile.
    - A banking organization provides banking services and products via mobile.
    - A health and fitness company that is reaching its end customers via a mobile application. This company acts as a companion in the daily walk of life of the individual to manage lifestyle and stay healthy and fit via the mobile application.
    - The entertainment and information industry provides a platform to consumers where the end users have access to content that is streaming, via a mobile application.
- An organization/group that creates tools and common frameworks to support developing mobile applications. These organizations develop a standard framework and tools that can be adopted by other organizations for developing mobile applications targeting multiple platforms. Examples of the framework include React Native, PhoneGap, Xamarin, Flutter, etc. This organization/group focuses on the following problem statements:
    - A single codebase for multiple platforms.
    - Framework and tools should work and support any kind of operating system.

In this book, we will be mainly dealing with the topic of enabling the mobile development role and how to succeed in it.

Note: **The frameworks React Native, PhoneGap, Xamarin, Flutter, etc. differ significantly in their underlying runtime architecture. Chapter 3, Cross-platform Versus Native, explores these distinctions in depth.**

Mobile operating system

The market has a variety of competing providers supplying mobile handheld devices. If one looks at device segmentation, there are two broad categories: privately-owned or open-source operating systems. In either of the cases, the provider gives a platform for end users to operate in the form of the OS, app store, and developer tools. In this context, the end user is an individual with any of the following personas: a mobile device user or a mobile application developer. The platform encompasses the operating system, app stores, and the **integrated development environment (IDE)**/framework/tools. The operating system and app store serve as a delivery mechanism for mobile applications to reach the end consumer; the IDE, frameworks, and supporting tools are used to build those applications.

Throughout history, there have been many players, and there have been ups and downs in the market for these players. In the current era, the prominent ones are iOS and Android.

iOS from Apple Inc. is an example of a privately owned operating system that powers all iPhones. Apple Inc. has full control of the release and lifecycle management of iOS. Apple Inc. has also provided the capabilities to the developers to operate in the restricted ecosystem. This ecosystem is powered by the framework from Apple Inc. to build, release, and deploy a mobile application that can be run on iOS devices.

Android, powered majorly by Google, on the other hand, is open source. This gives the flexibility to have a separate hardware manufacturer to take and customize the operating system to give a flavor different from the original. The open-source nature can result in competing hardware players without any logical coherence of certain features and capabilities supported, leading to inconsistent support for certain features and capabilities across devices. One of the side effects is the possibility that a feature working on a particular device is not guaranteed to work on devices by other manufacturers. The variation is not very common, but it is a possibility.

With iOS and Android, being well-versed in one platform can help with reasoning about another platform. In recent times, the different frameworks are becoming similar over time in their underlying principles and structure. An individual can draw parallels, and with some investment in the syntax and framework, one can gain proficiency in the other platform or tool. The ideology and syntax may require some level of practice to get embedded in muscle memory for the development of the skill. The conceptual parallelism can be drawn to build and architect a mobile application at scale. Flutter, Jetpack Compose, and SwiftUI, following a declarative style for UI development, are indicators to substantiate conceptual parallelism.

Understanding these operating systems and the tools for developing apps for these OS is the key to entering mobile application development. The mobile application development for all these platforms involves a separate skill set and proficiency in tools. For instance, the native mobile applications rely on Android Studio and the Android SDK for Android mobile app development, and Xcode and the iOS SDK for iOS mobile application development. The cross-platform framework is yet another choice that a developer can leverage to develop apps targeting multiple platforms in principle.

iOS and Android OS are the major players in the market for mobile OS. For having a better reasoning, looking at mobile operating system internals from a hardware lens could help. The current age mobile has minimal hardware keys and controls in comparison to the early days of the mobile generation. In both cases (Android and iOS), the similarity is that when the hardware device is switched on, a set of icons appears on the display, which the user can interact with. Performing an action of search, select, etc., is an example of interaction. Each different icon on the display is an individual app developed by another organization or part of the operating system. The operating system ensures that the individual apps have limited control over each other and are kept isolated to prevent meddling with each other's affairs. From the narrative, this would seem to be like any operating system, allowing application installation from different organizations. The key difference between a normal desktop OS and a mobile OS is that the latter must cater to performance optimization and compute throttling, ensuring a long battery life for the mobile device. The mobile OS has special applications, such as settings, Play/App Store, etc., to facilitate and help the user manage the lifecycle of other apps installed. The supporting app will help to manage the permissions used by the mobile application to access the capabilities provided by the operating system settings.

Figure 1.1 represents a topological view of the mobile device from interaction to the internals:

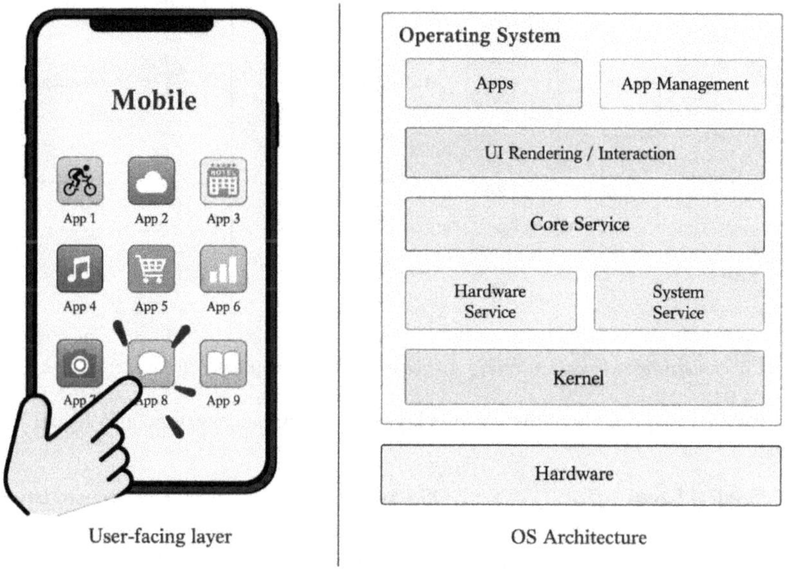

***Figure 1.1**: Topological view of a mobile device, from interaction to the internals*

The human interaction/input serves as the trigger to start an operation on the mobile device. This input gets processed by the underlying mechanism and will respond to the user by opening the application upon tapping the app icon. The internals of a mobile device depicted on the right side of *Figure 1.1* represent a formal view of the various OS available in the market. The label for each of the top boxes in *Figure 1.1* represents the component of a Mobile device. In the real-world, these would be identified by the names provided by the respective owners of the operating system. The key takeaway from the diagram is that the top layer a user interacts with will be the app or the mobile management touch points. The top layer uses the UI rendering pipeline and the capabilities exposed by the operating system. The capabilities are also exposed as different frameworks by which teams build the applications. The UI rendering system is followed by a core service. The core service layer thus serves dual purposes: functioning as the underlying mechanism for the top layer and acting as the abstraction layer for the toolkit to develop the mobile application. The layer even further is like a typical general-purpose operating system, where there are system services backed by the kernel, sitting on top of a hardware device. The two sections in *Figure 1.1* give the abstract view of iOS and Android OS, illustrating the two layers, the physical layer and the OS. The physical layer is where the end user of the phone interacts, and the OS layer is the vendor-provided hosting of the mobile application. There is a third layer, the development layer, where developers leverage tools and a development kit to build the mobile applications. The third layer (development tools and SDKs) is shown separately in *Figures 1.2 and 1.3*.

Additionally, *Figure 1.2* and *Figure 1.3* give a comparative view of how mobile devices differ from and relate amongst iOS versus Android. The diagram is intentionally simplified to help the reader encode a foundational idea of the two platforms. Additionally, the components listed in these figures are not exhaustive. The idea is to have a frame for reasoning when exploring the development toolkit for both Android and iOS.

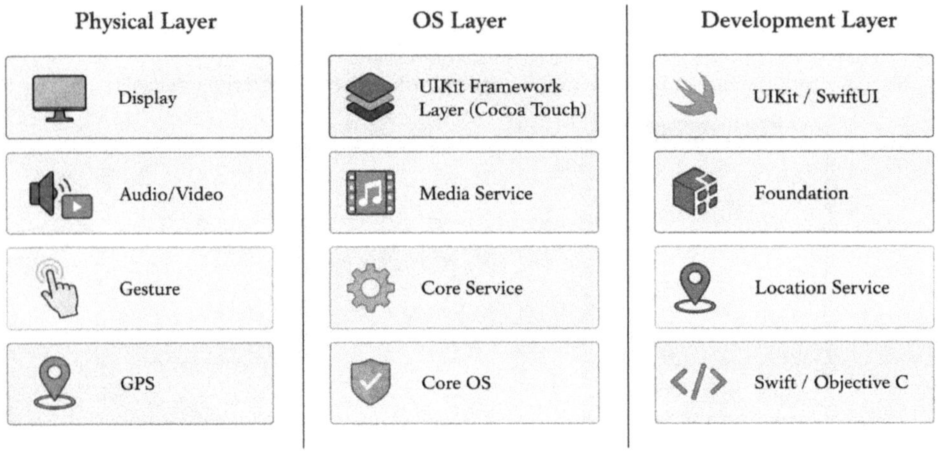

Figure 1.2: *Components of physical, operating system and development layer in context of the iOS ecosystem*

Figure 1.2 demonstrates the components of the various layers in the iOS ecosystem, and *Figure 1.3* explores a similar structure for Android:

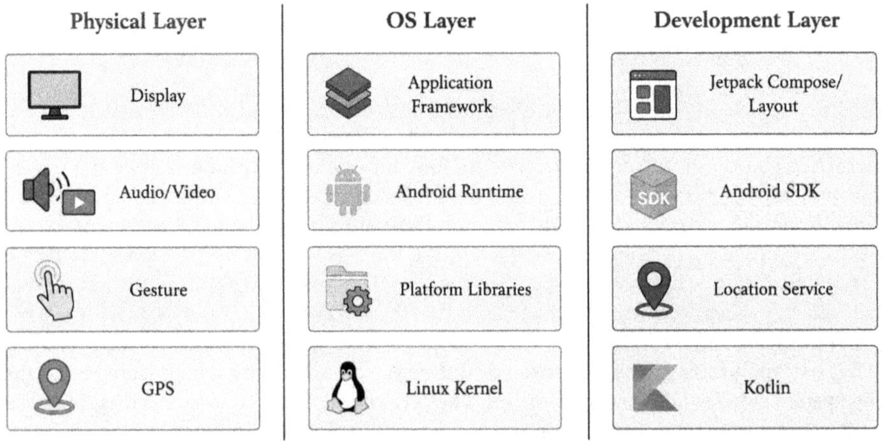

Figure 1.3: *Components of physical, operating system and development layer in context of the Android ecosystem*

Drawing parallels between the iOS and Android internals give a fair idea of the similarities and differences. The core principles of both platforms when abstracted out are broadly equivalent. However, the ideological difference of the respective platforms creators influence and manifests directly in the end-user experience that each platform delivers. These differences would thus influence the end user and the mobile application developer to practice and understand the idioms of the respective platform.

Consumer segment classification of mobile application

The mobile application, depending on the strategy adopted by the creator, can support a variety of segments of the consumer. One can classify this into three: B2C, B2B, and B2E. The product and the mechanism to develop these are the same. However, the business and the priority that will drive the mobile application will have differences. Now, let us explore the details of the three classifications:

- **Business to consumer (B2C)**: The mobile application developed by the organization is directly used by a consumer who does not have a formal contractual relationship with the organization. There shall be a terms-and-conditions agreement between the end user and the organization for the usage policy of the application and service therein. The organization for B2C apps cannot ideally force the user to comply with the use of the application. The applications mostly reach the consumer via the App Store/Play Store. An App Store/Play Store is a digital store powered by the OS/device proprietor to download and install the application onto the device. The store concept becomes an imperative choice as the trust for installing the software is guaranteed by the proprietor.

  Examples of B2C are retail ecommerce applications, banking mobile applications, messaging applications, and productivity applications such as Notes. In these examples, an individual uses the mobile application from an organization to leverage the service for their benefit.

- **Business to business (B2B)**: The mobile application developed by the organization is directly used by another business entity. Let us try to understand this case with an example. Consider a manufacturer of hospital equipment parts. The assembly and repair of this machinery is in most cases subcontracted to a third-party vendor. For installation and assembly, these subcontracted vendors will have individuals trained to be experts. Given the sheer volume that the team had to handle, managing the group of people would be a humongous undertaking. Training a flock of people and having a superior level of craftsmanship is an uncertainty that these organizations may have to navigate. Given the current technological advancement, having a mobile app that gives instruction and mixed reality features to instruct and give a live demo for supporting installation is a use case that the organization would invest in. The parent organization developing such an ecosystem is the true level of investment to support the supply chain of the product. This is an example where the parent company develops an application, and the application is used by a third-party organization to extend the capability to perform a function. This application can also be distributed via the App Store of the respective device.

  A more common example is the communication and collaboration applications that a company uses; for example, Slack, Google Chat, etc. These applications are developed by an organization that operate as a software as a service providers, leveraging a pricing model to enable communication and collaboration within a team. These have customized roles and features to manage the policy and usage of the application.

  It should be noted that there could be cases where B2B and B2C overlap, or where the same app may be available for both.

- **Business to employee (B2E)**: The example of a mobile application used for communication and collaboration, explained while discussing B2B, is used by the individual associated with the organization to perform the function of the organization. Such a use case thus gives rise to a subset of applications classified as B2E. Some examples of B2E use cases are applications for applying leave, help desk requests, HR operations, etc. In the early years, organizations had a strict device-management policies, and therefore, B2E applications were allowed only on company phones. However, in later years of technological advancement, organizations began allowing **bring your own device** (**BYOD**). All these gave rise to having a mechanism to manage the mobile device. In most cases, B2E applications are not distributed by the public application store of the device but instead are managed by privately-hosted application stores that will have access to only the employees or groups added by the organization.

Mobile-first and non-mobile-first strategies

An organization can adopt either a mobile-first strategy or have mobile as a supporting pillar for expanding the business. A mobile-first strategy is prevalent and tried out in organizations and markets where the end user predominantly uses mobile. The organizations adopting a mobile-first strategy understand that most consumers use mobile as a primary source to engage with businesses and services. The alternative channels can be a website, a desktop application, etc., for providing these services, where the channels will be with limited or no consumers. In the case of a non-mobile-first strategy, the mobile acts as a supporting pillar by enabling ongoing business by opening possibilities as additional channels for distributing services and products.

The mobile-first strategy adds risk, and the organization must now focus on reducing the failure points. If the mobile application fails, the time for the recovery mechanism to reach the consumer could be delayed due to the distribution process. Therefore, for critical services, some mechanism is required for providing alternative sources of access. An organization may also have to build the capability to compete and move forward at a pace that engages the consumer, maintaining the top edge in the market.

The key to keep in mind about the mobile-first strategy is that not every organization needs to take a mobile-first approach. Instead, there is a good possibility that having the mobile channel open for delivering the service and product of the organization would be an add-on to the existing one, complementing the other channels to reach consumers. In summary, be it mobile-first or an add-on, adopting a mobile strategy to reach end users would pave the way for revenue and business for the organizations.

Omnichannel strategy

The mobile-first and non-mobile-first strategies emphasize the use of mobile channels to reach the end consumer. However, when there is an equal split of consumer volume that adds to revenue for the organization via multiple channels, omitting a feature per channel may not be the right strategy. This would be a non-inclusive approach where the unavailability of a feature in a channel forces the end user to move to another. Ideally, this is not a great user experience.

Thus, a company distributing products and services with nearly the same features in all the channels comes under the omnichannel approach. An omnichannel strategy is not the same as using a cross-platform application where one tool is used to develop an app for all channels. It instead focuses more on the overall experience of the end user on different channels to be similar, even if the underlying development toolkit for each channel is different.

Mobile mindset

At times, one may get engulfed in certain fallacies formed from having a particular context. This thinking, biased by experience from developing other software, may not work well in developing mobile applications. The inadequate reasoning and logical structure to differentiate the constructs is the probable underlying driver for this bias. Added to this, individuals from different backgrounds have different perspectives on mobile applications.

The key to mitigating the bias from negatively affecting mobile application development is to invest in understanding the ideologies and constructs that define mobile devices and applications. The nearest software that follows a similar ideology is the standalone desktop application. Mobile devices generally operate leveraging restricted space and computational resources in comparison with desktops. Once the understanding of this ethos is acquired, having a check to see if the decisions are biased would be a great way to apply this thinking to the world of mobile development. The experience of developing web and backend applications would create a bias and would not be an optimal solution if applied as is. In the comparative analysis of web development versus mobile, one can clearly distinguish that there is an element of discernment required to make the optimal choice. Biased decision-making would be counterintuitive to the team from an operational and technological perspective. This thus leads to the section discussing the mobile mindset, which will draw out the technology's commonalities and differences. Having this would help the individual to adopt the foundational element of becoming an expert in mobile technology. The key mantra is that in a particular technology, one can follow some established ideas and constructs to navigate quickly and get the best outcome. It is not recommended to forcefully fit the constructs and ideas that worked elsewhere but are not contextually suited to mobile development.

Having a mobile mindset is an evolutionary process via experience. In a competitive world, learning from others will be more advantageous for progress. This could be accelerated by knowing the first principles that would help to lay the foundation for a mobile development mindset, which is the key to the path. The next sections in the chapter will focus on the factors necessary to enrich the mobile mindset.

Acknowledging platform differences

Different platforms are developed and maintained by competing organizations. This was discussed in the previous section. As a stakeholder, one should not be surprised or alarmed in a case where separate effort is required for each platform's development, release, and support. The way to justify the mobile platform difference would be to be at peace with the fact that different platforms can have independent standards that are different from each other. There could be similarities in the patterns when we look at the high-level view; this similarity could help in coming up with high-level solutions and approaches. However, regarding implementation details, each platform can differ regarding one or many factors. Cross-platform frameworks try to abstract these differences to a certain extent for the development phase. However, there shall be a considerable percentage of activity that will be platform-specific for the release of the application.

Adhering to platform standards

After adjusting and understanding the platform differences, the next step would be to follow the standards of the respective platforms. An individual using a particular platform would be habituated to the default behavior expressed by the platform. Building a habit is key to getting hooked to a product, which in turn gives consumer retention. Additionally, while introducing a new product, building familiar behaviors can also boost the adoption rate for the mobile application. The ideal product will let the user flawlessly operate to do what one intends without making the individual think. In such a context, deviation from these habits would become a reason for bad user experiences.

For example, let us consider the hard back button on Android devices. An Android user expects specific behavior inherent to the platform. A decision to block or prevent the behavior would be catastrophic and irritate the mobile application user, as the individual would think the application has gotten stuck.

Another example is of a file storage application that manages documents/files on the device and the cloud. The established norm in iPhone app guidelines states that an application should be responsible for the data it handles, and iOS does not give any capability to remove the data inside another application's sandbox. It is the responsibility of the application to provide a call to action that manages the document's lifecycle. Thus, while building an iPhone app, it would become the team's responsibility to add the data management capability, unlike Android, where the operating system provides controls without creating any feature explicitly. In the case of iOS, if the app does not provide a way for the users to delete or manage stored data, the effect could be catastrophic. If the app's storage footprint grows unchecked, the storage space for user's device could bloat and prompting the user to uninstall the application. The situation of file application is a far-fetched example. The intention of the example was to emphasize the adverse effect of misinformation and unawareness of platform strengths and weaknesses. Being unaware could thus lead to an unfavorable outcome and experience for the end user of the application.

Long-term goals for longer shelf life

A mobile application that introduces a new or competitive product for which the user base needs to be built over time is a bet that the owner would place. Stakeholders investing a large sum to build a parallel channel are subject to the strong market possibility of the product. Doubt about the acceptance of the application amongst end users would influence the stakeholder to prioritize the short-term goal and observe the growth to validate how the application is received by the end consumer. The team also would want to look at a quick time-to-market strategy to bootstrap and build functional products.

After a period of time, once the new product scales, there is a chance that the team will be unable to progress faster, reducing the competitive advantage. The technical debt and the choice made to develop the application would become the probable reason for this slowdown if the problem is with technology. The worst case may even lead to the sunset of the application and a possible rewrite of the mobile application if it is operationally relevant and helps in sustaining or growing the organization.

It becomes important to avoid shortcuts that have unknown side effects to prevent such a situation. The shortcuts, if taken, should be short-lived. The team should take preventive measures to avoid and mitigate tech debt. In the wake of achieving the short-term goal at an incredible speed, if the team makes suboptimal choices, it often forms one of the bottlenecks for growth. This pattern is a risk and an impediment to fostering the culture of a high-performing autonomous mobile application development team. The occurrence of such a pattern should be minimized.

Moreover, focusing on long-term goals does not imply that the team functions without any short-term goals. The idea is that the short-term goal should, in turn, map to the long-term goals. In an era where mobile development was in its early stages, the knowledge about the technology was in a silo. In modern times, knowledge and experimentation have increased with a variety of mobile apps in the market. Such a situation will present the option of collaborating with a subject matter expert, thus giving a head start rather than re-inventing or repeating similar experiments.

On the contrary, if the stakeholder considers the shelf life of the mobile application to be short-term and is certain about sunsetting the product, focusing on reducing the cost is logical. In this case, long-term thinking will be counterintuitive. In such a case, meeting the immediate goal could be the way to go forward. The stakeholder will be in the mindset to revamp when the need arises.

Embracing objective decision-making mindset

Individuals exploring mobile application development often come with a baggage of mental models that worked out successfully in previous software development. As we had discussed at the start, the closest that anyone can compare mobile products is with a standalone desktop application development or an IoT application. There shall be learnings that could inspire the mobile development strategies from previous experiences building software. One should exercise caution in the thought process and should not assume that the exact methods/strategy proven in other software disciplines will transfer directly to mobile development and make the development easy. For example, consider power consumption and resource usage; these two are critical for any mobile app and should be minimal. In contrast, in the case of a distributed system, power consumption and resource usage would not pose a bottleneck. In a distributed system, if there is an increase in demand, there are options to scale the system to meet the need. In the case of mobile applications, if there is computation-heavy work to be performed, it is not possible to increase the hardware capacity. This makes it important to address the compute-intensive work at an early phase of development. The development team can thus take an appropriate workflow that does not break the experience of the end user. A team must adhere to the standard practices while developing a mobile application to meet the power consumption and resource usage key performance criteria. Writing every line of code, keeping the performance criteria in mind, can help to have a scalable application architecture. If not done right, it could impact the user experience and adoption of mobile applications by end users.

In a nutshell, the best practice one should follow is to gauge any software design decision, weighing the pros and cons while adopting it for mobile application development. A mindset to categorize objectively would help achieve a balanced way of contributing while developing mobile applications.

Being objective in evaluating development tools

Mobile application development requires tools, as with any other software development. Each target platform for which the organization intends to publish an application would mean having a variety of devices on each platform to be supported. In most cases, a specific point of discussion amongst the stakeholders would be which technology should be the choice for mobile application development. The stakeholder can come with a strong point of view supporting tools that can be commonly used for multiple platforms. This point of view could be due to bias from previous experience with a particular tool. If the choice is biased, the team may often settle on a tech stack that later leads to unintended outcomes. Decision-making for a tech stack (framework) for developing mobile applications should be done by weighing and carefully understanding the pros and cons. In the context of the mobile mindset, the highlighted trait is that one should have an unbiased view and be open to factoring in contextual data to choose the right tool. Cross-platform internally uses and ultimately calls each platform's native APIs at some level. As a result, the platform-imposed restrictions by the platform's native layer can constrain the capabilities of these cross-platform frameworks and tools.

We have dedicated a separate chapter to discuss the different choices for development. *Chapter 3, Cross-platform Versus Native,* will give additional context on the factors to be considered for the choice.

Beyond dragging and dropping of components

Individuals can have a mental model that would pave the way for a perception that mobile application development is a simple facade. The individual would think that mobile development requires less engineering effort to build and maintain. Often, with superficial or limited understanding and incorrect logical structure, this thinking adds to the mental model supporting the statement that mobile development is thought to be dragging and arranging UI elements. This idea/perception misrepresents mobile development and is very far from reality. Such a closed mindset would not add value to a team building a mobile application. In most cases, the reality is that mobile development is much more than just arranging UI components to represent data visually. Mobile development in a typical enterprise involves a focused effort to engineer mobile applications that would scale and adapt to the changing market needs in terms of faster release, fewer defects, and parallel development for the feature; organizing the mobile application codebase with a clear separation of concerns, managing automated releases, and adhering to all the standard software practices to build a great application. In addition, if we club the computational capability and features provided by these handheld devices, we will see a whole new world where technology has revolutionized the way end users interact/respond to a service offered by a business entity.

Mobile development brings a certain kind of ecstasy to the developer. One can see the developer getting involved in aligning a button to writing programs that do complex processing. Being a mobile developer means having a mindset to write programs where an individual will have restricted resources to consume, but should strive for optimal output and experience. The key engineering challenges that a mobile developer deals with while engineering the app are having less memory to do complicated processing, writing mobile apps that will not drain the mobile device battery, reduced real estate to display information, and most of all, rules and guidelines controlled by the mobile manufacturers and the OS.

Optimal resource usage on a restricted sandbox

The organization developing a mobile application has the ethical and practical obligation to optimize resource usage by the app installed on the end user's mobile device. Resource usage can be seen as the use of hardware capabilities used by the mobile application to perform its function and provide the service to the end user. A mobile application running on a handheld device should maintain an experience that does not affect the handheld device negatively. For instance, battery performance, memory usage, security, etc., should be prioritized while writing the code. Deviating from the optimal usage for these can be catastrophic, where the trend of uninstalling the apps by the users for the mobile application can occur.

Cost-benefit analysis of platform differences

The understanding that there will be differences in the ways of implementation of ideologies on the ground level for different platforms is the first principle for having objective reasoning. A separate effort and focus for development, release, and support will also become essential to support each of these platforms.

The key mindset shift is to break the bias that different platforms are equal. The understanding is that until the underlying technology or the manufacturer's thought process and standards are identical, there will always be some level of separate effort to support and maintain each platform. One should never assume that there is always a one-to-one map of capability and features across-platforms. A subtle fact that needs attention and to be emphasized is that assuming equivalent behaviors as a working hypothesis is still an acceptable mindset. However, expecting a feature/capability in Android to work/behave on an iPhone the same way or vice versa would be a mindset one should avoid. An individual must always verify platform behavior through testing and documentation and never ship on the assumption that behavior is identical. This ideology applies to the development toolkit as well. Supporting multiple platforms would require the organization to have separate specializations and expertise. In the market, there is an advancement where toolkits/frameworks to support multiple platforms are available. The degree of effort required may vary for different cross-platform and, in theory, would be less than the combined effort of building and maintaining fully separate native apps for each platform independently. Irrespective of this, it still makes sense to have a percentage of individuals in the team who are specialized/aware of individual mobile platforms.

In summary, it is essential to reiterate the statement that *individual platforms have differences and similarities, and it is necessary to invest in understanding each platform's capabilities*. This would be the key to differentiating and preempting these use cases and adopting the appropriate strategy. It is essential for an individual, well-versed in one platform, to understand that the items that are easily doable on one platform do not imply the same for other platforms. For an organization, having some specialization and a dedicated focus would help in building mobile apps on multiple platforms.

Being ready to unlearn and relearn

On the technology and implementation front, getting into the mobile development space would mean being prepared to unlearn some of the prevalent patterns that have worked out well in other software applications. Trying to follow these patterns as-is is like force-fitting items that are counterintuitive for mobile application development. The network latency and computational scarcity are not a concern in the context of backend development in comparison to mobile application development. Another example: in the backend, if there is a failure or bug, one can deploy the fix with ease, as the process to change the source would lie within the organization. In the case of the mobile, the deployment has a gatekeeper to review the release to the app store. The app, after the release approval, then becomes dependent on the end user's choice to be downloaded or updated. This is thus an engineering problem to solve. Understanding these constructs would help the developer and the team to have a proper strategy. The takeaway to be re-emphasized is that one should be ready to unlearn old context and adopt what is contextually relevant for mobile development.

Concluding mobile mindset

The section *Mobile mindset* looked at non-negotiables that form the frame of reference to enable mobile development to scale and progress faster.

To empirically ground these, let us take a look at real-life examples and best practices that resonate with these principles:

- In iOS, it is not allowed to read the user's phone number. If the application requires the mobile number, there should be an explicit text field asking the end user to manually enter the phone number. If a product owner or an organization goes to the length where the developer must find a means to circumvent this restriction, the application, in all probability, will be denied from distribution via the Apple platform while trying to publish in the store. The mobile mindset is to be aware that the platform restriction is applicable to iOS. Thus, helping to make the decision, auto-populating of mobile numbers cannot be implemented in iOS.
- The organization does not own a mobile device of the end user in most cases, excluding a rare case where, for B2E purposes, mobile phones are supplied by the organization. The end user thus can influence the usage of computation capacity or capability of the mobile device by disabling these at the system level for the apps. In such a situation, the organization's ability to capitalize on the computational capacity of the mobile device will totally depend on the end user. If the end user restricts the usage of capabilities by the application, the functioning might become flawed. If we force users to comply, they may uninstall the app due to the side effects of excessive power usage and reduced battery life. An example of this is the mobile app using the background mode in iOS.
- In the distributed software, the computing machines are controlled and maintained by the organization. The cost of scaling and maintaining the computing hardware is owned and maintained by the organization itself. When it comes to mobile development, the application's hardware is not under an organization's control but rather the end user's. The mobile operating system also imposes restrictions that an application may not be able to override, necessitating the development team to understand what the platform offers and design accordingly. The platform capabilities offered by the system setting form the sandbox and, in most cases, cannot be overridden by the application itself. One should avoid force-fitting a feature from experience on other technology.
- The network calls triggered by mobile applications impact the device's battery performance. In contrast, for a backend or web application hosted on a server, it is the total number of requests hitting the server

that is measured. The network traffic thus defines the load on the server and thereby the cost incurred. For mobile, the load may not be applicable. Rather, the effect on the battery life would be the measure that the developer would be interested in. Understanding these subtle differences at the development and senior management levels is essential to create a strategic plan that would help to channel energy to what is optimal for mobile application development.

- The deployment depends on the rules of the store. For the platform providers, Apple and Google define the rules for iOS and Android devices, respectively. The private/enterprise app store is also an option. The private/enterprise store will have more flexibility for the app development organization on the apps uploaded. For iOS, there is still a set of processes to support an enterprise store. The team will have to adhere to the enterprise distribution process of Apple and obtain membership. In summary, one can see that, unlike a web application where an application is built and deployed immediately after verification, for a mobile application, it is different. The app deployment to a public app store must go through the respective proprietary platform validation before being available for the end user to download.
- Mobile applications provide various means to reach customers and provide an engaging customer experience. Business campaigns via push notification programs and customer loyalty programs are some examples where the business owner can leverage the capability provided by the platform to reach customers. Personalized user experience and offline experience are other examples of features. The mobile app can thus provide greater functionality by leveraging the mobile's hardware features. The stakeholder should have an overview of the features of the device to leverage these capabilities.

Table 1.1 shows the comparison of what a developer for the respective web, backend, and mobile thinks in the context of a certain keyword/feature:

Features	Web development	Mobile development	Backend web service development
Session management	Cookies, local storage, session storage	Secure storage (Keychain/Keystore), token persistence	Token-based authentication (e.g., JWT, OAuth), session management via API
Social login	OAuth redirects in the browser	Native SDKs for OAuth and social login. Browser redirection with deep link callback	OAuth 2.0, provider
Offline handling	Limited offline support, service workers for caching	Caching, offline data access, background sync, local database storage (e.g., SQLite, Core Data, Room)	NA (handled by the client-side/mobile app)
Network reliability	Assumes stable internet connection	Handles intermittent connectivity, retries, background network tasks	Server-side API design to handle network reliability and retry logic
Security	Browser security mechanisms (cookies, HTTPS)	Device-specific encryption, biometrics, app sandboxing, secure local storage	Server-side encryption (data storage, communication), API security
Push notifications	Browser-based push notifications	Native push notifications (APNs for iOS, Firebase Cloud Messaging for Android)	NA (act as the store and provide a trigger for notification)

Features	Web development	Mobile development	Backend web service development
Background tasks	Limited to background sync via service workers, minimal processing	Full background tasks, data sync, background processing for tasks depending on the capability exposed by OS	NA
Performance optimization	Optimized for desktop or mobile browsers, lower performance constraints	Highly optimized for specific mobile device resources (CPU, memory, battery)	Optimized API responses, database indexing, efficient resource use
User interface (UI) design	Responsive design (CSS, media queries)	Platform-specific UI guidelines (Material Design for Android, Human Interface Guidelines for iOS)	NA
Deployment	Deployed on servers, cloud platforms	Requires app store approval (App Store, Google Play)	Deployed on servers, cloud platforms
App lifecycle	Browser session lifecycle (open, close, refresh)	Foreground, background, suspended, terminated	NA (service availability could be nearest equivalent)
Access to hardware	Limited access to device hardware depending on the capability (e.g., webcam, microphone)	Access to all device hardware (camera, GPS, sensors, Bluetooth)	NA
App versioning and updates	Instant update	Updates require app store approval and users to download (should plan version management or provide force update feature)	Version management for API endpoints, backward compatibility

Table 1.1: *Comparison of feature development in web, mobile and backend web service*

This explanation should have given enough data to contextualize and form the mobile mindset and step forward to the world of possibilities, on a small real estate and a variety of computing capabilities at the fingertips.

Sharing experiences of aspiring mobile developers

This section lists some questions and their responses compiled in the context of mobile development. The idea is to cover the aspects and thought processes of individuals trying to get into mobile development from different backgrounds.

Question: What is so special about a mobile application, and why are organizations racing to adopt the same? What is the return on investment (ROI) for an organization building a mobile application?

Answer: Technology has reached a stage where an individual has access to information at every instant, at their fingertips. This technology shift is evolving and growing, thus presenting an opportunity for organizations to sell products and services via mobile. Compared to older times, when an individual had to walk into a store, mobile apps enable the individual to fulfill their aspirations in a few clicks, as discussed in the *Mobile-first and non-mobile-first strategies* section. Be it utilities, travel, health, or any other aspect in the walk of life, there is a high possibility of a mobile application supporting the cause. Individuals are also getting acquainted with technology to the extent that this new way of living has become part of life. As in any technology, there are ethical dilemmas that creep into mobile as well. The habit of using a mobile judiciously is the responsibility of the respective individual to make the right choices while using the same. The intent should be to pave the way for an enriching journey for the end user by using mobile technologies.

The strategy of promoting and sustaining a business in the past was circulating leaflets, advertisements, billboards, and technical people answering after-sales customer queries. With the advent of the mobile, retaining or growing consumer goodwill is a strategy that adds value to organizations. This provides an alternate means to get acquainted with services/products.

Zero digital presence may be counterintuitive, particularly if the volume of end consumers is high and diverse in nature. Let us try to decode the previous statement with an example of a retail organization and its business. The context considers a retail organization with a well-established chain of stores. People are rushing to each of these stores. There is always a possibility for a competitor operating from different locations to enter the market and capture a significant share of loyal consumers by providing online booking and delivery. A case where the retail store does not operate in an online mode gives the competitor the advantage to win over. This could cause a possible leak of loyal consumers as well. The decline of the business could be prevented with a proper digital strategy. Having the means to enable the consumer to shop from home is a convenience. There is enough evidence of this model working out in the market. The online presence equips digital strategy to incorporate a means to engage consumers and provide relevant and personalized information, bringing ROI to the retail organization through fulfilled orders. This can even be a booster for the in-store purchasing consumer in the form of loyalty programs, personalized offers, suggestions, etc., given via the mobile application. The mobile application in the digital strategy will also pave the way to improve the branding for the organization outside the physical boundaries of the store.

The intention was to communicate that mobile applications in the organization's digital strategy have the potential to improve business. A business, however, needs to thoroughly study and do market research on its user base to define the digital strategy, which would vary for different domains and groups of people. This study will help to understand the potential of the mobile application.

In a nutshell, the mobile application is the digital strategy an organization can have to complement the channel and extend its reach. Mobile application also provides a means of engagement for the product/service offered to the consumer, with the capability to potentially accelerate and provide a competitive edge in business.

Question: Are web, mobile web, and mobile application all the same?

Answer: There are different channels through which a business or individual can reach their customers. In the digital world, it can be a desktop application, website, or mobile application (as discussed in the *Mobile operating system* section).

A web application is software hosted on a remote server. It is accessed by a URL on a desktop or mobile device browser, which mandates the device to have internet connectivity most of the time to function. The web application uses technologies that enable the application to run in the browser. The capability of a web application is limited to the capabilities exposed by the browser on which the website loads.

In comparison, the mobile application is standalone software that operates entirely using the hardware of the device once downloaded and installed. The mobile application is built and developed with technologies closer to the platform. The mobile application will have direct access to the platform hardware via the APIs defined by the platform frameworks. These will allow additional capabilities beyond what a web app opened in a browser can do. However, these are restricted by the OS's sandboxing model, which limits what any third-party apps can do and requires them to operate under the guidelines laid out by the respective platform providers. The framework provides the mode to request access to capabilities exposed by hardware interactively to the user.

The underlying principles and technologies for websites and mobile websites are almost the same. The key difference between these is the form factor or the real estate available to present the information, constrained by the screen size of the mobile. The UI should thus cater to the small size and render the element appropriately to the real estate available. In most cases, the UI for the mobile website would remain similar to the mobile application. The website is generally built responsively to cater to multiple form factors.

Additionally, iOS/Android has the capability to embed browsers within the application. There exists an old cross-platform framework based on this in-app web browser. The usage of embedded browsers in apps is to redirect to a web URL within the app without leaving the context. This pattern is generally used as an intermediate go-to-market strategy of an organization where the feature rollout can be done until the native screens are built and released to the end user.

While web and mobile web have their benefits, some factors that differentiate a mobile application from the former are as follows:

- The mobile application forms a standalone software on a user device that operates much faster than a web browser.
- Performance and computation in mobile applications are faster by combining network data and on-device processing, sharing the load.
- While designing a mobile application, the team can compartmentalize the data and share the computation overhead across the backend as a system design choice. The mobile application can support offline capabilities.
- An offline app is best for businesses requiring less real-time processing; for use cases requiring capabilities where connectivity is less. Such a case will be better positioned to have a mobile app that goes ahead with the web as a digital strategy. An example of an offline application is a digital kiosk or point-of-sale application, which may require the application's end user to travel to remote places with limited connectivity.

To conclude, the mobile web is very different from a standalone mobile app. Once the internals of a mobile application unfold, embedding a web browser can be very handy for quickly building use cases and releasing them to the market.

It is essential to understand that considering one over the other from a web, mobile app, and desktop app should be an informed decision. Supporting any or all of these would be based on the business need and user segmentation, depending on the context defined by the stakeholder. Thus, it is important to understand that each channel has its pros and cons. They may serve a different purpose to give a collectively exhaustive outcome when used strategically to reach the end consumer.

Question: Building a mobile application will require sophistication. Does such a task require a specialized skill set? Does mobile development require any engineering effort to build and operate?

Answer: Mobile application development provides an arena for sharpening engineering skill sets. However, debating and comparing with the other technologies regarding what is best amongst the various engineering possibilities is very subjective. Such a discussion concluding in a single concrete answer acceptable to everyone is a far-fetched expectation. From a technological point of view, finding which development gives the best experience does not add any value to anyone. As long as the decision to develop a mobile application is part of the digital strategy of the organization, building a great mobile app will be the success criterion. One can expect the mobile development to encounter exciting challenges that a team has to carefully engineer.

The broad umbrella of the skill set required for mobile development is listed as follows:

- **Platform-specific knowledge**: The working of the device and the patterns followed in the operating system are some examples of the information in this category. The platform owner will define a manual or guideline that the team should adhere to. When this becomes the default psyche, the individual could take the path toward becoming a subject matter expert for the platform.
- **Mobile UI/UX design**: The experience that needs to be provided is a key skill required to define the interaction and representation of the brand. The right design is key to a functional mobile application that nurtures a great experience for the end user.
- **Mobile app architecture**: Deciding the structure of the code and ensuring the structure allows the project to scale is another key skill set. Choosing the right structure and understanding what works for the team building the mobile app has a critical impact on the time it takes to bootstrap and ensure the longevity of the application.

- **Performance optimization for mobile application**: Instrumentation and monitoring are areas that monitor the application's production readiness. Imagine the case where an app responsible for a critical action is not responding to the stimulus (touch). The degree of frustration in such a situation is huge. The performance optimization strategy could improve the app's behavior, making the end user happy, which can be achieved by having a skill set to use the different tools to do the analysis.
- **Mobile-specific development tools**: The supporting tools related to automation, linting, security, etc., are relevant to maintaining the sanity of the mobile application. Learning these frameworks and being aware of them could boost the developer's productivity, thereby pre-empting potential issues.
- **App store requirements and deployment**: The release process itself requires a special skill set, and having an individual with this awareness is critical to ensuring the application reaches the market.
- **Native code or hybrid solutions**: The choice of tech frameworks and the details of understanding how to build a mobile application in the framework are differentiators in the skill set of the mobile developer.

This list gives an idea of the skill set required to execute a mobile development project. This list is not exhaustive, and as the domain and complexity of the app increase, the framework and solution would become focused on the business context for which the mobile application is built and the capabilities of the hardware the app uses.

Now that we know some of the skills that could be required, let us look at some of the top items that counter the statement that *mobile development is only about dragging and dropping elements*:

- Writing performance-focused code while working in a constrained environment in terms of memory and power.
- Preventing any catastrophic event after shipping the mobile application.
- Presenting data on a minimal form factor that engages users.
- Using the hardware capabilities and triggers to process the information, which would otherwise have to be collected in person.
- Engineer to safeguard the trust established to prevent any security issues concerning the user, mobile application, and the device.

These are some of the ground realities faced by the mobile developer.

Knowing the dragging and dropping of components does not qualify as the only criterion for mobile development. Mobile application development requires a clear understanding of software fundamentals, tool usage, and accessing platform frameworks to capitalize on the capabilities of the hardware. In short, mobile application development requires the finesse of an engineer who knows the tools of the native platform and the strategies for deployment. All these would form the core strength. These can be acquired by investing in learning the tools and programming language. The *Beyond dragging and dropping of components* section of this chapter gives some examples of the skills required.

Question: Is it too late to enter mobile development in the AI-accelerated era? Is it the right decision to take the new mobile development as a career path?

Answer: The computing device that an individual uses is still largely a mobile device. AI accelerates mobile development; however, personas with a strong background in engineering are required to scale mobile applications beyond a minimum viable product, as discussed in the *Mobile mindset* section. An individual's intellectual capability needs to be built to handle enterprise-scale mobile applications. For an organization that thrives using a mobile application as its primary interface with consumers, having an individual or team who specializes in mobile development is critical.

The path chosen will be rewarding and present a different set of problem statements. There are different varieties of problem statements in mobile application development. This exposure gives the opportunity to reason and extend these lessons to other domains or technologies. For example, creating an HTTP server on a phone, creating a live video chat application, a Super App, etc., are some of the engineering manifestations of complexity that would challenge the system design thinking skillset of a mobile developer. The idea of the statement is not to belittle other technology but rather to emphasize the fact that a mobile application is not just a facade for showing data from the backend. All these could potentially instill curiosity and understanding of the underlying workings of how the rendering happens, optimizing the computation logic to reduce the frame drops in the render pipeline, using the hardware capabilities optimally without reducing the convenience provided to the end user, etc., are further examples of the kinds of challenges.

Choosing the right career path is a subjective element that depends on the person sharing the perspective. What one can guarantee is that building a mobile application is a game of core engineering, given that you are part of the right product. Having said that, there are organizations that build mobile apps that act as a facade for displaying and collecting information. Referring to such projects as the baseline to evaluate the challenges faced in mobile engineering shall not be the right yardstick.

Challenges faced in mobile development

The mobile industry has given unique problem statements for the individuals involved in development. Knowing these challenges will bring us closer to the thought process and help us reason well in mobile development. Here are some challenges:

- From an industry point of view, the short-lived nature and the diverse options to choose from for the development framework could create a dilemma. To make things worse, there will be conflicting and mixed opinions in the community about these technology frameworks.
- The varied set of devices out there in the market makes it impossible to test in every device. Thus the confidence that the feature will work for all the devices will not be one hundred percent.
- Control over the hardware is limited as the mobile application runs on a device that is not owned by the organization developing apps, in most cases.
- Given the niche nature of the technology, finding the right talent would pose a concern.
- The dependency on Apple devices for developing apps for iOS can incur costs for the organization.

Thought experiment

Need for mobile application: Let us try to explore a few use cases and evaluate the need for having mobile applications for these use cases. The idea for this section is to give a nudge to the brain to correlate the learning till now and see the relevance of mobile in each of the cases:

- **Use case 1**: A warehouse owner plans to reach out to you. The problem statement was within the large warehouse: an employee has to do the bookkeeping for the different incoming and outgoing products. The employees in the warehouse wrote the notes and made these entries in the office desktop computer.
- **Use case 2**: A retail business owner has a chain of convenience stores. They have considerable revenue. However, the company does not have any digital presence. The bookkeeping, etc., is managed by third-party software products, and with the help of vendors. New players in the market are rising to become their competitors. The competitors are excelling in process efficiency and convenience to the consumer, thereby promoting growth. Customer loyalty has been great with this retail chain, ensuring the business has been smooth until now.
- **Use case 3**: Consider the use case of a ride-hailing application. There will be two interfaces and user journeys, one for the rider and the other for the driver. In the driver user's journey, the sophistication involved is continuously tracking the driver's location and updating the information to keep the rider informed. This should happen when the rider has booked the ride.
- **Use case 4**: Consider the use case to build an analytics dashboard for an analyst to evaluate the company's product performance. An analytics dashboard supports the creation of reports. This dashboard helps the stakeholders to analyze the product performance of the organization.

Author's take on thought experiment

In the different use cases, except for the fourth one, all would benefit from a mobile application. The fourth use case of the analytics dashboard may need only a web application rather than a mobile app. The intended audience for the analytics dashboard will be business stakeholders. Obviously, mobile applications can act as a complement for a quick look at the data. However, this is a choice that the organization can make to invest, as the ROI may be less.

In use case one, having a mobile application to make the product entry and manage the inventory can be convenient to improve the efficiency of the warehouse employees.

The use case of a retail store looks at customer retention and engagement. The approach is to complement and enhance the business with additional channels. The team understands the competitive edge with such a strategy of bringing and providing the service at the fingertips of the consumer. This thus favors the need for a mobile app and the potential return that this can bring back to the business. The retail owner's business with a mobile application can improve the convenience of the customer who uses the service from the comfort of their home via an online delivery system.

The ride-hailing application leverages hardware features for safety and accuracy in locating the driver and the ride-hailing individual. The performance factor of the user's journey and the precision required would thus trigger the need to engineer a solution that best suits the portable version of the digital computing device, the mobile.

Conclusion

The objective of the chapter is to introduce the reader to the mobile development ecosystem, which has now reached its culmination. The idea shared will give the perspective that mobile application development is beyond just being a facade and requires a strong engineering mindset to enable an enterprise to reach end users via a mobile application. For a developer, there are choices of platforms such as iOS, Android, etc., and technologies to develop a mobile application. The reader shall now be aligned to the fact that, like any other tech role, the mobile application development role has its own sophistication that requires the team to engage and understand the underlying platform. This understanding would enable the team to engineer a scalable solution resulting in an optimal mobile application that adds value to the mobile users.

The next chapter is about planning a mobile application project. The perspective from a mobile development gives the flavor of how a project plan is curated and the key ingredient to make a viable and executable plan. The chapter also shares learning that helps mitigate the challenges faced in the planning of a mobile project as well.

Takeaways and reflections

Now that we have reached the end of the chapter, you have immersed yourself in the world of mobile developers and got an overview of the possibilities and mindset.

- From the narration, one can reason that the mobile is a clear winner over performance, personalization, leveraging hardware features, and offline access when compared with the web. On the contrary, the maintenance, time to market, and cost of development aspects for the web are better than those for mobile.
- We are in a world where almost everything has a mobile app, and in this case, it would be right to include the mobile app in the digital strategy to prevent missing out on any business potential.
- A mobile app is not a replacement for all the other channels to reach the customer; however, it is one channel that can potentially have a business impact.
- On the development side, different developers are fascinated by various aspects. For example:
  - Finding a fascination in developing and programming for mobile application user interaction and presentation layer.

    - Intrigued by using the small real estate to create lucid and fluid presentation layers that engage the user to use the mobile application.
    - The group that cherishes writing challenging programs using the hardware capability for optimal user experience.
- Individuals from different backgrounds have different perspectives on mobile applications. There is the possibility of many dimensions to these thought processes, which are categorized as follows:
    - The business opportunity
    - The technology involved
    - The capabilities and limitations
- The mobile is the most widely used and popular device to suit the business. However, other categories of devices, such as smart TVs, wearables, IoT devices, etc., are adding to the list of possibilities to reach a consumer. These devices thus bring opportunities for organizations in terms of business and ease of access to the individual in terms of services and products. The technological advancement and constant focus of the mobile device companies out in the market to improve the capabilities of handheld devices have been the key catalyst in taking technological progress forward.
- Channel refers to a medium through which an organization provides its service or product to the consumer. Understanding the channel is foundational to choosing between mobile-first, web or omnichannel strategies.

CHAPTER 2
Planning Your Mobile App Project

Introduction

The success of a project can be attributed to proper planning. Planning helps mitigate any risks and elements that may go wrong. The expectation of being omnipresent and knowing everything is hard. In such cases, preempting negative outcomes is difficult as the project engagement size increases. In such a case, having a plan could help hold the team together and navigate adverse conditions more smoothly. Planning can help the team to have a road map and a clear outcome that ties to the larger picture of the organization's goal. The chapter presents planning in the context of the iterative style development prevalent in the industry. Concepts such as requirement gathering, defining the backlog for the execution, and readjusting with a continuous learning and feedback loop will be the themes discussed in the chapter in the context of mobile app development. A mobile application project co-exists with the other platforms (e.g., web or desktop), and the chapter will focus only on essential parts of planning related to mobile applications.

Structure

This chapter covers the following topics:

- SDLC overview
- Planning and its purpose
- Ideal plan
- Determining raw velocity
- Creating a release plan
- Thought experiment

Objectives

After reading this chapter, the reader will have an in-depth understanding of how to create a project plan for a mobile application project. The process may have an overlap of knowledge if one has already practiced planning for other software development. The chapter starts with a comparative study of the evolution of two models of SDLC. The reader will be learning concepts relevant to creating a project plan, such as backlog, estimation, risk, and raw velocity, and practice these by applying them via thought experiments at the end of the chapter. The chapter will provide the necessary elements for planning and empowering individuals involved in mobile development projects. The chapter concludes with a practical walkthrough of creating a project plan, from the start to defining the go-to-market strategy and examining the challenges encountered.

SDLC overview

Before getting into the details of planning, it is important to understand the software development lifecycle and the evolution of the model. The whole planning for application software development could be baselined around these models, and one can leverage these principles to scale to the project needs. The timeline of adoption can be broadly traced back to Waterfall | Agile | DevOps, where DevOps complements Agile practices.

Consider the mantra: *Give the entire requirement and let me build software.*

It is a one-liner definition for the Waterfall model. The industry was operating in this model in the past. In the current world, there has been a shift to an incremental, iterative delivery in most cases. Agile will be a term that one can relate to the iterative software delivery model. The terminologies in SDLC are a precursor to understanding the planning process. The SDLC model chosen also influences the planning. In the introduction section of this chapter, the term backlog refers to a prioritized list of tasks, features, requirements, or user stories that serve as a repository of future work. The backlog generally evolves continuously and is updated throughout the project lifecycle.

Tip: **The first known usage and representation of SDLC can be traced back to a presentation in software engineering held by Herbert D. Benington at the symposium on Advanced Programming Methods for Digital Computers on 29 June 1956.**

Waterfall model

This is an SDLC model that is linear and sequential in nature. In principle, for this model, once a stage is concluded, the team does not return to the same stage. The name Waterfall becomes fitting to the context, signifying the unidirectional flow of water.

Software with stable requirements, a clearly defined scope, heavy documentation needs, and low technology risk is commonly seen in projects executed using the Waterfall model. An individual who has worked on projects that require rigorous validation, strict requirements that rarely change, and non-iterative critical tasks will likely have practiced the Waterfall model.

The rigid nature of the Waterfall model worked well to build concrete system software. At some point in time, the concrete structure became available to build auxiliary systems that support consumers. For the industry, the major focus area shifted to consumer software. This shift towards building application software required adaptability and constant change; thus, the problem statement emerged to find a methodology that works with a dynamically changing nature.

Agile

Historically, the first reference to Agile can be traced back to 2001, when a group of 17 engineers introduced a formal methodology with the publication of the Agile Manifesto. The key was to address the limitation of the Waterfall model, which is a traditional, heavyweight SDLC.

The interpretation of Agile as a methodology and a mindset is very critical. An organization can adopt Agile by aligning its practices to various frameworks. Examples of a few of the frameworks under Agile are Scrum, **Extreme Programming** (**XP**), Kanban, Crystal, Lean, etc.

In the context of Agile, a framework is a formal definition for the methodology. The team can adopt and follow this framework to practice Agile. All the frameworks follow the principles laid out in the Agile Manifesto.

Examples of a few frameworks are as follows:

- **Scrum**: The philosophy of Scrum is to deliver value in an iteration called a sprint. The incremental approach will give a sense of progress with the validation of the sample set of possible end consumers or stakeholders. The validation gives the opportunity to take feedback and evolve. The framework looks at a relative definition of backlog with plausible capacity to reach a stable burndown rate that reflects an autonomous, high-performing team. This framework works in a place where the outcome has to do with continuous value derived in an incremental fashion over a regularly defined interval called a sprint. The chapter uses Scrum as the reference Agile framework to explain the planning and methodology related to project execution.

- **Kanban**: The name came from a car manufacturing unit, that literally translates to *visual signal* or *card* in Japanese. The framework thus works well with the principle that the production unit will continue to produce outcomes if the supporting pillars and resources are available. If there is a drop, the outcome would proportionally reduce. Thus, for software development teams, Kanban is a framework that supports the software engineering team to deliver outcomes based on the prioritized tasks. The team member can pick up the task from the prioritized queue as the capacity allows. The total capacity available at a given point in time determines the number of tasks that are executed in parallel.
- **XP**: The engineering side of software becoming the pillar for the SDLC methodology is the core differentiator and underlying principle of the XP framework. The team following this emphasizes technical excellence, continuous feedback, and close collaboration among developers, customers, and stakeholders to produce a valued outcome. The framework has laid out the trio of principles, values, and practices that define the foundational theme driving the methodology.

DevOps

DevOps is not an Agile framework or an SDLC model. However, discussing DevOps in the context of the SDLC is relevant, and the reason is that it complements Agile frameworks. The central theme of DevOps is to ensure that the system with individual units can function at a larger scale with high quality and promote incremental change with ease. The siloed function of software development, when integrated, could create potential bottlenecks. The emergence of DevOps was a response to the problem statement.

Note: **A backlog refers to a prioritized list of tasks, features, requirements, or user stories that serve as a repository of work yet to be done. The backlog evolves continuously and is updated throughout the lifecycle of a project.**

Planning and its purpose

Planning is a continuous process involving the formulation of a strategy, roadmap, or framework to achieve specific goals. The purpose is to ensure all parties involved have a clear understanding of what, how, and when it is expected to be accomplished. Planning helps in proactively tackling risks, improving efficiency, laying out expectations, and ensuring successful project delivery. A project manager will ideally be continuously reviewing and adjusting based on the situation. The project plan should account for the effect of different phases of SDLC. The following are some key phases in SDLC that should be considered in planning:

- Understanding the requirement and defining the backlog
- Baselining and estimation of the user stories
- Determining raw velocity and creating a release plan
- Ready with proposal
- Execution
- Coming up with actual velocity
- Prioritization and readjustment
- Revisiting the project plan

An individual in a leadership role may have the direction and holistic view to create the plan. However, having the information across the team could give a structural and top-down view for the folks involved in planning, thereby improving the effectiveness.

Ideal plan

An ideal plan will have a clear project goal, breaking down the work, identifying and assessing the risks to plan, and allocating resources to create a realistic schedule with an optimal budget and cost defined to see through the successful completion of the project.

The measure of success of a good plan would be to have the ability to accommodate and rearrange the plan in case uncertainties unfold. A change in plan should happen without derailing the original outcome drastically. A good plan should have the dependency tracked. Ensuring the impediment or risk becomes visible to the team before creating a catastrophic shift in the way of working is another trait of a good plan.

A workshop to understand the vision and goal for the project would be ideal before any planning exercise. Engaging key stakeholders in the discussion with the group can set the stage and establish a common understanding among the group. This could be a green signal to start off the collaboration and create a better plan with collective wisdom.

Best practices for pragmatic planning

A project plan creation requires some level of groundwork to be done to get enough data to create a practical plan. The planning activity cannot be precise to the last detail, which implies the project plan may not be set in stone. One must adapt to the information that gets revealed over time. A ballpark time for completion with minimal deviation is what one can aim towards while creating a plan. This gives the option for readjusting as the team takes the journey. Be it Agile or Waterfall, any change requires readjustment. The impact and the way the risk is realized and accommodated will be different for Agile in comparison with Waterfall. Waterfall had serious problems with incremental addition and information getting changed. The occurrence of a change restarts the cycle in the Waterfall methodology. When the change cannot be deferred, the Waterfall methodology will not work, thus paving the way for Agile. The chapter focuses on planning a mobile project following Agile methodology.

The project plan requires the availability of a vision or objective for the project. The objective drives the team to collect information to formulate the details defining what the project is about and why the project is being undertaken. In case of iterative development, the details at which the team may have to operate need not be concrete for the planning phase, covering the full details. One should not misinterpret the statement that execution is done with incomplete information. The intent conveyed is in the context of planning, where the completeness of the entire scope is not mandated. The development of the entire system is broken down into smaller, logical units, which are combined to achieve the larger goal of the entire scope. The actual development of the logical unit, as outlined in the plan, will be carried out using concrete information that the team can iteratively discover in parallel, based on the priority of the planned feature.

Planning requires a level of preparation in which the team outlines the activities necessary to achieve the desired outcome. An estimate for these activities, based on a potential solution derived from past knowledge, is also required. Additionally, if the team tries to engineer or debate a solution in detail during the planning phase, this is also not a great use of time.

It is important to keep a watch on the time invested in the preparation process for planning. It should not go beyond the threshold that falls back to the Waterfall structure of requirement analysis. Following Agile on paper and practicing Waterfall is an anti-pattern. The illustration of creating a plan to build a chat application is explained next to better understand the impact of an anti-pattern.

A team building a chat application goes into the level of deep implementation in the estimation discussion. This consumes more time to conclude and is not the right use of time for the team during the preparation phase. The ideal next step for a longer discussion is to take a hard call to stop and timebox. The major activity is to define the list of epics, user stories, and the high-level solution as a preparation for planning. In the planning as well, the discussion can go on long and will be influenced by the knowledge of the folks involved. The goal to reach a common consensus and move forward faster may get derailed. Relying on SMEs is a better strategy, as they serve as gatekeepers to optimize and mediate the discussion.

For large projects, the organization often adopts a milestone-based approach for planning. The planning session in this case happens at every milestone level. The process is the same for milestone-based planning. Meeting multiple milestones will culminate in the churning out of the entire backlog for the product. A simplification of the case will be that the entire backlog for all different milestones is independently and incrementally tackled. The definition or outcome to meet each milestone will be the reference to start preparation for planning. This will then be used to create the backlog and repeats for further milestones.

For a mobile application project, it is not only about the development of applications. The development and readiness of the supporting systems should also be considered. While creating the backlog, it is essential to track the dependencies, as it will help to create a reliable plan by factoring in the dependency resolution date into the plan.

Understanding the concept of risk

Risk is the possibility of an uncertain event or condition that could have a positive or negative effect on the achievement of objectives when it occurs. The negative risks are a threat, and the positive risks pave the way for new opportunities. In the context of planning, once the backlog for the expected outcome is defined, the risk analysis should be done. Knowing the risk will help to accommodate the mitigation action or take stock of the causal effects on the plan.

A set of major possible risk categories that can derail the mobile development project is listed. The section defines possible questions that one can ask to understand the presence of risk in the said category. The questions are not exhaustive; rather, they will suggest the line of thought required to do a risk analysis during planning:

- **Design and wireframe**:
    - Does the project have a wireframe and a hi-fidelity design ready? Are these designs approved by the product owner?
    - If the hi-fidelity design is not available, there should be a delivery plan created for the finalized design for the development to start. Does the planning team have visibility for the same?
    - Does the team have stakeholder agreement on the delivery plan of the design artifacts?
- **External system dependency**:
    - What are the dependent systems (internal and external to the organization)?
    - Does the stakeholder have visibility for this system and their availability for development?
    - Does the system have an SLA and support mechanism that the development team can take support from when it does not work?
    - Are the dependent systems ready to be consumed to kick-start development?
    - Does the team have a connector and contract provided to leverage the dependent system? If not, is the documentation available to create the custom layer?
    - Does the dependent system have support to help with the issue?
- **Internal system**:
    - Are the backend services that need to be consumed by mobile ready?
    - If the backend service is not ready, how is the understanding of the system within the team?
    - Can the team proceed with the contract if the system is not ready?
- **Operational**:
    - What is the testing strategy?
    - What is the device metric to ensure the app is functional for most end consumers?
    - Is the team equipped with the necessary understanding of compliance and guidelines required for the domain?
    - How does compliance affect the release and the store approval process?

Modeling these risks is essential to creating a better plan. Next, the idea is to look at this classification and contextualize it to SDLC, projecting to ground facts.

Design and wireframing are critical workflows in the SDLC of mobile application development. The experience design itself has alifecycle of its own, from discovery to finalization of the UI representation. Design is a dependency for the development team, which is the specification that gets translated into the final mobile application. The design process also goes through multiple iterations before the final version is released to the development team. The answer to the questions listed in the design and wireframe risk category is a critical piece of information required to create the plan and define the release timeline. It is necessary to understand what the dates of the design deliverables are and see the possibility of what can be done in case the delivery of the dependency needs to be adjusted in the timeline.

In order to practice risk analysis, let us take an example of a banking organization ready to build a mobile app replacing the current version. This program aims for a digital revamp of the existing mobile banking ecosystem. The organization decided to outsource the work to three parties specialized in the skills listed as follows:

- UI/UX design
- Application development
- Auditing

The delivery plan of the UI/UX artifacts would decide the priority and order for planning the feature development. The failure to meet the mutually agreed delivery dates of UI/UX is the risk involved. The team should have an alternate strategy and understanding of the tolerance level of how far one can survive if the risk materializes.

Thus, in order for mobile application screen development to commence, the UI/UX artifacts should be delivered to the app development team with ample time to analyze and consume. A minimum of two to three weeks of analysis time is recommended, giving the developer adequate time to assess and plan implementation. This gives the developer space to think about the technology strategy to implement these seamlessly.

Similarly, system dependency, when not fulfilled, has the potential to derail any plan. Let us consider the case where there are multiple stakeholders with mutually exclusive interests representing the different systems that they are part of. The skin in the game for the primary product consuming this dependency may not be a priority for these stakeholders. To add to the burden, if the stakeholder of the primary product cannot influence the priorities of the team responsible for the dependent system, the risks of getting blocked are high. One strategy to mitigate this is to plan for parking lot items or shuffle the stories related to this dependency with other items that can be worked on. In case the third-party system is absolutely critical for the product, then pulling some strings or adjusting the release timeline will be the way forward. A similar situation that was narrated for the UI/UX is also applicable in this case, where the dependency, when delayed, will cause an impediment to the consuming product. A mitigation strategy will be to work closely with the team responsible and ensure the team meets the timeline, ensuring availability for consumption of the mobile application feature development without derailing the plan.

The third risk category is the internal systems, which are typically the backend services consumed by the mobile application. In most cases, the risk manifests when these are actively developed in parallel with the mobile application. The team can decide to develop the service first and then start the mobile application development. This approach of developing backend service first will not scale to support faster go-to-market; this approach also contradicts the *shift-left* principle, in which the development and testing of consumer-facing features begin as early as possible, enabling faster feedback for the API. An alternative to this is decoupling the backend and mobile by agreeing on a contract, which would make parallel execution possible. This strategy is termed contract-driven development and is followed in most cases. The risk involved can be seen as equivalent to that of external dependency. From the perspective of a mobile application, the backend service also comes under yet another dependency, which is HTTP/HTTPS endpoint or socket connections. The contract details of these dependencies, when delayed or not available to be consumed, can derail the plan.

Mobile development can move forward by agreeing on a paper contract of the dependent system and mocking the same. This is applicable to both internal and third-party systems. This strategy mitigates the risk of delay by having a clear, agreed-upon contract and expectations between teams, enabling parallel development, early testing, and better integration.

The fourth and final risk category is operational risk: the potential threats or challenges that could disrupt the smooth functioning, performance, and security of mobile applications during development or after release. This can occur at any point in the lifecycle of development. The availability of people is an example that demonstrates the risk. This would manifest when the unavailability of skilled individuals becomes a bottleneck for the development to move forward. Another example of risk in this category is the need to be vigilant and continuously monitor the systems for a crash or failure of an external dependency. The external dependency failure, when manifested, can be mitigated by having an SLA and a support structure in place. The risk manifested in the last category affects the system indirectly and may slow down the development. Risk mitigation depends on operational efficacy, influence, and coordination amongst different stakeholders within the team and from the team responsible for external dependency used.

This section has given the essence of risk and its effect. Having this knowledge as a toolkit can help an individual contribute to planning efficiently. Constantly evaluating the possibilities of what could go wrong can help catch issues early and thereby pre-empt them. This is an important practice that, when followed, would help to come up with a more accurate plan and release strategy for mobile application development.

Project execution archetypes

Execution strategy and project strategy are two terms that are often used interchangeably; however, there is a subtle distinction in the scope they represent. The project strategy is an abridged version of the plan that outlines goals and approaches at a high level, while the execution strategy is a detailed plan that expands the project strategy into an actionable plan. While creating the initial plan during the start phase, it will be ideal to lay out the project strategy, and over a period, as more data and maturity are achieved within the team, it will transform into a comprehensive execution strategy. It is worth noting that, irrespective of where the team is on the timeline of the projectlifecycle, there are a few execution archetypes that can affect the planning. As part of this section, the idea is to explore those archetypes and ways of planning around them.

At the board level, any project should be able to be classified into one of the following buckets:

- **Innovative/first-mover projects**: The product idea is new, and there are no other players in the market.
- **Legacy modernization projects**: Revamping the current product/service by either migrating to a new tech stack or rewriting the current platform, which is not scaling well.
- **Competitive response projects**: There is already at least one competitor in the market for the product/service that the team is trying to build.

These three form the foundational archetypes for most mobile development projects. The strategy to plan the above project types will have subtle differences. The next section is about the details of each of the archetypes, and their impact on the planning:

- For the first mover project bringing a new product to market, the discovery and the study for the viability of the product itself will have to be separate activities. The **minimum viable product** (**MVP**) approach could be an experimental strategy that the stakeholder could opt to validate new ideas. The discovery and analysis of the market should end by defining the vision. In the visioning exercise, the team will define the problem statement, goal, and what the product is solving. This is done by carefully studying and understanding the target market in the vision exercise. Wireframes, mockups, and the user experience studies are some of the items that need to be considered in parallel with the visioning exercise.

  Key milestones are as follows:

  - Market research and feasibility study
  - MVP development
  - Customer validation and feedback loops
  - Iteration and scaling
- The legacy modernization project focuses on migrating or revamping the platform to the latest trend, as the current version is not scaling. Mobile application rewrites to a new tech stack are mostly seen in such cases. The underlying reason for the rewrite is that the legacy system has become rigid towards change, and introducing new features is consuming time that is hindering the market position. Another reason that causes a rewrite could be that the underlying technology has been deprecated. A classic example occurred in 2024, when the Xamarin official support ended. In such a modernization project, it is recommended to

have a person who knows the legacy system well. In a case where the person with legacy system knowledge is unavailable, putting some effort into understanding the previous system would be a strategy that can benefit the rewrite. The investment to understand the legacy will serve as a reference to ensure parity for the features supported after the revamp. In the case of Xamarin, when the technology stack becomes obsolete, learnings from the past would help to reason the next step. The tech stack migration decision can be concluded by building smaller proof of concepts, validating the key feature, and evaluating current market trends and community support. Understanding the key points of failure or challenge in the legacy system shall also be one of the focus areas that feeds into the rewrite plan to ensure it is optimal and does not repeat the same mistakes.

Key milestones are as follows:

  - System audit and requirement gathering
  - Platform design and migration plan
  - Development and integration (e.g., new tech stack, scaling, performance optimization, better user experience)
  - **User acceptance testing** (**UAT**), friends and family migration, and go-live
  - Post-implementation review

- Competitive response project archetype is different, where the product already exists in the market, and a similar product is built as a competing product. The market will have experts who can share context on what is expected and what has not worked out. The differentiator and the market position required will be the primary concern for the organization building the competing product. Compared to the second archetype, which operates with an already established market position for itself, in this case, capturing the market becomes critical as it enables a company to tap into and capture the current market and maximize revenue potential. A quicker time to market offers advantages like early revenue generation, increasing market share, and the ability to respond quickly to customer feedback and emerging trends. A delayed release can lead to missed opportunities, increased competition, and potentially lower returns on investment. A visioning exercise could also be planned with the focus on defining key differentiators and the value offered by the new competing product.

  Key milestones are as follows:

  - Competitive analysis and market positioning
  - Feature development and differentiation
  - Product testing and feedback (beta)
  - Go-to-market launch and marketing campaign
  - Iterative product refinements based on feedback

These archetypes impact the planning differently. One can notice that the major difference amongst the archetypes lies in the initial project setup phase, how the team discovers, scopes, and validates requirements before development begins. The discovery phase of the feature for a new product is completely different from the other two. Building a competitive product may require the discovery of additional features that enable the product positioning in the market against competitors. Migration, on the other hand, may not require a detailed feature discovery, but rather will need a discovery of the user experience and evaluation of the tech stack.

The release strategy also differs and is operational in nature. The time at which the product or feature within the product needs to be released will be different across the three archetypes. The new product may go through the MVP phase and can go to market earlier with a top-hooking feature, which will bring more users to the app. The migration, on the other hand, should take time to build the minimum parity of the existing features available on the legacy system before releasing to the end consumers. Knowing the vision and having a fair idea about the key performance indicators will be required to start the planning phase in all the archetypes. The following table summarizes and compares the project plans for the different archetypes:

Project type	Focus areas	Plan components	Timeline
New product/service (no competitors)	Innovation, research and development, customer discovery	Extensive research, MVP development, market creation	Longer, more exploratory
Revamping existing product/service	Tech stack, scalability, system improvements	Audits, technology upgrades, operational efficiency improvements	Medium, focused on efficiency
Product in competitive market	Competitive differentiation, marketing, Agile execution	Competitive analysis, unique features, aggressive marketing	Shorter, Agile and iterative

***Table 2.1**: Project plan comparison through the lens of three archetypes*

This narrative is an ideal worldview of the mobile project type and those that can be seen for most of the domain. Based on the operating context and ground realities, mixing strategies across the actual project's planning and execution will enable the team to move forward in the journey.

Defining the backlog

The goal and requirement are key for any planning, re-emphasized multiple times in the narrative. An individual who is new to planning or from a Waterfall ideology could assume that a project can only start after the entire requirements have been finalized. This assumption is incorrect in an incremental SDLC. The chapter will help to pivot away from this thought process for an individual to accommodate a model supporting the incremental delivery and planning. The stakeholders define the vision or goal for the product or service offering from which the team identifies the high-level epic and backlog. This process, which will give the breakdown and realization of the vision, will be a list of user stories and tasks within the scope of the vision. This terminology might slightly vary from team to team.

In the context of the chapter, the following definitions are used:

- **Epic**: An epic is a group of larger functional modules. For example, login functionality, which includes frontend, mobile, and backend, is an epic.
- **User story**: The user story, on the other hand, is one level below the epic, an independent piece of functionality. An example of a user story could be the login page design, and if the login page itself is complex, it can be subdivided into login with username and password, or login with mobile number and password, etc. Multiple user stories will be under one epic.
- **Task**: An independent item used to logically define and understand the quantum of work within a user story.

Planning would be robust as long as the details available are accurate. The idea of coming up with very accurate details is a double-edged sword. Planning should not turn out to be a never-ending loop of discussion of things that delay the engagement. It would be ideal to time-box the discussion, ensuring the team continues making progress in the other areas as well. One can see this tactic replicated in operating system scheduling or threading, where resources are effectively utilized without requiring the hardware to wait, thereby minimizing idle time. The incomplete details are incrementally enriched by focusing only on the necessary details without affecting the plan creation.

Walking through a real-life example of creating a backlog for the Login journey for a mobile application will help the reader understand concepts better. The task of creating the backlog can take two routes: when there are unknown dependencies at the time of backlog creation, and when there are no dependencies. In this section, the design dependency is considered to explain the effect of the same in planning in the previous two situations:

- **Designs are not ready**: The possibility of coming up with an accurate plan would be difficult in this case. The best way to get to a realistic number is to have a stakeholder who has experience in building such a system to get a number that is not far off from reality. The team can come up with a ballpark number here, and once the designs are ready, these numbers could be revisited. The risk for the plan is that, as there is no visibility on how the product looks, the team may have to rely on the imagination of the stakeholder.

- **Designs are readily available**: In this case, the team can get a more realistic task breakup of the epic. The slight possibility of variance can be factored into the plan to accommodate any feedback after implementation. Compared to the situation where the team does not have the design, the variance in this case will be minimal.

Table 2.2 is a backlog for login when designs are not ready:

Epic	User stories	Task	Assumptions
Login	Login with mobile number and password	• Design the UI with two text fields. • Integrate the backend service.	• The screen will be simple with two text fields. • The screen will have validation. • On validation error or login error will be shown as simple alert.
	Login with username and password	• Design the UI with two text fields. • Reuse the backend service layer from the previous task.	Assumption same as above task for login with mobile number and password.
	Login with MPIN	• Single text field login • Integrate backend service	• Single text field • Show Static text • Allow number keypad

***Table 2.2**: Backlog when designs are not ready*

Table 2.3 is a backlog for login, when designs are ready:

Epic	User stories	Task	Assumptions
Login	Login with mobile number and password	• Design the UI with two text fields. • Integrate the backend service. • Switcher to be designed to change from mobile number login and username login. • Error shows as text field border change for validation with red icon on text field. • For server error, show as error label below the text field. • Login with mobile number has auto-population of country code **Out of scope item**: Forgot password.	
	Login with username and password	• Design the UI and behavior like login with mobile number in same page controlled via segment switch user interface. • Reuse the backend service layer from the previous task.	
	Login with MPIN	• Single text field login • There is reset MPIN button • There is a login with OTP button at the bottom of screen • Enable the biometric authentication button at the bottom of the screen. • Integrate backend service **Out of scope item**: Building the functionality for biometric, reset MPIN or login with OTP will be separate stories.	• Single text field • Show static text • Allow number keypad

***Table 2.3**: Backlog when designs are ready*

A pattern can be noticed in *Tables* 2.2 and 2.3, where the assumptions are more prevalent in the case of backlog without design. The number of assumptions is less for the backlog of *Table* 2.3, where the design is available. The level of concrete details that the team can come up with is higher for *Table* 2.3 with the design available. The best-case estimate for the item in the second table shall be more realistic.

Neither situation should stop us from creating the project plan. The planning should still go on. At some point, when the design is clear, the plan could be revised and adjusted accordingly.

Thus, in a similar fashion, a product owner, business analyst, and a tech person can collaborate to create the epic, user stories, and tasks for the mobile application, which is the data used for planning.

Estimation types

Estimation is a process to calculate an approximate value of the quantum of work based on the available information at hand, combined with any past experiences. The idea is to take an educated guess when the exact data is unavailable. Writing a software program is a creative and logical activity. The unpredictability of creative activity makes it difficult to calculate an accurate time to complete the activity, which is not ideal. In the software world, there is an alternate means of estimation that helps to create a project plan.

Time-based estimate

Consider the scenario of the vehicle traveling at a speed of 50 miles/hour. It must cover 100 miles to reach its destination. The speed does not change, and there are no interruptions. The vehicle, without making any stops, continuously travels at the same speed. One can confidently say that the vehicle will reach its destination in two hours.

Life would have been simple if a method similar to one used in the preceding example to calculate time to reach the destination, could be applied in the software development world as well, to determine the timeline to complete work. In the enterprise, there is a chance that the teams/individuals who have been involved in planning need not necessarily be involved in implementing. This could be due to the unavailability of an individual during the execution. Such situations can lead to a case where an estimation based on time is not accurate. A more subtle reason to look at is that the timeline-based estimate could vary from individual to individual. The context and the strength of the individual who did the estimation may be totally different from the person who is implementing the feature. Other than the people factor, there are factors such as organizational activity, team meeting, understanding of the system, and capability aspect that can influence differently for different individuals. All these have a nondeterministic nature, which supports the idea that different individuals take different times to complete this task. The implication is that if an individual says a particular task could be completed in two days, one cannot guarantee that someone else would complete the same task within the same time. A second scenario could occur where the same individual who has done the estimation picks up a story and cannot meet the timeline as planned earlier due to oversight. In either of the cases where an invalid estimation occurs, there is an effect on the plan, or it will need more time than regular work hours. In real life, there are situations where the team has even resorted to blaming the estimator for being inaccurate, which is not a healthy work culture. The time-based estimate, thus, is an anti-pattern for an organization and will work against achieving a self-organized, high-performing team. Thus, it is highly recommended not to think in terms of days while arriving at an estimate for a user story. The evaluation of the self-organized team's performance metrics should be based on value and quality delivered rather than just the speed of completion.

Relative estimation

The process of comparing and sizing the work relative to a predefined quantum of work and leveraging the same to quantify the total scope is relative estimation. In relative estimation, a yardstick will be defined to indicate the story's complexities instead of the time required to complete it. The yardstick is psychological in nature in comparison to a constant time value. Consider an example of the travel time like the example of a vehicle in the previous section. In the case of relative estimation, the idea of speed/velocity will be mentioned in relation to a reference, for example, the car travels faster than a person walking. There will be no mention of concrete speed. Instead, a perceivable baseline that an individual can relate to would be used, which can help make comparisons.

The following are the steps involved in the relative estimation:

1. Identify the base story and assign relative sizes to the story.
2. Define the task for the base stories.
3. To estimate a new story, compare the story with the base story.
4. Assign the relative size to the new stories for the comparison consensus.

Note: **Later in the chapter, there are sections that translate the theory to practice via an exercise-led explanation of the estimation. The idea of this approach in the chapter is to help understand the estimation technique better.**

Base story and relative size

A base story is a known piece of work that can be considered as a reference point. Consider an imaginary situation in which there are five boxes that weigh differently. You have the superpower to tell which box weighs more. This superpower gives the flexibility to arrange the boxes in the ascending order of weight. When a new box comes to the ecosystem, with this superpower, you will be able to gauge where the new box fits in. Defining the base stories will give such a superpower in the context of estimation. The estimation exercise involving multiple individuals who have the superpower will help in reaching a common consensus by averaging and minimizing the effect of any error. The value that denotes the complexity of a story is called the relative size. In the absolute start, where there is nothing to relate to, the base stories are defined by choosing reference stories from the backlog that anyone can relate to easily and assigning the story size to these. The story size assignment should be done by an SME who has the skill and experience to execute these stories.

This process of defining the user stories and agreeing on the size amongst the group is called the baselining of user stories. The baseline is associated with either of two popular choices of relative sizes: T-shirt sizing and story points. The intent is the same for both. In general, T-shirt sizing is more abstract in nature and can be used to provide a quick, high-level estimate without getting into too many details, whereas the story point estimation gives a quantitative scale. A story point size is typically a series of Fibonacci numbers. (e.g., 1, 2, 3, 5, 8) which is a general convention. The use of Fibonacci prevents the cognitive bias of going back to time-based estimation if the scale is linear in nature. The non-linearity of the Fibonacci helps offset the uncertainty that comes with larger stories with huge unknowns. The T-shirt size, on the other hand, uses XS, S, M, L, and XL as the convention instead of numbers. Using the T-shirt size benefits a person who is a novice in relative estimation and comes from a background where the estimates were mentioned in days. Using the T-shirt size has a higher probability of avoiding the possibility of falling into the trap of comparing the story sized in days. Creating a release plan requires an approximation of the number of stories that can be completed. This approximate number, which represents the total relative size of the stories, is referred to as raw velocity. Since the size is relative, irrespective of which story is executed or referenced, as long as the sizes are equivalent, the raw velocity ideally should not be affected. In case of T-shirt size, to do the planning to fit the release timeline, there should be some mechanism to quantify the T-shirt size that can be completed per iteration. An example would be to define the mapping as S = 1 point, M = 3 points, L = 5 points, and based on the same, the total capacity per iteration can be calculated and communicated to stakeholders numerically. Doing math only with T-shirt size and presenting numerical summaries to stakeholders might be a challenge.

Note: **For a release plan preparation, it will be better to use story points as it is easy to present a reference to stakeholders in terms of numbers, unless the estimate is for responding to a proposal where the details and planning are at a very high level. The chapter uses the terms story point and story size. Both terms mean the relative complexity value assigned to the user story.**

Defining the base stories for estimation

The idea of defining the base story is to pick five user stories that will be the reference stories. Five is a standard number that is prevalent in most projects. The implicit assumption is that there will only be five sizes required; any other stories that have greater complexity can be logically broken or split into smaller, logically coherent user stories.

These base stories should be such that anyone who is part of building a feature in the application shall be able to relate to these and compare the complexity. Any new stories that come their way should be relatable to these base stories and could be assigned to the nearest size. The largest story size is kept as a placeholder for very large stories that contain significant unknowns. *Table 2.4* depicts base stories and the estimates defined in both T-shirt and story point sizes. Once an individual reads the task associated with the story, they can clearly get a sense of the complexity that justifies the relative size. This can be used to compare and estimate other stories in the backlog:

User story	Task	Relative size		Comments/ Assumptions
		T-shirt	Story	
Login screen UI design	1. Design the layout with a button and two text fields.	XS	1	
Login with pin with backend integration	1. Design the layout with a text field. 2. Integrate a backend. 3. Design the static button without action for login with OTP and biometric login.	S	2	
Setting up push notifications on the mobile side	1. Creation of certificate. 2. Enabling permission. 3. Integrating the OS method. 4. Calling the backend service to pass the registration token. 5. Handle the receipt of the push notification. Showing the alert with a message will be the scope.	M	3	Deep linking will be out of scope.
Forgot password	1. Design screen to get the mobile number and email. 2. Integrate the forgot password initiation server call with email and mobile number. 3. If the forgot password service is successful then user is taken to the OTP screen. The field to enter the OTP received should be developed. There will also be a new password and confirm password text field after OTP validation. 4. Auto populate from SMS for mobile number field. 5. Integrate the backend service to take the OTP and new password. 6. Password client validation to be checked. 7. Show appropriate error message following the error convention of application.	L	5	The error convention will be designed separately.
Integrate biometric login	1. Register and enable the usage of biometric SDK for App quick login. 2. Handle the different biometric for different device. Example, Face ID, fingerprint or pattern lock. 3. Handle the failure scenario where biometric is disabled at mobile OS level. 4. Handle biometric authentication failure. 5. Keychain integration for storing the credentials. 6. Clear the keychain for forgot password flow and post error handling.	XL	8	

Table 2.4: *Baseline stories*

Estimating the remaining backlog

The key ingredient of a good relative estimate is to have a diverse group with enough context to estimate. If such a group challenges each other on the estimate, the possibility of amalgamation of wisdom to make the estimate effective is high. The team should collaborate and be powered by a respectful debate to come up with a common consensus on a story size in relation to the base stories created. A voting mechanism is used to estimate the story.

In practice, most teams estimate with five base story sizes as discussed earlier. The team should divide the user stories into smaller pieces of work with logical coherence. Even though the base stories are defined beyond 5 and L, the team can mandate practicing estimating stories up to the size of 5 or L. For those stories that go beyond this size, trying to split them into smaller pieces of work is recommended. The highest story point should be reserved for a user story that has maximum unknown or very high complexity. For stories with unknowns, the next step to enrich will be when clarity is obtained; these stories could be split.

For estimation, the first step for the group of developers is to get an understanding of the user stories and tasks. There will be a product SME who will explain the stories and answer any queries. The next step is to be familiarized with the base stories and the estimates. After this, the team can leverage any online tools to cast the vote after getting enough clarity. The SME could mediate the session for voting. Once the voting is done, the results are projected and debated if there is a difference. The debate should reach a consensus to finalize the story point for the story estimated. The diversity specified at the start of the section for the group is achieved by mixing the roles, and thus, various stakeholders can be part of this exercise.

In a voting session, there could be a possibility where votes are extreme from multiple individuals. For example, one developer might have cast a vote for a one-story pointer for a particular story while others might have cast a five-story point for the same story. The next step for such a case would be to discuss and debate within the group on the reasons and try to reach a common ground, and conclude. The story point that is unanimously agreed upon by the group shall be assigned to the story. The idea is to get unbiased and realistic relative estimates.

With the understanding gained so far, the reader will be equipped to estimate the stories in the backlog. With this knowledge, let us try to estimate a user story: order history list to practice the theory.

The following are tasks for the order history list user story from the backlog:

- Design the list.
- There are two sections, which are in the form of a tab listing the open and the completed orders, following the same design for a list.
- The single API will give the pending and completed orders. Filtering the data will be client-side logic.
- The two sections are a slidable tab where the UI component is readily available.
- On scroll, there is a header animation.

When the order history list story is compared with the base stories listed in *Table 2.4*, the complexity falls between a two-pointer and a three-pointer. Take a pause to put some thought into this statement. The conclusion can be reached by comparing the tasks for both, these will justify the statement. The team at this juncture, being in the estimation session, must conclude on an estimate to move forward by agreeing on one of the options.

> Note: **The story point shared is influenced by the empirical knowledge of the author. For simplicity in understanding the estimation process, the context of the author is used as the basis for the story being estimated. Someone may estimate the story with a different estimate depending on their experience. However, while working in the team the idea of coming up with the base story is to keep the estimate consistent with the rationale used and to compare it when assigning the new estimate.**

The next step is to get to the discussion. A conclusion could be reached by comparing the task with the base stories. In this example, one will find that the task, when compared to a one-pointer or a two-pointer story in terms of the amount of work, is more complex, and when compared to a three-pointer base story, it might seem the task for the order history list is less complex.

In this scenario, where team members are not able to precisely point out the relative story, the team can take one of the following approaches:

- Assign a closer estimate, if the team can debate and conclude.
- Assign the aggressive estimate and add some buffer to the plan.
- There might be multiple stories where the team might reach such an impasse. The team can adjust the overall for the plan. By choosing a lower bound in one story and choosing a higher bound in some other, so that the effect averages out, is a strategy the team can decide on.
- Ideally, adjusting story points will work out while choosing between the story points 1, 2, and 3. In cases where team members debate for story points between 5 and 8, or 3 and 5, where the margin between the two is large, the recommendation would be to split and break the story into smaller stories. The two parties involved in the debate should try to look at the different tasks to be performed and see if the complexity can be made more objective to be comparable with the base stories.
- In a case where a user story does not have enough clarity, the strategy best suited would be to record the best-case and worst-case estimates. The estimates will be in a range and can be appropriately adjusted when clarity is obtained.

Which of the approaches works best in all cases is a challenging question. The context of the discussion and the common sense of the group should dictate the choice.

Note: **In case there is only one person to estimate and create the plan, one may have to trust the experience the person brings to the table to make the right decision. The impact of biased estimates, if any, due to estimation done by a single developer, could be corrected in the raw velocity exercise as well, and the same will be explored more in the subsequent section of the chapter.**

Determining raw velocity

After creating a backlog and assigning the relative estimate for the user stories, the next step is finding raw velocity. Raw velocity is the ballpark number of user stories that a team would complete in a defined interval. In the case of Scrum, the defined interval is called an iteration.

Typically, to get the raw velocity, the list of user stories should be selected to create 3-4 groups of sample user stories. The following guidelines are recommended when selecting the user stories for different sample spaces:

- Each group should have a mix of all the different relative-sized stories.
- Each group should not have the same set of user stories.
- The user stories should be randomly selected and dispersed across the different modules the team is trying to build in the application.

Once the list is ready, a group of developers who were not part of the estimation, but are adept at developing these requirements, is selected. To them, the entire group of the user story is shared, keeping the estimated value for these stories hidden. The duration of the iteration will be shared. The developer should then pick from each list the stories that can be completed as part of the iteration. After the exercise, each of the developers will have three values of story size from the different sample spaces that can be completed. For each developer, compute the average number of story points they have committed to across three or four sample groups. This average per developer value multiplied by the number of developers in the team gives the raw velocity of the team.

Note: **Industry best practice is to discuss velocity at a team level. Later in the section, actual velocity and the reason for using velocity at the team level are explained.**

Creating a release plan

The building blocks required to create the release plan are the backlog (with epic and user stories), the estimates for the user stories, and the raw velocity. Every project has a tentative timeline to complete, which is the go-to-market date. The go-to-market date will be one of the aspects that drives the release plan.

The cumulative estimation data for all the user stories, divided by the raw velocity per iteration, shall give the total iterations to complete the work in theory. For example, if the total story points for the entire backlog are 1000 points and the raw velocity is 10, this would imply a case where a team will continuously take 100 iterations to complete the entire backlog. The stakeholder would want the product to be live in the upcoming 10 iterations. Theoretically, with the math, one can say that this will be possible if the size of the team increases ten times. The possibility of theory materializing into action will be the result of creating an alternate release plan with an increased team size. Creating the alternate plan to meet the time and taking up more parallel work will depend on the following items:

- How many epics are present that are not interdependent?
- How many parallel epics can be picked up?
- Will the dependencies of the epic be ready if there are any? The dependency can be either system or design.
- What is the timeline for the readiness?
- Even inside an epic, are there modules that one can pick up and work in parallel?

The answer to these questions should lead to the total number of parallel streams the project can run. The possible parallel stream will give the number of developers that one can onboard to the team to do the development in parallel. Thus, the max team velocity is a function of the number of possible parallel streams as well as the backlog.

In addition to the functional backlog, there will be platform-related activity, non-functional requirements, an additional buffer for unplanned unavailability for the developer, tech debt, release activities, bug fixing, etc. The plan should include a buffer to account for these contingencies. Generally, project setup and initial tasks that lay the foundation for the project to be developed in parallel would be suboptimal. These foundation activities are also mandatory to enable other items to be executed in parallel. A staggered team onboarding could help to reduce the idle time or duplication. The recommendation is to gradually increase the developer after each iteration. This will ensure the preparation and set-up time without making another team member wait or sit idle. The maximum number of recommended people required is two to four, along with the lead and architect, based on the project complexity. Until the initial project setup is completed, running things in parallel is ineffective, as the initial iteration capacity will be lower. This will gradually increase to attain the expected capacity. The lower iteration capacity ties back to the total number of parallel streams planned per iteration.

Table 2.5 shows a sample release plan where it takes 5 iterations from I0 to I5 to ramp up to a capacity of 5 streams per iteration. The release plan in the table indicates that only 5 streams can be run in parallel for this application. D indicates the development, and T indicates the testing phase. The release plan is created with the agreement that the dependency for an epic will be resolved 3 weeks before starting the development.

	I0	I1	I2	I3	I4	I5	I6	I7	I8	I9	I10	I11	I12	I13	I14	I15	I16	I17	FUTURE ITERATIONS
Initial setup	D	D	D	D	D														
Login		D	D	D	D	T	T												
Order					D	D	D	D	D	D	D	D	D	D	D	D	D	D	
Portfolio						D	D	D	D	D	D	D	D	D	D	D	D	D	
Account				D	D	D	D	D	D	D	T	T	T	T	T	T			
Home			D	D	D	D	D	D	D	D	D	D	D	D	D	T	T	T	
Place holder for other features which are not depicted in the table.																			
Total number of streams	1	2	3	4	5	5	5	5	5	5	5	5	5	5	5	5	5	5	
Legends: D = Development, T = Testing, I = Iteration																			

***Table 2.5:** Sample release plan*

Once the product matures to a shippable product, an intermediate release to production can be planned. The release plan will give the stakeholders the ability to get a perspective on the timeline of feature completion for the mobile application. The stakeholder can use the release plan to make decisions related to the following aspects:

- Go-to-market timelines.
- Check if the team can expedite certain activities to plan an early go-to-market.
- When the possibility of adding more streams is not an option. An alternate strategy by prioritizing the task and reducing the scope, to get a minimum viable shippable product, can help to go to market early.

Estimation for proposal

For an organization that works on a cost arbitrage model of operation, conceiving a project is preceded by a need to submit a proposal. The proposal is to showcase to the stakeholders the approach and the timeline for project execution in most cases. The proposal document has more details than an estimation; however, high-level estimation with a release plan is a part of it. The proposal will have an abridged version of the estimation exercises, with the budgetary details and assumptions, and a callout for any scope change from RFP details. Project sponsors reviewing the proposal document will get an idea of the project strategy at a high level, which forms the basis to approve the project and plan. This approval marks the kick-start of the project, and the corresponding team of project managers, team leads, architect, and developers will join forces to execute the project.

The core expectation from the proposal is to get an overview of the plan and the viability of the project. This would thus mean that an abridged version of the estimation would be enough. The exercise of backlog creation and estimation needs to be repeated to get enough clarity for the user story after the proposal is approved. In the case of the proposal creation, the expectation in the details required would dictate the level at which the estimation exercise may occur. For example, raw velocity computation, etc., may not be required if the individuals involved have been part of a similar product. The team can take up the previous value from the experience as the raw velocity to plan. The focus will be to get an almost accurate epic split-up and high-level user story list to create a release plan, giving a fair idea of the timeline.

Note: **In practice, the stakeholder can misinterpret the mandate in the proposal as the source of reference for the promise of completion and escalate in the execution phase. This is a prevalent pattern in a politically charged environment. Appropriate negotiation techniques to convey the reasoning for the change should be carried out in conversation to tackle such a situation.**

Execution strategy

As the project starts, the release plan becomes the baseline to be followed for each iteration, unless the priority and the context change. The release plan can change due to external factors, like systems or design not being ready. The team should respond to this by adjusting internally, reorganizing the plan, evaluating the possibility of shifting stories, or finding out independent items from the backlog. The worst case, where rotating the stories cannot help, would bring the situation where overall release shifts. The go-to-market date staying unaffected is one factor defining the success of the project execution. The change in the go-to-market timeline warrants a discussion with the sponsors. During the project's execution, performance is monitored by tracking the velocity and the size of the overall backlog. The increase in backlog size and the decrease in velocity are clear warning signs that the release plan's stability is at risk. These indicators would necessitate the need for replanning. The size of the story could change if the basis of estimation is incorrect or if the product scope changes. The factors that affect velocity are discussed in the next section.

Actual velocity

Velocity is a great idea; however, the team should keep in mind that computing velocity follows a non-deterministic and non-repeating pattern from project to project. A velocity is very specific to the current operating context/group. The top factors that affect the velocity are listed as follows:

- Optimum mix of expertise in development knowledge.
- People factor and learnability.
- Understanding of the domain and business to take an appropriate solution.
- Domain complexity.

It is not ideal to compare the velocity of one project with another. For example, if project A has a raw velocity of 10 points per iteration, the expectation for project B, of a similar nature, to have the same velocity might not be accurate. The 10 points defined for this context will not be equivalent for the separate projects.

After running a few iterations in full capacity, the iteration completion can mark three possibilities, which would be to achieve velocity less than, more than, or nearly equal to the planned raw velocity. From this data, one can come up with an average velocity or story size completed over this time interval. The new velocity that replaces the raw velocity will become the team's actual velocity. The release plan shall then be adjusted according to the new velocity.

During the project's execution, the raw velocity computed during the release plan is assumed to be the actual velocity for the initial set of iterations. After the iteration is completed, the team will get the number of actual story points completed. There is a chance that this would deviate from the raw velocity. A consistently repeated pattern emerges in the team after a few iterations, and this becomes established as the actual velocity. Once the actual velocity is established, the adjustment is made with the new velocity in the release plan as well. The team members bring diverse strengths. The collective wisdom avoids depending on an individual contributor. The diversity may also influence the variability in story completion speed amongst individuals. Setting individual targets by the team is not a great strategy for a diverse group. Evaluating individual targets shall not be ideal, as there could be a difference between the number of points completed by everyone. The reasons for the difference could be skill, experience, or context differences. Thus, it is ideal to follow team velocity instead of individual developer velocity. The ideal situation is that the choice of story will have some randomness. The effort thus will be evenly distributed amongst team members over time.

Preparation and grooming

In practice, being Agile does not imply that anything can change anytime without consequence. Application development in Agile also requires the details of the requirements to be finalized. The change management should be carefully done to ensure deterministic behavior exists during the execution phase. The key theme is to divide and conquer. Instead of taking a massive requirement analysis, dividing it into logical chunks makes it flexible to accommodate change. This also helps the team approach the problem statement with ease. The logical chunk, when connected, will become the solution for the larger problem being addressed.

The readiness of the logical chunk is very critical to ensure the team is efficient in the development. The readiness encompasses the availability of the dependency and the details of what the end outcome should be. The level of dividing the logical chunk is contextual to the team and can be decided based on the granularity expected to increase the possibility of parallelization. The core idea of ensuring readiness should be centered around enabling development to move faster. The team's velocity determines the minimum number of stories that should be ready for the development team to pick up. This will ensure that there are ready stories to fill at least one full iteration and so that team always has work to pick up. The relevant items that need to be picked will thus be scoped for the team with relevant details once ready.

Team readiness need not happen in a sequential manner. The journey to readiness is the **grooming** process. Grooming is to make the iteration items ready to be picked up. The relevant stakeholders contribute to this by sharing the respective knowledge collectively, thereby ensuring readiness. The groomed items are the outcome that captures the requirements for the team to read and develop against. These will have details such as the acceptance criteria for the feature to be called complete, UI/UX details, the backend service details, and any business validation or rule to be followed. This is not an exhaustive list; however, the intent is to capture the collective wisdom of different stakeholders across the business, product, and technology functions in one place, so that the development team has clarity of what is to be done. The groomed item is a source of reference for the functionality to be developed. The tech approach and the complexity details can also be a part of the story, which the tech team contributes. Anyone reading the story should be able to get the context to understand what needs to be done in the execution stage. With these details, the team can do a revalidation of the estimate and adjust the iteration items that can be picked up.

Note: **There is a possibility of almost all stories becoming bloated as the assumption went wrong, or there was a pivot in the requirements. Such a situation will lead to the re-adjustment of the plan.**

N minus X

One can see that the collaboration is required in the process of readiness. The technology and business team are interlacing to define and refine the problem statement, which can reduce any miscommunication or misalignment of product expectations.

The grooming activity, which requires time, is factored into the planning and velocity calculation. While calculating the velocity, one should understand that an individual performing development may also have other activities, such as coordination, documentation, and meetings. The grooming activity is one such responsibility, and factoring this into the velocity is essential during the planning phase so that timelines are not missed. The developer involved in estimating should ideally consider non-development activities involved in the velocity calculation.

The team, based on the operating context, can decide the time required to start the preparation. In the previous example, for the development of the login page, the team can say grooming is required to start two iterations ahead, and the dependency thus becomes imperative to be fulfilled ahead of the grooming. The lead time is expressed as N minus X for the grooming cadence. *X* represents the minimum iteration ahead of which the grooming should be completed and N represents the current iteration number. For example, if X = 2 and the team is in iteration 5, then grooming for iteration 7 must already be complete in iteration 5.

Prioritization and readjustment

Being pragmatic about the release plan and go-to-market timelines has a direct effect on shaping a better product and a sustainable team. The idea of increasing the iteration capacity just to ensure the go-to-market timelines are met is an anti-pattern. Similarly, trying to backtrack and fit in the complete stories or tasks to the release timeline with a limited number of people is also a serious anti-pattern. The effect of these anti-patterns is to achieve more than the average stable velocity for the team. This might be what a stakeholder without a long-term thinking will push for and the sole aim will be to go to the market faster. While it is essential to look at options to improve velocity, pushing beyond the stable number may not be ideal. The aftereffects of this decision should be thoroughly evaluated. The tradeoff of the different choices made should be weighed to understand if these are not introducing any negative effects.

Prioritization, combined with negotiating the scope, is yet another way to meet the timeline. The approach thus will start by prioritizing a thin slice of the very important functionally essential to be released to production. The additional feature will later be added iteratively. Different schools of thought exist around the prioritization aspect, such as business value proposition, customer-centric proposition, etc. One commonly used strategy around prioritization is to segregate the tasks based on value and effort. In this, the stories are bucketed into four categories:

- High impact (value), low effort
- High impact, high effort
- Low impact, high effort
- Low impact, low effort

Thus, bucketing the stories into these categories would give the necessary means to negotiate and readjust the release plan, thereby defining a realistic timeline for going to market. Low-impact, high-effort stories get the least priority.

Another approach to readjusting the plan is to increase capacity. This comes with the evaluation of the possibility of parallelization. The team should understand that parallel execution adds operational overhead of organizing and coordinating, and a corresponding support mechanism or role should be introduced to ensure the coordination.

Leveraging AI tools to improve the planning stage

In the current software industry trend, AI is more than a buzzword. AI is a definite strategy that organizations should leverage to improve productivity. Starting from curating and organizing the content, taking a summary, or finding a correlation almost accurately using AI products is now very much possible. This option should be kept open for the team to leverage and improve the efficacy, attaining faster delivery. A few of the key areas that have been directly impacted by AI are as follows:

- Market research and competitive analysis.
- Feature prioritization and requirement gathering.
- Testing strategy and test case generation.
- Summarizing meeting conversation.

Most organizations follow the practice of whiteboarding ideas during planning sessions or sharing sticky points in collaboration tools. Associating AI tooling with these will accelerate the possibility of finding patterns and relevant data from the content via a prompt.

Thought experiment

Planning example_dress.com mobile app: Applying the knowledge that has been explained till now via a use case shall give an empirical grounding for an individual. The name **example_dress.com** refers to a fictional company used for illustrative purposes. The idea is to create a plan with a use case of creating a mobile application for **example_dress.com**. Going through the journey would be equivalent to experiencing a real-life situation, and through this, the concepts will become a part of firsthand experience in planning.

Context

example_dress.com has been in retail and selling apparel for quite some time. They have the business and technology leaders to do the market studies and separately investigate the different trends in the market. The leaders understood the scope for building mobile applications to do their online business as the next growth path. Having the mobile application was predicted to be profitable, with the market analysis indicating a fair share of the user base. There was a percentage of users who preferred online purchases via other platforms, like desktop apps, the web, etc. An interesting data point indicated that a high volume of consumers preferred mobile platforms. Business leaders were also keen to ensure and devise strategies to ensure a seamless experience with all the platforms for the consumers. The data gathered from the market analysis led the executive of **example_dress.com** to be very clear in the decision and focus on developing mobile applications and the backend system to cater to the large audience and scale.

example_dress.com put forward a team to do the analysis for the initiative. The team came up with a vision for the product; this vision was to build a mobile application that allows users to buy apparel. The vision promised a seamless search and checkout option via mobile for the end users.

The project execution was confirmed, and having a mature solution at the granular level could now be done by the organization. The appropriate plan and resource allocation for those items that had clarity could be started to kick-start the execution. The business context was readily available, and the team could go into depth on functionality with ease. The technology **subject matter experts (SMEs)** from the Android and iOS channels for which the mobile application was targeted also helped to estimate and define the solution.

Key highlights

The leader at **example_dress.com** shared a list of features that were available on the website, and a few additional features specifically for mobile applications. These features were defined as a must-have for mobile applications to hit the market in a year. *Table 2.6* summarizes the features:

Module	Key features
Apparel listing and details	Home screen, product browsing, personalization, product detail pages.
E-commerce	Cart, checkout, payment integration, order tracking.
Account management	Authentication, profile management, loyalty program.
Inventory and product management	Product catalog, stock management, order management.
Shipping and logistics	Shipping options, return management, delivery tracking.
Customer support	Live chat, help center, push notifications, feedback.
Marketing and engagement	Email marketing, referral program, social media integration.
Analytics and reporting	Sales analytics, user behavior insights, campaign performance.
Augmented reality (AR)	Virtual try-on, size recommendations.

Table 2.6*: Feature breakdown for the example_dress.com mobile application*

To understand the possibility of meeting the release timeline to build the features, the team had to create a plan. The plan would give a projected estimate to understand whether the development would fit within the timeline, how many individuals should contribute and the possibility of doing the development in parallel. The creation of the plan happens in three phases as follows:

- Creating project backlog
- Creating a release plan
- Refining or replanning

Phase one is creating the backlog. The backlog will have the details at an epic and user story level. At this stage, the team should ideally not spend time on defining the tech solutions. The focus should be on ensuring logical coherence of how each feature fits together to form the larger expectation of the system. The implicit assumption is that these features are feasible from a technology point of view. The team will look at the dependencies related to the epic. The relation of one epic to another should be analyzed to check the possibility of parallel and independent execution. The dependency between various epics affects the kick-start for the development of each of the epics within the plan. In the case of **example_dress.com**, as the team had enough context from the business perspective and the know-how of the existing system to be mapped to the outcome expected, the team did not have a hiccup in finding the dependency and relationship of epics. The catalyst that enabled the team to be on the same page was to have a visioning exercise, and as an outcome, the goal and purpose of the engagement were defined. The insights from the visioning exercise were relevant to creating the release plan and understanding the business context across the stakeholders.

Visioning exercise highlights: The current backend system was evaluated for readiness to be consumed directly by the mobile application. It was identified that for most of the features, except AR/VR, the team did have the APIs or third-party systems ready to be integrated. There were some APIs that needed customization in the e-commerce and accounts module. The current UI/UX was not mobile-friendly, and the website was not designed intuitively to scale down for mobile web as well. Therefore, having a UI/UX was imperative to ensure the successful completion of the mobile application. The team had to finalize certain tools to take care of mobile-specific non-functional requirements, such as application performance monitoring, crash analytics, and security analysis tools. These were also incorporated in the plan.

With the knowledge of business context and expectations, the team was able to curate the backlog, which defines what is required as part of the product. An epic categorizing the non-functional requirements is also added to the backlog. *Table 2.7* depicts a part of the backlog created for the epics:

Epic	User story title and description
Apparel listing and details	**Title**: Product listing screen **Description**: Categories, filters, and sorting options will be displayed as part of the screen.
	Title: Product details **Description**: The product images, descriptions, and meta information for the buyer will be displayed as part of the details navigation from the product list.
	Title: Image zoom-in/zoom-out capability **Description**: The user should be able to zoom-in/zoom-out product images on the mobile application.
	Title: Dynamic content loading capability **Description**: The product screen will have details that change and need attention to attract different audiences; it should have the capability to customize the data presented.
	Title: Product variants (size, color) selection **Description**: The application should have the capability to switch variants in the product detail screen.
E-commerce	**Title**: Cart **Description**: Cart functionality enabling checkout should be developed, allowing users to add/remove items, adjust quantities, and view totals.
	Title: Payment gateway integration **Description**: Proceed to pay call to action taking to screen with credit card, mobile wallets, etc., options to pay.
	Title: Checkout screen **Description**: Enabling the user to enter the address, shipping options, and order summary.

Epic	User story title and description
	Title: Order confirmation **Description:** Display the order success or failure message, with details to connect to customer care in case of any issue.
	Title: Promo codes **Description:** Ability to apply a promo code in the checkout process.
Account management	**Title:** Login and signup **Description:** When returning to log in, the user should be able to sign up via email, social media, etc.
	Title: Personal profile **Description:** The personal profile screen should allow users to view and update personal information (name, address, payment methods).
	Title: Password reset functionality **Description:** The feature allowing to reset password when the user forgets.
	Title: Order history and track current orders **Description:** The page to display the status of orders placed and to track the current order.

***Table 2.7**: Example backlog for example_dress.com epic and user story*

Note: **The exhaustive details are not quoted in the table; the idea is to showcase the process. The details for items in Table 2.7 can be included based on the comfort level of the group. The description can be detailed or minimal; however, at the planning stage, it need not be exhaustive.**

Table 2.8 has two additional columns: backend readiness and UI/UX availability. These are external dependencies and prerequisites for starting the epic's development. The UI/UX screen for mobile was not available. For creating a release plan, the delivery date of each of the UI/UX was required.

Feature	Backend readiness	UI/UX readiness
Apparel listing and details	Yes	No
E-commerce	Yes	No
Account management	No	No
Inventory and product management	No	No
Shipping and logistics	Yes	No
Customer support	Yes	No
Marketing and engagement	Yes	No
Analytics and reporting	Yes	No
AR/VR	No	No

***Table 2.8**: Dependency matrix backend and UI/UX*

Note: **In the case where the dependency resolution date is not available, the creation of a release plan will be difficult. However, for the organization, if the plan is required to create the budget allocation, an alternative strategy will be to take a ballpark date where the dependency will be resolved and create the release plan.**

The backlog created is now the source for the release plan. The UI/UX team defined the timeline, which is summarized in *Table 2.9*:

Feature	Design delivery date [illustrative]
Apparel listing and details	28-Feb-2050
E-commerce	14-Mar-2050
Account management	14-Mar-2050
Inventory and product management	14-Mar-2050
Shipping and logistics	28-Mar-2050
Customer support	28-Mar-2050
Marketing and engagement	28-Mar-2050
Analytics and reporting	Not Applicable
AR	14-April-2050
Dates mentioned are intentionally fictional for illustration	

Table 2.9: *UI/UX readiness*

For the sake of simplicity of the thought experiment, the backend readiness is assumed to be fulfilled for all the modules. The dependency fulfillment date has a direct impact on when the mobile team can onboard to full capacity. The total parallel stream possible will also decide the max capacity. Readiness for the dependency on the feature will minimize the idle time for the team. The possibility of starting multiple features in parallel also depends on the dependencies among the features. For example, the shipping and order tracking feature can be tested end-to-end after the implementation of the e-commerce epic, which includes the checkout feature; therefore, even if these are developed in parallel, the shipping and order tracking must wait until the checkout is implemented. In the current use case, the decision to implement shipping and order tracking is to be completed after the checkout is agreed upon by the stakeholders.

From the UI/UX dependency *Table 2.9*, it is evident that 14th April is when the entire design will be available, and there is a minimum two-week gap between each epic. Ideally, there will be some additional time required to do the analysis on the design shared overlapping with the technology possibilities before starting development. If the timeline is aggressive, it is even more critical to have an intermediate and incremental release of the design, to do analysis, and pass on any early feedback. This will also help the technology team prepare for the approach and plan the activities before the start of actual development.

The dependency matrix has the fulfillment date of the dependency. The team can leverage the data along with the estimate for the backlog to create the release plan. The priority of the stakeholder was to understand if their aspiration is pragmatic and possible to achieve. Given the past expertise of the technology team in building a similar system, the stakeholder will get almost accurate information. The nature of estimating backlog with less information was an approach in the incremental SDLC. The mindset of adaptive planning, as the clarity is received, complemented by the expertise of the individual, ensured the effectiveness of the SDLC. The stakeholder and the technology consultant had an agreement that in the event of planning getting derailed due to some unplanned circumstance, the possibility of revisiting and taking an alternative strategy was open for discussion.

Table 2.10 depicts the total estimate for features at an epic level after analyzing the granular details for each of these:

Epics	Estimates (story points)
Apparel listing and details	130
E-commerce	120
Account management	100
Inventory and product management	110
Shipping and logistics	50

Epics	Estimates (story points)
Customer support	50
Marketing and engagement	70
Analytics and reporting	40
AR	140
NFR	100

***Table 2.10**: Epic estimates*

The raw velocity exercise gave the data that a stream can complete 5-point worth stories in a single iteration of two weeks. The team decided to operate with six parallel streams; thus, mathematically, the raw velocity of the team was 30 points per iteration. The velocity calculation is simplified to an ideal condition and on the premise that every team member is equal. Technically the team velocity will be computed for the team as a single unit rather than multiplying per person velocity. The stream was not able to operate at full capacity until the design was delivered to enable a parallel stream of work. Moreover, the max parallelization that was possible per epic was three streams.

The release plan, as depicted in *Figure 2.1*, was curated with the information:

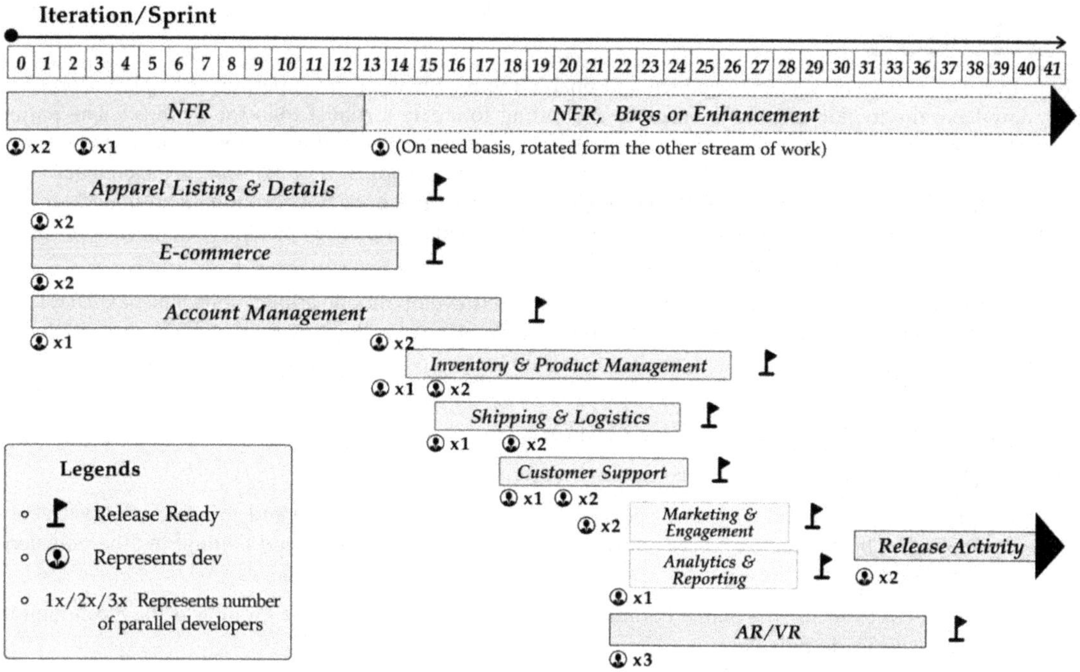

***Figure 2.1**: Release plan with sprint level mapping for the epic list for example_dress.com*

As per the release plan, an approximately 1.5-year (36 sprint) timeline was just enough to complete the development activities. The timeline incorporated the dependency fulfillment date to start the feature. Moreover, the timeline for the UI/UX did not allow the team to operate at full capacity on day one. In certain engagements, it is possible that the UI/UX is also developed in parallel. In such a case, the (n-x) cadence of the dependency resolution could be enforced to ensure the delivery is managed to give preparation time for development. Increasing the number of developers was an option under consideration; however, the operational overhead at the initial stage could have done more harm in the past experience of the team. Thus, in this case, the stakeholder decided to extend the timeline instead of adding more people. To ensure the testing and post-development activities are completed before release, each feature has a two-sprint timeline toward the end before release. One might possibly assume that it is only in the two weeks that the entire QA and post-development activities would happen. Such an assumption is incorrect, and one should understand what exactly happens. While testing and other activities will also occur in the last two sprints, the actual journey should have begun in parallel from day one and incrementally spread across the entire development cycle of the feature. The release and post-development activity is implicit and is considered in the release plan. The last iteration will conclude incremental testing and other validation mechanisms started along with feature development. The flag icon in *Figure 2.1* indicates the release readiness and marks the completion of all the development and testing activities. At this point, the team has the confidence to release the feature to the public.

In a typical project, which has a backend as an integration point on another system, the release can only be planned with a combined view of both backend and mobile. In the current narrative, the scope is limited to mobile only.

The plan that matches the stakeholder expectation determines the next course of action for execution. The expectation will be defined in terms of cost, time, and scope. When the plan is defined, there is an implicit quality factor that comes into play in the decision-making process. The plan defined for the use case in this chapter did not meet the time-to-market expectation. The stakeholder wanted the execution to be completed in 1 year. This implied the plan needed readjustment. Trying to optimize all three, that is, cost, time, and scope, will not be possible and will affect the quality factor. Negotiating to decide the order of priority amongst cost, time, and scope will influence the final decision of how the plan could be tweaked.

Conclusion

The objective of the chapter was to introduce and enable the reader with the superpower to plan a project. The readers now have the toolkit and the conceptual grounding to create a robust plan for a project. The pattern to keep a watch for during the planning for iterative delivery is a key focus area of the chapter. The reader should also take the contextual information and conduct experiments to evolve the journey of planning. The feedback from the journey should be monitored, and appropriate action to ensure that these are not becoming a bottleneck or overkill for the team should be taken promptly. Planning techniques defined are not a rule book; rather, guidelines to ensure a smooth journey and effective collaboration for the parties involved.

The next chapter focuses on the technology options available to develop mobile applications. The next chapter looks at a few key players in the market and explains the underlying principles that govern these. The information in the chapter will give the acumen to create a generalized opinion that helps to make informed decisions in a real project.

Takeaways and reflections

The following highlights key ideas presented in this chapter:

- Chapter narrative started with the importance and relevance of planning and correlated the Waterfall with Agile SDLC. The narrative covered an overview of these SDLC models and highlighted the prevalence of Agile methodology in the application software development segment.
- The key focus to ensure the plan is curated with the collective wisdom of a group was the recommendation to ensure efficacy in the plan.
- To accommodate risk in the plan, the modeling idea was presented in the chapter before the question and category to focus on in the mobile development project.
- Given the dynamic nature of the plan, the fundamental underpinning of the execution strategy will give a philosophical basis to create a plan. Understanding the project execution archetypes will help to create better plans.
- Creating and managing the backlog serves as the source of truth, outlining the goal and purpose of the engagement. To be effective in this, it is essential to focus on the critical and priority items. The yardstick will be the value this item adds to the product. The team emphasizes the importance of adaptive and

incremental maintenance to the backlog. The idea is to refine the content to subsequently replan and ensure iterative progress.

- Time-based estimation without enough data is sub-optimal. This goes against a highly collaborative environment bringing in a pattern of unnecessary pressure and inaccuracies. Relative estimation, combined with prioritization, shifts the focus to quality rather than just meeting deadlines. The team members must align goals and ensure that there is value associated with an action. Relative estimation also complements the creative side of software development, thus increasing the efficacy of the team.
- Raw velocity is the ballpark number of user stories that the team would complete in a definite interval. In the case of Scrum, the defined interval is called an iteration. Raw velocity while execution averages to an actual velocity, and the plan should be adjusted accordingly if there is a change.
- Velocity is contextual. For the same set of stories, if a different team estimated and repeated the planning exercise, the story points could vary. However, the overall release plan would remain the same if created by a group with equivalent collective wisdom.
- Leveraging AI tools is a key accelerator for the planning stage, with respect to analyzing requirements, summarizing the discussion, curating the action items, etc.

Chapter 3
Cross-platform Versus Native

Introduction

A mobile application can be developed in multiple frameworks, and for an organization, this presents a unique problem statement to think about even before the start of mobile development. The choice of technology to balance the business priority with the best result would be the responsibility one has to take on in the role as the SME in the mobile space. There is a need to shed personal biases and put oneself in the shoes of different stakeholders to decide the right strategy for the organization. The chapter presents the key ideas that one should have in the psyche to make an objective decision about the technology choice, ensuring that the grand scheme of things falls in place. The chapter will present information on some key players in the market and contemplate the underlying principle that governs these.

Structure

This chapter covers the following topics:

- Mobile development ecosystem
- Overview of a few cross-platform players
- Factors influencing mobile development technology strategy
- Evaluating a set of cross-platform toolkits
- Thought experiment
- Reusability in cross-platform
- Cost and timeline effectiveness
- Challenges, risks, and strategic trade-offs

Objectives

The purpose of this chapter is to provide a reasoning toolkit to make informed decisions when choosing from options for mobile application development. At the end of the chapter, readers will be able to facilitate conversations with stakeholders in the mobile application development process, in deciding on the development framework. The idea of the chapter is not to deduce the best technology choice. Instead, the reader will get the thought process and underlying principles that are foundational to governing the tech stack in mobile application development. Being judgmental can be avoided with the awareness of the idea presented in the chapter, and one will find peace with the idea that a tech stack working at one place does not necessarily imply it will work for all other cases. This chapter will empirically ground the thought process of the reader by sharing the point of view of a few cross-platform tools and experiences after using them. The major focus of the chapter will be on the two major players in the market, iOS and Android, as the target platform, examining how native and various cross-platform frameworks address these two dominant ecosystems.

Mobile development ecosystem

In the world of choice, a situation may arise where one cannot see the forest for the trees. The different choices and the biases in the development framework are some of the situations that a mobile development team would encounter. Quite often, for an experimental application where the effort and cost incurred may not be a concern but have the possibility to be recovered in the long run, the team can choose the most convenient strategy. The same ideology will not fit well for an application that requires targeting a regular and long-running business of an organization. Thus, the choice of technology becomes critical for such an organization. Technology choice is a careful decision that sustains the long-term vision. In the context of mobile development, terms such as development framework/tool and technology are often used interchangeably. In essence, the development framework or tool encompasses the ecosystem around the underlying technology that powers it. *Figure 3.1* depicts the ecosystem of mobile development in an abstract form. It focuses on different enablers that are part of the mobile application ecosystem.

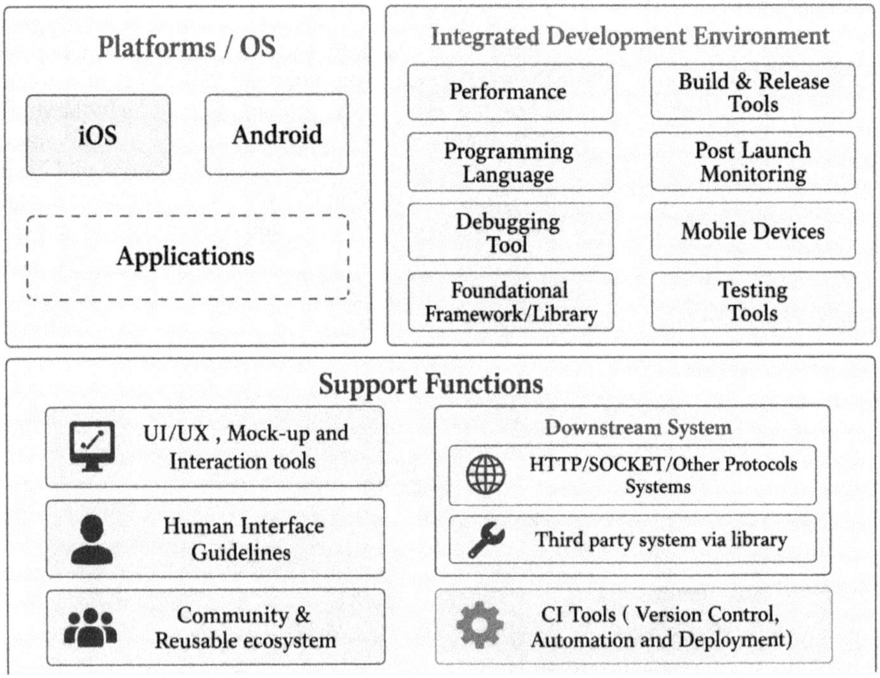

***Figure 3.1**: Mobile development ecosystem overview*

There are different development frameworks out there in the market that can be utilized to develop mobile applications. One of the prominent classifications segregates the frameworks into native and cross-platform. It is important to understand the functions each of these blocks fulfills at an abstract level, which will help the reader to relate to any mobile platform tool.

The meaning of the terminology used for a platform/tool need not be the same across. For example, the framework in iOS is equivalent to the SDK for Android, which represents the APIs for developing mobile applications. Additionally, in the iOS ecosystem, the term *framework* is also used to represent custom-built libraries and their equivalents from other development toolkits. In this chapter, the development framework is used in a broader sense and is more than just libraries. The usage of frameworks implies an ecosystem that encompasses a range of toolkits and accelerators supporting the development of software applications. These toolkits collectively empower developers to build applications for mobile devices faster without reinventing the wheel for a common or already-solved problem statement.

Native application

Native in the literal sense means closer to the origin, and in the context of mobile development, this translates to an application that is built on the tools and framework provided by the operating system provider. For example, an app developed in tooling provided by Apple for iOS. The code written for the mobile application gets compiled into the binary format equivalent provided by the native tooling and is mainly classified as a native application. This explanation is the most popular school of thought for defining a native application. The tooling surrounding the native application development forms the native framework for the platform.

For iOS applications, it can be done via Objective-C or Swift. One can build an application or framework in C or C++ for iOS as well, which is supported by the tools provided by Apple Inc.

For Android, similarly, Kotlin is the official Android development language. Android also supports NDK to implement parts of an app in a native codebase, using languages such as C and C++. The Android ecosystem application used to leverage Java; however, it is not the preferred language for development since 2019, as per the community sponsors. Kotlin, leveraging the Android SDK, compiles to an intermediate format called a DEX file, which runs on the application runtime environment in an Android OS.

Each platform has its own respective behaviors and nuances. In such a case, the best reasoning capability to emulate the larger picture would come from bucketing these items to logical equivalents. For a reader, it is important to draw parallels between the platforms. The process of comparison will help the individual to improve their reasoning capability and to think more broadly in an enterprise ecosystem.

Cross-platform

With native, the organization will be operationally managing different platforms and the diversity. This is the problem statement that leads to an interesting solution of a unified toolkit that enables the development of applications for multiple platforms. This toolkit comes under the classification of cross-platform frameworks. There are a variety of cross-platform players in the market, such as Cordova, Flutter, React Native, Xamarin, etc. The commonality of all these different options is that they are cross-platform toolkits addressing the multiple-codebase problem for mobile devices. The underlying internal structure for all these options in each of these shall be different.

Hybrid versus cross-platform

The terms **hybrid** and **cross-platform** are often used interchangeably in the context of mobile app development. However, in a strict sense, these are slightly different development approaches to building a mobile application. Let us look at the differences:

- **Hybrid mobile app**: A hybrid mobile app is one that is built using web technologies like HTML, CSS, and JavaScript, but is packaged within a native container (such as Apache Cordova or Ionic). This container allows the web-based code to be run on a mobile device as if it were a native app. Such an application has the capability to leverage the hardware features through a bridge, a mechanism within the native container that connects the JavaScript code to native code.

- **Cross-platform mobile app**: An app that uses a single codebase to target multiple platforms, allowing access to native APIs by directly accessing these without the intervention of the browser layer, comes under this category. These frameworks support iOS and Android, and even other distribution targets such as web, desktop, etc. The code written in this framework follows the strategy of writing the code once and deploying it for multiple targets.

In summary, one can say that a hybrid is a subset of cross-platform apps that use the web capabilities of mobile applications shipped within a container.

Overview of a few cross-platform players

Each cross-platform framework has a different ideology. Each framework follows a different approach for the problem statement; one platform to build mobile applications for iOS and Android devices. There are many players in the market. The idea is to look at and explore a few that present a unique set of ideologies possible in the cross-platform world.

Flutter

Flutter is a UI Toolkit, as advertised by Google, its creator, and is open-source, contributed to and maintained by a vast, growing community that continually updates and improves the platform. Flutter, as of 2025, supports web, mobile, and desktop platforms. One might be surprised to see the usage of the term UI Toolkit in the context of Flutter, and may be tempted to dismiss or underestimate the framework. The reasoning behind the advertisement of the UI Toolkit has largely to do with the nature of the ideology that backs it in developing mobile applications.

Flutter brings forward the cross-platform capability to develop mobile apps by creating a 2D drawing engine of itself. The code thus becomes platform-agnostic. Flutter's rendering engine draws the UI on a canvas provided by the host platform that is visually consistent across-platforms. The rendering engine will sit on top of the native layer exposed by the platform. The elements that are rendered are drawn on a canvas provided by the respective platform.

A mobile application that has a heavy presentation layer and collects information from users needs to focus on the interactive convenience. Bringing such an experience to their fingertips is the ideal use case that thrives very well with the Flutter framework. The catch here is that the vast amount of default patterns in UI is inspired by Material Design themes. An organization can decide to have a separate style other than Material Design . Even in such a case, Flutter has the capability to build user interfaces that are beyond those available default available within the framework. The community is active to keep the prevalent and widely used use cases readily available. In most cases, if the team is following any industry-standard design, there is a high probability of this design already being available as a ready-made solution.

Note: **The first version of Flutter, known as Sky for Android, was unveiled at the 2015 Dart developer summit with the stated goal of rendering consistently at 120 frames per second. In December 2018, Flutter 1.0 was released.**

Figure 3.2 represents the topology view of the Flutter toolkit:

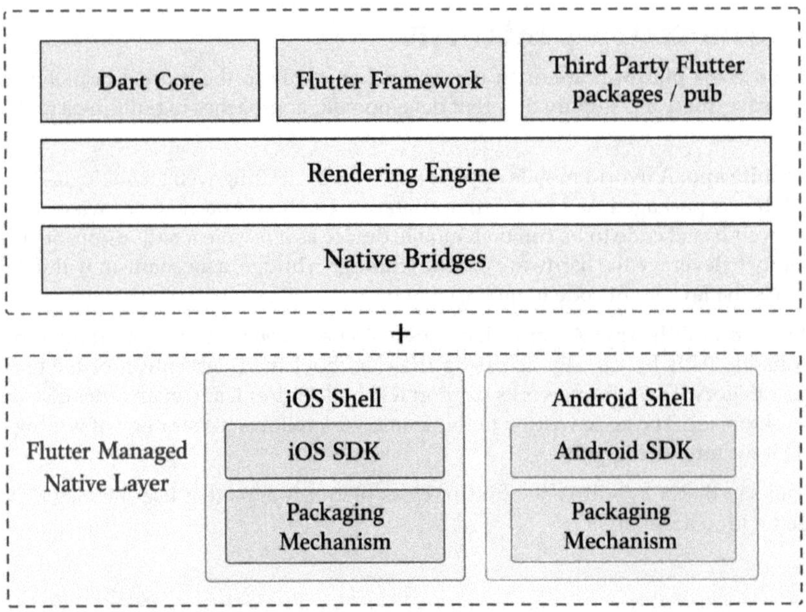

***Figure 3.2**: Flutter toolkit, topology view*

Internally, the framework Flutter renders the UI powered by the rendering engine Skia/Impeller using Dart as a programming language. The developer leverages the API exposed by the Flutter toolkit to write code. The compiled code runs on the rendering engine, which, when needed, communicates with the native via the channel to interoperate with the capabilities of hardware. Flutter is an open-source project. Skia was the name of the rendering engine used behind Flutter. On iOS, Skia exhibited performance issues with the dynamically loading shader function part of the rendering pipeline. Flutter introduced Impeller as a replacement for Skia on iOS (and later Android), providing a solution to the performance issue.

Flutter development is possible on Android Studio and Visual Studio Code. These IDEs have the performance tools to profile and evaluate the Flutter code. Flutter, when compiled, is hosted inside the iOS and Android shells written in native technology. This shell gets packaged to be shipped as an application with Flutter for the respective platforms. All these internal details are abstracted from the consumer of the Flutter development framework. The team developing the mobile application with Flutter does not need deep knowledge of the internal architecture. To be effective in day-to-day development, the team should be skilled with minimal information or configuration. In conclusion, for an individual who wants to build a cross-platform application, choosing Flutter will provide the experience of using the same codebase to create an application once and deploy to multiple platforms if the features are available in Flutter. Even though Flutter uses Dart, the code is compiled to the native binary equivalent. With the statement, a bigger question may be pondered in your head as to whether Flutter is a native framework. The answer is no. While Flutter compiles to native, the existence of the structure powering the Dart runtime and the rendering engine is the unseen layer in between, adding a small overhead when compared to the platform native framework.

Note: **Flutter has different mechanisms in debug and release modes. The Dart VM is present in debug builds, whereas in release mode, Dart is ahead-of-time (AOT) compiled to native machine code.**

React Native

React Native is an open-source mobile application framework created by Meta (formerly Facebook Inc.) and maintained by an open-source community. It has an increasingly growing community that contributes to and maintains the framework.

The ideology that powers React Native can be attributed to the usage of native platform elements to power the user interface and interaction, while segregating the common logic to be executed with JavaScript in a conceptual virtual DOM. There is a reason to call this a conceptual virtual DOM, which is unlike the React web version. In React Native, the virtual DOM maintains a tree to render the native UI elements for the mobile application. In contrast, in the web world, the virtual DOM can directly manipulate the HTML DOM. The UI components are exposed to a developer to consume as an API written in JavaScript or TypeScript. While the application runs, the native components send and receive messages both to and from the virtual DOM, coordinating the UI updates and event handling. The final package will have the JavaScript bundle shipped along with the respective platform dependency to function as a mobile application. The JavaScript bundle is the common piece that powers and does the magic to ship the cross-platform app.

As a React Native developer, most individuals may not worry about these nitty-gritty details in the day-to-day development. These are managed and abstracted to the consumers by the React Native platform tools.

React Native has a similar ideology, along with declarative style patterns in the web world. This thus enables individuals from web backgrounds to become mobile developers with the least learning curve. For a React developer to work on a React Native project, the investment required will be in learning the nuances of individual platforms to build and ship the products. An interesting feature unique to React Native is the possibility to update the JS-bundle at runtime, thereby supporting **over-the-air (OTA)** updates. Interpreting the possibilities of the OTA feature is important to stay informed about what can and cannot be done in comparison with other toolkits with the OTA. If there are any platform native features to be updated outside the JS-bundle, the capability shall not work. The reusability aspect of the code written for the React web project, if the architecture is right, is also an added advantage. Between React Native and React, the UI Layer cannot be reused directly; only the underlying logic written in JavaScript can be ported as is. For the UI, the conditional code, based on the platform, should be written.

This warrants the developer to be proactive in architecting and writing code in a fashion where the code can be reused to achieve the true code-sharing power of cross-platform.

Figure 3.3 is the topology view of the React Native toolkit. The figure depicts the React Native layer at the end getting compiled and bundled to the platform native host to be shipped as an installable for the respective mobile devices. The JS bundle layer, interpreted via a virtual DOM to define the layout for the native user interface on screen and host the business logic, forms the common React Native layer. The virtual DOM is an event-driven mechanism that interprets and coordinates the common code written in JS, unraveling the whole magic under the cross-platform.

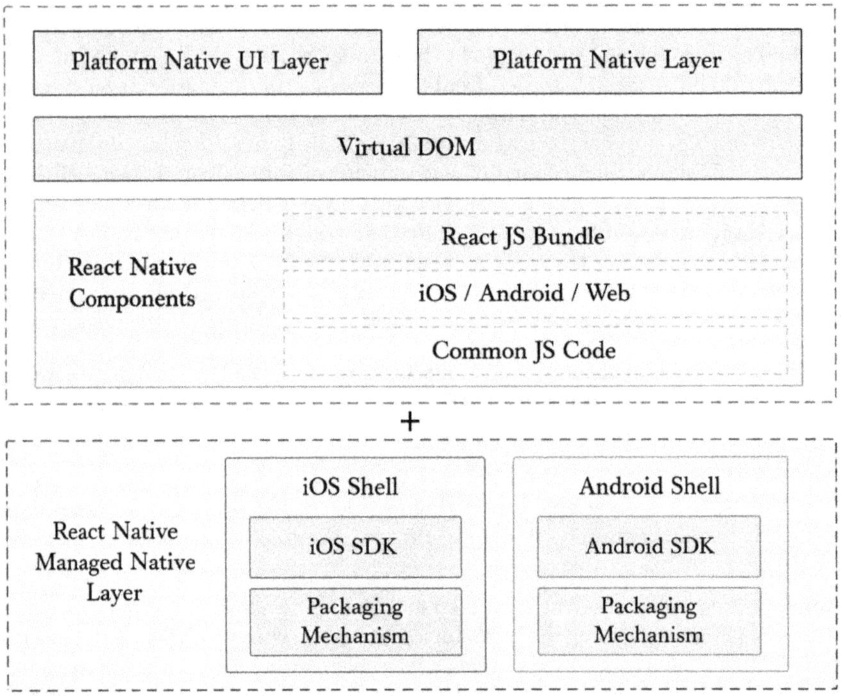

***Figure 3.3:** React Native toolkit, topology view*

An interesting occurrence in React Native was the introduction of TypeScript to improve the developer experience with a type-safe language. In the end, TypeScript is transcompiled to JavaScript. The popular opinion that a type-safe language implicitly prevents logical errors has driven the adoption of TypeScript in React Native projects.

Figure 3.3 depicts the React Native internal with virtual DOM. This was until the new architecture was introduced for the React Native community. The community has benchmarked the performance of the older version, and the result was not favorable. The shift in architecture has brought significant improvements to the performance of the application built in React Native. The reason attributed to the performance increase is the layer that allows the direct communication between the JavaScript and native code, eliminating the previous JSON serialization overhead. Turbo Modules enable lazy loading of native modules, reducing startup time. *Figure 3.4* depicts the new architecture:

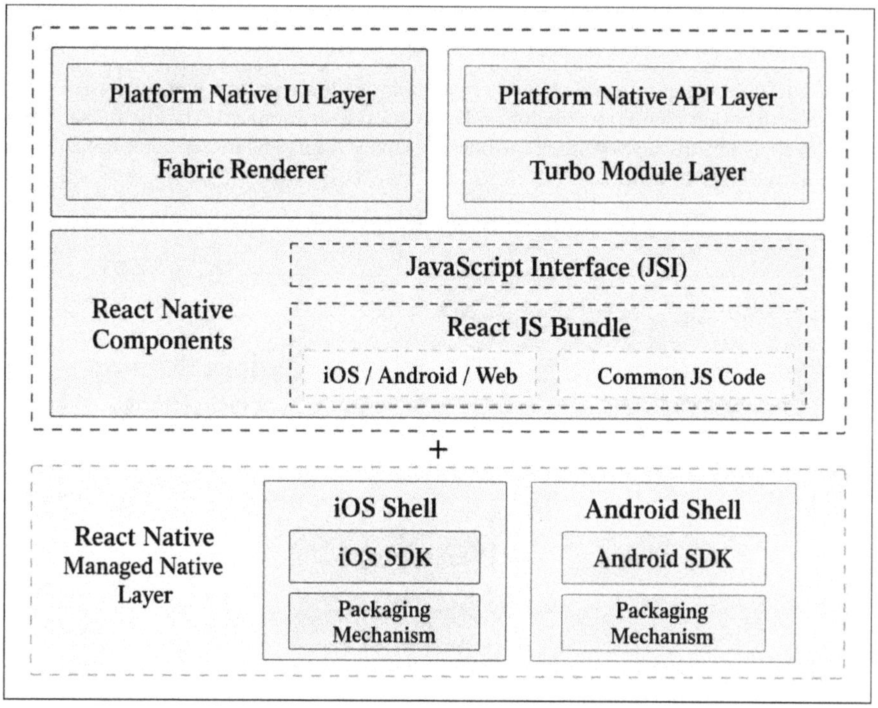

***Figure 3.4**: React Native latest revamped architecture, topology view*

In comparison with *Figure 3.3*, one shall be able to differentiate that the new architecture depicted gives the flexibility to compartmentalize rendering and API to be handled separately, leveraging an asynchronous event-driven ecosystem. This will enable the utilization of the computing power of mobile devices optimally without blocking each other. The new architecture introduces a mechanism that allows JavaScript to hold a direct reference to the native objects, and vice versa. This enables efficient bidirectional communication without serialization and deserialization overhead. This is made possible via the **JavaScript Interface** (**JSI**). The different module providing platform capabilities are exposed as module implemented via the JSI layer. Another component is the Fabric Renderer, the rendering engine which orchestrates native platform components. The communication between these layers is also managed via the JSI. The trio of JSI, Fabric Renderer, and Turbo Module layers ensure JavaScript code works for multiple platforms.

Note: **The new architecture became the default from version 0.76 (October 2024). Projects on earlier versions of React Native opt in to the new architecture. Migration steps are required to move to the new architecture.**

Cordova

Native platform supports WebView, thereby supporting JavaScript frameworks. WebView is a specific UI component that brings the capability to render and process HTML, CSS, and JavaScript within the mobile application.

The ideology behind Cordova is to build applications supporting the mobile screen sizes in web technologies with JavaScript frameworks and load these on the WebView. There are many JavaScript frameworks that are optimized for mobile. The entire UI and the logic layer will be developed in a JavaScript framework for Cordova.

The core platform features that are supported by the native platform are accessed by the JavaScript plugin system. Each plugin is a library bundled with Cordova that implements a bridge that maps to the underlying platform API to JavaScript. Cordova has plugins that take care of the native bridge. The plugins are inbuilt libraries that come along with Cordova. In the cases where the plugins are not available, the option would be to resort to writing a custom plugin wrapper to communicate with the native platform layer.

Using the web view will not be a good candidate for applications where performance is a priority. An app built in Cordova is the worst-performing compared to Flutter, React Native, or Xamarin. That being said, before the advent of some of the popular tools, Cordova was one of the best bets for a faster time to market for many organizations that were trying to establish a digital footprint.

Figure 3.5 summarizes the structure of a Cordova-based mobile application development:

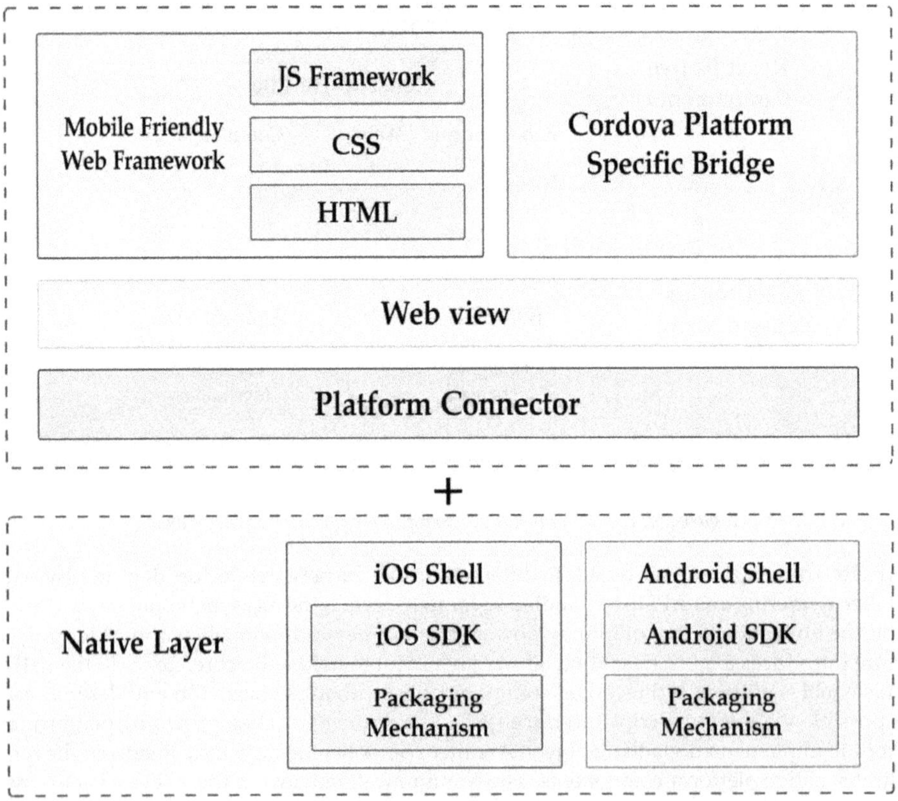

***Figure** 3.5: Cordova toolkit, topology view*

The platform connector exposes the functionality to access the hardware feature via the bridge, as depicted in *Figure 3.5*. The developer can consume this in the mobile-friendly web framework to create a web app codebase that will be bundled and packed to be shipped as a mobile app.

> Note: **The Cordova app behaves differently from a website. On the website, the pages are loaded on requesting the resources via a network. The Cordova app, on the other hand, bundles resources within the package and is loaded from the phone without the need for a network, thereby reducing the load time. The Cordova app has access to the native API to leverage hardware features via a bridge.**

Cordova is not currently the first choice. However, understanding the ideology can help an individual to reason about the cross-platform approaches in the industry. A similar toolkit is Capacitor by Ionic, which can be used with any web user interface. This is thought in the community to be a better version than Cordova.

Xamarin

Xamarin is a development toolkit based on C#. The main idea behind Xamarin was to enable developers with a C# background to build mobile applications. The underlying mechanism of how code runs is different for iOS and Android. The ideology of Xamarin can be attributed to two aspects, which are the Core C# framework and the C# wrapper for native API for the platform.

The C# framework is the one that can be commonly used for iOS and Android. The native wrappers are the ones where the framework provider has created a C# binding to native. This binding is a one-to-one mapping to the native function.

Xamarin applications are divided into Xamarin.iOS, Xamarin.Android and Xamarin.Forms. A developer will have to know both iOS and Android separately to build an application using Xamarin.iOS and Xamarin.Android. The common logic of an application that can be written in C# will be extracted and created as a library to be used inside the respective Xamarin.iOS and Xamarin.Android.

Xamarin.Forms, on the other hand, is built inspired by the .NET platform. The limitation here is that the UI design will be limited by the components and properties supported by Xamarin.Forms and will not be exhaustive.

The following is a historical timeline of the Xamarin evolution:

- **2001**: The Mono project begins (by *Miguel de Icaza* and *Nat Friedman*).
- **2011**: Xamarin is founded by *Icaza* and *Friedman*.
- **2011**: Release of Xamarin.iOS and Xamarin.Android for C#-based mobile app development.
- **2013**: Introduction of Xamarin.Forms for cross-platform UI development.
- **2014**: Launch of Xamarin Component Store.
- **2016**: Microsoft acquires Xamarin, integrating it into the .NET ecosystem.
- **2017**: Xamarin tools integrated into Visual Studio and Visual Studio for Mac.
- **2020**: .NET MAUI was announced as the successor to Xamarin.
- **2021-2022**: The release of .NET 6 was in 2021, providing the foundation for .NET MAUI; Xamarin was merged into .NET MAUI, which reached general availability in 2022.
- **2022 and beyond**: Microsoft continues to focus on .NET MAUI as the main framework for cross-platform development, with Xamarin becoming a legacy technology.

Internals of Xamarin.iOS and Xamarin.Android

Figure 3.6 depicts two ideologies within the Xamarin toolkit to support different platforms:

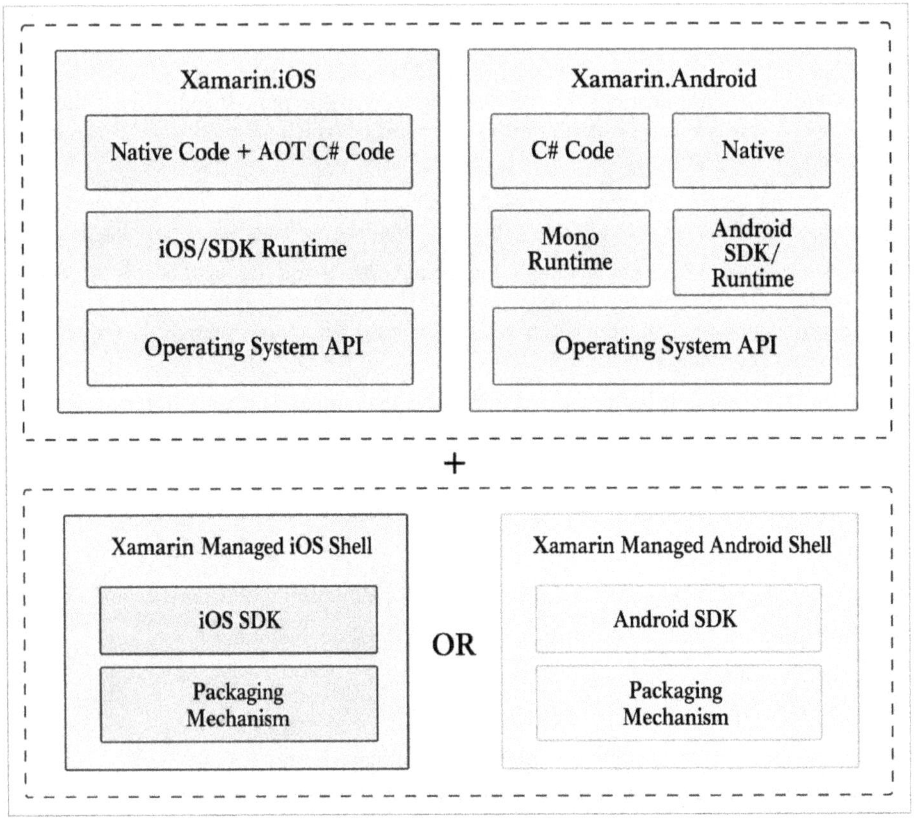

Figure 3.6: *Xamarin.iOS and Xamarin.Android toolkit, topology view*

One could find it counterintuitive to have designed two ideologies on a platform. The individual channels iOS and Android, being from different organizations, bring platform restrictions that influence the architecture or design of the cross-platform framework. The iOS ecosystem does not allow separate runtimes to be installed on the device, whereas Android does allow it. The influence of this difference is seen in the toolkit design. The Xamarin.Android works by leveraging a mono runtime installed on the device for C#, ensuring the compiled C# code is functioning on the Android system. On iOS, Xamarin cannot install a separate JIT runtime (as Apple prohibits it). Xamarin uses AOT compilation to convert C# directly to native machine code. Therefore, in iOS, this will remain like the architecture followed by Flutter, but without having a separate rendering engine, and the UI is managed by binding directly to a native layer, like the UI rendering on React Native.

Xamarin was heavily adopted by enterprises where the ecosystem was surrounded by C#. The toolkit has now stopped supporting Xamarin and has merged with .NET MAUI, which is a successor and improved version of Xamarin.Forms. The ideology behind the .NET MAUI centers on attaining near native performance by compiling the code to the platform binary equivalent, reducing the overhead associated with interpreted or bridged cross-platform approaches. .NET MAUI has exposed common UI components to build the screen and leverages the C# ecosystem to build a multiplatform app, sharing the code and leveraging a rendering pipeline by the .NET MAUI. The UI element specified will be mapped to a native counterpart for rendering, thereby abstracting the duplicated effort required for multiple platforms. This would be like a React Native from a top view, with key differences in near native compiled behavior.

Rapid application development frameworks

There is a different segment of cross-platform players out in the market. These cross-platform tools are very specific in catering to certain domains. Mostly, these are proprietary tools or frameworks from an organization supporting mobile application development. A proprietary framework for cross-platform development would need a support team to resolve the toolkit-specific challenges and queries. Like any product, the cross-platform framework will have documentation that defines the features available in the framework catalog. This documentation can be leveraged as a source of reference for developing apps. In contrast to an open-source cross-platform framework, the RAD frameworks need not necessarily have an active community, unless sponsored by the organization. The downside of not having an active community will result in the unavailability of ready-to-use libraries that can be consumed directly in the project. While evaluating the proprietary framework, one should consider the extent of features supported, matching the requirements of the mobile application that is planned. Enterprises can leverage a proprietary framework for the focused domain expertise of the framework provider and the comprehensive end-to-end solution for the domain-specific problem statement being addressed.

Nuances and similarities among cross-platforms

Now that we have looked at some of the players in the cross-platform world, we can identify a common pattern. The common pattern that one can deduce from all these frameworks is their shared reason for existence, that is, to eliminate the pain of writing and maintaining a separate codebase for each platform. This is the magic created by a cross-platform framework. The possibilities one can achieve with the cross-platform toolkit are limited by the restrictions enforced by the respective host operating systems supported. The intersection of features from the competing operating systems is what one can abstract via a common API. In the case where operating-system-specific features are needed, the cross-platform framework will provide means to bring in these capabilities. This will be either a platform-specific wrapper or a provision for extending the cross-platform, with the ability to incorporate operating system-specific features. Irrespective of the underlying ideology, in cross-platform, the core hardware feature will depend on APIs provided by the platform.

A cross-platform framework comes in one of the following archetypes:

- A virtual machine in between.
- Compiled to equivalent near native code .
- Native binding based.

These archetypes can be illustrated by categorizing Cordova, which falls in the virtual-machine-in-between archetype (via WebView). Flutter falls in the compiled-to-near-native archetype. Xamarin.Android in the virtual-machine archetype (via Mono runtime) and native binding for the user interfaces, while Xamarin.iOS uses AOT compilation and leans toward the compiled-to-near-native category for shared business logic and native binding for the user interfaces. React Native follows the ideology mix of virtual-machine-in-between and native binding archetypes.

The proprietary nature of the Apple ecosystem is a prominent challenge for cross-platform players to support or override device-specific features from the Apple ecosystem. For example, in iOS, the Apple ecosystem mandates that the release artifact be built or packaged by compiling on macOS and proprietary tools. This would mean the cross-platform team would be dependent directly on the Apple ecosystem. Some cross-platforms take care of abstracting these details from the developer. In this case, the configurations are specified at the cross-platform framework level, and the platform-specific commands get invoked by the cross-platform, exposing a common interface to the end consumer. Not every cross-platform needs to follow this design. There are cross-platform toolkits where the developer will have to explicitly follow the steps for the native application development for packaging. In such a toolkit, there will be two stages. The first stage involves the compilation and packaging of a cross-platform codebase, followed by the compilation required for native applications.

Note: The usage of the term near native is intentional, as the cross-platform does convert to platform native symbols for binary with the overhead to maintain the original language features.

Factors influencing mobile development technology strategy

A team will have to make the choice for development. The reasoning that the team shall depend on will be influenced by the operating context. A team should focus on exploring ideas that can bring objectivity to the discussion to decisively conclude and agree on the technology strategy for mobile development. Understanding the superset of factors influencing the preference between the two possibilities of native and cross-platform is the first step for the team. Going with native will not have further steps. However, in the case where the team has decided to go ahead with cross-platform, the team will be presented with the next set of choices within the cross-platform. Understanding the factors helps in reasoning the appropriate technology strategy from the myriad choices; concluding on what works is the crux of this section.

The reasoning that favors the choice of cross-platform over native will be our starting point. By swapping the pros and cons, a particular choice will suit well over another, as can be observed at the end of this section. One would see that these platform ideologies are from opposing schools of thought. The reader is encouraged to engage and leverage the ideas presented without introducing any bias into the mind. The key focus one should have is on the practical considerations and aligning these data with the purpose of the mobile application being built.

Factors favoring cross-platform

The following are situations where the choice of cross-platform shall be favored for the mobile development strategy for the team:

- The stakeholders would have postulated that operationalizing and mobilizing a team with different skill sets is a monumental task. The plausible reason could be the limited availability of talent in the market for native skills.
- For sponsors of the project, from a pure logical point of view, getting a tool that does the development for multiple targets, in principle, has a direct relationship with the reduction of timeline and cost of development.
- The organization is not planning to hire from outside but rather to leverage individuals within. In this context of the unavailability of skill sets within the organization, upskilling is required. Asking the team to take up the steep learning curve for two contrasting platforms may not be a great strategy for the organization with a low experimentation mindset and risk-taking appetite.
- Reusing the code across is another use case. For example, consider the case where using React Native can give an advantage of the JavaScript/TypeScript layer being reusable on the web or for the backend written in Node.
- Cross-platform can support more than iOS and Android. The organization would have a requirement to support multiple platforms, and thus, the operational overhead could outweigh the platform native benefit for the use case.
- An application that relies primarily on downstream backend services and makes use of only limited hardware capabilities is a strong candidate for cross-platform development. In such an application, the user flow and managing the state are critical pieces of work that the team shall encounter. Developing in a cross-platform environment gives the advantage of parity and reduces the risk of different behavior or bugs amongst the platforms. Interestingly, a side effect of the decision, the time associated, and the cognitive load associated with implementation and testing can be minimized.

- A minimum viable product or a proof of concept for a product idea, which needs validation to understand the viability and adoption, would benefit the cross-platform as the technology strategy. Choosing cross-platform plays an important part, where the investment needs to be optimal and limited.

Factors favoring native

The following are situations where the choice of native shall be favored for the mobile development strategy for the team:

- Given the opportunity, code written in the native language can attain maximum efficiency with respect to the platform's execution performance. The native platform does not have the bridge overhead of the cross-platform written to expose the contrasting capabilities of different platforms under one umbrella. Cross-platform would need a public API from the target platform and does not naturally allow the development team to leverage the internal framework. Thus, the cross-platform technology built on the capability exposed to the public via a native platform has little chance of excelling beyond native frameworks.
- Native apps offer direct hardware access, while for cross-platform, the *overhead* to access hardware features varies significantly. WebView frameworks are limited by the browser engine and communicate to native via bridge-based architectures. These architectures suffered from communication latency. Modern compiled frameworks like Flutter generate native compiled code, so the performance discussion shifts from bridge overhead to the efficiency of the framework's own runtime and rendering engine. As long as native runtime dominates the market, cross-platform will have to play catch-up.
- The brand and pattern associated with the device can create a natural habit for the capabilities exposed by the device. This could thus become implicitly expected behavior to the user, which, when changed, may not bring a great experience. Taking advantage of similar usage patterns reduces the cognitive load on the end user, thus making the experience better. The development toolkit provided by the mobile operating system provider will thus be closer to these definitions as long as the customization is minimized.
- If the application is focused on a rich user experience that aligns closely with the platform provider definition, going native would be an ideal strategy.
- When the engagement cannot tolerate the risk of technology becoming stagnant or failing to keep pace with native platform-released features, choosing native development will be the safer option. A recent example is Xamarin, where the stakeholder announced that support for Xamarin officially ended in May 2024. Following this update, the projects will not get any updates from Xamarin and will not have the option to keep pace with the evolving host platform changes. Thus, projects developed in Xamarin were forced to migrate to other mechanisms for development.
- An engagement that does not have the patience or appetite to choose the alternative for the cross-platform inefficiencies. An example situation shall help to go deeper to understand the same, and in this case, assuming the team is using react-native. In a later release of iOS/Android, an API was deprecated and had a keyboard issue if the code was not changed. Unfortunately, the issue is not identified or publicized in the community. The team handling mobile application development will never have a clue about what is happening when the component used inside is behaving weirdly due to this issue. This example shows the percolation of the bugs to multiple layers and the possibility for each layer to have its own bug. The issue present in the layer can have an impact on the application developed, and if the engagement cannot tolerate the manifestation of such risk, it is ideal to stay away from the cross-platform where there are layers of abstraction written to support multiple hosts.
- Engagement has failed once when executed with cross-platform for reasons other than an inadequate proficiency in cross-platform. A typical reason for failure is the inability of the cross-platform to match the feature support brought by the mobile operating system, affecting the profit and the organization's goal negatively.

- Particularly in the case of Apple devices, the platform provides means to promote the application in collaboration with Apple. To get such visibility and edge, Apple expects the incorporation of the latest tech released by Apple and leveraging the Apple platform's native tools. If the goal is to collaborate with Apple, the mobile application should be written in native technologies and tooling.
- The organization understands the revenue potential of the market and has the perspective that application experience is the key to gaining traction. For the organization, the ROI of providing a great experience outweighs the side effects of duplicate work and cost.

Factors influencing the choices within cross-platform

The options available when choosing native technology are limited, as the recommendation shall be dictated or influenced by the platform provider. However, in the case of cross-platform, there could be competing frameworks from multiple players. Once the team decides on cross-platform as the technology strategy, the next step would be to figure out the right option from the variety of cross-platform toolkits available. The cross-platform tools can be powered by open source or as a proprietary toolkit, as explained in an earlier section. These different choices have their own nuances. In most cases, the proprietary toolkit will be closed source, with the details of the internal implementation obscured from the consumer. The proprietary framework leverages domain expertise to get into the market, advertising the ease of mobile development and eliminating the need to reinvent solutions to match the industry's expectations. Additionally, there is a special category of proprietary tools built on extending open-source frameworks. The unique selling point that gets advertised is the ease of leveraging the framework to the extent that an audience with limited or no programming background can contribute to the development cycle. For example, a framework supporting visual design creation that can generate the mobile application UI code.

The remainder of this section explores the benchmarking themes used for the decision-making process within the cross-platform framework.

SLA or upgrade trends

The ability of a technology toolkit team to accommodate bug fixes in the native platform and the promise of moving to the latest version and updates released by the native platform are key considerations for the technology choice. At the operational level, when choosing a cross-platform, the condition will be that the toolkit is backed by a proprietary organization (with formal SLAs) or by an open-source community (where support timelines depend on community activity). If the toolkit is backed by a proprietary organization, then the team should start by understanding the SLA for the after-sales support for the toolkit and validate if it meets the expectations. For a proprietary closed-source tool, the obscurity in the technology could be a criterion, and the organization's appetite to accommodate this obscurity in the trust policy shall be a theme. On the other hand, for open-source toolkits, the trend in the community should be evaluated to establish a baseline and to check the trend of how fast the bugs are fixed or the upgrades to the latest releases for the target OS are met.

Community adoption and bug report

Feedback on the usage of cross-platform is the data that the team can leverage to validate the viability of the toolkit. All the toolkits address a particular class of problem originating in the minds of the creators of the toolkit. Therefore, the team should do the due diligence, evaluating the framework and giving the benefit of the doubt to the framework. For a team that is going to adopt the toolkit, the recommendation is still to evaluate independently in the context of the current project, without assuming that a framework's general reputation guarantees it will work for the organization use case. This will be a better strategy than simply following the popular opinion. The historical data from those who have used the toolkit and the stories of their journey using the toolkit could give data for decision-making.

Another theme is to look at the list of active bugs in the toolkit. The number of active bugs is one parameter, and the time taken to solve these bugs is another. There could be cases where the active bugs may not have any impact on the mobile application planned to be built as well. Having this information can give the perspective of what the team is getting into by adopting the toolkit and what possible technology debts the team may encounter.

The organization planning to adopt a cross-platform tool should look at the contributors and the supporting organization backing the cross-platform initiatives. These themes should be the data that help with the adoption of the framework. Evaluating the trends in the open-source repository can give a fair view of the adoption across the industry as well.

Availability of ecosystem around toolkit

The power of a toolkit is accelerated when there is a supporting ecosystem formed around it. The ecosystem helps in reducing the time required to reinvent the requirement. This could be better understood with an example use case of building an encryption library. Undertaking such a task requires a substantial investment and carries significant risk. An organization that wants to build a consumer product does not get the best leverage in betting on such additional tasks in most cases. Having a plugin/library that can be reused is a better strategy than developing these from scratch. The theme highlighted is the importance of having libraries and reusable solutions that can accelerate the usage of cross-platform solutions. This is a parameter to be looked at when comparing various options within the cross-platform in the context of the requirement and feature to be developed as part of the mobile application.

Extending capability

A cross-platform provider may intentionally/unintentionally skip supporting features from native, or there may be a case where a third-party feature available in native does not support the cross-platform. Additionally, the situation will be such that 95% of the use cases of the mobile application are fulfilled by the cross-platform. The question will be whether, for the 5% of use cases, shifting the technology strategy would be a wise choice. In such a situation, the decision-making would depend on the possibility of a cross-platform framework having the capability to integrate external features outside the cross-platform ecosystem.

Exit or migration criteria

Consider the scenario where the team reached a point where the cross-platform is not able to scale to meet the native feature. The team would want to move away from the current technology stack. For example, the use case of a product started as MVP, where the team is seeing the potential to grow. After evaluation of features, it is identified that native is giving the edge to build intuitive and performance features. In such a situation, dropping and discarding the MVP and starting a greenfield revamp is an option. Another option will be the reusability of the existing codebase and migrating gradually and incrementally. This shall be a better strategy. The capability of the cross-platform toolkit to be exit-ready, along with the ability to extract the part or extend the application to replace or remove the legacy features incrementally, forms the criteria to evaluate.

An ideal cross-platform with a good exit criterion should allow any codebase to be built as a binary that can be included in a different shell, a native shell in case of this example.

In conclusion, this section looked at the parameters that can be used to evaluate the various options in the cross-platform environment. These criteria are in addition to the base expectation of a cross-platform, which has led the team to choose cross-platform over native.

Evaluating a set of cross-platform toolkits

The idea of the section is to leverage the context shared till now and compare four cross-platform technology toolkits: Flutter, React Native, Iconic with Capacitor, and RAD. The RAD is a generalized version of a proprietary tool, as explained in the previous section. The intent of the section is to equip the reader with the prospective means of comparing the various cross-platform options. The section ends with a comparison of these four cross-platform choices.

Flutter offers an extensible framework with good community support and frequent updates for multiple channels. Flutter has a good ecosystem that is growing around, where there are a variety of packages available, preventing the team from reinventing libraries.

React Native is one of the most widely adopted frameworks with strong community support. The community support is higher than that of the competing technologies. The React Native community is focused on helping web developers get into mobile development faster. React Native has a relatively better ecosystem.

Iconic with Capacitor focuses on hybrid apps with a solid ecosystem for web-first development. It offers flexibility for web, mobile, and desktop apps, but is slightly slower in terms of updates and feature adoption. Capacitor components' responsibility is to bridge the native to the web ecosystem by providing access to the hardware and native capabilities.

A proprietary toolkit has a smaller community and vendor-specific constraints. The toolkit may offer solutions tailored to specific use cases; however, it lacks the flexibility and active ecosystem of the open-source options. One will have to depend on the toolkit organization to keep up with the trend. The same applies to any feature that is not available in the toolkit but is a requirement for the mobile application.

Table 3.1 provides a comparison of the cross-platform in the context of the SLA/upgrade theme:

Flutter	React Native
Strong community.	Strong community.
Roadmap-driven feature addition to the framework.	Regular updates. Community-driven patches and feature requests are common.
Backward compatibility has faced some level of code change.	Backward compatibility has faced some level of code change.
Limited dependency on native UI, however, as a consequence, replicating exact platform behavior has been challenging.	Dependency on native libraries has introduced breaking changes with OS updates.
Ionic with Capacitor	**Proprietary toolkit**
Supported by the open-source Ionic community and maintained by Ionic Inc.	Proprietary toolkit with fewer updates than open-source frameworks.
Updates do not match the pace of Flutter or React Native.	Updates depend on the vendor's roadmap.
Capacitor serves as a bridge to the native functionality.	Might not have rapid iteration compared to Flutter or React Native.

***Table 3.1**: Comparison of SLA or upgrade trends*

Table 3.2 provides a comparison of the cross-platform in the context of the community adoption theme. GitHub star counts in *Tables 3.2* are illustrative data points as of early 2025. It is recommended to refer to the official repositories for the latest figures.

Flutter	React Native
Rapidly growing ecosystem, with 168k stars on GitHub repo as of 2025.	Community where the web development knowledge can be leveraged with 120k stars on GitHub repo as of 2025.
Active GitHub repo and robust developer resources with great documentation.	Extensive documentation and active forums.
Bug reports are handled by the community.	Bug reports are addressed by both Meta and the open-source community.
Ionic with Capacitor	**Proprietary toolkit**
Popular in hybrid app development with a good community.	It is a smaller community than open-source frameworks.

Large documentation base, but less active than Flutter and React Native. The web knowledge will help, which is an advantage.	Documentation depends on the vendor of a proprietary toolkit.
Community support is available, but bug fixes and updates may take time.	Bug reports and updates might take longer to address, depending on the vendor's priority.
As of 2025, 51k stars on GitHub repo for Ionic and 12k stars for capacitor.	Limited community resources compared to more popular frameworks, unless the vendor opens marketplace with incentives.

***Table 3.2**: Comparison in lens of community adoption and bug report*

Table 3.3 provides a comparison of cross-platform in the context of ecosystem availability:

Flutter	React Native
Rich ecosystem with packages for almost everything.	Extensive ecosystem due to its long-standing presence in the market.
Excellent support for both mobile and web.	React Native support is limited for the web. The major web support is provided by React.
Growing number of plugins for native functionality.	Mature libraries for mobile and native integrations.
Ionic with Capacitor	**Proprietary toolkit**
Strong ecosystem for hybrid apps, with many plugins available for mobile and web.	Smaller ecosystem compared to the others.
Capacitor bridges the gap by enabling the toolkit to use native functionality.	Focus on specific enterprise solutions with limited general-purpose plugins specific to the domain.
Focus on web-first apps with solid integration across-platforms.	Integrations are more custom made for the use cases in the domain.

***Table 3.3**: Comparison in lens of availability of ecosystem*

Table 3.4 provides a comparison of the cross-platform in the context of extending the capability of the framework:

Flutter	React Native
Highly extendable with native code integration.	Can be extended with native modules in both Android and iOS.
Custom native modules can be added in both Android and iOS.	Limitations/engineering overhead involved with accessing deep native APIs.
Web support and desktop extensions available.	Web support requires careful architecting of code. Supporting web cannot be an afterthought.
Ionic with Capacitor	**Proprietary toolkit**
Extensible through Capacitor, which bridges the gap between native functionality and web code.	Extending capabilities might be more restricted, as this required support from the provider.
Supports native code extension for mobile apps.	Organization has the internal details to customize toolkit and is proprietary to the platform provider.
Extends easily to desktop, web, and PWA.	Customization requires more in-depth knowledge of the toolkit's capability, and the vendor defines the additional platform supported.

***Table 3.4**: Comparison in lens of extending capability*

Table 3.5 provides a comparison of the cross-platform in the context of exit/migration criteria:

Flutter	React Native
Can migrate to native apps (Android/iOS) but may require significant code changes due to platform differences.	Easier to migrate to native code due to JavaScript base.
Not fully compatible with every native feature. Migration may require rebuilding the app from scratch.	Migrating from React Native to native requires a rewrite.
Reuse possible. An incremental deprecation by incorporating the Flutter as frameworks with minimal engineering effort.	Reuse possible. An incremental deprecation by incorporating the React Native as frameworks with a significant engineering effort.
Ionic with Capacitor	**Proprietary toolkit**
Migrating from Ionic to native solutions (using Capacitor or Cordova) requires a rewrite and removal of the web layer.	Proprietary toolkits may make migration harder, especially if the toolkit's components are not directly reusable in other platforms. Vendor lock-in could make it costly to switch away from proprietary toolkits.

***Table 3.5**: Comparison of exit or migration criteria*

Thought experiment

The use cases discussed in this section present situations where the stakeholder needs to choose among the four options and define a technology strategy for development. Read the description of the use case and try to reason out what the developer would think based on the previous analysis of the four toolkits.

Which of the four options from cross-platform will have a better edge, from each of the use cases we will discuss ahead?

Mobile banking application for a global financial institution

A global bank aims to expand its operations by targeting mobile users. The idea is to provide seamless access to banking products to conduct transactions, manage the portfolio, and other features via a mobile application. The application shall support multiple mobile platforms (iOS, Android), integrate with complex backend systems, and meet stringent regulatory requirements. Security, data privacy, and compliance have variations with respect to the operating region. The time to market is a critical non-negotiable for the institution for this engagement.

E-commerce application

A startup wants to develop an e-commerce application offering a seamless shopping experience for customers on iOS and Android mobile devices. The team also wants to support both desktop and mobile web. The startup consists of a small development team with the aspiration to reduce the time and cost of building and maintaining separate applications for each platform. The team has exposure in development and leveraging web technology. Additionally, the organization wants to ensure that the app performs well and has a native-like experience on the respective platform.

Restaurant ordering mobile app

A restaurant requires a mobile app that allows customers to browse the menu, place orders, track their delivery status, and pay. The goal is to reach customers using iOS and Android platforms. The ask is to have a single codebase, saving time and resources for development and maintenance. These mobile apps are an additional convenience that the restaurant has planned to invest in.

Trading mobile application

A **financial technology** (**FinTech**) company wants to build a trading platform that allows users to trade stocks, cryptocurrencies, and other financial instruments. The application should offer real-time market data, secure transactions, personalized portfolios, and seamless access to global financial markets. The company intends to launch the app on both iOS and Android platforms but has limited resources and needs to develop the app efficiently while maintaining high performance and a native-like user experience.

Author's take on the use cases

The context of the operating circumstance and the experience of the author have influenced the decision-making explained in this section. The decision, when made as a collective activity, may be influenced by the diversity in the group.

Mobile banking application for a global financial institution

A RAD toolkit will be appropriate for a large-scale, highly secure, and regulatory-compliant mobile banking application. A RAD framework can be a potential choice due to its enterprise-grade features, out-of-the-box compliance, and banking-domain integration capabilities. An additional check that should be done is whether the vendor can demonstrate enterprise-grade SLA support. This toolkit is well-versed in the domain and has abundant exposure to the domain, and the features available will cater to most of the use cases relevant to the banking domain. If the bank wants to grow beyond just mobile banking, then the technology strategy option may be different.

Flutter and React Native are great for fast development with native-like experiences, but require more effort in security, compliance, and backend integrations for complex enterprise needs.

Iconic with Capacitor suits rapid prototyping of applications where a **progressive web app** (**PWA**) approach is acceptable, but will not meet the performance and security needs of a banking app without significant custom development.

E-commerce application

React Native is the best choice for a fully native-like mobile experience with the ability to easily integrate with native modules. The choice is ideal as the technology expertise that the startup needs to maintain could be leveraged from having a core team of web developers, which is operationally compact. Flutter is also a strong choice. However, as the team has expertise in web JavaScript framework, React Native seems to be a closer choice, optimizing the learning curve and faster time to market.

RAD tools are best suited for rapid prototyping or simple apps, but may not be flexible or scalable enough for an e-commerce application, as the inherent fee of the RAD may be an additional expense that could be avoided. Additionally, there is no domain expertise expectation to be met, thus not giving a great return on investment.

Restaurant ordering mobile app

For the restaurant ordering system use case, Iconic with Capacitor offers an excellent balance of cross-platform support, native access, and cost-effective development. It allows reaching a broader audience (iOS, Android, Web, and Desktop). The team can use a single codebase while leveraging familiar web technologies for faster development.

The need for native performance and a highly customized UI was not required, as the investment to maintain and build the tech should be kept low. Flutter/React Native might be a good alternative. However, finding the talent with the maturity to build for multiple platforms with web support would require a strong engineering-focused team and incur cost.

RAD tools are best suited for rapid prototyping or simple apps, but may not be flexible or scalable enough for a restaurant ordering system, as the inherent fee of the RAD may be an additional expense that could be avoided, and there is no domain expertise expectation to be met, thus not giving any additional benefit.

Trading mobile application

For the trading application, the expectation is to have high performance, real-time data updates, a native-like experience, and highly customizable UIs. The application is expected to be developed with a toolkit that can achieve complex charts and UI customization. The toolkit should offer a high degree of flexibility for both front-end and back-end integrations. Flutter fits the expectation as the performance with respect to drawing is more resilient and seamless than React Native. Unless the developer has difficulty learning a separate toolkit or has an advantage with JavaScript, Flutter would be a better choice than React Native.

The reasoning for Iconic with Capacitor or RAD remains the same as it would underperform for a high-frequency trading UI. A RAD tool would add the cost of proprietary tools without offering the specialized trading-domain feature, thereby not giving any added advantage.

Learning from the collective experience of the community or industry is the best way to make the most of technology. The further narrative will take the reader through some of the ground realities of native versus cross-platform development across several themes: reusability, cost, timeline, and strategic trade-offs.

Reusability in cross-platform

The measure of reusability would give insights into how efficiently the framework is able to reduce platform-specific custom code written to develop features. The reusability metrics can be used to get a measure of the percentage of code written once and deployed without modification to different platforms supported by the cross-platform framework. This will therefore help an individual to define the percentage of features that can be written without any platform-specific code and derive the value in decision-making to choose the cross-platform framework for development.

The factors affecting reusability are:

- The number of platforms targeted, how crucial a feature is, and the experience on these platforms.
- Architecting required in the code supporting different platforms.
- Percentage of platform-specific features in the application not supported by cross-platform.
- Availability of wrappers, libraries, or alternatives for platform-specific features.
- Separate user experience requirements for each platform.

The following is the list of some of the key learnings with respect to reusability:

- Consider the feature using a camera to capture images and upload. This would typically be implemented by the Camera Provider API from native. The underlying code to capture the image can be written independently for each platform. The upload of the captured image could be done at the cross-platform framework level. Alternatively, if this is implemented such that the handling of the image is also done at the native level, the use of a cross-platform tech stack will not serve its purpose. This will be applicable to all such features that cross-platforms do not support directly. Mostly, the package or library that comes along with the cross-platform would have considered this and would have made an effort to introduce abstraction for the common platform-specific features. Additionally, in most cases, the cross-platform framework has the ability for the team to write custom abstractions to create an in-house wrapper layer for the native API, giving the framework flexibility and adaptability.
- An organization will get more than 90% reusability if the application features are aligned with the capabilities supported by the cross-platform of choice. Consider an example of screen design aligning with the component from the library of the cross-platform, and another case of creating a custom version. A custom version may need a change of underlying implementation for cross-platform, thus writing code

for multiple platforms. This situation may reduce the ability to reuse. In such a scenario, being aware of what is possible within the framework and additionally educating the stakeholders on the impact of any deviation to enable them to make the right decision is crucial. The UI/UX team's awareness of the cross-platform framework and UI components could be a good strategy to bring the right balance to attain reusability. In most cases, this would end up restricting the native platform guidelines and might not be in the best interest of mobile applications. The stakeholder should evaluate the trade-off for the choices.

- Consider a scenario where a particular cross-platform faced an issue with a UI element that did not give the option to customize the border of the text field. The design team insisted on building the UI with the said requirement, which was not supported by the cross-platform. This added to the development effort to build the custom UI and write the cross-platform wrapper to interoperate. If the number of such occurrences is high, the benefit from using cross-platform decreases. The worst case will be if the team ends up writing platform-specific code, reducing the reusability.
- As the total number of platforms supported increases, the percentage of reusability will be proportional to the percentage of the core logic. The form factors are directly tied to the user experience, and therefore, reusability will also be a challenge if the UI is different. In a case where the main channel for distribution is mobile, and the percentage of users in other channels is minimal with respect to revenue, investing separately to build and maintain two different code bases might not be the best strategy, weighed against the return on investment. The suggestion in this situation would be to understand the channel where there is more incoming revenue stream and build primarily for that channel. For the other channel to ensure that optimal items are reused and complemented by making the design structurally equivalent to each other. For example, the usage of Material Design by Google is a reasonable default to develop apps in an Android-dominant user base since it aligns with users' established expectations on the platform. If the numbers are almost the same in all the channels, then it might be relevant to build what is best for each channel or a hybrid approach where the user does not feel a different experience in comparison to what is common.
- For each platform, the features and behavior are different. This brings us to a point where the cross-platform components are mostly designed to support the subset of features that all the platforms have in common. Enabling the unique features would be possible by introducing conditions based on the platform. Adding more platform-specific features would reduce flexibility by introducing more custom code. This is a pattern that the team needs to be watchful of, and should devise a pattern in code that can help reduce the impact by architecting and organizing the code optimally.

Cost and timeline effectiveness

Cost and time are very closely related in most aspects of software engineering. The section explores some of the facets of cost and time impacting a mobile application development project. The most important costs that affect mobile app development are operational and maintenance costs. There are other costs involved, like platform membership, tool license, etc., which will be one-time. A certain percentage of the one-time cost is unavoidable, and others, which are for the convenience of development, can be planned accordingly based on the budget possible for the project/organization.

The project's operation cost and maintenance should be optimized for the organization to sustain and scale. The project operation cost is where the cross-platform wins most of the time. The operation cost for a project that is developed from scratch typically gets a higher margin for development effort when developed with a cross-platform approach than native. The other contributing aspect is that the total number of QA, business analyst, or product roles needed for the project can also be reduced when the tool choice is cross-platform. The test suites can also be common for multiple platforms, which is possible for native integration tests as well.

In the context of the overall test pyramid, the lower layer, for example, unit tests, can now be written in the cross-platform layer, thereby reducing the repetition on multiple platforms. Take the example of Flutter, the package **`integration_test`** is the automation test suite that can be used to run automation tests for iOS and Android Flutter applications. Maintenance has a huge win only when there are no breaking changes from the underlying native platform. The code sharing for the cross-platform, however, gives the convenience of managing only one codebase, therefore reducing the cognitive overhead for the team during maintenance for an issue fix in the implementation of a functional feature.

Developing an application on native technology would mean having separate streams per platform, and each stream may have to track the functional features, test, and execute the validation for release. This certainly increases the cost as additional team capacity is required. The plan, dependency, and the tentative go-to-market timeline also influence the size of the team. The stakeholder should ensure that an optimal number of individuals in a team is thought through, to avoid the unnecessary burden of costs due to underutilization.

Consider a case where there is a bug for a particular feature or a case where an incremental change in the feature is required. Having a cross-platform would reduce the total number of developers required to investigate the issue or build the feature. The skill set required will only be that of cross-platform. The assumption here is that in the development phase, automated one-click deployment would have been set up, whereby in-depth platform-related aspects will not become a bottleneck for the cross-platform developer for release. The implementation being cross-platform would be applicable for multiple platforms, therefore creating a faster release cycle in the maintenance or post-production phase.

The preceding example also portrays how maintenance can become effective with a cross-platform approach. The pattern emerges where the cost can be optimized, reducing the number of individuals involved, which is a key selling point favoring the adoption of a cross-platform framework.

The timeline of development also follows a similar pattern to cost. In the initial phase, there may be challenges if there are features that are non-compliant/inherent to the cross-platform frameworks. Post-production maintenance can largely be achieved with a reduced timeline and development effort.

Not everything is perfect, and the alternate reality will be when the cross-platform has a limitation of a particular feature critical to the product. This situation delays the product time to market, which has a trickle-down effect on cost and timeline. The next option will be to revamp the entire product on another technology. Similarly, if the cross-platform tool development or support becomes obsolete and the provider discontinues the framework, the team will have no choice but to port to a different tech stack.

An optimal mix of developers can also be considered to balance the technology breadth required to operate in a cross-platform framework. The mix is required to support the resolution of the dependency of cross-platform on the native frameworks. The recommendation is that most developers with experience in cross-platform tools, along with 10-20% of developers who have native platform experience, should constitute a team to efficiently tackle any cross-platform mobile development.

In a nutshell, some key items to keep an eye on while considering cost and time are:

- Optimal percentage of experienced cross-platform developers in the team.
- Percentage of developers who know the individual platforms.
- The support and the feature availability for the cross-platform mobile app requirement.
- Awareness of different behaviors for cross-platform for each platform and of any features affected by framework issues or platform limitations.
- Understanding the pros and cons of a cross-platform to take a conscious call, defining the trade-off of a feature with respect to cross-platform, if any.

Challenges, risks, and strategic trade-offs

The following are a few points that look at some challenges, risks, and strategic trade-offs unique to the cross-platform technologies:

- Overcoming the learning curve with the help of subject matter experts in cross-platform or becoming the subject matter expert would be a key success factor for any cross-platform development starting from scratch. The subject matter expert should be mindful to make decisions that are pragmatic in the context of the organization's needs. When an organization is trying out a new cross-platform player in the market, the risk of getting stuck is there; adjusting to the alternative possibilities while using the platform or incorporating native for the item will be the way forward.

- The major players in mobile are iOS and Android, dominating the mobile consumer market. Given that these are from two different providers, there is also a chance for disparity in the features being built into these phones. In such a situation, the chances are high that a developer who has worked on a particular platform is biased when reasoning about the other. The individual with such a bias will be unable to see or acknowledge the disparity. The individual will expect the feature on one platform to be there and behave the same on other platforms as well. This could lead to the situation where an individual overengineers and incurs unnecessary costs in development to bring parity. An example of this will be an Android developer expecting background process control in iOS to be as flexible as in Android. In iOS, background capability is far more restrictive, and this platform-specific behavior and experience being different brings disparity. Acknowledging the disparity and focusing elsewhere would be ideal.
- The lifespan of the application is influenced by the technology decision. If mobile app life was supposed to be supporting a long-running business, the risk prevailing would be cross-platform technology becoming obsolete, and as said earlier, leading to a re-write of the application.
- If business leaders have an idea that needs to go to market with less time, and need validation cross-platform can be effective. The investment that one should ideally make for an early idea should be optimal in terms of cost and time. The choice of leveraging cross-platform in the MVP phase to cater to multiple platforms shall be favorable. Additionally, for MVP or proving an idea cross-platform is a real lifesaver, in cases where platform capabilities are used minimally.
- In a phase where the cross-platform is not scaling, or platform feature restriction kicks in, the migration to native could be planned. The migration could be an informed choice planned from the initial days. The migration happens after ensuring the business idea is validated and the product has gone to market on multiple platforms, keeping the cost optimal. In the case of migration, the cost to revamp is averaged and covered if the cross-platform with proper migration or co-existence with native is chosen for the development. The return on investment from the idea will be the major driver for the decision.
- A business will look at the in-house composition of the skilled individuals available. In a case where the team strength lies closely or is similar to a particular cross-platform technology, the adoption and operationalization of a team will become simpler for cross-platform as the technology choice. A 10-20% additional focus on the native skill will give the business the necessary team composition to advocate best practices on a particular platform. The bundling and packaging of the application shall be managed with the support of individuals having knowledge of iOS/Android ecosystem. Additionally, in extreme cases, awareness of the internals of the cross-platform would help to resolve the shortcomings or extend cross-platform.
- An application with UI that leverages the capabilities of a cross-platform uses few hardware or OS features, and does not have performance-intensive workload would be an ideal candidate for cross-platform as a technology strategy.
- One other problem statement that the team may encounter is the turnaround time for getting the latest platform (iOS/Android) updates to be supported by the cross-platform framework. One may have to rely on the cross-platform provider (open-source community or respective cross-platform companies) for bug fixes, support, and improving performance.

Case study 1: Revamping a banking mobile application

With a banking app created in a proprietary framework, the team was able to achieve around 70% reusability of the same codebase. 30% of the code in this use case was the main library, and the project had a dependency on a third-party system. This library was written on the native technology stack and had to be ported by writing a wrapper to be used in cross-platform. The current version of this banking application was built on a framework that interpreted the code communicated via VM to the native platform. The latest feature support was also limited.

The banking app was revamped from a cross-platform approach, as it was not scaling for the high-fidelity UI requirement. The app had subtle animation and effects that required precision and performance that could only be achieved on a native platform. At the time of the revamp of the application, circa 2022, Flutter was in the market, which was a promising player with respect to animation, and this could also be a choice. However, the failure incurred for app development using the previous cross-platform tool made the team risk-averse in trying a new tool.

Case study 2: Building a trading application

One of the success stories is building a trading application and scaling to support a huge customer base. The application targets iOS, Android, and Web, and there are roadmaps for desktop apps as well. Reusability can account for 80% of the three platforms. The UI design for the web, persisting data, a few libraries, payment mechanism, etc., were different and had to be handled separately.

Case study 3: Xamarin reusability across four platforms

The next mobile application that can be narrated is an internal application to monitor the fire panel device installed on a building connected via Bluetooth with a hardware interface. The app was built using Xamarin.iOS and Xamarin.Android. The app needed to be supported in Windows desktop and Windows mobile as well. The reusability was 50% of the overall code, which is a huge win because the target was four platforms. The 50% reusability was the only reusability, as the user interface was designed on the respective native framework. This use case was during the era when Windows mobile was also in use. Xamarin provided the binding to use the native API via the C# layer, thus the performance and syntactic similarity were less compromised.

Case study 4: Struggles with cross-platform

The following are some of the key anecdotes and inferences that came out from the experience of a developer who has had the chance to build a cross-platform application:

- When developing a document-based, offline-first application that targeted users in a region where iOS had higher penetration, there were struggles. The struggle was mainly around the inability to support features that were platform-specific as the application scaled. A cross-platform application that does not use the underlying platform's API will not scale to support platform-specific features. An example to quote would be for iOS when Spotlight integration was required. This capability works very well with the CoreData framework. However, typically, cross-platform will not use CoreData as it is iOS-specific. The preferred option for the database would be one that supports multiple platforms. This decision would reduce the ease with which the app can support or implement the Spotlight integration. Spotlight integration feature can be understood as indexing of the application data to be optimized for search from the iOS via Spotlight Search.
- One can see that a typical cross-platform in the initial stage takes only a relative cost of 30-40% less than a native. This is a generalization based on the author's empirical experience. The relative cost comparison is not an industry-validated benchmark.

  > Note: **This data is based on relative estimation comparing the two-approach native versus cross-platform from the different engagement from the authors' experience. The percentage shared previously is from the experience of the author not based on any industry benchmark.**

  The implicit assumption is that the cross-platform toolkit is mature, and the team is skilled.
- The application had a form-based user interface, and choosing cross-platform restricted the UI design to be within the capabilities of the cross-platform technology provided. If any customization was required

that the cross-platform did not support, then the team reverted to building pluggable components in native and using them alongside the cross-platform. This was the last approach if the alternative was not acceptable for the business.

- In general, a cross-platform application cannot match the peak performance of a highly optimized native application. However, modern compiled frameworks close the gap significantly for most use cases. The selling point of many cross-platforms is near native performance. However, for traditional **business to enterprise** (**B2E**) or **business to consumer** (**B2C**) applications, the performance needs could be optimized based on the tools by ensuring the perceived user experience is not impacted by the usage of cross-platform. The focus on engineering is required while developing such an application from the start of the engagement and should not be an afterthought.
- The cross-platform will have inherent issues, and for open-source platforms, one can track this in their respective repositories. These issues can span multiple platforms that are supported by the cross-platform framework. Another aspect is that when the mobile OS or SDKs have released updates, there will be inherent issues at the native platform level. For issues in the native platform, one can depend only on the platform to get the issue fixed. Now, given a case where a team is developing an application in a cross-platform environment, there is a high possibility that the final product will have issues from the native platform, cross-platform, and team-introduced issues, which is an overhead and a risk that cross-platform development brings to the table.

Conclusion

The objective of the chapter was to provide the reasoning toolkit for the reader. This reasoning ability will help to devise the technology strategy and make informed decisions when choosing from options for mobile application development. The chapter presents a few families of cross-platform tools out there in the market and covers the underlying workings of each of these. One can get biased by past conditioning and have alignment with a particular technology stack. It is critical to understand the business needs and challenges to make an unbiased decision that works best for the operating context when deciding the technology strategy for mobile application development.

The next chapter focuses on preparing for the journey toward a leadership role where one must operationally mobilize a team.

Takeaways and reflections

Now that we have reached the end of the chapter, the wealth of knowledge from the collective wisdom of experience is now acquired by the reader as a toolkit. This can be applied to the decision-making process for mobile development. The following are the highlights from this chapter:

- It is our professional duty as engineers to be unbiased in technology choices and make decisions appropriate to the context. Thus, the data and examples in the chapter should be treated in abstract form to evaluate the technology choice.
- The chapter started the narrative of the development ecosystem and its components, moving to the options available in the market to develop mobile applications. Two prominent categories are native and cross-platform toolkits.
- The narrative compared different cross-platform players: Flutter, React Native, Cordova, Xamarin, and RAD. This narrative gives the unique ideologies that drive these cross-platform toolkits.
- The idea of taking the pain to create an abstraction to unify the complexity of multiple platforms is the central theme of cross-platform.
- The technology choice for a mobile application development is an undertaking. Making the right choice can help to have a longer life span and a high-performing team with great outcomes. The chapter has given various frames of reference to quote and evaluate the choices.

- The factors affecting the native and cross-platforms gave a contrasting point of view. This narrative shows that individuals can always come up with a counter-narrative for a claim. The collective wisdom should challenge to ensure that the claims genuinely help the operating context of mobile application development, and are not based on the biases of individual choice.
- The thought experiment to evaluate the different choices within the cross-platform has given the reader a first-hand experience and practice to make such a choice in a real situation in future encounters.

CHAPTER 4
Organizing a Mobile Development Team

Introduction

When an organization tries to leverage technology to accelerate business, the likelihood of making early mistakes should be assessed and planned for. This will help plan mitigation and prevention strategies, reducing the adverse effects of such mistakes. Understanding past strategies is the wisdom one can leverage to adapt appropriately to the given context. For a mobile developer, the chapter presents insights from a decade of wisdom from the industry. This chapter focuses on the operational side of project execution rather than the technology. Reading this chapter will equip the reader with operational wisdom to calibrate a mobile development team.

The narrative proceeds on the premise that the strategies will work well for a team size of seven developers working in parallel on the same codebase. The corollary of this assumption is that a subset of these ideas can be adopted for a smaller team. The magic number 7 is an empirically observed benchmark among the Agile practitioners. Additionally, Miller's Law in cognitive psychology states that an ideal range for communication efficiency is seven individuals in a team, give or take two. As the team size increases, there is exponential growth of communication channels, and thus, the recommendation is to work with an optimal team size.

Structure

This chapter covers the following topics:

- Team
- Core roles and responsibilities
- Facets of team setup
- Team split
- Central team
- Challenges in operating a team
- Thought experiments

Objectives

The chapter aims to explore the foundational principles and considerations enabling the journey toward a leadership role in a mobile development team. These principles will help to set up the team. An operationally stable team is essential to reduce chaos and ensure the quality of the software being written does not deteriorate. The key idea is to share the experience with respect to the operational considerations and insights that can be applied to have a positive impact on the team's dynamics. People management itself is a topic for a separate book. In this chapter, the focus is primarily on the context of the mobile development team. A few of the ideas shared shall be generic and may find similarity with other software development aspects as well. The chapter explores some thought-provoking ideas. These are based on past experiences and incorporate first-hand information from the experience and learning. The best practices to be used and anti-patterns that need to be avoided in the journey of software development shall be a key takeaway for the reader.

Team

The word team implies a small or large group of individuals working together. A collaborating team is the backbone for building a great product. The individuals involved may be in multiple roles, such as developers, designers, product owners, program managers, etc. These individuals shall work towards attaining the common goal of developing the product.

People management is subjective. The intent of this chapter is not to cover the entirety of the subject, but rather to focus on two perspectives with respect to:

- Focus area for managing the development of a mobile app with a sizable team.
- Bottlenecks that one may encounter while managing a sizable mobile development team.

Note: **The usage of principle and rule has subtle differences and understanding the difference could help an individual make a choice that is optimal for the context. The rule is absolute in nature and should be followed at all times to get the desired result. Alternatively, a principle is the generalized observation that has worked out for most of the sample set. For an outlier, these principles could become an anti-pattern and may not give the expected outcome. The ideas presented in the chapter are, by nature, principles, and readers are advised to practice caution while contextualizing and taking them as guidelines. Every statement proposed as a best practice or a solution should be verified to see whether it is a rule or principle.**

Core roles and responsibilities

In a large engagement, making a single individual take all the responsibility is not pragmatic. There will be groups of individuals who, based on the organization's operating model, share different responsibilities. Each group can take multiple responsibilities as well. The roles and responsibilities defined shall be collectively exhaustive, ensuring the overall functioning of the team to reach the expected outcome. The section looks at archetypes that define the ideal behavior for various responsibilities required to ensure the smooth functioning of the project.

Note: **In an organization, the ontologies used could vary from one another, and there could be a local version of the labels for the role. The section focuses on some of the core universal roles that are directly involved in or influence the feature development.**

Program management for strategies and coordination

Program management exists to ensure operational readiness and enable the successful delivery of mobile application development. The **program manager (PM)** role owns the coordination and the responsibility to operationally set up and sustain a team. For an engagement, there could be multiple PMs with hierarchy among the roles. The following are some of the key expectations of the role:

- **Stakeholder management and alignment**:
  - Coordination with relevant businesses and technology stakeholders to align the vision for the mobile application. The role should ensure alignment across stakeholders and bring all the stakeholders to a common ground with respect to vision and execution strategy.
  - Constantly connect with the stakeholders and advocate for a balanced approach to be effective and efficient. For example, there could be cases where requirements or expectations might be an overhead or counterproductive to implement from a point of view of technology, or it could be an anti-pattern that would detract from the overall vision. A PM role should ensure the product owner, **user interface/ user experience (UI/UX)**, and technology team are aligned and make the right choices.
  - The role serves as a conduit for information radiation, making the relevant details available and accessible for the respective roles within the team.

 - Ensure there is communication across the stakeholders about the progress of various strategies for the team.
 - Optimize the ways of working to be effective in collaboration by monitoring the vision and priority evolution and using these insights to adjust the team's workflow.
 - Keep the conversation alive with the stakeholders (project sponsors or decision makers) regarding the value proposition of the activities performed in the **software development lifecycle (SDLC)**.
 - Weigh must-have and good-to-have against the time-to-market constraints for activities that affect the SDLC.
- **Facilitation**:
 - Advocating and taking ownership in defining sensible defaults and patterns relevant to the program.
 - The defaults and patterns could be evolving data. The role should keep track of the information and ensure it is not obsolete and is updated to the current context.
 - Ensure individuals do not operate or make decisions based on personal bias in a cross-functional team.
 - Typically, a team with two opposing strong personas would balance out the decision-making. For example, one who prioritizes speed and one who prioritizes quality bring contrasting perspectives to balancing decision-making. The role of the PM will be that of a mediator, preventing the discussion from escalating or going into a loop. In a team where there are no opposing powers, empowering the team to have contrasting discussions will be the role that the PM may have to fulfill.
- **Risk and issue management**:
 - Plan for potential risks that can affect the program and have a mitigation strategy for these. Identifying early indicators for any delay or challenges in the plan is a standard operating procedure for this role.
 - The human element involved could be a potential source of error. Acknowledging this and factoring the time needed to address the errors that occur into the plan is essential.
 - Plan to minimize the adverse effects of the risk identified.
 - PM is responsible for creating the priority definition for post-release issues and the escalation metrics for the reporter to address the issue.
 - PM is responsible for creating the post-production support service level agreement and defining the process for these post-release issues to be incorporated in the regular projectlifecycle. For example, creating priority and severity definitions for issues reported.
- **Operational efficiency and process management**:
 - Setting up the governance with multiple stakeholders. For example, consider the case of a risk or issue occurring in the system repeatedly. The business and tech stakeholders may have different perspectives and opinions. The governance will help to ensure that the stakeholders come to a common ground.
 - Keeping track of dependencies and adjusting the plan in case they are not met. This will involve coordinating with the relevant stakeholders. For example, design deliverables, tooling, process to maintain and manage changes, etc., will be coordinated by this role by reaching out to the respective individual.
 - Mediate and ensure the business stakeholder is aware of the factors that enable the technology team to move faster and the trade-off. This would enable the team to make informed decisions.
 - Watch for duplication of effort and take ownership to ensure there is a mechanism that nudges and guides individuals to be optimal and efficient in an autonomous manner.

- **Team strategy and knowledge distribution**:
  - Set up the strategy to define the team composition. The role should cultivate a mechanism to leverage the strength of the personas in the team by complementing their growth.
  - Ensure that knowledge silos do not exist by ensuring the optimal context is shared across team members and that an individual does not become a bottleneck. Reducing dependencies on specific individuals is possible by planning the team structure, balancing the experience factor, and ensuring there is a leader-follower structure operational within the team.

Note: **The overview of key responsibilities under project management is concluded. This is not an exhaustive list, but rather the top and key responsibilities in the context of a mobile development project.**

Additionally, the PM role may operate directly, by taking support from **subject matter experts** (**SMEs**) or by delegating the ownership of one or many of these items. This would depend on the organization's structure and the expertise of the individuals fulfilling the role.

Leads or architects enabling technology governance

The mobile application is mostly consumer-class software. As narrated in *Chapter 3, Cross-platform Versus Native*, there are various technology options to build a mobile application. In such a case, to bring the best outcome for the product, a cohort that possesses the collective wisdom to do the right thing, balancing the technology with the product expectation, is required. These individuals advocate best practices and keep a constant watch on the tech parlance of the team. These individuals should create an influence circle to follow the right practices from top to bottom and should plan to enforce enough mechanisms for the team to adhere to these. On the ground, when the team faces a problem, getting feedback on these practices to course correct, improve, and change the strategy from the bottom-up execution will reduce the friction in the team. The organization identifies these individuals as the leads/SMEs/architects for the team. Generally, for a mobile development project that relies heavily on the downstream system to do the data processing, a specialist for mobile playing the role of the system architect is rare; rather, the role shall be more cross-cutting in nature. The deviation where there is a mobile-centric architect role arises in a core mobile product when the mobile client itself is the primary product and business differentiator. In such an engagement, the mobile application itself shall play an important part in the economy of the organization. The following are some of the key responsibilities that the role requires to fulfill:

- Articulate and design the solutions, giving direction to what is ideal and appropriate for implementation.
- Define the right practice along with a sensible default and tolerable minimum for any deviation to get things moving.
- Constantly look at and suggest the adoption of tools and techniques that enable and empower the team to mitigate anti-patterns.
- Communicating the risks, pros, and cons of a particular approach to the team and mediating the discussion to finalize the approach. In the case where there is an equally agreeable solution, the final decision-making could be part of the responsibility.
- Recommendation from technology to product and business stakeholders to make informed decisions and raise awareness of capability in the ecosystem. The PM role may act as a conduit in this discussion.
- Define the mechanism and the gatekeeping strategies for code.
- Keeping track of and having constant vigil on the codebase quality, practices, and team dynamics. Take appropriate action if there are any anti-patterns slowing the team or execution. For example, when a tech debt is identified, it is the responsibility of this role, and it must be converted into a value proposition to present to the business to get the task prioritized and planned to be taken up for execution.
- Ensure a regular cadence to monitor the health of the codebase and mobile application. **Root cause analysis** (**RCA**) of the issue will become the input for devising strategy improvements and preventing

future potential flaws. For example, organizing activities such as group/mob code review to bring all the groups into the same mindset.

- Taking ownership to establish common norms and patterns across the team, which will serve as the operational expectation for the development team. Ensuring adherence within the team becomes the responsibility. Another strategy will be creating awareness amongst the group about the theme. Programming, being a creative task, has more than one correct way to solve a problem. However, for a large engagement, it is essential to have a common way followed across the team to be efficient.
- The role should keep a check on over-engineering and ensure the team does only what is optimal and necessary. The role should ensure there is a delicate balance between cost, technology, and business, and influence in forming a collective decision.
- Define the mechanism to continuously advocate for the importance of non-functional requirements, which are often ignored or less prioritized by businesses. For example, tasks such as analyzing the pattern of bugs, performance analysis, building components, and ensuring the right practice is followed throughout.
- The role should establish a mechanism ensuring the team is accountable for end-to-end observability. In certain organizations, these activities are coordinated by a roster-based support team. To achieve the same, the leads should ensure that on the execution side, the team should implement structured logging, distributed tracing, and real-time monitoring dashboards to proactively detect performance, regressions, and production anomalies.

Like the PM role, even in the case of the lead role, the responsibility laid out could be shared or handled by a single individual, depending on the organization's workforce strategy. Additionally, this list of activities is not exhaustive; rather, it mentions the top ones.

Mentors

A diverse team will bring collective wisdom and could do wonders in bringing out the best solution for a problem. In such a team, stakeholders should also cultivate means to promote individual growth. Motivation for the team is one of the key factors that translates to better productivity, and in this case, a great mobile application.

Earlier in the section, while discussing the role of a PM, the responsibility of planning the team with proper leverage (meaning, a mix of different experience levels) was highlighted. This would also make it essential for individuals to help each other to complement their strengths and weaknesses, and the entire team will collectively power the execution speed.

There is a subtle difference between a full-time trainer and someone in a mentorship role. Mentoring may not be a full-time role, and can rather be seen as an investment that compounds its return to the team with time. The effort taken to sustain a high-performing team can be optimized with the leader-follower model of operation.

The role will have the following key responsibilities:

- To bring new joiners up to speed.
- To give direction, support, and feedback to mentees.
- Identify core strengths and share observation that could function as input for defining the team's leverage.

Other roles

A mobile application team will have other supporting roles as well. An enterprise mobile application is not a standalone app; rather, it interacts with downstream systems. The other input for developing the mobile application is the user experience. These are the mockups and design specifications created by the UI/UX experts along with product managers. The quality assurance, production support, and DevOps-related activities also form some of the responsibilities that are associated with mobile application development. The mobile development itself is done by the SME of the respective development framework. The lead/architect will ideally also be an SME in this development framework.

Note: **The definitions mentioned here, of these roles and responsibilities, are to lay out the archetype prevalent in a mobile development project. The organization can define who should do what based on the context and workforce strategy. The key intent is to provide insight to the reader on the superset of the roles and responsibilities that, when fulfilled, could be a catalyst for the smooth functioning of a mobile application development.**

Facets of team setup

The section explores some of the key themes that one may encounter while operationalizing a mobile development team. The aim is to give the operational acumen that complements the technology journey toward a leadership role. The setting up of a team is an iterative process. Once the initial structures are put in place, a series of experiments operated with a feedback loop in a project specific environment is what it leads to a stable team. A diverse nature of the individuals forming the team could bring up a case where the strategy used in a particular team may not work as a rule for all cases. The operating context should be calibrated and will influence the team setup.

General structure for technology organization

An organizational structure can be sliced into three pillars, namely strategy, operation, and engineering. If the organization is into consulting or service, two additional hybrid role emerge, i.e., management consulting (a blend of strategy and operation) and techno-functional consulting, which is a blend of operation with engineering. These roles will pan out to be the advisory structure for a client. The structure, focusing on engineering, translates to the following roles:

- **Architects**: Responsible for setting up the technology direction for the organization.
- **Vertical developers/engineers**: An individual who has deep expertise or specialization in a particular platform or technology. Alternatively, this represents domain-specific or focused specialization.
- **Horizontal developers/engineers**: Individuals who are polyglot programmers who will focus on cross-functional or system-wide concerns.
- **Other supporting functions**: Examples include UI/UX, product management, etc. The roles under the strategy and operation will have an overlap with this role in engineering.

All these roles will enable the activities within the organization for the various stages in SDLC. Depending on the organization and its business, the activities could be consulting, solutioning, product development, platform engineering, etc.

This role definition is from a technology point of view. There are additional roles for the organization, which are the project sponsors, executives, etc. In principle, the additional roles the organization has have an indirect influence on the execution. This additional roles are project sponsors and executives who primarily focuses on the outcome and means of achieving the goals, including profitability and growth.

Mobile development falls under the category of a vertical skill, where the developer can specialize in a particular platform or framework.

Setting up a mobile development team

The important information that one should understand and analyze to be effective in setting up a team would be the product plan and the high-level roadmap. The awareness of the scope and structure of work, dependencies, and the go-to-market timelines is what one can know from the roadmap. Defining an independent parallel stream after evaluating the possibility is requisite for minimizing the idle time within a team. Typically, for any project, the team should never start at full capacity. Rather, the team members should be brought in incrementally to reach an optimum capacity. The reasoning for the staggered increase is to get the lead time, logically create reusable structures, and set up the foundation for a mobile application codebase. The staggered onboarding will ensure there is no overlap and conflict of responsibilities.

The possibility of parallels and independent streams is critical in defining the number of individuals within a team. Adding more developers to increase stream than the optimal number of parallel streams can have adverse effects on the project. Parallel execution requires additional operation overhead on the coordination, and if the number of individuals increases more than the possible parallel stream, the task division will be difficult and will cause idle time, as mentioned earlier.

The technology of choice for development, either native or cross-platform, will have an impact on the team structure and composition, where, in the case of a cross-platform technology, the team size will be reduced. An optimal team shall have a mix of developers with different levels of seniority. The reason for considering seniority is to focus on optimizing the cost and not on the hierarchy in an organization. In a case where the cross-platform framework is used for development, it is also good to have a mix of 10 to 20% of developers who have awareness of both native and cross-platform and have a strength in the native platform.

Factors affecting team size for mobile development

A pragmatic answer to the question, *what is an ideal team size?* is that an ideal team size is difficult to standardize, as it depends on the operating context. Mobile application development can happen with a single individual or any number of developers. At the start of the chapter, Miller's Law in cognitive psychology was discussed. Therefore, having a five to nine-person team is efficient. The number of features to be developed and the time to market have a major influence on defining the team size. If the time to market should be earlier, the stakeholder could try to add capacity to increase the speed of feature development. At first glance, the stakeholder will thus have the two options of either going with the possible time to market or going against the ideal team size based on Miller's Law. An alternative strategy to meet the timeline will be to increase the team size without breaking Miller's Law by logically separating the team into much smaller units, which are autonomous in nature. The smaller units are called squads or pods. One hundred percent autonomy in mobile application development with the squads/pods will be difficult, as there will be a coordination effort required, as the mobile application is shipped as a single application compiled from all the squad codebases together.

A typical medium complex mobile application with 100 to 200 screens, which displays and sends data from a web service, on average, takes six months to one year to complete the implementation with five to seven developers. These teams also have multiple streams for parallel development. If the development target is for multiple mobile operating systems and the development is on native technology, then the streams will be doubled, each for iOS and Android separately. This ballpark estimate does not consider the development effort of other interacting systems, but rather only considers the effort to consume the service from the other systems.

In the market, there is a class of mobile applications that fall under the category of multi-module applications, also known as Super App. *Chapter 12, Use Case of Developing a Super App,* goes into detail about the same. However, in the context of the team structure for the organization, developing apps that follow a Super App strategy is seen to divide and conquer by having multiple dedicated units or teams for each product. Here, the team size will be large based on the number of products.

Another case study of a banking application with international presence will give more insights into the factors affecting team size. The banking application needed the capability to customize features based on the region. The possibility of the features being totally different or non-existent for a particular region was there. One of the possible options was to have a different team based on a combination of region and common feature, and the other was to build multiple versions of the application per region. Having a single codebase that can generate a build flavor for each region and conditionally packaging the region-based feature was the goal. It is suboptimal to maintain separate teams for each region and duplicate the work if there is a great percentage of commonality between regions. This use case demonstrates the possibility for the team size to be large and can be operationalized based on the feature that can be run in parallel. This example also demonstrates the effect of operational requirements to support multi-region, influencing the team setup.

A mobile application, after release, would require production support where there could be hotfix requirements. Evolved organizations do frequent releases, and the hotfixes can go with the mainstream release unless it is a blocker or critical issue. The team can de-prioritize the mainstream work and leverage the existing capacity to do support activity. However, if the number of production issues is high or the current feature implementation has equal priorities, then having a dedicated capacity to address production issues is recommended.

One can conclude from the section that a mobile application can be developed by a few individuals, a small team, or a very large development team. The team size for a mobile application depends on the scope of the application being developed and the availability of the individual. The team size for the entire mobile application development is thus a function of time to market, combined with the possibility of parallel execution of features. However, in case of a large team size causing inefficiency, ideally, dividing into pods/squads is followed.

Challenges to scale or ramp up a team

As the team grows, it could get organized into a single team or split into small squads. Irrespective of the choice made, the common side effect of adding individuals to scale the team is operational overhead. The operational overhead comes in the form of additional need for people management, technology leadership, and product scope management to match capacity to pick up tasks for execution, thus managing a large group of individuals. Splitting the team into logical squads could reduce the communication complexity; however, the impact on the operational and strategy will still be there. The coordination amongst the individuals/squad to build a feature that should function together can be factored as the major contributor to the operational overhead. Operational overhead thus becomes the necessary evil and should be handled gracefully while scaling the team. Improper coordination can create mayhem in the development cycle. The following section explores some of the key areas that will affect the scaling up of the team. These insights provide the reasoning toolkit to pre-empt and prepare for ensuring the journey is seamless.

Democratizing information

A large team size implies parallel execution possibility. There will be a proportional increase in the scope and functionality of the product being developed. The stakeholder should ideally not expect everyone in the team to know every aspect of the product, as there will be a division of context. The context becomes concentrated in a few individuals creating information asymmetry that paves the way for information silos. For sustaining any team, preventive measures to reduce the information silos formed where context gets limited to only one or two individuals should be devised. Generally, having a forum to share information across contexts that would otherwise be siloed could be practiced. In summary, for a large team, expecting everyone to know everything will be unreasonable. Ensuring the context is accessible via the forum is the first step. The stakeholder should cultivate a culture and habit where the team shares information across, which should be the goal.

Note: **The short-term information silos in a sliced team are inevitable; however, there should be mechanisms, such as a decision record and other knowledge hubs, created to democratize the information.**

End-to-end feature ownership

Typically, in smaller groups, individuals would have better visibility of the roadmap of the product/service. As the team grows, there is a high chance that the team may drift away from being aware of the holistic goal. In such cases, individual's focus would shift to their own scope and may become an anti-pattern, breeding less collaboration. This situation needs to be addressed and should not be allowed when the team ramps up. Ideally, having a group with an optimum ratio of feature owners, tech leads, and stakeholders ensures the disconnected information is tied together and helps to avoid the anti-pattern. These groups should be proactive in ensuring that they are on top of the aspects that are beyond the individual scope to bring the context and the broader picture closer to the individuals, ensuring the implementation scale for the larger goal or codebase. This brings a proper balance to tie application priorities together, along with the long-term goal of the product.

Regression code changes

In a smaller team, testing the effect of the changes in the affected area for the code changes and other features is easy. Now consider the case where there are multiple small teams working on the same mobile app code base. The possibility of one team introducing side effects on the features of the other is present. Innately, the team may not even think or anticipate such a regression bug. Most commonly, this occurs when the architecture tightly couples the features across teams. Another reason could be if the team modifies a common code without discussion with others, potentially breaking the other feature. The occurrence of such a situation could send a faulty app to production, thus bringing a bad experience to the end user. Such cases of broken features are called regression bugs. It is important to have a sanity and regression test run for any change. Impact analysis done before implementing a feature to get a sense of the affected areas of the codebase will give the focus areas to perform the testing.

A regression bug can range from a cosmetic issue to a critical issue. A worse situation would be if the defect is missed in the early stage of the development cycle and gets reported from the field. In the case of the occurrence of issues, the RCA and its rectification are required. In a large team, the initial analysis can be taken care of by the developer who has context on the feature for which the defect is reported. In a case where the RCA identifies the issue as a side effect of a feature introduced by a sub-team, coordination from multiple sub-teams may be required to resolve the issue. If each team is isolated operationally and defines its own priorities, a situation could arise where either team tends to pass the bug by delegating the responsibility to fix to the other. The worst-case situation will be a blame game within the large team, and the issue will lie unattended in the backlog. The organization should curb such occurrences where the sub-teams detract from the larger vision.

Investing in a strong test strategy and mechanism to propagate the regression issue would be a mitigation strategy to prevent the side effects of the code change. Focusing on the collective ownership of the mobile application and resolving issues in an early stage would be an ideal thought process that the team should inculcate within itself.

Managing dependency between squads

Consider a case where two squads are dependent on each other. The dependency could be one-sided or two-way. If the team does not prioritize resolving the dependency, it could become a bottleneck. This could be due to bandwidth or capacity constraint, or the time required to address the dependency. The risk of derailing the current priorities could be another reason. Stakeholders will have to keep watch for such situations and intervene to take appropriate action. The action that adds value to the holistic goal of the product should be the core theme driving the team.

Normalizing opinions

Irrespective of the team size, conflict can arise between individuals and within a team, in the case of multiple teams. Most conflicts fall into either the priority of developing a dependent feature or an approach to be followed. Stakeholders should have strategies or systems established where the conflict could be addressed and resolved to align with the best interests of the project. The regression bugs or managing dependencies are two cases where conflict can arise in a large team. Another common source of conflict is disagreement between an individual or sub-teams over which pattern or coding approach should be adopted within the codebase. In all these cases, having a governance committee that looks at the pros and cons of multiple options, weighs the ROI, and takes the best-suited option for the context is the mitigation strategy.

Team split

Managing the system as a smaller logical unit will allow for leveraging a divide-and-conquer strategy. The smaller units will simplify and localize the operational scale and give better visibility and operational efficiency. However, there is an inverse relation where the smaller unit may not align with the greater goal. This strategy could be used in the mobile application development lifecycle as well. As the team grows, the question of whether the organization should split into smaller teams or remain a single entity is explored in this section. The section expands on the following ideas:

- The pros and cons of team split.
- The ideal time to team split.
- Overhead and challenges in team split.
- Anti-patterns to avoid for the team to be effective after team split.

Note: **Mobile application is a single codebase; even if the team split happens, there will still be a necessity of collective ownership and responsibility to ensure the sanity of the entire codebase. This is essential and non-negotiable, even if the code change is local to a squad.**

A team split is to compartmentalize the functioning of a large team. A simple analogy to relate to this situation is to compare taking a group of individuals in a single room versus the same group split into five different rooms. The individuals in the same room have an open space for communication; however, when a team split occurs, there will be a need for operational coordination to keep the information in sync across teams. This requires someone to go beyond the wall to communicate with one another. The mismanagement in the coordination can severely impact the throughput of the outcome expected from the entire group. Alternatively, the possibility for single larger teams to end up in increased time spent in meetings, reduced focus, and potential inefficiencies in execution is high. This situation can be attributed to communication overhead, coordination complexity, reduced focus on critical tasks, bureaucratic process, decision-making delays, conflicting priorities, and loss of individual accountability.

Every team starts as a single entity. As it scales, the team encounters the previously mentioned patterns, which could become the trigger for splitting the team. In the case where the team split is delayed, the operational efficiency of the team could be adversely affected.

After a team split, the lack of coordination can hinder productivity. Splitting a tightly coupled sub-team could create mayhem in operation. The mobile application is still a single artifact; thus, if the sub-team ignores the cross-cutting feature, the common pattern to be followed is not ideal. This would reduce efficiency in the application development and could affect its functionality and scalability. There is another case where the product backlog is blocked due to dependency fulfillment within the sub-team. In such a case, if the team cannot find alternative tasks, there could be idle time, which may result in a loss of capacity and increased cost to the organization.

Patterns to watch for

Top-down thinking in an operational model, defining the guidelines for ensuring consistency throughout the team, is required. This would help to efficiently manage multiple teams contributing to achieve a collective goal of mobile application development. Giving feedback from the bottom up can incrementally course-correct the defined guidelines. In the case where the change does not align well with the other team, a means to override for the localized scope can be practiced. The top-down nature would make this choice a collective informed decision agreed by stakeholders at multiple levels rather than a siloed decision.

Dividing the team based on features with independent capabilities will reduce dependencies. This would act as an accelerator for creating self-organized sub-teams. A cross-functional team, by having all individuals representing the different functions and systems (mobile, backend, quality, etc.) involved to develop features end-to-end, is a recipe for a self-organized team. This strategy of forming a self-organized cross-functional team could be adopted as a consideration for team splitting up. The sub-team formed with a cross-functional role beyond mobile will make the operations and coordination easier. The sub-team in such a case is a cohesive unit with all the capabilities required for the end-to-end feature delivery of the entire system, from requirements to mobile, backend, and infrastructure development. In principle, the strategy looks ideal; however, in practice, cost, people's availability, and the quantum of work for the respective tech stack will also influence the decision. For the mobile application, the different sub-teams still must collaborate with each other, as the final mobile application will still be a single application. This would necessitate having a separate focused group that coordinates this collaboration. Generally, the separate group called the central team, explained later in the chapter, coordinates to add to the effectiveness of the team split.

The cross-cutting features can span across sub-teams. Randomly assigning the cross-cutting feature to a sub-team is another anti-pattern and should be avoided. There should be some logical relation and continuity in organizing the task assignment. At times when the workload is uneven across the sub-teams, available capacity may dictate the task assignment. Assigning tasks based only on capacity should not be a long-term arrangement, as the cross-cutting feature could be a cognitive overload as these are not directly related to features the sub-team has to build. This situation causes miscoordination within the teams and these patterns discussed would also be the signal to rethink whether the sub-team should remain separate as discussed next.

Note: **Cross-functional and cross-cutting are two terms introduced in the section. The former deals with the end-to-end functional role of the team, and the latter is about the internal dependencies and factors impacting the mobile application.**

Another case is where the operational roles are not fulfilled to effectively balance the team split. The organization might decide to run the show with the existing set of hands. The organization could decide that the same stakeholders are held responsible for two teams. The necessity of a team split should be revalidated. Managing the time spent for each team and mixing of the facts between the teams can cause human errors and contribute to reduced productivity.

Note: **The chapter has presented two contrasting ideas of equal importance. One is that Miller's Law, presents the idea of an ideal team size to be five to nine. Miller's Law asserts team size beyond the range of five to nine can create communication inefficiency. The other idea is the disadvantage of splitting teams too finely has the potential to fail. The intent of such a contrasting narrative is to present an unbiased and neutral point of view. The data shared should ideally empower the reader to make the right decision valid for the localized context of the project.**

Central team

In the narrative about the team split in the previous section, the idea of having smaller units of independent functional teams was conveyed. Additionally, the mobile app being a single artifact and developed on a codebase to which all the sub-teams contribute is the ground reality. In such a case, the occurrence of a cohesive cross-cutting requirement that the team may encounter is imminent. The ownership of the cross-cutting feature should be managed and controlled, or else it would be dangling without focus. This would adversely affect the mobile application development and the scaling of the team. Most projects, when they become large, are therefore best managed by a cross-functional central team. In the central team, individuals may have a dual responsibility where they are responsible for the project achieving its goals and are also responsible for ensuring that the project complies with the standards and best practices established across the organization.

Top-down thinking is one of the key ingredients to operating at scale for a large team. Some form of mechanism enabling debates and discussions to validate the idea will complement top-down thinking and help in making the right choice. Having governance to keep these in check would lead to a high-performing and self-organized team. This can be orchestrated by having a central team that brings a strategy to reduce the disconnect within a team as it scales.

The members of the central team would be the primary guardians. They act as gatekeepers, coordinating together to keep a watch on the entire mobile application, ensuring the patterns, quality, and standards are met. The central team could curb the side effects of information or feature silos formed in a large team by being the torchbearer for the idea of thinking beyond just the local optima and focusing on how each decision can affect the whole mobile application.

The size of the central team would vary based on the phase of the project being executed. In the initial phase, there would be more work involved in the setup, and even establishing the pattern would require more capacity. As the team moves forward over time, the capacity required for the central team can later be reduced, and the individual could be reassigned to any feature team.

It is essential to ensure that the central team is kept isolated and given the power to make decisions for the overall project. The autonomous stature of the central team prevents individual sub-teams from diverging from the agreed architectural and coding standards, thereby ensuring the long-term scalability of the shared mobile application codebase. The autonomous nature does not mean awarding absolute power to the central team. The dynamics of the team should be such that there is a symbiotic relationship, preventing misuse of power. The central team should promote a platform for objective, unbiased decisions to be made for the collective good of the entire team, product, and organization. An organization can adopt a strategy to have individual representation from each sub-team to form the central team. In such a case, the individual shall be responsible for features as well as the whole project standards, patterns, and quality. A central team operates like any other team, where the cross-cutting tasks shall be prioritized based on the priority agreed by the representative from each sub-team.

The following is a list of a few activities coordinated by the central team:

- Setting up the folder structure and coding guidelines.
- Debating the architecture and defining patterns for the project.
- Setting up the automation and key security tools.
- Mediation of tech decisions and approaches amongst teams.
- Keeping watch of the latest trends.
- Managing the release in coordination with individual sub-teams.

Note: **The central team has alternative labels amongst the industry, and the most common ones are platform team or core team. Irrespective of the name, the fundamental responsibility remains the same as explained for the central team.**

Chapter 12, Use Case of Developing a Super App, will look at the platform team in detail in the context of a special category of mobile application called a Super App.

Challenges in operating a team

It is important to understand the challenges in the software development team. The recommendation when an issue occurs is to diagnose the root cause , followed by creating the appropriate course correction or proactively monitoring the stimuli to ensure there is a mitigation strategy that serves as the means to prevent any issue from escalating. Understanding the operational levers could help the stakeholder create a robust execution strategy and platform.

Examples of situations that one may encounter in a development team are listed as follows:

- **Aspirations versus monotony**: There can occur a case where the individuals in the team lose interest when aspirations are not met or when work becomes repetitive. It is important to balance ambition and long-term vision for a team member to ensure a long-running team. For a larger organization, it may be impractical to cater to the needs of each and every individual; however, the key point highlighted is to be pragmatic about what can be done best by the stakeholders. The continuous growth/rotation strategy for individuals in the team would be an ideal theme to be considered in a project plan.

- **Push versus performance balance**: The constant micromanagement, along with over-pushing an individual, can lead to burnout. Similarly, in the opposite situation, under-pushing could possibly lead to stagnation. It is essential to manage and balance this tension between motivating and pushing teams to work smart while maintaining consistent and sustainable contributions to the project execution.

- **Leveraging strengths, understanding interest and fitment**: The positioning of an individual by validating the expectations of the role that aligns with the individual's strengths and interests is a key ingredient while setting up a team. This would ensure the individual is able to function without much friction. The difference between strengths and expected outcomes from the individual could lead to disengagement, adversely affecting the goal. Assigning individuals to roles without considering interests and strengths could reduce effectiveness and engagement. In a temporary situation, an organization could take the risk that does not cater to the fitment; however, the stakeholder should be cautious of how long this could continue. Ensuring the support ecosystem to enable the individual to be effective should be a proactive strategy. The aspiration and the choice of the individual resonating with the expectation will be the key to the success of the role.

- **Unavailability of feature/item for team to engage**: If the capacity is not planned properly, there will be a case where the team member's availability is more than the actual amount of work. This will result in idle time, thus increasing the cost incurred by the organization. The reason for such a situation is improper planning and could stem from the unpreparedness of the product itself or the sequential nature of the associated task.

- **Scaling without a roadmap**: A team can randomly start developing a feature without a structured worklog, which could affect collaboration. Such a situation opens the possibility of duplication. Managing team growth and operationally scaling without a clearly defined strategy or plan would affect the quality of the product percolating to the implementation layer and to the consumer experience, making it worse.

The examples are not exhaustive but are some of the top ones that demotivate a team. The diverse nature of the team that one may encounter in the journey makes it difficult to keep track of every item. Thus, defining a universal strategy as a solution for all team-related issues would be difficult. It is best to look at the localized context along with the lens provided in the chapter to improvise and tackle these situations.

Thought experiment one

As part of the thought experiment, a use case will be presented to consolidate the ideas shared in the chapter and to help understand how these can be applied in a real-life situation. The use case presented involves an organization planning to modernize its mobile application.

Bootstrapping a team in new technology

Consider a case where an organization must modernize the mobile application, where the individual available within the team does not have expertise in the framework chosen for the modernization. The ratio of the expertise and experience within the team should be optimal and balanced, according to the organization's requirement. This would mean that the number of individuals with varying levels of hands-on years of experience in the mobile ecosystem should be in the team, spread from shorter to longer tenure in industry experience. There are existing developers who have exposure to the tech stack used in the legacy application. The organization might consider hiring a cohort of individuals skilled in the target tech stack as the most immediate option to initiate the engagement. The downside is that the existing people in the ecosystem will become redundant. Thus, the pragmatic and win-win strategy would be to upskill the team members and bring in a temporary external expert.

Putting on the hat of the primary stakeholder in the situation, give a try to think of a potential strategy to handle the scenario effectively.

Author's take on the thought experiment

The team, when new to a technology, will require some preparation and groundwork. To deliver and learn in parallel, divide and conquer would be one of the strategies. Becoming an expert will be a sizable task; however, if the team's collective knowledge meets the required threshold, it provides a solid bootstrapping mechanism to initiate the engagement. Reading between the lines of the thought experiment, one can deduce that there was a product already available in the market, which means an existing mobile application development expertise is already within the team. The closer the new framework for modernization is to the existing technology, the faster the learning will happen.

Alternatively, as a learning strategy, the team can divide the learning into multiple segments and democratize the learning to the entire team via mob-programming. The sponsor of the project would consider this activity to be cost-intensive. If the overall cost of hiring and bringing in expertise to replace the current team is looked at, this strategy of upskilling would leave the organization in a better position due to the business context available with the existing team.

Thought experiment two

A second use case is presented to consolidate the ideas shared in the chapter, and to help understand how these can be applied in a real-life situation. The use case presented is for an organization developing a mobile banking application.

Banking application

A mobile application built for a banking domain, providing core banking capabilities in the **minimum viable product (MVP)** features, should now be transformed to include an ecosystem of other products. The mobile application in this phase is planning for an overhaul of the UI, along with the other digital services added to the mobile application. The additional features, such as managing portfolios and products, such as cards, family accounts, etc., will now come under one umbrella on this mobile application. The organization wants to go to market faster and has decided to increase the team size to get maximum parallelization post-MVP.

Being the stakeholder for the engagement, try to map the probable fan out of the team structure in the situation.

Author's take on the thought experiment

A typical banking application can have *login, registration (onboarding), banking accounts, banking products,* and *profile* as the top categories of features, and the narrative indicates these features were built in the MVP stage. The following context is assumed, which resonates with an ideal scenario for this banking mobile application. This banking application team plans to run two parallel streams, which is a result of the hiring capability limit of the organization, along with the time to market not being very aggressive for the post-MVP modernization. Login, registration, and the profile are closely related to each other, and the possibility of reuse is highly likely with respect to the user interface in this flow. The team member who has worked on the login and registration flow will have a better handle on the business context. Similarly, the core banking feature and the different products would be separate features altogether and would be different from each other. The downstream system that manages these different features could be different, depending on the banking capabilities.

Based on this context, there are two additional possibilities of team structure influenced by the choice of technology. If the team decides to go with native technology, two developers, one each for iOS and Android, a quality analyst, and two backend developers per stream could be the composition of the team. There will be one program manager looking at the overall application and the two streams for executing the post-MVP. In such a setup, there will be a designated technology lead per stream to mediate and ensure collaboration that aligns with the larger product. The UI/UX and the product-related operational role will be additional to the technology team.

In the case of the stakeholder wanting to reduce the time to market, and if the feature remains the same, the team can, at a maximum, increase the stream to three streams because the products introduced as part of this banking application are not very complex in implementation.

Conclusion

Operationally organizing a team is a subjective topic and can take multiple dimensions. The prime objective of the chapter was to look into this topic and explore the ideas to form collaborating teams. The intent of the chapter was to break the entry barrier for a technology-focused individual to operational thinking. The operational thinking is required to ensure a team is collaborative and high-performing in an engagement.

In the situation where the product development is complex and requires more time to develop, and the stakeholders want to go to market, it would call for a strategy to have more parallel streams of work. In a large team where the team is contributing to the same codebase, additional focus is required to be effective and bring a qualitative outcome. The reader shall now be equipped with the idea that, when practiced, will help to reduce points of failure in an engagement. As a stakeholder, it would be effective to identify and channel the strengths of various individuals in the team to get the best outcome. An efficient team has equal opportunity for growth for everyone. Supporting everyone to become a superhero would be something that an organization should ideally strive for and can reap a long-term positive impact.

While the entire theme of the book is to empower the reader in technology leadership, this chapter specifically focuses on the operational acumen that complements the technology leadership that a mobile developer should have. The reason for the shift is to emphasize that an individual's efficacy can be improved by having operational acumen. This knowledge is necessary for vertical growth in an organizational structure.

In the next chapter, we will discuss how to establish effective quality assurance strategies for mobile application development. It covers testing methodologies, best practices, and practical insights that enable teams to deliver high-quality applications.

Takeaways and reflections

As the narrative reached the end of the chapter, the reader should now be equipped with insight into the purpose of why certain structures exist in an organization. The reader will now be aware that there are strategic tools and techniques one can leverage to empower a team.

The following are some key highlights from the chapter:

- A team is a large or small group of individuals working together to attain a common goal.
- Enterprises should have an individual specialized in the nuances of the native mobile development frameworks to build a scalable, intuitive, and performant application. This is irrespective of whether the enterprise uses the native frameworks directly to build an application or not. The knowledge of native behavior is important to get the best from the device's capabilities.
- For any organization, the more detached the individuals involved in development, the better the business continuity plan. For example, consciously rotating people and ensuring the project does not rely on a single person can be one strategy to reduce dependency on an individual.
- Laying the groundwork for having a platform for context sharing or conducting tech sessions across teams can improve collaboration and pave the way for a high-performing team.
- An increase in possible communication channels (number of people interacting) can bring inefficiencies; however, if the time to market is short and critical, the challenge of meeting the timeline for the product can be achieved by adding more capacity, splitting the task among parallel teams.
- The concept of a central team is employed to have a top-down model to ensure there is cross-cutting equivalence in ways of working. This is essential when a large team is logically separated into squads. The central team will also help to optimize the communication effectiveness and focus.
- Operational acumen for a mobile developer would contribute to an individual's efficacy in being proactive and is an essential element to grow vertically in the organization's roles.

Join our Discord space

CHAPTER 5
Quality Assurance for Mobile Development

Introduction

Quality assurance (**QA**) is an integral part of any software or product. A software failure can have a catastrophic effect on the end users. It is very important to take QA as a discipline to be adhered to by any team. In mobile development, quality is the key component that drives success and brand retention. Quality will ensure the product gets the competitive edge in the market. QA for the whole product is a separate domain. To do justice in covering the depth of content requires a separate book covering the whole gamut of topics under QA. The focus of this chapter is not to be exhaustive or to cover the entire landscape, but rather to focus on the items relevant to a development team building a mobile application.

Structure

This chapter covers the following topics:

- Quality assurance
- Purpose of testing
- Quality assurance strategy
- Unit test coverage
- Challenges, risks, and learnings
- Testing and defining the QA strategy case study
- AI in context of quality assurance

Objectives

The purpose of this chapter is to provide insights into setting up the strategies to ensure the quality of the mobile application being developed. The topics covered in the chapter will be specific to mobile development from the perspective of what a development team should do. The chapter shall discuss topics covering an ideal test pyramid, different possible test strategies, the benefits, and the time impact of testing, qualitative tests, and the examples of a few ground experiences from projects. Practicing the theory and deploying the knowledge to production concludes the chapter, solidifying the know-how required for a developer.

Quality assurance

QA is the umbrella terminology encompassing all the forms of testing and gatekeeping mechanisms to ensure the quality of the product under development. Often, testing and quality assurance are used interchangeably; however, in a strict sense, QA is a process-focused approach to quality, while testing is a specific strategy to execute and verify the various touchpoints of quality.

Testing is the process of evaluating any system, product, or idea. Testing ensures that the functionality meets expectations of defined standards and performs as intended under various conditions. If one looks back into history, one can see that it was during the eighteenth and nineteenth centuries that testing became a more organized discipline in manufacturing and science, and standards started popping up. In software development specifically, the mid-twentieth century marked the beginning of structured testing practices, coinciding with the programming languages becoming more accessible. Testing started with informal means for error detection and debugging to become an organized discipline. The establishment of the first ISO standards for software testing (ISO 9000) happened in the 1980s and can be seen as an outcome aligned with testing becoming a discipline.

Purpose of testing

It is expected of a developer to do a sanity check on the functionality that each individual has developed before calling out the completion status. In a large application, the developer will have an extra responsibility to ensure that there is no side effect created by the code change to an existing functionality. This is the first time the quality of the mobile app being developed is checked, and the ownership lies with the developer.

In an ideal world, this should be good enough to ensure that the mobile app has met quality standards. However, the ideal case is very far from reality. The possibility of software having side effects leading to improper functioning of the mobile app is the ground reality.

Once the developer completes the functionality, the QA team takes control. Breaking the system and finding the problems in the functionality would be the main aim of the testing team. The mobile app goes through these software development lifecycle stages and reaches the end customer. Each of these stages has the probability of failing to serve the purpose. The severity of the failure can vary from case to case. Moreover, such failure can create a bad reputation for mobile applications. If these failures are at the end customer stage, the user can go to the extent of deleting the application from their mobile.

This catastrophe needs to be avoided, and testing is a means to preempt this by ensuring the correctness of the mobile application before reaching the consumers.

Testing through the lens of SDLC

Multiple phases of the **software development lifecycle** (**SDLC**) were quoted in *Chapter 2, Planning Your Mobile App Project*. In a normal sense, one would tie the testing to be part of the execution phase. This idea may even limit the QA stage to only a part of the execution stage. However, the mindset to ensure the quality should start from the very moment a product idea is realized. The product idea is converted into actions in the various stages of SDLC. The mindset of quality, along with structural thinking, forms the foundation for building world-class software. A QA strategy for an enterprise would thus be an essential ingredient in SDLC.

Table 5.1 lists examples of QA activities in various stages of SDLC:

SDLC stages	QA activities examples
Understanding the requirement and defining the backlog	Requirement review, defining QA strategy, test case creation, and test planning.
Baselining and estimation of the user stories	Test case estimation, test data planning, and test plan creation.
Determining raw velocity and creating a release plan	Velocity testing, recalibrated during execution, release plan validation, risk assessment.
Ready with a proposal	Test scope review, proposal review, and readiness check.
Execution: Development, delivery, maintenance, and upgrade	Unit testing, integration testing, functional testing, automation testing, and other mechanisms.
Coming up with actual velocity	Test execution metrics, defect tracking, regression testing, performance testing.

SDLC stages	QA activities examples
Prioritization and readjustment	Test re-prioritization, impact analysis, and retesting.
Revisiting the project plan	Reviewing progress, test case re-evaluation, and risk evaluation.

***Table 5.1:** Example of possibilities of testing in SDLC*

Gatekeeping mechanism

The primary goal for a developer is to build a great mobile app. There are other aspects that the developer should give appropriate weightage to keep the mobile application sustainable. The cost of refactoring, the maintainability, the ease of scaling, or adding new features are a few aspects a developer can have control over and impact on the longevity of a mobile application.

There are factors like maintaining clean, readable code, following best practices, etc., that the team must ensure. The most critical aspect from the consumer's point of view is the quality and functioning of the application. These test mechanisms can act as the gatekeeper for refactoring, preventing side effects and regression, and can be used to do sanity checks on the application. The popular testing mechanisms and the purpose that each of these serves in the context of mobile application development are explored further in this section.

Manual testing

Testing applications by having human intervention to validate the various functional flows is termed manual testing. The mobile application developed can be shipped as an artifact to be installed on a real device or a simulator. An individual performing these tests can use either a simulator or a device to validate the functional accuracy. The accurate means to ensure the correctness is to test on real devices with an equivalent or actual production-ready setup.

Unit test

A unit test is a test done on the smallest scope of functionality identified as a logical unit. A unit test would only worry about an input and the expected output for the unit under test. A typical mobile application project mostly has an object-oriented or functional programming language with a supporting framework for writing these unit tests. The classes that encapsulate the logic and the function inside the classes are the candidates for unit tests. By writing the unit test for a functionality implemented, it solidifies the accuracy and gives confidence in the functioning. The unit test also serves as the foundation to automate and validate to catch any side effects that might come in future code changes.

Automated unit tests can be the gatekeeping mechanism to safeguard the mobile application code base from erroneous functional behavior. This benefit comes with the catchphrase *The developer should write it right*. The accuracy of the thought process while writing the unit test, and the coverage obtained via these tests, will be the factors that ensure the team gets the full benefits of the unit test.

Here are some recommendations while writing a unit test:

- Ensure best practices and patterns for unit tests are followed when writing.
- Ensure each test is readable and independent of other unit tests.
- Write unit tests such that they serve as the documentation to understand the system.
- Ensure unit tests are written by the same developer while developing functionality.
- Practicing **test-driven development** (**TDD**) would be a great step toward the quality of the product and code. A developer should be able to wear both a developer and a tester hat alternatively; in the process of development, the core idea enables the TDD thinking.
- Do not write an empty or purposeless test for the sake of improving coverage.
- Ensure brittle tests are not present in the test suite.

These recommendations are not exhaustive; however, they are the prominent ones that must be strictly followed.

A better unit test can be written if the developer invests time to understand the scenarios to be tested. Writing the unit test by the same developer ensures the context and the relevance of the functionality are available to the developer, enabling them to write better unit tests. An ideal practice is to write a unit test case along with the functional development, rather than deferring to a later stage. The development frameworks have adapted to accommodate, support, and enable writing unit tests. Additionally, there are third-party frameworks and libraries to reduce boilerplate code as well. Together, built-in framework support and third-party testing libraries form support ecosystems to ensure there are strong test suites as the guardrail for the quality of the application.

Component test and integration test

For an end user, a mobile application is a collection of **user interfaces** (**UI**) that provide an experience that helps the user achieve certain objectives via interaction. These are composed by combining different UI elements provided by the framework and customizing the properties to suit the application's behavior.

A mobile application can have a custom UI element used once or as a reusable UI element. Similarly, there can even be a certain flow or large components developed from multiple smaller UI elements reused. On these components, the styles and colors applicable to the brand of an organization are applied to form the interface that the user interacts with.

Every development framework comes with the base UI components. As the development frameworks change, nomenclatures for these UI elements also differ. Some frameworks call these views/sub-views, while others call them widgets. Components is also a popular name to represent these.

The base elements provided by the framework are tested and proven to work on the platform itself. These components will not require separate testing while used inside the application as is. However, the ones that teams develop by combining these would have different states and behaviors. In such a case, there is scope for testing to ensure the accuracy of the behavior. For reusable components, specifically in a large project, any developer can change the behavior at random, intentionally, or unintentionally. If the developer is unaware of the impact on other areas where this component is used, it would cause an adverse impact and is not desirable. This warrants a gatekeeping mechanism to validate and keep the behavior of the component intact.

The UI element developed can be tested independently or as part of a user journey. This decision is taken by the team based on the complexity of the UI Layer. This thus translates to component testing for independent UI elements and integration testing for a journey as two strategies one can use to test.

Component testing, also known as a widget test or headless test, is a test that is written for smaller UI elements developed to design the mobile application screens. These can be tested independently or along with the containing page. The component testing is a slight variation of an integration test for mobile applications. The scope, possibilities, and capabilities of the component test depend on and are influenced by the development framework itself. For example, in Flutter, tests can be done to validate the value assignment to the field, the overflow factor, the state changes, visibility, etc., on an independent widget. On the other hand, for native iOS (as of the time of writing), there is no separate framework provided by Apple for component testing equivalent to Flutter's widget test; rather, the component or subview must be tested as part of the unit test framework itself. In native iOS, the test can be written for any of the subviews, views, or view controllers implementation for validating the behaviors associated with these.

Integration test suite, on the other hand, is a collection of tests that run to verify user journeys in the mobile application. These tests will focus on the multiple negative and positive user journeys within the application. The integration test suite will cover the journey from an end-to-end perspective.

Component tests can be preferred over integration tests for faster feedback during the development phase. The overhead associated with executing the component test is much less than that of the integration test. Integration tests are run on actual devices or simulated devices. Running a test on a device or simulated device has a higher impact on the time taken to execute the test, due to the non-deterministic nature of the downstream system. This non-determinism will also impact the fragility of the test.

It is always best to avoid writing logic inside the view or UI layer. A clean code should strictly adhere to this principle. Avoiding logic inside the UI layer gives the advantage of reducing the impact of UI layers undergoing frequent changes. Keeping the moving parts separate could really be beneficial to reduce the cost caused by the change. The costs of execution associated with the UI test are also greater than those of unit tests and are dependent on the framework used for development. Later in the chapter, where the ideal test pyramid is explained, it will help the reader to understand the percentage of components or integration tests that a developer should incorporate in the gatekeeping mechanism for a project. The *Test pyramid* section in this chapter will explain the different layers of testing. The component and integration tests form the minimal set of tests in the top layer of tests, and should cover the scenarios and cases that cannot be covered by the lower layer of unit tests. The critical journey of the mobile application will be the focus area covered by the integration test.

The end-to-end integration tests are generally owned and written by the testing team; however, organization to organization, this would vary. The focus for the development team would be to ensure maximum coverage at the unit test layer and reduce the reliance on integration tests.

Screenshot testing

In the context of mobile testing screenshot comparison is used to refer to the matching of the outcome rendered on the device with an expected reference image. This could be the entire screen or at an individual component level. Now the testing can happen at a pixel-level visual verification or matching code generated as composition tree presented to the rendering engine. In frameworks such as Jest (React Native) or Flutter's widget-test, *snapshot testing* is a term related to the technique that compares the component tree composition via code.

The question to ponder would be how one can ensure the UI components developed are intact for rendering on multiple screens where it is used. Being intact would mean ensuring that there is no code change, intentional or unintentional, that alters the visual appearance of these components from an established reference.

The conventional way to find and verify the accuracy of the component would be to install the application and test it manually. Checking the critical journeys inside the mobile app and ensuring the areas where the UI component is used are functioning is the expectation of manual testing. The manual effort required for more such components would impact the overall release timeline and is proportional to the number of features in the application.

An alternative means to reduce the manual effort is to introduce screenshot testing. The approach is a pixel-by-pixel comparison of a UI component. The reference of the expected UI Component is created and stored, and for subsequent runs, these references are used for comparison to validate any impact due to code changes.

The coverage one can plan in screenshot testing will be the different possible states that the UI component can render. These can be verified for different possible canvases as well.

Screenshot testing does not guarantee the consumer of the UI Component the correctness of the functionality. One should note that the component itself is a higher-level abstraction. These components combined will represent an application-specific UI layer, which in turn becomes the functional features. Thus, it is the responsibility of the developer to configure and use the component in the right way to get the functional accuracy. Screenshot tests do not compare the screen with the mockup provided by a user experience team; rather, they can be considered the gatekeeping mechanism to ensure that the look of the already developed component is not modified unintentionally.

Screenshot testing is relevant for mobile application projects that have UI components that are built as common components and reused at multiple places. Screenshot testing serves the purpose of pixel-to-pixel comparison to catch any unintentional UI changes from the expected reference image.

The team can organize these UI components as libraries or common packages. These packages are UI libraries or toolkits that would be used to build the entire screen for a mobile application. This library is labeled a **design language system** (**DLS**). DLS is a design strategy to ensure a common brand across organizations. The team converts the specification from a UI/UX team to a design language system library in code. Such a library can leverage the pixel-to-pixel comparison on the expected reference image, and the component under test could be used to ensure and safeguard the accuracy of the functioning and rendering of the component.

The important consideration one should be aware of is the different sets of devices with a variety of sizes and dimensions in the mobile space. In such a case, screenshot testing should be under the same set of parameters used to create the reference screenshot.

Contract testing

For mobile applications that are transactional in nature, the information is either presented or collected. This is coordinated with a computer system in a network to collect or be serviced to provide information. Consider the example of account opening, purchase of any goods, money transfer, account details, etc., which happen with the support of the respective backend system. In each of these cases, the mobile application and the integrating system communicate via an agreed protocol and format. The agreement between the mobile application and the integrating system on a certain format and pattern is a contract. This section uses the label integrating system to represent the software/computer that the mobile application communicates with.

Either in the case of getting the data from the integrating system or sending the data to the integrating system, there can be bottlenecks that cause failure. These failures can disrupt the user using the mobile app. The failure could occur due to either an issue related to the connected system or incorrect implementation on the mobile application codebase. The important takeaway is that these bottlenecks should be handled gracefully to ensure a great experience for the user.

An integrating system will send data for mobile apps to consume in an agreed format, or the mobile application sending the data to the integrating system in a consumable format is the key to ensuring successful integration of both systems. Any change in the format that either the mobile app or the integrating system does not understand would be a potential cause for undesirable behavior in the mobile application.

A software system evolves over time and the agreed communication contract between a mobile application and its backend is subject to change. This may cause failure. To handle the failure of a contract in such cases, the developer can build backward compatibility by retaining old integration while releasing a new version. Alternatively, to handle the failure, the organization can block old versions of mobile applications while the release of a new version occurs. The mitigation strategy is not foolproof, as there could still be a case where the end user cannot upgrade to the new app.

The mitigation strategy holds true only when both mobile applications and the service provider are aware of the contract change, which implicitly means that there should be backward compatibility and the old incompatible version of app should be blocked. In the case where there is an oversight from the service provider, where the contract is changed, or vice versa, the effect can be catastrophic. If the mobile app fails or if any critical functionality of the app cannot be performed, it can lead to a bad experience and cost reputation loss for the organization.

Examples of frustrating moments are:

- When a user cannot transfer money or get account details in a banking app.
- When an online shopping app is not allowing users to track details or process a refund request.
- When a stock trading prevents the user from placing an order.

Imagine being the end user in each of these cases, and the impact on personal life will be daunting to go through such pains.

Thus, for ensuring the stability of a system, it is important to have early-stage failure-detecting mechanisms. The information from the failure detected will help to take appropriate corrective action before end users are affected. This proactive approach will have a positive impact on the consumer experience and, thereby, the brand.

Contract testing is one such approach where there would be an automated test suite that will be run on a predetermined schedule. The end goal would be to ensure that the critical integration points are working as expected. For any failure in these tests, the appropriate team can be intimated to respond to the situation. Having the failure information at hand can even help the customer service team to ensure they communicate the disruption of service to consumers up front, reassuring them that the remedial action is in progress rather than being clueless.

Performance testing

The mobile application development team shall encounter the following feedback regarding the app performance:

- It is taking too long for the application to launch. In certain platforms, if the app launch takes too long, the OS would prevent such apps from launching.
- The mobile app user is experiencing jitter or jank while using the mobile application.
- App is not responding while scrolling or navigating inside.
- Upon returning to the mobile application from the background, the mobile application does not remember the state where the user had left the mobile app.
- Battery is draining while the application is in use.
- Mobile app crashes.

This list is not exhaustive; however, it should be prevented and fixed when they occur to provide a better experience for mobile application users. A developer ideally should consider these aspects while developing the mobile application. From time to time, it is also highly recommended to use the tools and instrumentation techniques to keep track of these in the mobile application. To get similar feedback while the mobile application is in the field, strategies should be engaged to capture and evaluate the relevant metrics on application performance.

Each platform provides tools to capture and analyze these bottlenecks that hinder a great mobile app experience. This form of analysis done on the mobile application can be collectively called performance testing. The performance testing shall be done considering various factors such as the lower-end device to be supported, the network bandwidth being limited, the background usage, etc.

Running the performance tests will help identify the following issues with the mobile application:

- High memory usage
- Incorrect memory clean-up
- Unnecessary usage of mobile hardware features
- Unnecessary computation
- Longer computation blocking the UI rendering operations for the application, causing frame drops.

Fixing these issues and ensuring the team understands the best practices to avoid such issues would play a key role in building high-performance and resilient applications.

Static analysis

A programming language will have best practices for the usage while writing code. The aesthetics and readability could be improved by following these best practices. There are tools that can be used along with different frameworks to catch the deviations. The process of analyzing the code in its raw form to capture the deviation from the standard and potential flaws is called static analysis. The static analyzer can be configured to capture custom rules defined for a particular team as well. The static analyzer will give an indicator to improve the performance of the code by pointing out incorrect usages in the code base for any pre-encoded anti-patterns in the scanning tools.

One can comprehend that till now the theme discussed covered some of the potential strategies to ensure quality checkpoints at the development stage. Setting up these has an impact on cost and time. However, in the long run, the benefit coming from the extra investment will outweigh the cost factor.

A team can make use of the benefit from the test only if there is a habit of executing these when changes are made. After writing all the unit test cases, if the individual developer does not execute the test suite before promoting the changes to the source control, the setup may not deliver the expected results. This topples down the purpose of having the unit test. The developer forgetting to run the test cases could be due to the misconfiguration of the hooks in the local development system. The best practice for any team would be to configure hooks for the source control for individual developers that automatically trigger the test execution for the source control action. These hooks will ensure that the necessary tests are run and, on success status, promote the changes. The hook can also incorporate tools that would auto-correct some of the errors or warnings in the code. The static analysis can be configured at various stages of SDLC. It depends on the automation requirement and the scope where the static analysis is triggered. Generally, the static analysis is configured as a pre-commit Git hook in the development machine and as an additional gatekeeping mechanism in the CI/CD runner. The details of the workflow are detailed in *Chapter 8, Scalability in Mobile Development: Part 2*.

Other testing terminologies

There are other variations of testing, such as integration testing, regression testing, user acceptance testing, sanity testing, etc. Some of these variations may have overlapping responsibilities as well. Incorporating these strategies based on the need ensures quality at various stages of software development. As defined in the objective, the chapter does not focus exhaustively on all the different testing ideologies and strategies. However, having an overview of different mechanisms at a high level relevant to mobile application development will be beneficial to the reader. *Table 5.2* summarizes the additional testing strategies relevant to mobile application development:

Testing type	Description
UI/UX testing	The testing ensures the app's UI and **user experience (UX)** meet the design specification. This is done by ensuring pixel-to-pixel comparison of the screen with the original design artifact referenced for development.
Functional testing	This testing ensures the validation of the correctness of the feature built by the team, matching the requirement.
Load testing	This is a subset of performance testing relevant to the backend. As mobile application is the consumer of backend, this test will also enable the developer to validate the behavior of an application for an occurrence of delay, failure, or unresponsiveness when the backend is under heavy workloads.
Chaos/stress testing	Tests the app under extreme conditions (e.g., very high network traffic or low resources) to determine its breaking point and recovery capabilities. The idea of the chaos test is to break the system by inducing a situation that will affect users on rare occasions. Another example is to test the behavior of an application during an incoming call on a mobile application.
Compatibility testing	Testing to verify if the app works seamlessly on different devices, operating systems, screen sizes, and hardware configurations relevant to the target audience.
Security testing	This testing will help to find vulnerabilities in the app and pre-empt the possibility of any malicious activity. The data from this testing for the vulnerability detected will help the team to harden the mobile application.
Localization testing	Testing will ensure the app's accuracy in different languages and cultural contexts. Additionally, this testing strategy will also ensure that as the language changes, the characters are not misaligned or cause any UI to break.
Regression testing	Testing to ensure that the new code changes or updates to the app are not creating an unexpected or erroneous side effect to existing features or functionalities.
Beta testing	Testing which involves closed group users (outside the development team) in real-world conditions to identify the functioning of the application before the official release.
User acceptance testing (UAT)	Testing that involves a user equivalent to the end user's persona to confirm the app meets their requirements and expectations before being deployed to production. This could be done by the stakeholder to sign off on the release as well.
Network testing	Test the app's behavior under different network conditions, particularly in low-bandwidth situations, to ensure that the app functions well across various network speeds.

Testing type	Description
Crash testing	Testing to identify any situation where the app may crash or freeze. The idea is to handle errors gracefully without impacting the user experience.
Accessibility testing	Testing to ensure that the app is usable by people who are differentially abled. This testing also ensures that the app is adhering to accessibility guidelines.
Installation testing	Testing the process of installing, updating, and uninstalling the app and its effect on the target device. An example is the case of data migration in an application.
App store testing	Testing if the app meets the guidelines and requirements set by app stores for successful submission and approval.

***Table 5.2:** Other testing mechanisms prevalent in industry*

In most organizations, the needs and focus area will drive the team to use a combination of these testing strategies as a gatekeeping mechanism. In some cases, these testing strategies are combined under a single label to perform different responsibilities. An example one may see in real life is the use of label performance testing to encompass the expectation of crash testing, installation testing, network testing, etc., along with the actual expectation of performance testing. In short, employing every testing mechanism is not mandatory, and the context relevance should be considered to define the tests required to ensure quality for the application. The next section focuses on defining the quality strategy and considerations while prioritizing the required test mechanisms for a project.

Quality assurance strategy

In SDLC, the QA strategy defines the different kinds of testing mechanisms. A team, while defining the QA strategy, decides which stage a particular testing mechanism should be used. Defining the optimal testing mechanisms for the project, defining a plan of action, and segregating different kinds of gatekeeping mechanisms will be part of the QA strategy. A project with a QA strategy ensures execution has the right checkpoints to prevent leaking of inadvertent behavior to the consumer side of the mobile application. QA strategy also improves confidence to release. Additionally, the testing should not be overkill, causing unnecessary slowdowns. One should avoid duplication of effort, and this will be a factor to consider while defining the test mechanism in the QA strategy.

Ensuring the right mix of quality mechanisms

As part of defining the QA strategy, it is essential to ensure the right mix of mechanisms is included to ensure quality. Overdoing or adding unnecessary test mechanisms will attract cost without adding any value to the QA. Investing in knowing the purpose served by each testing mechanism will give the decision-making group the insight to define the right QA strategy for the project's SDLC. Right from the kickoff of the project until the very end, testing should be an essential part of any project.

For example, consider the case of designing a screen starting from the user experience stage until release to the end user. Validating the design with a potential set of users on the visual experience is the test mechanism that is required at the stage of experience design. Once the designs are validated and finalized, the next step is the implementation and the gatekeeping mechanism to ensure the implementation is as per design and functionally correct. Once validated, the release occurs, and there could be production issues reported. These production issues are fixed and validated with the gatekeeping mechanism at the post-release stage as well. All these mechanisms form a cycle in the mobile application development SDLC.

The testing mechanisms can overlap with each other. Ensuring the overall outcomes are mutually exclusive for each mechanism within a QA strategy is ideal. A QA strategy defined for the application with the right level of testing mechanism will help to get a holistic and exhaustive coverage, ensuring the quality of mobile applications being developed. The usage of the right level is intentional to emphasize the fact that employing a repetitive strategy to validate an already validated feature is an anti-pattern. Each testing mechanism can have its own and different overheads. These overheads have a direct impact on the time to set up, execute, and maintain. Understanding this overhead is critical to devising the appropriate mix and to contextualizing the project's relevance of a test mechanism. For example, in a medium-sized system where the backend team and mobile team are collocated and working closely together, the contract testing does not need to be mandated in the QA strategy. Focusing on ensuring better collaboration and communication would be more beneficial for an organization than mandating contract testing.

Cost of defect

The development time a team spends creating a functional software has a direct relationship to the cost of the software. One of the success factors for the project is keeping the operational cost at an optimal level. A defect in the system also affects the project cost. The time spent correcting the defect would be a cost that adds to the project. If the defects are ignored, it will influence consumers, which would add to the indirect costs. Consumer feedback has the power to tarnish the goodwill of the mobile application as well, thereby affecting the organization's growth.

The narrative further explores the time and resources consumed by the development team to identify and fix defects that is direct project cost. Identifying a defect, if any, before reaching the consumer is the core responsibility of QA. The defect can thus be fixed, and the repercussions can be curbed. Interestingly, the time at which the defect is identified in a system also plays a role in determining the cost of fixing. The later a defect is identified, the higher the cost. The major factors that increase the cost would be the loss of context for the requirement or code and the time taken to reproduce the issue in the developer environment, derailing the current pipeline item. Consider the case where a developer is working on a particular feature and has a great context for the feature while developing it. As the developer moves on to another task or after a long duration when the same developer is not available to fix the issue, analyzing the issue and finding the root cause could become time-consuming in most cases. This may bring a situation where the current item or feature that the individual must work on needs to be reprioritized. The summary from the example is that the overall time required to resolve the defect will increase exponentially with the time factor and complexity.

A defect crept in as a side effect of code change made for a new feature introduced would be another situation. There are chances that these defects are easily missed. The probability of the defect getting missed is high in a project that does not have enough gatekeeping mechanisms. The cost of such defects can be more. These defects can be silent killers to the brand itself if the impact is high on the consumers.

In summary, a defect found in the development stage will have a lesser cost burden than one found in the testing stage. The cost could be the highest if the defect is found once the mobile app goes live. Thus, preventing defects and mitigation at an early stage is effective in reducing the cost.

Shifting left

The whole theme of QA strategy has a close connection with the concept of the cost of defect and getting early feedback. The strategy which advocates moving the quality activities closer to the development lifecycle to ensure defects are caught closer to the point of introduction is termed shift left. Getting early feedback can bring tremendous efficiency in the execution with respect to cost and stability of the mobile application. The idea of shift left signifies having a mechanism closer to the start, ensuring the maximum coverage for testing of the functionality. As one move further up in the development lifecycle, the additional layer of testing mechanisms should complement the lower layer and try to cover functions that are not possible in the lower layer. The top layer of the test pyramid can remain lean avoiding duplication of the scenarios already covered for the testing in the lower layers. The idea of shifting left and having the right mix of testing will give the pyramid shape structure. The testing pyramid is one of the key outcomes of the QA strategy.

> Note: **Layers of testing indicate the different test mechanisms corresponding to the stages in SDLC. The next section will give more insights into the same.**

Test pyramid

Not all testing mechanisms need to be done with equal weightage to ensure quality. In other words, any project need not necessarily have an equal number or percentage of different kinds of test mechanisms. The QA stages that are not relevant to the context can very well be avoided if the business finds no value in them.

For a stakeholder, the key is to identify the team capable of defining the right QA strategy for the project. The ideal mix for different test mechanisms is combined based on the context of the project. The test mechanism that takes the minimum time to give feedback and is easy to implement gets the higher weightage. The team should ideally depend more on such a test mechanism. This criterion is used to prioritize the different test mechanisms in the QA strategy. The unit test is a lightweight mechanism in the development phase of SDLC and is the clear winner across all platforms to be the most effective mechanism to catch early feedback. The integration tests take a back seat as integration tests typically require more time to write/maintain the script, along with the execution time being longer compared to the unit test. The fragile nature of integration tests for changes may also become a bottleneck, causing false alarms. Relying on an integration test log will also be counterintuitive.

The prioritized test mechanism gives rise to a pyramid structure for the testing mechanisms employed in the project, as depicted in *Figure 5.1*:

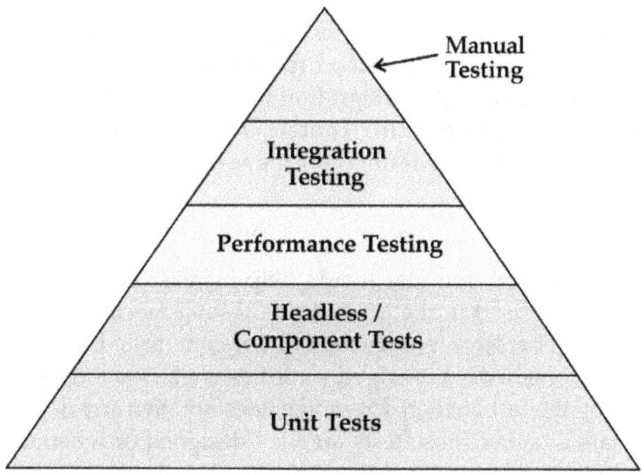

***Figure 5.1:** Ideal test pyramid*

The different kinds of test mechanisms for a typical project are depicted in *Figure 5.1*. The lower portion would indicate the test having a higher concentration with respect to the different scenarios or features being covered. As one moves up to the top in the test pyramid layer, the coverage or number of tests decreases. An ideal strategy would be in the top layer to cover the cases that cannot be covered at the bottom layer; thus, collectively, the test pyramid gives exhaustive coverage for the entire application.

The pyramid structure is also indicative of the cost and speed of execution for each kind of test. The top layer of the pyramid depicts a higher cost. For example, manual testing is above the integration test, which indicates the manual test as a cost and time-intensive process, attributed to longer feedback loops, prone to human error, being a labor-intensive process, etc. Therefore, it is always recommended to have maximum coverage in the lower layer and to keep the top layer lean. The pyramid structure, when inverted, becomes equivalent to an ice cream cone. *Figure 5.2* depicts the inverted cone structure of the test pyramid. This is an anti-pattern to be watched for and corrected. The unit test is intentionally omitted to show the worst-case situation where the testing is delayed as a post development activity, against the shift left strategy. The problem one can see in the ice cream cone is a defect identified later in the stage, increasing the cost to recover.

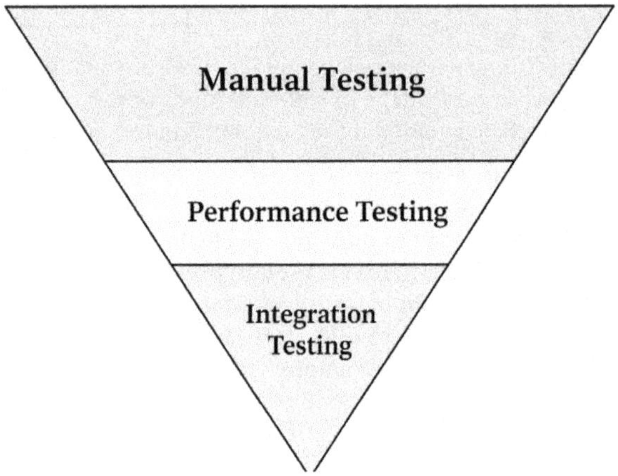

Figure 5.2: *Ice-cream cone test strategy*

Note: **The test pyramid does not include screenshot testing and contract testing. They are suited for special business use cases where the UI is built as an artifact to be consumed. The amount of the screenshot and contract test would be somewhere between the integration test and the unit test. The example highlights that every test pyramid is customized for the operating context. The combination of testing mechanisms would vary for different projects, affecting the layers defined for the test pyramid.**

Coverage

Coverage is an important piece of information that would help increase confidence in the stability of the mobile application. Coverage in the section is used in the context of a testing mechanism. Coverage as the metric would be an indicator for stakeholders to get a sense of functionality or code tested. The stakeholder can get hooked on this metric. Getting hooked can become a double-edged sword as well. Coverage gives the efficacy of the number of lines covered with the feature by the test written. Coverage does not give any details on the quality of the test, by which one will be able to evaluate whether those tests are well-designed or whether the right scenarios are being validated. Coverage should be holistic in nature and should not be localized to an individual testing mechanism as a metric for the entire project. Ideally, the expectation to meet the coverage should be a collective nature of the entire test mechanism. The team, when under pressure, can take a shortcut in the code to inflate the coverage number. This pattern is majorly seen when the top-down hierarchy of organization does not have an operational structure that understands that the test mechanism also must be carefully crafted and maintained. In such a situation, the team does not care about quality but will focus on getting the coverage number. This occurs when there is pressure to achieve the coverage without giving the required time, which affects the stability and accuracy of the mobile application test written and the features themselves. The recommendation is that the team should follow the test patterns. Test patterns ensure the test suite remains purposeful rather than becoming a showcase for coverage metrics.

Coverage when the test is written correctly can be considered as the measure of the overall feature that is covered in the testing suite, with reference to the totality of the features in the mobile application.

Unit test coverage

Each test mechanism can be used to compute the respective individual coverage. The unit test is the one that the team should maximize on to get a stable QA strategy for any project. Unit test coverage is a metric that is captured for the unit test execution. Unit test coverage helps to understand the lines of code traversed in the entire project when the unit test is executed. The unit test coverage report generation is provided as a capability of development tools in most cases. The time taken up for execution shall ideally be less compared to the other kinds of test mechanisms. The unit tests get the highest priority to be maintained in mobile application development from the stakeholders of the team.

Leveraging unit test coverage as a parameter to measure the quality of the test is an anti-pattern. The developers writing the unit test should never have the thought of meeting the coverage number as a priority. The quality of the test should be developers' priority, and meeting the coverage should be a side effect of quality unit tests. It is also important for the decision-making stakeholders to understand the coverage for the project at the test pyramid level when focusing on the product quality. The decision-making stakeholder should not push for 100 percent coverage. For the unit test, the quality of the test and focusing on faster turnaround time for development and release should be the key goals. The unit test coverage can, however, be used by a stakeholder to have an eye on the health of the system at a very high level. A stakeholder who is further interested in understanding the quality of the test should go thoroughly through the report than just using the coverage. The quality of the test is affected by multiple factors, such as a reduction in the total number of bug counts being reported after development, the overall reduction of issues, the confidence of the team to make the code changes, and the confidence to sign off on the release after executing the test suite. All these will define the quality of the unit test suites.

Educating the developer on the advantages of the unit test suite and bringing the culture to the team where relevant unit tests are written could be a theme that every organization should focus on and invest in. This idea should be the key purpose that drives the testing strategy.

Defining QA strategy

QA strategy, in most cases, will be defined at an enterprise level for the entire software suite. The decisions are largely influenced by how an organization is structured. Mobile development, in most cases, for an enterprise, goes hand in hand with interacting systems. The downstream systems with which the mobile interacts may also be going through changes and implementation; therefore, the QA strategy defined for end-to-end development for an engagement is optimal for the organization. As part of this chapter, the focus is mainly on defining the mobile QA strategy for a project. The stakeholders defining the QA strategy prepare comprehensive details on the items described in *Table 5.3*, thus defining the QA strategy:

Component	Description
Testing objectives	The QA strategy should have a definition of the testing goals.
Scope of testing	The QA strategy should have the definition of inclusion and exclusion, specifying the boundaries of testing.
Testing levels/types	The QA strategy should describe different levels/types of testing, thus forming the test pyramid. There could be multiple test pyramids based on the separation of different systems of technology. Examples of types of testing are functional, non-functional, black box, etc.
Test environment	The QA strategy should detail the hardware, software, and configurations required for testing. The device matrix is the key factor to evaluate and baseline the sign-off process.
Test data	The QA strategy should detail the data to be used for testing, including production, anonymized, or synthetic/mock data.
Roles and responsibilities	The QA strategy should detail the roles of team members and their specific responsibilities in the testing and escalation matrix.
Test deliverables	The QA strategy should define the artifacts and reports produced during the testing process (e.g., test cases, reports, coverage data, etc.).
Defect management	The QA strategy should detail the mechanism around defect triaging, with details such as where defects will be reported, prioritized, tracked, and resolved throughout.
Entry and exit criteria	The QA strategy should detail the start and sign-off strategy to close the testing.
Test tools	The QA strategy should detail the tools used for test management, automation, performance testing, and defect tracking.

Component	Description
Test schedule	The QA strategy should detail timelines for test planning, execution, and reporting across testing phases that go hand in hand with the development. The team should also define the capacity required to do the testing.
Risk management	The QA strategy should detail potential risks to testing and how they will be mitigated or managed.
Operational details	The QA strategy should detail the matrix and tracking of testing efficiency, along with the process for defining feedback collection to review the QA strategy based on the project plan.

Table 5.3: *Components of a QA strategy*

Unit testing as developer's focus area

The tendency of developers to delegate the quality responsibility entirely to the QA team cannot be ignored. This pattern should be avoided. Quality, being everyone's responsibility, is the idea that should drive any team. This would help the team to be autonomous and collaborative. The school of thought advocated in this section agrees on the need for a specialized role of QA. The emphasis is on the importance of a collective responsibility of the team to ensure quality. Such a setup, complemented with clear segregation of responsibility of who owns a particular segment of the testing mechanism, will ensure the actions are not orphaned.

Note: **There are other schools of thought as well. The organization contesting the need for a specialized role of QA is an example of another school of thought. In this case, the responsibility of ensuring quality is divided among roles in the team. This format will be effective when each role in the team wears multiple hats of responsibility.**

In any case, the developer is responsible for taking up some of the testing mechanisms to ensure the quality of the software developed. The unit test is the crucial piece that the developer completely owns. In mobile development, when UI is involved, there will be business logic which transform and decide the state how UI is rendered. These logic and UI behaviors are expected to be tested by developer with automated script. There will be cases that cannot be adequately covered alone by the unit tests; these may become the area to be covered in the top layer of the test pyramid. These get covered in headless or integration tests. In practice, the integration test is the sole responsibility of a QA role. However, the headless test, which leverages the unit testing framework to write tests at the component level, would be better handled by a developer.

Note: **In principle, the developer is responsible for writing the unit test following the right pattern. The unit test should ideally evolve with the change in the code base. Throwing away existing tests, particularly, should be kept to a minimum when the functionality itself is enhanced, not replaced. The existing test should be intact to ensure the functionality introduction has not caused side effects that change previous behavior and does not add complexity to maintain and rewrite for every change, which does not alter the entire old functionality, as discussed in the next section. Unit tests should be written as a guardrail and not for the sake of meeting the coverage number. The anti-pattern - writing tests purely to meet a coverage number is quite prevalent. This often defeats the purpose of unit tests, as discussed in the coverage section.**

Brittleness of unit test

A failing test is a good sign to get early feedback. If these unit test failures are a false positive, the feedback would be counterproductive for the purpose served.

A non-deterministic behavior in test results is unproductive and challenging. For a team, the investigation on the **root cause analysis** (**RCA**) will be challenging. Understanding the pattern and cause in such cases will be time-consuming, and it will derail the capacity for feature development as well. A unit test execution results behaving differently each time it is executed is an example of non-determinism.

The tests that randomly fail due to random or unknown reasons are brittle tests. One should always avoid writing and depending on such tests in the gatekeeping mechanism.

A code change to add features can trigger modification of the existing unit tests. This can be considered counterproductive in the case where the old features are intact. These tests should ideally function as is, which will be the expectation. When such a situation occurs, the team can evaluate to check whether the unit test code is written with the right pattern or if the code itself is architected to enable unit testing. Thus, the observation of a brittle test could be a hot spot to look for a code smell in architecture or a unit test. It would be a good checkpoint to revisit and evaluate the approach in such cases to refactor these.

The following are examples of some practices that the team can follow to avoid writing brittle unit tests:

- One should avoid writing environment-specific unit tests. For example, if there is a test that depends on the date and time zone of the system, the test would fail if the system date is changed.
- One should avoid writing unit tests that depend on other unit tests. A common oversight by the team is the usage of state information shared across multiple tests, causing a race condition in test execution. In such a case, independently the test may pass; however, when executed as a suite, it shall fail.
- Leveraging proper mock dependencies for non-deterministic hardware and framework features for testing. Examples are network-related classes, geo-location, etc., that should be mocked while the unit test cases are written.

Unit test suite execution time

The time of execution of a unit test affects the developer's overall productivity. This also has an impact on the time consumed in the release cycle. Thus, it is important to keep track of the factors affecting the test suite execution time. While writing unit tests, the team should think about the means to optimize them.

Consider the following two scenarios while working in a large team. In this case, the team uses source control to manage code collaboration:

- In one scenario, an individual, before committing the changes, should run the unit test suite to ensure other parts of the application are working as expected.
- In the other scenario, each individual, before releasing the completed feature, should follow certain predefined steps such as executing automation unit test suites, preparing the build and artifacts, beta testing, and going live when test results are positive.

In both cases, the larger the time taken to execute the unit test suite, the more it will have an impact on the time of completion of the activities. The overall productivity will also decrease as these are not one-time costs. For example, an individual developer running the unit test suite at a higher frequency will be waiting for a long time to get feedback if the test execution time is high.

Frameworks provide support and capability to optimize the test execution faster. For example, the Xcode test framework provides means to do parallel unit tests.

In a nutshell, it is always recommended to proactively invest in optimizing the time taken for unit test execution. For the mobile app project, the unit test layer being less time-intensive can be a guard for most features. The theme in this section ties back to the test pyramid explained earlier in the chapter. The time execution is one of the factors considered in positioning the various test mechanisms in the pyramid.

Challenges, risks, and learnings

There are challenges, risks, and tradeoffs while maintaining unit testing in an ecosystem. Having this insight shall help to pre-empt the overhead associated with the journey. The team can then use this insight to structure the test ecosystem to mitigate these challenges and overhead. The section ahead explores some of the past learnings and takeaways from the project that had a unit testing mechanism in the development workflow.

Unit testing complementing development workflow

The premise circles around the story of a developer who has never written unit tests as part of the development. The individual was new to writing and using the unit test framework. The learning of developers when moving away from the inherent inertia of not writing unit tests to completely depend on unit tests is the crux of this section. The outcome expected from the unit test was to ensure the stability of functionality. This transition of mindset is a great journey that establishes the potential of leveraging unit tests in the development workflow.

This was in a team of ten developers building mobile apps using the Flutter Framework. The personality traits of the team in the section can be seen as individuals who want to ensure that whatever contribution they make to the codebase, functionality, or any other things should be perfect to the dot. The team members were working on a parallel feature. However, post-development, there were features that broke in the testing cycle continuously. The root cause analysis was done for understanding why the number of defects was increasing across the team. The pattern was found where the reused common codes are changed by other developers in the team, and the impact is percolating as a side effect, introducing unexpected behavior. Due to the sheer size of the codebase and the development team running against the clock, there were cases when the team missed validating the impact of the code changes, creating issues in other places in the existing functionality. The mitigation action was to communicate to every developer who repeated the mistake of change for common shared component and educate them with the risk of modifying shared component without checking the side effects. However, this mitigation strategy was not scalable. The solution was not worth the effort and time, and it was not future proof. Another bottleneck that was prevalent in the team was when the feature and the nitty-gritty details started fading from an individual's mind for older features. The code changes in the older features were becoming a source for the side effects that could not be controlled or preempted by the team. The fact that the detailed context about older features will be vague or lost which makes it harder to assess the impact of the change to the code. The team also had to invest more time and effort to carry out the impact analysis. All these were in parallel with the development of new features. The developer thus had to work on both the issues that popped up in the old module and the new feature, increasing the amount of work involved. All these became bottlenecks, delaying and slowing the development of new features. This repeated in the team, and the respective individuals who had the context started becoming the bottleneck to fix the issue. Eventually, this had an effect on the morale and, in extreme cases, added to frustration, reaching its peak. The important observation to note is that this issue was not because of the inherent flaw of the codebase, but was the result of a lack of exhaustive testing.

This marked the turning point at which the team rethought its strategy and began writing the unit test case. Initially, UI was not covered. However, later, the team even started investing in widget tests that helped to cover the UI as well. This shift helped to reduce the total number of occurrences of the issue post development of a feature and prevented side effects caused by changes to the codebase.

One of the key functionalities in the application was to convert a large number to a short format in a specified range, for example, 1000 to 1K, 10000 to 10K, 1000000 to 1M. There was a large combination of input and output, and manually testing for this was tedious. The entire logic was implemented with the help of unit tests by simulating multiple inputs.

In addition to writing the unit test, the team also sought the support of QA to review the unit test. The confidence of the scenario covered was mutually reviewed with the QA team and developers. The QA effort was to write tests for the incremental scenarios that are not covered within the unit test.

While there have been many patterns for writing unit tests, the one that helped the team in the story narrated in this section, followed the given sequence of arrangement:

1. Setting up the data (mock or fake), dependencies (mock or fake), and system under testing.
2. Invoking the functionality for testing.
3. Writing the assertion.

This structure helped in ensuring readability for the unit test suite. The test was organized into a group of unit tests covering the various functionalities to ensure confidence in the accuracy of the software and complement the documentation required for functionality.

Test-driven development with a proper mindset

TDD is a mindset shift in development where the team writes tests to drive the functional development. For individuals coming from different schools of thought on testing, it may be difficult to digest the idea of following the test-first approach in development. The main bottleneck for a developer will be to have a mindset shift to think ahead about the end-to-end details of the feature and to write tests for these incrementally alongside the development. In most cases, for developers who have not practiced this, the brain will never be wired to shift to this mindset easily. Thus, a team that looks forward to following the TDD approach should tackle this by educating the developer. The developer to be effective in TDD should take off the hat of a developer and wear the testing hat. Initially, to overcome the inertia, the scenarios can be written as pseudocode, then converted to test and actual code. This helps to align the mind to start thinking of tests. The red-green refactor pattern is a strategy followed, where the test case with the expectation was written, which would fail at the start. The failed test is fixed by navigating back to the code to refactor and ensure the test is passed. This pattern would be repeated to get a suite of tests and fully functional features.

The difficulty of taking the test first can be alleviated by having a proper mindset. This comes with practicing the same.

Hundred percent TDD would be counterproductive

The previous section introduced TDD. Understanding the ground realities by knowing the experience of other teams will help make the right decision for any project.

Mobile applications use the layout mechanism on the respective platform to develop UI. The work involved for a development team is to choose the appropriate component from the framework and configure the rule and properties in the layout mechanism. These rules would be followed for developing the UI, and once complied with, will render in the mobile application. From the perspective of the user, an action or user interaction on the mobile device will trigger the event. The event, in the context of a mobile application, processes information from the user or sends info to a connected system via the operating system capabilities to process. The response of the processed information is relayed back to users. The cycle of this interaction and response is the crux for the functioning of a mobile application.

Consider the Sign-In feature implemented in any application. This feature will have a UI with two input fields and a button. The sign-in page has other functionalities as well; however, the same is left for readers to explore themselves beyond the scope of this book. On tapping the login button, after entering the value in the input field, the input for the rules of username and password would be checked, and on successful validation, the login service would be called. On success, the user would navigate to the home page. The UI for sign-in shall be developed in the mechanism provided by the framework to build the layout. The logic for validation, service call, etc., will also be part of the code.

Designing the sign-in page with TDD will be a challenge. The difficulty can be attributed to the limitations of the tool, as these tools are unable to create the test suite for UI tests before its existence. A case of chicken-egg problem where test framework cannot render the UI before it exist. This makes the *test first* requirement of TDD impractical for the UI layer. Additionally, the UI is the most dynamic part of the development; therefore, maintaining the suite after the UI is developed will involve a huge effort, which may affect the time to market.

TDD is ideally suited for the logic-layer for a mobile application code base when writing unit tests. UI tests should be minimal in number and applying TDD for UI test is not recommended as the overhead exceeds the benefits.

Perspective from mobile app team lead

The section explores an experience team lead enabling their team. The experience took a route where the team had to be enlightened about how to write a better unit test, what patterns to use to ensure the code is unit testable. There were different kinds of personas in the team, listed as follows:

- Developer who was vocal about and interested in writing tests.
- Developers who considered unit tests or automated tests not worth investing time. The school of thought advocated by these personas was that testing was the job for a separate, dedicated testing team.
- Other personas who have not tried unit testing frameworks.

Interacting with each of the personas and enabling was a great experience for the lead. The summary of key learning from this interaction is as follows:

- Unit tests would add value if done correctly. If unit tests are written for the sake of delivery or coverage, the team may not reap their benefits.
- The total percentage of the members who are specialized in QA in comparison to the development team is lower. This adds more burden on the testing team to do sanity checks and sign off before release. When there are last-minute deliveries of features, the situation of the testing team will become worse. The automated testing is done as part of both the testing and development phases. The adoption of a unit test suite increased the confidence of the testing team.
- Initially, for those who were new to writing unit tests, the time taken to write unit tests was considerable. However, after familiarizing themselves with the patterns and leveraging the reusable setup that the project had, the average time taken to write unit tests reduced. A 20 to 40% of additional effort is required to include unit tests. This data with respect to effort is empirically grounded, drawn from the author's experience and peers who have held lead roles in mobile projects. This figure varies depending on team maturity, codebase architecture, and the testing framework in use. However, the overall effectiveness of the quality releases offsets the cost of writing unit tests.
- The developers who were reluctant to write the unit test came from a background of building small mobile applications. This developer had experience in working at a smaller scale with respect to the complexity of the development lifecycle. For some of the individuals, the mobile application that the team had experience with never saw beyond their minimum viable product phase. These factors indicated the inexperience of the individual and the lack of exposure to build an application at scale which can be seen as the prime reason that caused inertia, that prevented writing unit tests.
- The developers who have never written unit tests had initial learning curves. The applicability of software principles became clearer to them. These principles are essential to write the code that enable unit testing. The developer learned that if code is not structured in an optimal way, writing unit tests would be a bottleneck.

Incrementally increasing coverage for any misses

Consider the situation where a project is developed without any unit tests. The value of writing unit tests is later understood by the team. The team, originally, when it started, due to time pressure, succumbed to ignoring setting up and writing the unit test. Once the importance of unit testing is understood, the question arises of how one needs to handle the unit testing of legacy code as well. The stakeholder would like to know if it makes sense to write the missed unit test.

The point of view would be that if the code base is functional and working fine, writing unit tests is not worth the investment until a change occurs. Investing in minimal integration tests for critical flow will be a better strategy. The idea to highlight is that the coverage should not be the sole aim. There is no business value coming out of writing unit tests for already functioning code that is not affected by any change. However, for any changes to fix bugs or code refactoring to occur in the codebase, it would be a good starting point for adding the unit test. This can later be extended to bring more coverage for the changing features and code. The risk of finding the side effects on the existing code cannot be mitigated with this additional test. However, the stability of the new code base could be guaranteed to be safeguarded from future changes.

Avoid deferring unit tests to latter stage in development

There is a tendency in the team where the unit tests are written as a separate activity post development. Such a practice is an anti-pattern, and this should be avoided. The effort of writing the unit test later in the project development cycle is high when compared to writing it along with the development. Additionally, if two separate developers write the unit, the time could be even longer. The major factors affecting the effort for writing unit tests are:

- The need to refactor and the effort to make the functionality testable.
- The lack of tacit knowledge that the developer who originally implemented the feature would have acquired post-development.

Automation for improving productivity

Imagine doing the redundant, monotonous task repeatedly. Most of the team members could get bored with the repetitive work. Such a situation can cause the team to slowly get less interested. The creative element of work also starts diminishing if it is repetitive. This situation is not great for a high-performing team. Investing in automation is the ideal strategy to ensure individuals on the team grow. With the automation, the benefits and effectiveness start showing up over time, with its impact percolating to the organization as well. The cost associated with the initial investment in automation is covered by reducing the extensive manual effort required in the later stages of SDLC. Once the automation is set up, there will be minimal dependency on individuals for executing and maintaining these. Automation could be scheduled for any interval defined by the team. The risk of the automation is the critical failures and errors in the automation scripts itself caused due to infrastructure flakiness or misconfiguration rather than genuine defects. These errors, when timed incorrectly (such as just before a release), could create noise amongst the stakeholders that might cause the team to burn the midnight oil. Automation taking care of recurring and monotonous tasks gives the testing teams and developers space to focus their attention on core business processes and revenue-generating activities. The narrative does not imply that the automation, written once, never changes. Over the course of time, the automation script has also improved, and the missing piece in the automation has been added, for which the effort will be minimal.

Testing and defining the QA strategy case study

The team decided to create a toy project that has only one function, which is to log in. The login mobile application has a single page that takes two values, username and password, and validates with a backend service. Based on the response, a success or failure message is shown. In the application, there is client-side validation checking that the username and password are not empty and have a minimum of eight characters. Additionally, a valid password field was required to contain at least one capital letter, one special character, and one number. The team had to decide on the QA strategy for the application.

The application has two fields and a button connecting to the backend server. The backend server is a black box and is not considered to be in the scope of this QA strategy. Developing the mobile application will have the following top-level tasks:

- Create the UI layer.
- Write the client validation.
- Connect the UI to send the request to validate input with the backend.
- Receive the response and show the appropriate message.

The UI will have a test that is headless in nature. The headless test will check to ensure that the error/success message is displayed.

The unit test layer can validate the following cases:

- Client-side validation logic to check the business rules for a valid username and password.
- Propagation of the valid input to the backend layer.
- Propagation of the success and failure state to the UI Layer based on the server response.

Given the small use case, the UI test and the unit test have enough coverage to confidently release the application. Being on the consumer side of the login API provided by a third party, the mobile team must treat the backend as a black box. Thus, the consumer expects the API provider to do the due diligence to test and expose the functioning API. The mobile team may, however, depend on the integration test to verify the end-to-end journey.

In the real-world, if the reliability of the backend system that the team trusts is low, it is critical to include integration tests as part of the overall QA strategy. The team should ensure the feature is working end-to-end, and the validation should happen every time there is a new deployment/release. The integration tests, along with the unit test and headless test, serve as an end-to-end validation of the system, confirming that the frontend and backend components work together as expected.

Extending this requirement, the team decides to add the sign-up feature as well. Take a moment to imagine the possibilities of what testing strategy will be beneficial. The sign-up feature is like the login page, with the button names changed, and the backend server is invoked for registration. In this case, the UI headless test and the validation layer may be present. The integration test could be written to validate the end-to-end journey of sign-up, followed by the login.

Decoupling backend and mobile development

Consider the case where the backend service is developed separately and in parallel. One option for the mobile team is to wait until the backend is ready, thus making the development sequential. In this case, the wait period affects the time to market of the product. The other option is to make the development parallel. The contract agreed is the means to enable parallel development. This contract can be used as a stubbed response to continue the development. The mobile development team typically creates a dummy endpoint serving the backend response as agreed in the contract to continue the development. The same dummy endpoint can be used to write integration tests that validate the functional flow in the application for a journey is working as expected. Integration tests, as discussed earlier, are heavy in nature to maintain and execute. This major reason highlighted earlier was that the non-determinism of how the third-party system behaves is not in control of the mobile app, as the factors such as network delay, server behavior, etc., can vary. Now, with the dummy endpoint and predefined data, which is stubbed, this integration test execution can happen in a controlled environment. In such development, when a production-ready backend becomes available after completing the development, it can be configured on the mobile with the endpoint URL change. This is possible as the dummy endpoint mimics the expected backend and the integration tests written against it serve as a regression suite. Once the real backend is available, the development team can release the app with only a subset of targeted tests as long as the contract remains unchanged. Running the same or a subset of integration tests written as sanity tests will give confidence as well. This setup gives the flexibility to decouple mobile development from the backend system. The team following this approach can be confident that the mobile application is production-ready before the backend is fully developed. In most cases, both the mobile team and backend team should maintain their own test pyramids to ensure quality for each. The integration tests between the mobile and backend will ensure that data flows between the mobile app and the backend are functioning as expected.

Thus, for the use case referenced in the case study, the QA strategy will be to have the application tested for the logic written with the unit and the effect of logic on the user interface via the headless test, ensuring the functional accuracy. The developer is responsible for the unit and headless tests. Integration test/manual test before deployment will give validation of functionality end-to-end. The data creation and the access to the internals of the backend, being a black box, may not be part of the strategy. Any bug will be categorized based on severity and will be triaged to be looked up by the team and fixed. The re-deployment will trigger the testing cycle again, and once the functionality is fixed, it will be released to the end users.

The scale for the case study is very localized to a single feature. However, when the application scope grows, the same ideology can be scaled by including additional layers and mechanisms to ensure the different gatekeeping mechanisms provide confidence to release the application.

Practicing unit testing

Every programming language will have a testing framework. The testing framework provides the ecosystem to assert and execute tests. As a developer, one should be aware of how to write tests using the capabilities of the respective framework. Understanding at least one testing framework will give the benefit of correlating with others, as the structure of how to write a unit test remains the same across frameworks.

Concepts such as using dependency injection, libraries that help to mock/stub, are other areas that the development team should be familiar with to write better tests.

Returning to the case study provides a concrete baseline for writing the unit test. The first test can be to validate the propagation of the success and failure state to the UI layer and the effect the response has created on the UI layer.

The following code is for the class handling the backend service invocation logic, which has callback handling success and failure:

```
class Login {
  func login() {
    let username = self.usernameTextField.text
    let password = self.passwordTextField.text
    //Validation and error handling logic is not added for simplicity of
explanation
    LoginService()
      .invokeLogin(username, password) { success in
        self.messageLabel.text = success ? "login success" : "login failed"
      }
  }
}
```

The **login** class takes the input value and passes it to a **Hyper Text Transfer Protocol** (**HTTP**) network handling logic. Based on the response, the message is displayed to the UI. This function should be tested, and the class **Login** is the system under test. If carefully observed, there are two anti-patterns in the original code that make writing unit tests non-deterministic and tightly coupled. The code anti pattern are:

- Direct references to UI elements create tight coupling between the logic and the view layer.
- Direct instantiation of **LoginService()** introduces a non-deterministic network dependency that cannot be controlled in a test.

The first principle of writing a unit test is to write a code that is testable. In the codebase, removing the UI layer dependency and the non-deterministic element of depending on the HTTP call is the first step.

One of the many possible strategies is outlined as follows:

- To use variables in the function signature instead of **self.usernameTextField** and **self.passwordTextField** and return text instead of setting **self.messageLabel.text**.
- To pass the **LoginService** instance as a dependency that can be mocked to control the behavior of testing:

```
class Login {
  private var loginService: LoginService
  init(loginService: LoginService) {
    self.loginService = loginService
  }
  func login(username: String, password: String) {
    //Validation and error handling logic is not added for
simplicity of explanation
    loginService
```

```
            .invokeLogin(username, password) { success in
              return success ? "login success" : "login failed"
            }
        }
    }
```

In the refactored code, the logic is decoupled from the UI. The network layer is passed as a dependency using constructor dependency injection to the **Login** class. The **Login** class is now in a shape to write unit tests deterministically.

Note: **The code being deterministic gives more edge to predict an outcome and can encompass the different possibilities. This ensures that the team has space to cover the maximum list of cases that could potentially occur for the system under test. 100% adherence to this, getting the different situations tested will sometimes not be possible. However, being closer to the maximum possible cases is the best that any programmer should strive for in an application development.**

The unit test for the **Login** class is depicted as follows:

```
class LoginTests {
  var sut: Login  // sut = system under test
  func setup() {
    //Do any setup before test execution
  }
  func tearDown() {
    //Do any cleanup after test execution
  }
  func test__login_success_returns_success_message() {
    var mockObject = MockLoginService()
    mockObject.succeed = true
    sut = Login(mockObject)
    assert(sut.login("username", "password"), "login success")
  }
  func test__login_failure_returns_failure_message() {
    var mockObject = MockLoginService()
    mockObject.succeed = false
    sut = Login(mockObject)
    assert(sut.login("username", "password"), "login failed ")
  }
}
```

The test is written to assert the response returned by the login function matches the expected outcome. The expected outcome and the behavior are controlled by the **MockLoginService** class. **MockLoginService** is passed as the dependency to the function externally, and this gives control to simulate the behavior of **LoginService** and to test how these affect the logic in the system under test. The core principle is that the login service, being an external entity, should not create any side effects that will derail or affect the logic of the **login** class. Adhering to this principle will ensure the **Login** class has focused and self-contained responsibility and can now be externalized to remove the network dependency on the **Login** class.

The code used to explain is influenced by the Swift language. However, the idea is universal and applicable to other languages as well. With the advent of declarative-style UI development, some of the tight coupling of the UI elements is now removed by the framework itself. Additionally, *Chapter 10, Introduction to Swift, Kotlin, and Dart,* will get into the Swift language in detail.

AI in context of quality assurance

The growth of AI tools can complement the time factor that typically acts as an impediment to investing in the testing strategy. A startup or an aggressive organization focusing on time to market and having less audit trail can get sucked into the rat race of feature completion. This thought process would pave the way for stakeholders to ignore the pillars that ensure long-term sustenance. However, with the advent of AI tools, some of these tasks that become overhead can now be achieved with ease. The generation of test scenarios, data, and code suggestions for tests will make the life of a developer better and can help move this faster. Adopting an AI culture with human intervention to prevent spaghetti can help accelerate the journey.

Conclusion

The objective of the chapter was to enable the development team to get the perspective of what testing means and the importance of having a test strategy for the enterprise. The chapter has provided insight to the reader, solidifying the idea that building software with minimum defects does not happen naturally. Achieving quality is an intentional and planned activity. The entire QA domain requires a separate book for itself; however, the theme that is discussed in the chapter focuses on the gatekeeping mechanism with respect to mobile development and treating the other interacting systems as a black box.

The next chapter focuses on the means to establish great collaboration between the two roles, UI/UX and engineering. The engineering team that translates the idea to a seamless experience leveraged by the end user should be able to do this optimally, balancing the cost and intent. The chapter will give insight into establishing such a balance in a mobile development engagement.

Takeaways and reflections

Now that we have reached the end of the chapter, the reader should be able to leverage the knowledge to understand and structure the QA strategy for a mobile application project. This chapter lays a strong foundation that can be contextualized in any other situation that the reader would encounter, to have enough mechanisms to ensure quality. The following are some of the key summaries from the chapter:

- It is necessary to invest in approaches that reduce overall cost in the long run. However, this comes with the disclaimer that the ground realities need to be evaluated to ensure the approaches align with the business cause.
- Unnecessary overhead may not be of value to the product. For example, writing screenshot tests or integration tests may not be relevant for a mobile app that has not started incorporating the high-fidelity design.
- The chapter started with the purpose of testing, followed by looking into the popular test mechanisms and an ideal test pyramid.
- The chapter delved into the QA strategy definition and the various themes around the same that will help the reader to define and set up a QA strategy for any project.
- The role of the developer in ensuring quality and unit tests are closely aligned to the development cycle was established from the perspective of the chapter.
- The chapter established the theme of the quality of unit test cases.
- The unit testing case study gave an idea of how to bring the unit testing practices to the project. The case study also looked at defining the QA strategy and gave a hands-on flavor of unit testing.

Join our Discord space

Join our Discord workspace for latest updates, offers, tech happenings around the world, new releases, and sessions with the authors:

https://discord.bpbonline.com

Chapter 6
Balancing Design and Engineering

Introduction

Mobile applications need to be visually elegant and seamless, along with functionally accurate. Design thinking is a trait that plays a crucial role in developing a mobile application, alongside engineering requirements. Design thinking has a varied meaning based on the context in which it is used. The reference to the design thinking in the current chapter will denote the ideas and strategies that ensure a mobile application adheres to the user interface guidelines. These guidelines are established by the platform and the product research. This chapter focuses on the intricacies that a mobile developer should be aware of to effectively collaborate with the **user interface/user experience** (**UI/UX**) team. One of the artifacts that the developer consumes is the outcome of the work done by the UI/UX team. The various ideas presented in this chapter will also help any individual from a technology background to understand the thought process of the UI/UX team and vice versa.

Structure

This chapter covers the following topics:

- Design
- User interface and user experience
- Design thinking
- Design outcomes
- Factors affecting interface design and engineering
- Design language system

Objectives

The objective of the chapter is to introduce design thinking from the perspective of user interfaces for mobile applications to an engineering team. The chapter starts by introducing common terminology in the UI/UX process, the persona, and the workflow in the mockup creation. Further in the chapter, the narrative explores the best practices the team should follow to address the major challenges faced by the two parties (the technology and design teams). The chapter concludes by looking at the design process through the lens of building a design language system and its details. One of the key outcomes of reading the chapter is to think effectively in both design and development perspectives. The team will now work towards a collaborative environment. This will help the team increase operational efficiency. The approach will also scale as the UI/UX and engineering ideologies collaborate closer with each other.

Design

A design is a specification defined for portraying an object or an abstract concept. The definition can be demystified in the context of software as two facets - codebase design and interface design. The codebase design is generally called the **software design,** which looks at architecting a scalable system from a code point of view. This chapter focuses on the second facet, which is the user-facing interface design. The second facet, interface design governs the aesthetics, interaction pattern and feedback mechanism of the mobile application.

The user-facing design that involves the sensory side of the consuming individual is the interface design. The user-facing design would have a bidirectional impact. The design is used to get the attention and provide a means for the end user to trigger an action. The term where the consumer responds to the sensory trigger is called the interaction. The response to the interaction is termed the feedback. In most cases, the interaction or feedback is visual in nature. However, there are other forms of feedback and interaction, such as sound, haptics, and touch. These contribute towards ensuring a holistic and seamless experience for the appropriate functionality or feature exposed.

Example of an interaction:

- Voice command to the application.
- Mouse/trackpad pointer actions such as click, hover, etc.
- Touch events on the mobile screen, such as scrolling through a page, button tap, etc.

Example of feedback:

- Visual feedback in the form of alerts, information changes, page navigation, etc.
- Haptic feedback gives a physical sensation, particularly in mobile devices.
- Audio feedback, for example, includes the ringtone of a mobile phone.

The individuals involved in defining these specifications form the UI/UX team. The team that converts these into working software forms the development team. The development team labels this layer of code managing interaction and feedback as the presentation layer for the application. A developer refers to the specification and leverages the development tool to write code that brings the interfaces to life. The functional behavior makes the interface ready to deliver the service provided by the organization to the end user.

For a UI/UX team, it starts with an idea, discovery of the product, sampling with the audience, and coming up with a final mockup. This process is a continuous cycle with the involvement of multiple individuals. The following list demonstrates some examples of an individual's involvement in the journey of creating the mockups:

- A domain expert's involvement would be required to validate that the mockups designed are functionally correct and have the right intent.
- A domain expert could validate if the mockups corresponding to the application are compliant with the guidelines defined in the regulated software industry.
- A technological person would look at the mockup and share a perspective on the feasibility or time required to develop the feature.

User interface and user experience

A mobile application is primarily the **graphical user interface (GUI)** delivering the service to an end consumer. The literal meaning of user interface is an area on a screen with which the end user interacts. A broader term, as described earlier in the chapter, for the user interface is interaction and feedback. The user can provide input or get a response using various other capabilities for hardware, for example, voice, haptic, or visual. The intuitiveness and the accuracy of the application are the key expectation to be fulfilled. The mobile application feature should align with the end user's intention. Given the versatility of human nature, having a design that satisfies every end user may be tricky. The goal of any team, however, would be to design and develop an application to be likable and accepted by the maximum number of users. The journey, starting from conceptualization up to the deployment to the end user for any product, will go through different stages. In this journey, the stage where the idea is represented as mockups of the application is the high-fidelity design or user interface design stage. A mockup can be seen as a replica portraying the end state for the mobile application. The team will finalize high-fidelity designs after a series of ideation. The team in the ideation stage would ideally start with a whiteboarding session to come up with a simple line sketch. These line sketches are transformed into a black and white box diagram, and as the idea matures, they move closer to how the actual product would function. This process, starting from ideation until defining a skeleton of the mobile application, is called **wireframing**.

A team that does the wireframing for the mobile application is responsible for the final design as an outcome. The outcome also goes through a series of validations, feedback, and corrections with the relevant stakeholders. One may find it interesting to understand how an organization can validate something that is not out there in the market and get any feedback. The level of validation in this context can be seen as the verification of intermediate output, the wireframe. A wireframe is showcased to the stakeholders or a sample set of potential end users to take feedback and get a perspective on the usability. The potential sample of users is expected to validate focus areas such as the user interface, the functional journeys, the ease of using the application, etc., which are the prospective features planned for the mobile application. The team will iterate over the change, feedback, and validation to make the product effective. The experience for the product is managed by the team of UX specialists. The key focus areas for UX team members will be experimenting with different choices. The team then discovers the best by sampling the hypotheses amongst the probable personas of end users or domain experts. The result of the experiment will contribute to defining the high-fidelity design for features. The team members whose role is to create these designs are UI designers.

The UX team specializes in product and interaction research to discover how a mobile application should behave. The UX team defines the value delivered by the mobile application through interaction and design for the targeted end user. This end-user-centric approach would, in turn, get tied to a robust product. Essentially, the better the acceptance of a product, the better the return on investment to the organization. The UX team evaluates the means to increase the engagement and reach of various features offered in the existing product and the product itself. Discovery is where UX explores and defines the features to be implemented. These features should ideally enhance the experience of the mobile application. The discovery process happens via user research. User research is the field of study targeted to understand the end consumer behaviors. The user research happens within the context defining the need for the product. In the case of a mobile application, the user research will investigate how the mobile application can make the life of the end consumer convenient. The user research will factor in how the product affects operation and the business potential. After the user research, the team will have the structure and a concrete idea, which translates to a mockup and a high-fidelity design.

The UI and UX will be closely intertwined. One can summarize that the user experience is the feeling that the end user gets, and the user interface is the look and feel.

A UI/UX expert need not necessarily be a domain expert. This implies the need for roles that bridge the domain and product expertise with the product design at early stages. The user experience should follow the business rule and guideline, ensuring adherence to the dos and don'ts of the domain. The product domain expert and the UI/UX team thus collectively would ensure the app follows the accepted standards of the domain and make the experience convenient for the end user. In the regulated industries, such as banking, healthcare, etc., the law of the land can create rules that the team should follow in implementation. In such a regulated application, there is no chance for violation, and if such an occurrence happens, there could be severe penalties for the business. In conclusion, one can see that the functional feature definition of business will come from an SME of the domain. The aesthetics of the usability and intuitiveness of the mobile application that hooks the user will come from UI/UX.

Design thinking

It is essential to find the right balance between engineering and experience design. This ensures the product idea is transformed into a seamless mobile application experience for an end consumer. Design thinking is a balanced approach in which the stakeholder provides the best possible value to the consumer by ensuring the solution remains feasible and financially viable for the organization. Generally, when multiple stakeholders are involved, there could be debate and multiple options to choose from. Evaluating the options and weighing the pros and cons is best done when all the key stakeholders involved in the discussion are on the same page for the expected outcome. The challenge an organization faces is the competing design and technical requirements. This is a common situation that mobile development teams may come across. This situation would bring potential conflict between the UI/

UX and developers in the team. Encouraging close collaboration between the UI/UX and the engineering team and resolving the differences is essential to avoid any side effects affecting the product.

Conway's Law states that the system mirrors an organization's communication structure. This translated to a situation where a siloed team produces siloed products. For an organization to scale, it is essential to have all parties empowered in decision-making to build a unified product that feels consistent and connected across all parts of the user experience. A practice called Inverse Conway Maneuver is employed where an organization intentionally structures the team to match the desired system architecture. Such a strategy ensures that the collaborator gets an equal voice to come up with a mutually agreed best possible solution. The UI/UX would not compromise on the precision required for mobile applications and will have a strong emphasis on attention to detail for the screen to be accurate and faithfully reproduce the intended mockup. The technology team, on the other hand, ensures that the design is as per the platform standards. When UI/UX designs call for solutions that exceed what the chosen platform or framework can support efficiently, implementing these designs would require investing in over-engineered and complex solutions and drain the profitability of the business. The engineering team and design should have healthy debates about how to mitigate such a situation.

For an individual representing the technology side, acquiring design thinking would mean drifting toward understanding the nuance in the ideologies around the UI/UX world. For the UI/UX team, the design thinking would be to understand the guidelines and possibilities of the technology choice made for developing a mobile application.

Design outcomes

In the journey from the idea to the creation of the mockup, there are a series of outcomes that need to be collated. Having traceability for these outcomes could be useful to retrospect and learn. As in any software development, the life of the outcome generated need not be infinite; the artifact that forms the outcome could become obsolete and thus could be deleted or archived. This section focuses on the outcomes in the journey of the UI/UX team.

When starting with the product discovery, the key outcomes will be as follows:

- User map, which defines the persona and the traits of the possible set of end users of the mobile application.
- The journey map (general flow), which defines the way the personas will interact with the application. The focus is to determine the potential pain point and key hooking features.
- The notes from the interview form the sample persona of the proposed product. The interview note will consist of how the end user would feel if such a product were available, and their wants and expectations.
- Research into findings about the product and competitor analysis.
- A flow of the functionality. This may not have the component detail for each page, but it will baseline the hierarchy of the flow of the application.
- All these will be summarized and collated as the UX strategy document.

The culmination of discovery would lead to the creation of wireframes. These are the levels of the document defining the application flow. In this, the screen layout starts materializing. The wireframe will be evaluated by the design team, product stakeholders, and a sample persona to give feedback. This may go through multiple iterations and get finalized. The wireframe thus becomes the blueprint for developing the high-fidelity design.

High-fidelity design (**HFD**) is the version where the brand color, typography, spacing and alignment, components, etc., get added. HFD will become the reference that the technology team can leverage to build the application. The HFD also goes through a review with stakeholders. The tools have advanced, thereby providing capabilities such as allowing the simulation of micro-interactions and the application flow for these designs in the tools. The HFD thus allows the stakeholder to get a simulated experience of the product even before being developed and deployed.

Platform guidelines

The platform provider defines guidelines that resonate with their unique ideology. The expectation for the team is to adhere to these guidelines while developing a mobile application. Adhering to the guidelines laid out by the respective platform ensures the mobile application is familiar to the end user. There is a possibility for the platform provider to restrict and disallow an app during the review for not meeting the guidelines and standards of the app store. The rejection due to the mismatch is not prevalent; however, the possibility is open from the platform provider of the mobile application marketplace.

Knowing the guidelines from the platform becomes critical for getting up to speed with design thinking. In the case of a product design, there will be different channels for which the application is targeted, for example, mobile devices, desktop web, etc. With a mobile device, there are different providers. Additionally, there is a regional influence on the percentage of users on each of these channels. There will be segmentation in the percentage of the different versions or kinds of devices being used. For example, there will be regions where there is a higher percentage of Apple device users when compared to Android, and alternatively, there could be possibilities for the vice-versa of device composition or having an equal ratio as well. These are some of the key aspects that affect the decision of the design being used.

In the case where the end consumer market user base is heavily concentrated on Apple devices, leveraging the platform guidelines defined by the iOS ecosystem would be the better choice for shipping the iOS application. In contrast, if the Android ratio is high, the design should align with the Android ecosystem. If there are high-value customers in both platforms, the choice to go with one platform may be tough. The design specification on iOS also has restrictions for use on other platforms; for example, the fonts on iOS cannot be used elsewhere. This brings about the additional operational overhead for an organization to maintain two versions of a design system. Such a situation could become a bottleneck to scale in the long run. Most organizations that have an equal importance of multiple platforms are seen to take a hybrid approach, with essential and crucial platform-specific elements and behaviors kept as per the respective guidelines.

The design guidelines defined by the platform provider will cover multiple devices and different modes, such as dark and light modes. The components defined in the platform design guideline are open to modification to bring in the brand identity of the organization. The organization thus can extend these guidelines, keeping a check and ensuring that the don'ts defined in the guidelines are not violated.

Each platform has undergone a journey of evolution in developing its guidelines. For Apple devices, guidelines started with realistic interactions. These gave the feel to the end user that aligns with real-world equivalents. The approach was called **skeuomorphism**. This later moved to flat design with iOS 7. A community-driven trend known as **neumorphism** (or **neomorphism**) subsequently emerged. Neomorphism is a soft blend of skeuomorphism with flat design to give a soft three-dimensional look and feel. This was never adopted as official design by Apple though. The design system is continuously evolving as the different platforms evolve. In recent times, as augmented reality is in the picture, the trend is moving toward designs that are 3D space-friendly. These designs are evolving to be uniform for device type in the ecosystem. Liquid Glass for Apple devices is a recent design guideline introduced in 2025.

Android did not have such formal documents in the early days, until the Material Design guidelines came out around 2014. Material Design follows a flat design with realistic depth and motion using shadows and elevation. Material Design aligns with the ideology of modular, customizable, and flexible user interface. The outcome of this philosophy will come in the form of different components with focused responsibility defined in the Material Design guidelines.

Factors affecting interface design and engineering

The ideas introduced so far are common terminology one may encounter in the interface design world. This section pivots to look at some of the key factors that influence the design and engineering team. Understanding the factors that affect the collaboration between mobile interface design and engineering is important. The following sub-section explores these key factors.

Customization possibility of UI components

A design team should have insight into the technology possibilities. This becomes very important when the framework chosen for development has limitations. The design team, coming up with the layout outside the possibilities in the development framework, adds cost and is suboptimal. A certain framework does not give the customization capability, which becomes challenging as the team will not be able to build the custom component.

It is a fact that mobile developers are the consumers of the API provided by the development framework. These APIs provided by the framework are composed together to create the required experience for the feature. This inadvertently means that anything beyond the API will be time-consuming to build. If the time to market does not align with the effort involved, then it will become a roadblock. The platform also controls specific capabilities of the mobile device, thereby limiting the features that can be developed.

The classic example of a platform for restriction is the inability to achieve the product requirement to customize the camera control or change the system app rating pop-up. These requirements may not work even with additional time given to the development team, as the platform will not allow it. The understanding of what is possible and what is not possible should be there with the design team to be effective in designing the mobile application flow within technically feasible boundaries. The collaboration between the engineering team and UI/UX will thus be effective in exchanging information, understanding, and ensuring both parties are on the same page. The collaboration will also be a forum to convey such intricacies that are platform-specific. Another example is in the case when the team uses cross-platform technologies to develop applications. If the requirement is to develop a user interface that is not supported by the common design defined by the cross-platform framework, the team will not be able to move faster. For example, in the Flutter framework, there are components that do not mimic the exact platform behavior. If the UI/UX team defines the mockups that are expected to be platform-specific, a situation would arise where the team would end up implementing platform-specific code. This defeats the purpose of using cross-platform. The UI/UX team, knowing the possibilities of Flutter, could ease this situation.

These examples show the importance that the awareness of the capabilities of the framework brings. The awareness helps the team be effective in coming up with the designs that adhere to the development framework, whose usage does not impact the time to market.

Design for multiple screen sizes

The organization will have multiple targeted channels such as website, tablet, mobile device, etc. The product, when designed, ideally should provide an omnichannel experience. Pragmatics of the degree of user experience presented to the end consumer would depend on organizational aspiration and the investment capability. For mobile applications, there are different variations of device size and market segmentation. All these put the design team in a position where the team must ensure consistency in the look and feel while catering to the nuances of the respective channel.

The design should handle different screen sizes and have an adaptive structure, ensuring that the smaller screen does not break. The user experience for a larger screen should not be odd in the look and feel. If the target device consists of multiple form factors, it becomes essential to support the adaptive design and the development team should be given the requirement to be considered at an early stage. If the design team initially comes up with a mockup without considering the form factor variations, the code written may not be flexible enough to adapt to these multiple screen sizes easily. The assertion is based on the historical data, considering the nature of work involved in designing screens for multiple screen sizes. A general trend seen that slows development for multiple device screen sizes is the design coming as an afterthought. Such a case has a high probability of bringing an antipattern of the user interface components designed not to be logically composable.

An example would help in understanding the necessity of considering multiple screen sizes ahead of time in design thinking. Consider the case of building a **Login** page in the context of the form factor changing with respect to orientation. The space available for different orientations will be drastically different, and one should leverage the canvas as much as possible wherever needed. *Figure 6.1* represents the mockup for the expected behaviors in the portrait and landscape modes:

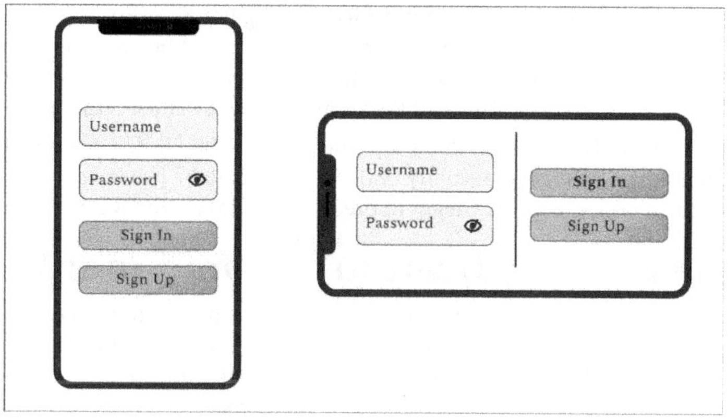

Figure 6.1: *Login screen mock-up*

Two possibilities can come into play. In the first case, the design team will share both landscape and portrait designs. In the second case, the design team will share the portrait version first with the development team to implement the same. Later, after completing the portrait implementation, the design team delivers the landscape version. In the second case, the developer, while designing the portrait version, does not have a clear idea how the landscape version of the screen will look. The second case is where the landscape version of the design comes as an afterthought of development. The login screen should support both orientations. The positional change depicted in *Figure 6.1* for the text fields and button will be the behavior in the application when orientation changes. Developing this would ideally require a separate design for each orientation. In the best case, the text fields, and the buttons are grouped inside a parent container, two separate vertical stack containers. These two vertical stacks become two sections, and these sections will be placed in another page container. Based on the orientation, the page container hosting the component group can be designed to toggle between a horizontal and a vertical stack thereby shifting the expectation depicted in *Figure 6.1*. The functional working will be standard and does not change, as there are no new interactions involved. If the developer has not implemented the container approach and the design comes as an afterthought, refactoring to modify the implementation will be required. This is an additional overhead.

The idea of the preceding example was to showcase the effort on a small screen. When it comes to complex screens and multiple device sizes, considering the strategy as an afterthought will compound the effort required and is not cost-effective.

Figure 6.2 is another example depicting a broken screen for the details page of a customer service application:

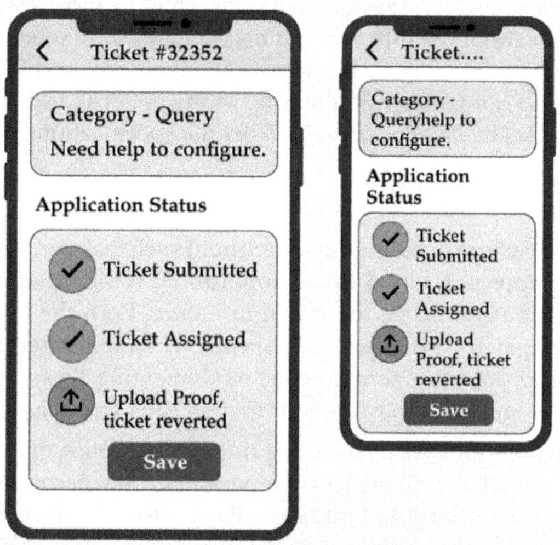

Figure 6.2: *Broken UI for the same code rendered in a different form factor*

The UI/UX team considered the most significant form factor and gave a design where the card will fit into the screen. The team developed the application testing in a larger form factor. When tested in a different variation of the device size, the user interface is broken for a smaller form factor, as depicted on the right. *Figure 6.2* shows a worst-case scenario. However, such cases are plausible, and the team needs to be considerate about such cases.

The smallest possible size should always be factored into the design. The UI/UX team should ideally give design for smaller form factors. It is equally the responsibility of the developer to be proactive in discussing such anomalies possible ahead of development with the UI/UX team to preempt and take effective decisions, reducing rework.

Tight coupling and duplication in components

Screen design without proper planning can bring duplicate code for repetitive patterns across a mobile application. This adds a lot of redundant code. The pattern is not prevalent in smaller teams or applications. However, when building a large-scale mobile application in a distributed team, the communication may not be seamless and continuous across the team on a day-to-day basis. Such a team will have a smaller squad focusing on smaller units of work. The task will have a localized scope within a very large codebase. If the organization does not have a top-down mechanism to control the duplication in the overall codebase, the squad will diverge from the common patterns. The checks and balances that each squad will do will be different in nature. The visibility of the larger scope may not be there, or will not be practical for the individual to look at the global level. In a larger team, the possibility of individuals not resonating with each other and not aligning with the larger goal is high. Consider an example situation with a screen with a list, which has a row showing the products in a retail shopping app. The lists of products will be repeated in various pages, such as home, search, cart, summary page, etc. The design is the same for the row item. Imagine a case where the row item, when designed by the team, is created multiple times and separately for each page. Such redundancy is not ideal and does not help to scale the code base when repeated frequently. If the designs are totally different, the code will be separate; however, in any other case, the code repeated multiple times is harboring an anti-pattern. The development team creating a UI component closely coupled to a feature should be avoided. The component could have been built such that the same can be reused on multiple screens by abstracting and delegating the changing part of the feature. In the preceding case of the product list page, the row item being built also has the functionality of navigating to the details page. The same row should be developed to be usable on all screens. In short, the tight coupling and duplication in components should be avoided whenever the same functionality appears in more than one place. The preference should be to build reusable, decoupled components from the start.

Inconsistencies in mockups and design artifacts

One should expect that the design artifact delivered can have errors. The reason could be oversight of the team. A typical example is the value of the style or the spacing being different or inconsistent for multiple screens. Now, if the developer blindly follows these and if the differences are glaring, the app screen and experience will be affected. In most cases, the issue is prevalent when a new developer joins the team, and the familiarity with the ecosystem is limited. As an individual who has not gotten into the habit of the patterns and the common theme in design, one would tend to miss the finer details. The developer may follow the specifications that are incorrect.

Composability in engineering

Composability is a design approach where the components are built such that they can be combined and reconfigured. A team that does not follow this approach could cause duplication. While designing the presentation layer for a mobile application, the tech decision should be top-down in nature. Both the interface design and development should have the components segregated, and these components, when put together, form the screen. If the design prototypes are not clearly bounded, reusable components, implementing these designs in code with composable architecture will be a challenge. An anti-pattern to avoid is to treat each screen as a single indivisible layout.

Example: Consider a banking application where there are different varieties of banking products, such as a loan, fixed deposit, demat, credit card, wallet, etc. To explain composability, the discussion will focus on the footer design for different screens. The wallet will have an **Add Funds** and **Pay** button, the fixed deposit screen will have an **Open FD** button, or the credit card will have a **Pay** button with the processing screen. *Figure 6.3* depicts these screens:

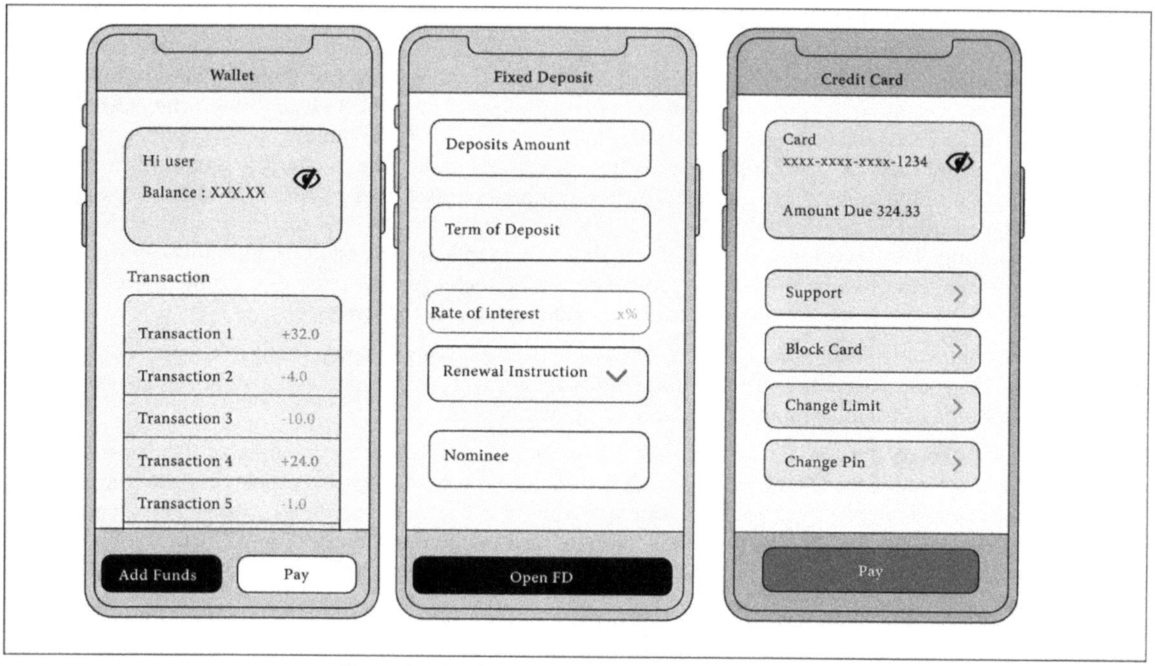

***Figure 6.3**: Product screens from a banking application*

In the preceding figure, there are multiple footer kinds. As a developer, one can implement this for each page separately. If the team is doing parallel development of features, the possibility of duplication in component development is high. However, in the case where architecture decisions are made collaboratively as a team, even when the team is running parallel tracks, the duplication could be avoided. A more structured approach will be to have the interface design team define the possible superset of the footer types. The proactive thinking required to identify such a combination is an example of the top-down execution. In this case, if the pattern is enforced at the user interface stage, it will drive the reusability at the implementation.

In the aforementioned case, the footer type and button can be defined as depicted in *Figure 6.4*:

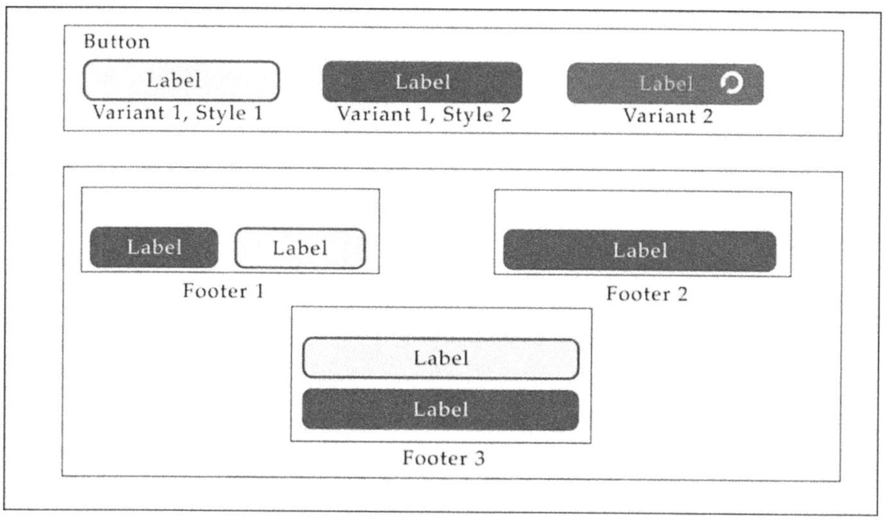

***Figure 6.4**: Button and footer components*

Figure 6.4 depicts the footer type and button. The button has three kinds, and even amongst these, the first two are just a style variation. The buttons are used within the footer. In the case where the UI/UX team confirms that the preceding combination of footers is the superset of possible combinations out there in the entire app, for a team, it is a matter of creating the three different footer components. The respective actions for the entire banking application will differ based on the target screen where the footer is used. When building the component, the option to configure this action separately will help to scale the usage of the footer component throughout the application. The implementation of the footer will be to use a button component inside the container, stacked horizontally for *Footer 1*, the single button inside the container for *Footer 2*, and vertically stacked for *Footer 3*, with the required margins and padding. The developer can make the style and variants of the button configurable externally to the footer. This approach will provide the flexibility to configure the footer for any page, and for the preceding *Figure 6.3*, you can use the footer container instead of using a button directly on the screen.

This strategy of composing style, button, and the container is an example of composability. Composability comes into play where the component can be divided into a button, a footer component, and a style. As one can see, the mentioned footer types are a mix and match of three components.

This strategy for composability worked out in the above example due to the fact that the superset of the possible footer was defined. In a case where the team had no clear direction, then it would become a problem where composability would become an afterthought, which requires refactoring effort. If the organization is in a rush and the focus is to hit the market faster, some of the focus on the scalability of technology may go unnoticed. The development team should have a clear strategy and should proactively invest in building or refactoring the individual components that can be composed and reused.

Note: **The components division in the use case of the footer is one of the many possibilities. The team can come up with multiple levels of granularity. The idea was to introduce composability and help the reader think of how one can bring reusability.**

Composability should be there in engineering and design philosophy. Composability gets the best outcome if not done as an afterthought. In real life, however, one can commonly see that the time between development and UI/UX design is too thin. Therefore, building such a structure in the codebase will be a challenge, and such a case will incur rewriting and refactoring some of the components in multiple iterations.

Other UI/UX and engineering challenges

The design team's expectation can create turbulence and challenges for the development team on various factors, such as time for delivery, technology feasibility, etc. Examples of a few obstacles and anti-patterns were covered in the preceding section, such as tight coupling, duplication, or inconsistent mockups. In addition to these, there are other challenges that the team may encounter. The following list looks at some of the major ones, along with the means to mitigate or control:

- An anti-pattern in the design that undermines the composability is when the development team tends to hard-code the style or configuration along with every component used. This pattern in code creates scalability challenges in the development cycle. Altering the style across the entire codebase will become an enormous task. The recommended approach is to use the style maintained as a shared code or configuration for similar and repeating components and designs.
- An anti-pattern affecting collaboration is when the user interface team publishes continuous changes without notifying the development team. If the change is in the components that are actively being developed, or if they receive a complete overhaul or become irrelevant, that would not be great for active development. This communication ineffectiveness can cause disturbance in the overall collaboration. The side effect of this situation can percolate to affect the functioning of the product being built. Such situations are seen when the designs are also evolving along with the product. The mitigation strategy is to have a versioning system for the design delivery and plan the development work iteratively to accommodate the incremental changes, discussing the priority and impact.

- It is essential to consider designing screens to cover positive and negative cases for a use case. The best practice for error states, is to be managed in a common place. Similar patterns should exist across the entire application for the component and page level to manage the errors at a common place. This should be a consideration for the UI/UX design team to adhere to. The component-level errors seen in a typical application are validation errors for text field inputs, data fetch errors on pages, network errors, etc. There could be page-level errors that define the behavior of the overall page, and these shall be either a combination of multiple component-level errors or a separate page-level error. This error shall prevent users from proceeding with the next call to action. A common example is the page expecting users to fill in some mandatory details, designed such that the save or call to action is enabled only after the valid input field is fulfilled. Another example is the behavior of the user interface during page transition or loading of the data. These patterns should be considered in the early stage. The development team should cater to the behavior early in the coding consideration, which implies the UI/UX team should be proactive in coming up with a design. Such a strategy could reduce the need for refactoring.
- The design team can leverage micro-interaction to bring an appealing nature to the feature in the mobile application. Organizations leverage micro-interactions as either business opportunities or to use them to engage the end consumer. An example of micro-interaction can be seen in a food delivery app showing the status of the weather in the order confirmation screen via the artwork and animation. The feeling that the end user gets from this animation is empathy for the delivery persona who must work in harsh weather conditions. A fact check on the current delivery time and information about harsh weather will give a visual indication, bringing a natural tendency for the end mobile user to anticipate a potential delay. This is achievable with the subtle indication on the user interface. There are other similar micro-interactions as well. Micro-interaction should be aimed at enabling the right level of visual indicator to convey the information. These micro-interactions should not become an overkill, hampering the experience and performance of the application. Other examples of micro-interaction are the loading screen, shimmer, pull-down to refresh, etc.

In the next section, the focus will be on a means to unify the design thinking of the engineering team by creating a design language system. The UI/UX team, following the strategy, will enforce a top-down structure, thereby bringing scalability and substance to the presentation layer of a mobile application.

Design language system

Reusability of the user interface component is an essential factor that drives the scalability and sustainability of a mobile project. For a mobile development project, the presentation layer is the major code written. Therefore, it becomes essential that there is reusability at the presentation layer. The reusability shall become better if the presentation layer components are developed as smaller composable units, as explained in the preceding section. The development also moves faster by having smaller composable units acting as the superset of UI elements. The element should follow a plug-and-play approach with configurability to accelerate development. Anyone hearing the statement could ponder as to why a team would need a special superset of elements, as the development framework itself provides these capabilities. The answer to this could be understood by looking deeper into the ground facts. The development framework provides a simplified and thinner version of the user interface component, and for this reason, a special superset of customized user interface is required to bring the context of the organization into the design. Styling and customizing the behavior that meets the branding standard of the organization will require additional development effort. These styles should be planned to be reusable. The superset of components is the DLS for the product. Organizations that have multiple products can even take the DLS as a standard across the entire organization.

Dimensions of DLS

The DLS has two dimensions: a specification and the implementation. The specification for DLS starts from the central idea, where the components are defined. The specification will have the details of the component documented, denoting reusability and explaining the behavior. This definition will generally be for the entire platform, covering the nitty-gritty details for all individual channels exhaustively. In most cases, organizations take hybrid cross-platform components compatible with multiple channels whenever possible, which does not violate the platform guidelines. The specification thus forms the source of truth that contains the details for the user interface expectation in the digital ecosystem within the organization. The emphasis on cross-platform capability when defining the specification is crucial. This should be noted as a key characteristic of a scalable and efficient design strategy. The specification should ideally be platform agnostic, and the component will have a similar behavior for all the supported platforms. The diversity in the platforms presents unique challenges that work against having similar behavior in all cases. Therefore, a certain set of specifications will be platform-specific in nature. The implementation of the component defined in the specification will take the shape of separate libraries that the respective technology team for the channel can consume. The specification can thus host documentation for a reusable library or framework that the respective platform consumes. The outcome of the implementation will produce three key outputs:

- The artifact published with version history.
- A codebase of the component library where individuals can contribute.
- The details for usage made available for the consuming entity.

Case study of a practical DLS

The section explores a basic DLS through the eyes of a hypothetical organization that is in the retail business. The team at the organization wants to build a unified branding guideline. The idea is to use this across the web and mobile applications. The retail organization was going through the digital transformation journey. The team assembled to curate the digital specification to be followed by the development team. This became the trigger for the organization to decide on the DLS as the strategy. Building the DLS implies the team goes through three stages, listed in the section:

- Defining DLS
- Execution or development of DLS
- Standardization, and ensuring accessibility

These stages need not be chronologically completed in a strict sequence. These could be iterative, cycling through each stage in a round robin manner, logically chunked into a group of smaller units, for each stage.

Defining DLS

The team would start by defining the composition for the DLS by dividing it into three: the foundational elements, components, and documentation, incrementally evolving these.

Foundational elements

The foundational elements are those that will complement and decorate the component, which form the superset of the style definition, listed as follows:

- **Color palette**: This includes a set of colors that should be consistently used across the web or mobile application. The palette can be categorized into primary and secondary colors and may be further organized based on different states.
- **Typography**: These guidelines govern the text elements used throughout the application. The typography definition covers:
    - Primary font family
    - Type styles and font weights (e.g., italics-700, regular, etc.)
    - Line height
    - Character spacing
    - Font sizes (e.g., *small* = *14px*, *large* = *56px*, etc.)

- **Breakpoints**: Breakpoints define the points at which the layout and styling of the application should adapt to accommodate various screen sizes and devices. This is mainly required if there are screens that can be resized, prevalent in tablet or desktop web.
- **Layouts and spacing**: This encompasses rules and specifications regarding the arrangement of elements on the screen and the spacing between them.
- **Iconography**: This forms the list of images and icons used. The definition and purpose of the context in which these icons should be used will be defined as well.

Component

The components in the DLS, on the other hand, will have the purpose to interact or provide feedback to the end user. These form the reusable and composable UI elements built, which can be decorated with the foundation elements. The following lists a few components and examples of states associated with components:

- Buttons, inputs, modals, cards, tooltips, etc.
- Define states which the user interface will transition through (default, hover, active, disabled)
- Ensure accessibility (focus states, color contrast)

Documentation

The third composition of DLS, the documentation will explain to the consumer the purpose and rationale of the DLS component. Documentation will also have the trail of iterative evolution of the DLS managed via versioning. Good documentation will also be the key parameter that measures the quality of the DLS specification. The documentation will fulfill the responsibility of giving clear usage guidelines, code snippets with visual examples, and best practices with dos and don'ts. The DLS implementation is a continuous evolution and evolves with the contribution from the entire team. The process for the designer and developer to collaborate would also be the key information captured as part of the documentation.

Note: **The case study does not explore an exhaustive list of components. The intent was also not to be exhaustive, as the context of the product will influence the kind of components. The theme represented, however, can be emulated to be followed as a pattern for other components as well. This learning could be leveraged in the journey of any mobile application development.**

Execution or the development of DLS

Defining DLS can be seen as an experimental stage evolving to a logical state. Once the definition is at a logical state, the execution of these for the target platform will kickstart. The backlog of the defined elements and components will be converted from design to code in the execution stage. The backlog need not be exhaustive but will instead be evolving as components are iteratively added or modified. Getting immediate feedback from the developer on usability, ease of development, and adherence to the standard defined by the development framework will help the DLS evolve and mature. The execution can also be influenced by the feature requirements, which are identified later by teams consuming DLS. In such instances, the reprioritization of the component not used immediately can happen in the execution stage and will take a backseat to the new component to be developed.

The execution stage produces the outcome as a library that can be consumed. Once consumed, the feedback from the adoption will add to the backlog in case of any observation. Analyzing the feedback and incorporating the relevant items would enhance the DLS. The design team and the engineering team should have proper governance until the DLS reaches the maturity and stability as expected.

The execution strategy while developing a DLS platform depends on the organization's budget and leeway on the available timeline. The organization could either have a separate focused team or the same team member investing in parallel tasks along with the feature development. In either of these cases, the commitment to being a technology-first company and the mindset of doing the right thing are essential to scale. *Chapter 4, Organizing a*

Mobile Development Team, explains the benefits of having a central team, and the DLS will be one of the cross-cutting functions owned by the central team. A hybrid approach will be to maintain a separate team to come up with DLS at the start of a project, and once it reaches maturity, the team could slowly ramp down. Some organizations have taken the community's support by open-sourcing to enhance the design library. Such an approach has the indirect benefit of spreading brand awareness of the organizations with the external tech community and attracting talent. The indirect benefit is additional to the direct benefit of community contribution to improve the DLS.

Note: **For small-scale applications with fewer developers, investing in a separate DLS may not be financially viable. Building components with a DLS mindset will still benefit from the architectural efficiency of the project. The specifications with documentation and versioning, etc., are overhead that will not suit the small-scale application or organization.**

Standardization and ensuring accessibility

The key practices that would enable the team to be efficient in building and scaling the DLS are discussed in this section.

Access management for tools and artifacts

Access management essentially emphasizes that the documentation should be access-controlled and audited to prevent any unintentional issues. Managing and updating the DLS requires appropriate access control and role management. As the organization grows, permission and contribution guidelines become essential. Such a system would streamline the chaos where an individual cannot make changes unintentionally. The access can be for documents and usage details, editing the design, editing the codebases, etc. Access management becomes very important in case the DLS is open-sourced. The contribution to the ecosystem should be audited, which can be designated with the help of access management.

Naming conventions

The proper naming convention goes with its literal meaning. The name to identify should be closer to the domain to be effective in readability and usability. Such a name will help the individual to operate without much cognitive overload. A standard convention is good for preventing any chaos and reducing the learning curve. Leveraging the common convention will bring all the individuals to the same page and thus reduce the communication chaos and gaps. The name, when used without a logical pattern across the codebases, documents, the UX artifacts, etc., will be difficult for an individual to follow through. This might even lead to the case where the team is not adhering to these. The naming convention for the components is thus an important focus area. Making these naming conventions generic would provide abstraction from the underlying implementation and an easy-to-understand structure for a team. While implementing DLS, such practices should be strictly adhered to.

Example: The following are some possible naming conventions:

- red10, red20, red30, red40, red50
- primaryRed, secondaryRed, lightRed, backgroundRed, textRedH1
- primary, errorText, headerBackground, pageBackground, titleText
- #880808/rgb (136, 8, 8), #AA4A44/rgb (170, 74, 68), #EE4B2B/rgb (238, 75, 43), #EE4B2B/rgb (238, 75, 43), #800020/rgb (128, 0, 32)

In this example, the second and third cases seem to be more convenient, which reduces the cognitive overload on the developer compared to other options.

Logically structured ecosystem

The logically structured system is essential to easily find and navigate within any ecosystem. This will help in both consumption and contribution to the DLS codebase. The versioning details, the status of the component developed (for example, in progress, available for consumption, beta, deprecation status, etc.), and the ideology of decision-making are essential details that the development team looks at while consuming the library. These details also help make the right architecture choices while consuming. The details are also essential to make a contribution to DLS. The logical structure defining how DLS is organized becomes one of the key traits of DLS. The naming convention used by the UI/UX team, followed across all the layers of DLS implementation, reduces the cognitive load on the developer. This will provide an effective structure that can be consumed by the application codebase easily.

Conclusion

The chapter achieved its objective by introducing the design thinking from a user interface perspective to the engineering team. The chapter has provided enough depth to equip the reader with the considerations required to develop design thinking. The points discussed help the reader to keep a checklist of the best practices. These practices could help to be efficient in collaborating with the UI/UX team. These ideas will also help the team to be prepared for the development of a scalable mobile application.

In recent years, the design tools have made significant progress, and the availability of generated code in the interface design tool, along with the advancement in GenAI capabilities, has brought together the prototype and the code representing the UI. This has reduced the bootstrapping time for developing the components. The readiness of this generative technique to build an entire user interface for a mobile application needs a human in the loop to review and validate output quality and correctness. The MVP may work relying totally on a generative AI tool. However, the responsibility and validation of being 100% accurate is a guarantee that GenAI is yet to attain.

The next chapter focuses on techniques that, when leveraged, ensure operational efficiency and serve as a means to scale a mobile application development.

Takeaway and reflections

Interface design and engineering are disciplines that operate with different cognitive structures. The individuals involved would get the best outcome when these differences are unified. This needs the team to foster deliberation among these individuals to collaborate. The idea of the chapter was to help the reader put themselves in the shoes of both these disciplines to understand nuances in the journey:

- The interaction and feedback form the major elements of any design philosophy.
- The user interface design is a means for portraying an object or an abstract concept for an individual, serving as a blueprint. A user interface design should be designed to achieve a specific purpose. A design that does not achieve the purpose while adhering to platform guidelines and remaining technically feasible is a good design whereas the one that fails is a design required to be revisited.
- User experience is emotional in nature, addressing effectiveness and usability, while user interface defines the look and behavior of the product.
- For an individual representing the technology side, acquiring design thinking would mean drifting toward understanding the nuance behind the ideologies of the UI/UX world. For the UI/UX team, design thinking would be to understand the guidelines and possibilities of the technology choice made for the development.
- The UI/UX team produces outcomes in the form of an artifact. These are either consumed by relevant stakeholders or used for historical bookkeeping. One can use this as one of the reasons for the design philosophy choices. Some examples of these artifacts are user maps, journey maps, notes from the interview, flow of the functionality, UX strategy document, and high-fidelity design.
- High-fidelity design or the interactive design is the mockup consumed by the development team as a reference for development.
- Reusability of the component when applied to a mobile project in interface design will help to maintain the scalability and sustainability of a project.

Join our Discord space

Join our Discord workspace for latest updates, offers, tech happenings around the world, new releases, and sessions with the authors:

https://discord.bpbonline.com

CHAPTER 7
Scalability in Mobile Development: Part 1

Introduction

Development teams often underestimate the impact of operational excellence. The underestimation negatively impacts the sustainability and scalability of a mobile codebase. In addition, the platform provider comes with yearly updates, which, if not planned or anticipated, shall delay the development. For the team to gear up and ensure a smooth development experience, it is crucial to have the foundations laid out correctly. Thus, the team will be able to keep up with the change and ensure business continuity. The bounded context can limit the team. As soon as the team realizes the limits in their approach, it is recommended to course correct. Software development is an activity that may involve learning acquired through mistakes or failures. Recognizing that operating with bounded context can lead to hasty generalization helps the team avoid making irrational choices. Acquiring learning from experience and knowing past use cases can help the team to understand some of these patterns and, accordingly, without procrastinating, act on these indicators. The ideas discussed are divided into two chapters, *Chapter 7, Scalability in Mobile Development: Part 1* and *Chapter 8, Scalability in Mobile Development: Part 2*. This chapter will give techniques that, when leveraged, ensure operational efficiency and scalability for the team while developing a mobile application. Part 1 primarily expands on ideas around the knowledge hub and code workflow, with occasional intervention of other topics that ensure seamless operation of mobile application development at scale.

Structure

This chapter covers the following topics:

- Sustainability and scalability
- Knowledge hub
- Software entropy
- Branching strategy and workflow
- Code reviews
- Qualifying the choices
- AI assisted delivery in mobile development

Objectives

The purpose of the chapter is to present to the reader the factors that can help a mobile application development team thrive. In general, the mobile application codebase is affected by the functional expectation of the product and the capability of the associated technology in the ecosystem. In all practicality, it is rare to have the same team member present for the entire lifecycle for long-running mobile application development. There could be operational or aspirational reasons for the movement of individuals involved. The theme in the chapter will be foundational in creating a logical structure and mechanism, empowering anyone who has a role to play in the mobile development team. These will enable the individual to contribute and collaborate toward the sustainability of a mobile application project. The chapter employs a series of thought experiments to contextualize each concept and give a model to support technology decision-making and conclude by introducing the AI-assisted delivery in mobile development workflow.

Sustainability and scalability

For an organization, when a mobile application software becomes a legacy, the plan for modernization kicks in. However, redoing the same thing repeatedly in the name of modernization is not optimal and financially sound.

This situation is the hook to introduce the terms sustainability and scalability. These two terms can be seen as the ability to maintain a system over time while also allowing it to grow and adapt beyond its current capabilities. For a mobile application, sustainability implies being relevant. The relevance can have two dimensions: the product relevance and the technology relevance. The chapter focuses on ensuring technological relevance, which involves the code written, tools, etc., that enable the development team. The technological relevance has a direct impact on the scalability. Scalability explained in this chapter is all about how easily a codebase can be managed and extended as the mobile development team grows. This scalability in the backend refers to runtime scalability for handling more users or data. This is not the concern addressed and has less relevance in the case of mobile application. In all these cases, maintaining a high-performing team requires ensuring operational continuity, where the mobile application has a role to play, as it ensures the business reaches the end user.

Knowledge hub

Product development at scale is a collaboration between individuals. It is necessary to share context and information across the team to ensure the efficient functioning of the team. Setting up an organized knowledge hub is a great way to help individuals independently explore the context of the project.

In an abstract form, mobile application development is a cycle of three stages: initiation, execution, and maintenance/ enhancement. The third stage will also be a seed for new ideas for the mobile application. The third stage will thus become a conduit for repeating the cycle. In the case where there is no new idea, it will be running in maintenance mode, addressing any feedback or minor optimization. When the team goes through changes, such as an individual moving from the team, the action will be to find a replacement to ensure the continuity of the development cycle. Retaining and transferring the context information will thus become very important to sustain the development cycle. Another situation is when the team grows by adding more team members. In this case, where additional team members are added, the available workforce will increase, boosting overall output. The team thus will have to plan tasks and features that can be developed in parallel by all the team members. Parallel development opens up the possibility of releasing the features faster to market. Parallel development will also need the context to be shared with a wider group, who shall be part of the development cycle. The onboarding of these individuals will now become the key factor to attain balance and efficient parallelization within the team. A balance within the team implies a situation where everyone speaks the same language and is on the same page. In a nutshell, the key theme narrated is about having a means to preserve context without any loss. As the team progresses, having the ability to enhance the knowledge hub pertaining to the context, adjusting the new data is necessary to ensure sustainability.

The knowledge hub ensures that there is a centralized information repository to consolidate information. This will give rationale to the decision formed within the team. The knowledge hub will promote collaboration and a positive trigger for the team to curate collective wisdom, whereby the information asymmetry of the team is reduced. The side effect of this will be faster problem-solving and even reusing the tips and tricks across the team. The team having a common frame of reference is operationally effective for any organization by bringing in consistency. The chance of miscommunication or having incorrect rationale can also be avoided with this setup.

The teams that have a knowledge hub ensure knowledge retention along with monitoring and tracking of relevant items in the historical timeline of the mobile development project.

In a team with different individuals, there is a definite possibility of different sets of ideas. For a larger team, as discussed in *Chapter 4, Organizing a Mobile Development Team,* if the team split occurs, the total amount of work would be divided into smaller, logical squads. This individual segment of work owned by each team would later be incorporated and integrated into a single product. An organization should strive to ensure that there are common sets of patterns and standards that act as the guidelines for individuals to get maximum efficiency within the organization. In mobile application development, a standard naming convention, following coding guidelines, etc., forms the ingredients for ensuring uniformity within the team and across the organization. Thus, to invest in building a collection of knowledge repositories would be relevant and necessary for any organization. This collective wisdom is specific to the engagement, thus forming the context. The context, therefore, is the information that is not available outside the ecosystem, a treasured possession that needs to be safeguarded by the team to be handed over to the next heir.

Ideally, maintaining the context would be a continuous process. The context can be maintained in various forms of documentation. Maintaining should happen organically, where everyone contributes. There will be an initial investment to set up a system and process for collating the information. This setup should ensure the individuals in the team are motivated to contribute to these documents. The developer joining the team should be educated about these best practices to prevent any deviation. In an alternate reality, there could be a situation where the business leader's focus would be to get the features or product out as early as possible. The pressure mounted by the business priority can trigger a deviation where the new individual is not getting the necessary onboarding. Such an individual, without proper onboarding, will not have enough details to operate efficiently in the project. The organization must decide the priority for the choice between short-term wins and long-term scalability for execution so that the individual is positioned to do the right thing for the organization.

These knowledge hubs address the problem of information asymmetry. The team will have a unified information center. While the intention of the knowledge hub is to reduce the information asymmetry, in an organizational setup, there will always be deliberate divisions of information by role-based access control definition from organization policy; for example, strategic roadmaps visible only to leads, or credentials restricted to the DevOps team. For the knowledge hub, it is essential to adhere to the organization's policy; the access management of the various documents must be considered while setting up the knowledge hub. The modern project or collaboration tools have the option to configure these.

For a project, any context information should be a part of the knowledge hub, and the context can be bucketed into the following functions:

- Decision
- Past knowledge
- Onboarding
- Learning material
- Best practices

There are some formal means to structure the preceding item as part of any project. The format and way of representation may differ depending on the project management tool licensed by the organization. However, the intent and relevance of each item would be the same in all cases. Next, the idea is to look at key items that could be part of the knowledge hub.

> Note: **A document in the context of a knowledge hub could be any form of content leveraged for information sharing. For example, the document could be videos, text notes, a PDF, a presentation, or any other format that is accessible to the team.**

Vision document

The reason why the mobile application exists and the problem being solved by the mobile application is a key piece of information that gives a broader perspective to the individual contributing to the development. The understanding of the purpose of developing a mobile application can act as a catalyst for any individual to align with the goal. The individual would thus become more efficient in their day-to-day activities. The context of what the mobile application is addressing and the audience whose lives are being impacted is a key piece that binds the team by defining a purpose. This document that captures this info is labeled as the vision document for the engagement. In a long-running engagement, the vision document shall be updated as the priorities change and when new learning becomes part of the product definition.

Team structure with roles and responsibilities

The definition of clear roles and responsibilities can give operational efficiency to the team. The data in the document, maintaining the roles and responsibilities, also represents the baselining of effectiveness, growth path, and the point of contact within the team. The growth path and responsibility of the role represented by the document are an archetype. Essentially, this will be the source for an individual to look at and reflect on the effectiveness of the role and responsibility performed in the respective role. Another side effect of having this document is when an individual realizes that a particular archetype warrants all the innate strength the individual possesses. With this realization, one can be proactive in leveraging these strengths to make the product better and promote self-growth. An individual who is either not positioned correctly or wants to grow to the next level in a team can talk to stakeholders to transition to a much more effective role. Such a situation is a win-win for any project, accelerating the larger goal.

One should clearly distinguish this document from a typical rulebook that defines hierarchy and responsibility. Unlike the rulebook, the document will just be a guideline and reference point for a team to have conversations in relation to the effectiveness of the team's structure.

Decision record

The team comprising diverse individuals can have a varied set of options. Such a setup should have the capability to discuss and collectively agree on a decision. A formal means to capture the details is called the decision record. The interested party is responsible for creating the narrative with the various options and comparing the pros and cons of each option. The team can then look at the decision record to debate and put forward an opinion. This approach is more democratic in nature, where the collective decision would win when operating in a flat hierarchical team structure.

In the technology space, the decision record is known as an **architecture decision record** (**ADR**).

Other documents

Exploring the exhaustive list of documents is not ergonomic and will not be the scope of the chapter. The intent of the chapter is to bring to the forefront the relevance of maintaining a knowledge hub for a project to ensure sustainability and scalability. *Table 7.1* lists a few other document types and their purpose:

Document name	Purpose
Overview document	This document is the consolidation of the various documents maintained in the knowledge hub. The core summary with appropriate logical grouping would be maintained as part of the document.
Learning and training documents	A team can have two layers of individuals: those with experience in the technology and those who are adopting. Enabling the latter is key to increasing their contribution to the outcome. The knowledge hub can have documents that act as checklists, tool access, team policies, resources, and details for ongoing team training, skills development, and internal learning opportunities.
Standard operating procedures (SOPs)	A team operating in the helpdesk will have a case where mobile applications require support for incidents that occurred in production. The document with the details of the SLA, the priority definition, and the contact information for reporting is key to ensuring the support team can collaborate with the development team. This document will have the instructions and details defining the operating procedure to execute when an incident or production issue is reported.
Project management documents	The definition of the project timeline, milestones, initiatives, and some examples of project management documents.

Document name	Purpose
Guidelines and policy document	SOPs are more externally facing in nature. Within a team, how can collaboration be effective, and what are the sensible defaults around the same forms that some key insight to be maintained. For example, communication guidelines and best practices, version control practices, etc.
Templates and forms	A repetitive activity for information curation and radiation can be templatized. Such a document forms the template that can be used to populate details in a unified manner for the class of information. For example, reports, meeting agendas, feedback forms, etc., are common documents that can be copied from a template to fill in the instance-specific information

Table 7.1: *Document types and their purpose*

AI for knowledge hub

AI can be leveraged by personas with the intent for either content generation or content assimilation. Content generation is when the team must contextualize an existing idea to the current use case and document these details. An example of content generation is when AI is used in the case of detailing the best practices or dos and don'ts of the mobile development ecosystem.

Content assimilation, on the other hand, is a case where a large, overwhelming context can be prompted by a stakeholder to get specific and concise details. This ensures the team efficiently optimizes the usage of time. In the case where AI was not integrated as part of the ecosystem, an individual could get overwhelmed by the sheer volume of information at hand. The volume of data now is reduced to a source to be assimilated via prompts using AI tools to get focused and relevant information.

Evaluating an AI-powered work assistant connecting all the organization's knowledge to bring the answers an individual needs is the first step. After this, using enterprise search and RAG technology, the organization exposes information for LLMs to respond to prompts. The tool, in general, generates answers grounded in the organization's own knowledge hub. This ecosystem will be with access governed by the same role-based policies already in place. This makes it more than a conventional search mechanism. The response is contextualized to the specific knowledge rather than drawn from public sources.

Efficient usage of knowledge hub

A knowledge hub that merely serves as an archive of past war stories, rather than an active resource, is not healthy for any organization. The knowledge hub acting as the catalyst and reference for a cultural transformation shall be the key performance indicator for evaluating its success. For instance, practices like enabling static code analysis in the development setup, enabling source control hooks to prevent non-adherence to best practices, etc., can be documented to give the details of why and explain the rationale behind the choices of tools. This detail will establish and instill the relevance of these tools. The document, organized under the umbrella of the knowledge hub, is the source of intellectual growth and skills required for individuals to succeed.

The knowledge hub can have information from the collective intelligence of the team. The learning and experience from the team, including anti-patterns and modus operandi that can be adopted by others to be efficient, are examples of such information. The developer should actively contribute back to update and add information to this knowledge hub as long as the information has the potential to help other team members. Contributing back as a practice should be advocated as an expectation from the development team, thereby ensuring the knowledge hub thrives with relevance.

The key points for the lifecycle of the knowledge hub content can be summarized as follows:

1. Define and agree on the document list and content collectively.
2. A group of designated stakeholders will mediate any discussion.
3. Keeping track of the critical information that has an action item.
4. Ensure continuity by setting up audits that enable periodic evaluation of deviations or bottlenecks.
5. Aligning and educating the team to leverage the content of the document.
6. Repeat these steps when there is a change in the contents of the document.

Note: **Step 3 is not mandatory if the documentation is serving as an information source.**

Thought experiment one

Let us set the stage first and understand the example that we are tackling. The idea is to look at a use case and see how a knowledge hub would help add value to an engagement as part of the thought experiment.

Modernize mobile application

The banking institution was having serious challenges with the legacy mobile application. The application was creating a bottleneck while releasing competitive features, hindering the time-to-market expectation. The situation was not so positive for the institution, where even bug fixes took a lot of time to reach the market. The team decided to revamp the application. The institution did not have the technological capability within, which led to partnering with an external entity. The larger goal was to transition and slowly build the in-house capability. The team has people who were foundational in the product and its roadmap. The project was the modernization of the banking system end-to-end. To add to the context, the banking organization was losing market share to the competitor, thus it was very critical to preserve parity in the feature for modernization. As part of this narrative, the focus will be on the mobile team and how the knowledge hub helped in sustaining and making the project transition to meet the vision.

As a consultant assigned to the engagement, take a shot at answering the following problem statement:

- What does the banking institution expect from the partner organization?
- What are the challenges that will be faced by the consulting organization?

Author's take on thought experiment

The value that the consulting organization should deliver is to be the technology partner with the highest quality of deliverables. The consulting team should ensure the transition of the knowledge when the in-house team starts. The key success criteria for transition will be that the banking institution is enabled to sustain, and the in-house team can move ahead independently. In such an engagement, the team shall ideally be structured to have staggered onboarding. The starting team members will set up the baseline, and when the banking organization introduces the in-house team members, the slow replacement of the consulting team, marching toward the transition to a fully in-house team, would start. Now, there are two unique reasons where the information asymmetry can occur. When the consulting team is onboarded in a staggered fashion, the later-joined member will not get the advantage of the past context and may pose a challenge to be effective in achieving goals. The second occurrence of information asymmetry is during the transition of the context to the in-house team. The cognitive overload of keeping track of the entire context would be a challenge if the team put this onto a dedicated group of individuals due to the coordination and information loss. Having a strategy to organize the information is required, and this will complement the organization's value and goal, along with the project context and expectation being preserved and propagated. Such a setup ensures the organization delivers technology excellence from the organized catalog of information.

Software entropy

The deterioration of a software code base is termed software entropy. Software entropy is likely inevitable in the evolution of software. Software entropy applies to mobile codebases as well. It is important for an organization to focus on introducing a culture within the team that promotes measures to mitigate and delay the effects of software entropy.

Software entropy is a conceptual model that can be leveraged to define the frame of reference for an organization to comprehend the scalability and sustainability of a codebase.

Before we talk about software entropy, let us try to understand a few challenges that are encountered in day-to-day projects:

- Every code that any individual writes becomes a legacy the moment they complete writing it.
- As the day progresses, the readability, quality, and maintainability can deteriorate.

- Establishing a baseline for the team to quantify the readability and quality of the code is difficult, as this is subjective.
- As time progresses and the technology evolves, the software may take a path where it can become obsolete.
- The code change creates a side effect and breaks the functionality. These side effects start occurring in unrelated functionality. These unrelated features will start showing errors. The individual will not be able to identify any logical relation and such a situation is challenging in nature to resolve or act on.
- The team is taking more time to add small features to the application.

The listed scenarios are not exhaustive; however, the premise of this section will be based on this theme. From the point of view of an organization, these items are generalized observations or perspectives that are common and should be addressed. Addressing these can have a positive impact on improving the software lifecycle.

For an organization, it is essential to keep track of software entropy and understand if it increases. If software entropy reaches a stage where it is undesirable, this would be the signal to revamp the software.

A sensible metric that an organization can use to measure the software entropy could be to keep track of the time to complete similar functionalities over different periods of the development lifecycle. The metrics, normalized to remove the external factor affecting the time to complete a feature, will give a perspective on the rigidity of the codebase. The codebase being less rigid, it is easy to adopt any new changes.

Note: **The stability of the codebase is measured in the outcome. The outcome of a codebase is software, and the randomness and uncertainty affecting the software justify the name software entropy.**

Graphical representation

The four broad possibilities of software entropy in an ecosystem are as follows:

- Undesirable
- Bad
- Pragmatic
- Ideal

These four possibilities can be visualized in *Figure 7.1*:

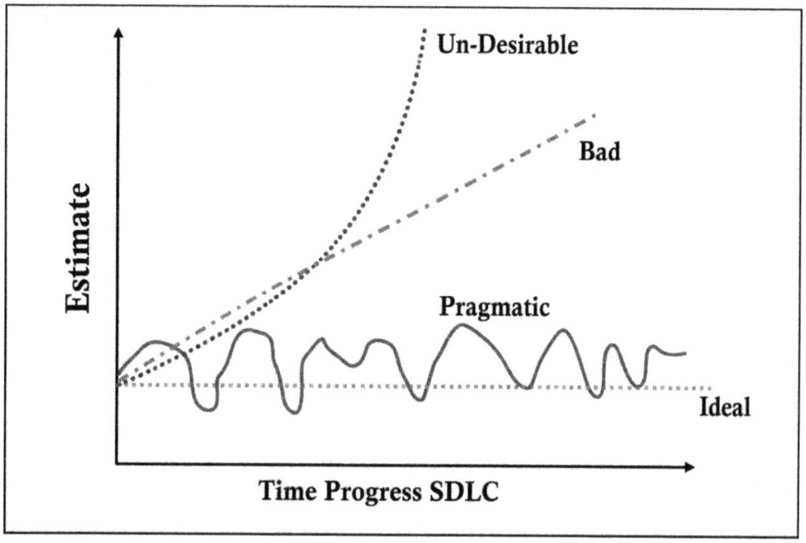

Figure 7.1*: Graphical representation of prevalent software entropy patterns*

Undesirable software entropy

The *Undesirable* curve is an indicator where the feature development time grows exponentially and signals the organization to invest in rewriting the software. If the development team sees an exponential increase in estimates for subsequent development of similar features, it is a situation that is undesirable. It can lead to a huge financial loss in the long run.

Let us try to understand this with an anecdote from a product company, where the team has identified their codebase as undesirable. There could be either a case where software from the product company is used by clients who are dependent only on bug fixes, or a case where the software is used by clients who are expecting constantly evolving features and customization for the product. In both cases, the possibility of the product encountering the side effect of errors or delays in the product development is prevalent. The common problem is the turnaround time to get the fixes and features. This will accelerate the notion of moving away to a competitive product that suits the current needs of the organization. The stakeholder will bear the pain of being the consumer for a faulty or delayed product. This will push the stakeholder to think of breaking the shackles of relying on the product. A typical product comes with an SLA guarantee. However, the undesirable software entropy in the product codebase will impede the entire chain. The situation may even lead to nonfulfillment of the SLA.

Bad software entropy

Bad indicates a software entropy that is slightly less severe than undesirable, however definitely not a great indicator for a codebase to be in. The basic difference is that the time is not exponential here, but rather linear. The codebase is in this stage that could potentially transition to undesirable if unchecked. An organization in a bad entropy state cannot remain viable long-term. Taking steps to course-correct this would be key. Bad software entropy could lead to progressive decline of growth and profit, leading to undesirable outcomes that may culminate in the closure of the business or the product itself. A suitable course-corrective action is to modernize the codebase. Evaluating the possibility of code reuse without a complete throw-away of the existing code base, unlike in the undesirable stage, will be an option here.

Pragmatic software entropy

Pragmatic, the third curve, is the one that every organization should strive for. This curve indicates the most practical and best possible state for a sustainable codebase that an organization can be in. The organization can stay in a pragmatic curve by focusing on the proper practices. Ensuring and enabling the team to follow these practices is an outcome that the team should target. The pragmatic software entropy depicted in *Figure 7.1* is equivalent to short spikes of ups and downs without a recurrent pattern. Even with these spikes, the time to build features that are similar in nature should be equivalent. The spike in the estimate will not have any pattern. The reason for this is that the underlying cause for the spike is not repetitive. The spike in the estimate could be attributed to the outliers that would not have occurred in execution. Exercising control for these spikes in estimates to prevent them from accelerating to a higher intolerable value is important to maintain pragmatic software entropy. The organization should ensure that the spike in estimates is within an acceptable limit. Taking proactive and reactive measures is required to prevent and control outliers while maintaining the equilibrium of a stable codebase.

Ideal software entropy

Irrespective of all the measures taken, the probability of achieving a very flat or stable curve is rare in a software development cycle. Non-deterministic factors impact the software entropy and thereby the estimate for any feature. *Figure 7.1* depicted before has a straight line that indicates, at any point in the software lifecycle, the time taken to build a piece of functionality is constant, which represents an ideal software entropy pattern.

Leveraging the software entropy model in practice

An organization should keep a constant watch on the development cycle to identify where the codebase falls in the software entropy. The steps and actions to be taken would depend on the current software entropy state of the codebase. The team will either course correct or stay put, depending on the software entropy state. Ensuring the codebase falls under the pragmatic curve would be great for sustainability. An organization should aim to be in a state where software entropy follows the pragmatic curve. The following are two means to keep a check on the software entropy:

- A routine reporting mechanism automated via script to pull up similar tasks from multiple timelines in the development cycle and compare the completion time. This could be part of the governance or cadence call amongst the stakeholders.
- A routine polling amongst the developers to periodically evaluate task completion time and compare with the past data could give a trend. This is repeated to multiple individuals in the team, and taking an average can provide a number closer to ground realities without the bias of individual weakness or strengths.

Factors influencing software entropy

There could be many combinations of factors influencing the timeline for completing a feature. Examples of these factors could be development environment or infrastructure, people, requirements, dependencies, testing data, and others. Each of these shall have a varied degree of influence. The factors need not have the same impact in different timelines.

The usage of past data to do the causal analysis of the software entropy and carefully calibrating with the current reality and context will help to define the current state. This will help to keep track of the influence of these on the codebase.

Looking at a case study of a banking app could help understand the software entropy better. The application development for the banking app, when conceived, started with folk who did not have enough technology specialization and were going through a learning curve. After a certain period, a set of individuals with specialized skills was brought into the team. The specialized individual was able to deliver much faster than the individual who is new to technology. If the team uses the task completion time of a specialized individual compared with that of an individual new to technology to measure software entropy, it could give incorrect data. In short, the idea of software entropy represents the difficulty level of adding a feature or modifying the codebase as long as the factors not related to the codebase remain similar.

Having the knowledge of the factors influencing the software entropy is essential to understanding the state of the codebase. This understanding will also help to keep a check on the false alarms. The perspective that external factors will have a constant effect on the team is a fallacy. This means that the effect of the factors need not necessarily repeat. However, keeping a tab on the different factors and by observing, retrospecting, and identifying the root cause could foster an objective decision-making regime. This will also help identify any noise or false alarms. The next section looks at some of the common factors that can affect software entropy.

People factor

People are the key pillars in any project. In the current context of factors influencing the software entropy, the individuals who are involved in mobile development are referred to as people. The possibility of individuals hopping within the project lifecycle with reasons such as resignation, growth aspirations, or a change of role in the project affects the time of completion of the task. Irrespective of the reasons for the team changes, the side effect of this factor can percolate into the team. The worst possibility is that during the transition, the context gets lost when passing through multiple hands. The frequency of context switches can contribute to the project lifecycle taking a bad or undesirable state. The code would start becoming legacy, and each time a new individual takes over, there could be cumulative information gaps. This, at some point in time, would make the organization rethink the strategy and decide on revamping the application.

Lack of common norms

Random patterns caused by a lack of common norms or agreement within a team do not scale well for a large team. The situation is a deal breaker, and the effect will be seen instantly. This situation would be severe if there were no mutual exclusivity and isolation between the two developers. The severity increases when communication within the team is weak. Such a situation will lead the team to start crossing each other's toes. Thus, the situation shall turn chaotic, affecting the reliability and quality of the software.

Environment and infrastructure

The environment and infrastructure that the developer interacts with are the machine setup, the interacting system, or the testing device. The stability, performance, and availability of this have a direct impact on the development time for a feature. Let us take an example where a team is developing an authentication feature, which is the first screen to access the inner functionality. Now, if the developer has not factored in the possibility of the login service getting broken and has not implemented an alternative mechanism, the entire team working on other features can get blocked. This case is an example of an increase in effort due to the idle time waiting for a block to be resolved. This may not directly be the reason that affects the quality of the codebase; however, in the context of the entropy, the time taken to accomplish a task would be perceived as longer. This will affect the computation of software entropy, thus the comparative estimate for tasks with similar complexity will be skewed.

Dependency

In mobile development projects, there are different kinds of dependencies, for example, a downstream system that the mobile interacts with, the library that the mobile codebase uses (substitute to a functionality instead of reinventing), the requirement, etc. The term dependency in this section refers to the broader choice of framework that can be leveraged to develop the application. The framework could be any one of proprietary, open source, or native to the platform, as it was explored in *Chapter 3, Cross-platform Versus Native*. In each of the cases, the choice of these frameworks ties the project team to the framework, and the development would be in a bounded context of what is possible with the framework of choice. This creates an indirect impact where the software entropy of the framework percolates the effect to the consuming mobile application codebase.

An example of software entropy creeping into the system can be quoted in the case of the libraries inside the frameworks having a strong possibility for breaking changes introduced later. If the library is the core dependency that powers most features of the application, and in the case when the maintenance team does not provide backward compatibility, the team will be forced to update the codebase, and could potentially block the feature development dependent on the frameworks. Similarly, in the case when there is a critical vulnerability and the time for the fixes, or SLA, is not in favor of the release timeline of the consuming codebase. The effect of vulnerability could even lead to loss in business. Another situation is the case when the development framework itself introduces deprecation of the API, which can possibly prevent support for an existing feature. This trend is majorly seen in certain cross-platform development frameworks where the community support is not active. All these situations showcase how the development framework affects software entropy.

Case studies evaluating software entropy

A system that does not get affected by software entropy is a utopian dream. Therefore, what a team should strive for is to plan and execute a realistic goal to balance and reduce the effect of software entropy.

Depending on the state of software entropy of the project, the aim and strategy would differ. For a project that falls into the pattern of a *bad* or *undesirable* curve, the idea will be to take steps to achieve the pragmatic entropy curve. The project, which falls in the pragmatic curve, has the expectation to maintain the state and strive for the ideal. A few case studies to understand the approach to handling situations for various cases of software entropy will help the reader to empirically experience the concept.

> Note: **The ideas shared in these case studies are indicators carved out from the perspective of the author. It is the prerogative of the reader to contextualize the information. The action should be finalized by evaluating alternative approaches and weighing the pros and cons when encountering such situations. The possibility of other solutions to a problem that give a similar outcome does exist.**

Case study one

The premise surrounds a billion-dollar enterprise that has a mobile app with a worldwide presence. The enterprise operates in a structured manner such that different teams maintain and develop the mobile app for different locations across the world. The feature parity, time to market together for different countries, and the cost of maintaining multiple teams are increasing as time progresses. This led the organization to re-evaluate the tech strategy, and the data was collected. This data indicated the need to re-evaluate the operation to optimize the spend. There were instances where the mobile was operating with software entropy between bad and undesirable in multiple locations. In the root cause analysis, there were many factors at play. People, distributed disconnected teams, and reduced focus on tech excellence were the top three that came out of the analysis.

For the enterprise, experimenting to revamp the existing codebase was worth the risk associated with the approach. The factor at play against the revamp of the existing code base was the stability of the features in the current version. The codebase context was spread across multiple geographies and teams, preventing a complete rewrite by a centralized team. A drastic change could impact the regular business, and a rollback strategy shall not be there. The alternative to this approach will be to invest in a parallel track to develop a **minimum viable product** (**MVP**). The MVP will have the most critical features carved out from the existing mobile application to address the common features. Incrementally, there will be multiple MVP releases in a closed customer group until attaining parity. After the parity of current production features is achieved, migrating a larger customer base and slowly sunsetting the old version becomes a viable strategy without disrupting the regular business operation.

The case study is an example where software entropy is affected by the decision of a disconnected team. The enterprise had developed a similar product with multiple teams duplicating the effort for different regions. This added the cost burden. In this case study, the best course of action was to rewrite. This case study is an example where the software entropy was not controlled and reached a state where rewriting was the most viable option. The key accelerators for the rewrite engagement were:

- Ensuring automation is the first preference for all possible redundant activity.
- Ensuring proper test layers and optimal strategy.
- Reusability of the component.
- Abstracting the dependent downstream system to have minimal breaking changes.
- Keeping an open channel of communication across and ensuring to share feedback.
- Setting up a central team structure with cohorts of **subject matter experts** (**SME**) to define, coordinate, and establish the guidelines for the entire team.

Case study two

The premise surrounds a banking app that started with the focus of incorporating the latest tech stack and industry practices to ensure stability and a faster release cycle. In the initial phase of the program, the developer invested in building a proper gatekeeping mechanism to get faster feedback. As time progressed, the number of developers contributing to the development increased. All the developers were given the context about the best practices and strategy of the program, and the patterns that need to be followed. However, after some point in time, there was an early indicator that the program was leaning away from the pragmatic software entropy curve. The factors that led to these were attributed to people aspects, where the pattern and best practices were not followed by the team.

A few examples of the situations are as follows:

- Ignoring the gatekeeping requirement while developing features and pushing the code that is not tested to the remote repository.
- Disconnected team members are adding redundant code to the system, affecting the behavior of the application.
- Adding random code to the system to meet the deadline of the task without considering the code design and the effectiveness of the solution.

This case study is an example of a code with pragmatic software entropy deteriorating to undesirable.

The situation was addressed by the stakeholders by creating a focus group. The focus group had the following responsibilities:

- Identify, remove, and refactor the redundancy introduced.
- Ensure to educate and promote best practices via feedback and mechanisms like group code review.
- Emphasize why certain ways of working are important and educate the team on misses.
- Debating and discussing in an open forum for any concerns about the ways of working and accepting any relevant feedback to bring in the changes.
- Creating a knowledge hub for avoiding repetition of context.

There was friction while bringing all these changes to the system; however, educating the why helped. Reducing this friction helped to get the best of the individual driving towards a high-performance sustainable team structure, and this returned to pragmatic software entropy.

Conceptual model on software entropy

Defining a single rulebook to tackle software entropy seems to be difficult due to its subjective and contextual nature. One can invest in identifying the factors and start experiments to get early feedback that would help in controlling the software entropy creeping into the system. In this section, the idea is to explore a conceptual model to monitor the software entropy.

Software rigidity

The proposed model is based on the term **software rigidity (SR)**, which represents the impedance in the system that accelerates the software entropy to undesirable and bad. The calculation of SR would be based on the following data:

Time required to develop a feature(x) on current day = T_Current

Time required to develop a feature(x) in past = T_Past

Ideal business time to develop feature(x) = T_Ideal

Mathematical notation: SR = (T_Current - T_Past) / T_Ideal

Note: **Feature(x) denotes a feature of defined complexity type x; T_Current and T_Past must be measured for features of the similar complexity type to ensure comparability.**

A negative SR value will come in the case where current estimates are lower than past ones indicating a great code base which is easier to work with and not affected by software entropy. Teams should also ensure that improvement is not merely the result of the developer's familiarity with the same code over time. A positive SR value on the other hand indicates an increase in rigidity in the code base. There could be a possibility of a false alarm when there is a one-off case. The stakeholder should evaluate and reflect on the cause for the alarm. The team should wait to see if the pattern is repeating. Building a feature as time progresses should ideally have reduced estimates. This could be explained as the side effect of the base patterns, context, and reusable components being established and available.

A larger positive value is a red flag, and it would be time for the organization to revisit the program and plan a future strategy for the application.

Factoring external dependency

External dependency would increase complexity and thereby the estimate. The previously depicted notation is in raw form for the ideal case and is the uncorrected baseline. The formula assumes no external overhead affects either the current or past measurements. However, adjusting for the factor in play to correct the error factor is important. Therefore, the previously mentioned mathematical notation would be error corrected (calibrated) as follows:

Time required to develop a feature(x) on current day excluding the dependency overhead T_Current_Adjusted = (T_Current - Extra_Time_Current)

Time required to develop a feature(x) in past excluding the dependency overhead T_Past_Adjusted = (T_Past - Extra_Time_Past)

Mathematical notation: SR = (T_Current_Adjusted - T_Past_Adjusted) / T_Ideal

Note: **The conceptual model should be treated as a toolkit to evaluate the software entropy, and it is important to keep in mind that software entropy is difficult to quantify precisely with the non-deterministic factors affecting it.**

Branching strategy and workflow

In a world where a large group of individuals is collaborating on a single codebase, it is a prerequisite to have a system to enable source control. The operational practices laid out to be followed to manage the source code with the help of version control and other techniques are an essential strategy defining the workflow of the team. In modern software, the prevalent source control is Git. Git is a third-generation source control software that enables developers to collaborate and work efficiently on a single code base. Git tracks changes in any set of files, and its strength lies in ensuring speed, data integrity, and support for distributed and non-linear workflows. Git is a great software/technology that enables collaboration. Like any other tool, if used inefficiently, it can create chaos in the team. The inefficiency manifests after a certain timeframe as the cumulative effect of incorrect Git practices in teams. Overcomplicating the Git norms can create inefficiency that makes the team rigid, slowing outcomes. This section will focus on the ideologies and toolkit to keep the codebase in control without any degradation in quality.

Quite often, the team uses a strategy to isolate incomplete code. This technique will help to optimize the development workflow. A small detour looking at ways to isolate incomplete code is explored next, before getting into the main topic discussed in the section.

Isolating code from affecting release

The existence of source control makes is practical to commit code incrementally. This would mean that the case where a part of the code that is incomplete by itself may get regularly moved to a centralized repository. In due course of time, the code forms a fully functional feature, committed as smaller chunks of incomplete code to the central version control system by different individuals. This forms a cycle, and the central repository is the source of truth for the codebase, which will have all the features. These smaller, incomplete chunks flowing in should not ideally disrupt the existing release features. One may have the question as to why an incomplete code should go to production. In the case where the feature development post-release is complex and takes more time to complete, along with the case where there are bug fixes, the release should be a priority. The team will have to decide to keep a separate copy for feature development, separating bug fixes. If the team does not want to take the overhead of two copies of the codebase until the new feature is implemented, the situation would arise where bug fixes are available to production only when a release happens. An alternative approach is to push the changes to the source control without affecting production. This uses the toggle approach to conditionally hide the incomplete features.

The toggles are classified mainly as a **remote toggle** (configured server-side) and a **developer (dev) toggle** (also called local toggles, configured in the codebase itself). *Figure 7.2* depicts the feature controlled with a flag to be switched on and off when the application is shipped. Turning off the flag will switch off the feature, and the feature will not be available for the end user, even though the code exists in the development ecosystem.

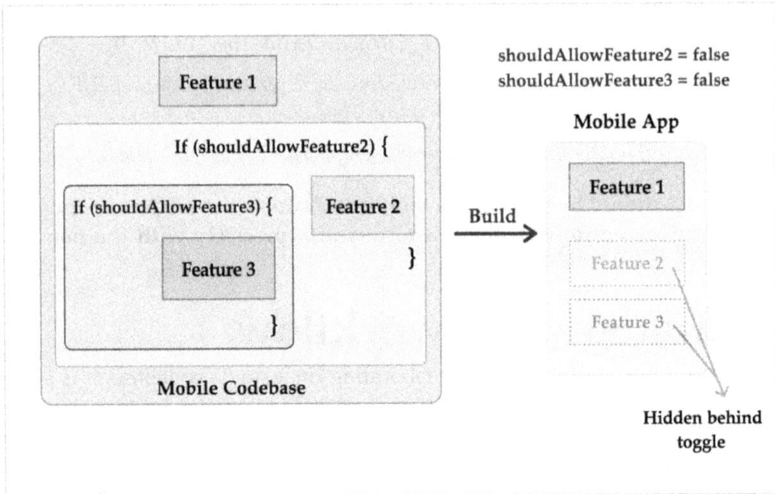

Figure 7.2: *Code to deployment toggling feature ON/OFF with flags*

The remote and the dev toggle are differentiated by the place where these are configured. For the remote toggle, the values are configured in a remote server, which can be fetched by the mobile application via a network call. The advantage of remote toggle is that the value can be changed from the backend without redeploying the mobile application. The dev toggle, on the other hand, leverages configuration in the codebase to manage and define the values. Any change in these values will require a rebuild of the application that is to be reinstalled on the mobile device. The special version for the dev toggle is the usage of the pre-compiler flag, which will not compile the code itself, thereby not packaging it with the build. Multiple versions of the app will be there in the field, and thus turning the flag to true will also make the feature visible in the old version of the application. The remote toggle must accommodate the version-specific configuration. This is important because the end user has the flexibility to choose whether to update to the new app version, which can create app fragmentation. When changing the value for remote toggle the older version should still receive the older value ensuring the backward compatibility.

The local toggle, on the other hand, will lose the flexibility to switch off a feature if the shipped feature turns out to be broken and a rebuild and redeployment are required. In most projects, the combination of these two is used to have a controlled and stable release.

Note: **The incompleteness of the feature can also be caused by the incompleteness of the dependent downstream system. In such a case, the usage of the remote toggle has more advantages over the local toggles, where the feature could be toggled on with a configuration change as soon as the backend system is ready, without releasing the mobile application.**

Workflow

The norms established for managing the codebase maintained in source control are classified as development workflow. In any application development project, team collaboration is the key to success, and it becomes essential to adopt practices that suit and act as a catalyst, enabling collaboration across the teams. The collaboration within a team working on the same codebase would be efficient and less chaotic when common norms are established. These norms would enable the team to work without much friction. These norms, by themselves, should not impact the speed of the individuals negatively, but rather should complement them as well.

Different formats of workflow are followed across industries. In this section, two kinds of development workflows are being explored. It is recommended to invest in understanding key factors to consider while choosing the development workflow. The team can reap the following benefits by practicing the appropriate branching strategy:

- Faster, independent, and controlled releases
- Lesser defects
- Focused feature development
- Smoother code review
- Proper collaboration

The two different workflows narrated in this section are trunk-based development and feature branches. Each of these strategies suits different needs and types of projects. The idea conveyed would help to understand the aspects that should be considered while making the choice of workflow between these two. The other workflows are mostly extensions of these two. Focusing on the patterns and antipatterns in workflow and understanding them is important to be effective on the ground. This awareness will enable the team to make informed decisions and avoid any inefficiency while practicing workflow.

Covering every possible combination is not the scope of this section. However, the major areas that need attention will be covered. These will be applicable for most of the cases. The narrative will be explored through the following two lenses:

- A relatively small codebase with fewer than 15 developers collaborating.
- A team with more than 15 developers and a large codebase, which has separate modules and sub-teams.

Feature branches

In the feature branch workflow, a codebase is bifurcated to create branches from the main in a source control system. Each branch is created to add the new feature or enhancements. The time instant at which the split happens will be the state of the codebase that gets copied to the new branch created. The individual can make the changes to the codebase without affecting the mainstream codebase. The team will merge these changes back after enough checks and balances, verifying if the change has not caused any side effects to the mainstream features. When there are more changes added to the main source, the responsibility of the new branch is to keep it in sync with the latest mainstream. The current working branch should update from time to time from the main branch.

The individual independently contributes to the branch for a feature development or bug fix. Once the development is completed, the team creates a pull request to the source. The pull request is a formal means to promote the changes back to the main codebase. The team can review and approve the pull request to be merged with the main source. There are different variations to this workflow across the industry. The underlying ideology is the same for all the variations, that only a logically complete and accurate feature should ideally go to the main branch. At any point, the main branch ideally will be ready for taking the build to be released to production. *Figure 7.3* depicts the feature branch workflow and illustrates two strategies. One with two parallel branches for release and development, and the other with a release tag using a single branch named main and called as trunk.

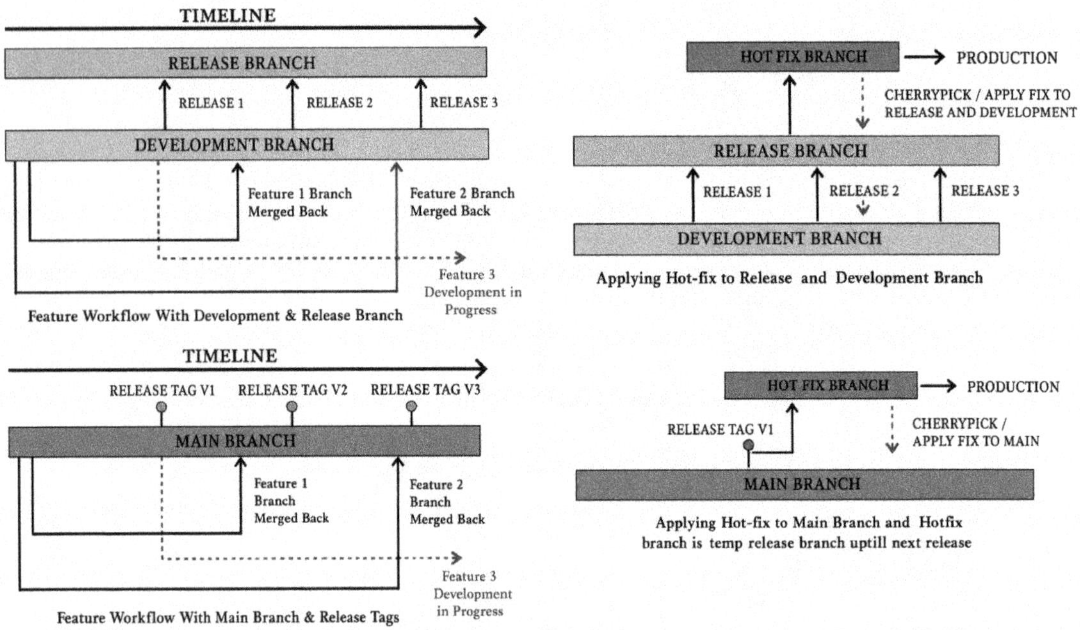

Figure 7.3: *Feature branch workflow*

In the case of both strategies, the feature branch created from the development is merged back into the source. One can notice that these branches can be long-running in nature, depending on the complexity of the feature being developed.

A separate release branch is to keep track of the software being released. The code in the release branch is sourced to branch out and apply any future hot fixes. Hotfixes are generally the response to issues from production support. Hotfixes are applied by evaluating the criticality of the bug. The issue is fixed on the release branch, and an intermediate patch version of the app is released. A short-lived hotfix branch is created and merged back to the release branch. The same hot fix is also applied back to the mainstream to keep the fix in sync with the active development version of the codebase, thereby not missing subsequent releases.

For any release, the development branch will ideally go through rigorous quality analysis. The quality assurance team should sign off on the promotion to the release. Once the release is finalized, the development branch is ready to be merged back to the release branch using a standard merge or rebase.

An alternative approach without having a parallel release branch could be followed. This approach is to keep track of the commit on which the release build was generated and use the release tag on this commit. The release tag will be numbered and shall be used to identify the release commit. In this approach, there will only be the development branch. Each approach has its own pros and cons based on the operating context. The stakeholder can decide the strategy to be used. For example, the usage of the release tag may be limited by the source control tool, where a commit cannot be tagged. Another example is the case of maintaining the older version for B2B applications for the different vendors. The different vendors consuming the application will have different feature requirements or will not be ready to take up the updated features. In such a case, the organization cannot use the development branch for releasing the fixes. The provider instead will have to use the codebase released previously as the base on which any improvements could be made. Thus, the incremental release happens on the respective release trains for B2B consumers, which diverged from the main release.

The feature branch created from the development branch is live until the completion of the functionality identified in the feature. The functionality is labeled as a user story, or a task, which is the smallest piece of work in the SDLC terminology. The developer would work on the same branch, and once a feature is completed, it is merged into the source branch. The merging happens via a pull request created to the source. The pull request is reviewed, followed by an approval process by peers or an authorized team member for merging with the main branch. This review is one of the gatekeeping mechanisms facilitated by the pull request feature.

Typically, a team's needs and operating context can determine the various stages of quality mechanisms required before merging. For example, automation, test approval, static analysis, etc., are to be passed before merging.

The feature branch workflow addresses the problem of collaboration with a large team. For every approach, there are pros and cons; understanding these would help the individual to reason better and decide or take preventive measures against anti-patterns during the execution.

Table 7.2 gives an overview, providing an example of the challenges involved in the feature-based workflow:

<table>
<tr><th>Challenges</th><th>Detail description</th></tr>
<tr><td>Long-lived branches, divergence between branches and merge conflicts</td><td>A branch that has diverged and remained out of sync with the source branch for a long time can cause conflicts that delay feature integration. If there are multiple teams working on the same area of the codebase for different features, conflicts will occur, which will cause the delays.
Mitigation strategy will be shorter commits, with minimal code changes focusing on small logical independent features (mutually exclusive features). This will help to ease the pain of merge conflicts.
The long-lived branch is a pattern prevalent with feature branch workflow. This increases the risk for the team to endure complex merges.
The feature branch can get outdated easily. If the individual does not put conscious effort to keep track of the change in the main, the feature being built will be on outdated code.</td></tr>
<tr><td>Delayed integration and feedback</td><td>The merging of the feature can happen only after development is completed. This would potentially mean a longer period of isolation. Multiple such features in the pipeline could lead to merging hell and big-bang integration. This could cause late discovery of issues due to the side effect of the integrated code.</td></tr>
<tr><td>Code freeze</td><td>The code freeze is inevitable before the release stage. The code written for features to be released later should not be merged until the release branch is cut. This ensures the regular workflow of the team is blocked until the release branch is cut.</td></tr>
<tr><td>Overhead with branch management</td><td>Managing the branches is an overhead. The team should have the discipline to do the reviews in a timely fashion. The overhead of coordination can cause potential disruption to individual task completion. The following are a few example situations leading to delays in merge:<ul><li>Awaiting pull request approval from a peer. The peer reviewer will have a large number of pull request lined up.</li><li>Waiting for green status for the automation test suite before merge.</li><li>Wrath of conflicts; regular rebase/merge being absent will mean more work during the time of merge. Particularly if the changes are massive, this would mean a lot of testing and refactoring effort to resolve conflicts.</li></ul></td></tr>
<tr><td>Testing and validation complexity</td><td>When the developer works in isolation without worrying about day-to-day changes from other team members, the possibility of integration issues at the time merging is high.</td></tr>
</table>

Challenges	Detail description
Overhead of taking hotfixes to mainstream	Managing hotfixes is tedious. The release branch may have an old version, and coordination may be needed to bring this to the main branch. This situation worsens with multiple hotfixes and deteriorates further if the developer fails to merge the fix back into the main branch.
Reduced parallel execution possibilities	Consider two tasks, A and B, which have a subset of features that are common to both. In the case of branching, the team will have to wait until A or B is completed to avoid duplicate effort.

***Table 7.2**: Potential challenges in feature branching workflow*

Table 7.3 gives an overview of the potential benefits while leveraging the feature-based workflow:

Benefits	Detail description
Isolation and completion control	The individual working on a feature can work independently without disrupting others, thus minimizing the risk of breaking the main code and blocking others. The features are merged once they are fully completed and tested thoroughly.
Clear versioning and easy rollback	The isolated nature of the feature ensures versioning and prevents the release of an untested feature. The feature branch approach makes it possible to track and revert changes.
Parallel development and improved collaboration	The team can work on multiple items, and if the features are independent of each other, the productivity will be high.
Easier code reviews	The structure of the pull request in the workflow tools provides an interface for code review and thereby catches the hot spots in the code changes.
Minimal risk to the main branch	The main branch will have minimal risk of breakdown. Anyone who is starting a new feature will have the least effect.
Flexible releases	A controlled merging of features to the main can enable releases with minimal risk and reduce the overhead of regression issues.
Faster hotfix management	The hotfix can go faster. The team with no automated quality testing mechanism may only focus on the area affected by the incremental change for the hotfix and release the app after minimal end-to-end sanity testing.

***Table 7.3**: Potential benefits in feature branching workflow*

One may see that there are a few points that are repeated across the pros and cons and in some cases contradict each other. When a particular project requires the workflow etiquette defined in the pros of the feature branch, the cons become an accepted norm that the team will have to live with.

For example, consider the case of a takeover of a legacy project where the codebase does not have enough gatekeeping mechanisms. In this case, having the feature branch will enable a seamless code review. Similarly, for hotfixes, the team can go ahead with the fixes on the latest release codebase without the interference of any side effects introduced by changes in the existing codebase. The confidence of a developer to predict the accuracy of any change introduced in the legacy code will be low. The feature workflow will be more appropriate for the organization to ensure sanity of the codebase, ensuring the review of code is performed for the feature developed. An in-house codebase developed from scratch should ideally have a strong gatekeeping mechanism that provides proper checks and balances. An individual who is well-versed in technology may find the branching to be a waste of time; however, they may have to adhere to this for the collective good of the overall team.

Trunk-based development

Unlike the feature branch workflow, in **trunk-based development** (**TBD**), branches are not created for every feature. In TBD, there is a main branch of the codebase to which the development team will continuously add changes. Now, one would be curious to know how the continuous release happens while following TBD. While following the TBD, it is expected that the branch is always production-ready for every commit at any point in time.

TBD is best suited for self-organized and high-performing team. The team should plan to achieve the level of discipline and competence before adopting the workflow. The belief is that an individual in the team is competent to ensure the code committed to the main branch is of the highest quality and does not break the system. Trust amongst the team, where everyone will do the right thing, will be the outcome of practicing TBD. There is always the possibility of human error; however, to catch the issues upfront and proactively, the TBD workflow will be complemented with strong gatekeeping mechanisms that give early feedback.

TBD enforces self-discipline within the team, and without which it will be flawed.

The fact that the trunk is expected to be production-ready raises the question of whether the incomplete code should be pushed. The team will leverage a mechanism to toggle the functionality affecting the system. The means to isolate the incomplete code was discussed earlier in the section. The toggle approach will help to hide the feature from surfacing or affecting the production-ready application.

The release in the TBD will be tagged with a version number or using the commit-ID. For case where there is a need for a hotfix and production support, the team shall not be required to keep track of the previously released version of the codebase. For the happy path the trunk is always production-ready, and a separate release branch is unnecessary. However, if the trunk contains an in progress major commit, team may fall back to most recent release tag to add the fix and release the build. Thus the release tag or keeping track of commit ID for the recent release will become important.

TBD is complemented by practices such as pair programming. Teams whose members are experienced and work independently find TBD to be most effective. The team, however, will take time to gradually reach an equilibrium and common consensus of practice, which requires conscious effort while following TBD. With TBD, the inefficiency of waiting for someone to review can be avoided. TBD helps in bringing down the cognitive overload from late feedback when compared to the feature branch workflow. The team following TBD can move the individual to the next feature without idle time or context switch while waiting for review and the other gatekeeping mechanisms to be completed.

The TBD workflow is depicted in *Figure 7.4*:

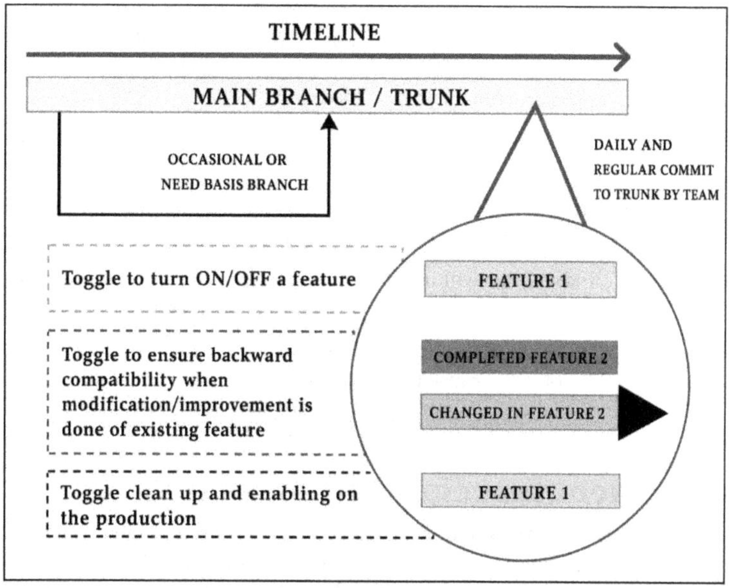

Figure 7.4: *TBD workflow*

Table 7.4 gives an overview of the benefits of TBD collating the data from ground experiences:

Benefits	Detail description
TBD in teams with experienced developers or pair programming	TBD is effective when teams have people who can confidently integrate the work frequently and collaborate effectively. In an organization the confidence is also gradually built over a period. The team formed should have a proper leverage mix to enable and cultivate the trait within the team.
Gradual improvement of practices	Different minds will have different ideas. These ideas may even conflict with each other. As time passes, the team will reach an equilibrium through conversation and debate. Some of the difference becomes the mutually agreed norm for the team.
Avoiding inefficiency of waiting for reviews	The delay for waiting for code review is avoided, and the practices to address the quality by doing pair programming, etc., complement the TBD. The recommendation is to have smaller and more frequent commits.
Minimizing cognitive overload	The codebase is maintained with a strong gatekeeping mechanism; therefore, the team can confidently commit with the testing done for future changes. The reduction in the cognitive overload of causing any side effects is an outcome of the gatekeeping mechanism. This, therefore, helps the individual to stay focused on the task at hand, complementing the effectiveness of the TBD workflow.
Feedback comes sooner	The feedback comes sooner and will help to maintain continuity without many context switches. Unlike the feature workflow, TBD does not have idle time, breaking the natural flow of an individual.

***Table 7.4**: Good parts of TBD workflow*

Table 7.5 gives an overview of the challenges of TBD collating the data from ground experiences. It should be noted that *Table 7.4* and *Table 7.5* are not mutually exclusive and will be applicable mostly when there is a similar context.

Challenges	Detail description
Pipeline and infrastructure constraints with large teams and the ask for frequent builds can be overwhelming, causing slower feedback loops	In large teams, shorter commits, frequent commits, and associated gatekeeping mechanisms that run on every commit can be resource-intensive and overload the infrastructure. This can strain the system, causing potential system failure in a resource-crunched environment.
Build failures can be overwhelming	In mobile, generally, the test mechanisms are time-consuming. A previous commit causing a failure can prevent any future build. This will create panic in the team.
Challenges with non-technical team members	Individuals without much technology expertise may contribute to leaking inefficient code into the system. This can lead to confusion, inconsistency, or delay.
Improper practices and discipline can create chaos	Ignoring the best practice can break the whole purpose of TBD, which will be chaotic and cause the project's failure.

***Table 7.5**: The bad parts affecting TBD*

Workflow requirement for regulated software

In the industry, there are businesses that are regulated and have strict audit requirements. For such an organization, the rulebook will mandate the PR requirement. However, for operational efficiency, the team may see TBD as the strategy. In such cases, a hybrid approach for short-lived feature branches, along with the principle of TBD, could be followed.

The lifespan of the branch in such an approach is until the completion of the smallest unit of work. This ideally should not take more than an iteration in an agile execution. The smallest piece of work will be developed in the feature branch. After completion, the branch is rebased and merged into the main. The pull request raised will be applicable to facilitate the code review.

Recommendation for team practicing TBD

Here are some recommendations for teams practicing TBD:

- Every incomplete feature will be under a toggle (remote or dev), and code should be checked in daily to source control. This could help facilitate faster collaboration, and keeping the changes behind the toggle will make them safe.
- If an existing feature is modified or changed, ensure that there is a release flag to maintain two sets of code for backward compatibility. This would mean that until the modification or change is complete, the released changes will be under the toggle. When a production release is made, the old functionality will be visible to users. This is essential as part of continuous delivery, where incomplete code is in the system without causing any issues.
- If there is a production bug and a hot fix is needed, then the main trunk will be used for the release. In the worst case, if there is a major issue with the trunk, which is not ideal in TBD, then the release tag will be branched, and a hot-fix build will be released. The developer should ensure the hotfix changes are merged into the main branch as well. This case is a deviation from the ideal principle laid out by the TBD workflow.
- Feature toggle cleanup should be on the back of the mind of every developer. The clean-up should be proactively prioritized and should be done as soon as the feature is released to the public.
- If there are large features that cannot be done as part of the release flag, like Flutter upgrade or major language feature updates, etc., the release flag may not help. In such a case, backward compatibility will not be possible. This case will only have the possibility for branching.

> Note: **Practicing TBD does not mean that the team shall never create a branch. However, the idea is that in principle, the team would tend to avoid branching from the main trunk.**

Thought experiment two

Let us set the stage first and understand the example that we are tackling. The idea of the thought experiment is to understand the inertia for a team when moving toward TBD as a branching strategy.

Team shifting to TBD

The premise for this thought experiment is around a team where most of the developers were new to TBD. The team members were not aware of toggle usage and came from a background of feature branch workflow. Stakeholders anticipated skepticism and inertia in the team to adopt TBD with toggle. The discussion and questions that came up within the team are as follows:

- TBD seems like a workflow that does not use the full capability of Git.
- Will developers be able to ensure the commit does not break the existing code? If this cannot be guaranteed, how can the team maintain a codebase that is stable?
- The team was already comfortable with another Git workflow. TBD was alien to the team. What are the issues associated with other Git workflows?
- How can the team do code reviews without any pull requests? In such a case, how can the team ensure sanity for the code?
- Maintaining and cleaning up release flags is an overkill and additional effort. Is it worth spending extra effort?

As part of the thought experiment, imagine you are responsible for advocating the choice of TBD to the team. The problem statement at hand is to prepare for influencing to get acceptance. The details presented in the chapter can act as the source to answer the above questions.

Author's take on thought experiment

Some of the questions that are asked in the thought experiment are already answered in *Table 7.5*, and the data can be used. The individual who recommends the adoption of TBD should ideally start with the rationale of why TBD suits the context. This perspective would give the logical foundation for the answer to the questions. The idea of TBD is well-suited for a time-to-market-critical mobile application where the entire team must collaborate independently as a cohesive unit. Such engagement cannot allow the developer to waste time and effort in reviewing each other. The team is expected to be writing good and efficient code. TBD will enforce this idea, and it becomes imperative for individuals to do the due diligence of being efficient, effective, and accurate in doing the right thing independently. Individual outcomes, when done with cohesiveness, help to attain the larger collective goal.

Thought experiment three

Let us set the stage first and understand the example that we are tackling. The idea of the thought experiment is to understand the effects of feature parallelization on the development workflow.

Feature parallelization

Organizations are very much interested in the faster time to market when building products in a competitive market. One of the strategies to enable faster time to market will be to maximize parallel development. The parallel development should be sustainable and optimal as well. The team in such a situation will have to rely on conceptual contracts. The conceptual contract will help in internal collaboration and setting the boundary of the feature to limit duplication and overlap. The integration will be done at the end with minimal effort as the entry and exit will work seamlessly if the contract is adhered to.

Consider an example of building a login feature. A probable situation played out in the team involved is depicted in *Figure 7.5 (a)*. The login feature will have the main page with multiple functionalities: sign up, forgot password, and login. The entry points are on the same page. Additionally, there are many reusable pages and controls. If the team decides to sequentially develop these, the time taken to complete the feature will be stretched. The team wants an alternative to reduce the timeline, and the team is ready to add more folk if that would help in reducing the development time. Running parallel streams can reduce the overall feature release timeline. The team decided to divide the entire feature into three parallel streams of work: login flow, signup flow, and the forgot password flow. For this strategy to be effective, the team must agree on the following:

- The skeleton of the app with the placeholder for enabling parallel development should be implemented with minimum effort.
- Each individual stream should continue development independently on top of the skeleton.
- Effective communication and operational optimization to prevent duplicate effort are required.
- Efficiently dividing the common component amongst parallel streams will reduce code clutter.
- Proactively planning features that can be developed in parallel.

The underlying theme is to have the skeleton codebase with an entry point based on the contract agreed upon. This strategy opens the possibility of maximizing the parallel execution, and the ideology can be extrapolated to any feature being developed. *Figure 7.5 (a)* depicts a glimpse of the office conversation played out for the situation of login feature parallelization:

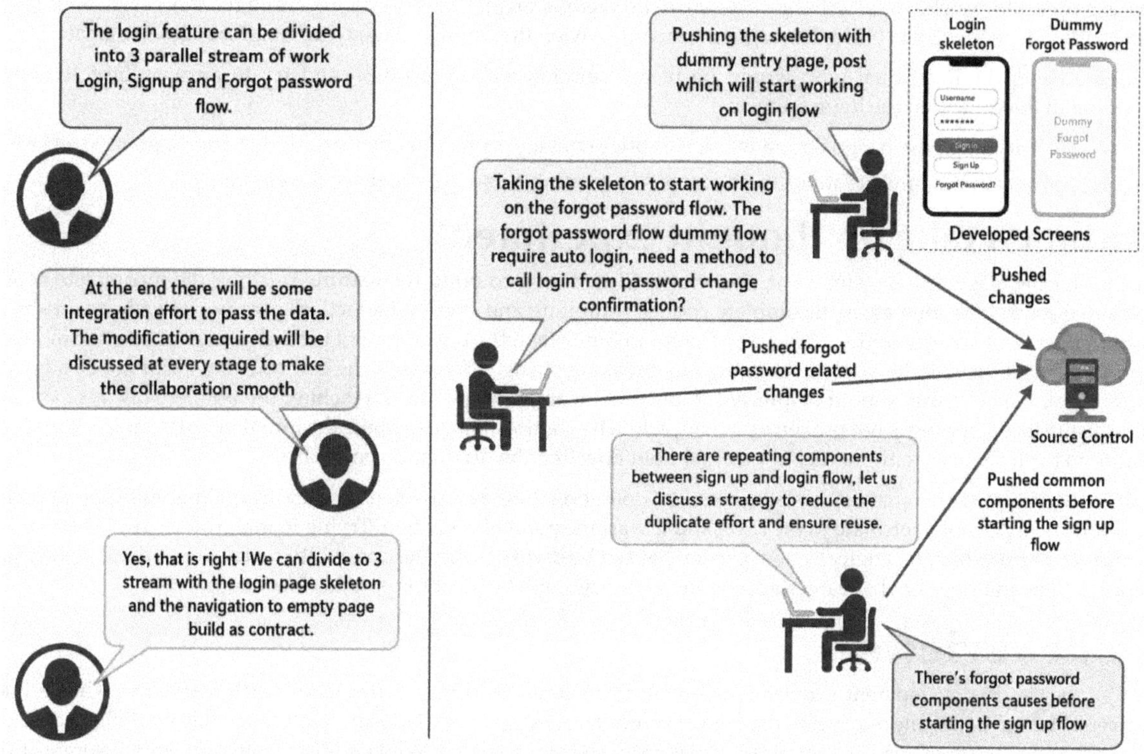

Figure 7.5 (a): Sneak peek at a plausible office conversation

The parallelization can only be effective after the first story is developed, which will have the skeleton and the dummy page. This would enable parallel development and collaboration. *Figure 7.5 (b)* zooms in on the skeleton with the necessary integration points defined:

Figure 7.5 (b): Developed screens zoomed in view

For example, the skeleton has the **Forgot Password** link redirecting to the dummy page, and the other team members can work independently to build the forgot password flow on the dummy page without affecting other areas.

Imagine being the individual who would be in the decision-making position and try to answer the following question in the context of the login feature:

- What could possibly go wrong when the above strategy is used for any features developed after the release?
- What are the considerations or challenges in running a parallel stream of development?

Author's take on thought experiment

In the starting stage of a development, the team will be trying to build the feature, pushing the incomplete code to source control. As long as the incomplete code is compiling and does not affect other code bases, the team shall continue without any disruption. After some point in time when the development reaches a stage where the mobile app shall be released to the market, releasing any breaking change that affects the end consumer will not be a great experience. A mechanism should be present to prevent incomplete code from reaching the public. This mechanism will ensure that shipping is not broken or incomplete. The team will have to make the initial investment to set up the ability to push changes to the source control without affecting the production codebase.

Parallel development comes with an increase in operational effort. Any inefficiency in maintaining operational coherence can possibly percolate to the team and thwart the parallel execution. Trying to make more parallel streams is also counterproductive. Logically, the feature that can be divided with the possibility to develop independently in separate files and does not have overlapping dependencies will be ideal for parallel execution.

Code reviews

For any software development problem statement, there could be different means to reach a solution. This is the universal freedom that one may get in the field of computer science. Formulation of a solution while working in a team to build a larger system needs a common norm agreed upon by the team. When multiple individuals collaborate, it is important to follow common patterns in the codebase, which enable the organization to scale and sustain.

In such a setting, the code review is an integral part that ensures the common norms are curated and validated for adherence. The team will start with a baseline, and over a period, the baseline will mature to become a general rule of thumb for the team to follow. An informal means to ensure adherence is socializing the learning with the team and advocating the relevance. A formal mechanism is to take sessions or perform code reviews. In the source control workflow, code review has a great role to play in an organization and a certain regulated sector, as narrated before, code review and approval are mandated and cannot be skipped.

Table 7.6 lists a few forms of the review types in software development:

Types	Description
Peer review	In peer review, the developer reviews the code of other team members. For an efficient peer review, having the context of the codebase and the feature being built could help. Peer review is generally done in a smaller team. In peer review, the developer sits alongside other team members to do the review post-implementation of the code. There could be multiple iterations of small review sessions if the feature is complex and has many changes.
Pull request (PR)/ merge request (MR) review	This is a form of peer review that extends the tooling capability of the version control system to raise requests to merge the changes. The reviewer from the team can self-assign on the tool and can find the differential changes to review. The tool can be configured to adhere to rules to define the list of designated reviewers.
Formal code review/ checklist-based review	This is a form of peer review with a set of agreed-upon principles. These principles are documented and referenced as part of every review session. The document acts as a checklist of items to be adhered to. Automating such a review process can be easily achieved by configuring a lint tool to do the static analysis.

Types	Description
Pair programming	Pair programming is a practice within the extreme programming agile framework. The main idea is not about code review, but rather two brains working together to solve a problem. However, in the context of TBD, this practice has a greater role to play where the code pushed to the main is agreed upon by two team members, which gives a greater probability of being accurate in implementation. Pair programming acts as a review mechanism as well.
Over-the-shoulder review/quick review/ lightweight code review	This is an informal review of a smaller codebase or approach to be implemented. The review will be focused on identifying major issues (bugs, security vulnerabilities, design flaws) without deep inspection of end-to-end code.
Third-party review/ external review	This involves bringing in a **subject matter expert** (**SME**) from outside the organization to review the codebase for patterns and architecture, typically when in-house expertise is limited.
Automated code review	Leveraging linter tools and the AI mechanism to scan for patterns that could be potentially of bad quality without the intervention of individuals is prevalent. This review can be complemented by a mechanism to send periodic reports, where any high-risk items are identified.
Walkthrough/reverse code review	In this review format, the individuals give a walkthrough of the code. The reviewer plays the role of interviewer as the developer walks through the code base. This practice is relevant in mentoring, cross-training, or knowledge transfer.
Mob review	The team will do the review in a group where features will be decided and conduct walkthroughs with a larger team. Anyone interested can join this review session. The practice of mob review promotes thinking of cross-cutting concerns and helps to normalize the knowledge base across the team.

***Table 7.6**: Various formats of code reviews*

Qualifying the choices

In the myriad of possibilities, it is interesting to understand the structure that one can leverage to make the choice. The idea for this section is to bring a logical structure to reason effectively when presented with multiple choices. In mobile development, there are various choices starting from the technology framework, the libraries to be used, the products that need to be integrated, etc. All this can culminate later in the SDLC stage for the team to realize that a particular choice was not appropriate. When the failure is bound to happen, it is important to do the due diligence required to analyze the options to reduce the risk of failure. During the start of any journey, the effort to evaluate other options would be disheartening, demotivating, and overwhelming to one's mind; however, it will benefit in the long-term.

Figure 7.6 is a graphical representation of the various possible stages in the lifecycle of potential dependencies/choices:

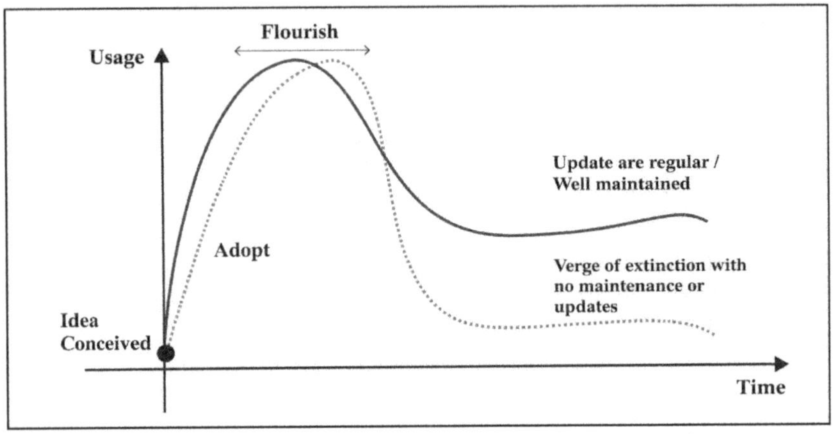

Figure 7.6: *Pictorial interpretation of a lifecycle for a choice made*

At an abstract level, this can be applied to any technology choices at hand. In this model, technology is classified through the following stages: conceived, adopted, flourishes, updated/maintained, or extinct. The longer the stay in the *flourish* stage, the longer the life of dependency, and thus can maximize the life of the consuming system. For any individual, looking at the data from the above lens can give a better structure and soundness to the judgment in deciding the technology.

The preceding graph is a representation of the path of technology from introduction to the journey thereafter. The graph can be seen as the outcome representing the introduction, followed by the adoption and acceptance of the technology by the community. The analysis and positive results of the proof of concept will lead to adoption. This could also be triggered by the traction created by the technology in the community. There is a possibility that the technology may not bring the value, causing the failure to meet the expectation. Multiple such occurrences will bring down the adoption, thereby putting the technology on the verge of extinction. The positive results of the technology to solve problems will increase the relevance and extend the traction to expand the usage by a wider community, thereby supporting the widespread adoption. The trajectory then goes on to be stable usage or extend capabilities in parallel. The gradual desire for the adoption of competing products can put technology on the verge of extinction as well. The stability and regular updates to a library or technology will ensure the consuming enterprise progresses and is able to keep up with the trends.

For certain cases, organizations would be in a position where the business is continuing without much change in operation. A revamp of the product is not monetarily viable and does not add any value. In such a case, the team will have to use the technology to ensure the solution is maintained. For the application to sustain, the underlying technology should be maintained, and support should be in place. The cost of maintaining will become the responsibility of the consuming enterprise. This is an example of how legacy technology helps to sustain the business, and there could be a case where, outside the ecosystem, the technology itself has become extinct or obsolete.

Thought experiment four

Let us set the stage first and understand the example that we are tackling. The idea of the thought experiment is to practice decision-making when presented with different choices.

Choosing Flutter

Deciding on the technology for developing a mobile application is critical for any team. *Chapter 3, Cross-platform Versus Native,* has given details on a variety of choices. The cross-platform itself has multiple options. As part of the thought experiment, the idea is to explore the usage of graphical representation to help in decision-making for the technology choice. If the team looks at the historical data for Apache Cordova, jQuery mobile, Sencha Touch, Xamarin, etc., the life of these cross-platform technologies in mobile has gone through various stages, as depicted in *Figure 7.6*: introduction, adoption, flourishing, and extinction.

As part of the experiment, the reader is expected to take Flutter as an option and try to map the stages, evaluating the data available in the community to do this analysis. Flutter, which was initially built for Android, then added support for iOS, and the web channel is actively used by organizations to build production-grade applications. The million-dollar question will be to check if Flutter fits the above four stages for the model of technology choices. In the context of the lifecycle of Flutter, what path it can take, and the possible risks associated with the choice.

Author's take on thought experiment

Flutter is in an adopt and flourishing stage. The community's contribution to making the framework better is also a trend one can observe. This provides confidence to adopt Flutter technology for building products or offerings.

Whether Flutter can be called a true cross-platform is still debatable and subjective to the context. Time will decide the lifecycle for the Flutter frameworks. However, for a large-scale enterprise that has B2C or B2B mobile apps where only less than 20% of hardware capabilities are used and the rest is an intuitive user interface, Flutter seems to be a potential choice. The ideology of focusing on creating platform-agnostic layout and interaction mechanisms has positioned the framework against the odds of becoming obsolete. The design is such that this layer will not be affected by any platform changes. Even if the framework cannot fulfill any promise, the entire platform capability that Flutter provides techniques to hook into native capabilities to interoperate. Flutter had performance issues on iOS. However, the team had addressed the same by changing the 2D drawing engine to address the shortcomings. The updated rendering engine is called Impeller. *Chapter 3, Cross-platform Versus Native*, narrates at length the data to be considered, and leveraging this framework along with this data can bring in rationality to the decision-making to understand the risk associated with the choice.

Choosing third-party dependency

A similar thought process can be used for making the choice of a library that is the third-party dependency for the project. This choice also goes through the four stages. The evaluation of the criticality of the effect of dependency and the possibility of isolating the usage with abstraction may give an operational cushion when the dependency meets its end. Additionally, factors such as the GitHub stars for the open-source dependency, the number of open issues, the community activity, and the adoption will complement the decision-making. This will help to understand where the library falls in the stages represented in the graph depicted in *Figure 7.6*.

AI-assisted delivery in mobile development

AI can play two roles in the context of the mobile development lifecycle. The first role will be as a provider, and the next will be the consumer. In the provider role, the developer will be using the framework provided by the platform to create AI/ML-enabled features accessible to the user via the mobile application. A pose detection application by a health provider for monitoring and guiding an exercise regime, a language translation feature within an application, etc., are some examples of the mobile application features providing AI/ML capabilities. Smart prediction and providing personalized services are additional examples of the provider behavior with which both the organization and consumer benefit.

The consumer role, on the other hand, is when the team leverages products, frameworks, or toolkits that assist in the delivery to accelerate the end outcome. AI, as of 2025, has grown to be a tremendous companion that can accelerate and enhance skills. It is important to note that, for a team, AI cannot replace creativity. Rather, it can turn an intellectually sound idea into reality faster. The key is that the individual handling this should have the ability to reason about the idea; otherwise, there is a high probability that the usage of AI may not lead to an actionable outcome.

The following are some of the prevalent presences of AI in the consumer role:

- Getting a review on the implementation.
- Generating code for a complex codebase in agentic mode.
- Reasoning and trying to correlate a legacy codebase.
- Debugging a code snippet when there is a logical flaw.
- Generating boilerplate and starter code.

- Generating mock and stubs for testing.
- Reducing the entry barrier for technology-focused folks to product/domain expertise.

In short, leveraging AI can complement the efficacy in the development lifecycle. One of the points that would come up while integrating the AI tools into the development workflow will be security concerns about the data being exposed outside the organization. There are means to self-host the AI tool within the enterprise so that data remains within the enterprise. For an independent developer, there are means to run the LLM locally and leverage the solution to integrate into the development workflow as well.

Note: **AI is continuously evolving and a separate book would be required to cover end to end scope for AI. Appendix has elaborated on how to enable oneself to accelerate AI adoption and the meta model one should encode.**

Conclusion

The objective of the chapter was to look at the area of helping the mobile application development thrive. The terms scalability and sustainability in the context of mobile application development are different from the development of distributed software. The knowledge hub, software entropy pattern, branching and development workflow, decision model and AI-assisted delivery are the main themes explored in the chapter. These themes form the process-related aspect essential for enabling the technology elements of the team. The combination of skills from the breadth of these ideas presented in the chapter will help to scale a mobile application development project.

The next chapter is the second part, narrating ideas to scale a mobile development project. While this chapter focused on key processes, the next will be on capabilities to be built to ensure operational efficiency. The themes discussed in the next chapter are around automation in mobile, folder structure, and environment management in mobile.

Takeaways and reflection

Now that we have reached the end of the chapter, the relevance and the idea that need to be practiced to scale a mobile application development codebase are now etched. Here are a few takeaways from the chapter:

- Knowledge should be democratic within a team, and the win would be garnering the collective wisdom to reach an equilibrium of common understanding. Curating the context within a knowledge hub is a means to achieve this in project execution.
- The formats and standards for knowledge organized across different organizations may vary. The key outcome on which the stakeholders should focus is the purpose served by the knowledge hub to sustain the context.
- The software entropy pattern is to be watched. The team should take steps to reduce and delay the impact of software entropy. This will ensure maximizing sustainability in the ecosystem, preventing the execution from going chaotic.
- A **software rigidity** (**SR**) model evaluates the deterioration of the software system by comparing the time to build a feature today against the time required for a similar feature in the past.
- People, lack of common norms, environment, and infrastructure dependency are some of the key factors that influence the software entropy.
- A branching strategy and workflow define the mechanism for code transformation from ideation to deployment.
- Choosing feature branch versus TBD could go for a heated debate. Both can serve a unique purpose. Weighing the context to define what is appropriate and ergonomic. Making a decision based on the facts available is logical.
- AI is used as a provider or in a consumer role. The provider role will be to build an application that leverages AI to help the consumer. Alternatively, the consumer role will be to consume the product or leverage it to bring efficiency in the mobile application development lifecycle.

CHAPTER 8
Scalability in Mobile Development: Part 2

Introduction

This chapter is the second part that takes off from where we left off in the context of scalability in mobile application development. The focus of the previous chapter was on process excellence. The themes discussed in the previous chapter, when leveraged, ensure collaboration and enable the team to be efficient and maintain the rigor and energy throughout the execution of the project. This second part expands on the capabilities forming the support structure to ensure scalability. These capabilities act as practices and mechanisms that the team should use. These will also be built as part of the project lifecycle. Automation to reduce the repetitive load and release-related strategies will be detailed in the chapter. These techniques, when followed, would ensure discipline and bring cadence within the team. All these will be achieved by having a workflow of successive progression towards deployment. The techniques described in the chapter, when followed, reduce the risk of any unwanted side effects creeping into the mobile application being developed, thus ensuring stability.

Structure

This chapter covers the following topics:

- Automation in mobile development
- Pipeline in mobile application development
- GitHub Actions
- Release process overview of iOS and Android
- Folder structure and naming
- Environment management

Objectives

The purpose of the chapter is to introduce ideas enabling the reader to know the techniques to build capabilities to reduce the redundant and repetitive tasks prone to error due to human intervention. Offloading these to machines will ensure predictability, and the team shall now focus on other areas of the business requiring critical thinking to grow the product. The possibilities of leveraging automation in the **software development lifecycle** (**SDLC**) of a mobile application project, along with the patterns and nuances that a team should be aware of from the coding to the release stage of an app, will be the major topic discussed in this chapter. The aesthetic beauty of a codebase would help a new individual to self-learn and recognize patterns. Organizing the code and the relevance of the folder structure in organizing the code is another theme introduced in this chapter. The chapter concludes by looking into the strategy in the development cycle that enables a team to switch the environments, defining the deployment context of the application.

Automation in mobile development

In mobile development, when a technology or software tool is used to perform tasks without requiring manual intervention or with minimal manual intervention, it represents automation. Generally, the overall experience is improved with automation. Automation is used along with the script written for testing. One should know that automation testing is just one piece of the puzzle, and the possibilities are beyond that. As part of this section, we will explore the innate view of automation possibilities in mobile development.

Possibilities in automation

Imagine a world where the mobilelifecycle is managed manually, and there is no automation at any stage. A high-level workflow for a feature development would include the following:

1. Write code and develop the functionality.
2. Commit the codebase to the repository.
3. Generate a test build and publish the release note.
4. The testing team can take up the build and continue the testing.
5. After feature sign-off, plan for release and create the production build.
6. Beta / pre-prod testing and sign-off.
7. Publish the production build and update the release note.

In an automation-averse world, this workflow shall be the steps an individual in a team has to perform for stages between coding and release. These manual steps exert cognitive load on individuals and are likely to be error-prone. Additionally, the stages that require manual testing have a sharp increase as the features in the codebase increase. The extent of testing required would be way higher to ensure the mobile application functions as intended in all combinations of a journey. The increase in features will have a direct impact on the number of possible combinations and the edge cases.

If the mobile application being built is a small proof of concept or one having very similar features that can be tested in less than half a day, and the team knows that the feature may not grow, it may not make sense to invest in automation. However, if the team is involved in a long-running engagement and is spending significant time to release the application updates frequently, it would be advisable for the organization to invest in automation. The automation looks at the possibility of offloading steps from manual effort to machines and thus gets the benefit of being precise with minimal maintenance. Automation advocates for reducing the reliance on manual effort and cognitive load on the developer for large mobile applications. The idea is to illustrate a world where automation is not a focus.

The preceding narrative indicated the challenges in an automation-averse world. One can deduce that creating strategies to reduce the manual intervention for repetitive tasks or processes is one of the key characteristics of a high-performing team. Automation would enable the team to shift the focus and energy elsewhere to make the product or service better. Automation is also the key that would optimize the operation cost and speed up the time to market in the long run.

The typical areas one can automate are as follows:

- Setting up the tool, frameworks, and dependencies.
- Access management, granting / revoking.
- Setting up gatekeeping tools, such as static analyzer, syntax correction, commit hooks, automated testing, etc.
- Observability, monitoring, and reporting.
- Build release.

The development framework comes with utilities to be used in scripts. The possibility of writing a script makes the tool more adaptable for automation. These scripts, combined with the triggers of the machine, will be used to sequence and set up the stages for automation.

Automation can be done for the development setup. An organization, by embracing automation at the onboarding stage of a developer, can ensure the individual and teams are using a controlled and carefully audited software setup, avoiding the security risk, software version conflict, and legal implications of unauthorized software dependencies, which would otherwise fall to each individual developer to manage.

The individual joining such a team also gets a lightweight onboarding process where the development machine is ready with a few clicks and minimal documentation to go through, which would otherwise be daunting.

Automation in the testing strategy is a value-add to any organization. An application with a large codebase, in all probability, is a candidate for numerous interdependencies and points of failure. The SDLC addresses this by having a testing strategy to maintain the quality of the application. Continuous monitoring of the test result is required to keep a check on the stability of the application. The testing script, scheduled to run in an automated and timely fashion, is a great way to offload the **quality assurance** (**QA**) onto the machine. *Chapter 5, Quality Assurance for Mobile Development* details the specifics of testing.

The deployment stage starts after the process of compiling the code base and generation of the artifact. At this stage, the first level of quality of using the test should also happen. Deployment is the uploading of the artifact to an app store or release channel. Automation at the release stage involves delegating the upload process to be done without manual effort. In the mobile development world, the products are the shippable packages or bundles, which are either mobile applications or a library (third-party SDK, e.g., payment SDK). Mobile application bundles are uploaded to the Apple, Google, or private stores; there will be an approval mechanism once uploaded and post approval will be made available to the end user.

In a typical mobile application development by an organization, the sheer number of total builds generated in the projectlifecycle is a very high number. Thus, it becomes important to understand where all these processes get automated. Manually accomplishing the release task is clearly an anti-pattern that organizations should avoid because it thwarts efficiency when operating at scale.

Automation is the best ingredient that accelerates the journey to the following outcomes:

- Setting up a high-performing team.
- Bringing the benefit of cost and time effectiveness.
- Enhancing the workflow with accuracy and consistency.
- Reducing the dependency on manual effort.

Note: **As a result of short-term thinking, if an organization substantiates the choice of an automation-averse strategy, highlighting the time commitment needed to set up automation, it becomes the duty of a team to present the counter-narrative that, as time progresses, the investment for automation will pay off.**

Key success metrics for automation

Automation is an activity that goes through iterations, feedback, and correction. In such a case, the organization should do due diligence to monitor the success of automation and ensure it is serving the intended purpose. It is necessary to understand the key success metrics that need to be attained in automation to baseline the expected outcome. The points discussed in the following subsections are key success metrics of an automation strategy.

Stability with predictability and consistency

For a seamless automation strategy where the team does not complain, it is essential to have stability with predictability and consistency. Imagine the case where the organization has invested in automation, and the automation scripts are failing intermittently. As the frequency of the failure increases, the operation costs also start to increase. This pattern will be counterproductive and break the promises made by automation. In a nutshell, stability, predictability, and consistency represent the qualitative aspects of automation that need to be ensured and achieved.

The stability and predictability of an automation imply a case where, for each automation execution, there is a guaranteed outcome. The consistency of automation is defined by the success rate of each execution. The factors that affect each of these parameters are the infrastructure, configuration, and accuracy of the automation strategy or script.

Inconsistency is the case where the automation test suite gives different and unexpected test results in each run. The test case randomly alternates between success and failures in multiple runs. An example of this pattern is when the test depends on non-deterministic factors in the ecosystem, for example, network, date, and time, improper state sharing between test cases, etc., causing the inconsistency. The following are a few cases of interruption in automation:

- A classic example of infra-related issues is the unavailability of build agents to run the automation script. This could be attributed to any reason, from power failure, OS crash, max utilization, or any other build agent failures.
- The case where the script depends on the absolute path instead of a relative path, the dependency for the build machine, time zone configuration, which may change in the distributed server, different configuration for build runner pool, etc., are examples where the development machine being different from the runners takes a toll on the automation stability.
- False alarm in the test automation suites. This is generally an aftereffect of having an anti-pattern or brittle test.

Note: **The build agent is explained later in the chapter. A build agent is a machine on which the automation is coordinated and executed.**

Attaining stability, predictability, and consistency is a continuous process that can be targeted iteratively. There will be learning, failures, and takeaways. An organization should nurture the flexibility in a team to revisit and do the right thing to progress and improve iteratively after each iteration and data from feedback.

Time for execution

Optimizing for the minimal time for execution for an automation is a metric that is the key goal to be achieved. The effect of these metrics could manifest in the following areas:

- The time to market for a feature developed.
- Ease of rolling out the application to production.
- Developer productivity by reducing wait time for feedback.
- Optimize the defect feedback cycle with early failure.
- Creative utilization and channeling the team energy to other avenues.

Any automated task should be designed with an optimal time of execution. The strategy would be either to scale the infrastructure and bring in parallelism in the task or to optimize automation scripts to be faster.

Utilization

The adoption of automation by the team and promoting the culture of an early feedback cycle play a major role in favoring the increase in efficiency. After investing in automation, if the adoption rate is low within the team and the team is having inertia resisting change, sticking to the manual process would be counterproductive. Stakeholders should intervene to find the cause of the same and take steps to mitigate such occurrences, promoting the adoption of automation. Lack of understanding of the operating mechanism, fear of losing the roles, and the learning curve associated could be the reasons associated with the inertia.

Monitoring and alerting

Monitoring and alerting shall not be the success metrics. However, it is important to understand that these factors elevate the purpose of automation. Monitoring and alerting are means to give feedback to the stakeholders. Monitoring ensures that the place where the information is collated is the source to understand the health of the system. The monitoring side of automation is to have a dashboard to view the activities and outcomes of the automation. On the other hand, alerting is to ensure that any failures are brought to the attention of the relevant stakeholders. Monitoring and alerting have two areas of responsibility:

- Monitoring and alerting for the automation infrastructure.
- Monitoring and alerting for the mobile application.

In both cases, the purpose of employing these is the same. The automation infrastructure will have mechanisms to catch failures and send an alert for any failure to the development team as early feedback. The alerting for the mobile application, on the other hand, is based on a rule configured to operate on the data from the event pushed onto a system by the application. The layer where the system consumes data from mobile is responsible for monitoring and executing the rules configured. This data also serves as the trace logs for any future failures to debug and analyze.

Pipeline in mobile application development

Automation in mobile is accompanied by a topological structure defined as the **pipeline**. The terminology pipeline is used in other software development, and there is similarity and overlap of constructs across the development.

The pipeline for mobile will have the following outcomes:

- Automated trigger to the QA stages.
- Publish the monitored result or reports for the QA stage.
- Automate or provide an option to deploy/publish.
- Capability to configure roles to perform controlled/audited deployment.

Unlike the distributed system, mobile development does not require managing the deployment infrastructure. The deployment happens on the device of the end use via a hosting service. The automation ends after the build is published to the app store. The infra requirements for the mobile application team would be to cater to the following:

- Artifact generation for different environments
- Hosting codebase and artifact
- Manage the pipeline for release
- Publishing the different reports (test, code quality, etc.)
- Security scanning
- Enabling the virtual/connected devices for testing via distributed infra
- Release management for different environments
- Project management tool integration with workflow

A typical mobile application codebase generates multiple installable packages for different environments. These installables have their respective target audience. The rules should be set to define the deployment strategy to share the installable with the appropriate audience. For an organization, the segregation of the environment to which the mobile artifact connects may be different. The recommended set of environments for each team could be: development, user acceptance, pre-release, and production. Later in this chapter, environment management is discussed in detail.

A pipeline is a set of stages, which are sequential or parallel in nature. The stages start from an input transforming into an output. The outcome is the mobile app getting published in the store. Each stage will be a combination of input, transformation/operation, and outcome. *Figure 8.1 (a)* and *Figure 8.1 (b)* represent a standard mobile application pipeline representing code to deployment:

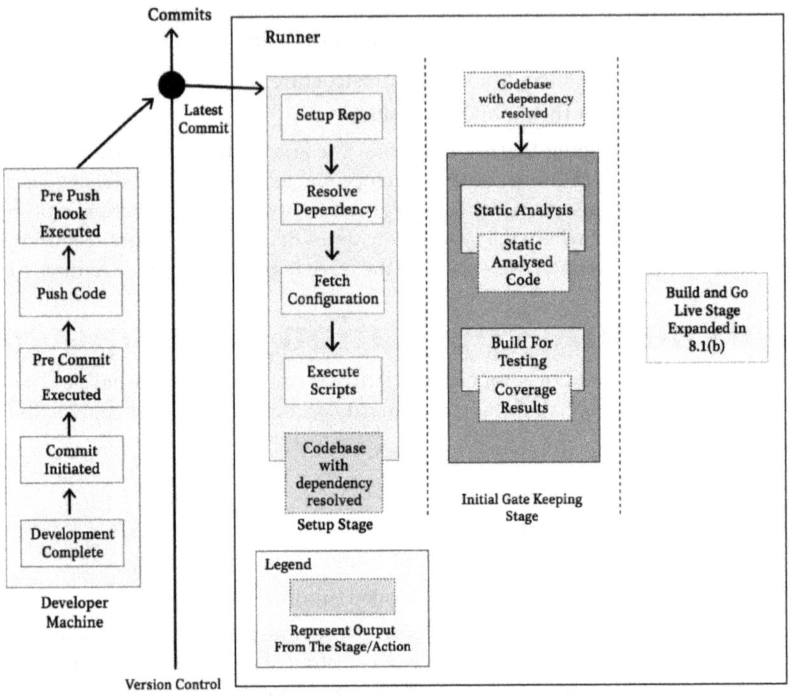

***Figure 8.1 (a)**: Mobile pipeline stages*

Figure 8.1 (b) zooms into the steps in the build and go live stage represented in *Figure 8.1(a)*:

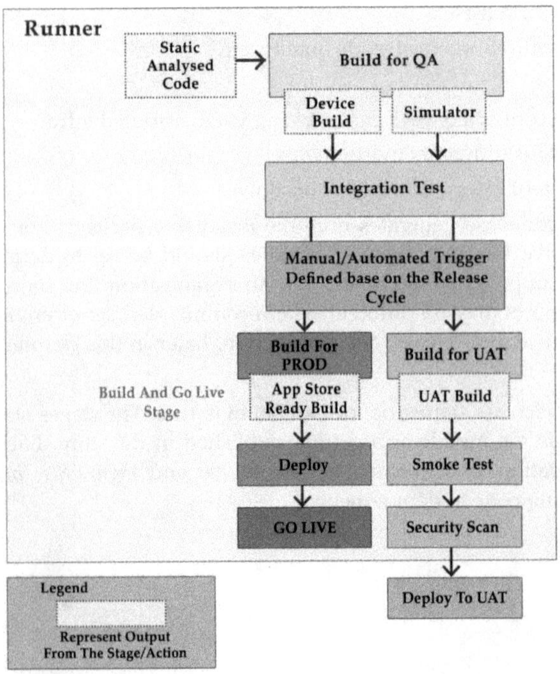

***Figure 8.1 (b)**: Build and Go Live stages of mobile pipeline*

From the figures, one can see that the trigger to automation in development starts when a developer decides the code is ready for the source control repository. At this point in time, the developer, after the due diligence to verify, will commit and push the changes. The Git-based source control has commit and push actions, which synchronize the local changes with the remote version control system. The figure depicts the stage where there is a pre-commit check that does the source code style validation and static analysis. The reason for doing this in pre-commit is to address the cases where the code has not been formatted or has any errors that need correction before commit. Once the code is committed, before pushing, it is essential to ensure there are no side effects created on other functionalities. A basic sanity check by executing a subset of the automated test suite for critical flow will ensure the quality is unaffected. All the stages meeting the expectations mark the completion and are typically referred to as the *stage being green*. For any failure in the stage, it is referred to as the *stage being red*. A stage, when completed, will essentially hand off to the next stage or, in the case of the developer machine, to the pipeline as depicted in *Figure 8.1 (a)* and *Figure 8.1 (b)*. The push action happens on a developer's machine, which hands off the trigger to run the pipeline in the automation infrastructure.

For every new commit, the build machine triggers the rest of the pipeline. The primary intent of the build machine is to vet the quality of the codebase, generate reporting artifacts, and publish the app on the store. Alternatively, the build machines have the capability to trigger these stages manually as well. The build machines are configuration-driven. The pipeline can expose these configurations, which can be edited to suit any specific need. This gives the flexibility to externalize the moving part in the automation stages between code and deployment workflow, thus enabling the customization of the stages. The pipeline thus can be architected to cater to the different needs of the project, and the team must decide what stages are must-haves and good to have while designing the automation strategy.

The stages depicted in *Figure 8.1 (a)* and *Figure 8.1 (b)* give an overview of almost all the relevant activities from a code check-in up to publishing of an artifact to the app store. The complexity and implementation details would vary from one project to another; however, the skeleton remains the same in almost all mobile application development processes.

The section further drills deeper into key stages and components represented in *Figure 8.1 (a)* and *Figure 8.1 (b)*.

Artifact

An outcome of a stage in automation produces artifacts or consumables. Not every stage will have artifacts to be published for the actual end user of the product being developed. There will be stages for which the output is picked up by subsequent stages. Such stages mainly modify or massage the input to a different format, which will be required for the execution of further stages. The artifact associated with mobile development can be one of two categories: one supporting the project governance, or one that is a shippable product to end users.

The artifact for project governance presents the information that denotes the efficiency, performance, and other indicators for the project lifecycle. The shippable artifact, on the other hand, gets released and is shipped to be used by other projects or installed on a mobile device. The following is a list of major artifacts that come under either of the mentioned categories and are relevant for a mobile development project:

- Installation bundle for each target platform, also known as a mobile application
- Automation testing/analysis report, which includes unit test, security test, integration test, etc.
- Documentation for SDK
- Publishing library for SDK
- Massaged codebase

Shipping artifacts directly to production without validation has its risks and is not recommended. In practice, for every project, there are different environments where different quality checks and validations are done for the product. After testing in an environment, the team signs off on an artifact to be ready for deployment into the field.

The number of installable artifacts depends on the number of different environments on which the application shall be tested, governed by the deployment strategy defined. In the case where the outcome is SDK instead of a mobile application, the situation would require only one artifact with separate configuration for each environment, unlike the mobile app.

Setup

The build machine is unaware of external factors. Therefore, it needs to be set up based on the configuration to execute further steps. Once the trigger is received, the build machine goes through the following steps:

1. Set up infra-dependency for the codebase to execute
2. Code checkout
3. Set up third-party dependencies on the code

The build machine would check out the code for the commit (or configuration) when the pipeline trigger is received. In the mobile pipeline, the dependency required to build the code comprises the development framework, build tools, and third-party libraries. The third-party libraries are those that form a part of the code or are involved in generating code that will be compiled and shipped. The setup stage will resolve all these and ensure the code is ready for the next stage, which is to repeat the steps of linting and code formatting. The setup stage also ensures appropriate versions of software and tools are part of the build machine.

The pipeline execution requires other tools and utilities that are used for supporting functions such as creating test coverage reports, setting up project dependencies, etc. These tools may not be available prepackaged in the machine, but rather should be configured separately. The setup stage also addresses the installation of these.

An optimization technique for a pipeline would be to retain the state of the build machine, as some of the installation activities are time-intensive. The ability to do manual overrides to reinstall on a need-to basis will still be there as an option.

The requirement to cache, the time to invalidate, and the frequency to check for updates are specific to a project. All these will be configurations that the team can control without rewriting the setup scripts. The setup stage thus generates the transformed codebase with the dependency and configuration fulfilled to be used by the subsequent stage. The transformed codebase is then picked up by two parallel stages of static analysis and build. Needless to say, in the case of parallel execution, the response to failure for one of the parallel tasks will typically initiate a cancel request for the running pipeline. The pipeline can be architected to have mandatory and non-mandatory parallel tasks. However, all these combinations would be an operational decision based on the team's requirements and would influence how the pipeline is configured to handle failure or progression of stages. Thus, the three steps take the code from the setup state until the packaging as a bundle to be installed, tested, or released.

Pre-packaging, compile, and build

This stage deals with the creation of an executable that will be shipped. The stage kickstarts when the previous stage of setup is successfully completed. This could be configured as a parallel stage to the static analysis in the pipeline. The stage is a combination of multiple steps, comprising pre-packaging, compilation, and build. Examples of the prepackaging activities involve pulling of secrets and configuration to be bundled along with the app, enabling build options such as obfuscation, setting up certificates, signing keys, etc. Like any programming language, the compile and build stage will convert the project into an executable for the target.

Execute the test and publish the result

This stage validates the accuracy of the features developed. There are multiple facets of the test stage. The validation of features can happen with the unit test and the integration test. In the case of mobile application development, unit testing is different from integration testing. The testing framework gives the flexibility to run the various tests in parallel.

A certain development framework does not allow the test to be executed in an isolated fashion; rather, the entire build will have to be run. For example, the unit test gets executed on an iOS simulator, which requires the build and compile to happen before the test.

In the pipeline, such a situation where the build is required for testing is handled independently as a separate step for testing. Some of these steps do not have strict guidelines to be sequential. The choice will be based on the team's preference and the appetite to either absorb the increased cost of the parallel compute required or to be okay with the increased time required to complete the sequential steps pipeline.

The unit test forms the first facet of the testing stage. There are other testing mechanisms, such as security testing, integration testing, and dynamic analysis, that may happen after this and will not require a separate build, as the previous stage build artifact could be reused.

The artifacts from this stage include the quality report for governance of the project. The pipeline can be configured to follow a layered promotion strategy. In this, a build is promoted from the lower environment to production stage by stage after passing each stage's quality checks. For example, the execution of unit tests on the simulator/emulator successfully for the development build is an indicator of the readiness of the build for the QA stage. A similar pattern of each stage giving the green signal showing the readiness for the next higher environment can be seen as the build promotion.

Publish artifact

Once the build is completed, the artifact generated is published to a common location in the pipeline. This artifact will be picked to run the test and can be leveraged to be downloaded to install on the device to do a manual test. The common location will not only have the build, but also the report generated for the various quality mechanisms in other stages. All these can be arranged onto a dashboard to make it accessible to various stakeholders without any hassle.

The production build is deployed to the respective stores provided by the target platform once there is a sign-off from the necessary checks defined in the release workflow. The app distribution service provided by the platform to upload the artifact is configured by the pipeline to upload the production artifact generated. Once the build is approved by the store, the end user shall be able to download and install it on the mobile device.

Every commit may not require a release to production. This leads to the pipeline design consideration, where, in this stage, an option to trigger the build and publish manually is available. The manual trigger in design is an optimization strategy to have production built only when needed.

Note: **Running a fully automated test suite is not advisable for a production artifact. Ideally, testing in production should be limited to quick sanity checks or tests targeting specific issues reported. There should be a lower environment that has an equivalent production setup, where extensive testing can be done, and the production issues reported can be replicated. Automation testing on the production environment may reduce the operational overhead of maintaining a dummy user for testing; however, the organization should be able to absorb the extra workload on the production server.**

Release workflow for published artifact

Once a build is signed off by the testing team, the next step would be to publish to the store. The store would be private or public. Once uploaded to the store, there could be an approval process. The approval process is seen in the public store managed by the platform organization. The application will be made available for the end user to download and install after the approval process. Once the application is available on the store, the user will be able to download, update, and use the application. Before taking the build to production, which is production-ready or even the lower environment build, it can be shared with the team using a private app store. The alternative approach is beta testing frameworks coming along with the development ecosystem. This constitutes the release workflow stage of the pipeline. The various artifact generated in this are made available to the respective target audience.

The release workflow has concluded the journey of an artifact. All these points showcase the value that automation can bring. The one-time setup of the pipeline thus reduces the otherwise manual effort that the team must do. An organization must invest in automation to optimally handle redundant tasks for a machine. This ensures that there is minimal cognitive load on the individual wherever the maintenance shall be done on the pipeline. Creating a simple comparison or a mind map of the manual effort versus the benefit of automation will provide the perspective needed to make the right strategic decision.

Hands-on with GitHub Actions

Creating a pipeline for a mobile application project is about an understanding of the following three constructs:

- Agent
- Runner
- Command line utilities for setup, build, testing, and publishing/deployment

In most cases, the majority of platform-related configurations are abstracted by the build agent. The developer designing the pipeline may have minimal steps involved by using the capability exposed by the build agent, for example, setting up the repository, defining the stages, configuring the compile, build, test, and publish. This section attempts to define a pipeline for a Hello World Flutter project on GitHub Actions. The CI/CD platform shall influence the way in which the stage can be configured. Flutter shall give a flavor of the two prominent platforms, iOS and Android. Understanding the agent and runner is key to an effective understanding of the pipeline.

Note: **One should understand that the concepts here are tool-agnostic for most cases and can be used to understand any other pipeline tool. The learning curve will be the naming convention used in the configuration to represent the pipeline stage.**

Agent and runner

The agent and runner are the core components of the CI/CD platform. The agent is the workspace where the stages are configured, and the runner takes the responsibility of execution. There are two possible modes of operation: CI/CD self-hosted inside the enterprise, where the compute infrastructure is self-managed, and the other, where the CI/CD is hosted on the cloud by the provider who manages the infrastructure. The latter is the convenient choice, which could fast-track setup time. Irrespective of the mode, the fundamentals and operating structure are the same. The agent has the responsibility of channeling and delegating the responsibilities of the pipeline to a runner machine. The agent can be installed on the same runner machine or a different machine that acts as only a runner. The other responsibility of the agent is to listen to the operation being performed and mirror the progress onto the dashboard for the stakeholders to view. The role-based access can also be provisioned on the agent, which gives the capability for the team to configure the pipeline to limit the kind of operation that can be performed based on role. For example, in the case of multiple teams in an organization, the dashboard for one team should not be visible to other teams. In another case, in the same team, only designated team members will have access to trigger a production-related task.

A runner machine or a build machine is where the build phase for the codebase and other operations for transforming the code into an artifact and getting it deployed is performed. A developer involved in setting up the pipeline is responsible for creating the configuration on the agent for the different stages executed on the runner. The runner machine enables execution and requires processing power. The processing capability required for a runner machine would start becoming a bottleneck to efficient running when shared across a larger team. This could be to match the parallel computing required for the total number of simultaneous executions. The number of runners should be increased to scale the pipeline. Later in the chapter, strategies to optimize and scale pipelines are explored.

Capabilities of GitHub Actions

The specifics of what the agent and runner explained earlier hold true for all CI/CD platforms. For the CI/CD platform, there are some unique thought processes and components that the individual should know of to configure the pipeline. These can be seen as features and capabilities of CI/CD. The following list summarizes the capabilities or features of GitHub Actions:

- **Workflows**: This is a group of configurable automated processes. In the terms described earlier in the chapter, workflow is a group of various stages. Workflow can be configured to listen to GitHub events (e.g., pushing code, opening pull requests). When any of these events occur, the respective workflow will get triggered to get executed on the runner. Workflows are defined in `.yml` files located in the `.github/workflows/` directory of the repository.

- **Runners**: These are the build machines. A build machine can be one of different OS, e.g., Linux, Windows, macOS, provisioned on cloud, or the team can set up self-hosted runners on their own infrastructure. The OS requirement for the workflow depends on the kind of workflow requirement. For example, if it is compiling to build for iOS, then macOS is mandatory, whereas if the code is developed on Flutter and one must run only the unit test, then a Linux/Windows version would suffice. The development framework and the target can influence the OS requirements for runners.
- **Events**: Events in GitHub, such as a push to a branch, a pull request being opened, or a scheduled time, can be used to trigger a workflow. These events can be configured to trigger based on rules as well.
- **Jobs and steps**: A workflow is divided into multiple jobs. Each job can be configured to have multiple steps. Each step represents a task that can run commands or actions.
- **Actions**: A code/configuration snippet that performs a specific task, such as checkout code, setting up languages or frameworks, deploying to cloud platforms, etc. The packages from the marketplace can be used to configure the actions. One can install utilities onto the runner to set up the command-line tool used in the actions or steps defined in the workflow. The step and action will seem to be the same; however, the subtle difference is that the action is a reusable piece of code used in a workflow configuration, while the step is a small unit of work directly used in the workflow.

Steps for configuring GitHub Actions for Flutter project

The following steps serve as a guide to configure GitHub Actions for a Flutter project:

1. Create Hello World Flutter and add to the GitHub (*Chapter 10, Introduction to Swift, Kotlin, and Dart* has details on how to create a Flutter project).
2. Create a GitHub Actions workflow file. The configuration for GitHub Actions is stored in a YAML file located in the **.github/workflows/** directory of the codebase repository connected to GitHub Actions. The developer will have to create a new file, for example, **.github/workflows/flutter.yml**, to define the workflow.
3. Add the configuration to the workflow. This section details the essential configuration one by one. Setup is done by instantiating the runner by defining the **runs-on** parameter with the required OS. The following figure depicts the workflow configuration for the Flutter mobile codebase:

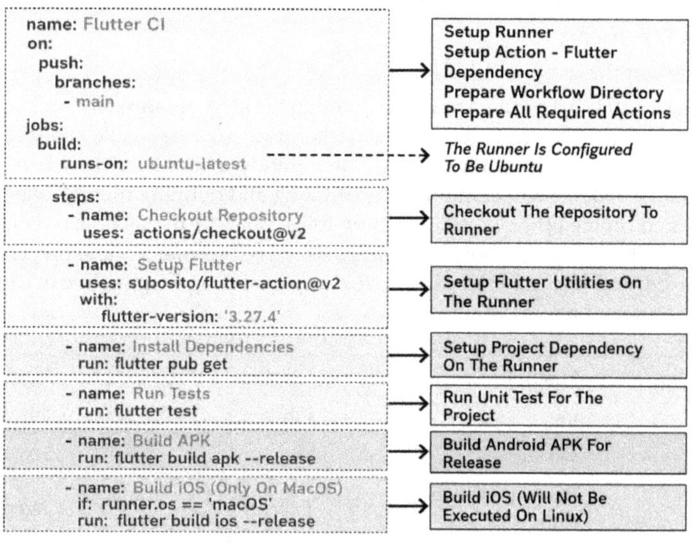

Figure 8.2: *GitHub Actions workflow configuration: iOS and Android for Flutter codebase*

4. The last step to build iOS will be ignored in the preceding execution, as the runner configuration is Ubuntu. For the same last step to be executed, the **runs-on** should be updated to macOS as depicted in *Figure 8.3*, and the rest of the steps can be kept as is:

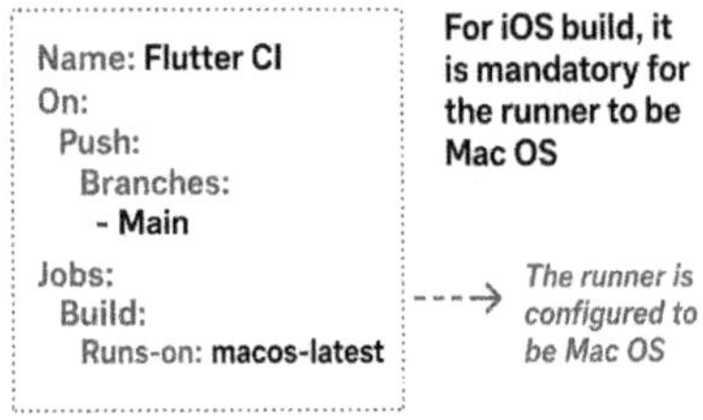

Figure 8.3: *Change in workflow config required to run the iOS build on agent*

The scope of configuration possible in the workflow is much more than depicted in Figure 8.2, such as creating multiple jobs, running integration tests, linter, and format checks, etc. The pattern to configure remains the same and will be an extension to the above workflow. This section explores a beginner version that gives a GitHub Actions introduction.

The efficiency of the workflow can be measured by the following parameters. The pipeline should be optimized based on the scale of the mobile application project.

- Separation of concerns (modularity) of workflow
- Optimized resource usage
- Parallel execution
- Custom trigger for different events
- Custom permissions
- Environment-specific workflows
- Better failure isolation
- Easier debugging for workflow and failure
- Run different jobs on different OSes or runners
- Improved CI/CD efficiency
- Cost-effectiveness in the usage of CI/CD

One can see that extending a GitHub Actions is all about defining the steps required for the pipeline and the command configured to execute these steps. The GitHub Actions marketplace gives reusable actions that can be used to add these to the workflow with the required configuration. The individual should add a job and configure the steps in the GitHub Actions workflow. All this will culminate in designing and defining the pipeline for the project. A similar thought process is mimicked on the other CI/CD enabling tools. *Table 8.1* depicts the parallel terminology for other CI/CD enablers in the market. The logic of how to organize the CI/CD remains the same. The parallel labels used in each ecosystem are depicted, and one may have to practice implementing the pipeline in each of these:

GitHub Actions	GitLab CI	CircleCI	Jenkins
Workflow	Pipeline	Pipeline	Pipeline
Job	Job	Job	Job
Step	Job step	Step	Stage step
Runner	Runner (GitLab CI Runner)	Executor	Agent

GitHub Actions	GitLab CI	CircleCI	Jenkins
Action	Job/Script	Command or Orb	Build step/Plugin
Matrix strategy	Parallelism	Parallelism	Matrix/Parallel jobs
Artifact upload/download	Artifacts	Artifacts	Archive/Publish artifacts
Environment variables	Environment variables	Environment variables	Environment variables
Triggering events	Triggers	Triggers	Triggers
CI/CD configuration file (`.yml`)	`.gitlab-ci.yml`	`.circleci/config.yml`	`Jenkinsfile`

Table 8.1: Parallel in terminology for four CI/CD enablers in the market

Note: **The matrix strategy defined in the table is the ability to replicate a workflow for different configurations. Parallelism in the matrix strategy would be to run each workflow independently. A CI/CD supporting matrix strategy, thus, can also be made to behave in a parallel manner, reusing the workflow. The matrix strategy is seen while generating builds for multiple environments.**

Strategies to optimize the pipeline

Pipeline is a compute operation. The more the compute, the higher the cost. For an organization with more developers, it is essential to optimize the pipeline for operational efficiency. Just imagine the case where the pipeline execution is slow, which becomes the bottleneck of a developer's progress. In such a case, the whole benefit of automation becomes redundant. Horizontal scaling and on-demand/schedule artifact generation are two key optimization strategies explored as follows:

- **Horizontal scaling**: Horizontal scaling adds hardware cost. However, as the number of developers increases, if there are not many parallel runners, the number of sequential stages could kill the efficiency. Defining an optimum number of runners per platform would depend mainly on factors like total number of developers, runner specification, branching strategy, number of environments to be built per commit, the size of the codebase, and execution time for each stage of the pipeline.
- **On-demand/schedule artifact generation**: Generating artifacts may not be required for each commit. In this case, the configuration to defer the generation of artifacts to a later point in time when it is absolutely required can reduce the compute. This strategy can thus enable the other tasks to leverage the computation capacity. Additionally, there are artifacts that are required only on a particular schedule; identifying such cases and ensuring that such artifacts are generated only on the required schedule can support optimization of the pipeline.

  For example:

  - A build that is tested in the QA environment will only go to UAT or production. Therefore, generating a UAT or production build may not be immediately required and can be deferred once the QA signs off on the build.
  - A production build is not required to be generated for each commit and can be generated based on release cycle timelines. The organization can weigh these parameters to create a schedule in automated stages to publish the artifact accordingly.

Mobile application deployment

The deployment is the critical piece in the list of **non-functional requirements** (**NFRs**) that need to be accomplished as part of any mobile project. Without the deployment of the artifact to the distribution channel, the end user will not have access to the application. The process of deployment of an artifact is termed a release. Understanding and planning for release should not be an afterthought. Release being automated brings stability to the workflow. The focus of the section will be to understand the nitty-gritty of the deployment.

A user can install mobile applications on the device via specific platforms, which are referred to as stores. App Store for Apple and Play Store for Android are the proprietary stores, which are maintained by Apple and Google, respectively. These are the major means for accessing the publicly distributed applications, **business to consumer** (**B2C**) apps. For a **business to employee** (**B2E**) application, there are private stores that each enterprise can host to control where the artifact is made available to be downloaded and installed on the device of the end consumer. There are pre-packaged software products for managing thelifecycle of the B2E app from installation, updating, revoking access, etc. One can classify the private or public store under a common label called Go Live Platforms. The deployment strategy defines the path by which a production-ready artifact reaches the Go Live Platforms after the quality checks.

Release process overview of iOS and Android

The section focuses on the release process of the mobile. *Figure 8.4* depicts the journey of the code to the deployment stage. The figure depicts a parallel comparison of entities associated with the build and artifact generation stage for Android and iOS:

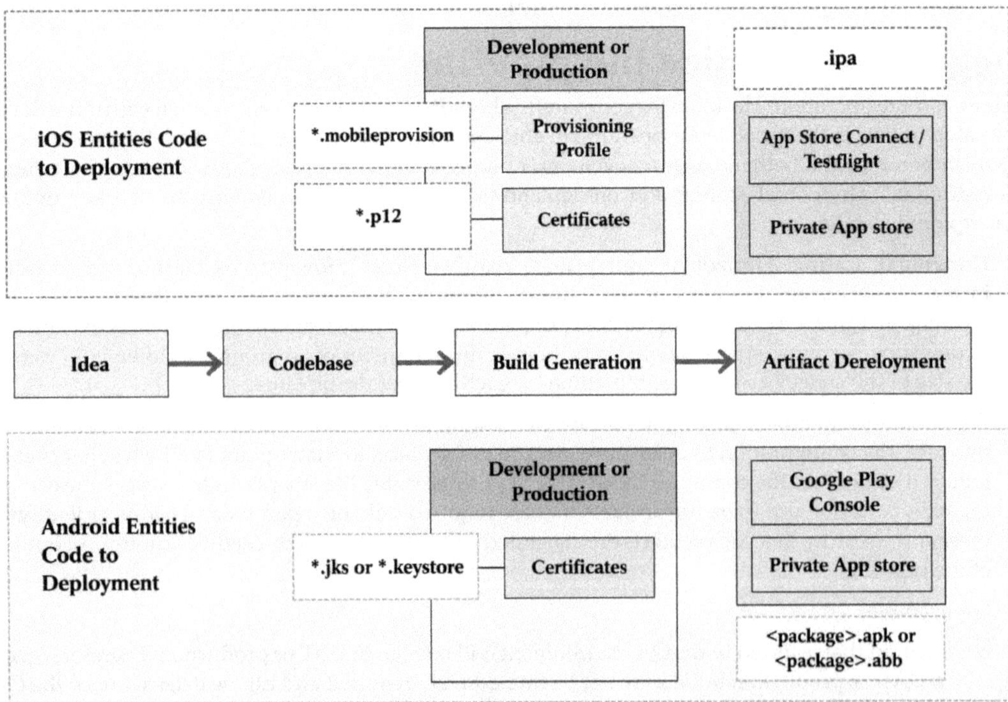

Figure 8.4: *Code to deployment stage overview with entities in iOS and Android*

For each of the platforms, deconstructing the preceding block diagram will give an understanding of the release process. In a broader sense, the release process has three transformation layers from code to publishing in the store:

- Idea to code base
- Code base to signed binary (artifact)
- Binary published to app store

Release process in iOS

The documentation and the extensive information to understand the release process in iOS are available on the official website. The scope of this section is to cover the key facts, focusing on the critical constructs that one should be aware of and know. These constructs shall add to an individual's intellect to reason about the release ideology. The details from the official documentation can further help an individual to excel and contribute seamlessly to the release workflow. This section will present the ideas an individual should have when approaching the release of a mobile application to consumers.

The iOS ecosystem is regulated and has restrictions imposed. This is closely tied to how the release of a mobile application can be approached following the Apple release guidelines. The rule and principle laid out would be limited to what Apple Inc. has defined, and the team may have to operate within this context, adhering to the guidelines. iOS application development happens on a computer (Mac machine), which can have totally different hardware and software architecture than the actual device (iPhones). Thus, the build generation on Mac machine happens via the compiler toolchain by cross-compiling the code. The cross-compiled codebase is packaged and shipped as a mobile application. It is important for a final test to be done while installing on the physical device, thereby ensuring the accuracy and functioning of the application for the target hardware types.

The installation of the software onto a device is mediated via the ecosystem provided by Apple Inc. The ecosystem mandates the individual to have access to the developer portal to run on a device while developing the apps. An individual should sign in to the Apple Developer portal to build and ship the application. The developer portal access has two modes, one of which is free and another with a subscription. The free account has limitations on the capabilities, and to get the full capabilities for development and shipping a production-grade application, enrolling in the Apple Developer program is a must. The installation via the free developer account is called **sideloading** (introduced in the Apple ecosystem in 2015).

Apple's ecosystem has created a clear distinction between enterprise and public release. There is a further separation one layer down that differentiates between the development and production environments. Based on the purpose that the application is used for, the entities used to generate the build will be different.

After enrolling for the membership, an organization gets either enterprise (B2E apps) or public (B2C) release programs. If an organization has both requirements, then separate subscriptions for both memberships would be required for enterprise and public release. It is also possible for an individual to publish an application to the app store and fall under the category of a public app. An independent user can only get access to the B2C application; for enterprise membership, it is mandated that the requesting entity be an organization.

Bundle ID as app identifier

An application released to the store will be uniquely identified by a bundle identifier, which is a string, and the team should define the unique identifier. The convention used is the reverse domain name of the organization with the app name. In the Apple development portal, these domain names should be registered as app IDs, which should be used to create the digital entities called a provisioning profile. This provisioning profile would be used to package the artifact that can be installed on the device or released to the market. As pointed out earlier, the development and release profiles are to be separately created. The process after the building and compilation for generating the artifact is known as archiving. This is followed by **app signing**, which embeds the certificate and provisioning profile. App signing is a mechanism to establish digital trust, leveraging the principle of asymmetric encryption using a combination of public and private key pairs. One should know that creating duplicate bundle IDs across the globe registered in the Apple Developer portal is not allowed. When the creation of an app ID is tried for an existing string, developer portals will throw an error if there is a conflict in the name. In practice, the reverse domain name prefixed to the app name helps in keeping this conflict under check.

Note: **App Signing workflow involves a developer signing with a private key and uploading the binary to App Store. This binary is verified by the public key associated with the developer on the Apple app submission portal, post which there is a review of the artifact leading to approval or rejection. In this process once the review guidelines are cleared app store has a mechanism where the binary is resigned by the private key on the AppStore side and is made ready to be published. The organization then can choose to release the application to public. The publicly available app then gets downloaded and has verification mechanism where the public certificate on an iPhone device verifies the signing identity of the downloaded application.**

Digital entities in Apple ecosystem

The main digital entities required for packaging are the certificates and the provisioning profile. A certificate is the signing key, whereas the provisioning profile is the entity that ties the codebase, certificate, and the device specification. A provisioning profile can be seen as the file that collectively defines how and where the app may be installed and run. The provisioning profile ties together the App ID, the signing certificate, a list of authorized devices (for development profiles), and the app's declared entitlements. A provisioning profile also plays the role of defining whether the app is supposed to be built for debugging/testing or for release to the market. It should be noted that Apple has mandated certain capabilities to be specified as part of the provisioning profile. For example, enabling data sharing with two apps, access to background capabilities, using the wallet, etc.

Not every capability needs to be defined or registered in the provisioning profile as certain capabilities are managed at the framework level. All these capabilities may still require the end user for permission when used in the application. The development team must implement the check required to ask and validate to ensure explicit permission is granted to use the capabilities. When using these capabilities, the team should also implement the on-demand prompt to the end user displaying an alert to get explicit permission from the end user for using the capability.

In the Apple ecosystem, the digital entities are separated by development and production. To test the code, it should be packaged with the digital entities associated with the development environment, and to ship to production, the latter would be used.

Archiving

The artifact generated from the development digital entities (provisioning profile and certificate) can only be installed on a restricted set of devices registered in the portal. The process of generating the installable is termed as **archiving**, which happens after build and compile. The installation can be done via a macOS-enabled machine or the development tool. The artifact for release should be generated with separate digital entities for production. The production artifact, on the other hand, will be uploaded via the developer portal for review in case of B2C. For B2E, the production artifact will be uploaded to the private store. In the case of B2C, Apple has a mechanism to distribute via TestFlight, where the release build can be planned for beta testing with a restricted set of users.

Distribution to non-tech stakeholders

There will be personas in the team who are not tech-enabled. The individual will not be skilled to use the tools or equipped with the knowledge available to developers. Expecting the stakeholder to install using tools may not be ergonomic. This would mean setting up a simple distribution strategy, which is limited to clicking on an external link and installing the application on the mobile. Such a mechanism, having an option to get notified for every release made to the development environment, would be a value addition. Previously, before TestFlight, third-party services to distribute were prominent. However, with the availability of TestFlight, it is the preferred choice. In the case of the enterprise version of the developer account, TestFlight will not be enabled. In this case, the organization will have to depend on a third-party service. Such a service will be there when the organization uses a **mobile device management** (**MDM**) product as the enterprise strategy.

Device restriction in Apple ecosystem

In the Apple ecosystem, installation is allowed only for devices registered in the development entity. Only a certain number of devices can be registered on the developer portal. Now, for an enterprise, the limitation on the number of devices is an operational overhead. Additionally, there could be a case where the organization tends to test the mobile application on a controlled set of end users outside the organization, called crowd testing. Crowd testing would require distributing to a larger number of users. In such a situation, having a limited number of devices or even the expectation of the device being registered on the developer portal is challenging and not realistic. This is where an organization can devise a strategy by leveraging the beta testing option in TestFlight or signing up for Apple enterprise membership programs.

The use of a production profile in enterprise developer accounts gives the option to be released via a private app store. The strategy of using a private store for testing will reduce the operational overhead of an organization when supporting multiple operating systems released via a single platform. The onboarding and offboarding overhead for the crowd can now be managed in one place.

Release process in Android

The Android ecosystem takes a different route, and being open source, it comes with flexibility and uniqueness. In comparison with iOS, the deployment process of Android artifacts is not difficult. This applies even for the artifact to be shared for development, testing, or to the App Store. While there is essentially a requirement to sign the application and get access to the developer portal, the operational overhead is much simpler compared to iOS. The concept of Bundle ID is the same for Android as well. Android SDK is available on the most popular operating systems, unlike Apple, which mandates macOS as the operating system where the code should be compiled to generate a build and create artifacts. The Android application packaging also uses digital entities; however, unlike the signing process in Apple, only a certificate pair is used to sign the application. The installable created does not have a restriction imposed by the platform, where only a select configured device can install the development build. The Android build can be installed on any device freely, and obviously, with the permission of the end-user of the device.

The bundle identifier is required for Android, and the rules are similar to those of the Apple ecosystem; the need for it to be unique is enforced by the Google Play Store.

Beta testing channel for mobile application

Beta testing is an essential part of software development, and it is similar to a field test. The hardware segmentation makes it even more important and, at the same time, difficult to test on a wide array of devices. Testing on a large set of devices will increase the time required to cover all these, and is sub-optimal. In mobile, the alternative strategy would be to test the mobile application before release in a closed user group. There are organizations that source user groups to test the application. Such testing, where a random group of individuals is given access to a pre-release version of a mobile, is termed crowdsource testing. The individual ideally will be outside the day-to-day development team that tests the application and gives feedback on the mobile application's correctness. In any of these cases, the key factor would be to manage and make applications available to the end user via some channel. The choice is on the organization to either use third-party distribution services or the inherent platform provided service (TestFlight or Google Play Console).

The following are the key considerations while deciding on a distribution tool:

- How easily can the distribution channel integrate with CI/CD tools and automation.
- How easily can the distribution channel integrate with the project workflow.
- Analytics and user access group support in the platform with roles privilege and access mechanism setup.
- Costing for the tool coming within the budget.
- Security
- Convenience and ease for the team to enable the beta testing channel.

Version management

The bundle identifier explained earlier helps to uniquely identify an individual application within an app store. For the same app, when there are multiple releases, the unique means of identifying a release artifact is by following a build number. In mobile, there are two distinct identifiers that are typically used; one is the build version and the other is the app version.

The following terms will be introduced in this section:

- App version major
- App version minor
- Patch version
- Build number

All the preceding terms are different from each other, and when combined, help in uniquely identifying an artifact. This could be used to trace back the codebase version from which the build is generated.

The format used for the app version in most cases complies with the **semantic versioning (SemVer)** specification. The build version will be different for each artifact. Every build generated need not necessarily go up till production. There could be various reasons, such as inadequate quality, incomplete features, etc. When a build is ready to go live, the team uploads it to the store. The version that identifies the Go Live release is the app version. The following are some of the common version representations:

- **App**: (Major version) (.) (Minor version)

  For example, 0.9, 3.6, 39.0, etc.
- **App version with patch**: (Major version) (.) (Minor version) (.) (Patch version)

  For example, 1.0.8, 3.6.5, etc.

Note: **SemVer strictly requires three segments, `MAJOR.MINOR.PATCH`. Two-segment formats such as 0.9 or 3.6, are a platform convention and are not SemVer-compliant.**

The three segments of the version distinguish what the team decides to be a major change in a feature being released versus a minor patch/hotfix release and appropriately incrementing to the next number.

Exploring a real-life example could help to get hold of the concept of versioning. Consider a mobile application where the live app version is 1.1.3. The team decides to release a new app with version 1.1.4. The app with v1.1.4 goes for testing and beta testing. Before the app is released to the public, an issue is found and needs to be fixed, after which there will be a redo of the build generation. Given that v1.1.4 is not yet public, the new fixed artifact still represents the next version 1.1.4. However, this could create confusion about multiple artifacts for the same version. In the mobile ecosystem, this case is handled by the additional configuration of the build number. The combination of app version and build number thus helps identify an artifact uniquely, by incrementing only the build number without incrementing the app version.

A build number, thus, is an identifier for representing multiple build artifacts for the same app version. The build number is mostly internal numbering that will not be relevant for public app store display and will be used in the pre-production stages.

While uploading the build to the platform store, there are restrictions and validations on the app version and build number. The app version should be incremented at the time of upload to the store; otherwise, the store will reject the upload. Before the app is released to the public, the app store provides a means to upload multiple builds in case there is any issue with the uploaded build. In such a case of uploading the app version, incrementing once for the first time will be sufficient; however, the build number should be incremented.

The common convention is that the initial public release is given the version 1.0.0, though teams may choose otherwise based on their beta and pre-release history.

App version and build number automation

App version uses semantic versioning, as discussed earlier. It should be a unique number, and when uploading to the store, it should be greater than the previously uploaded number. The team should adhere to this constraint. Manually updating the version for an enterprise is not scalable, as it may be difficult to keep track for a larger team. Alternatively, a number generation algorithm meeting the rule and constraint could be used to automate the version management. An example of a simple number generation algorithm would be to take the integer representation of the current date when the build was triggered to be used as the build number. The build number and the app version can thus be automated.

Folder structure and naming

For a mobile application project, the aesthetics of structuring code is an important factor that an organization should focus on. It would be very subjective to define what is right or convenient for all the individuals in the team. However, what an organization can establish is a set of common norms and agreed-upon terminologies or conventions that the team can follow while writing code. When multiple individuals are collaborating, having such common norms helps in easy switching or backfilling any absence. The onboarding would be smooth, as the common pattern is what one may have to explain and get used to. The repetitive strategy reduces the additional overhead of learning for the new individual, as there will be an existing code reference.

The development framework of choice will have the definition recommended by the community or the platform defining the agreed convention for the naming to be followed. The team can additionally decide on rules or patterns to be followed for the project. Another composition of a mobile application codebase is resources such as images, strings, and other platform-related resources bundled in a package and shipped to the consumer. For a developer, having these files (resource and code) organized ensures a readable and well-structured codebase. This is one of the parameters that impacts the maintainability of the codebase. The architecture chosen to develop the mobile application influences the naming convention and folder organization of a mobile application project. Along with these guidelines, the team can decide on a convention as well. The top items to consider for defining the folder structure are as follows:

- Defining the purpose in the context of the entire project. For example, test, source, helper, dependency, etc.
- Separating and grouping the functional differences and similarities. For example, Login, Payment, etc.
- The responsibility of the files and folders with respect to architecture choices.
- Based on the type of file. Configuration, artifacts, assets, codebase, scripts, etc.
- Modular abstraction of and extraction capabilities. E.g., Folder organized as separate reusable libraries.

Based on the technology and associated tool, some of the boilerplates for these folder structures would be provided by default. The developer shall adopt and modify the structure that logically suits the project, which the development tool supports.

Further in the section, the idea is to explore two use cases and the folder structures in action for these. The reader will gain an empirical grounding in modelling the folder structure of a mobile application codebase. At the end, the reader would ideally be able to reason effectively and define the folder for any engagement that the reader may operate in. The use case will not give an exhaustive list of possible folder structures, but only the key parts. *Chapter 13, Introduction to Mobile Architecture,* discusses the architecture options involved in a mobile project. The relevance of folder structure and the naming convention is one of the key ingredients. While reading the latter chapter, it will be evident that the architecture choice will enforce folder structure and convention defining programming constructs and the responsibility of the components relevant for the project. The folder structure is one of the key NFRs that needs deliberation and focus on the technology decision of a mobile application codebase.

Mobile application developed in Flutter

This is the first use case to explore the nuance while defining the folder structure. The use case mimics a mobile application developed in Flutter in the real-world. *Figure 8.5* represents a high-level view of the folder structure from the outside view of the development tool:

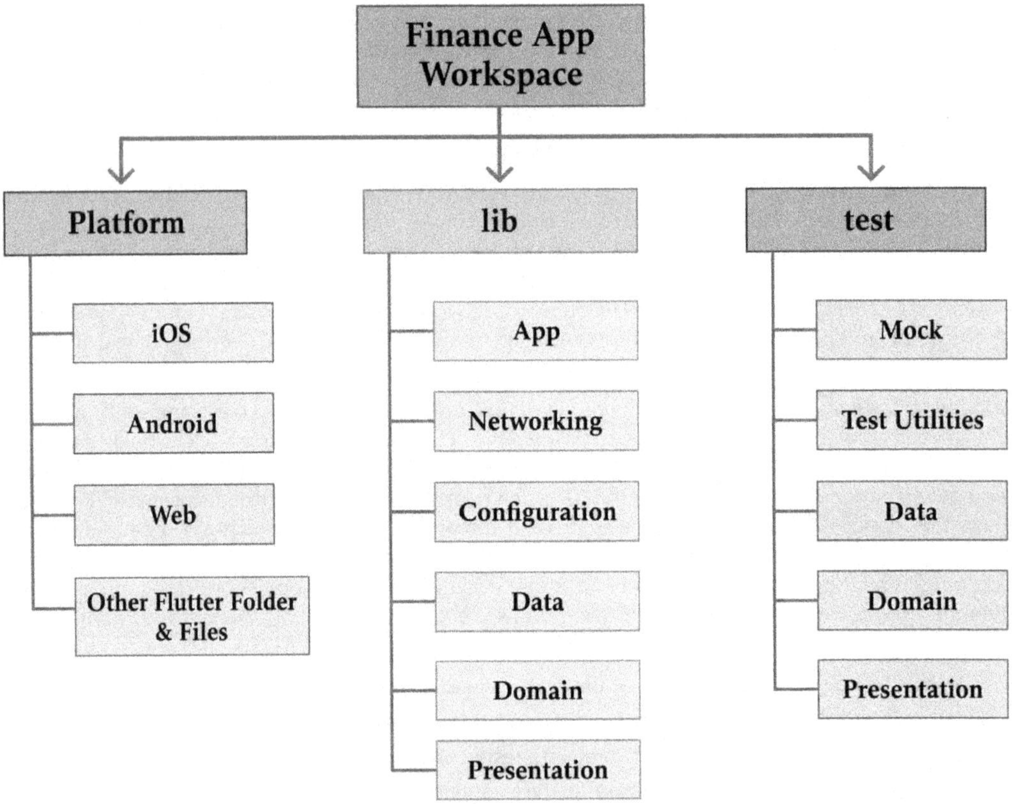

***Figure 8.5**: Folder structure for mobile application developed in Flutter*

The structure divides the codebase horizontally with respect to the commonality in the codebase. The major categorizations (platform, lib, and test) are provided by the Flutter framework as default. These are accompanied by a few others that form the project dependencies and framework-related files, such as build caches, configuration, native library dependency definition file, etc.

The focus for the development team would be on the two-folder lib and test, which will have the codebase developed and managed by the team. The remaining folders and files are provided by the platform, and the reason to change these will be for integrating native features or for any build-related config. The test folder will mirror the structure of the lib folder with additional helpers specifically required for the test script execution, such as mock, test utility, or helper class.

Let us take a closer look at the lib folder. The entire project in *Figure 8.5* is logically divided into six components: at the top layer is networking, followed by app main, configuration, data, domain, and presentation. The networking folder has the codebase that deals with the networking client and abstractions and connects with third-party systems. The app folder has the file with the entry point for the first page of the application after app launch. The configuration folder contains environment-specific configuration that would be compiled based on the choice of environment for which the build is generated. For the lifetime of the project, all these folders are not regularly modified, nor will they be a major area of interest for the day-to-day programming. The data, domain, and the presentation folder inside the lib are where the day to day development happens; their responsibilities are explained in detail next.

Responsibility of data, domain, and presentation

Figure 8.6 is a zoomed-in view of the data, domain, and presentation layers:

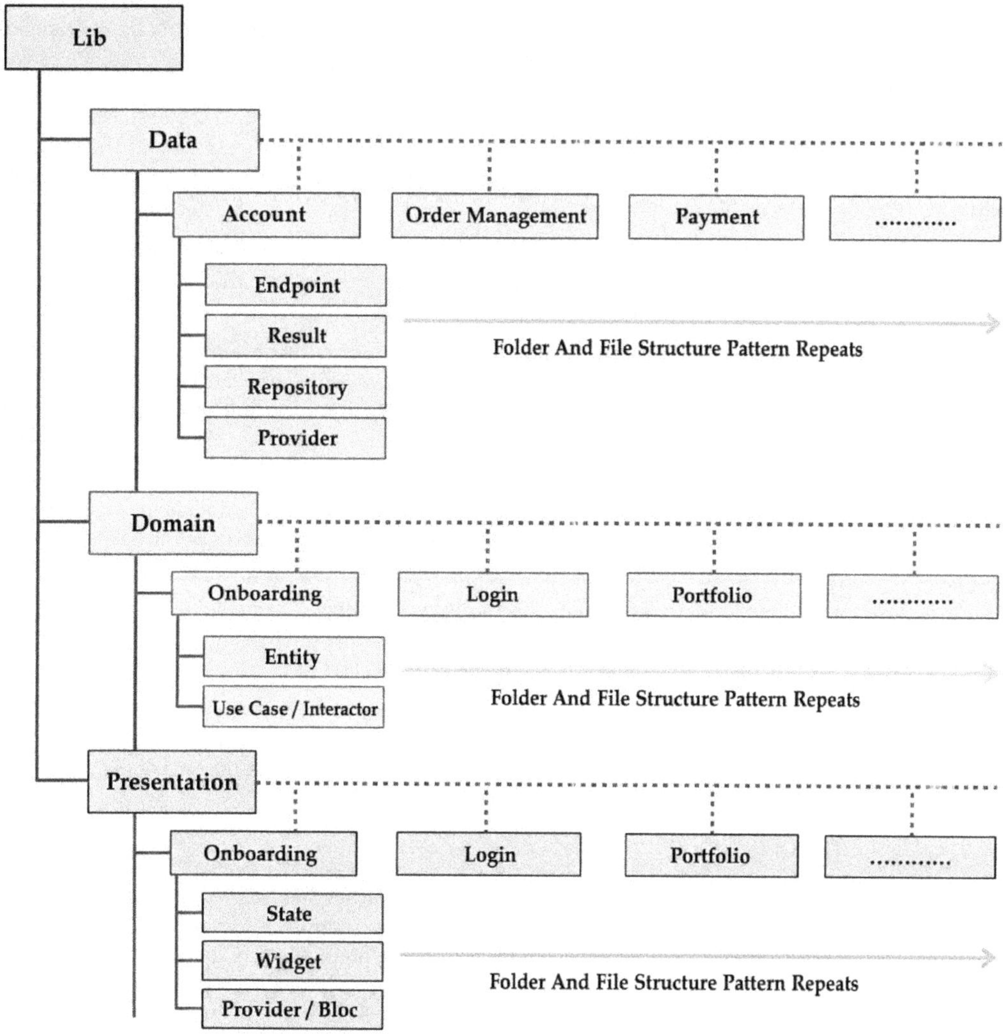

Figure 8.6*: Inside view of data, domain, and presentation*

Figure 8.6 can be interpreted considering the example of the onboarding journey in the application. Onboarding, as the name suggests, involves a new user trying to get access and sign up for the service provided by the application. The onboarding will involve registration, setting credentials, and account creation. In the preceding diagram, the account folder in the data layer has the code written to handle the backend service call related to the onboarding functionality. The code in the data folder does deal with network call, other than the account as well. In such a folder setup, the Account stands as the parent business function. A business function is a segregated backend service as a single unit, and the mobile data layer will mirror the same. From the point of mobile development, the data layer is a wrapper or connector to the backend services. This pattern repeats for all the different business functions exposed by the backend service. The data layer is consumed by the domain layer.

The domain layer can be seen as the layer where the logic and business rules are written. The domain layer will use the appropriate code component from the data layer to fetch and send the data. The domain layer thus coordinates what the presentation layer requests and expects as a response. The domain folder in *Figure 8.6* contains onboarding, Login, and other folders. Among these, the onboarding uses a subset of the code components from the Account data layer, and similarly, the Login will use a different subset of components from the Account data layer. Depending on the complexity of a feature, the folder in the domain layer can rely on multiple data layer components as well. The domain layer sends a request to the backend via the data layer and receives the response. The response is massaged applying the business rule and forwarded to the presentation layer. The trigger to send the request can come from the presentation layer. The domain layer mediates and determines whether to process data at the same layer or forward it to the data layer and responds appropriately to the presentation layer. The components of the domain layer include:

- Entities, which are the abstraction transformed from the raw responses from the data layer.
- The business logic, which involves the validation, submission details, and other onboarding-related functionalities that the presentation layer invokes.

The presentation layer has the state and reference to the domain layer. Together, the presentation layer and the domain layer coordinate the UI presentation logic and state management for the mobile application in the various journeys. The UI component, which uses the state to interact with the user, and the interaction reaching the component from the device are managed by the development framework. The narrative thus gives a template of how code is logically divided and grouped amongst these three layers.

To recap, the data layer is responsible for the codebase for backend network calls. The data layer logically organizes a group of network call code into readable and logical segments of functionality, mirroring the backend system.

The domain layer is a one-on-one map to the functional requirement that the mobile application provides to the user. This layer is closer to the functional features that a user will see or utilize via the mobile application. This layer will convert the response into an intermediate abstraction and will be used at the presentation layer. The abstraction helps to reduce the tight coupling between the presentation and the data layer.

Additional files in the data layer include the endpoint, provider, response, and input type. Provider in this context is different from Flutter's Provider state-management package. Provider is an abstraction responsible to cache or persist the data received from the backend service. The endpoint holds the configuration to connect to the backend service and the network client mediating the connection.

Retail domain iOS Application

The ideology presented for the folder structure in this use case is to separate the different code components written vertically. In the structure, the overall code base is divided into a combination of logically independent features. Organizing folder groups of related screens could be a means to decide on the feature division. An option the team can choose is to maintain a collection of screens organized within a parent folder, segregated into multiple smaller subfolders, maintaining a hierarchy and modular structure. Alternatively, the team can decide the feature to be a smaller module only, which is less than a maximum of three to four screens, with no nested structure. *Figure 8.7* depicts the two folders for the mobile application:

- Option one is depicted in *Figure 8.7*, where the feature is divided into groups of three to four screens. In this case, the number of files required to be maintained per feature will be less for fewer screens. For example, payment confirmation, payment history, login, sign-up, etc., will be considered independent and individual features. Now, for each feature, there will be files and folder structures that fulfill the role of the presentation, data, and domain layer responsibilities.

- Option two is where a feature is grouped into a larger umbrella. For example, the whole payment-related screen itself will be a single feature. This structure will segregate the feature into domain, data, and presentation.

Additionally, there are other common components beyond the feature, which in both options are organized in separate folders that could be utilized by each feature, e.g., theme, common UI, network client, etc. Take a look at *Figure 8.7*:

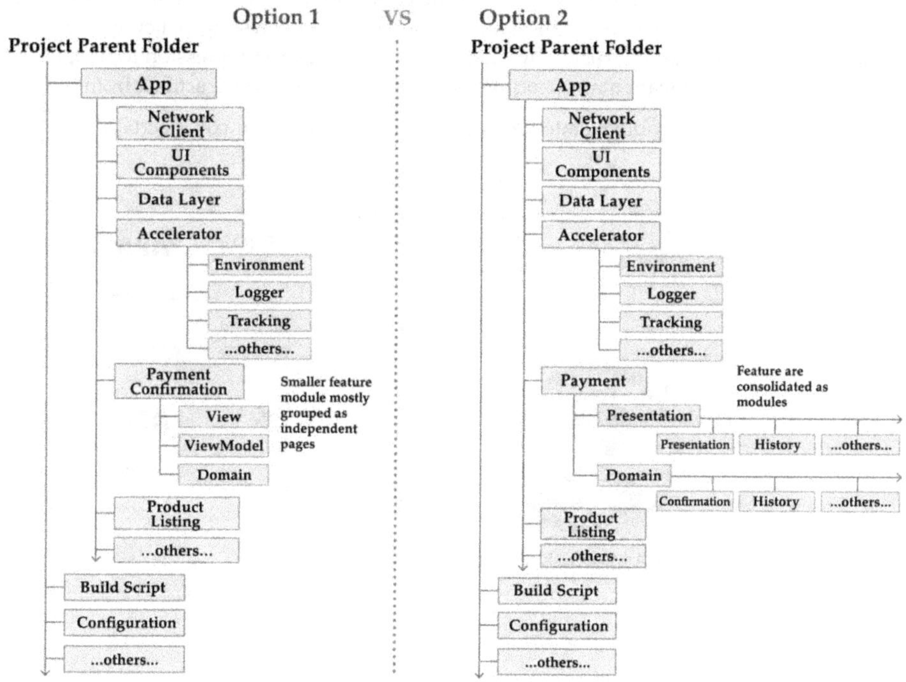

***Figure** 8.7: Vertical slicing with folder structure options*

The folder structure distinction in *Figure 8.7* has two different ways for organizing the codebase. The team can choose what appeals to the groups and follow the collective opinion mostly based on heuristics. For example: prefer Option 1 (fine-grained features) when screens have minimal shared state; prefer Option 2 (umbrella features) when multiple screens share domain logic.

Environment management

A mobile application connects to downstream systems with locators (URL endpoint) as an identifier for the system. The recommendation would be to separately test the application on a lower environment. Having a lower environment ensures the safeguarding of the confidentiality of production data and prevents the maligning of the production environment by unnecessary requests.

There could be a case where a team is developing the downstream systems as well, in parallel with the mobile development. Providing stability of the environment to the consuming entity (the mobile application development team) could be a challenge due to active development. The production service will not be there until the quality check is complete. A stable downstream system for development is required to continue the mobile development without any disruption. The disruption can be avoided by having a segregated environment strategy, ensuring the active development of the backend does not affect the consumers in most cases. An organization can decide the ideal number of environments serving different purposes, such as development, testing, performance testing, UAT, and production. The strategy of managing the data and the specification of these different environments shall depend on the purpose. The problem statement addressed in this section is from the point of view of mobile application development. The ability to manage and switch connections between different environments efficiently is therefore a key concern in any mobile project.

For a mobile application, by design, the environment change should be just a base URL change. One may ponder why simple URL management needs more discussion. The environment management impacts the effectiveness of the QA team. By this, one should know that a mobile application code base is generated as an artifact to be installed on the device, and the configuration of the URL will be a part of the code base in principle. Every time the URL changes, a new build is required to reflect the change. A QA team with a conservative testing policy will consider any change of artifact that has been rebuilt cannot be trusted by default and would expect regression to happen. There are other conversations that the development team may encounter, specifically on the mobile artifact from the QA team.

Figure 8.8 provides the two unique problem statements that the QA team might come across:

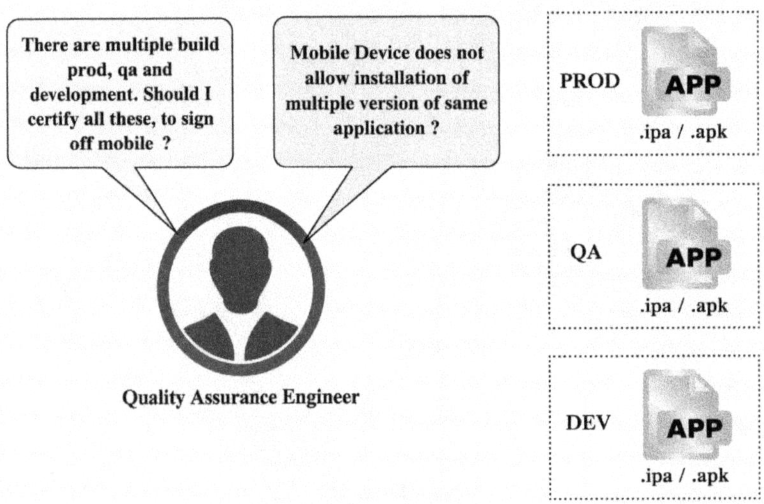

Figure 8.8*: Multiple artifact related challenges for mobile QA*

Figure 8.8 depicts the dilemma of testing multiple artifacts. A single bundle ID, when used for all three artifacts, will not allow the installation of all three on the same device. The preceding figure is the reality that one may encounter while testing a mobile application on devices. It is imperative to understand that the build generation is a platform-provided mechanism, and any change in the URL configuration would ideally not make any difference as long as the downstream system behavior is identical in all the downstream environments. As the artifact changes, the only change in the case of environment change will be to verify if the mobile is connecting to the right endpoint by observing the log. The second problem statement, where the artifact cannot be installed together, could be solved by using a separate bundle ID and digital entities, thus allowing installation of multiple environment versions on the same device.

Remote fetch of configuration

Up till now, the narrative provided the solution where the configuration change needed was bundled. By having the possibility to externalize the configuration, the artifact generation could be reduced. *Figure 8.9* depicts the conceptual diagram of the internal working of using external configuration. The underlying theme to achieve such a setup is by employing a service to remotely fetch the configuration. The problem with the approach is that there is another URL or downstream system that the app is dependent on to externalize configuration, and the reliability of the system is critical, as any failure can have a ripple effect on the functioning of the mobile application. Take a look at *Figure 8.9*:

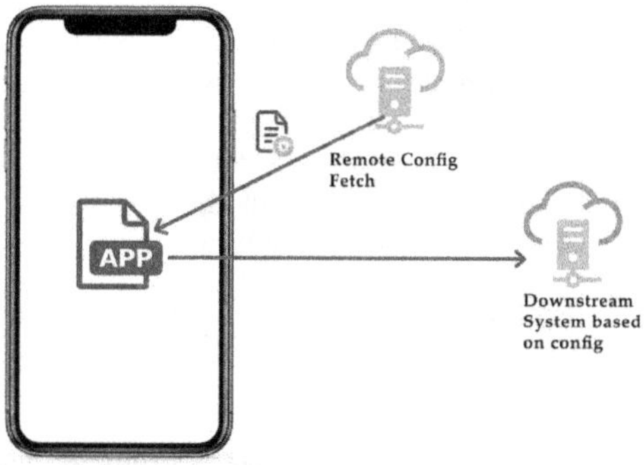

Figure 8.9: *Remote Config Fetch to externalize the backend base URL and configuration*

From a QA point of view, the approach of remotely fetching configuration guarantees that only the digital entities required for signing change across the production and the lower environment, and the rest of the code remains the same. The remote fetch of production configuration can be implemented by supplying the environment's URL from the backend. This approach decouples and adds flexibility to update the environment configuration without going through the app release process. This can be extended beyond the URL for other configurations as well. Such a strategy helps in avoiding the delay to release any config change, which otherwise would have happened only with deployment in B2C applications to the app store.

Embedding configuration during packaging process

In remote fetch, there will be a common service invoked to fetch the configuration. The remote fetch is a runtime endpoint resolution strategy. This section discusses the strategy applicable in a situation where the team wants a solution that supports compile-time resolution of the endpoint without hardcoding or manually changing the code every time a build is generated. The automation at compile time to introduce a config change is a means to provide confidence for an individual wearing the QA hat by ensuring that the build generation happens without manual intervention for different environments. The fact that there will be two artifacts does not change. The code change when generating a build for the different environment can be perceived to be limited to the compiler conditional check. At compile time, the script automates the bundling of the appropriate environment-specific configuration. *Figure 8.10* depicts the flow diagram for the build generation with conditional compilation for bundling the config into the artifact:

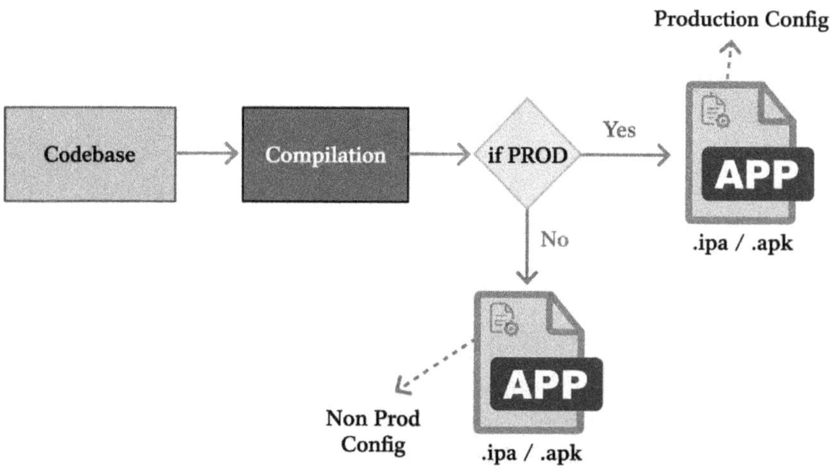

Figure 8.10: *Compile time decision-making to bundle config to the application binary*

In conclusion, with the topics discussed so far, the reader has enough details to comprehend the environment management. The choice is either having client-side logic to select the configuration or an embedded configuration before the build generation. Both approaches have their pros and cons. One can note that in the case of remote fetch, which is calling a backend API to fetch the configuration, there is a probability for failure (network or API errors). And embedding the configuration at compile time would mean generating a new build for any configuration change. The final decision for the approach to be followed should be weighed by the team, debating and discussing based on the operating context of the mobile application being built.

Note: **The environment management is an NFR to bring convenience to the QA team.**

Environment switcher

As the number of environments increases, the number of artifacts generated will increase as well. The regular clean-up for older versions would remove the size overhead. However, from an operational standpoint, keeping track of different artifacts and the challenges of environment-specific bug reporting creates a cognitive load for the team. Therefore, reducing the number of builds by providing an environment switcher in the development build could be an option.

Environment switcher is a lightweight approach that reduces operation, computational, and space overhead while managing multiple environments. The implementation will be the same on the build generated for development and testing. There is a temporary screen where the environment to be connected can be selected. The configuration required for that environment will be loaded, and the application will function by connecting to the selected environment.

There will still be two versions of the artifact for production and development. Care should be taken to ensure that production application artifacts do not have any configuration for environment switching.

The environment switch strategy is a convenience for internal maintenance and operation, and can be used along with either remote fetch or bundling the configuration strategy. *Figure 8.11* shows the wireframe for the environment switcher screens:

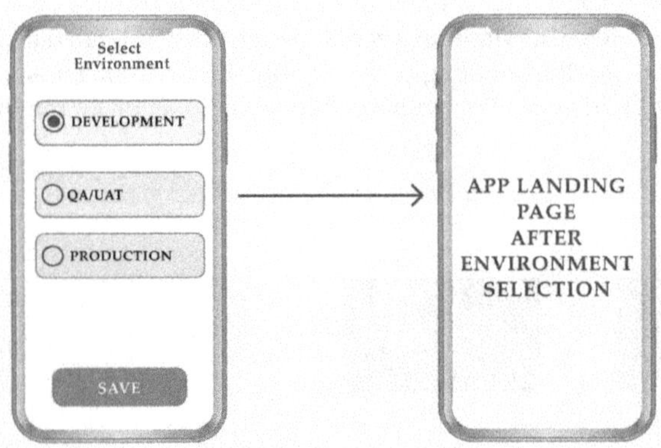

Figure 8.11: *Environment switcher wireframe*

The environment switcher introduces a code change with reference to the additional screen required for a lower environment in comparison with production. Thus, the rule of no code change will not be strictly followed in the lens of QA when promoting or signing off on an artifact in a lower environment. The logical reasoning that the environment switcher is only there in the debug build and the convenience provided in operation would give weightage to prioritize the environment selector approach over the conventional approach.

A lightweight pseudo-code implementation of the environment selector is depicted in *Figure 8.12* as a class diagram:

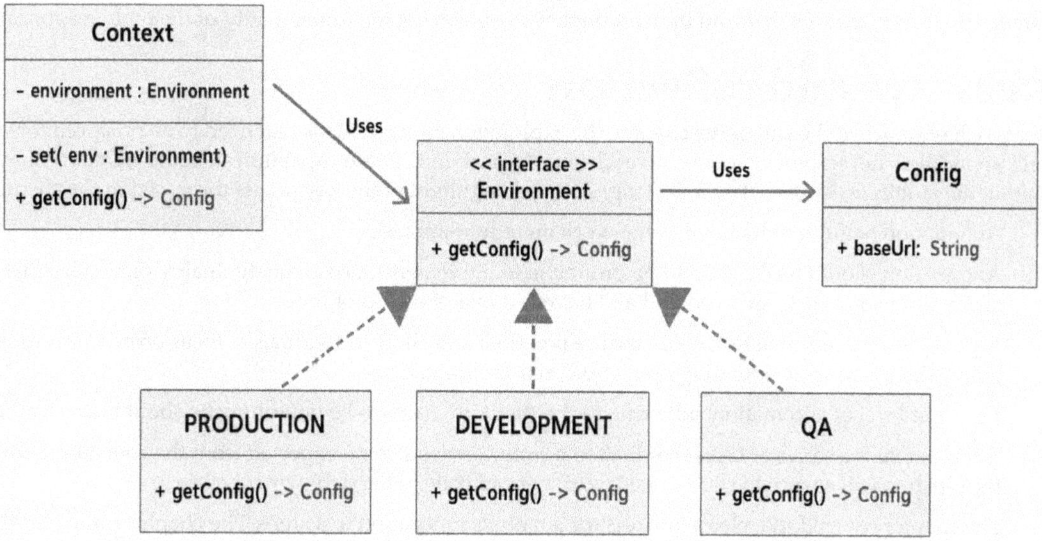

Figure 8.12: *Class diagram for environment selector implementation*

Figure 8.12 is an application of the Strategy design pattern. The implementation has each environment (PRODUCTION, DEVELOPMENT, QA) as a concrete strategy implementing a shared Environment interface. This will allow the environment change to be straightforward to swap at runtime without changing the consuming Context class.

The following is an explanation of *Figure 8.12*:

- **Context (or EnvironmentSelector)**: The class that has a reference to an interface environment responsible for calling the appropriate **`getConfig()`** method from the selected environment strategy. The **`setEnvironment`** method allows you to change the environment at runtime (QA, dev, prod). This class will be used by the environment selector page to set and save the chosen environment for the application.
- **Environment**: This is an interface that defines a method **`getConfig()`** which is used to return the configuration for a particular environment.
- **Concrete strategies (QA, dev, prod)**: Concrete classes are respective implementations of the environment interface.
- **Config**: This class holds the specific configuration values, such as baseUrl, etc. These configurations vary based on the context of the application and can be segregated or extended to multiple responsibilities.

Conclusion

The chapter equipped the reader with the knowledge needed to ensure the mobile codebase scales effectively and remains sustainable. The capability to automate and set up the pipeline will ensure redundancy is handled without any human intervention, which provides the flexibility to be deterministic and get early feedback. The environment handling mechanism and having the aesthetics of code maintained would be critical to ensure a mechanism is set up, providing convenience for testing and reading code with reduced cognitive overhead. The release process is a topic that is often seen as too heavy to be assimilated. The chapter provided the details that ensure the reader has the logical structure to decode the details in a jiffy with the official documents.

The next chapter is about bringing some cross-cutting themes under one umbrella that benefits the reader in mobile application development. These techniques form the non-functional requirement, which means those requirements of a mobile application that will have an indirect impact on enhancing the functionality of the mobile application.

Takeaways and reflection

Now that we have reached the end of the chapter, the exploration of major ideas that need to be practiced for scaling a mobile application development codebase reaches its logical end. These capabilities should be advocated to be built within the mobile ecosystem. The following is a quick highlight of the key points discussed in the chapter:

- Automation helps in reducing manual work on redundant tasks.
- Automation should be checked to be profitable to implement. A cost-benefit analysis indicates that setup and maintenance costs are averaged and balanced over a period of time.
- Automating the repeated task could reduce boredom and allow individuals to focus on other priorities and innovations instead of operating on manual, redundant items.
- The right level of automation, adhering to the standard, helps to be deterministic about the task at hand.
- The pipeline is a series of tasks that lead to a cumulative outcome expected from the codebase. Setting up the pipeline will ensure the automated journey from code to the deployment cycle.
- The chapter covered the release process for a mobile application to a store. The chapter compared the iOS and Android release process. It highlighted the usage of the reverse domain name with the app name string as the bundle ID, which serves as a unique identifier for a mobile application package/binary.
- Semantic versioning is used as the standard for mobile apps for managing the app version. The format used is (Major).(Minor).(Patch) for app version combined with a unique number called the build number. The build number is used to differentiate between separate builds for a particular app version before getting released to the public.
- It is relevant to think about and define the naming conventions and folder structure. The different possibilities at a broad level are horizontal slicing and vertical slicing. When sliced horizontally, the folders are organized with respect to the responsibility of the code module, whereas in the case of vertical slicing, the different features dictate the top directory.
- The mobile application should be compiled and packaged separately for any code or configuration change. To configure the URL in the codebase, which is the configuration for multiple backends for different environments, requires a separate build or a conditional logic written in the code unless the configuration is externalized during runtime.
- For a production-ready code, it is advised not to ship the conditional logic that handles configuration for the lower environment.

Join our Discord space

CHAPTER 9
Mobile Application Development and Cross-cutting Themes

Introduction

The accuracy, ease of using the application and presentation provided by the mobile application impacts the end user experience. To achieve a great experience, the development team can capitalize on techniques that complement the functionality of a mobile application. Such techniques are broadly categorized as **non-functional requirements** (**NFR**) or **cross-functional requirements** (**CFR**). There is a super set of such requirements in a mobile project lifecycle. Based on the context, the team should prioritize and implement those which align with the respective goals expected in the SDLC. The scope and functionality of NFR for the mobile application could be divided into must-haves, good-to-haves and do-not-haves. Implementing the NFR can aid and accelerate the mobile application development and thereby benefit the organization's business.

The techniques listed in the chapter are those that might get ignored by the business/feature focused teams. In such a case, incorporating these techniques might get less priority over the functional aspect of mobile application. Ignoring the NFR is an anti-pattern. Ignoring NFR would lead an organization away from sustainable technology excellence. Such a situation should be preempted. It becomes imperative for the team to understand this technique to be effective on the ground. The team should strive to change the perception and negotiate the importance of these non-functional requirements. The strategy adopted by the team shall be to give equal importance to functional features and non-functional requirements, in order to deliver an effective product.

Structure

This chapter covers the following topics:

- Recap of mobile application development
- Shelf life
- Force update
- Accessibility
- Error handling
- Logging
- Deep linking
- App size
- Screen rendering performance
- App startup time
- Market segmentation in mobile device
- Data lifecycle

- Multi-language support
- Efficiency and reliability
- Security consideration

Objectives

The purpose of this chapter is to bring under one umbrella the techniques that are often ignored or diluted in mobile application development. The topics discussed in the chapter shall be independent of each other. However, holistically tying these together and implementing the relevant items bringing about a collectively exhaustive outcome, empowering the mobile application to be efficient.

Recap of mobile application development

Mobile application development goes through a series of stages before it reaches the end consumers. The following *Table 9.1* recaps the respective deliverables for different stages in SDLC. These lists of different stages and the outcomes were discussed in *Chapter 2, Planning Your Mobile App Project*. Have a look at the following table:

SDLC stages	Outcome/deliverable
Requirement	Backlog, Wireframe, or Prototype.
Preparation	Hi-Fidelity design and interactive mockups, Architecture, Tech Choice, and Decision, etc.
Development	The product and its requirements are developed. The end outcome will be the artifact ready for testing, followed by production release.
Testing	Certified usable product meeting requirement.
Deployment	Ship the artifact and end user start using the product.
Maintenance and enhancement	Incorporating the feedback to the product or enhancing the feature of the product. The task conceived in this stage will trigger the repetition based on the listed stages, forming a cycle.

***Table 9.1**: Deliverable for stages in SDLC*

In the journey of idea to product the transformation of an abstract thought to a concrete expectation is called a **requirement**. Fulfilling the requirement happens in the execution phase. The business team is responsible for defining and laying out these requirements. The explicit definitions of what the product encompasses is called the **functional requirement.** The hidden structure that strengthens and binds these functional requirements together is called the **non-functional requirement**. Often these hidden structures are known to be invisible in the eyes of a business. Addressing these is crucial in ensuring the success of the product.

Consider a situation where the mobile application jittering will deteriorate the end user experience. Jittering in a mobile application is the case of the screen becoming erratic with jerky reactions when the user interacts. The jitter often is perceived as a screen non-responding or a sudden jump in an element. Such interactions cause the response to user actions to be very slow, signaling a performance issue. Ignoring these and similar cases will be catastrophic and would work against the brand. Such an issue can bring down the adoption rate of the mobile application. Engineering the mobile application to prevent such issues is the key ingredient for a great mobile application.

In *Chapter 1, Stepping into Mobile Development*, the classification of mobile applications as B2C, B2E and B2B were discussed. The context of NFR will mostly be the same for all three deployment contexts: B2C, B2E, and B2B. The difference will be around the deployment and data handling influenced by the policy laid out. The organization and the rules of the operating demography define these policies and guidelines.

Before looking at the NFR it is essential to understand the uniqueness of mobile application development. The following items describe the uniqueness. These will reinforce the relevance of NFR discussed throughout the chapter.

- Mobile applications are deployed into hardware which are controlled by the end user. An organization will only have limited control for phone owned by end user. The case may be slightly different for an enterprise managed phone, where the organization rules can be enforced onto device. Enterprise managed phone will be provisioned with configuration or profile that restricts the phone usage. The user will have permission for the mobile app usage based on the policies set via the mobile device management strategy.
- Deploying mobile applications can happen in the public app store of the respective operating system provider for B2C apps. iOS and Android platforms dominate the market. Most organizations focus on either of these. Apple App Store is for iOS and Google Play Store is for Android. These stores act as the marketplaces for publishing mobile applications.
- Each platform has its unique deployment rules, development tools and dependencies. While there are cross-platform technology and framework leveraging a common code base, the commonality is only for development, the resulting build artifacts must still be compiled and deployed separately for each platform as there is no single universal binary support. The end deployment is unique and needs to be done separately for each platform.
- At any given time, the plausibility of version fragmentation of application exists. Version fragmentation is a case where there are different versions of the application actively used by end users. The mobile application deployment happens via app store, and the end user has the choice to decide if update is required or not. If the user chooses not to update to the latest version and if the pattern repeats for multiple users, it results in the phenomenon called version fragmentation. If the end user does not have the hardware supporting the latest release, this will also lead to version fragmentation. An organization should have strategies to handle multiple-version support.
- There are specific OS and tool dependencies for the development. The platform providers can enforce these to be proprietary to a platform. The proprietary nature is primarily seen for Apple ecosystem. Apple platform enforces the end packaging and compilation mandatorily done on a Mac machine. On the other hand, Android, being open source, supports the build packaging in multiple operating systems.
- Mobile application development can be done with various frameworks. This was discussed in *Chapter 3, Cross-platform Versus Native*. The choice of platform has its effect on the ecosystem of the tools supporting the development. A separate learning curve will be required for each of these tools to understand the usage. Irrespective of the cross-platform tool the developer should know the nuance of the target platform. Knowing the inside details of target platform would be essential as the native platform tools perform the end-packaging in all cases.

NFR is crucial to ensure the application is at its best given the uniqueness of the mobile. The development team should constantly balance evaluating the effects and trade-offs of the NFR. The NFR discussed in the chapter will bring the various traits such as security, usability, maintainability, availability, reliability, compliance, performance, compatibility, scalability, correctness and accessibility into the mobile application and the development process.

Shelf life

Shelf life defines the lifetime of an application. The stakeholders should think a priori of the shelf life. The expiry date of the mobile application is a very subjective topic and can be difficult to predict. The mobile application can become obsolete due to multiple factors. The section explores the factors that affect the shelf life of the mobile application and the impact on the digital strategy for the organization.

When the shelf life is reached, discontinuing the application or revamping the application could be the next step. A revamp can be done either by starting from a clean slate or reusing the existing code. The clean slate versus building on top of the legacy code with incremental deprecation or migration of legacy features has respective pros and cons. Comparing the two approaches can bring to light these pros and cons. The clean slate approach is not chosen as it is cost-intensive. The need for maintaining the old code until the new development reaches the parity along with the difficulty of understanding the legacy mobile application is the reason that adds cost in clean slate approach. The reuse of legacy is chosen as time to market is less and release should happen ensuring parity with the existing legacy mobile application. The following factors affect the shelf life:

- **Obsolete service/product offerings**: If there is no demand for the service/product offerings provided via the mobile application, the team can decide to discontinue the mobile application. There are cases where application has multiple service/product offerings. If only a subset becomes obsolete the entire application may not be discontinued, rather, the features that are irrelevant will be removed and stopped.
- **Bottleneck in adapting to market needs**: The mobile application is backed by a technology to build. An organization can select the appropriate technology from multiple options out in the market. If the organization has adopted technology that does not keep up with new changes the risk of falling behind the latest trend prevalent in the market will exist. This will limit the progress of organization and underlying limiting factor will thus be the technology. Such a situation will be a clear case of revamping the application. A typical strategy used to minimize disruption to the end user is to invest in parallel in the revamp. The team would adopt a new technology to modernize and after the required parity is reached for the product the user is migrated to the new application. Eventually the old application becomes obsolete and can be discontinued after all the user migration is completed. Depending on the context and risk appetite of the organization, the migration strategy could vary from phased or one-shot migration of entire users. The organization would think of modernization when the maintenance cost is exponentially rising. Another reason would be when competing with market peers becomes challenging, caused by an inherent flaw in the technology.
- **Negative reviews and ratings**: Consider a scenario where an organization did not do due diligence researching the mobile application development or the case where the mobile application was built in a haze. In both the cases if the application does not meet the quality or market standard, it could prove to be a problem for the organization. Such a poor-quality app can only thrive if it provides an essential service or if it is a monopoly. Any mobile application that has alternative option with poor quality should reconsider and take the next course of action. Providing the optimum quality of usage to the end consumers is a must for such applications.

Force update

Force update is a means to gracefully present the end user with the notification on the availability of newer version of application. The user is presented with either a prompt that can be dismissed or a mandatory requirement to update before continuing. This represents the two flavors: soft update and mandatory update. An organization would need this capability when deploying new version with critical fixes, feature deprecation or shipping changes. When a new version is deployed force update gives the provision to ensure end user discontinues the old version of the app. The soft update will give the indication that there is a new release available. In soft update the end user can continue using the application without updating. The mandatory update on the other hand would prevent the user from using application. The old version would stop working in this case. The user will have to update to the new version to continue the usage of the service provided. The mandatory update is generally preferred when there is a critical vulnerability or issue with the older version. Using mandatory updates would be counterintuitive with respect to user experience. Personas who are not fond of updating the application frequently will find it irritating.

Version fragmentation discussed earlier can occur when the end user chooses not to update. In a large user base there could probably be multiple versions active. Version fragmentation brings operational overhead. The classic example of operational overhead is customer calling and reporting an issue in the application, leading to the development team being clueless about the version of the application. The customer support team can direct the user to update to the latest version and react to the situation. The organization providing a proactive measure to notify user to update the application could be a better implementation from an end user experience. The hassle that end user should endure for the resolution via customer support also thus get avoided.

The recommendation is that the force update feature should be implemented based on the data on version fragmentation. If the end user behavior analytics has a large percentage of user using older version of application and if the application needs to be deprecated, the force update could be leveraged. Force update is a powerful feature. The team must exercise due diligence to devise the strategy that defines the required frequency. Applying the force update balancing the user experience will become an NFR to be planned.

Lightweight force update

A typical force update can be implemented either by writing validation logic on the client or validation done at the backend. *Figure 9.1* depicts the two approaches and the wireframe for force update in mobile application:

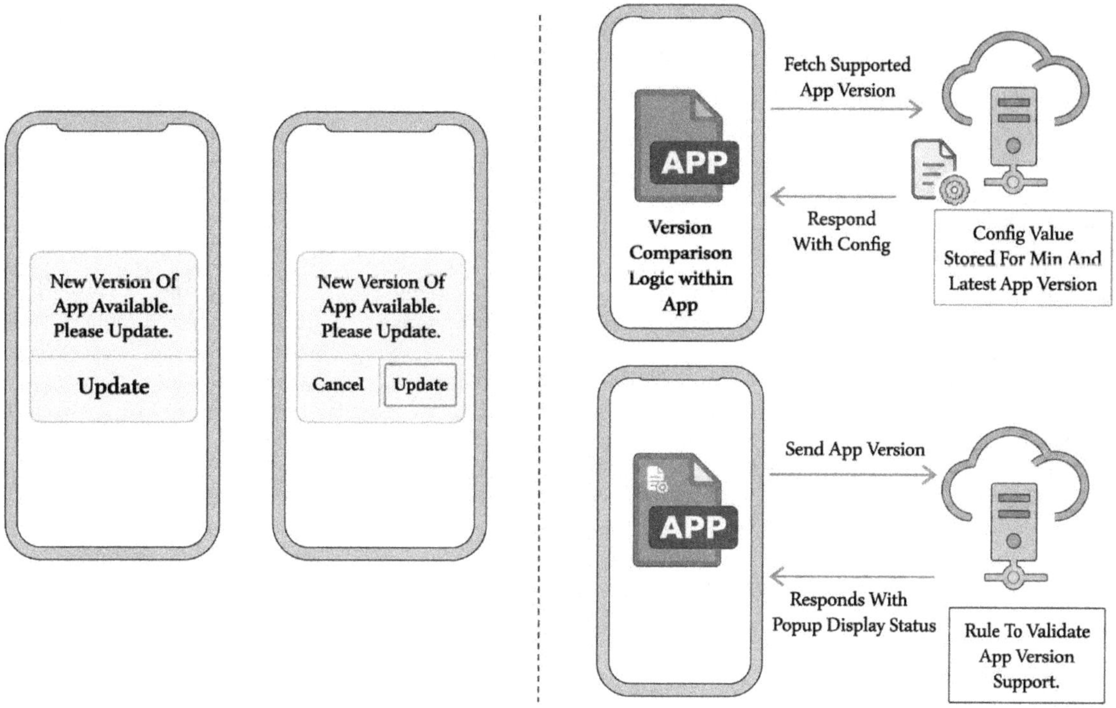

***Figure 9.1**: Force update wireframe and implementation strategies*

Irrespective of when the validation happens the logic will be similar. The logic will have following two values compared to the current version of the mobile app:

- **Minimum support version**: Any version below is not supported.
- **Current stable version**: The active version in production recommended for use.

Table 9.2 depicts the logical rules and the respective popup (soft or force update) will be displayed to end user:

Client version	Update
Client version < minimumSupportVersion	Yes (Mandatory update)
Client version == minimumSupportVersion	Yes (Soft update)
minimumSupportVersion < Client version < currentStableVersion	Yes (Soft update)
Client version == currentStableVersion	No
Client version > currentStableVersion	No

***Table 9.2**: Update popup display rules*

The client version in *Table 9.2* is the mobile app version.

The logic follows the given rules:

- If the client version is less than minimum support version, show the mandatory update and prevent the user from using the application.
- If the client version is between minimum support version and current stable version, show a soft update where the user will be able to cancel the update and continue using the application.
- If the client version is greater than the current stable version no popup is shown.

For force update feature implemented via network call to backend, the best practice is to have a minimal and optimal number of invocations. This would prevent battery drain. Even for the client-side version checking force update should be throttled to avoid unnecessary compute usage. Throttling the force update checks can be achieved by invoking validation in app starts or on resume from background. Further optimization can be done by limiting the frequency of checking, for example once in a day.

A probable edge case that can occur in force update is when the mobile application relies only on network calls and the internet is turned off. The internet unavailability would give rise to a situation where a fallback should be implemented. The fallback could be restricting the application or allowing the user to continue. Restricting the application should be implemented on the mobile side if the operating domain has critical need of blocking older versions. Consider the use case where a banking application detects a vulnerability in the account listing screen. The user should not be allowed to login to the application which is having the vulnerability. Ideally, the organization would shut down any version below the version that has vulnerability. If the organization implements the logic like explained earlier in app startup, it may create a blind spot where the user will not see the warning. The right strategy will be to prevent users from entering the app and blocking the user at the login service. This implementation is one level above the flow explained earlier. This strategy is recommended for financial applications to prevent and tackle any fraud or vulnerability. *Figure 9.2* depicts the block diagram for such an implementation strategy:

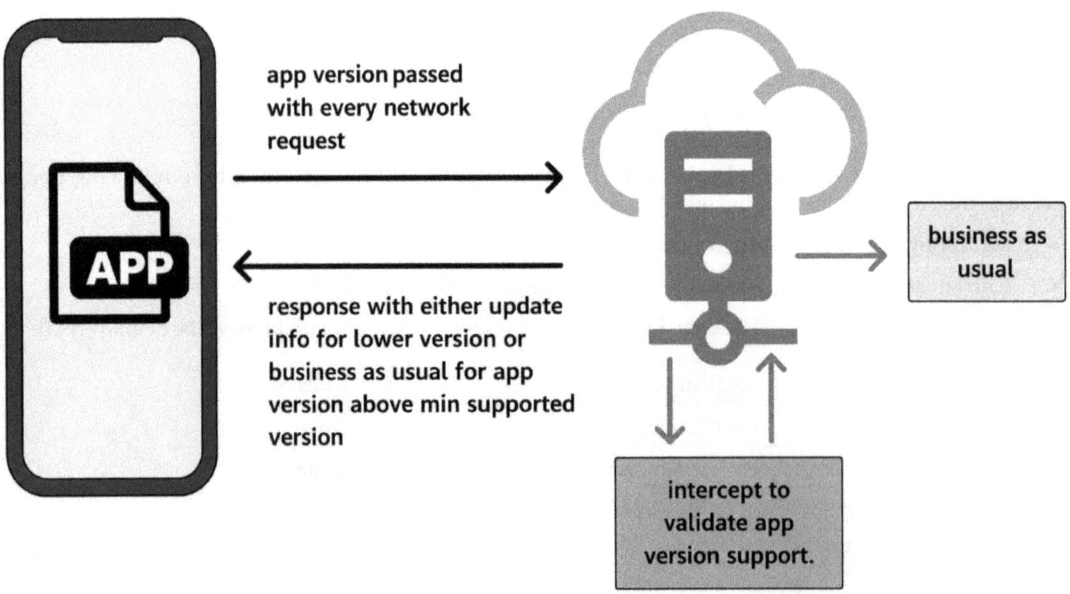

Figure 9.2: *Force update implementation strategy with every network call*

Accessibility

For a mobile application, supporting accessibility and inclusiveness should not be a design afterthought. It should be considered from the start. The mobile app being presentation-heavy, should factor these in from the UI/UX design phase. Themes such as color contrast, dynamic sizing, audio descriptions or captions are a few examples that relate to accessibility. Other examples where accessibility consideration is critical are designing and developing app for the users with visual difficulty. The solution will be to use haptics, voice over and compatible visual design elements. The mobile platform has APIs that can be leveraged to support accessibility. With the support from the platform increasing for accessibility, the life of developers has become easier to incorporate accessibility related features. Setting up of haptics and voice over can be achieved with minimal effort.

Let us look at a case study where spatial audio is used to solve for accessibility. Spatial audio is a technology simulating sounds on the earphone or headphone connected to device in a way it is heard in real life. In the case study spatial audio is used to provide audio feedback to the mobile user. The audio feedback will help user to navigate in a 3D space. The individual wearing a compatible device could get feedback via sound intensity. The intensity of sound can be changed to give the end user a sense of direction thereby aiding in moving around.

Another example is the usage of screen design following color contrast and text sizing appropriate for visually challenged user. Such an app will be developed with the capability to responsively adjust based on the text size phone setting. The text size thus could be adjusted to the size which the end user is comfortable with. The topic of accessibility is a separate product capability to be considered. The chapter introduces the concept to establish the relevance of accessibility. The following are some examples of common use cases prevalent in mobile application where accessibility is applied:

- A button should have the frame size of minimum 44 x 44 points. This is mentioned in the interface guideline. Following the guideline ensures the click area for the user is large enough and spaced appropriately to recognize an action.
- If the color theme used in the mobile does not factor the color blindness the app would be unusable for those individuals. The team should design screen using multiple strategies such as ensuring the color convey an intent, using the high contrast colors which are color blind friendly or ensure the design are tested for color blindness fitment.
- Mobile applications support interaction via multiple touch gestures. If the designs and interactions are such that using the gestures becomes complicated, it would not be a great experience. Enabling conflicting gestures would create confusion in the usability. Using standard guidelines provided by platform or simple gesture should be the ideal practice.
- A navigation application used by vision impaired end user would need voice over and voice input command support for using the application. The platform provider has implemented these in the map's app available in the industry. When the team is developing custom maps, the development team should ideally use the APIs to ensure the support for the voice input and voice over is present.

Error handling

A software application has the probability to behave differently from the intended functional expectation. For a mobile application, the error from the downstream system may manifest on the consuming side, affecting the end user. It is ideal during the development time to anticipate the possibility of an issue. The issue that could potentially trigger such behavior should be handled gracefully. It is essential to preempt any possible error and exception that can fail the functional behavior of the system. When a failure occurs in the system, the feedback should be propagated to the upstream layers through each layer for a multilayer codebase. The presentation layer logic can give an indication to the user if recovery is not possible. The presentation layer will give enough context to take appropriate action. In a case of planned unavailability for maintenance, sharing a note to wait would keep the end users informed. This strategy can be applied for long running unplanned issue as well. Such a strategy will give a better experience.

The following are few examples of common failures/error scenarios:

- Network related error which could be due to the device connectivity or internet.
- Third party system to which the mobile is connecting to would be down.
- The third-party system that the mobile application is connecting to does not abide by the contract which the mobile is expecting.
- User-entered input does not meet the requirement or validation rules.
- Mobile OS related failure or the restriction imposed due to denial of permission by the user. For example, disable location access, disable camera access, etc.

These errors should be proactively handled at the development stage. An application should not be left in an unknown state. The occurrence of these errors should be minimal for a great user experience. If the errors do occur, the app should be capable of gracefully handling the same displaying a message or workaround for the user to progress. Investing time to handle the error should be weighed against the time to fix, criticality and ROI of the issue. Such an analysis will help to get the prioritized list of error handling required for the application.

The following are two examples of error handling strategies:

- Grouping the common and repeating patterns of error. For example: text field validation, the internet outage, response data from backend failure, etc.
- Building a common UI with the possibility of dynamically changing the relevant content. For example, message or any words that are injected based on the context.

Figure 9.3 depicts wireframe for common error patterns in a mobile application:

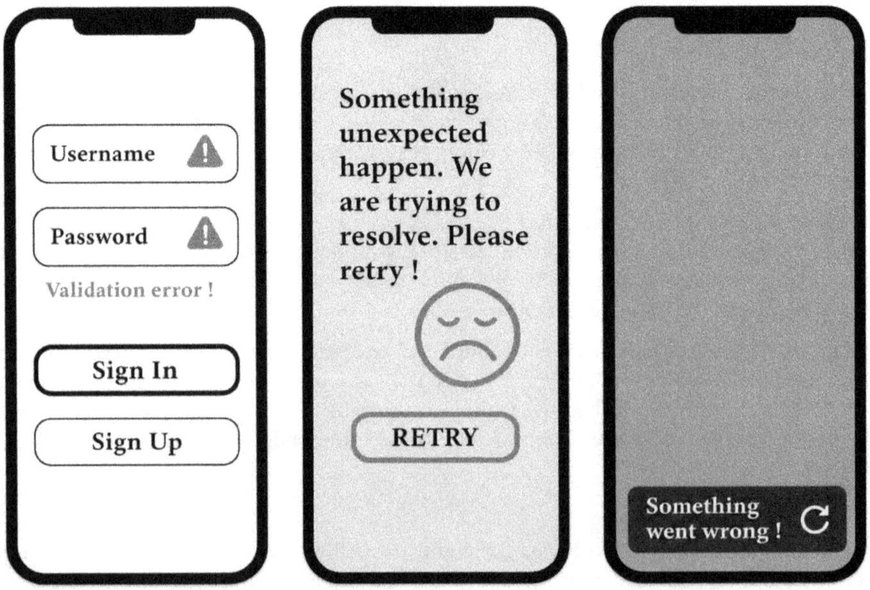

Figure 9.3: *Wireframe of common error patterns*

Logging

Logging is a means to provide additional information. Logging provides a mechanism for traceability for an event. Logging is very useful for diagnosing events that should not have occurred. Logging would serve to be a tool that provides data to analyze, isolate and gather information on a behavior which has occurred and requires debugging.

The logs can act as the audit trail for an issue which has occurred and could help to recreate the scenario. Logs are useful for the post development events occurred on a mobile application in the field.

The mobile application is a standalone software installed on a device. As discussed, in the start of the chapter, the organization does not have much control over the end user's device and usage. In the industry there is strong market segmentation with a wide variety of devices. A situation would arise where the application running on a particular device is facing an isolated issue. In such a case logs are the means for the development team to get clues to debug and analyze the root cause. The logs become even more important if the issue is not reproducible consistently on any other device. Device-specific issues shall be prevalent after the application is live and used on a wide array of devices. Logs are used during the development cycle. Features developed could be tested by individuals who do not have the setup or tool like development team. Getting deeper insights into what is happening inside would be difficult if internal logs are inaccessible. The manual testing team is an example who will have to endure such a situation. Access to the logs becomes important for the testing team and will help to reduce time to report an issue. Testing team with access to logs will be able to do the initial analysis. The initial analysis will help the test team to categorize the defect for the respective owners, downstream or mobile development team who have context. The visibility of the log to testing team will give additional insights such as crash logs, service call response or request structure and other information which is logged. These data act as the insight for accelerating debugging process. As the complexity of the system increases the necessity of stricter logging becomes more important. The development team along with the stakeholder thus should decide and add logs for required information.

Note: **The decision of what should be logged and what should not be logged is an engineering decision. The decision should be agreed by the whole team and should align with the team's logging strategy. A log should have data without noise and jargon. The purpose of the log will be to help to debug an issue faster.**

Platforms provide a mechanism that can be used to print messages to the console. These APIs can thus be used to bring out additional runtime and dynamic information to the console log. The console will require developer tools to view. It would be counter-intuitive for a non-developer to use development tools to view and share the logs. For non-developer having the log outside the development ecosystem will be convenient.

Development logs: The console logs can help the development team. The information can be used to find the logical issue from downstream system to debug issues. Care should be given to prevent any platform log to be present in the production or release artifacts. Team should ensure any sensitive data leak is curbed. The platform default logs are an output function that pushes the string message onto a console.

The purpose of the development log is to get additional information to track an unanticipated behavior. These logs can be exposed to the non-development community to share any evidence or get a quick understanding of what is happening behind without any hassle. In an issue reported which is not reproducible or with an unknown cause, debugging would become incredibly difficult without logs. These logs could give visibility with which the developer can speculate on probable cause of failure based on logs added.

Implementing simple light-weight development logger

There are open-source libraries that can be included in the source code to support logging. Getting insight of internal working of a logger could give an epiphany. The section looks at a lightweight implementation for the logging mechanism. Logger is implemented by exposing a function by rerouting the data to the console log or to a screen as a list. The behavior of the logger and the level of log is controlled by configuration which can be changed at runtime. The logger entity is appropriately instantiated with the required configuration by the development team in the start of app lifecycle. Logger entity can be a simple class which needs to be called with the log message and type. These logs will be captured in a store (LRU cache). The implementation to simultaneously print on to console can also be enabled driven by configuration. The stored data can be displayed to the end user. A backdoor on a testing build can activate the display listing the captured logs on the screen. The backdoor could be a unique gesture such as a shake or triple-tap edge of the first screen. The backdoor should not affect any existing functionality. All the logic and code associated with the logger should not be a part of the release build. This can be achieved by writing precompiler conditional statements to exclude the logger related code on release build.

Logging in production environment

Logging in the production environment can bring a conflicting point of view in the mobile development team. The preference should always be to build an application with zero bugs. Device segmentation for mobile phones makes it difficult to test for all the constraints or combinations of varieties available in the market. A case would arise where the functionality does not work as intended on certain mobile devices. When the issue is device specific or not reported by any other user, it would be hard for the development team to get insights easily. Having production logs could be very useful for the team to fix the issue. Logging necessary details to debug in production would be very useful. The scope of necessary is very important and in the case of production, the data that is exposed via log should be handled with caution. Only data that aids debugging without exposing sensitive user information should be logged. The data that could be leveraged by someone with malicious intent should not be logged.

The production logs could become a monitoring mechanism to act on issues before the consumer reaches customer care. This would be a delightful customer experience where the solution of an unanticipated issue occurs even before the consumer raises complaints. An alerting mechanism and automated resolution strategy thus bring operational efficiency in the production support workflow. An example one can think of is a user facing a payment gateway failure. The user getting a message of automatic reversals or reconciliation process initiation without raising support ticket is a better user experience.

It is not mandatory for application to log all the data to the production environment. The team should decide on data based on the operating context of the features and the purpose to be fulfilled by logs. The mobile application sending log involves computation. The data that is logged must be stored, which adds cost for maintaining storage space. The team should be cognizant of the fact and should optimize the logs. The logging mechanism can also be configured to be enabled from a remote flag. In such a design the team can enable the log reacting to an issue reported. Once the issue root cause is identified the team can turn off the log thereby reducing the overall logs sent from the mobile.

Let us explore another real-life use case where the mobile logs were a life saver. The application was continuously failing in production. There is an error caused by a field which is not adhering to format agreed in contract. The incorrect value is creating a potential failure in mobile. This should have been caught in the contract test. The value was correct in the lower environment and this issue only happened in production for a particular user. Having the production log will be important for the development team, which has to do a quicker analysis. The development team without logs will have no clue as the issue is user-specific and occurring only in production.

Implementation consideration of a logging framework

In a development environment, sharing of the logs would be relatively easier. The development team will have direct access to tools. When the application is out in the field, the team must depend on an end user to get the logs. The logs from the production to reach the development team have to go through many channels if stored in the end user device. It would be manually extracting the file from the device and sharing it via support ecosystem. This is counter-intuitive for a mobile application user. Alternatively, the mobile application can send the log to the server, without involvement of the end user. The logs should be posted to a backend storage. A best practice to adopt is to use a batch processing mode for sending logs instead of sending each log one by one in separate request to the backend. Sending in batch is optimal for the battery efficiency of mobile device. The mobile application will implement network call to connect to the backend storage and publish the logs. Logger can be designed to have various levels. This can be the configuration which the team shall set. The level of the log will determine the severity and the importance of the log. The log level configuration will help to prevent too many logs. Enabling the log level to be controlled from a remote service would offer more flexibility for the production logs. With the remote configuration to control the logger, team can selectively switch ON/OFF, the logs. Such a strategy will provide an optimized experience and performance for the mobile application. There is a pattern seen in the industry where certain organizations use analytics product repurposed for logging.

Another design consideration is to prevent any duplication of logging mechanisms. For example, a payment failure due to invalid input or unauthorized user can be logged at the backend and in mobile as well. However, if the log is sent from the backend for payment service, then mobile need not send the same information again from mobile.

Logging security consideration

When logging any data, the following principles should be adhered to. These are security considerations to ensure the misuse of data is prevented:

- Data that is logged should not contain sensitive data that can be exploited by a malicious entity.
- Data logged should be traceable.
- Access to viewing logs should be controlled and audited.
- Prevent unauthorized use or a client application to publish to log.

Mobile application availability

A key performance index of a service/product is its availability. The availability can be defined at different layers of the systems involved. For mobile applications the unavailability of any downstream system will disrupt the mobile app's functioning. An organization would want to track the overall timeline where the system was unavailable at each of these layers. Mobile connects to the downstream system via the internet. Internet could be a potential failure point, where a mobile application operating in a poor network will not function well. A logical error in the mobile application also could cause unavailability. Team should build mechanisms that help to track the downtime and ensure enough data for analysis is available with the team when in need. There could be separate dashboard that summarizes the health of various system. The availability status gives the live update. Any system failure will be highlighted in the dashboard, and the team can work towards resolving the same.

To understand the impact of availability let us look at a use case building a login feature. The development team's success criteria are to build a system that has zero downtime for login. The end user has a mobile application to login to the system. The reason for potential failure could be poor network connectivity of the end user. The end user would probably call this as downtime. From the development team's point of view, the underlying issue was at the mobile network. Availability of mobile network is not an issue which can be resolved by the development team. Ignorant of the fact, if the stakeholder comes and states that the development team was not successful in building a zero-downtime system, it would create a logical dissonance. At this juncture, a new problem statement arises on how a development team can track these cases and remove the false positives that skew the performance index on availability. Ensuring that the events from mobile are logged will give these insights. The data could be correlated and analyzed to understand if the mobile failure was due to an issue in the request response of the backend or due to an issue on the mobile application itself. This data could clearly be used to single out the problem and whether it is specific to any system. This data also gives the team a kick start to work towards mitigating the issue.

Deep linking

An oversimplified definition of deep linking would be a feature that would provide a mobile application the power to easily navigate to pages using simple identifier. The data can also be encoded as optional input parameters along with the identifier. This feature is known by different names in different platforms such as URL scheme, app links, universal link etc. For each platform level, the means to implement would differ. There are multiple mechanisms with which a team can configure deeplink capabilities in mobile applications.

Figure 9.4 depicts an overview of the functioning of the deeplink feature:

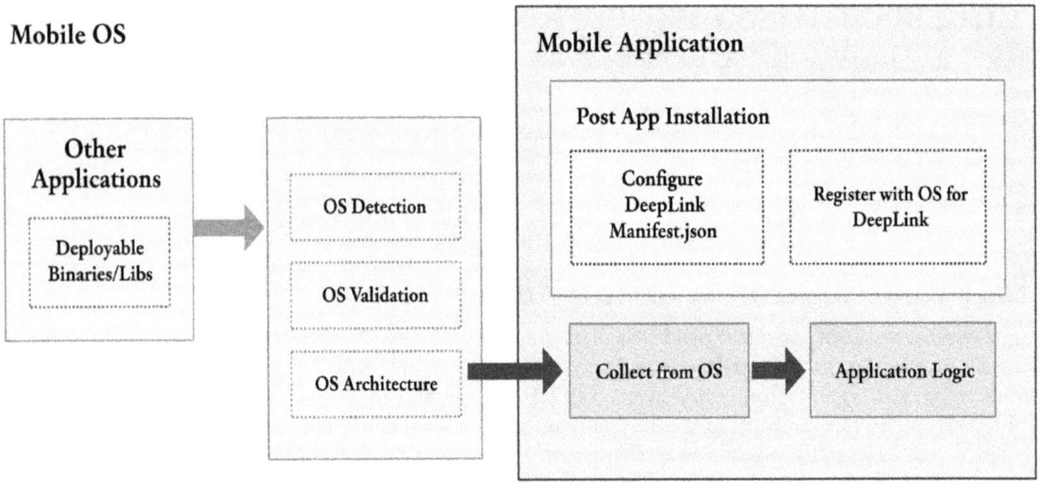

***Figure 9.4:** Deeplink functioning overview*

Figure 9.4 depicts different components and actions performed when a deeplink invocation occurs:

- The deeplink mechanism has two parts: registering and invocation.
- The configuration done by development team while shipping the mobile application is used to register a unique identifier with the **operating system** (**OS**). The format supported by the individual platform should be followed.
- The unique identifier gets registered with OS as the end user installs the mobile application on the device.
- When there is a deeplink invocation, the OS detects the invocation. The OS validates and redirects it to the appropriate application.
- Once the control is transferred from OS to application, it becomes the application's responsibility to take the next course of action that needs to be executed by the mobile.
- The deeplink will have the necessary details for the application to take the next action. If the deeplink invocation is not meeting the definition that the application expects, it would be a clear case of responding with error. What happens inside the application can be controlled programmatically. The deeplink invocation should not ideally cause any side effect.

Deeplink invocation

Deeplink invocation is when a deeplink trigger transfers the control to the mobile application. The deeplink can be invoked from email, message, notification, or other application installed on the device. As the invocation occurs the OS intercepts the same and passes the control to the registered application for the deeplink.

Sneak peek into iOS deep linking mechanism

iOS provides two means to support deep linking: URL scheme and universal link. Universal link was introduced at a later stage. Universal link is an improved version addressing potential flaws in the URL scheme. The section compares both these.

The URL scheme functions by defining a custom string as a scheme. The scheme adheres to the format specified by platform. Scheme is the identifier which can be used to interact with the application. URL scheme will be recognized by OS only if only the application configured with the respective scheme is installed on the device.

The universal link on the other hand is like URL scheme. In universal link there is an additional layer of validation done by the OS to check with a configuration hosted in a server. The configuration is mapping for a routes supported by the mobile application. The universal link is sent to the user via the same channel as URL scheme. The development team must follow the guidelines and instructions defined by Apple platform to set up universal link. In principle universal link brings forward the idea that the pages in website will have mobile native counterpart. The route for website when invoked as the deeplink will open the same feature on the mobile if exists. Universal link thus is a polished URL scheme which provides the means with which an organization can map the different functionalities provided by website pages to mobile counterpart. Universal link thus accessed from mobile will open the app.

Sneak peek into Android deep linking mechanism

In Android there are three variations: implicit deeplink, explicit deeplink and App Links. The underlying mechanism of the handling is similar. However, the key difference is the format of the deeplink URL each type expects: implicit deeplinks use custom URI schemes, explicit deeplinks use HTTP/HTTPS URLs verified by the application itself, and App Links use HTTP/HTTPS URLs verified against a server-hosted configuration file

Table 9.3 lists the example of the deeplink format supported in Android:

Deeplink variation	Deeplink invocation example format
Implicit deeplinks	**exampleapp://custompage**
Explicit deeplinks (uses HTTP URL)	**http://exampleapp.com/custompage**
App Links (uses HTTPS URLs)	**https://exampleapp.com/custompage**

***Table 9.3**: Android deeplink invocation format*

App Links is equivalent to universal link where the verification with a website is managed with the Google service. Implicit deeplinks are equivalent to URL scheme explained earlier for the Apple platform. The explicit deeplinks are http link which is configured to be recognized by the application. The internal implementation of deeplink in Android is using intent filters defined in the app's manifest. Intent filter can be registered to detect specific URL schemes or paths by the application.

Deep linking exposes a potential attack surface

Deep linking exposes a potential attack surface on the mobile application. Any entity with access to mobile (including other applications installed in the mobile) can invoke the URL scheme. Precaution should be taken to validate deeplink invocation. Any malformed URLs identified should be discarded. Limiting the actions that exposes accessing the user's critical data is important to reduce any risk. An example case would be a deeplink allowing direct deletion of content. A malformed deeplink can cause crash is another example of a catastrophe, an example of serious vulnerability which can be exploited by a malicious actor to destabilize application. The recommendation is to write automated test with the negative scenarios to keep check when changes are made to the deeplink logic.

Deeplink validation

There are two layers of validation that a deeplink feature must pass on invocation. The first is at the mobile operating system level and the next at the mobile application level. The first layer of validation ensures that a valid deeplink recognized by the operating system is processed. Typically, invalid deeplink which OS cannot recognize is ignored with no action at the OS level. The source application can influence the behavior for unrecognized deeplinks. The second layer of validation starts when the OS passes the control to the targeted application. To get the invocation details, the deeplink URL and the associated data are received as URL params. The application as the next step should validate the accuracy of this data and parameter. The application code should take steps to prevent any malicious action targeted towards the application. The validation at the mobile layer is very critical and is the responsibility of development team to implement. Handling the action triggered by the deeplink is fully under the control of mobile codebase. The development team should do the due diligence to keep track of what is exposed by the mobile application. Deeplink feature development should be accompanied by the necessary safety nets to prevent any malicious intent.

App size

In the world of mobile applications, the total size of the application can be measured through the following three perspectives:

- Artifact to store
- Downloadable size
- Installation and post-installation size

Each of these sizes can impact the end user experience of the mobile application. The team should clearly understand the relevance and impact of the different app size. Team should be cognizant to keep check on these app sizes and take steps to have an optimal size. The upcoming sections focus on each of these and their impact.

Artifact to store size

The mobile application code base is compiled and packaged as artifact. The artifact then gets uploaded to the store. The store takes the artifact through the approval process. Once app store standards are met then the uploaded artifact can be released to market. The size of the package/artifact which is uploaded to the app store would be the combination of the codebase and the resources. The resource would include image, fonts and other platform related files. The codebase and the resources are the items which the development team has control on and has the potential to be optimized. The factors that significantly increase artifact size are suboptimal resources or images, duplicate resources, resources to support multiple device resolution etc. Another factor that affects app size is when using third party cross-platform frameworks for mobile application development. The framework overhead will get added to the package size.

An artifact uploaded will have to cater multiple targets of device type in the market. For example, iPhone and iPad in case of an Apple device. Even within iPhones as the hardware changes the code should be recompiled. A similar situation exists for Android devices as well. This indicates that the app size is directly proportional to the number of device type targeted. For an end user the artifact to store size does not have impact as the app store optimizes the binary and only the specific binary and resources for the target is downloaded.

For an organization the artifact to store size will be a factor to consider. The artifact adds up the internal space to store the historical binary of the different app version released. The team can opt to remove older versions along with the optimization to keep the storage size in control.

Downloadable size

The artifact released would be available to the public. The artifact uploaded in the store is a compressed package of multiple targets. As discussed previously, it is not necessary that the size of the artifact uploaded to the app store and size that the end user downloads are equal. The download size should be less than or equal to the uploaded artifact size. App stores provide the means to selectively supply the necessary components for a particular device when the application is downloaded. The redundant files are not downloaded at the time of installation request. This strategy in the platform is known as **app thinning** which includes app slicing (delivering only the relevant binary slice and assets), bitcode recompilation, and on-demand resources in Apple ecosystem. On Android, the equivalent is achieved through **app slicing** via the Android App Bundle format, which allows Google Play to deliver only the device-relevant APK. The underlying methodology used to optimize the download size would be owned by the respective platform. The developer will have to understand and adhere to the guidelines defined by the platform to capitalize and reap the benefits by respective platform vendor.

Installation and post-installation size

Once the mobile application is downloaded from the store, the OS would install the application and perform the necessary initialization. The user can then start using the application. In a typical mobile operating system, an application has a space allocated called a **sandbox** and the application is equivalent to any other executable on an operating system. The operating system takes care of necessary security aspects to prevent any malicious intent by an unauthorized executable. The permission allotted to an application is restricted to the space allocated on installation and not beyond. The space occupied by the artifact post installation, after decompression is known as **install size**. As the usage of applications increases, the app and user data may start adding up. The application logic implemented influences the post-installation size. The sandbox expands, occupying and consuming the space available on the device. Optimizing post-installation size thus is important. Team should ensure that the code written does not add unnecessary data that increases installed size. There should also be a provision to clear the data.

For a mobile application, it is advisable to give control to the user to clear this additional data, like a file management application. In Android, the OS provides this feature to clear cache and application data. The Apple platform on the other hand has set the expectation for the development team to provide an option to manage application data. If the option to delete data is not provided, the user would be forced to delete the application when there is a space crunch. Such a case is potentially a bad user experience.

Managing assets

When a mobile application is developed there would be several images, fonts, text files, etc. These would be packaged as part of the application and are essential for the functioning of the mobile application. Embedding these files has an impact on the download size of the mobile application. Images/artwork are generally the major assets in most cases that add to the application size. The development team should ensure that the files are optimally sized. Optimizing size should not affect the fidelity of features. Another way of managing assets would be to enable on-demand download along with caching the resources post installation.

App size as an NFR is critical. The section gives enough context for the team to have a mindset in place to optimize app size. If the mobile application should be made available in a region where network speed is limited, and the data transfer cost is high, it would really be efficient to have a minimal size mobile application.

All app store optimization applies when B2C apps are released via the App Store or Play Store. In B2E, the capability provided by the platform app store may not be available to optimize the artifact. For B2E it would depend on the application development team to optimize the application size.

Screen rendering performance

Mobile application development is all about the presentation of features to end users. The success criteria of a feature depend on adoption by end users. The app responds in the form of visual, sound, or haptic cues to a user's action. For an action, any delay in response would trigger an uneasiness for end user. The mobile application should be engineered carefully to avoid such delays. An app that responds faster creates a great experience. Out of the three, the most used mechanism is visual and thus UI rendering of mobile applications should be at its best. The label for performance metrics for the user interface is the screen rendering performance. Haptics and sounds are a means of extending these functionalities to be inclusive and more immersive. In this section, the idea is to investigate the guidelines and strategies followed to ensure the visual screen change meets the optimum standard for a mobile application. The section explores the techniques to track the same on the field.

Understanding the refresh rate

In a typical 2D world, animation is a deception to the human eye. Animation occurs when continuous images are played one after the other at a certain speed. This technique of rendering the continuous sequence of image is the job of a rendering pipeline. The rate at which the frame or image change occurs for a mobile is called the **refresh rate**. There are different standards for refresh rate and the most common ones are 60Hz and 120Hz. These numbers indicate the rate at which the frame changes on the mobile device. For example, 60Hz means in one second there will be 60 frames that get rendered in the mobile device display. For an application, the frame change is equivalent to change in the rendered pixel on a screen from the initial state to the next expected state. During this process, any noticeable discontinuity in-between the frames will cause jitters. The mobile device also receives input from the end user. The input should be processed, and the app should respond appropriately. If the device is unable to process an external input from end user and is unable to respond, it is termed as **unresponsive behavior**. The rendering engine that gets the state information to determine what to draw is generally blocked due to main thread becoming busy thus skipping the frame redraws causing jitter and unresponsiveness. The jitters and unresponsiveness can be avoided by looking at the computational time available to influence the state change responsible for the upcoming frame. A typical program has a time window defined by refresh rate between each refresh. For a 60Hz refresh rate, the time window between each refresh is 16.67ms which can be derived from 1/60 second, the time interval between consecutive frames to render. This would mean that if the refresh or computation takes more than 16.67ms, the frame redraw will not occur. This leads to the **frame drop**. In mobile application the standard practice to handle computation that takes more than the mentioned time is deferring to a different thread unblocking the main thread responsible for the rendering.

Consider the case for an end user trying to drag a view from the bottom to the top. In an ideal scenario the view should move along with the interaction when the user drags. In this case if the computation is a heavy operation running on the main thread, let us say for one second due to an oversight in codebase, the frame redraw will be blocked for that entire second. This will cause the frames getting skipped from rendering for one second. Thus, the user interface when dragged will start changing the position abruptly. This will not be a smooth experience. Visually the mobile screen would jump position in the interval of one second. The end user will feel that the app is not responding to the cue which is the touch drag. Such an app experience would irritate the end user. The right step would be to bring down the computation to less than 16.67 milliseconds and ensuring that there is continuous frame update.

The technologies are continuously evolving, and the development team should be aware of the tools and best practices. The team should ensure the rendering pipeline is not blocked in any way. The platform tools measure the screen rendering performance by sampling the screen employing test run on the mobile applications. These samples will give indicators of such bottlenecks and frame drops. These tools will give insights and highlight the functions that are suboptimal and that have gone beyond the allocated threshold blocking the main thread. Such functions should be optimized or moved to a different thread to ensure the app is stable without rendering issues.

Screen load performance

A mobile application that consumes data from external system could be affected by network or any other delay due to complex computation or processing. The downstream system taking time to respond to request will manifest as a delay on the mobile. This delay has direct impact on the user experience. Implementing loading screen pattern is prevalent in mobile. The loading screen informs the user via visual feedback for any delay. A longer delay or overuse of loading screen is not a great experience. The time taken for a screen to redraw with the received data, including the time for the backend system to respond, should be optimal. This is an important performance metric. The team should monitor this metric to optimize the mobile application usability. The team should aim to design and develop systems with minimum delay. The network delay is an external factor affecting the performance. A mechanism to measure the time taken to load the screen with and without the network delay could give data which will indicate if screen design approaches need optimization. If the delay is from network, the downstream system can be notified to check the bottleneck. The screen load performance thus, will give a hint where the user experience needs to be improved or if it is performing at the optimal threshold.

Tracking every screen could be a choice that team can decide, however it may not be required. A team can start by tracking the critical features. Finding the operation which are computational heavy in these paths will give the data to kick start the optimization. The screen load is measured by finding the time between creation of screen and end of a loading of the screen. The time calculated for the screen load can thus be observed for multiple runs to analyze the screen load trend and performance. The team could even configure to send alert to a group if the time goes beyond a certain threshold. There exists a plethora of devices; the practicality of testing on every device during development stage is limited. In such a situation the team can capture the screen load data while the application is deployed in the field. Capturing data for in production will give more coverage. If the load time goes above the threshold for a considerable number of users and if there is a pattern formed, then the team can investigate. The screen load data will become a reference for deviations and steps to correct the issue. The screen load tracking mechanism usually catches most of these screen load issues. The data from a wider array of devices and OS which might not be covered in the testing phase gives data corresponding to actual impact. In general, the recommended screen load time is less than 1.5 seconds with network calls and for screens which does not have external network calls should load in 500milliseconds.

The difference between screen load and screen rendering performance is that screen rendering measures the processing overhead in the main rendering pipeline whereas screen load looks at the delay in the screen to load due to any processing, computation or fetch done for preparing the data to load the screen.

App startup time

The time a user takes to see the first screen of the application is called startup time. This is an important performance consideration that the team should optimize. There are tools provided for the platforms to measure and keep track of the app startup. Tracking and optimizing the startup time should be done along with the development with these tools. The mechanism to capture the app startup post release could be done to keep a check. The section looks into the different possibilities of app startups that one can measure. It should be noted that there are different names used to represent startup kinds in different platforms. In the section the classification which is commonly used and labels that can be mapped across different platforms is listed as follows:

- **Cold app startup**: Cold app startup is when an application launches for the first time after the mobile is restarted or after the application is installed. In this, the application has to majorly deal with all the processes associated with the initialization of dependency which are external and internal along with the standard app startup process. Example of external dependency is language runtime or library which is part of the operating system that get dynamically linked. The total time taken for cold app startup would depend on and is influenced by the factors inherited from these dependencies of app. The inherent structure within operating system will affect the cold startup. The operating system decides how these dependencies are loaded to the memory while running the mobile application.
- **Warm app startup**: A warm startup is a platform capability where the OS will allow the application to retain a particular state so that the additional initialization overhead could be optimized. In the warm app startup the full step required for cold app startup will not be performed, resulting in faster launch time.
- **Resume stage/soft start**: The mobile application typically can go to the background stage when it is not in use. This is an ideal time which the OS can optimize and channel the computing power to other important tasks. The user can bring the application back to do the required action. This transition from a background state to active can be termed as resume stage/ soft start.

Optimizing app startup

The goal of optimizing and keeping app startup in control should be a priority for any mobile application development. The time recommended for any mobile application as the upper bound is five seconds for cold start, three seconds for warm startup and one second for resume stage or soft start.

The app startup could be delayed by the downstream system. However, the recommendation is that network calls which are synchronous in nature should be avoided during app startup. In an unavoidable circumstance, an interactive and engaging screen indicating progress and providing a wait indicator should be leveraged. The wait indicator should temporarily engage the user. The platform also adds constraints for startup time to ensure the app start-up is optimized. If the app load time exceeds the suggested threshold, the app will not be allowed by the operating system and will crash. Thus, it becomes a functional requirement to adhere to the platform specification and optimize the app startup.

Market segmentation in mobile device

The mobile phones variation out in the market are huge in number. The permutation of OS versions in combination with the device will increase the market segmentation. This increases the number of target device for the mobile application. For a mobile development team, this would become an important parameter to validate. The team can create strategy to ensuring the application is usable for most of the devices. The specification of the devices may not be the same. The team may encounter a situation where certain feature has separate implementation in code and the behavior is different in these specifications. Different behavior is seen in Android ecosystem where the hardware manufacturers customize the operating system. In most cases the compatibility for different device specifications is handled at the platform layer when developing app in native technology. A cross-platform framework on the other hand may target multiple platforms and encounter a situation where a feature available on Android is not available on iOS. The application programmer in such case may have to ensure the right configuration is used to build and the necessary checks are in place to activate any conditional logic for specific targets.

Let us take an example image management, the device has various sizes and pixel specifications, each image asset must be provided in the appropriate resolution for each target device. An image loading well in a MDPI device may not render well in XHDPI.

Note: **Dots per inch (DPI) is the construct that indicates the screen resolution of an Android device. The DPI represents and determines the clarity and sharpness of content displayed on the screen. Android has different buckets of DPI across devices. The developer must add different resource versions to cater to each of these. Alternatively, Android codebase can use vector-based images which scale for different DPI.**

Now, a few important questions arise:

- How can the team logically conclude testing and ensure the application will work on the field on every device?
- What are the best practices to come up with an optimal number of devices to be tested?
- What is the minimum number of devices the team must test to ensure the application will be stable in the field?

While developing a mobile application, it is essential to know the probable percentage of device used by targeted end users. For the platform, the strategy to ensure the wide spectrum of device versions are covered in testing is different. Therefore, the strategy for iOS and Android separately are explored separately.

iOS has a relatively smaller set of devices and operating system fragmentation when compared to Android. The trend in operating system adoption indicates that the end users are very prompt in the Apple ecosystem. As soon as an update is released the end user is highly likely to update and be on the latest release. This reduces the cost overhead to support multiple OS versions as the organization can decommission the support for lower version of OS. It is a possibility that there are users who have not updated to the latest OS. The organization can decide and define the strategy to support or deprecate the support for mobile application on older versions of OS. The organization should decide if catering to a hundred percentage of consumer is important. This should be further validated to check if the ROI is affected with this decision and will it create bottleneck for a sustainable growth.

The following are some potential options when deciding support for different iOS devices:

- **Option 1**: Support above 95% of devices out there in the market.
- **Option 2**: Support only the latest version out in the market. In this case, the end user will be forced to update to the latest OS to continue using the app.

Option 1 has implications on cost. The development effort, testing effort, post-production defect management effort for all the versions of devices adds to cost. The goodwill of the organization to ensure the reach of the product to the maximum possible customer is what stands out. Even in option 1, the rule of (*n*-2) should be followed. This translates as 2 versions lower than the latest version released by Apple. This rule will still give coverage of more than 95% which can be derived from the statistics Apple publishes on the adoption of the latest OS. Supporting lower version more that this will be suboptimal and not recommended unless there a strong business reason.

The option 2 on the other hand is a slightly aggressive option. The number of audiences that will have access to the application will be based on the market share of people who have update to the latest OS. The organization could go for this option if there is data showing all the user are on the latest OS versions. Another potential reason that would force the organization would be the cost and time constraint to accommodate the different version.

Option 1 and option 2 are situations that which resonate with the Android ecosystem as well. The impact of choosing between the option is way higher in comparison with Apple devices. The variation of Android devices out there in the market is very large and becomes one of the major reasons for this impact. The impact manifest in the form of increased cost and time in comparison with iOS. Android operating system being open source gives possibility of OEM version which can have custom behaviors. With all these complexities the team will have spent separate development effort to ensure the different device are supported.

This section now has given enough familiarity of the ecosystem. In either case of iOS and Android the organization can either choose option 1 or option 2. The count of physical devices that need to be tested to be foolproof is quite a big number. A better strategy would be to identify critical segments of device with respect to various features of both hardware and software being used by application. Example of the hardware feature would be the support of fingerprint, device resolution, etc., in comparison to software version which would be mainly OS version. The team must then categorically come up with a subset of devices which covers the major variation of the devices available in the market. Testing in these subsets of devices should provide confidence that most of users out there in the market will not have issues. This number of devices which can be afforded for testing will be limited by the budget an organization can spend.

Another factor to consider when curating the device subset would be the popular devices in the region where the application is being released. This should be correlated with the features that are most essential to the business or functionality supported in the application. For example, what is the minimum display resolution used by a majority of population or what is the brand which is most popular amongst the targeted users.

Android devices can be from multiple manufacturers. As explained earlier there will be various combination of device feature or OS specification. The strategy employed for covering OS specification would be to validate if the mobile application works on a subset of manufacturer. This data shall give the confidence that the application will work in similar software specification. In the case of hardware specification, it would be recommended to ensure the required phones are present is the testing strategy. The hardware features that are critical to business will need to be mandatorily tested on the actual device.

Consider the example where team have decided to support all the screen resolutions. Procuring all devices may not be practical. In this case the strategy would be to test in minimum one lowest resolution device and on highest resolution device. This act as the subset and from this one can confidently conclude that the intermediate resolution will not have major issues.

The ideas discussed till now in the sections are structures that helps in the decision-making. These ideas will help to come up with a logical and pragmatic set of devices to be tested before application hits the field.

Physical device or simulator/emulator

Development tools come with simulators/emulators. The team would have to decide on how many test devices an organization should procure for the team. Procuring all device for everyone in team will add to cost. The logical and pragmatic approach will be to have a device distribution across the team where collectively the coverage of devices could be attained. The strategy works well in a co-located team with the advantage of exchanging the devices amongst each other when needed. The organization thus can ensure the exhaustive list of device matrix curated to ensure the production readiness is covered. An organization should take into consideration the budgeting aspect to procure the devices and can decide the number. The device matrix is the list of devices on which the team should test before going live. These devices form the exhaustive list of agreed subsets of device which the team must ensure the mobile application is stable. An organization limited by budget will use simulator/emulator to substitute the device matrix.

The simulator and emulator are meant to test the mobile application and should not only be restricted to the development team. The testing team can also leverage the simulator to verify the function of the mobile application. Ideally the behavior exhibited in the simulator/emulator almost would be recurrent in actual devices and vice versa. Thus, if getting a physical device is difficult the fallback could be to have a mix and match of simulator/emulator with physical devices.

Defining a hard and optimal number of devices in the device matrix is challenging. It is always subjective and can be decided based factors such as budget, features, etc. The team can use simulator/emulator when physical device is not available. For a small team, it is wise to have one device per developer and one per tester. For a team which is larger in size the recommendation is at least 40% of the team size (developer + tester) should have one device per platform with the assumption that the hardware dependent features are minimal.

Device specific issues development versus production

Every issue needs to be fixed. However, as a business, it is always essential to weigh the priority and severity for any issues. For an issue occurring only on a particular device or a group of devices, it is recommended to check the priority and severity of the issue weighed against the other items at hand. The prioritization looks at the impact of the issue being present for the long-term and short-term. If the return on investment of fixing the issue is low along with not many users affected by the same the priority and severity of a defect will be low. A defect that which affect many users or break the main functionality affecting business will be an example of high priority and the team should start investing to analyze the root cause and resolving the same. The root cause analysis will give additional clarity. The product along with tech team can decide on when the bug fixing should kickstart amongst other item being handled.

If an issue occurs in development, it would be easy to address an issue as the device would be there with the team. The team can validate and debug a specific issue in real-time along with the development. The same will not be true for the production issue. The issue might occur in the device that was not considered in the test devices planned during development. Consider the case when the business categorizes such an issue to be a top priority. The worst part if the issue is that it occurs only on the particular device. The team should first check if issue can be replicated on a simulator/emulator which have same specification as the actual device. In the issue is not occurring in simulator/ emulator procuring the device at least temporarily becomes mandatory to tackle such an issue. Until the device is procured the developer would be in a tight spot to comprehend the issue. The probable fix will happen via trial and error. When it is not feasible to procure a specific device the team alternative are to use speculation, logs and trying to replicate in simulator are the alternative option. Replicating the issue and debugging will be a challenge until the said device is available. The recommendation will be to reconsider the priority and criticality by accessing the need to endlessly do trial and error.

Minimum SDK and OS

Every platform matures and new software updates are released from time to time. There will be deprecation and even discontinuity for support of older versions. This is applicable for mobile operating system and the development environment. The decision of minimum and maximum version support for mobile operating system will influence the effort required for development. The testing device matrix should also cover the min and max version of operating system. The farther minimum value will bring a larger complexity for both testing and development. The development team therefore, must agree upon the minimum version of the device and OS that would be supported for the application. The maximum support would always be the currently available latest at the time of development and when the new release happens, an analysis would be done to make the necessary changes. In most cases, the breaking changes in software updates will be minimal. The adoption of the new feature could be planned to be developed as per the business priority. The definition of min version is generally done based on the market segmentation and the platform sensitivity of the geography targeted.

For iOS, the general rule of thumb is to keep the minimum version of OS as the *n-2* version (*n* is current latest version of operating system supported on device), unless the market data aligns where the users are using the lower version of mobile.

For an Android, no minimum version will cover all Android devices, as the ecosystem is highly fragmented. The recommendation will be to choose a balance comparing device compatibility, feature availability, and security. If a mobile application has special needs or regions where older devices are prevalent, the team may want to lower the minimum version slightly. This choice should be weighed against the trade off in terms of security and feature limitations.

In both Android and iOS, supporting a lower version of SDK and OS will end up bringing the inability to adopt new features introduced in the ecosystem. The developer will have to put more effort to ensure compatibility in all versions. Defining the optimal and appropriate minimum version of the OS and SDK is thus very critical.

Data lifecycle

A mobile application is the conduit to represent data in an aesthetic manner on the palm sized device. The data being dealt in the mobile application can be broadly classified into three categories: transient, persistent and secure. Among the three classifications, each classification can take various forms when used inside the mobile application. For a mobile application a mix and match of the three classifications of data are used. Let us investigate each of these in detail.

Transient data/runtime memory data

This data represents the information present in control of mobile applications for the runtime of the application. The max validity or expiration of the data is until the application is exited or quit. Typically, this data could be locally scoped a state or shared singleton state. The locally scoped state is the data that gets allocated and deallocated as part of the object lifecycle in the code. The state or data used inside any logic also falls in the same category of transient data/runtime memory data.

The data stored as singleton is shared state across application which is required to be retained and modified at different points of time of the mobile application lifecycle. A typical example is the access token for authorizing the service call sent as request header post authentication. The developer must take care of the lifecycle of the transient data. The data scope should be restricted to the place where it is used and should ensure the data is cleared from memory if unused. Consider the case where the token data is not cleared after logging out of the application. On subsequent login without killing the application the possibility of older token sent via request header is there if developed incorrectly. This could give access to the system and data and a malicious actor who was able to get possession of the mobile and application will be able get details. The probability of this happening and the attack surface is quite far-fetched. The issue described is likely not to happen as well. The idea to highlight is the presence of potential vulnerability while handling transient data. Transient data increases the runtime memory usage which is another reason to reclaim the memory consumed by the unused data.

Persistent data

The data stored for the lifetime until the data is erased comes under the ambit of persistent data. Persistent data could be a simple file or a database which is relational or non-relational. Each platform has their respective implementation for the persistent store. Library or frameworks are available that covers the complexity that managing the file storage and database for the platform. The developers can utilize the capability to interact with the storage solution provided by the mobile devices.

While using the persistent data, the potential challenge that the development team may face is in the migration. Migration is required when the application is updated and the latest version has changes in the structure of the data stored. The simplest technique to ensure the latest version of application work is to remove the old data and start from a clean slate. This will prevent from any format from causing issue in the application. The experience associated with deleting and reinstalling the application would not be great. It is ideal to employ migration of the data to ensure the app update retain data and convert to new structure of the persistent data.

Let us explore another example showcasing a situation which forces the user to uninstall the application. The persistent data stored incorrectly is causing a functional issue which prevents the user from using the application. The functionality of an account lock out for multiple number of failed login attempts is not resetting after cooling-off period. A cooling-off period is a time until the user is restricted to perform any interaction. This restriction is the case where account lockout screen persisted over the quit and relaunch of applications. The user will only be greeted with an account lockout screen until the cooling period is over. After the cooling-off period the application has logic that resets the persistent data controlling the account lockout screen. Due to some reasons, the development team did not handle the scenario where the account lockout data should be cleared after the cooling off period. This was clearly a defect that did not surface in the early stage of the SDLC and thus became a bug that led to reinstalling the app for a user who is locked out. This resolution resulted in a poor experience, and the team took the learning to be stringent in the quality process.

Another potential failure that the team can encounter is the redundant data being stored in the application sandbox. A continuous growth of data consumes disk space bloating the usage and constraining the storage availability of overall device. The development team should employ a strategy to remove the old data or should provide options to the end user to the clear the data. Providing explicit option to clean up is primarily applicable for Apple devices. Android is providing cleanup options at the operating system setting level. For Apple mobile OS, if the developer does not provide the option, it would mean that the end user must delete and reinstall the application, which is not a great user experience.

Secure data

Data can be misused by a malicious entity. The data thus should be safeguarded. Securing the data thus is necessary while building a mobile application. Secure data can be transient or persistent in nature. The platform will provide different means to secure the data. For Apple devices, there is a separate hardware module to store the secure data, and the user can save and retrieve data from this space using Keychain APIs. An alternative strategy for the data being handled is to use custom encryption and decryption algorithm to secure the data. The algorithm should be compliant to standard development and security practices. The team should also avoid unnecessarily adding the security overhead for trivial data. The decision of securing the data should be strongly debated for the pros and cons. Such a strategy can help to reduce the compute overhead of securing data.

Multi-language support

Multi-language support for a feature is a means of adapting to different languages, regional peculiarities and technical requirements for different locale. For a global application, these languages could be any from around the world.

Each operating system provides the framework to support multiple languages. The framework supports out of the box for rendering of the languages which is written left to right. The developers must ensure that the API and configuration provided by the development frameworks is used. The different translation required for the multiple language should be supplied at the development stage in the required format.

The following are the use cases that the team could potentially encounter when supporting multi-language:

- **Difference in the length of text in different languages**: A text when expressed in a different language can have a different length. The size of the string, the encoding or the expressive nature of the language could contribute to the size difference. A developer's life would be convenient if the text size is maintained same across different supported languages. If the similar size cannot be maintained the UI should be developed to support dynamic text size.
- **Text inside of images or artwork used in the application**: An application can have images and artwork. There is always a possibility of these images and artworks having text. As part of localization, these images may require multi-language support. The team should try to minimize such occurrence to optimize the app size.

- **Parameterized string**: The string with dynamic parameter or format specifier are prevalent. Such string will have a use case to support singular and plural variation.
- **The total number of keys which adds to the size overhead associated with translation**: An end user may not be interested in all the languages. If the application supports many languages the overhead of downloading unnecessary files not relevant will occur. This additional overhead is an area that needs to be optimized in the multi-language support.
- **App release required for any text change**: The default platform provides multi-language support by bundling the different language strings with application package. This would mean that any change of text would require a separate release of the mobile application. Later sections explore the means to achieve string change without an app release.
- **Possibility of missing or having incorrect value for a particular language**: The multi-languages support is achieved by having key value pairs for every language supported by the application. If the value is missed or the value is incorrect for a particular language, the error is propagated to the consuming layer. The development tool may not have the capability to validate the string resources at compile time to ensure the complete keys are encoded. An alternative gatekeeping mechanism that the team can build is by leveraging unit tests for the key and comparing the values.

Remote multi-language support

Opposed to the bundling of the string literal, localization can be achieved by downloading the language asset from a backend service in the runtime. This would give the business team control to change the value in languages after the deployment. Building the remote multi-language support has its own complexity. The problem statements like when to invoke or fetch the text file, when to invalidate the localization files, performance optimization while downloading the file, download failure impact on mobile application, etc., are to be solved to support the remote version of multi-language support. Remote multi-language would require additional infra and a one-time cost of defining the rule to add new text. The development team can take an approach to download and cache the file and resources at app startup. App startup to trigger the download may not be optimal for a large size file. Another issue that may pop up due to the version fragmentation of mobile application is synchronizing the language value with the appropriate app version. The keys expected by the app and the key supplied by the language configuration should match to ensure the app functions accurately.

The language files of smaller size and the user downloading the files may not seem to cause a bottleneck in the user experience. For larger file an incremental and on-demand language file update would be an option. This approach is used for applications that serve multiple geographies and are multilingual in nature.

The language values are typically defined by business stakeholders. A common excel where the stakeholder maintains the string as the source of truth for localization of all supported languages is important to manage the string addition and modification efficiently. The technology team can write a program to parse the excel and create literals in the format that the codebase requires. This thus would be a great way to automate one layer of manual work.

Efficiency and reliability

The mobile application running on a device should ensure that it is built for optimal usage of device resource. The application failing to fulfill the intent which the application promised to achieve is not ideal. Efficiency and reliability are two key pillars the team should strive for. Efficiency focuses on aspect such as minimizing battery consumption, memory and processing power, data usage and minimizing the usage of unnecessary background capabilities. Reliability on the other hand looks at consistency, data integrity, error handling and avoiding crash. This section looks at the theme in the context of battery performance, crashes in mobile applications, and background behavior.

Battery performance

Imagine using a mobile application that drains the battery of the mobile. It would create such a havoc that the user may never use the application. The development team should pay attention to optimizing the battery life to ensure the retention of end user. During the development phase, the team can follow recommended practices laid out for the platform. For example, following practices such as reduction in the network call, optimizing the location fetch, optimizing computational overhead, and judicious use of the hardware features that consume more battery. Additionally ensuring that regular battery performance analysis is performed, or that data is captured to report the average power consumption analytics will help to keep watch on the performance.

Tracking crashes

When there is an exception or unexpected behavior, the mobile application crashes. In an ideal scenario, a team should address these at the development stage. In the case where the application has gone live and the crash occurs there should be an efficient way for the business to track these occurrences. Solving this problem statement will help to get insights to stabilize application.

The crash creates a log within the device. With access to these logs, the team can trace the crash back to the code. The tracking requires the crash log to be available with the development team for further analysis. The log that is mentioned in the context is the trace logs generated for crash by the operating system. These are not the equivalent of the logs explained in the logging framework. By default, the mobile platform has analytics of crashes in the app store console with data for the crashes. Alternatively, an organization can invest in a custom solution that does the crash analysis and reporting.

Note: **From a technical point of view, compilation is a transformation of code to an executable where there is loss of information encoded in the codebase. Therefore, mapping the trace log to code will not happen directly. This will require an intermediary data mapping generated during the compilation process by the respective platform. This data is used and correlated with the trace log to pinpoint the line of code where the crash occurred and debug the issue.**

App behavior in background

The app behavior in the background is the function of the capability exposed by the platform. Depending on the mobile platform, there are restrictions that the team must be aware of while leveraging the background capability. The resource hungry approach toward computation will not get well with writing programs on a mobile platform, as when the application enters the background the operating system restriction kicks in. Additionally, the mobile OS is designed, to maximize the battery efficiency and balance the workload. The operating system will take corrective action to prioritize the execution regime when there is a resource crunch. The ideology of background capability of mobile is way different in comparison to high-end directly powered systems with a background processing capability. In mobile, the intent of background capability is to give the application control to logically perform minimal operation that would enhance the user's experience of heavy processing. Heavy processing on mobile should be intentional when the user is actively using the application in most case.

Some examples are as follows:

- Clean up any unfinished task when the application is moved out from focus.
- Prefetching information based on the user behavior to get the latest data for the user next launch.

Security consideration

Security in mobile is critical as it is for any other software. The security can have different tiers in context of mobile application. The following section signifies the various levels where a mobile app is secured:

- Inherent to host platform
- Device mandated

- Development team integrated
- Industry/business mandated
- Other statutory body mandated

The first one is the one where the host platform operating system/device has built-in capability to secure the end user interest. For example, the concept of app sandbox where every app is isolated from each other and cannot access the content inside one another or the app signing for release. A development team does not have any role to play as these are inherently available in all apps by default.

The **device mandate** is where the operating system provides means to customize and override some of the inherent host platform layers. In this case, the development team must be explicit about the intent and configure the mobile application to have these capabilities. The possibilities of what can be done is still defined by the operating system's capabilities. Data sharing between multiple applications under the same organization is an example. The explicit request to the end user for accessing location, camera, files etc. is another example.

The **development team integrated** are those security practices that team follows in implementation to secure the mobile application. Based on the feature and potential attack vector where a malicious actor can affect the team will implement capabilities to prevent these. The decision made by team for usage of encrypted data base, secure store for personal identifiable and critical data, SSL pinning, preventing apps installed on a tampered operating system, avoiding the hardcoding of secrets in the artifact and using https over http are some of the examples in this level.

The field of security is evolving, where researchers and contributors are monitoring the exploits and attack surfaces. There are communities that discuss this and come up with best practices to ensure that these does not affect the application. This community build around in the software industry has become the place of wisdom to be referenced. The insights can be borrowed and inculcated in any software development engagement. The organization aligns, contextualizes and curates these as best practices the team should follow, which forms the fourth layer: **industry/ business mandated**. This level falls in the same category where the development team must build and integrate in code the techniques to secure the application.

Mobile apps from a regulated industry can have a mandate from the statutory body acting as governing entity for the domain. When an instance of non-compliance occurs, the organization will face repercussions. The governing body defines the rule books which need to be incorporated by an organization. Typically, in such cases, the rules defined in industry/business mandated layer will act as the rule book derived by the organization from the statutory body. The region in which the mobile application is deployed and where the organization operates can also have mandates which the development team and organization should adhere to. Examples of this layer are **General Data Protection Regulation (GDPR)**, **Payment Services Directive 2 (PSD2)** in Europe, **Health Insurance Portability and Accountability Act (HIPAA)** in the U.S, **Federal Communications Commission (FCC)** in the U.S, SEBI mandate for trading application in India, RBI mandates for banking apps in India, etc.

Security by obscurity

The theme of not giving an option and reducing the attack surface is known as **security by obscurity**. There is an inverse relationship when implementing security by obscurity with respect to the app experience. Strict security by obscurity will make more features restricted whereby reducing the attack surface and as a result these features will become less accessible for legitimate users. The team should be sure of the attack surface and the impact or the probability of occurrence while making a feature obscured. Consider a simple data displaying application where there is no personal identifiable application. In such a case, if team decides to implement all the security expectations of a banking mobile app, it does not seem to be a logical choice. The example is a classic over engineering anecdote and would sound a far-fetched example in real life. However, the key idea emphasized is about weighing the pros and cons of a choice of solution. The team should look at the requirement expectation from a security lens and validate necessity and criticality while developing a mobile application.

Dynamic analysis

Dynamic analysis monitors the behaviors of an application while in execution (or run). Some of the examples of the behaviors include observing system call execution by the application, the interactions with the hardware features, analyzing data traffic to the server, analyzing data stored locally etc. Finding potential attack surface and corresponding vulnerability in the application's workflows is the key outcome of dynamic analysis. The static analysis also exists which inspects the source code without executing. The dynamic analysis is done on a real-world simulation and gives a real-time assessment of application interaction and attack surface being exposed. Security is one of the responsibilities of dynamic analysis. Examples of security testing include buffer overflow, remote code execution with dynamic injection, validation of input source to downstream system, man in the middle attack etc. Sending of plain text for the private key or password is one of the critical vulnerabilities identified with the analysis.

Note: **The topic of security is a different beast, and this section is the entry to the domain. The section establishes the fundamental themes that the development team should be aware of.**

Conclusion

The chapter presented a variety of themes that often get ignored when prioritized against the functional requirement. These are termed as NFR or CFR which need to be planned. NFR are necessary, as they make the overall experience of mobile apps better. NFR also increase the operational efficacy while implementing the functional features. It is the responsibility of the technology team to advocate the importance of the NFR. NFR without fail should be prioritized along with the functional requirement.

The next chapter closely examines three popular programming languages and their ecosystems, comparing their similarities and differences. By doing so, the idea is to understand how each platform works and how developers can effectively move between these and cross skill.

Takeaways and reflections

Now that we have reached the end of the chapter, the readers are immersed in the breadth of cross-cutting concerns in mobile development. The following are some of the key takeaways in the chapter:

- The chapter presented ideas that will strengthen the efficacy of a mobile application from a cross-cutting lens.
- The version fragmentation where multiple versions of application existing in the field cannot be controlled by the organization. Force update is a means to deprecate and be operationally efficient.
- Deeplink feature is a double-edged sword. This feature can be leveraged to build an application that can be modularized by reducing the tight coupling in navigation.
- Building applications that are inclusive is important. Bringing accessibility as an afterthought will be much more complex than having these considered from the start.
- Handling error by following a common convention is ideal for development and less annoying to the end user.
- Multi-language is built on the strategy to manage static text from a centralized manner. Multi-language will enable the app to scale for different locale.
- There is a major cross-cutting function that a mobile application has to take care of ensuring screen transitions are smooth. Examples are frame drops should not occur, battery usage should be optimal, application should not get crashed and app startup should be optimized.
- The security in mobile application development has different levels which are influenced by host platform, operating system, development team, community or a statutory body.

Chapter 10
Introduction to Swift, Kotlin, and Dart

Introduction

Fear often holds back individuals, making it harder to gain the confidence to become a polyglot in programming. The chapter explores what it really means to be a polyglot in mobile development.

A programming language is meant to express the intent of a programmer. An intent written as code gets transformed through a series of stages to produce an executable. The executable will be deployed to the target. The target is a machine, in the context of the book a mobile device hosting a computational ecosystem. The computational ecosystem is the operating system, runtime libraries and the hardware drivers that provide the environment which the executable runs on the mobile devices. The chapter will give three perspectives for a mobile engineer: the programming language syntax, a toy project, and the language nuances.

Structure

This chapter covers the following topics:

- Overview of programming languages
- Abstraction in OOP
- Polymorphism in OOP
- Generics
- Flutter framework

Objectives

By the end of the chapter, the reader will be able to shed any fear around learning multiple languages. Mastering one platform can boost an individual's confidence to tackle others. Being technology-agnostic and having the ability to choose the right tool for the job would be an ideal state one should strive for. This mindset allows developers to approach challenges with flexibility and confidence. Knowing that the skills acquired in mobile development frameworks are adaptable and transferable will be one of the key takeaways. The chapter will focus on the programming structure with occasional references to the inner workings of the ecosystem.

Note that the chapter comes with a codebase which the reader can check out from the repository. The link to the installation instructions for setting up the tools (Flutter SDK, Swift toolchain, and Kotlin/JVM) is provided in the appendix of the book. However, to run the codebase, a separate setup of tools is not mandatory. Any online version of a compiler should give the arena to test and play with the code in the chapter.

Overview of programming languages

The programming language learned at the grassroots level, focusing on the essence and the underlying philosophy, gives an edge. An individual with this approach can reason about a problem in multiple language constructs. This is essentially the polyglot way of approaching any programming language. For example, an individual who is skilled in, say, the programming language Swift, will have a head start in acquiring Kotlin.

Note: **The principle of reapplying the skill in one programming language is well-suited in the case of traversing to learn the same family of programming languages. The family of programming languages can be defined based on the underlying ideology each of the programming languages represents. Languages such as Java, Kotlin, Swift, C#, Dart, etc., are primarily object-oriented programming languages. There exist other families, such as logic programming, prototype-oriented language, functional language, etc. These follow a different set of paradigms.**

A program in its simplest form can be considered to be a set of instructions. A program will have data on which transformation and computation are performed to produce results or outcomes. The programming language acts as the medium for writing the program. The broad structure that forms the language construct to organize the program is objects/values and functions. *Figure 10.1* depicts the model for any program in its simplest and abstract form. One can imagine this to be a conceptual unit computing system:

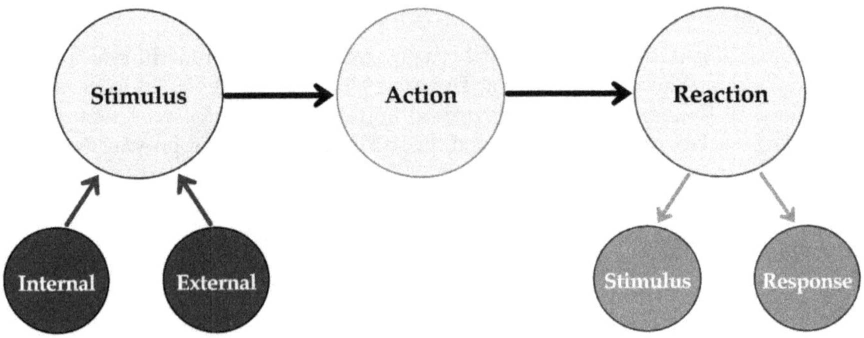

***Figure 10.1**: Abstract model for computing system*

Creating multiple units of computing, depicted in *Figure 10.1,* and composing these together in an organized manner is the approach to solving a large problem. The fundamental role description for any developer will also resonate with the previous statement. The developer has to leverage the programming language and the ecosystem to fulfil the role. A program can be as simple as reading a value and printing to the display. On the other end, a program can be as complex as handling the mobile device interaction, triggering an animation presented to the end user. All of this complexity can be broken down into smaller pieces of multiple units of the model depicted in *Figure 10.1*. Together, the separate units can be combined to serve the complex task.

In most cases, the lower-level details of any computing system will be taken care of by the development framework. For an application developer, it will be a higher-level programming interface that needs to be used to build the system. Irrespective of the API being used, the foundational model, which is described here, is applicable to every software problem statement. A higher-level API itself internally can be represented as components defined in *Figure 10.1*. The developer combines multiple such APIs and writes logic around them to build a mobile application. The responsibility of stimulus, action, and outcome maps directly onto the abstractions the higher-level API expose. In this chapter, the programming languages Dart, Swift, and Kotlin are explored. The following is the basic definition of these three programming languages:

- **Dart**: It is a general-purpose, object-oriented programming language developed by Google. It was first introduced in 2011. Dart is primarily known for being used in the development of Flutter for cross-platform application development.
- **Swift**: It is a programming language released in June 2014, which was part of the Apple ecosystem. Swift has expanded its adoption to multiple platforms with the support from the open-source community.

- **Kotlin**: It was announced as the platform default for Android in Google I/O 2017. The language was there even before this and was the flagship project as a new language for JVM.

OOP versus functional programming

Object-oriented programming (**OOP**) is a paradigm for designing and developing code. This is based on modeling the real-world problem as an object/class. The imperative concepts of function/method are used to perform operations/instructions on these objects to get to an outcome. The OOP is based on the four pillars: encapsulation, inheritance, polymorphism, and abstraction. The chapter explores the programming language in the context of this paradigm. The key focus will be on the feature that enables developers to write object-oriented programs.

Functional programming, on the other hand, is a declarative style approach toward a problem statement. One can imagine functional programming to be a series of transformations, from an input to reach an outcome. Functional programming is based on pure functions, which do not create side effects. The immutability thus becomes the guiding principle with the support of the first-class function in functional programming.

The three languages discussed in the chapter support multiple paradigms and are not purely functional.

Note: **The Flutter framework described later in the chapter will show similarity to the functional paradigm applied in the way the user interfaces are developed.**

File extensions

The file extensions used by Swift, Dart, and Kotlin languages are listed in *Table 10.1*. The file format will be detected by the respective development toolkit to process and enable developers with features to write and read code faster. The compiler also looks at the extension to process the file for compilation.

Language	File extension
Dart	`.dart`
Swift	`.swift`
Kotlin	`.kt` or `.kts`

***Table 10.1**: File extension for different languages*

Hello World!

Adhering to the customary practice of the first program of any software developer, we shall look at Hello World! as the first program. Add the following code to a **`hello.dart`** file and execute it with the command **`dart run hello.dart`** would do the trick for running the first program:

```
//hello.dart
main() {
  print("Hello, Dart World!");
}
```

Add the following code to a **`hello.swift`** file and run with the command **`swift hello.swift`**. It should do the trick for executing the first program:

```
//hello.swift
print("Hello Swift World")
```

Add the following code to a **`hello.kt`** file and run the command **`kotlinc hello.kt -include-runtime -d hello.jar`** to compile. The compilation command produces the output which is a self-contained executable jar. This can be executed with **`java -jar hello.jar`** to see the output:

```
//hello.kt
fun main() {
  println("Hello, Kotlin World!")
}
```

The terminology function is used to name a block of code. In the code previously discussed, the **main** function is an example of a block of code. The block of code can take two forms, either declaration or invocation. The declaration is where the function is defined, and the invocation is where the function is used. The usage of **print** is an example of the invocation of the print function. The same block of code can also be referred to as *method*, and quite often, the term function and method are used interchangeably. The subtle difference between these two is in the declaration scope. A method will be inside the scope of the type, for example, inside a class, whereas a function will be independent and not inside the scope of a type.

The main function is the entry point for the program, kick-starting the execution. The operating system ideally gets a launch signal for a mobile application to start. Once the signal is received, the operating system initializes the necessary dependencies and passes control to the main method of the application. Once the control is received to this point, the chain of control for the mobile application gets initiated. The code execution inside the app takes the execution thereon. Swift language in isolation treats the function written in the global scope as the entry point. A Swift program does not require an explicit entry when running in isolation as a command-line program.

In the Hello World code, one can observe that the print statement in the Dart code has a semicolon as a terminator for the statement. The Dart language syntax mandates the statement to be terminated using a semicolon. This marks the end of a statement, and is enforced by the language for the code to be syntactically correct. This makes Dart a semicolon-based language. Swift and Kotlin do not mandate the statement to end with a semicolon.

Keywords

A word that has a special meaning in the context of a programming language is known as a keyword. The programming language authors are responsible for defining and creating the set of keywords. The developers leverage keywords to write the computational structure to build the software. The compiler treats these keywords as markers with predefined meaning and ensures the code follows the rules defined for the language.

Keywords can be classified into five major categories:

- Control flow
- Type related
- Functions and closures
- Access control
- Error handling and miscellaneous

A logical flow for input transforming to output can be represented and written with the combination of these. A control flow represents a node presenting a decision. A type-related keyword, on the other hand, defines the blueprint and encodes the data. The function and closure form the keyword to write a computational transformation operating on the data and control flow. Error handling and other forms of supporting keywords give the programmer the ability to handle the unknown and bring convenience in the development ecosystem and the program itself. This explanation holds true for any program written in an object-oriented language. The role of the developer is to define the blueprint (data) to process input and provide a response.

Dart

The keywords for Dart have been discussed in the following table:

Group	Keywords
Control flow	if, else, switch, case, for, while, do, break, continue, return, yield

Group	Keywords
Type-related	class, mixin, enum, interface, extends, super, is, as, void, dynamic, var, final, const
Functions and closures	function, async, await, yield, typedef, call
Access control	private, protected, public
Error handling	try, catch, throw, on, finally
Miscellaneous	null, true, false, this, super, assert, static, abstract, rethrow, operator, await

***Table 10.2**: Dart compiler keywords*

Swift

The keywords for Swift have been discussed in the following table:

Group	Keywords
Control flow	if, else, for, while, switch, case, default, guard, continue, break, do
Type-related	associatedtype, enum, extension, protocol, typealias, is, class, let, var, lazy
Functions and closures	func, inout, mutating, rethrows, return, self, set, async
Access control	fileprivate, private, internal, public, open
Error handling	catch, throw, throws, try, try!, try?
Miscellaneous	defer, continue, break, fallthrough, return, nil, true, false

***Table 10.3**: Swift compiler keywords*

Kotlin

The keywords for Kotlin have been discussed in the following table:

Group	Keywords
Control flow	if, else, when, for, while, do, break, continue
Type-related	class, interface, enum, data, object, sealed, typealias, in, out, reified
Functions and closures	fun, val, var, return, lambda, inline, crossinline, noinline
Access control	private, protected, internal, public
Error handling	try, catch, throw, finally
Miscellaneous	null, true, false, this, super, lateinit, companion, by

***Table 10.4**: Kotlin compiler keywords*

Type

A computer program is a series of data transformations from an input to an output. Any program should represent data in a meaningful way to be effective in computation and readability. A computer can perform any algorithmically solvable computation with data. The limits may be due to the hardware resources. A computer will work fine with any form of encoded data as long as the mechanism for decoding is known. In contrast, for the human mind, it will be difficult to cater to the cognitive complexity if the data is not organized and readable. It is important to organize the data into a meaningful representation called types. The programming language is a first-level language that helps to encode human language into idioms that the machine can understand. The types in a programming language will help the developer to model the data. These data thus reduce the cognitive load on humans. Further, with other software and toolkits, the encoded idioms can be lowered to what the machine understands, which are ones and zeroes.

At this point, one might wonder why someone cares about meaningful representation. The reason for this lies in the fact that day-to-day software development is an incremental and continuously evolving journey. The requirement could come up for the software evolution for an infinite amount of time. There will be nuances and feature additions that the software lifecycle will endure and go through in this journey. The humans involved will have to make the code written readable, meaningful, and manageable to make continuous modifications to the code with ease.

There are different classifications of the type system, and not every language necessarily supports all these. In most cases, the following classification will be relevant to reasoning about a programming language:

1. Primitive/built-in/language-defined and user-defined.
2. Value type and reference type.

Dart and Kotlin do not explicitly support user-defined value types. Dart and Kotlin can have code programmed to have value semantics. The value semantics approach is to design a reference type to mimic the behavior of a value type. The data types, though they use reference semantics, will mimic pass-by-value behavior. The primitives in Kotlin and Dart are value types. Swift supports both value and reference types as a language feature. A user-defined type is the data that can be modeled by the developer. The class, enumeration, struct, actor, etc., are examples of user-defined types in the languages.

Class

The class forms the blueprint of the object. A class constitutes an initializer or a constructor with a member function and a member variable. A typical class definition has a name identifier and a body. The body of the class constitutes the method, and the variable definition associated with the object.

Dart

The **class** keyword is used to define the blueprint of an object in Dart. The following is the pseudo code for the class with the variable and the method definition defined previously:

```
class <name of class> {
  /*
  Variable definition
  */

  /*
  method definitions
  */
}
```

The block of code or state that is independent of individual objects created from the blueprint can be achieved by marking the variable and method as static. Marking a method static would mean that the method has the capability only to manipulate or operate on static states or instances within the scope of the static method. Static functions generally serve the responsibility of quick computation, transformation functions, etc. Use the **static** keyword before the variable and function name in the syntax, as depicted for a person class, as follows:

```
//person.dart
class Person {
  String name;
  int age;
```

```
 static int maxLifeExpectancy = 100;
 Person(this.name, this.age);
 _speak(String content) {
  print(content);
 }
 speakName() {
  _speak(name);
 }
 static int averageAge(List<Person> people) {
  if (people.isEmpty) return 0;
  int totalAge = 0;
  // Sum all the ages
  for (var person in people) {
   totalAge += person.age;
  }
  //Return the average age & used .round() to project to an integer
  return (totalAge / people.length).round();
 }
}
```

Note: **List is a data structure defined inside the Dart core package, which, when used with generics, can hold multiple person objects.**

The method in the class in Dart uses the following format. The angle bracket in notation is used to demarcate the component in the syntax.

```
<Return Type> <Space> <Method name> (<input value/signature>) <Method body inside curly brace>
```

In the Dart ecosystem, there are no special keywords to mark a type as private or with lower visibility outside a scope. Prefixing an underscore (_) would do the trick to mark a type private. The **person** class in the previous example has the **_speak** method, which is an example of a private method. An interesting fact about the Dart language is that it does not have any special keywords defining the access modifier (private, protected or public) unlike Swift, or Kotlin, which provide explicit keywords for controlling visibility. This is a design choice by the language's author to support dynamic invocation capability in Dart.

Note: **Dart language support for dynamic invocation and not allowing explicit access modifier does not imply that these two-language feature are mutually exclusive to be implemented. The overhead associated with the implementation to support dynamic invocation in the compiler is much less complex in the current structure of the Dart compiler. The Dart language is able to serve the purpose and intent without an access modifier.**

Swift

In Swift as well, the **class** keyword is used to define the blueprint for the object. The pseudocode specified in Dart is similar for Swift as well. The following code depicts the **person** class in Swift:

```
//Person.swift
class Person {
 var name: String
 var age: Int
 static var maxLifeExpectancy = 100
 // Initializer
 init(name: String, age: Int) {
```

```
   self.name = name
   self.age = age
  }
  // Private method to speak a content
  private func speak(content: String) {
   print(content)
  }
  // Public method to speak the name
  func speakName() {
   speak(content: name)
  }
  // Static method to calculate the average age
  static func averageAge(people: [Person]) -> Int {
   if people.isEmpty {
    return 0
   }
   var totalAge = 0
   // Sum all the ages
   for person in people {
    totalAge += person.age
   }
   // Return the average age and round it to the nearest integer
   return Int((Double(totalAge / people.count).rounded()))
  }
 }
```

The Swift implementation draws a parallel with the Dart implementation. The notable difference between the two is the syntax. The method definition in Swift uses the following notation:

```
<func keyword> <Method Name>(<input signature>) < arrow operator with return type> > <Method
body inside curly brace>
```

The keyword **`private`** in the preceding code, written at the start of the **`speak`** method, is the access modifier. The access modifiers are the keywords that define the scope in which the property/method can be accessed. The visibility of a method or variable marked with the **`private`** keyword will be limited to the scope within the parent type. In the preceding example, the scope and visibility of the **`private`** variable/method will only be within the class **`Person`**.

Kotlin

In Kotlin, the **`class`** keyword is used to define the blueprint for the object. The pseudocode specified to represent a class in the Dart section applies to Kotlin. Kotlin, however, has an additional companion object declaration for defining static variables and methods. There is no separate static keyword for Kotlin as in Dart or Swift. There can only be one companion object declaration per class. The following is an example of the **`Person`** class in Kotlin:

```
//Person.kt
import kotlin.math.roundToInt
class Person(val name: String, val age: Int) {
  companion object {
    var maxLifeExpectancy = 100
    // Static method to calculate the average age
    fun averageAge(people: List < Person >): Int {
```

```
      if (people.isEmpty()) return 0
      var totalAge = 0
      // Sum all the ages
      for (person in people) {
        totalAge += person.age
      }
      // Return the average age and round it to the nearest integer
      return (totalAge / people.size.toDouble()).roundToInt()
    }
  }
  // Private method to speak content
  private fun speak(content: String) {
    println(content)
  }
  // Public method to speak the name
  fun speakName() {
    speak(name)
  }
}
```

The method definition in Kotlin has the following notation:

```
<fun keyword> <Method Name>(<input signature>) < : with return type> > <Method body inside curly brace>
```

Variable

The variables are identifiers to hold the data in a program. The identifiers can be seen as the labels for the container holding the data. The variable gives the capability to read, write, or modify the value stored inside, which the program can manipulate during execution. The variable thus represents the state of the program. The keyword to define the variables would depend on the respective programming language. The variable declaration can be decorated with other keywords to add special meaning/restriction, such as making the variable read-only, constant throughout the application lifecycle, etc., depending on the feature supported by the language.

Dart

The variable declaration follows the given notation in Dart:

```
<Data Type> <Space> <variable name> = <Assignment Value>;
```

Example: `String stringValue = "Test String";`

For a variable where the initial value can be determined during the declarations, the usage of the keyword `var` shall be possible instead of the actual data type. The type-inference capability of the Dart compiler will kick in to infer the type. The compiler in the following example infers the `stringValue` variable to be of the type `String`.

Example: `var stringValue = "Test String";`

The following code will produce an error at compilation. This can be attributed to the strongly typed nature of the Dart language:

```
//hello_variable.dart
main() {
 print("hello world !");
```

```
  var stringValue = "test string";
  stringValue = 1;
  print(stringValue);
}
```

In the previous section, the **class** keyword was used to declare the user-defined types in Dart. These user-defined types can be instantiated as a variable. The Dart language treats every type as a class and is inherited from the base type **Object**. **Object** is the type defined in the core library of the Dart language. One exception to this is the null value, which does not inherit from object. The Dart language does support primitive types as seen in other languages.

Dart supports dynamic typing using the keyword **dynamic**. The dynamic keyword can be used to define a variable. The **dynamic** typed variable does not require an *is-a* relationship for assignment. The variable, which is **dynamic**, can take any type in the lifetime of the program, and the compiler would not complain about the assignment for any data. For example, the compilation error in the previous code snippet, where the value assignment was different, will not be affected if the code is changed, depicted as follows:

```
//hello_variable_corrected.dart
main() {
  print("hello world !");
  dynamic stringValue = "test string";
  stringValue = 1;
  print(stringValue);
}
```

The strongly typed nature is a mechanism to ensure type safety at the compile stage. This is a feature of the programming language. The details of the same are explained later in the context of Swift and Kotlin variables. The Dart programming language is strongly typed for all the other types, which are not defined as **dynamic**.

Swift

The variable declaration for Swift follows the given notation:

```
<keyword var/let> <variable name> : <Data Type> = <Assignment Value>
```

The following is an example code:

`var stringValue: String = "Test String"` or **`var stringValue = "Test String"`**

In the example, the second version leverages the type inference capability of the compiler to infer the type to be **String**.

Keywords **var** or **let** signify if the variable can be changed in its lifetime. The keyword **let** prohibits mutability for the variable declared. Swift is a strongly typed language, which means once a variable is defined, the type of the container for the variable cannot be changed. The container can only store the value of the defined type. Trying to assign values of another type will cause the compiler to throw an error. For example, a variable of **Int** type when assigned a **String** value will cause an error in Swift. The criteria to assign a different type to the variable can occur if there exists an *is-a* relationship between the value and the type of variable.

For example: If **class A** inherits from **class B**, the variable of **class B** can hold the value of **class A.**

Kotlin

The variable declaration for Kotlin follows the given notation:

```
<keyword var/val> <variable name> : <Data Type> = <Assignment Value>
```

The following example denotes the declaration for a Kotlin variable:

var stringValue: String = "Test String" or **var stringValue = "Test String"**

In the example, the second version leverages the type inference capability of the compiler inferring the type to be **String**.

Keywords **var** or **val** will define if the value of variable can be changed in its lifetime. The keyword **val** prohibits mutability for the variable defined. Kotlin is also a strongly typed language like Swift. Once a variable type is defined, the container is restricted to support only the same type or a type with an *is-a* relationship.

Functions

A function is a reusable logical block of code that performs one task and may return a value. A function can be identified to have four key components: a return type, a name or reference, a scope, along with the body of the function, and the signature.

The **void** keyword (in Dart) is the return type for a function that does not return any value. Swift uses **Void** to represent no type, however it is a **typealias** of the empty tuple Swift type. Kotlin uses a class called **Unit** to represent no return value from a function. The following code represents the **Void** type specifics in Swift:

```
//void_type.swift
typealias Void = ().
```

The function and method are syntactically equivalent within a programming language. However, the scope of usage will be different. A more accurate definition is a method being a subset of a function declared inside a type in an object-oriented paradigm. The method can be marked as static or instance. The static function operates at a class level and does not have the ability or responsibility to influence any changes to the state of an instance. In this section, the label function is interchangeably used and will represent both.

In programming languages where functions are first-class citizens, there exists a classification of functions as closures (aka lambda) and named functions. Internal implementation for closure in most cases is its dynamically dispatched nature, which means the execution is resolved at runtime. The named function is statically dispatched, meaning the resolution of the functions is done during compile time. The parameter to any of these functions is called a function signature.

Dart

The following is a syntax example for *named function* and *closure*. It is an example with a void return type:

```
//function_examples_without_return.dart
updateIntValue(bool increment) {
 int intValue = 20;
 if (increment) {
  intValue = intValue + 1;
 }
}
Function functionVariableExample = (bool increment) {
 int intValue = 20;
 if (increment) {
  intValue = intValue + 1;
 }
};
```

The next up is the syntax for *named function* and *closure* with a return type. For both cases, the return type is **int**. The operation performed is adding the input parameter passed and returning the result. The input parameter that forms the signature to the function is also depicted in the following example:

```
//function_examples_with_return.dart
add(int a, int b) {
 return a + b;
}
Function functionVariableAdd = (int a, int b) {
 return a + b;
};
```

Swift

The following is the Swift example for *named function* and *closure*:

```
//function_examples_with_return.swift
func add(a: Int, b: Int) -> Int {
 return a + b
}
var add = { (a: Int, b: Int) -> Int in
 return a + b
}
```

In the case of Swift, the syntax will differ for the function and closure. The closure has the definition of signature followed by the return declared and the `in` keyword as a separator for statements to be executed. The return can be void as well.

Kotlin

The following is the Kotlin example for *named function* and *lambda* (alternate label for closure following which is based on the functional paradigm terminology):

```
//function_examples_with_return.kt
fun add(a: Int, b: Int): Int {
  return a + b
}
val addClosure: (Int, Int) -> Int = {
  a,b -> a + b
}
```

The syntax is similar to Swift. For Kotlin the difference is the usage of arrow operator to separate the body from the signature in closure. The closure also does not have its return type explicitly specified.

Constructor

Constructors are special functions defined in the class. Constructors are responsible for initializing an object. The section explores a constructor in declaration for Dart, Swift, and Kotlin.

Dart

Dart allows defining a constructor either as the same name as the class or as a named constructor. The named constructor is a Dart language feature that gives developers the ability to add clarity and readability to the class instantiation in certain contexts. The signature of a constructor could be used to set the initial state for the object. The following code depicts an example of both kinds of constructor:

```
//location.dart
const double zeroLatitude = 0;
```

```
const double zeroLongitude = 0;
class Location {
  final double latitude;
  final double longitude;
  Location(this.latitude, this.longitude);
  // Named constructor
  Location.zero() : latitude = zeroLatitude, longitude = zeroLongitude;
  // Redirecting constructor
  Location.pointInPrimeMeridian(double latitude) : this(latitude,0);}
```

The constructor syntax in the Dart ecosystem comes with the design philosophy of fulfilling responsibilities, such as redirecting constructor, constant constructor and factory constructor. A redirecting constructor serves its purpose by redirecting to another constructor in the same class. The implementation of redirecting will be with an empty function body and have the **this** keyword appearing after a colon (**:**) which is a call to existing constructor depicted in the above code example. Prefixing the constructor syntax with **const** will allow the creation of a compile time const. The class which does not have const constructor cannot create instances that are compile-time constant. The instance created from constructor should also be marked with const keyword in the variable for it to be compile time constant. There is another keyword **factory** which when used before a constructor provides the capability to add the factory pattern to a class. The factory pattern can be used to implement lazy or cached instances for the object.

Swift

The constructor in Swift is defined with the keyword **init**. The code for the same is depicted in the **Location** class below. The constructor can be seen as a special function. The signature for the constructor has the values that need to be passed externally to set to the member variables. The concept of multiple initializers exists in Swift. In Swift, an invariant exists whereby the compiler checks and ensures that all the non-optional values are initialized within the constructor. The usage of function and its invocation before setting the initial value is not permitted by the compiler and throws an error.

Swift has a concept of a failable constructor (Swift's official term is *failable initializer*). A failable initializer returns a nil object. Such use case is required when the initialization cannot proceed. A case where the input value has not satisfied a condition or rule for initializing the type will cause the initialization to fail and return nil. Like redirecting constructor in Dart using the keyword **convenience** will allow an equivalent in Swift. The following example is a reimplementation in Swift for **Location** class defined earlier in Dart:

```
// Location.swift
let zeroLatitude: Double = 0
let zeroLongitude: Double = 0
class Location{
  let latitude: Double
  let longitude: Double
  // Regular initializer
  init(latitude: Double, longitude: Double) {
    self.latitude = latitude
    self.longitude = longitude
  }
  // equivalent to `Location.zero()` in Dart
  convenience init() {
    self.init(latitude: zeroLatitude, longitude: zeroLongitude)
  }
  //equivalent to `Location.pointInPrimeMeridian()` in Dart
```

```
  convenience init(pointInPrimeMeridian latitude: Double) {
    self.init(latitude: latitude, longitude: zeroLongitude)
  }
}
```

Kotlin

Kotlin has two kinds of constructors: primary and secondary. A primary constructor is one that is written along with the class declaration. The primary constructor is a compact syntax followed in Kotlin. For any logic in initialization phase a separate **init** block can be used. The following code depicts the primary constructor with **init** block. The keyword **constructor** is used to define the secondary constructor.

```
//Person.kt
class Person(val name: String, var age: Int) {
  init {
    println("Person initialized with name: $name and age: $age")
  }
  // Secondary constructor with default age value
  constructor(name: String): this(name, 0) {
    println("Secondary constructor called. Default age is 0.")
  }
  // Another secondary constructor with a custom age value
  constructor(name: String, age: Int,
    default: Boolean): this(name, age) {
    println("Secondary constructor called with custom logic. ")
  }
}
```

The rule for secondary constructor is to mandatorily use the primary constructor for initializing the member variables and ensuring these are initialized through a single code path. The following code represent an alternative to write the primary constructor:

```
//Person.kt
class Person {
  val name: String
  var age: Int
  // Primary constructor
  constructor(name: String, age: Int) {
    this.name = name
    this.age = age
  }
  // Secondary constructor with default age value
  constructor(name: String): this(name, 0) {
    println("Secondary constructor called with default age.")
  }
}
```

Null safety

Modern programming languages are evolving. The focus of the evolution is to complement and enhance the developer's experience. The developer energy should ideally be focused on the functional features and the stability.

The theme advocated in any programming language evolution is that it is the compiler engineers who shall focus on language features. Compiler engineer is responsible to make the programming language intuitive. The success criteria will be the reduction in programmer making mistakes. The compile time checks will become rigorous to ensure the code is free from errors caused by oversight or incorrect usage of language feature by the developers. Dart language is designed with the same foundational thought process. The feature *null safety* is an example for the ideology. The null safety ensures unintentional null exception are handled. Thus, application will not crash during the execution of the program. The null safety mandates the development team to be specific about the value that should be null. Unless a variable is explicitly declared null, it can never hold a null value . Thus, the responsibility and onus is on the development team to make the intent of the code clear while defining any data type.

Null safety prevents unintentional assignment of a null value for any type and will give an error at compile time. Thus, any error will be caught during the development phase itself, and the unintentional behavior can be fixed earlier in the development.

Dart

In the initial version of the Dart language there was no null safety. The Dart compiler never performed a compile-time check for the nullable nature of a variable. The compiler did not give any indicator to the developer to convey that the value could potentially be null. The developer had the possibility to miss checking the case when the variable is null as well. The null safety was introduced later into the Dart language. After the introduction of null safety all types defined are non-nullable by default. For example, defining a variable of type **int**, should always contain a value. The rule is enforced and wherever the variable is used the compile time check is performed.

The case where a code requires a value to be null is also supported in the language. The developer must specify the variable that can accept null. A variable of type **int** can accept any integer or the value null only if the question mark (**?**) is added after the type syntax. A **?** changes the type of variable to a nullable type. The following notation represents a nullable value declaration:

```
<Data Type>? <variable name> = <Assignment Value>;
```

The following code represents the null safety usage in Dart:

```
//null_safety_variable.dart
main() {
 int? nullableType = 10;
 int nonNullableType = 20;
 nullableType = null; //Nullable type can have null value
 nonNullableType = null; //This assignment will cause compile time error
}
```

Swift

In Swift, the null safety feature is called the optional. The **?** and **!** symbols are used in the syntax to define a variable that accepts null. The **!** declaration is implicitly unwrapped optional and the **?** declaration represents an explicitly unwrapped optional. The implicitly unwrapped optional tells the compiler that in thelifecycle of the type the possibility of using the variable accidentally as nil is not there and thus can ignore the type checking therefore the safety now depends on the developer explicitly. The **!** is used to force unwrap an optional value as well. The notation for nullable value in Swift is as follows:

```
<var/let> <variable name>: <type>? = <Assignment Value>
```

The following code represents the null safety usage in Swift:

```
//null_safety_variable.swift
var optionalVariable: Int?
var optionalVariableExplicitlyUnwrapped: Int!
```

```
print(optionalVariable!)
print(optionalVariableExplicitlyUnwrapped) //The code will crash
```

Kotlin

Kotlin has a similar declaration as Swift by using the symbol `?` for marking a Kotlin type as optional. The force unwrapping is achieved with the symbol `!!`. The following code represents the null safety usage in Kotlin:

```
//null_safety_variable.kt
fun main() {
  var nullVariable: String ? = null
  print(nullVariable?.length ? : "no value")
  print(nullVariable!!) //The code will throw exception
}
```

Force unwrapping a value should be done when developer is certain that the value will be non-null at the point of execution; otherwise, it will cause a runtime error. A case with no value available will end up in a null pointer exception causing crash. Kotlin has shorthand syntax `?:` used to assign a default value for a null variable in assignment. In Dart and Swift, the equivalent is `??` operator called as null-aware operator and nil coalescing operator respectively.

Abstraction in OOP

The chapter classifies the three programming languages as OOP languages. In OOP, there are four pillars and abstraction is one of them. Leveraging abstraction will help to write code with clear separation of concerns. An individual who designs a software system should start from a contract. Contract to code strategy would enable the software design adhere to the law of parsimony. An individual when starting from contract will cater to the minimal details exposed outside the unit being developed. This strategy of exposing only necessary details required for the consuming entity is the abstraction. To understand full power of abstraction let us explore implementation details for a feature with multiple payment modes for making a payment via mobile application. An app user can select one option from the available list to complete the payment. From an implementation point of view, the contractual obligation for the app codebase will be as follows:

- Initiate the order and create an order ID.
- Load the payment user interface with the prefilled values for order.
- On success/failure of payment and passing the handle back to the main application.

Note: **The payment ecosystem follows the pattern where authentication and authorization are handled by the provider. A consumer can only initiate a request.**

A payment feature being built would look at the preceding three aspects to be fulfilled. The system should scale to add and onboard new payment methods as the time progresses with minimal change. Designing the system with an interface representing the contract between the payment mode on client and the downstream system is a better design. As long as the downstream system adheres to the contract, the team can integrate any payment solution without affecting the code that initiates the payment request or the one that handles success or failure. The mobile application thus need not care about underlying implementation of downstream system if the contract is adhered to.

The following pseudocode is for a class written for mobile application to display the payment page using an interface to process different payment method:

```
//Interface: PaymentStrategy
interface PaymentStrategy {
  func getInputFields() -> [String]
  func processPayment(data: [String: String]) -> PaymentResult
```

```
}
//Class: PaymentResult
class PaymentResult {
  var success: Bool
  var transactionId: String?
  var errorMessage: String?
}
//Payment Implementations
class CreditCardPayment: PaymentStrategy {
  func getInputFields() -> [String] { /* ... */ }
  func processPayment(data: [String: String]) -> PaymentResult { /* ... */ }
}
class WalletPayment: PaymentStrategy {
  func getInputFields() -> [String] { /* ... */ }
  func processPayment(data: [String: String]) -> PaymentResult { /* ... */ }
}
class UpiPayment: PaymentStrategy {
  func getInputFields() -> [String] { /* ... */ }
  func processPayment(data: [String: String]) -> PaymentResult { /* ... */ }
}
// MARK: - Payment Strategy Factory
enum PaymentMethod {
  case creditCard, wallet, upi
}
class PaymentStrategyFactory {
  static func getStrategy(for method: PaymentMethod) -> PaymentStrategy { /* ... */ }
}
// MARK: - Controller: PaymentPage
class PaymentPage {
  var selectedMethod: PaymentMethod?
  var strategy: PaymentStrategy?
  func renderPaymentOptions() { /* ... */ }
  func onPaymentMethodSelected(method: PaymentMethod) { /* ... */ }
  func onPayButtonClick(inputData: [String: String]) { /* ... */ }
}
```

The payment page in the above pseudo code is not aware of the different payment mode. The payment page will do the operation via **PaymentStrategy** which is an interface acting as the abstraction. The abstraction hides the details of how the individual payment mechanism is implemented.

To support this behavior, the language can use constructs such as inheritance or interface. Dart, Swift and Kotlin support their respective syntaxes.

Polymorphism in OOP

Polymorphism is another pillar for OOP. Polymorphism is the design philosophy in programming language that allows controlling the behavior of an operation within a type. Method overloading or compile time polymorphism and method overriding or runtime polymorphism are the two kinds of polymorphism. Dart in its language semantics does not support method overloading directly. However, it can be achieved using the dynamic keyword or generic type. Swift and Kotlin support both kinds of polymorphism. The multiple inheritance support is not there for any of the three. A class can implement multiple interfaces to mimic partially the behavior of multiple inheritance.

The following code is an implementation of the overriding and overloading for the Swift and Kotlin.

Swift example:

```
class Animal {
  // Overloaded method
  func speak() {
    print("The animal makes a sound")
  }
  func speak(times: Int) {
    for _ in 1...times {
      print("The animal makes a sound")
    }
  }

  // Method to be overridden
  func makeSound() {
    print("Some generic animal sound")
  }
}
class Dog: Animal {
  // Overloaded method in subclass
  func speak(loud: Bool) {
    if loud {
      print("The dog barks loudly!")
    } else {
      print("The dog barks softly.")
    }
  }

  // Overriding the method
  override func makeSound() {
    print("The dog barks!")
  }
}
// Usage
let dog = Dog()
dog.speak()          // Inherited from Animal (Overloaded)
dog.speak(times: 3)     // Overloaded in Animal
dog.speak(loud: true)    // Overloaded in Dog
dog.makeSound()        // Overridden method in Dog
```

Kotlin example:

```
open class Animal {
  // Overloaded method
  open fun speak() {
    println("The animal makes a sound")
```

```
    }
    fun speak(times: Int) {
      repeat(times) {
        println("The animal makes a sound")
      }
    }
    // Method to be overridden
    open fun makeSound() {
      println("Some generic animal sound")
    }
}
class Dog : Animal() {
    // Overloaded method in subclass
    fun speak(loud: Boolean) {
      if (loud) {
        println("The dog barks loudly!")
      } else {
        println("The dog barks softly.")
      }
    }
    // Overriding the method
    override fun makeSound() {
      println("The dog barks!")
    }
}
// Usage
fun main() {
    val dog = Dog()
    dog.speak()        // Inherited from Animal (Overloaded)
    dog.speak(3)        // Overloaded in Animal
    dog.speak(true)      // Overloaded in Dog
    dog.makeSound()      // Overridden method in Dog
}
```

Generics

Generics enable a programming language to support type agnostic code. This is a feature of programming languages. Generics support the reusability of common behavior across types. Generics are an example of a basic metaprogramming. The compiler or runtime is responsible for resolving the actual type, and this process is known as **reification**. A generic feature has three major components: the placeholder, the implementation, and the usage. All three languages (Dart, Swift, and Kotlin) support generics, and the implementation ideology is similar.

Dart supports this generic feature and can be seen in various inbuilt classes. Some examples are future, stream, and list. Implementing a stack data structure in Dart would help to familiarize oneself with the constructs behind the generics. Before diving to implementation lets us hypothesize about a case where generics are not available as a language feature. In this case, the possible solution for implementing stack will be having to create multiple implementations for storing each type by repeating the same code. In such a case, one may have to write code separately to handle a stack for each int, double, string, or any other custom type. An alternate solution will be to use the base type **`Any`** in Kotlin or Swift and in case of Dart using the **`dynamic`** keyword. The downside of the usage of Any or **`dynamic`** keyword is that the type information will not be available for the compiler. The developer should be explicitly aware of the type and should cast the type to use it. Such a programming model breaks the inherent type safety paradigm and will not scale.

The generics feature of a programming language thus will be ideal in designing a much more scalable solution where the common behavior is extracted to create a generic class. The generic class, in turn, will get associated with the type to be stored inside of the stack when it is initialized. The following is an example implementation of stack in Dart:

```
//stack.dart
void main() {
 var intStack = Stack<int>();
 intStack.push(1);
 var stringStack = Stack<String>();
 stringStack.push("string1");
}
class Stack<T> {
 List<T> _list = [];
 int get count => _list.length;
 push(T item) {
  _list.add(item);
 }
 T pop() {
if (_list.isEmpty) throw StateError('Stack is empty'); return _list.removeLast();
 }
}
```

The preceding example has an angle bracket expression represented by `T`. The `T` here is a placeholder expression to be replaced by actual type during the definition as represented in the example where two types of stack (**`int`** and **`String`**) are declared.

The usage of generics is not restricted only to a class, it could be used to define reusable independent function, typedef etc., as supported by the language. A single class can have multiple placeholders as well to represent separate types in generic implementation. It is recommended to keep watch on where generics are used. For case which does not have a use case of repetitive logic, force fitting generics may not be the right strategy. The following is an example of generic pair data structure with multiple placeholders in Swift and Kotlin:

```
//Pair.swift
class Pair<T, U> : CustomStringConvertible {
 let left: T
 let right: U
 init(left: T, right: U) {
  self.left = left
  self.right = right
 }
 // Custom description for the Pair class
 override var description: String {
  return "Pair(\(left), \(right))"
 }
}
func main() {
 // Create a pair with an integer and a string
```

```
  let pair = Pair(left: 42, right: "hello")
  // Access left and right values
  print("Left value: \(pair.left)")
  print("Right value: \(pair.right)")
  // Print the pair
  print("Pair: \(pair)")
}
main()

//pair.kt
data class Pair < T, U > (val left: T, val right: U) {
   override fun toString(): String {
      return "Pair($left, $right)"
   }
}
fun main() {
   // Create a pair with an integer and a string
   val pair = Pair(42, "hello")
   // Access left and right values
   println("Left value: ${pair.left}")
   println("Right value: ${pair.right}")
   // Print the pair
   println("Pair: $pair")
}
```

Generic type constraint

A generic placeholder in the preceding case is used to represent a type. In practice, often the case would be to invoke the methods or access the relevant states from the placeholder. For a compiler understanding the possible types applicable for the generic placeholder gives a better context while writing reusable logic. The additional information will give more flexibility in building advanced generic types which are compile time safe. Additional information can also be used to constraint a generic class to have specific behavior. These constraints can also be based on some conditional logic. Generic placeholder of such type will be constrained by rules enforced on the generic types. These rules associated with generic place holder is restricting the behavior of the generic type substituted. These rules are called the generic type constraint.

In Dart one shall define a generic type constraint using the **extends** keyword with the placeholder. The use of **extends** differs from class inheritance: here it means that **T** must be a subtype of the type following the **extends** keyword. The syntax for Dart will be to write the constraint inside the angle bracket declaration, **<T extends #some type#>**. Such declaration tells the compiler that T type defined as the placeholder is in an *is-a* relationship with the type declared in the generic constraint. This declaration also exposes method and properties of the constraint type. The method and properties will now be accessible for the usage of placeholder T inside the scope where the definition of placeholder T is valid.

A similar structure is present in Swift as well. For example, constraints specified using the placeholder T followed by the protocol syntax (e.g.: **T: <protocol name>**), where it is implied that T must conform to a protocol. In Kotlin the similar code will follow the pattern **<T: Some Interface>** to define the generic constraint type. This implies for any T applied to the generic class it should implement the interface specified in the constraint.

Note: **In Swift, protocol is equivalent to the interface construct found in other object-oriented programming languages.**

Error handling mechanisms in programming

Being deterministic about the outcome is the best state to be in when writing code. This ideology would help a team in preventing any unintentional side effects. Adhering 100 percent to this ideology is not practically feasible. The example for such a case is the dependency on downstream system and their behavior not in the control of the consuming program where predicting outcome is difficult. The unintentional side effects manifest in the form of bugs, blockers preventing usage of the software or a cosmetic issue deviating from the expected screen layout of the application. Such issues should be handled and the team should aim for preventing the occurrences.

In programming languages, the provision to prevent these unintended side effects comes under the umbrella of error handling mechanisms. Examples of errors are arithmetic error, parsing failure of data, unresponsive downstream, etc. It may happen that these error scenarios may or may not occur in the application lifetime as it involves a non-deterministic trigger or input. An example case is that unresponsive downstream causing error in the list backing a screen. As the list depends of the data from backend an internet or the server failure will mean the data cannot be shown rather one should display a mindful communication to the end user. The internet or server being stable would imply the downstream system will never face such an issue, however the system cannot only be designed to handle positive use cases. Preempting errors and adding condition in the code to handle how to respond should be practiced in day-to-day development activities. This will ensure the application behavior is in control without affecting the user experience adversely. A developer ideally should prepare and handle for the application's behavior for a worst-case scenario. The action could be as simple as projecting downtime information or alert that are user friendly with a predicted time for restoration of service. Such an alert would be less of an annoyance to the end consumers than the application crashing or being unresponsive. A mechanism to trigger a recovery action such a retry would also be a better experience to end user. An application shall design mechanism that throttle the user interaction to prevent pattern identified with malicious intent. This optimization strategy is majorly seen in critical features such as payment, login etc. Such design is also under the error handling strategy of mobile application. The example situation is for login feature for a financial app, when multiple attempts fail due to invalid credentials, the account would be locked as a precaution to prevent brute force by an intruder. Such a feature is implemented in code by designing the login feature to throw the error (either backend or client-side logic), which the mobile presentation layer handles by locking out the user from the mobile application.

Error handling has the following three blocks of code:

- Block for execution
- Block for catching the error
- Block to propagate the error gracefully to upstream

A combination of the preceding three components would be used to design code that handles errors. To conclude, one can see that error handling mechanism takes the responsibility to induce the need for team to take proactive steps to handle any deviation from an intended behavior or response. In its fundamental form one can define error handling as means to address an exception thrown at the runtime which gets intercepted on occurrence to be handled gracefully accompanied by intimating the user in an appealing manner. Without error handling, the application will crash and exit.

Next, let us explore the error handling mechanisms for the three programming languages.

Dart

Dart programming language has provided for error handling mechanism using the try-catch keywords. In Dart the `Exception` and `Error` are the base interface types available as part of Dart-SDK for error handling. When designing the code, a team shall extend these interfaces to create more meaningful error types based on the context. For mobile application development, the API or library written on top of the Dart language form the surrounding ecosystem. These API will have various predefined error types depending on the feature used. Any individual leveraging the programming library must handle the functions that throw an error.

A function which throws an error is handled by defining the boundary with the try-catch block. These are the error handling keywords. The **catch** block can be customized by the team using **on** keyword. The **on** keyword is used to specify the error type and can handle multiple errors in the same block.

The language also provides a mechanism to design APIs that raise error signals to the upstream consumer. The keywords used to raise errors are **throw** and **rethrow**. The following code depicts the error handling in Dart:

```
//error_handling_sample.dart
class MyException implements Exception {
 String message;
 MyException(this.message);
}
void riskyFunction() {
 throw MyException('Something went wrong');
}
void main() {
 try {
  riskyFunction();
 } on MyException catch (e) {
  print('Caught MyException: ${e.message}');
 } on Exception catch (e) {
  print('Caught a generic exception: $e');
 } catch (e) {
  print('Caught an unknown error: $e');
 }
}
```

Swift and Kotlin use a similar mechanism for error handling. The **try** and **catch** keyword syntax is also present in Swift. The syntax is different across language, however the structural similarity of the error handling, custom error declaration and propagation can be seen in the three. The code snippets in the upcoming sections depict the same.

Swift

The following code replicates the error handling in the context of Swift. The definition of an error, marking a function to throw error and the error handling mechanism when the invocation occurs is depicted in the following code:

```
//ErrorHandlingSample.swift
enum MyError: Error {
 case somethingWentWrong
}
func riskyFunction() throws {
 throw MyError.somethingWentWrong
}
do {
 try riskyFunction()
} catch MyError.somethingWentWrong {
 print("Caught an error: Something went wrong.")
} catch {
 print("An unknown error occurred.")
}
```

Kotlin

The following code is the Kotlin version of the error handling:

```
//ErrorHandlingSample.kt
class MyException(message: String): Exception(message)
fun riskyFunction() {
  throw MyException("Something went wrong")
}
fun main() {
  try {
    riskyFunction()
  } catch (e: MyException) {
    println("Caught an exception: ${e.message}")
  } catch (e: Exception) {
    println("An unknown exception occurred: ${e.message}")
  }
}
```

Framework/Ecosystem around languages

A framework is a collection of pre-bundled utilities that perform a certain function abstracting the internal workings from the end consumer. Understanding the programming languages is the first step in garnering the skillset required in developing apps in any framework. Next would be to understand the framework itself and the surrounding toolkit. Let us take the example of Flutter which fits the description of a framework. Flutter uses Dart as the primary programming language. The individuals/teams use Dart to develop software. Configuring the Flutter framework by installing Flutter SDK on to the development machine would give access to Flutter cli, pre-built packages, Dart SDK, packaging, monitoring, and debug tools. These form the ecosystem supporting the development. The activity explained in Flutter is applicable for any other frameworks as well.

In the software industry, as a new tool or framework gets introduced to the market, there will be two forms of entities. First entity will be consumers and the second will be the providers. The provider entity is responsible to add capabilities extending or customizing the framework. Setting up this third-party entity would require additional steps. In case of open source, the providers play an important role by creating software that enhances the original tool. In the case of Flutter, the providers could offer a vast array of libraries available as **pubs**. Another example is an AI code generator that convert the UI/UX designs to code or other similar entities. All supporting frameworks will extend and accelerate the capabilities of the any framework. Having such a group of capabilities to form a strong ecosystem is the key parameter that favors choice to adopt a framework.

Similar is the case for Kotlin and Swift, which have the surrounding ecosystem of development frameworks and toolkit for developing mobile applications. The ecosystem powering Apple devices uses the label framework to represent equivalent of library in another ecosystem. The label SDK is used instead as the label for the entire gamut of development ecosystem. The naming convention difference is called out to avoid the confusion that one may encounter.

Further in the chapter, the idea is to focus on Flutter framework and to build a toy project. A similar approach to build a mobile application in Kotlin and Swift will be discussed in the subsequent chapters, *Chapter 11, Kotlin Multiplatform for Mobile Development* and *Chapter 12, Use Case of Developing a Super App*. The code walkthrough in these chapter will provide the foundational exposure for becoming a mainstream mobile developer leveraging the development framework.

Flutter framework

Chapter 3, Cross-platform Versus Native had given enough head start on what Flutter framework is all about. The current chapter introduced the Dart programming that power the Flutter development. The best way to understand further working of Flutter is to dive into the initial requirement the seed team would have hypothesized while creating the Flutter framework.

Following is the list of capabilities required for a cross-platform framework:

- Library or code that will abstract the hardware specific API. A developer having the ability to access and interact with the hardware from different manufacturers with these common API's. The common APIs could be leveraged to build feature while developing mobile application without knowing the internal details of each hardware. Example for capabilities: screen rendering, gesture recognizer, touch sensing, camera access etc.
- Cross-platform code should get transformed to an executable compatible for different OS supported. The compatibility should handle user interface, interaction and ability to respond seamlessly to the end-user.
- The cross-platform tool should have capability to bundle the code as packaged to be deployed onto specific OS channels.
- Monitoring and debugging capability should be supported by the cross-platform framework. Having the provision of live feedback will help the team to fast track the fixes causing the bottlenecks in the application.
- The cross-platform framework should enable third-party developers to publish reusable libraries. This will help teams to use them without reinventing the solution and move faster.
- The cross-platform should allow extending the capabilities to add support for features that are not inherently possible with cross-platform. This should be allowed across multiple OS.

The Flutter framework fulfilled the above requirement, and these capabilities were implemented using Dart and C++. A consumer of the Flutter framework uses Dart as the primary language along with the API exposed to develop cross-platform application.

The central idea put forward by Flutter framework was the creation of a canvas on which the UI elements were drawn. The underlying technology that powers the canvas was separate for each channel (iOS, Android, web, desktop, etc.). This allowed the development team to write common code for drawing the user interface on channel which became the common layer. The underlying means to implement canvas for each channel was different. Thus, building canvas compatibility became the one time overhead for the Flutter framework development team. Additional effort for any incremental maintenance also was required if the operating system changes affect the respective canvas. The details of the rendering engine has been discussed in detail in *Chapter 3, Cross-platform versus Native*. The common code written in Dart which leverages the Flutter framework forms more than 80% of the code written during Flutter app development.

Any Flutter application is a composition of the five functional units - Dart App, Flutter API (Framework), Engine, Embedder and Runner. The `flutter` command from the **command line interface** (**CLI**) is part of the Flutter framework. The command is used to generate the project structure which has all the other functional units.

The Flutter framework has a platform-specific and platform-agnostic functional unit. The platform-agnostic features are written in Dart and C++ majorly leveraging the capabilities independent of the underlying platform. The platform-agnostic unit of the Flutter framework has to access the host specific feature for development. All these are exposed via common API wiring internally to respective host. The wiring of API's is done at the Dart/Flutter engine which keeps the registry of the platform specific implementation and the platform agnostic Dart API. At compile time, the relevant platform-specific implementations are bundled into the executable, and at runtime, invocations of the platform-agnostic APIs are resolved to their respective implementations during application execution. This behavior is similar to a contract and promise between the Dart application and the Flutter engine. If the contract is not abided by the host platform, for example, missing a required platform channel implementation, the application will encounter a runtime error.

Figure 10.2 is a pictorial representation defining the boundary and responsibility each of the functional units:

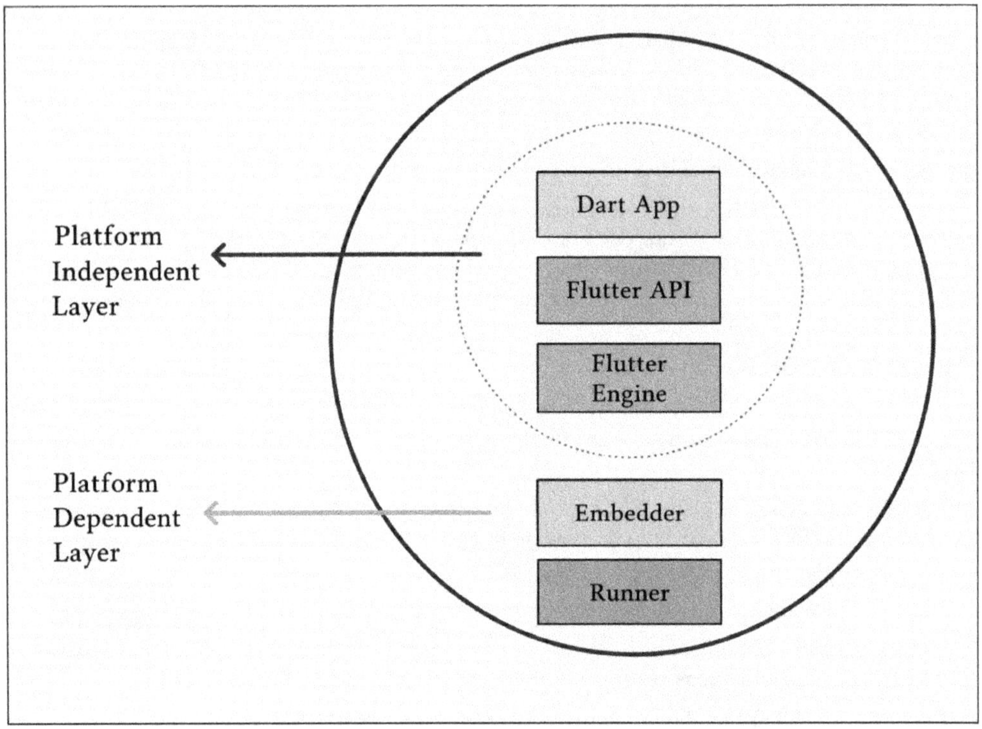

***Figure 10.2**: Flutter framework responsibility rings and components*

The component of the rings can be described as follows:

- **Dart App**: The application code developed by the team.
- **Flutter API/Framework**: The pre-built packages and the higher-level API exposed by the Flutter and Dart ecosystem used to create the Dart App.
- **Engine**: Convert the Dart app into mathematical renderable information displayed by the render pipeline to the end user. This layer is also responsible for redirecting or delegating platform capability invocation.
- **Embedder**: The layer coordinates with the underlying OS to access the service. Thus, the engine passes the invocation to the embedder. The embedder also has a role in managing the overall lifecycle of the framework's runtime.
- **Runner**: The team owns the template generated by Flutter CLI and acts as the wrapper that will become the container to package the Flutter app on the respective platform.

Note: **Flutter is an open-source ecosystem, and the team can always customize the behavior of the development frameworks. This opens up the possibility of using a custom version of Flutter framework. There are organizations that provide custom Flutter frameworks as well. Caution should be exercised while deviating from the publicly available version.**

Capabilities of Flutter

In any Flutter application codebase, the logical entry point to the app is the main method. When the application developed in Flutter frameworks is installed onto an operating system start up, a series of events gets triggered. The series of events includes the instantiation of an application object on the native platform and transferring the control to the embedder component of the Flutter. The embedder component is compiled along with the runner app acting as the host layer connecting the Flutter with native. The runner app host for respective platform packages the Flutter code as a single executable. The runner app is essentially the skeleton and wrapper codebase which provide the canvas for user interface rendering. The runner app also has the mechanism to execute compiled Flutter code. The native entry point (the platform-specific main method in the runner app) initializes the embedder passes the control to **runApp** Dart method, which is the starting point of every Flutter application. This method is ideally the starting point of a Flutter application where the first widget is defined. The first widget is presented to the user who can interact and use the application. One can debate the splash screen to be first screen however it is separately handled by the operating system in parallel to the initialization of the application. From the point of view of Flutter, the first screen will be the one configured in the **runApp** Dart method.

Widget terminology is used in Flutter to represent a class that acts as the blueprint of the UI element rendered on the screen. The beauty of the Flutter framework lies in treating everything on the UI as a widget. One may be intrigued to see a class that represents margin applied between two UI elements as a widget itself. A person coming from an imperative style of UI development may find this odd. One may see various types of programming paradigms inherent to Flutter framework. For UI development declarative style is prevalent.

Note: **The difference between the two styles, imperative and declarative, is that the imperative style follows an approach where detailed instructions of what should be accomplished are given. Providing detailed instruction will be the responsibility of the individual writing the code. In contrast, in the case of declarative, the focus will be on the outcome by composing the ingredients in a certain way and adhering to specific rules. The nitty gritty details gets handled by the framework implicitly.**

Let us explore the key capabilities that make the development in Flutter framework unique in its own way.

Box model for UI development

The UI development in Flutter at its core follows a box model. In box model different components are arranged and packed inside a parent/container box. The box can have nested boxes. Every box is designed as a logical group of UI elements rendered on a screen. Each box fulfills a purpose and may have different capability. The various special types of widgets along with the box model form the perfect recipe to create any high-fidelity screen. The box can span three directions represented in the screen: horizontal, vertical, and Z-stacking. Z-stack is arranged one widget on top of another in the z index from the perspective of the display.

Abstractions unifying platform native feature

The existence of embedder in the Flutter framework would assert the fact that there is layer which is the platform specific components of Flutter. Embedder is separately written for each operating system. The **dart:ui** library in the Flutter framework is the underlying API that act the abstraction hiding the low-level implementation of Flutter's APIs responsible for channeling to platform specific features. The widgets and components are written on top of this framework. A regular mobile app developer may never encounter the requirement to direct usage of the low-level implementations in most cases. The individual may only have to look at the high-level APIs to develop the feature. This ability makes the framework Flutter truly cross-platforms when evaluated from a UI development tool. The other reason that supports the statement is the development team can work with single skill set on multiple platforms.

The Flutter framework gives the ability to build the reusable code to be distributed to a third-party development team. A large variety of libraries can be published to a common place which can be consumed by any team. These are published in the official package repository of Flutter. The provider may define additional terms and conditions when publishing package. The official package repository of Flutter is **pub.dev**. The **pub.dev** was established to promote the contribution to create reusable libraries thus adding capabilities to the Flutter ecosystem. The **pub.dev** will also be a good place to search and find reusable libraries for the capability required for development. The open-source community is very active in writing and maintaining respective platform/OS capability that is not available by default in Flutter framework. These reusable packages make the day-to-day development simpler for team adopting Flutter.

Support for host platform layout styles

The OS manufacturer in the mobile ecosystem audits the apps that can be installed on the mobile device. This happens when the app package is published to App Store. There are guidelines and recommendations that the application should adhere to. Non-adherence could be a potential reason for the rejection of applications from going live in respective app stores. The ideology projected in the human interface guidelines is backed by the usage data from the diverse end user base amalgamated with the ideas advocated by the organization owning the operating system. Choosing any pattern at will that deviates from the default platform behavior is not ideal. A new pattern introduced will break the consistency and familiarity of a particular style with the end user. Reusing the default style will create a seamless adoption. Such a mindset is beneficial and essential to penetrate the market successfully and reach maximum user. In Flutter, the team has tried to resonate with this ideology in most cases. One should note that the product development team has free will to disrupt and still achieve the best result, however mostly in instances where it will be a success will be in the case of long tail.

The prevalent design style supported in Flutter ecosystem is the Material Design. The Material Design language was created for cross-platform, not limited to one channel. A `MaterialApp` in Flutter is a widget that is configured as an entry point hosting the landing page. The `MaterialApp` instance handle the basic setup required for a mobile application. It has the same look and feel on all devices as defined in the Material Design guideline including iOS.

If an app has a requirement to follow a standard iOS-style, the team can use the Cupertino definition from the Flutter framework. The material widget has equivalent widget with Cupertino behavior. In some case the same widget has different behavior. One can technically run a Cupertino app on either Android or iOS, but (due to licensing issues) Cupertino will not have the appropriate fonts on Android. Writing a Cupertino app is thus recommended only when the application is targeted for iOS-specific devices. Alternatively, if the application required support platform specific behavior in both device the developer can write conditional code decided based on the platform type. The Flutter framework provides the provision to configure a conditional statement to set up a widget to be rendered based on the platform.

In most cases it would be rare that one may have to write platform specific code. It is recommended to take platform neutral approach to get the best out of the cross-platform strategy. Given the community driven nature of the Flutter evolution, there is a possibility of innumerable solutions out there to cover most of the common use cases that meet the need for the development for enterprise grade mobile application.

In short, Flutter supports host platform style. The recommendation is to go with neutral approach. This decision is mostly in context of UI/UX. When the platform specific behavior is required, the specific case could be conditionally handled and it is important to keep such occurrence minimal.

Multi-paradigm programming model

The beauty of Flutter framework lies in the multi paradigm. The optimal pattern respective problem statement is adopted by framework. The complexity to know multiple patterns will be an overhead for the developer. The benefit of the multi paradigm outweigh the complexity encountered by the developer. A pattern prevalent and repeating in nature become a paradigm or norm. In Flutter, there are various paradigms that are core ideology influencing how the application code shall be developed and organized. Some of the pattern may get enforced by the Flutter framework for example, the widget tree and declarative UI model are mandatory. There are others set which are left to the development team for example the choice of state management pattern, The possibility to be extending or choose alternate for capability exposed within Flutter may exist. However, this will lead to re-implementation. In case of the re-implementation the guiding principle will still be limited by possibility defined within Flutter or dart framework. The Dart programming language exerts influence on the pattern which the team may use within the Flutter framework. The official Flutter document has listed a set of the paradigms prevalent in Flutter framework. Some of these are composition, functional programming, event-driven programming, class-based object-oriented programming, prototype-based object-oriented programming, imperative programming, reactive programming, declarative programming, generic programming and concurrent programming.

Hello World Flutter

As a part of this section, the idea is to explore at an already created Flutter project. The intent will be a code walkthrough to understand the different nuances in Flutter ecosystem.

> Note: **The flutter.dev portal contains the necessary details to setup the development environment and CLI to run the application. For the Hello World application in the section, the website dartpad.com can also be used.**

A Flutter project directory comes with the folder structure for different platform runner/host apps, a lib, and a test folder. There are other configuration files and directories as well, however the preceding three are the main ones that a developer shall deal with most of the time. The release related configuration such as version number, signing identity, etc., necessary to deploy the code in the respective platform will have to be separately configured for each targeted channel. The focus for application development team will be the lib folder where the Dart file with the code for all the features will be maintained. The test folder will contain the unit test suite. By default, when the project is created the main file with the boilerplate code for a simple page will be present. The team can start editing this file and add others to take the application development further. *Figure 10.3* depicts the structure explained for an example **`hello_flutter`** project:

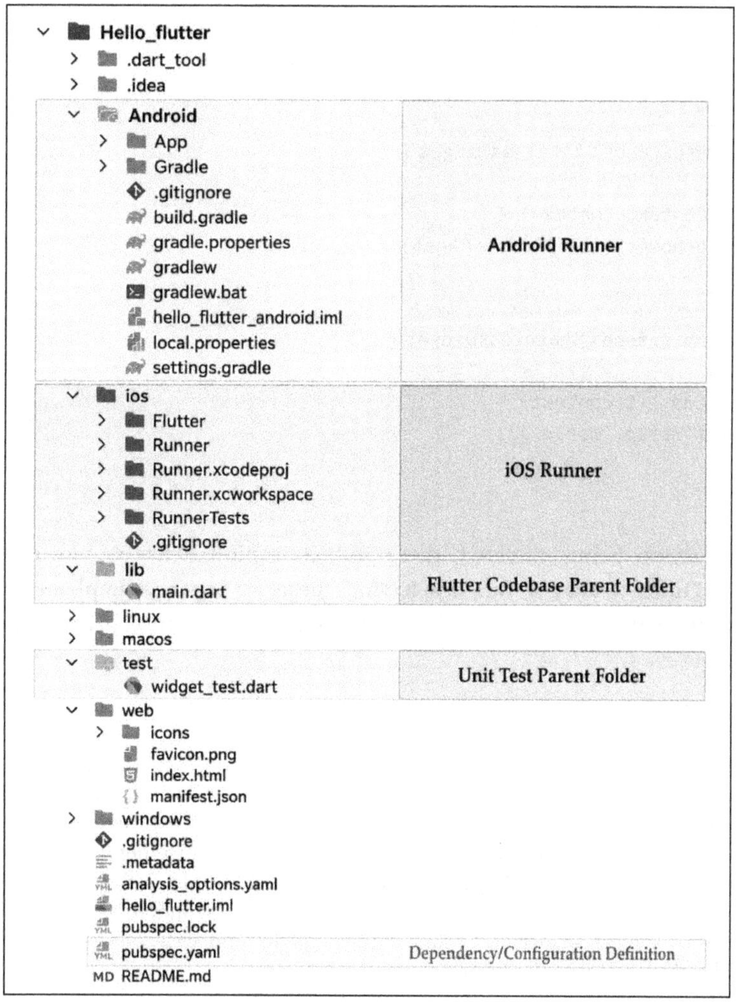

Figure 10.3: *Rendered code on iOS device*

The project lib folder where code for Flutter application gets written. This code written will use the reusable libraries which are either in-house or available in the public added as dependency to the project. The project specification file **pubspec.yaml** will have the dependency details and configuration used by the project. The other folder that the development team deals with is the test folder. The unit test and the widget test are in this folder.

Let us look at the code inside project in the **hello_flutter.dart** file. It is the boilerplate Flutter code created by default. The code represents a page displaying the text **Hello, World!**. The file can be dissected into the header which import the necessary dependency followed by the **main** method invoking the **runApp** method. The input param for the **runApp** method takes the first widget. The **runApp** is the entry point for the codebase and on execution it transfers the control to draw the widget on the canvas. The first widget is the container hosting the inner child **MaterialApp. MaterialApp** has parameters that take another Flutter widget that is the home page in the sample app with the **Hello, World!** text. For any mobile application that uses Material Design needs the **MaterialApp** widget in the hierarchy. **MaterialApp** sets up the theme, navigator, and the **context** that the underlying widgets rely on. If the **MaterialApp** is not present, there will be runtime error. For a Flutter project it is essential to have a class in hierarchy which takes up equivalent responsibility **MaterialApp**, for example **CupertinoApp**:

```
//hello_flutter.dart
import 'package:flutter/material.dart';
void main() {
 runApp(FirstFlutterApp());
}
class FirstFlutterApp extends StatelessWidget {
 @override
 Widget build(BuildContext context) {
  return MaterialApp(home: FirstFlutterPage());
 }
}
class FirstFlutterPage extends StatelessWidget {
 @override
 Widget build(BuildContext context) {
  return const Text('Hello, World!');
 }
}
```

Note: **Based on the platform being rendered, these widgets exhibit behavior like platform native iOS or Android respectively. Flutter manages this by having these as separate implementations. The package import 'package:flutter/material.dart'; and import 'package:flutter/cupertino.dart'; are example of platform specific widget sets.**

Flutter widget

The Flutter widget along with the functional logic of application written in Dart is the crux of any Flutter application. The smallest logical unit that any developer has to encounter on a regular basis is the widget for UI design. Widget gets rendered onto the screen. There are two kinds of widgets used majorly for development, stateless and stateful widgets. These are the two variations which developer has to inherit from when creating a UI control. If the UI behavior of the widget changes based on logic, the individual should opt for the stateful widget. In the Flutter ecosystem, the various widgets for data representation and inputs are available as part of the framework. These widgets can be used as is by setting properties to control the behavior and style. Based on the responsibility fulfilled the Flutter widget can be classified into the following:

- Defining the layout/structure

- Control arrangement/positioning
- Displaying content
- Getting input or facilitating interactivity
- State/data management

The following are some examples of the few widgets in the Flutter ecosystem:

- Container leveraged to group other widgets and to create boxes with padding, margins, decoration, and other styles.
- Column provides the capability of arranging its children vertically.
- Row provides the capability of arranging its children horizontally.
- Stack provides the capability of allowing to stack widgets on top of each other.
- TextField is for entering text input.
- Checkbox is for toggleable selection (true/false).
- Align, wrap, margin controls the positioning.

Note: **The given examples are not exhaustive. Additionally, in the Flutter there are many widgets that does not directly inherit from the stateful or stateless widget as well. Some of these are only used internally. Widget is the common abstraction for all the UI component in the rendering hierarchy in the Flutter framework.**

Hello Flutter example code shared is a simple application which renders a hard coded `'Hello, World!'` text onto the screen. In the example one would have noticed the pattern where the text is defined inside hierarchy of custom widget classes inheriting from `StatelessWidget`. The instance of `Dart` class named `FirstFlutterApp` is passed as the input param to the `runApp` method which renders the first widget. As stated earlier this widget is the entry point to the app. The `FirstFlutterApp` class is a stateless widget which act as the container for the `MaterialApp` widget. The `Dart` class `FirstFlutterPage` which is yet another stateless widget passed into the `MaterialApp` constructor is the first page configured and rendered onto the screen with a simple `Text('Hello, World!');` widget.

In an abstract form, the entire Flutter app is a group of nested widgets which get recreated and redrawn based on the logic managed by state changes. Thus, for a Flutter developer, the work involved will be to leverage the box model to compose UI and architect the codebase to control the transition and the redrawing of these widgets based on the data and the rules governing the feature.

Example of stateful widget

The themes discussed in the chapter with respect to Flutter framework could be brought together by exploring a stateful widget. The structure of the entry point and the setting up the first page is same as the preceding example of stateless widget. In the following example, a notable difference will be the usage of `CupertinoApp` and `MaterialApp` as two separate implementations. The `CupertinoApp` widget has the same responsibility as `MaterialApp`, setting up the application with a Cupertino (iOS-style) application.

Note: **The usage of the CupertinoApp and MaterialApp will trigger the ripple effect on the inner widget used in the view hierarchy. Some of the inner widgets are style agnostic. Some are style specific thus will only support the respective parent. These are the areas where conditional logic will come if the team decide to favor platform specific behavior.**

The following code has the class `MyPage` that inherits from stateful widget. `MyPage` class has only one method returning the instance of the class extending from abstract class `State`. `State` is defined in Flutter framework.

Note: **The Flutter source code defines the responsibility of the class `State` as information that can be read synchronously when the widget is built and might change during the lifetime of the widget. It is the responsibility of the widget implementer to ensure that the [State] is promptly notified when such state changes, using [State. setState].**

The class **_MyPageState** that extends the **State**. The class **_MyPageState** is responsible to manage the widget hierarchy and the logic of retriggering the rendering. The **_MyPageState** is depicted in the following code has three main components **TextEditingController**, **String** and **_updateText()** method. The three components coordinate together to capture the input from the **TextField**. The state also has the build method which returns the widgets to be displayed on the UI. The **setState** method triggers the redraw. User defined state thus can be programmed to control the behavior of the stateful widget.

The difference while using **CupertinoApp** versus **MaterialApp** is depicted with the separate implementation for the **MyPage** stateful widget. The recommendation is to go through the code and return to read the preceding explanation shared once again to solidify the understanding:

```
//main_cupertino.dart
import 'package:flutter/cupertino.dart';
import 'package:flutter/material.dart';
void main() {
 runApp(MyApp());
}
class MyApp extends StatelessWidget {
 @override
 Widget build(BuildContext context) {
  return CupertinoApp(home: MyPage(), debugShowCheckedModeBanner: false);
 }
}
class MyPage extends StatefulWidget {
 @override
 _MyPageState createState() => _MyPageState();
}
class _MyPageState extends State<MyPage> {
 // Controller to capture the text input
 TextEditingController _controller = TextEditingController();
 // Variable to hold the text that will be shown after button press
 String _displayText = '';
 // Function to handle button press
 void _updateText() {
  setState(() {
   _displayText = _controller.text; // Update the displayed text
  });
 }
 @override
 Widget build(BuildContext context) {
  return CupertinoPageScaffold(
   navigationBar: CupertinoNavigationBar(
    middle: Text('Stateful Widget Example'),
   ),
   child: Padding(
    padding: EdgeInsets.all(16.0),
    child: Column(
     mainAxisAlignment: MainAxisAlignment.center,
     children: <Widget>[
```

```
      // Text field for user input
      CupertinoTextField(
       controller: _controller,
       placeholder: 'Enter text',
       decoration: BoxDecoration(
        border: Border.all(color: CupertinoColors.black, width: 1),
        borderRadius: BorderRadius.circular(8),
       ),
      ),
      SizedBox(height: 20),
      // Button to trigger text update
      CupertinoButton(
       onPressed: _updateText,
       color: CupertinoColors.black,
       child: Text(
        'Update Text',
        style: TextStyle(
         color: Colors.white,
        ), // Font color for the button text
       ),
      ),
      SizedBox(height: 20),
      // Display the text entered after button press
      Text('You entered: $_displayText', style: TextStyle(fontSize: 20)),
     ],
    ),
   ),
  );
 }
}


//main_material.dart
import 'package:flutter/material.dart';
void main() {
 runApp(MyApp());
}
class MyApp extends StatelessWidget {
 @override
 Widget build(BuildContext context) {
  return MaterialApp(
   home: MyPage(),
   debugShowCheckedModeBanner: false,
  );
 }
}
class MyPage extends StatefulWidget {
 @override
```

```
 _MyPageState createState() => _MyPageState();
}
class _MyPageState extends State<MyPage> {
 // Controller to capture the text input
 TextEditingController _controller = TextEditingController();
 // Variable to hold the text that will be shown after button press
 String _displayText = '';
 // Function to handle button press
 void _updateText() {
  setState(() {
   _displayText = _controller.text; // Update the displayed text
  });
 }
 @override
 Widget build(BuildContext context) {
  return Scaffold(
   appBar: AppBar(
    title: Text('Stateful Widget Example'),
    backgroundColor: Colors.white,
   ),
   backgroundColor: Colors.white,
   body: Padding(
    padding: EdgeInsets.all(16.0),
    child: Column(
     mainAxisAlignment: MainAxisAlignment.center,
     children: <Widget>[
      // Text field for user input
      TextField(
       controller: _controller,
       decoration: InputDecoration(
        labelText: 'Enter text',
       ),
      ),
      SizedBox(height: 20),
      // Button to trigger text update
      ElevatedButton(
       onPressed: _updateText,
       child: Text(
        'Update Text',
        style: TextStyle(
          fontSize: 20,
         color: Colors.white
        )
       ),
        style: ButtonStyle(
        backgroundColor: MaterialStateProperty.all(Colors.black),
       )
      ),
```

```
            SizedBox(height: 20),
            // Display the text entered after button press
            Text(
              'You entered: $_displayText',
              style: TextStyle(fontSize: 20),
            ),
          ],
        ),
      ),
    );
  }
}
```

Figure 10.4 depicts the rendered version of both the preceding code (Cupertino and material) on an iOS simulator:

Cupertino Material

Figure 10.4: *Rendered code on iOS device*

The key difference in the two version is visible in the widget rendered. The widget follows the respective style of the design system.

Note: **In practice most organization follows a customized design guideline that suit the branding guidelines. This decision has an impact on the kind of widget to be used during development. A hybrid UI/UX design that has overlap in design philosophy of material and Cupertino would be optimal when choosing Flutter for development.**

Flutter test framework

In the context of mobile development, the test strategies and tools that ensure the quality of mobile applications developed have been discussed in detail in *Chapter 5, Quality Assurance for Mobile Development*. In this chapter, the focus is on introducing the Flutter test framework. Any unit test written leveraging the capabilities of the Flutter Test library is essentially yet another Dart program. The test file which has the unit test for any Flutter application has to import the package **flutter_test**. The test cases are written inside the main method. This boilerplate repeats for each unit test file written. The individual unit test is written inside function with the expect matcher function as depicted below in the **Calculator** example. Consider the Dart class **Calculator** with the implementation for basic arithmetic operation of add, subtract, divide and multiply. The file naming convention for Dart ideally will be **calculator.dart** placed within the lib folder of a Flutter project. The best practice to name the test file is to start with the name of the file which has the class followed and adding the suffix **_test** to the same. The name recommendation for the unit test file for the class **calculator.dart** will be **calculator_test.dart**. The suffix **_test** is file name pattern used to identify the test file. This rule is configured by default in flutter unit test execution command-line tool.

Running the command **flutter test** would be sufficient to execute the unit test. All the test file inside the folder where the command is run with the pattern **_test** in the file name will be executed. If one must run only test for particular file the command to explicitly run would then be **flutter test <path to test file>**. The IDE of the flutter gives option to run the test via user interface click instead of command line as well.

There are various command line options available in context of the test. The exhaustive list can be obtained by typing **flutter test -h** on the CLI which has the Flutter configured. The following is the code for the **calculator.dart** and **calculator_test.dart**:

```
// lib/calculator.dart:
class Calculator {
  int add(int a, int b) => a + b;
  int subtract(int a, int b) => a - b;
  int multiply(int a, int b) => a * b;
  double divide(int a, int b) {
    if (b == 0) throw ArgumentError('Cannot divide by zero');
    return a / b;
  }
}

// test/calculator_test.dart:
import 'package:flutter_test/flutter_test.dart';
import 'package:hello_flutter/calculator.
dart'; // Import the Calculator class (adjust the path to your project)
void main() {
 group('Calculator Tests', () {
  Calculator? calculator;
  // Before each test, create a new instance of Calculator
  setUp(() {
   calculator = Calculator();
  });
  test('Addition of two numbers', () {
   expect(calculator?.add(5, 3), equals(8));
   expect(calculator?.add(-5, 3), equals(-2));
   expect(calculator?.add(0, 0), equals(0));
  });
```

```
    test('Subtraction of two numbers', () {
      expect(calculator?.subtract(5, 3), equals(2));
      expect(calculator?.subtract(3, 5), equals(-2));
      expect(calculator?.subtract(0, 0), equals(0));
    });
    test('Multiplication of two numbers', () {
      expect(calculator?.multiply(5, 3), equals(15));
      expect(calculator?.multiply(-5, 3), equals(-15));
      expect(calculator?.multiply(0, 5), equals(0));
    });
    test('Division of two numbers', () {
      expect(calculator?.divide(6, 2), equals(3));
      expect(calculator?.divide(5, 2), equals(2.5));
      expect(() => calculator?.divide(5, 0), throwsA(isA<ArgumentError>()));
    });
  });
}
```

The following is the list of the key components along their responsibilities in the unit test written in the preceding flutter codebase:

- **flutter_test** package is part of Flutter's testing suite and should be imported in every unit test. This package provides the APIs and the mechanism that the developer can leverage to craft the unit test.
- **setUp()** is the function that runs before each test and the above code uses it to initializes the **Calculator** instance before each test.
- **test()** function defines individual unit test cases and in the above codebase verifies the implementation of addition, subtraction, multiplication, and division of the **Calculator** class.
- **expect()** is the method that asserts the output with the expected outcome and is used to check the function's correctness.
- The **throwsA()** matcher function used inside the expect method verifies if the code under test throws an exception. The expect method in the above code validates the condition if an exception is thrown for division by zero.
- Like any Dart program one can notice the test file also has a **main** method as an entry point.

Conclusion

Learning a language is a continuous journey, however having the strong foundation will help any individual to take this journey with ease. The chapter presents a comparative overview of Swift, Kotlin and Dart, equipping the readers with similarity and nuances across the three languages laying a strong foundation. Acquiring speed will be a matter of practicing these concepts. Any advanced topics will now be an easy read which can be built on top of the current ideas. Learning is limitless as there are innovations and nuances coming out every now and then. The key modus operandi in a change driven world will be to have the ability to reason with abstract ideas. A top-down learning model where idea can be extrapolated and converted to action items while leveraging the skill on the ground could be ergonomic for individual.

Note that the chapter provides the entry to journey toward a polyglot and multilingual thought process in development. A polyglot programmer is the one who could think in terms of the host language. A polyglot programmer ideally will not translate construct from different language rather will be thinking in idioms and pattern of the language which the program is written. A polyglot programmer will have the capability to write the code in multiple programming languages. When changing a language an individual should not force-fit constructs from one into another; instead use the knowledge from one to find equivalent or alternative prevalent in the other. This would help in becoming a polyglot.

The next chapter focuses on introducing **Kotlin Multiplatform for Mobile** (**KMM**). The idea will be to understand the nuances of the framework and build a sample application.

Takeaway and reflection

Now that we have reached the end of the chapter, the reader shall be equipped with a familiarity with the three prominent languages in the mobile ecosystem with an overview of the Flutter framework. The following are some key themes discussed in the chapter:

- The programming languages Dart, Swift and Kotlin have a similarity in concepts and being proficient in one can help an individual transfer knowledge and skills to the other, to make learning faster.
- Each of the languages have keywords which have a special meaning which can be leveraged to build a logical program.
- Each platform uses the respective languages along with the framework to give the capability to the developer to build a mobile application.
- Dart does not directly support method overloading. However, one can mimic the behavior using the dynamic keyword or generics.
- The three languages provide mechanisms to design the code to handle an error/failure occurrence in the execution. The error thrown by a function can be handled with the try/catch keywords.
- Flutter framework is composed of Dart App, Flutter API (Framework), Engine, Embedder and Runner.
- Flutter UI development follows a box model layout. The developers must organize and write code to arrange the widget in row, column and z-index boxes to design UI.
- Flutter frameworks support the platform specific style, Cupertino and material. The Cupertino font will not be available due to licensing restrictions on platforms other than those of Apple devices.

CHAPTER 11
Kotlin Multiplatform for Mobile Development

Introduction

Mobile applications on the Android platform are built using Kotlin, the official language of the Android ecosystem. The Android **Software Development Kit** (**SDK**) is the API ecosystem that enables the development. The capabilities and tools provided with the Android SDK are used by developers to build **user interface** (**UI**) interacting with downstream systems. Thus, the application developed uses mobile computing power to connect the users with business functions. A developer working with the Android ecosystem in the early days used to develop the UI with an imperative layout mechanism. The developer in the imperative style of UI development had to explicitly specify the intent. With the advent of Jetpack Compose, there has been a shift towards a declarative style.

Kotlin subsequently expanded support to be compiled for other platforms under the umbrella name of Kotlin Multiplatform. Initially, the idea of supporting multiple platforms was not extended to UI. Kotlin with Android SDK for UI was only written specifically for the Android platform. When the capability of Kotlin Multiplatform is amalgamated with the idea of Jetpack Compose, the UI support extends beyond Android. This brought to the world the Compose Multiplatform UI framework. With the advent of Compose Multiplatform, the paradigm shift of building multiple targets and platforms came to the Kotlin ecosystem. This approach of cross-platform development got to be known in the community under the brand of **Kotlin Multiplatform** (**KMP**). Throughout this chapter, KMP refers to the broader cross-platform framework. The subset targeting mobile development on iOS and Android came to be known as **Kotlin Multiplatform Mobile** (**KMM**).

Structure

This chapter covers the following topics:

- Kotlin Multiplatform Mobile overview
- Render pipeline in Compose Multiplatform
- Hello KMM
- Movie app in KMM
- Challenges with KMM

Objectives

The chapter aims to serve as the entry point for building a mobile application with KMM. The theme followed throughout the chapter also serves as a broader context giving an introduction to Jetpack Compose for Android native development. This chapter intends to give insight into the KMM philosophy with relevant history. This chapter will help improve the reasoning capability of an individual. The awareness of cross-platform capabilities coexisting with the native framework of the Android ecosystem is the uniqueness that stands out in KMM.

Note that the code depicted in the chapter available in the companion repository of the book uses version Kotlin Multiplatform (2.1.0), Compose Multiplatform (1.7.0), Android Gradle Plugin (AGP) (8.5.2), Kotlin language version (2.1.0) and minimum Android SDK (24).

Kotlin Multiplatform Mobile overview

Kotlin was developed as a new language for the **Java Virtual Machine** (**JVM**). The language was made open source in February 2012. The language Kotlin was adopted as the official language supported by Android and announced at the Google I/O conference on May 17, 2017. The JetBrains team has evolved the language to add support for multiple platforms. KMP is the outcome of the team's ambitious goal to create a cross-platform development framework.

Note: **The language can be used to build software beyond mobile; however, in this chapter, the major focus will be on the iOS and Android platforms.**

The Android ecosystem was originally supporting only the imperative style of development for mobile apps, where the UI was developed on an XML-based layout, which had a one-to-one mapping with the programming language Java. Two years after the introduction of Kotlin, at the Google I/O event, the first preview of a declarative UI development framework was introduced, called Jetpack Compose. Jetpack Compose was the declarative alternative to the XML format for UI development in Android. There is a series of name transformations that have happened within this new framework. The names Compose and Kotlin Multiplatform have been used in multiple contexts with different interpretations. As the framework evolved to new names, the understanding got consolidated. A logical map of the evolution of the name is captured next. In the context of mobile, the latest categories of development possibilities grew, as follows:

- **Android native app with Jetpack Compose**: This category is an Android native mobile codebase that does not have shared logic for other targets. The codebase is fully based on the dependencies optimised and supported for Android.
- **iOS and Android app with Compose Multiplatform UI framework**: Mobile codebase with shared UI and logic is the second category. This project is referred to as Compose Multiplatform. The non-UI dependency used in the project is supported through Kotlin Multiplatform. The UI in the Compose Multiplatform follows the same principles of Jetpack Compose. Essentially, Compose Multiplatform extends Jetpack Compose to have multiplatform support.
- **iOS app with SwiftUI and KMM**: There is a third category where the codebase will only share the logic amongst multiple targets. The UI in this category will be written in platform native frameworks. For example, SwiftUI for iOS.

As of mid-2025, the Compose Multiplatform UI framework for iOS was marked as stable and production-ready. The feature around the core platform API of the native device requires the native layer access. The Compose Multiplatform cannot write shared logic for such a native API that will work across different platforms. The native platform API will be unified for multiple platforms via a bridge or wrapper. Developers expose native APIs to shared code by writing a platform-specific adapter using Kotlin's expect/actual mechanism explained later in the chapter. The internal working of Android for rendering is via Skia. Skia is the rendering engine and has been used even before Compose Multiplatform. The Skia Graphics Library is a 2D graphics API that works with the **graphics processing unit** (**GPU**) for rendering and is used for Compose Multiplatform as well. *Figure 11.1* represents the internal functioning of different kinds of KMM apps:

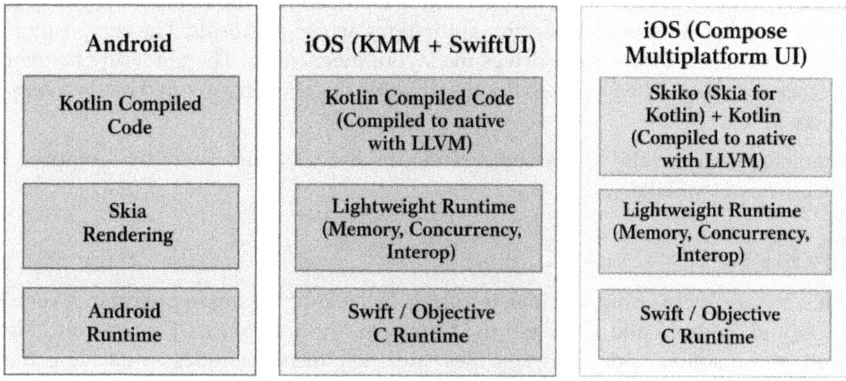

***Figure 11.1**: Components enabling KMM on iOS and Android*

Android works with **Android runtime** (**ART**). ART is not the same as JVM; rather, its function is to do the ahead-of-time compilation of the bytecode to native machine code during installation. ART thus plays a role similar to the JVM, but it is not literally the JVM. However, unlike Android which relies on ART, iOS has no **virtual machine** (**VM**) equivalent. Kotlin is natively lowered (compiled step-by-step) via **Low Level Virtual Machine** (**LLVM**) infrastructure to machine code that can interoperate with the Swift or Objective-C runtime. After lowering the machine code, the Kotlin executable still requires a lightweight runtime that helps manage the foundational structure, memory management, concurrency, and compatibility with the platform's native language. This ideology thus enables the native iOS app to interoperate in the KMM world. The iOS app with the Compose Multiplatform UI framework, on the other hand, has two components: the Skiko (otherwise known as Skia for Kotlin) and the natively compiled Kotlin codebase for logic. Skiko is a low-level library that uses the Skia rendering engine for the screen. Skiko glues the Compose Multiplatform UI to the rendering context, drawing the screen components while running on iOS.

Render pipeline in Compose Multiplatform

In the Compose rendering model drawing can be abstracted into four fundamental blocks. These blocks are:

- Canvas to draw primitives
- A collection of primitives (shapes)
- A scene graph for applying transformation to shapes
- States that control which content is rendered

Composing these blocks will give the necessary UI. The UI is controlled based on data, which are called states. The state is the data that can be changed to trigger a re-rendering of the content of the composable UI. The state can be used to decide what combination of the composable UI should be composed together to render a UI on the screen. This explanation is the abridged workflow of any code used for the presentation of elements on screen. The workflow is encapsulated and exposed as the API of the UI library called the Compose UI. The fundamental element a developer will use in the Compose UI is the **`composable`**. **`Composable`** is the label given to different types that can be combined, representing the code to draw a user interface onto a screen. The platform does the heavy lifting of the common usable composable elements for any project. These form the foundational UI components and can be used as is in the codebase.

For a Compose Multiplatform project on Android, the entry point activity inherits from the **`ComponentActivity`** class. The first or entry composable acts as a top-level container for the application. The first **`ComponentActivity`** class will have this first composable set as the content. The **`ComponentActivity`** has a member variable that accepts the type **`AbstractComposeView`**, and the first composable gets attached to this entry activity. The **`AbstractComposeView`** hosts the responsibility to channel and connect Skia with the Compose engine. The layer also translates the UI onto the canvas. Skia does the heavy lifting of all the graphics operations for Compose UI.

Skia handles all the low-level 2D graphics operations, making it possible for the Compose engine to efficiently render graphics, manage complex UI layouts, and perform animations across-platforms. The composition tree, which is a compiled encoding for the composable view, drives the layout mechanism. The rendering happens next, which is powered by the Compose engine. The Skia executes the drawing instruction provided by the Compose engine, and thus the UI is rendered.

For iOS, the mechanism is structurally the same for rendering the UI written with the Compose UI. The internal working uses APIs powered by Skiko.

Hello KMM

As is customary in software engineering, the idea is to start by creating a sample project in KMM. The HelloKMM project caters to iOS and Android and leverages the Compose Multiplatform UI framework. *Figure 11.2* depicts the folder structure of the source code with key files and their responsibilities in enabling the cross-platform development for iOS and Android:

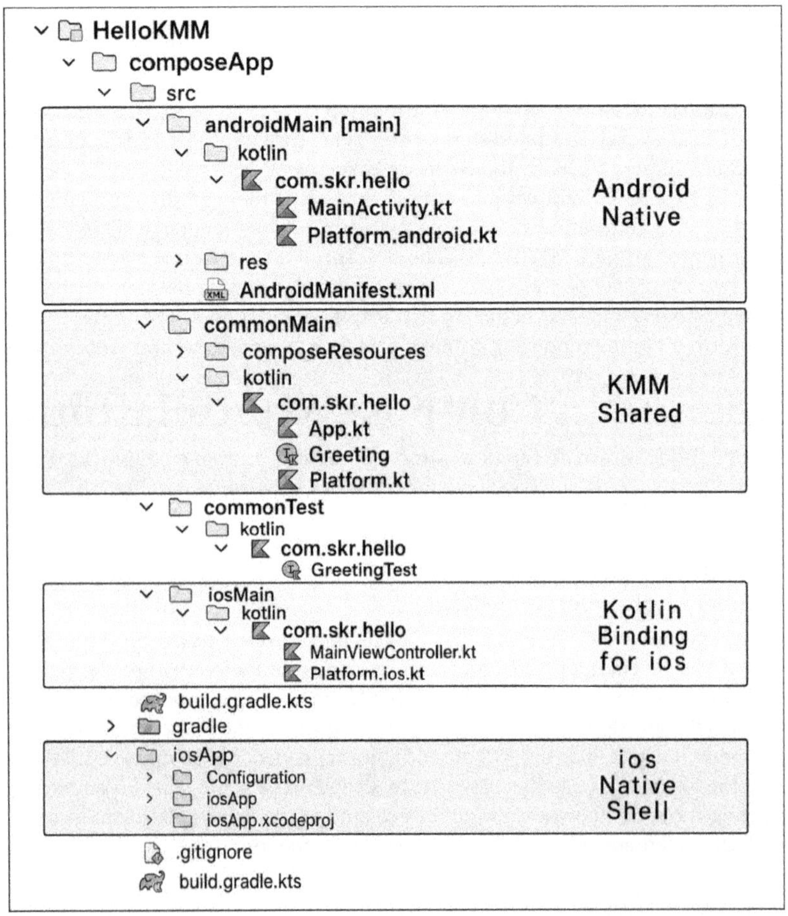

***Figure 11.2**: Project folder structure of HelloKMM*

JetBrains has provided a Kotlin Multiplatform Wizard to create the boilerplate project starter. The appendix has a reference to the website. The name of the project, details, and the target platform can be selected with the appropriate option mentioned previously for iOS and Android to generate the base project. The KMM project can be created from Android Studio as well; however, the templates available may not be identical to those generated in the Kotlin Multiplatform Wizard.

Most of the codebase should ideally be in the folder **commonMain**, which hosts the Shared UI and the business logic. The **androidMain** and **iosMain** have the entry point to the first composable view registered with Android and iOS, respectively.

In the narrative, the usage of the term source set may startle the reader. The same is used interchangeably to reference a particular folder in the HelloKMM project. Source sets are folders with a logical grouping and means to organize codebases that are logically together. The codebase in the source set can be targeted to one or multiple platforms and holds Kotlin code and other assets. The source set could be platform-specific or shared components. The **commonMain**, **androidMain**, and **iosMain** will be found in the folder structure within the KMM project, and represent examples of a few source sets. Each of these has the respective test folders as well, which are themselves additional source sets.

Let us explore the code inside **MainActivity.kt** and **MainViewController.kt**. These files have a composable function **App** set as the initial view for Android and iOS, respectively:

```
//MainActivity.kt
package com.skr.hello
import android.os.Bundle
import androidx.activity.ComponentActivity
import androidx.activity.compose.setContent
import androidx.compose.runtime.Composable
class MainActivity : ComponentActivity() {
   override fun onCreate(savedInstanceState: Bundle?) {
       super.onCreate(savedInstanceState)
       setContent {
           App()
       }
   }
}
```

MainActivity.kt file has the code that connects Compose Multiplatform UI with the Android application. Once the application starts, the entry point to the user interface originates from this activity class. The composable function **App** is attached using the **setContent** method on the main activity. Along similar lines, the iOS application has the **ViewController** configured as the root and initial controller. In the case of the KMM, a custom class **ComposeUIViewController**, which is packaged as part of the KMM framework, is used. The initial **ViewController** is an instance of the same. The composable function **App** is attached as the content for the **ComposeUIViewController** class. The code for the same is written in the **MainViewController.kt** file depicted in the following code. The file is part of the **iOSMain** source set specific to the iOS platform.

```
//MainViewController.kt
package com.skr.hello
import androidx.compose.ui.window.ComposeUIViewController
fun MainViewController() = ComposeUIViewController { App() }
```

Note: **A simplified definition of the ViewController is the controller class that manages the UI in the iOS ecosystem. The base class provided by the iOS framework is UIViewController.**

MainActivity.kt is in the **androidMain** source set, and **MainViewController.kt** is in the **iosMain** source set. This source set is appropriately compiled and bundled with the respective targets. The underlying native tools are used along with the necessary project dependencies to build and package the code. *Figure 11.2* shows the project folder structure, which includes the iOS native shell (the iosApp folder at the bottom of the tree). The native shell, along with the Kotlin shared code, gets compiled and packaged, which is shipped as the mobile application. **ContentView.swift**, depicted as follows, represents the code that connects the native iOS to the KMM runtime:

```
//ContentView.swift
import UIKit
import SwiftUI
import ComposeApp
struct ComposeView: UIViewControllerRepresentable {
    func makeUIViewController(context: Context) -> UIViewController {
        MainViewControllerKt.MainViewController()
    }
    func updateUIViewController(_ uiViewController: UIViewController, context: Context) {}
}
struct ContentView: View {
    var body: some View {
        ComposeView()
                .ignoresSafeArea(.keyboard) // Compose has own keyboard handler
    }
}
```

In the preceding codebase, the **import ComposeApp** line of code represents the reference to the compiled version of the **commonMain** source set along with the **iosMain** binding. The symbols from KMM are now available for the native Swift to consume inside the iOS native codebase. The import **ComposeApp** inside the iOS native codebase exposes the method **MainViewControllerKt.MainViewController()**. The code invokes the **MainViewControllerKt.MainViewController()** and connects the KMM entry UI with iOS. When the code is executed, the native layer passes control to the composable function **App** by the method invoked inside the **ComposeUIViewController,** as explained earlier. The responsibility further lies with the code written inside the **commonMain** shared source set, handling the functioning of the application.

Expected and actual keywords

Kotlin has the capability to write platform-specific implementations. The adapter pattern is used to expose platform-specific functionality to share code. There will be an adapter exposed as an abstraction to bridge the respective native implementation. The Kotlin language has two keywords to achieve the same. The **expect** keyword defines the abstraction, and the **actual** keyword is used to connect the implementation for each of the different platforms. The **HelloKMM** project has an example for the usage of these keywords.

The interface **Platform** is defined in the **Platform.kt** in the **commonMain** folder, and in the same file, a function, **getPlatform**, to return the instance of **Platform** is written. The **getPlatform** is marked with **expect**. Essentially, the **expect** keyword conveys that there exists a function **getPlatform** returning an instance of the type **Platform**. The **expect** keyword gives the indication that the method does not have implementation written in **commonMain;** rather, each target platform separately implements the respective code in the platform layer. In summary one can see that the **expect** keyword declares the abstraction in shared code, and the **actual** keyword marks each platform-specific implementation. The following is the code for this simple abstraction. In the following, a string value **name** is defined to have a separate value on each of the target platforms:

```
//Platform.kt
package com.skr.hello
interface Platform {
    val name: String
}
expect fun getPlatform(): Platform
```

The **Platform** interface defined can be used as any normal Kotlin interface elsewhere in the code. The **HelloKMM** project uses the **Platform** in the **Greeting** class, declared as a variable depicted in the following codebase:

```
//Greeting.kt
package com.skr.hello
class Greeting {
    private val platform = getPlatform()
    fun greet(): String {
        return greet(platform.name)
    }
    fun greet(str: String): String {
        return "Hello, ${str}!"
    }
}
```

The greet method, when invoked, will call the implementation, which gets compiled and bundled on the respective platform. The actual specific implementation will be in both **androidMain** and **iosMain** source sets, respectively, in the project. The compilation maps the respective platform implementation to the abstraction. The following is the codebase for implementation for Android and iOS in the respective source set:

```
//Platform.android.kt
package com.skr.hello
import android.os.Build
class AndroidPlatform : Platform {
    override val name: String = "Android ${Build.VERSION.SDK_INT}"
}
actual fun getPlatform(): Platform = AndroidPlatform()

//Platform.ios.kt
package com.skr.hello
import platform.UIKit.UIDevice
class IOSPlatform: Platform {
    override val name: String = UIDevice.currentDevice.systemName() + " " + UIDevice.
currentDevice.systemVersion
}
actual fun getPlatform(): Platform = IOSPlatform()
```

The two files **Platform.android.kt** and **Platform.ios.kt** have the implementation of the **getPlatform** method. The method is prefixed with the **actual** keyword. The Android and iOS return the respective instance of the native API implementation. On Android, the **name** property is set to the string 'Android' concatenated SDK integer version (e.g., 'Android 35'). On iOS, it is set to the device's system name and version (e.g., 'iOS 18.0'). These details come from the package **android.os.Build** and **platform.UIKit.UIDevice.** The package **android.os.Build** is compatible as is with the KMM ecosystem. The package **platform.UIKit.UIDevice**, on the other hand, is the bridge and exposes the native API for the toolkit supporting iDevices. Their API is made compatible with the KMM ecosystem and is accessible from Kotlin code. A pattern similar to this can be followed to expose the native API to the **commonMain** source set. The maturity of the KMM platform will evolve as more such adapters become available. The convenience of using the cross-platform will also improve with the availability of adapters, as the team will be able to consume without reinventing from scratch.

The philosophy of the highest common factors applies to such native API abstraction. The preceding code is an example where a single API is a bridge to provide platform specific implementation. If one platform did not support a particular feature, writing an API common to all platforms cannot be achieved. As noted earlier, the KMM has

Kotlin that is lowered to platform native symbols to interoperate with Swift and Objective-C, in iDevices, thereby enabling access to the API and framework exposed by the native ecosystem. Invoking platform code becomes necessary in the case where the capabilities are not available in the **commonMain** source set. The capabilities that are hardware-specific will also not be accessible as a common API, by default. The **android.os.Build** and **platform.UIKit.UIDevice** are examples of such an API that is not accessible commonly. These packages are the result of contributors who undertook the effort to write the abstraction bringing these together, with the help of **expect** and **actual** keywords in Kotlin.

KMM build lifecycle and ecosystem

Every project or workspace is a collection of code working together. The project, when compiled and packaged, transforms into the mobile application for the target platform. The IDE and the associated ecosystem form the support system, providing convenience to developers while developing an application. The transformation of code to artifacts is called the build lifecycle. The build lifecycle in KMM is coordinated through Gradle, which has the script and configuration that can be modified to tweak the lifecycle as per the project's needs. *Table 11.1* summarizes the responsibilities of the Gradle script:

Responsibility	Details
Setting up project configuration	The project structure and configuration for the various targets supported by KMM are handled by configuring Gradle.
Managing dependency with versioning and synchronization	The dependencies for the shared and target-specific codebase are defined in the Gradle file. These can be separately configured for each source set. The versions of these dependencies are tracked and kept in sync. Gradle ensures the targets have the correct versions available during the build process.
Compile and build a project	The Gradle coordinates the compilation of the Kotlin to the respective target, and in the case of iOS, produces a framework or app bundle.
Packaging and distribution	Gradle manages the packaging to create the artifacts and distribute it for targets. The Gradle shall internally use the underlying native tools for the respective platform, abstracted from the end user.
Build flavors and customization	The case where one codebase is used to create multiple artifacts for the same target can be configured with Gradle. In a typical development, the build flavor is used to separate the production and lower environments.
Defining target configuration	Gradle can be used to define a target with separate configurations for each. The platform-specific settings for the targets are also configured. The platform-specific settings for the respective targets are defined and applied according to the project's Gradle configuration.

***Table 11.1**: Overview of Gradle build tool responsibilities*

Table 11.1 covers a subset of the various responsibilities of Gradle, listing those relevant to KMM.

commonMain

The **commonMain** source set is responsible for hosting the shared logic and the UI within the Compose Multiplatform UI framework. A true cross-platform application should place the maximum code written for the application in this source set. The **App.kt** file has the implementation of the entry point to the UI. The entry point to the UI is the first occurrence of a Composable view in the Compose Multiplatform application. This composable function gets attached to the **MainActivity** for Android and the **MainViewController** for iOS. The codebase inside **App.kt** is depicted as follows:

```
//App.kt
package com.skr.hello
import androidx.compose.animation.*
import androidx.compose.foundation.*
import androidx.compose.foundation.layout.*
import androidx.compose.material.*
import androidx.compose.runtime.*
import androidx.compose.ui.*
import org.jetbrains.compose.*
import hellokmm.composeapp.generated.resources.Res
import hellokmm.composeapp.generated.resources.compose_multiplatform
import org.jetbrains.compose.resources.*
@Composable
fun App() {
   MaterialTheme {
       var showContent by remember { mutableStateOf(false) }
       Column(Modifier.fillMaxWidth(), horizontalAlignment = Alignment.CenterHorizontally) {
           Button(onClick = { showContent = !showContent }) {
               Text("Click me!")
           }
           AnimatedVisibility(showContent) {
               val greeting = remember { Greeting().greet() }
               Column(Modifier.fillMaxWidth(), horizontalAlignment = Alignment.
CenterHorizontally) {
                   Image(painterResource(Res.drawable.compose_multiplatform),  "Compose
Multiplatform logo")
                   Text("Compose: $greeting")
               }
           }
       }
   }
}
```

The code in the file starts with the **`@Composable`** annotation after the import statements. The annotation is attached to the Kotlin function named **`App`**. Marking the function with this annotation is the first step for writing any Composable. The composable function acts as the parent block, which can host other composable views. In principle, any application should start with **`MaterialTheme`** Composable as the top node in the view hierarchy. The **`MaterialTheme`** composable, which is the entry point, serves as the container to host the hierarchy of views that are constructed in the declarative structure. The developer shall combine the other composable views (custom or inbuilt) to build the screen required for the application. This approach is similar to the box UI model approach explained in *Chapter 10, Introduction to Swift, Kotlin, and Dart*, in the context of Flutter.

After running the codebase written in the file, **`App.kt`**, the UI will be rendered to a screen. The preceding code will have a vertically aligned button, image, and text. The logic written in the above code hides the text in the initial load of the composable. The button click triggers the state to change and display the text and image.

The button, which is a composable view, has an **`onClick`** action to specify the logic and the composable content to be rendered as UI for the button. In the codebase previously discussed, the text with the **Click me!** string is configured in the code to be rendered for a button.

Every composable view has data associated. This data is static or dynamic in nature. The data decides how a composable behaves and defines the content, which is called its state. The state is used to coordinate the user interaction and feedback in an application. The state management for the composable view is done with the concept of captured value with the respective APIs such as **`remember`** combined with **`mutableStateOf`.** The following is the syntax from the previous codebase depicting the state value usage:

```
var showContent by remember { mutableStateOf(false) }
```

Any change in the captured value is listened to, by the composable, and the change triggers a redraw of the screen for the specific section for the modified state data.

The next section gets into **`@Composable`** and its internal working. The idea is to look at the schematic description that logically represents the physical implementation of a **`@Composable`** annotation. Understanding this will give a clear picture of how the Compose UI functions.

> Note: **The annotation feature is supported in Kotlin. An annotation enables a developer to add meta information to a code structure, thus adding more meaning to it. The annotation is used as a mechanism to reduce the boilerplate code. By annotating code, the responsibility will be on the compiler/runtime to leverage the pre-written logic added to the annotated code. The prewritten code otherwise should be manually repeated in multiple places, which is now achieved with a one-line annotation.**

Composable internals

The syntax structure of composable is an example of **domain-specific language** (**DSL**) written using the Kotlin language structures. The Compose DSL, when compiled, gets lowered to the Skia drawing instruction or commands. The Skia drawing instructions are then transformed to the format rendered on the screen. The literal meaning of composition is the nature of something's ingredients or constituents. A composition can be seen as the way in which a whole or mixture is made up. A parallel can be drawn in the context of composable as well. A composable is used to create a visual screen appropriate for a mobile application screen representation by bringing together and mixing many other composable views.

Referring to the official documentation, one can find that **composer** is the core of any Composable. Composer is implicitly passed to every **`@Composable`** function by the **Compose Compiler Plugin**. The composer has the following three responsibilities:

- Create the composition as a tree.
- Keep track of the data and detect the changes to the data.
- Re-compute the composition based on the data changes.

The format of the composable function is represented in the following pseudocode:

```
@Composable
fun ComposableView() {

      OtherComposableView {
        SomeOtherComposableView {
        }
      }
      OtherComposableView {
        YetAnotherComposableView {
        }
      }
}
```

This pseudocode has the function marked with the **`@Composable`** annotation. There are other composable views nested at the peer level. The composer runtime will do the magic of converting the declaration to a version that can be rendered onto the screen. The pseudocode does not depict the state. The following rewritten version adds the state to the composable view, which has the captured value to control the data represented on the screen:

```
@Composable
fun ComposableView() {
        OtherComposableView {
         var stateForOtherComposableView by remember { mutableStateOf(someState) }
    SomeOtherComposableView {
          var innerState by remember { mutableStateOf(someOtherState) }
         }
        }
        OtherComposableView {
   YetAnotherComposableView {
   //Other composable view
         }
        }
}
```

Every composable cannot have a nested structure and act as a container. Some of the composable serve a single purpose, such as interaction or representing information. *Table 11.2* lists some examples of the composable types along with the responsibilities:

Type	Examples	Responsibilities
Basic UI	Text, Image, Button	Display content
Layout	Column, Row, Box, LazyColumn	Arrange elements
Interactive	TextField, Checkbox, Slider	User input and actions
Scaffold based	Scaffold, TopAppBar, BottomNavigation	Full-screen structure
State and effects	remember, LaunchedEffect	Handle state and lifecycle
Animations	AnimatedVisibility, Crossfade	Add motion effects

***Table 11.2**: Composable UI types, examples, and responsibilities*

Unit testing

In a cross-platform application, the majority of code will be written in **commonMain**. The unit test, thus, should also be primarily on the logic within the **commonMain** source set. The unit test for the Kotlin file **Greeting.kt** is depicted as follows:

```
//GreetingTest.kt
package com.skr.hello
import kotlin.test.Test
import kotlin.test.assertEquals
class GreetingTest {
   @Test
   fun testGreet() {
       val greeting = Greeting()
       val result = greeting.greet("Kotlin")
       assertEquals("Hello, Kotlin!", result)
   }
```

```
    @Test
    fun testGreetWithEmptyName() {
        val greeting = Greeting()
        val result = greeting.greet("")
        assertEquals("Hello, !", result)
    }
}
```

The package **`kotlin.test`** is added as a dependency to the **`commonTest`** source set defined in the **`build.gradle.kts`**. If the **`commonTest`** folder is not there by default, it is recommended to create the folder at the same level as **`commonMain`**.

The test annotation is used to mark the function as a test. The test declaration, act, and assertion are the three components written for any unit test and are depicted in the preceding code. The same structure can be followed to write unit tests corresponding to other implementations in **`commonMain`**.

Movie app in KMM

HelloKMM was the exploration of the default starter boilerplate created with the KMM Wizard. Next, the idea is to expand the learning by creating a simple list backed by hardcoded data. A Search text field will be added with the logic to do a simple text search on the title value of list items. The search will filter the list, and the result will be displayed to the end user.

To begin with, follow the KMM Wizard to create the project named Movies. Open the project in the Android Studio IDE. It is recommended to check out the code associated with the chapter for reference. The major focus in the section will be on the **`commonMain`** folder. *Figure 11.3* depicts the end outcome for the application:

***Figure 11.3:** Android and iOS movie list page*

The view depicted in *Figure 11.3* can be divided logically into a **Container** view hosting two sections. The top section is the search **textfield**, and the other section is the movie list. The movie list has repeating items, the **MovieRows**. The data backing the movies list in this codebase is a hardcoded list of **Movie** objects with name, description, and image URL. In an actual use case, this could be fetched from a backend service or a database.

The following code is written for the **MovieRow**:

```
//MovieRow.kt
@Composable
fun MovieRow(movie: Movie) {
    Box(
        modifier = Modifier
            .padding(4.dp)
            .border(2.dp, Color.Gray, shape = RoundedCornerShape(8.dp))
            .padding(8.dp)
    ) {
        Row(
            modifier = Modifier
                .fillMaxWidth()
                .padding(8.dp),
            verticalAlignment = Alignment.CenterVertically
        ) {
            Box(
                modifier = Modifier.size(40.dp)
            ) {
                PlaceholderMovieImage()
            }
            Column {
                Text(
                    text = movie.title,
                    style = MaterialTheme.typography.h6,
                    maxLines = 1,
                    overflow = TextOverflow.Ellipsis
                )
                Text(
                    text = movie.description,
                    style = MaterialTheme.typography.body2,
                    maxLines = 1,
                    overflow = TextOverflow.Ellipsis
                )
            }
        }
    }
}
@Composable
fun PlaceholderMovieImage() {
    val painter = painterResource(Res.drawable.video_file_icon)
    Image(painter = painter, contentDescription = "My Image")
}
```

There are two composable views in the preceding code: **PlaceholderMovieImage** and **MovieRow**. The **PlaceholderMovieImage** is used as the image icon for the list, which takes the **Res.drawable.video_file_icon** resource added in the drawable folder of the **commonMain**. The **MovieRow** takes a data class **Movie**. The **Movie** object has the title and the description set to two **Text** components. The **Text** component is set with the style and other properties. The code has a composable component **Column**, which helps in vertically arranging multiple child views, and the **Row**, which helps in the horizontal arrangement of the children. The combination of these **@Composable** is configured inside **MovieRow**. **MovieRow** represents each item in the list.

Note: **Android does not support scalable vector graphics (SVG) directly. The image should be added as the ImageVector with the Android Studio IDE. In KMM, when using Compose Multiplatform, the same method to configure the vector asset could be followed to add resources to the commonMain. Adding to commonMain makes these available for shared development for all platforms.**

The **MovieRow** will now be iterated over a list of data. The following code is the **MovieList** composable:

```
@Composable
fun MovieList(movies: List<Movie>) {
    LazyColumn {
        items(movies) { movie ->
            MovieRow(movie = movie)
        }
    }
}
```

The list of movie items is passed in the signature inside a **LazyColumn** composable. **LazyColumn** is provided by the framework. Unlike the **Column**, the **LazyColumn** is designed for loading items as they appear on the screen instead of loading all the items of the list together, which is memory-intensive.

The following code is for the search section composable view. The composable function has its signature as a string and a closure function. The signature ensures the search view is configurable to bind the text entered by the user. The closure function is to observe the value change action. The action is triggered when the user enters or modifies the **textfield** value, as follows:

```
@Composable
fun SearchBar(query: String, onQueryChange: (String) -> Unit) {
    OutlinedTextField(
        value = query,
        onValueChange = { onQueryChange(it) },
        label = { Text("Search Movies") },
        keyboardOptions = KeyboardOptions.Default.copy(
            imeAction = ImeAction.Search
        ),
        modifier = Modifier.fillMaxWidth()
    )
}
```

Combining all the composable views together in the container view, as depicted in the following code, will produce the expected page shown in *Figure 11.3*:

```
@Composable
fun MovieAppHomeScreen() {
    var searchQuery by remember { mutableStateOf("") }
    var filteredMovies by remember { mutableStateOf(movieList) }
```

```
    Column(modifier = Modifier.padding(16.dp)) {
        SearchBar(query = searchQuery, onQueryChange = { query ->
            searchQuery = query
            filteredMovies = movieList.filter { it.title.contains(query, ignoreCase = true) }
        })
        Spacer(modifier = Modifier.height(8.dp))
        MovieList(movies = filteredMovies)
    }
}
```

The **MovieAppHomeScreen** in the preceding code is the container that hosts the two-section search text field and the list. The filtering logic is implemented in the **onQueryChange** closure. The state change will trigger the closure, which filters the data, reloading the content in the list.

Challenges with KMM

The following are the top challenges to KMM adoption:

- Early stage for iOS ecosystem support. KMM is in the catch-up race with alternatives as of September 2025.
- Tooling and IDE support have not reached the finesse for all the supported platforms.
- Learning curve for non-Android developers.
- Third-party library compatibility.
- Binary size.
- Community and documentation compared to existing cross-platform players.

KMM is evolving. A team that decides to choose KMM as the technology strategy may face a shortage of readily available reusable components that support all the platform features. As the ecosystem evolves, the expectation is that the maturity of the KMM will grow. Only time will determine the adoption rate of KMM. KMM may or may not get the fair share of cross-platform development adoption. The core theme of cross-platform for KMM is that the native Android official language and its surrounding toolchain are extended to target iOS. Such an ideology ensures that even if cross-platform does not prevail, the technology underneath, backing the native Android, will be a worthwhile learning that can be carried forward by learning KMM. This makes the KMM unique as a technology to learn.

Conclusion

Kotlin and the surrounding development ecosystem are topics worthy of a separate book. However, the idea of this chapter was to give the reasoning toolkit and familiarity with the Android ecosystem. The journeys from introducing the Kotlin language in *Chapter 10, Introduction to Swift, Kotlin, and Dart,* to building a one-page sample application using KMM, covers significant ground. This lays the foundation for deeper exploration in the topic. The next step for the reader will be to take this learning forward and build additional features on the sample project shared. Exploring the other APIs of the development framework will enrich skills in KMM. Such an approach will thus empirically ground the concepts learned and build the platform-specific nuance for an individual to anchor their journey toward becoming a specialist in KMM.

In the next chapter, a special classification of mobile application called the Super App will be explored, and in the process, we will build a Toy Super App for iOS, leveraging the frameworks provided by the native platform.

Takeaways and reflections

This chapter has given familiarity with the KMM ecosystem and kick-started the journey into the world of KMM and Jetpack Compose as well:

- KMM adoption as of 2025 is in the phase of growth. As the community surrounding the ecosystem contributes to reusable capability, it would aid the reach of KMM to a critical mass of end users to build production-ready applications. Such a situation will be a win that promotes the adoption.
- An organisation that would not have the budget leverage to contribute back to the ecosystem should weigh the use case of KMM adoption in its early stages.
- An organisation with a strong Android market with relatively fewer iDevice users could benefit from the KMM approach.
- The language semantics and the benefit of the native development and the tooling are directly available without migration overhead.
- Composable is the smallest unit of UI that can be combined to create the experience for the end user of a mobile application. @Composable is an annotation that can be marked on a function or closure to transform it into a Composable view in KMM.
- Anything that comes with the commonMain source set is the shared codebase. In order to maximize the benefit of the cross-platform approach, the application developer should aim to develop within the commonMain source set.
- An iOS shell (Xcode project) will package the binary created from the common shared Kotlin codebase from the KMM.
- KMM has built the capability to write an abstraction to access the platform's native functionality. The platform's native features, which use the API of a closed-source platform, require the abstraction created with Kotlin to be invoked via native bindings.
- The build generation process and the deployment process would remain the same as those for the respective platform.
- Gradle is the tool used to manage the lifecycle of the build. Gradle is where the dependency, the key configuration, and the version of the tools and dependencies involved are defined.

Chapter 12
Use Case of Developing a Super App

Introduction

The Super App is the buzzword that revolutionized mobile development. The name Super App in the chapter denotes a mobile application which is an all-encompassing self-contained service or product offering from an organization. One should not misunderstand the Super App name to its literal meaning of being a great app. Super Application takes a platform approach towards building a product and services provided to the end consumer via mobile app. Building a Super App requires a strong will with technical and operational acumen for an organization. Typically, the organization targeting Super App as the strategy should prioritize long-term strategic position over short-term success. There is a possibility of encountering setbacks and learning when taking this journey. The organization needs to either accept such a situation or find alternatives for problems encountered without taking shortcuts in the Super App journey. An organization thriving in current business with a simple mobile application may plan to extend the growth by developing Super App. In such a case the established team should focus on optimizing the technology layer and add additional product that attracts users or enhance the feature provided in the application. Such a strategy should be adopted to ensure the growth.

The organization started as an early bird in the industry with Super App vision would have to ensure many cycles of experiments. These players in the market would have had their fair share of setbacks and success in building Super Apps. Learning from such a group could provide an edge with a good head start for a successor. For any new organization having individuals who have gone through the journey previously can accelerate the efficacy while building a Super App.

The themes explored in the chapter are centered around the challenges one may encounter and the best practices that one should follow while developing a Super App. The chapter gives awareness of the subtle difference while devising strategies to build a mobile app that scales to a monstrous-sized codebase. The challenges encountered while developing a mobile app that provides interconnected services vary from those of developing a mobile application that provides multiple independent services. The variation is primarily in the ways of working and coordination. The mobile application with multiple independent products is analogous to an aggregator mobile application. The chapter will give a top-down overview of building such an application.

Structure

This chapter covers the following topics:

- Topology of Super App
- Components of Super App
- Unique learnings from past
- Dependency management
- Toy Super App

Objectives

By the end of the chapter, the reader will become aware of the term Super App and the intricacies surrounding it. In the mobile world, getting to build a Super App from the ground up is a once in a lifetime opportunity. The chance of working in such an engagement will push forward the intellectual maturity for an individual in mobile development. This chapter will be the stepping-stone for such a journey. The last section of the chapter will be to build a Toy Super App using SwiftUI for iOS. The chapter ends by ensuring readers leave with an empirically grounded understanding of the Super App.

Topology of Super App

Super App is an overused term as any organization can make the audacious claim where the mobile application built by their team is a Super App. In some cases, the organization will be focusing on the literal meaning of the word *super* to indicate that the mobile application is something great. In the strictest sense of technology lens, the audacious claim of being a Super App gets satisfied when there is a monstrous sized code base managed by a large sized team of individuals developing features.

The technology definition explained above can be visually ascertained from the topological view of a hypothetical Super App as depicted in *Figure 12.1*:

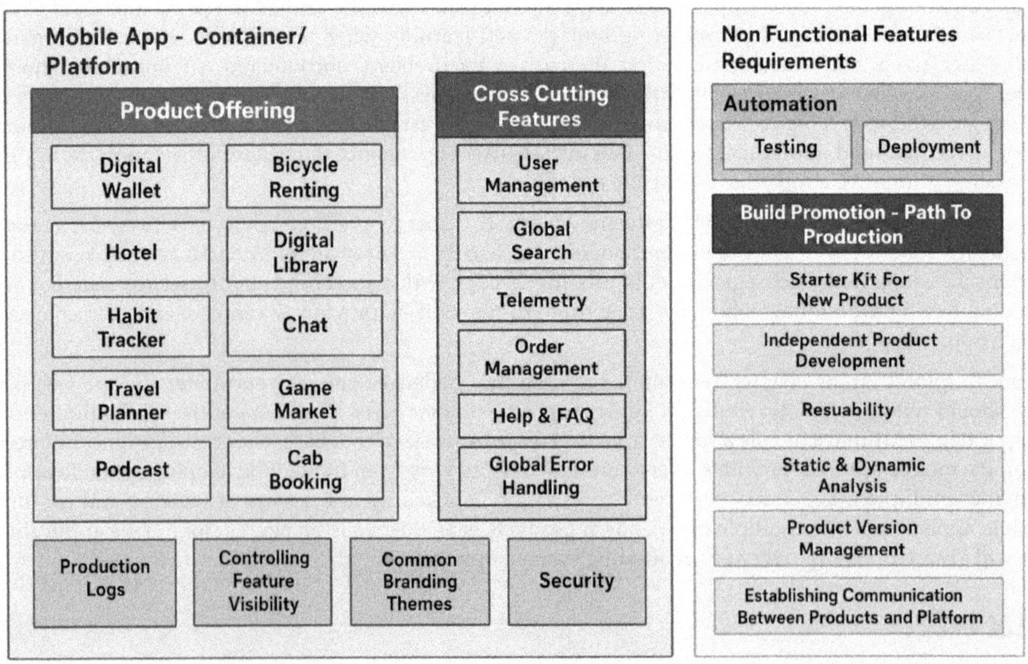

***Figure 12.1**: Hypothetical Super App: topology view*

Organizations typically starting from a small product offering targeting growth will look at mobile as one of the channels to expand the business. Such organizations tend to play the infinite game in the industry by expanding the reach of the product or adding additional product offering. The above depicted hypothetical Super App is a representation of such an idea. The interesting aspect to understand is that any organization can acquire the technology required to build such an offering. However, to be operationally relevant in the market the organization should have a strong product strategy. In short such an engagement should have a strong foundation in the business model along with the technology stability. A top-down nature of execution and repeating patterns will be the trait required for the engagement. If a strong business model foundation and technology stability are not maintained, it could pave the way for an unsustainable state affecting the existence for the organization. A top-down nature of execution implies structuring boundary and the super set of practices to be followed in the codebase first. The implementation of these along with the features shall happen within the boundaries adhering to the practices. The implementation shall happen bottom up within these guidelines.

There was a time when mobile applications were smaller in size and served a minimal set of functionalities. However, those times have passed, and nowadays mobile applications go through sophistication within themselves. The size of codebase is also huge where the demand for releasing the product in shorter time to market pushes the leader to adopt strategy of adding more people and getting the work done faster. This strategy of parallel stream of work necessitates investing in the factors that make such a journey possible in the development phase.

This now brings an interesting correlation for creating two possibilities: a mobile app with a separate independent product and a mobile application which is monster-sized but offers related services. The challenges encountered while developing a mobile app that provides interrelated services differ in comparison with those of a mobile application that could serve a totally independent product. The mobile application which serves totally independent products is analogous to an aggregator mobile application whereas the mobile app that provides interconnected features will be a single codebase having closely knit services and possibility of inseparable dependency with each other. The latter will be operationally challenging and can be compared to a standard mobile application but at an enormous scale, with a far larger codebase and team. If the operational challenges are excluded and looked at both these kinds of mobile applications through a technology lens, a common problem statement emerges. The problem statement in front of the team will be to manage monster-sized codebase and to be able to run parallel stream of development on the same. Both application kinds will have strategic and implementation similarities at the technology layer.

Retail domain example app

A retail organization selling apparel had a flourishing business in the area with a strong customer base. The organization wanted to grow horizontally. The idea is to leverage technology to bring additional products to end user, improve standard of living of the customer and bring returns to the organization. The current ecosystem of the organization was equivalent to a large store selling apparels with both digital and walk-in stores. The existing mobile development team had ten developers. With the new direction, the organization aspired to scale towards a path where a team size of 50+ was anticipated. This growth path triggered the tech stakeholder to revisit the strategy of mobile development. The top items which the stakeholder thought about in the start are as follows:

- Revamping existing code to scale to multiple products.
- Finalizing the decision to have multiple apps for each product or single app.
- Reusability to be established amongst the growing team and avoiding duplication.
- Steps to be taken to establish a common pattern across the team.
- Enabling easy movement of people across the team without much learning curve.
- Improve productivity and manage lean and peak periods by rebalancing people across different products.
- Managing independent release cycles for different products.
- Continuing development or production support for each product.
- Collaboration across the team to manage dependency.
- Build an ecosystem to do experiments to introduce and decommission a product without much hassle.

This became the baseline to define the vision that the organization was aiming to achieve. From these, the stakeholders curated the following end goals:

- Identification of ten products to be incorporated to the existing application. These products should be modularized (made independent and separate from each other) and loosely coupled to progress independently.

- To build the platform hosting individual products. Platform shall ensure redundancy or duplication is minimized. The code could be organized as modules with clear separation of concerns.
- To set up the structure and process that helps the product to thrive. The smaller unit within the ecosystem should adhere to the structure laid out to achieve semantic equivalence.
- To ensure the same brand identity is retained in every product.
- Enable independent product lifecycle. Each product team can focus independently on their growth, marketing, features addition and enhancement associated with their products.
- The mobile application shall have common functionality, and this could be maintained by a platform team. The product teams thus can focus on their respective goals.
- The organization should emphasize autonomous decision-making across. The product team should have the freedom to influence beyond the working group. The co-creation and overlap where members contribute to shared concerns beyond their own scope of work are essential for a stable and scalable mobile application. This setup will ensure the team works towards the collective good rather than competing internally.
- Any team member should be able to ideally pick up task related to cross product integration or to add features/customization related to the other products with minimal learning. Even though different products are served, the products are still under the same organization. This overlap enables the moving around of an individual to support critical capacity requirement across. Such a setup is important theme that will optimize the utilization of team.
- The organization emphasizes the expectation to be known as a pioneer in technology in building and running such a business. The organization also has the ambition to contribute to the community by sharing these learnings and getting feedback in return. Such contribution will also enable others to take inspiration from these learnings. The organization has a plan to open-source a reusable framework to build and setup a similar mobile application ecosystem.
- The general guideline is for products to be functionally isolated from each other. In all practicality, the possibility of interacting with each other exists and the team has to build a mechanism to cater to it. The technology team must ensure the ecosystem supports the means to internally allow the product team to expose the service amongst each other to consume in a controlled and loosely coupled architecture.

The preceding list became the goal to be achieved for mobile application. The aim was to use the goals to create a flat functioning structure in conjunction with an ecosystem of guidelines. These will thus enable managing of smaller team. Each team will be responsible for production or logically independent components of the Super App.

Financial domain example app

A financial institution had an existing mobile application supporting a large customer base. Their presence was in multiple regions/geographies (eight to be exact). The application supported various banking products and personas, and the codebase was of a monstrous size. Feature release and bug fixing took an eternity. The cost incurred was high and the patience of the stakeholder and end consumers was killed. Being an essential service and due to the lack of alternative, the consumer succumbed to the atrocities of the application.

The team had plans to expand and revamp the software. The financial application had to follow regulations from the governing body for a financial domain-related software. The mobile applications had to adhere to these. Being present in multiple geographies led to a situation of region-specific regulations influencing the development of regional flavors of the mobile application.

The current setup had separate teams building different mobile application for each region. The financial institution saw that almost 70-80% of similar features were built multiple times by different teams. This meant additional cash was burning from the organization's profit. The organization was keen on optimizing the operational cost by reducing duplication. Having a centralized team build the application's common features and reuse them in multiple regional flavors was the seed idea. This idea transformed into a vision of revamping the application.

The goal aimed at developing a central framework that could manage every region's feature. The framework was also expected to act as the source to ship the mobile application for the different region. This central framework was expected to have all the necessary capabilities and tools to support all the regions.

The financial application also showed trait similar to retail domain application explained earlier. The following list relooks at the specifics of trait for the financial application:

- Revamping existing code to scale for large sized teams working in parallel.
- Reusability established amongst the growing team and avoided duplication.
- Steps to be taken to establish a common pattern across the team.
- Enable easy movement of people across the team without much learning curve.
- Managing release cycles without breaking and ensuring shorter release cycle with fixes and feature.
- Continuing development or production support.
- Collaboration across the large team and coordinating dependency.

This use case shows a clear overlap in the expectation and problem statement in comparison with the retail domain app. While the goals are similar, the operating context of this application brought a different nuance to be tackled. The reason for the revamp was not horizontal growth by adding new products. The goal was rather to ensure that the vertical growth is seamless where the maintenance cost incurred in the current setup is optimized. There were eight different codebases to be looked at. The team had to consolidate the reusable parts from these. The prerequisite for the revamp and consolidation was having strong functional idea for each geography. This functional context was required to get the clarity of the common features. Without the functional context, the execution of the idea for having a single source for generating build flavor for 8 geographies would be difficult.

Figure 12.2 can be seen as the ten-thousand-foot view of the expected outcome of the financial domain app:

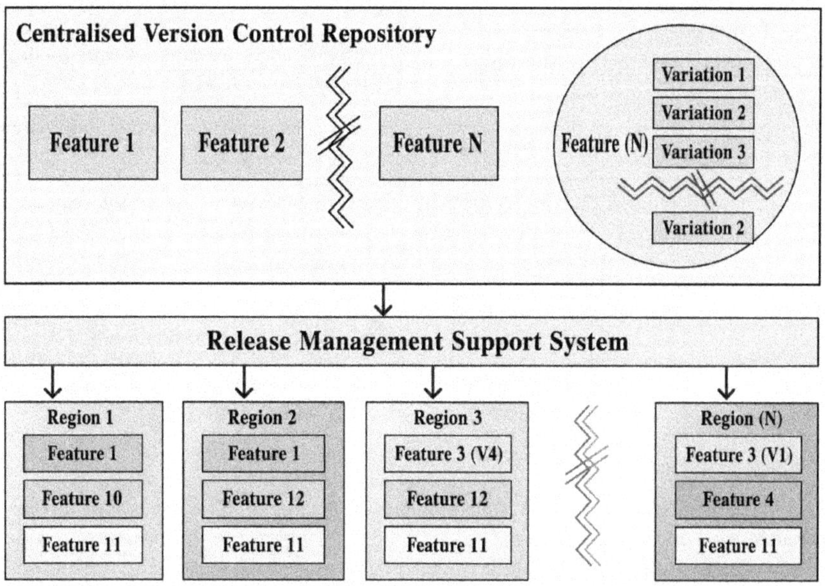

Figure 12.2: *Vision overview for a multi country application*

The organization aimed to build a single framework that supports reusability of the functionality and features supported by the mobile application across the world optimizing the cost. One of the other motivations for the organization that led to the decision was to create focused and strong business units that can hold the expertise on a particular area of financial organization. The organization did plan to have cross-cutting groups with the responsibility of holding the business unit together. In short with the framework a single technology team working on a single codebase responsible for 8 geographies. While the number of codebases to manage has shrunk, the team size may not proportionally reduce. The team size will still depend on percentage of geography specific customization required. Such an app will have complexity greater than a simple mobile application and is an example of a case where the codebase is considerably large and requires parallel development capability with large team size. The financial application thus serves as an example where the philosophy of Super App will be required.

The two use cases that are looked at are classic examples that need technology and operational excellence of a Super App philosophy. The use case 1 may however need additional product excellence to streamline the introduction of different product. By the end of this section the hope is the reader gets equipped to comprehend the possibilities of the mobile application. Now one can formally label these two under the label as **Multi-Product Super App** (**MPSA**) and **Multi-Module Super App** (**MMSA**). *Table 12.1* gives a comparative overview of both. From the table one shall get an understanding of how to track and look for patterns to identify a *Super App*:

Multi-Product Super App	Multi-Module Super App
A mobile app hosting multiple, independent products with minimal interdependency.	A mobile app where products and services are tightly integrated and interdependent.
Codebase is monstrous-sized, loosely connected components and features with minimal interdependency and operating independently.	Codebase is monstrous-sized, interconnected features dependent on each other and may even not function without each other.
Each product is an isolated business function with separate roadmaps and success criteria.	Features cannot be isolated as they rely on other features to function. These features behave as part of a unified business model where their success is interlinked.
Removing a product has minimal impact on the app.	Removing a feature can introduce inefficiencies and disrupt the overall system.
Easier to scale with separate business entities and independent teams for each product.	Higher complexity due to tightly integrated features that require constant coordination.
Consumers who need different services but can access them through a single platform. Consumers see multiple services but treat them as separate products within one app.	Consumers who need a tightly integrated suite of services that work together. Consumers see a seamless experience with interconnected services as one unified product.
Scalable as different products can be added or removed independently.	Challenging to scale as features are interdependent, requiring careful coordination.
Independent products can function alone without much issue.	Features cannot stand alone, creating challenges if isolated or disconnected.

***Table 12.1**: Comparative overview of Super App varieties*

MPSA and MMSA have similarities for several implementation strategies. The navigation pattern, design thought process, sensible default and coding pattern will be equivalent for both. The approach followed will work exactly the same way for both. The feature can be isolated from each other in MPSAs, reducing the tight coupling. However, for MMSA, the feature will be dependent on other features. The code could be modularized in this case as well. The team must have efficient communication and dependency management mechanisms to separate the feature in MMSA. The manifestation of these concepts in a real-life project will be influenced by a contextual flavor of the people involved. At an abstract level, there will be a great chance for equivalence in the technology and architecture used. The parlance to execute such a project is a skill that can be replicated across multiple engagements if one possesses familiarity in building at least one such application.

Components of Super App

A mobile application is identified as a single package installed onto the device of the end user. For an organization, a product or service delivered through the mobile can either be shipped as a single installable or separate installable(s) for each product and service. Maintaining separate installable may invite operational overhead such as separate release management for each product and duplication for common functionalities. If properly planned, the team can build reusable assets to reduce the effect of duplication when maintaining separate installable(s). However overhead of release management cannot be avoided.

An end user installing multiple applications on a device gives a disconnected experience while using the different service provided by the same organization. This disconnected experience does not seem to be intuitive to hook the end user and create a brand loyalty. An alternative school of thought brings forth the perspective that if the end user does not use a particular service, the user would lose the benefit and flexibility to keep the mobile device light. An organization should weigh both the choices and do a comparative analysis looking at the pros and cons of the two options to take the next course of action. If the analysis indicates the value provided to the end user outweighs the overhead of slightly larger installable, then shipping a single app for multiple products becomes the recommended outcome.

Understanding the concept of micro frontend will give an additional familiarity with Super App. If looked back in history one may see emergence of technical ideas that later became the choices for architectural decisions for multiple software kinds. One such idea was to build software with clear logical separation and as independent modules. The independent module was expected to have a lifecycle of itself. This structure in backend came to be known as microservice. In front-end web application this came to be known as microfrontend. The same idea got extended to the mobile application. However, the idea did not fit in as is when compared with the web. There was a subtle difference amongst the web versus mobile. The difference was in the deployment. The deployment for the web could be done independently for each micro frontend. However, in case of mobile, the deployment for any update in the independent micro frontend required a recompilation of the entire application and redeployment. This eliminates true independent deployment and requires all modules to be versioned and released together. In mobile app development however the code structure of micro frontends could be replicated, which are independent from each other.

In short, having multiple units of micro frontend team working together orchestrated by the platform became the central theme of building a Super App ecosystem in mobile.

Any Super App code has the following listed three components:

- Platform/Container
- Feature/Product module
- Driver/Reusable common module

In this structure, there is exactly one platform/container component. However, the feature/product modules and the driver/reusable common modules will be multiple. *Figure 12.3* depicts three components of the Super App:

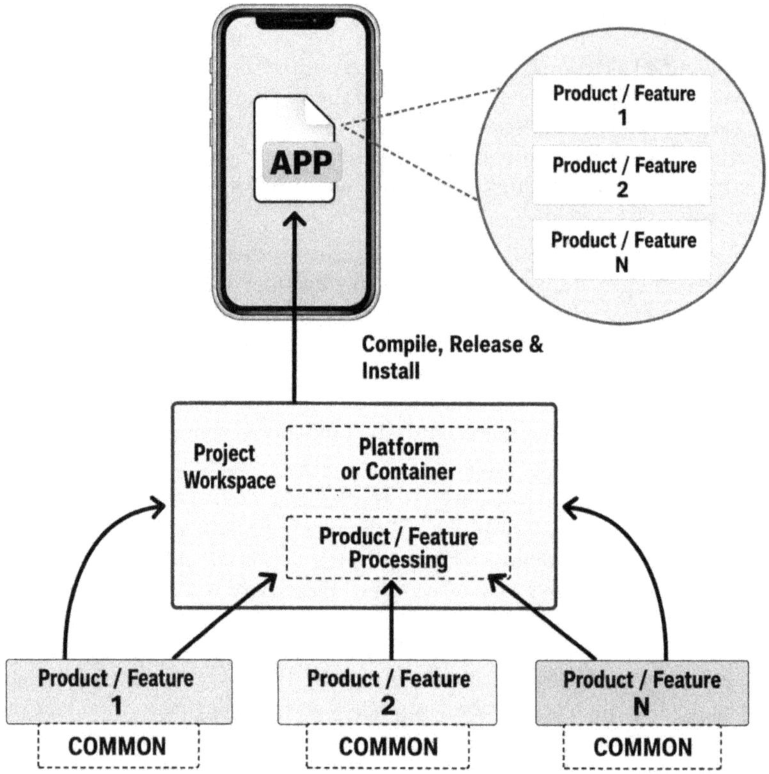

Figure 12.3: Super App components

These components are applicable for both MMSA and MPSA. The platform/container represents the component that has the app related functionality and is responsible for hosting the product/feature. The container will do the necessary orchestration, coordination and ensure the cohesion required for the product/feature module. The product/feature registration is required to ensure the individual modules are bundled and integrated together. Appropriate dependencies shall be set up for each product. In the *Figure 12.3* this responsibility is depicted in the **registering** block and is closer to the platform/container. The third component, the driver/reusable common module, is responsible for holding the reusable functionalities of the application. For example, the UI components, network library, etc., reused in app products. These common features may also be used by the platform or container.

After looking at these components, one may ponder over the question: How can code/module segregation be possible for MMSA since it is a tightly integrated system? Additionally, one could possibly think why do we even need MMSA, since it seems to be like any normal mobile application. In the first look, the statement would seem to be true. However, the MMSA is not evident or an application which operates with a smaller team and the preceding modularization would even be an overkill in such applications. The scheme of things for MMSA will become relevant when the mobile code base is big, and the number of team members is large. Keeping the team size small has advantages with respect to coordination and focus. When the team grows, a squad wise split up would be beneficial, thereby necessitating the need for logically independent functional breakdown of code. Segregating into components thus becomes important.

For MMSA the tight integration ideally represents the close association of the business requirement of the feature. At the code level separating to independent module could still be done by using the principles of abstraction. Such a strategy would lead to design loosely coupled code where smaller feature is divided and modularized. These features are connected to form a single application. For example, consider the onboarding and banking account feature from the financial Super App mentioned in the earlier section. Onboarding seems to be quite a complex journey with login and digital sign up. The account screen will be another journey and a separate journey in a different flow. Other than the need of an authorization token specific to the login session, the account related feature does not have any dependency on the onboarding feature. Since there is no dependency, one can possibly develop the two features in parallel. The onboarding feature is to be developed in parallel. The account feature can have a temporary hard coded authorization token used to connect to the account backend system and the development can be kickstarted in parallel. The bank account screen for mobile can be integrated later to the token from onboarding journey removing the hard coded value. Thus, both features are completed in parallel with additional effort or dependency only on the integration. The divide and conquer strategy brings slight operational overhead to manage the context and communication across the parallel stream. However, the strategy will help to parallelly add feature speeding up the time to market. The possibility of a focused, logically separate and almost independent teams will open up. The organization with this setup can have a balanced pool of subject matter experts driving independent business areas.

Platform team

From the three architectural components, the key piece for ensuring stability of product or feature integration is the platform component. Once the platform is established the independent teams can focus on respective products while platform team continues to evolve and enhance the common reusable component. The reusable library will grow and mature as time progresses where features or products are added or enhanced. The feedback cycle to enhance the components shall be a continuous journey. If the organization does not focus on the platform, it could hit a roadblock to scale.

Setting up a central platform team is a critical piece for the Super App project. It is important to ensure that there is a dedicated tech focus and planning done to setup and enhance a platform where different products are hosted. The responsibility of the platform team will be beyond merely providing a host platform/container. This team must define the tech strategy, best practices and the guidelines that each product team can take forward to be incorporated in the products. The platform team will be the epicenter where the decision-making equivalence across products should be established. This will ensure the mobile application is coherent. The product being part of the same mobile app would want the experience to be uniform across. Such a team setup ensures the top-down nature expected for Super App is established by defining the guidelines, best practices and convention to be followed.

In summary, the responsibility of the platform team is to create and maintain an ecosystem supporting the construction, integration and functioning of the entire mobile application that hosts the various products.

Ten-thousand-foot overview of platform team activities

Following is the list that summarizes the activities that the platform team must undertake. These are the major items to be planned from starting stage, assigned priority and executed. The following list is not exhaustive, but it encompasses the major activities involved for the platform team:

1. Build a host/platform responsible to bring together all the different products/features. This should be done along with incorporating the common cross cutting functionality that supports products/feature.
2. Initially one may think that the platform team would be a team that will be focused on the technology area that support the nonfunctional requirement of the mobile application. The statement shall not hold true as the common features identified will be functional in nature. The login, the order summary, notification, help and resolution of a particular product, etc., serve as examples of cross-cutting features that are functional. These features would be ideally be driven by business specialists. The platform team thus defines, owns and executes these common features along with other nonfunctional requirement common across the application.
3. There was a very close collaboration amongst the platform team and product team. If a particular product team wanted certain common capability in the platform team, it ideally should be planned ahead in the

task to be completed by platform team. A provision for individual product teams to contribute to the platform codebase and raise a merge request to take forward is also an option.

4. The primary responsibility for the platform team will be to own the host/container. The nature of organization can define the collaboration or way of working appropriate and optimal for the operating context.
5. Build the starter kit framework to add new products. It would be repetitive to add the boilerplate codes for every new product added to a mobile application. For example, the retail use case quoted in the start of the chapter had 10 products identified. It was definite that this number would go higher as the time progressed. The platform team should invest in creating a tool that generate the boilerplate and setup required for adding new product without much overhead. The folder structure, the communication mechanism and access to the functionalities exposed by the host application and the product registration are example of items that needed to be achieved via the starter kit. All these could now be created with a few clicks using the toolkit, abstracting the complexity from the developer.
6. The platform team should have backlog to implement capability to decommission a product from the mobile application easily.
7. Setup process and strategy for version management and collaboration amongst the team. For example, organizing the release cadence, change management process for interconnected products, process followed to change platform feature or common reusable components etc.
8. Building the common frameworks and modules which will be used by products or the platform:
   a. Crash analytics
   b. Authentication and authorization
   c. Networking client and abstraction
   d. Logging - debug and production
   e. Analytics
   f. Remote config and feature flag
   g. Data sharing - secure and non-secure
   h. Image and asset management and sharing
   i. Common reusable UI Layer - a design language system
   j. Localization framework
9. Building pre-login and post-login products' entry pages.
10. Building capability to allow inter product navigation. For instance, deep linking capability, navigation container, etc.
11. Setup framework to enable light weight independent product testing. For an independent product development building, the entire application could add an overhead for a large sized codebase. Therefore, having a mini lightweight host for an individual product could make the life of the product team simpler. This address the worst-case scenario, where host application itself is having an issue, the individual product team can continue without any dependency. The day-to-day activities other than release will always be independent.
12. Configure environment management techniques and build flavors for the mobile application.
13. Set up the automated pipeline covering activities between the development to deployment. These activities include automated build and verification stages.
14. Take the ownership in defining the guideline for the test strategy.
15. Define mechanism to review the permission enabled for hardware and mobile operating system capabilities in cases where the specific product would require the same to function.

16. The nonfunctional requirement that affects the entire mobile application will be ideally part of the platform team. If the scope is specifically related to the product, then the product team will be best placed to tackle the requirement.
17. Constant monitoring of the non-functional feature and aspects of the application.
18. In an ideal scenario platform team would be the core team focusing on research and development for improving the overall mobile application. After the experiment, the aspects that add value are incorporated to make the system better.
19. In some cases, the individual tends to see the platform team as a team to park those items which are becoming an overhead. Such pattern is seen when multiple squad teams work on same application with tight timeline. Team should not dump all the items to the platform team. This is an anti-pattern; the responsibility is orphaned potentially and no team clearly owns the item and making the platform team responsible to absorb these diverting from their core responsibilities. The platform team has the full power to decide and take up and define the priority of the task rather than succumbing to external pressure to meet the timeline.

The platform team will be responsible to coordinate and collect feedback from the other group to improve the pain points identified in the platform. These data should be analyzed, and actions should be prioritized to be taken up. The team can come up with viable approaches to mitigate these pain points. In short, the ownership of the evolution of platform gets handled by this team.

Unique learnings from past

As part of this section, the idea is to explore a set of such learnings and choices that stakeholders have encountered while building a Super App. A Super App is yet another mobile application and thereby the challenge discussed will have overlap with regular mobile application development. The intellectual maturity to make better decisions in a future Super App engagement is the purpose of understanding these. The reader will be able to propose these learning without doubt to the team and help to come up with a robust decision in such situation.

Reuse codebase versus rewriting codebase

Oftentimes, an organization will already have a mainstream product that either needs to grow or may need modernization. In this case, the existing codebase is an investment that the organization has already incurred. A simple logic could trigger the thought to evaluate the possibility of reuse, either for making the time to market faster or for cost advantage.

Such a choice will come up where there is an existing codebase. It is essential to do an evaluation for the codebase to arrive at a conclusion. The subject matter expert in the technology should look at the readability, technology stack of choice, ease of extracting functionalities or modifying the code, confidence factor to make changes on the codebase, gatekeeping mechanism available to capture any side effect due to code change etc., as the key parameters for the evaluation. In some cases, if the organization is having multiple versions of the codebase for a multi-country application, this evaluation will become tougher. If there are red flags that will make the reusability costlier, rewriting from scratch becomes the key recommendation as the evaluation outcome.

The following are a few examples of anti-pattern or non-reusable code one may see in legacy codebase that detract from the decision to reuse and are red signal:

- The legacy codebases have a different style that cannot be used for the revamp.
- The style which are tightly coupled with the user interface as hardcoded and non-uniform value maintained is not a great pattern.
- There is unused code or code using deprecated APIs.
- There are duplications within the same codebase for similar functionality.

- The bugs reported for the codebase are way higher than the acceptable number for a team to own and improve.
- The automated testing layer to provide the confidence is limited and does not cover the end-to-end journey. There are no additional test layers and these end-to-end automated tests cover only major and critical flows representing less than 50% of the entire application.
- Poor readability causing the increase in time to onboard and understand the codebase.
- Separate libraries used for similar functionality.

When such anti pattern exists and the inherent overhead is high reusing the existing codebase to get an early start would potentially damage the vision. Particularly for Super App the effect will be multifold. The code base needed to sustain Super App vision should allow democracy and autonomy for the developer. A codebase with a lot of anti-patterns will bring rigidity and will be difficult to change without investing considerable effort. The possibility to reuse those parts which can be extracted out from the codebase is still open instead of reusing the entire codebase.

Feedback mechanism to prevent software entropy

A sizeable team has the potential to drift away from the original goal and vision. The codebase over a period will grow to a sizeable shape. The team size working on the same codebase may grow as well. All these could become unmanageable. A constant vigilance over the situation and a feedback mechanism will help to prevent such occurrence.

To get early feedback the following practices could be leveraged:

- For codebase the feedback could be received via establishing a test strategy.
- For measuring the ease of making change to the code one may compare the time to delivery of similar features over time. The model on software entropy discussed in *Chapter 7, Scalability in Mobile Development: Part 1.*
- Evaluating and tracking the patterns of bugs at different stages of mobile application - pre and postproduction.
- Having a clear role and responsibility to channel the feedback.
- The code should have mechanism where boundaries are agreed in a large codebase when team is divided to multiple smaller squads. This also would enable control, ownership and enable quick resolution for conflict.

Dependency management

The mobile application development will have significant number of external dependencies. These dependencies could be on the readiness of the requirement, high-fidelity design and interaction, and the contract for the downstream system are the major ones. A development team only can function effectively when there is enough clarity on these dependencies. To add to the complexity, since multiple developers are working in functional silos, it would be essential to pre-empt dependency between the parties involved before starting a functionality. Deferring or delaying the dependency analysis could cause rework. Finding mismatch in the expectation by the consumer and provider would be chaotic. In the case of mobile applications, the developer should know the contract to collaborate across the different integration points. The contract is necessary while multiple teams/developers are working on the same codebase where there are two features that connect with one another. In the Super App the feature/product split will ideally help isolate functionality in most case. However when the feature/products are combined into a single app there will be some level of integration. There could be overlap in functionality or configuration to be implemented in such integration. The teams in such case must mutually decide and agree on the ownership. The common interest of the success of the whole app will drive the team to have a reduced friction between the team in decision-making. In an event of disagreement , the stakeholders can intervene to mitigate the conflict.

Programming is a creative task. Any creative task requires some amount of preparation. In coding, this comes in the form of designing a solution. The space to think is quintessential for reducing the cognitive load of uncertainty on the development team. Additionally, having clarity on features would help the leads to pre-empt any cross-team reusability or dependency. The recommendation in an engagement is the product owner to be ready with the requirement and functional stories at least a month ahead. The developer with this can get early visibility and do analyses incrementally to figure out any dependency.

The clarity in requirement is the expectation to be fulfilled. These would be the baseline for the expected outcome. Post analysis the requirement is transformed into the visual design and acceptance criteria which is the blueprint team can refer. The team leverage these details to build the mobile application and these form the source of truth for the expected behavior. The development team shall devise solutions based on these inputs. This information being available much ahead would give flexibility to invest and come up with the tech strategy at an early stage. These inputs will help identify dependencies within the development team when dividing the features. It is in the best interest to prevent any back and forth during the development. Spending time upfront on analysis of the features thus should help provide enough clarity to devise a robust solution. Such a strategy would help in creating a better plan. The development team will be effective and move forward as planned, resulting in more predictable progress.

Backend services can be built either ahead of the mobile development or in parallel. In the case where the downstream system is built earlier, the team can consume these directly without delaying development for mobile. In the case where downstream system is developed in parallel, a dependency for the upstream system exists. The mobile development will either follow the strategy to have a contract-driven development or wait to have the backend ready. The development can start with the defined contract finalized. The consuming side will either hard code or temporarily mock the data which later can be integrated with minimal change to be fetched from actual downstream.

In an engagement, if the dependency affects the delivery completion of parties involved, it should be tracked. The dependency should be fulfilled on the agreed date to take the next step or else there will be delay meeting the goal. The dependency being tracked is maintained as the dependency matrix and is an essential tool for collaboration.

Preventing information silos

Super App thrives on optimal reusability. Platform team does maintain the top down nature to promote reusability. However, the feedback should flow in the reverse direction of where the implementation can influence and refine the top-down decisions from platform team. Such a strategy where there is bidirectional influence would help in preventing any information silos and promote diversity in the larger ecosystem. To foster such an ecosystem, it is ideal to have a forum where the cross-team contexts are discussed. The individuals in the team should plan for rotation across teams. This approach should be encouraged by the organization. Such rotation can help the individual to get to know repetitive pattern across the entire codebase.

Testing, environments, sign off strategy

The journey of a feature from the ideation to deployment should be controlled and effectively monitored to get the best product out. This means having a test strategy that will continuously and gradually validate the feature and promote from one stage. The feedback from the previous stage should be positive to promote to next stage. Depending on the complexity and the convenience of the organization, there could be a separate environment for each stage. For example, development, QA, UAT and production corresponds the possible different environments.

The team should define the test pyramid to ensure that the defects are identified early in the development. *Chapter 5, Quality Assurance for Mobile Development* talks about the test pyramid. The developer must ensure that the unit test are part of the completion of a feature. The feature once completed is moved to the testing bucket. The testing team would evaluate the scenarios covered in the unit test done at the development stage. The scenarios not covered in the development cycle should be focused in the automation written by the quality assurance team. The layer in which a particular scenario could be tested is a mutually agreed decision based on the relevant context and constraint from each feature. The recommendation would be to have near to lower layer of test pyramid which is the unit test. The developer can have access to all the environments. The lower environment may not be exposed to public internet. In production, the login credentials that the developer has signed up would be restricted. If it is regulated industry the rules and norms could be strict.

To make development easier and to have the ability to cover different scenarios the development server could be an express server that serves the mock data based or an actual backend application serving hardcode test data. Such a setup will bring the data closer to the development team and can be modified to mimic the expected behaviors and do multiple experiment or test. Having separate lower environment provides stability for the respective testing or development team to do isolated experiments or test. The developer completes the functional development, and move the features developed to the testing phase. The consuming downstream dependency which have their own lifecycle should be ready and integrated into the mobile application for the feature to be complete.

Once the development team hands it over to the quality team, validation happens on the build artifact pointing to the QA environment. Once the build meets the required completion criteria, it can be planned for the next stage, UAT. The user acceptance test, aka UAT, for any organization, would be a focused group with a pool of users to take the mobile application and do the next round of testing. The expectation of the actual end user is validated in the UAT. The UAT environment will be very close to the production environment, with simulated data matching the production. The anonymized data dump from production may even be ported to the lower environment. When porting production data to lower environment one should ensure that all personal identifiable data or private data is not exposed and anonymized.

Figure 12.4 depicts the typical artifact generated for mobile application:

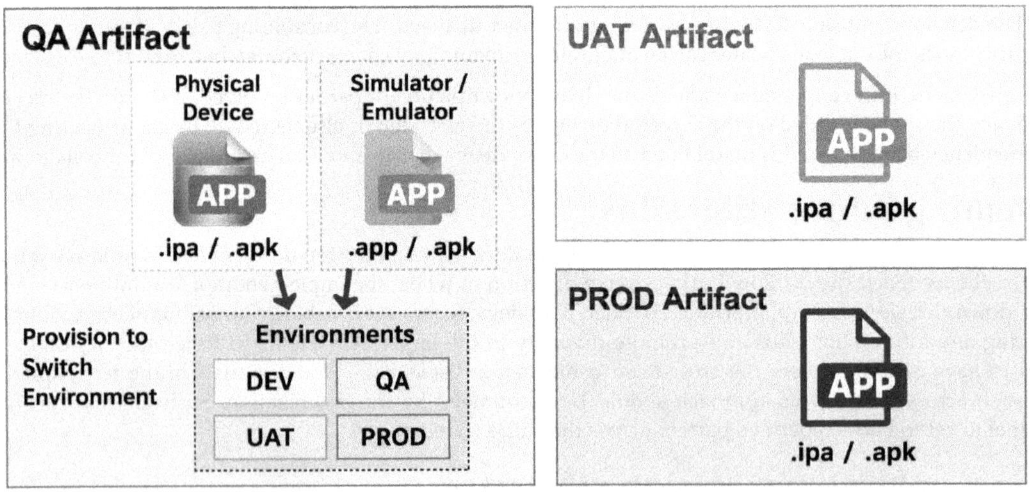

***Figure 12.4**: Build artifact for mobile application*

The developer could also use the QA artifact. The developers will have a tool to generate the artifact and would be skilled thus the automation tool ideally avoids generating artifact for the development stage. On the other hand, the artifact generated in the QA stage should have a mechanism to switch between different environments. There are various solutions to implement the environment switcher, and the developer can choose what works best for the context. *Chapter 8, Scalability in Mobile Development: Part 2* has the details talking about for environment management.

The entities who owns the quality mechanism defined for particular stage will give the sign off. The sign off will promote the progression of build to next stages. These stages can be classified broadly to the following four:

- **QA sign off**: QA validates the development accuracy. Deeper testing and feedback of any major flaw. This stage should capture the issue missed by the development team.
- **Product/business owner sign off**: Product/business owner validate if the feature has met the requirement envisioned by the business.
- **UAT sign off**: The application is production-ready and working well with the downstream systems will be validated at this stage.

- **Compliance sign off**: The business risk evaluation before the application Go live to the consumer. This stage also ensures that the application does not have any behaviors causing violation affecting the organization and the consumers.

After all these signoffs, the product is ready to be shipped. The trigger for deployment to the store will be the next step. Then, it goes through the process associated with the app store to reach the consumers.

Note: **Team structure and squad composition talked about in Chapter 4, Organizing a Mobile Development Team of the book shall be relevant for Super App development. The reader should go back to the chapter and revisit the same to solidify the learnings.**

Toy Super App

The convention of introducing any new concept in programming with hello world for SwiftUI is where this section starts. Later after the hello world the next is to jump to build a thin version of a Super App. The core objective is to give a flavor of what does it mean to be part of a team developing a Super App. The section will leverage the native iOS toolkit in this journey. The section follows a structure focusing on the walkthrough of a Toy Super App codebase. The code is built for iOS with a home screen and a few dummy products. The codebase depicts the different components of a Super App described earlier.

Essentials of SwiftUI

As part of this section, the idea is to look at an already created SwiftUI project and do a code walkthrough to understand the different nuances. The project structure created will have the boilerplate that includes the entry point with the first page for application, unit test and the UI-test folder. In Xcode there are various project templates that the individual can choose from. Further during the project creation with Xcode the developer will be presented with the option to add offline data capability, XCUITest, etc. as well. This narrative will look at the thin version of the iOS codebase. *Figure 12.5* represents the folder structure for a simple SwiftUI application:

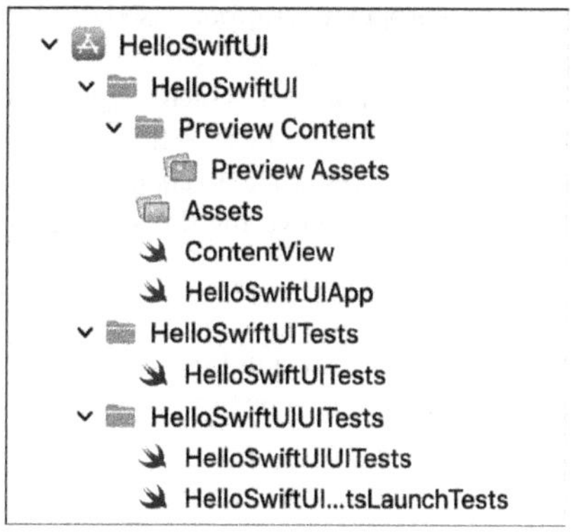

***Figure 12.5**: Simple SwiftUI project folder*

The **HelloSwiftUIApp.swift** file is the key that defines the entry point. The **@main** attribute is the syntactic minimalism brought in the Swift compiler that marks the **HelloSwiftUIApp** struct as the entry point. The **HelloSwiftUIApp** struct should extend the **App** protocol as well. The following code depicted is the entry point. The **HelloSwiftUIApp** struct set up the screen with the window group that loads the **ContentView** which is the first SwiftUI view on to the canvas.

```
//HelloSwiftUIApp.swift
import SwiftUI
@main
struct HelloSwiftUIApp: App {
  var body: some Scene {
```

```
    WindowGroup {
      ContentView()
    }
  }
}
```

SwiftUI also follows the box model of UI development described in *Chapter 10, Introduction to Swift, Kotlin, and Dart.* In this box model the UI elements are composed and grouped together to form a functional UI that presents information and provides options for the user to interact and navigate through the different features. The **ContentView** is defined as the following which implements the SwiftUI **View** protocol and the **body** variable has a vertical stack holding an image and text, as depicted in the following code:

```
struct ContentView: View {
  var body: some View {
    VStack {
      Image(systemName: "globe")
        .imageScale(.large)
        .foregroundStyle(.tint)
      Text("Hello, world!")
    }
    .padding()
  }
}
```

The SwiftUI framework provides APIs that can be used to control and coordinate the application state. These come in the form of property wrappers. The property wrappers can be used to implement binding of data. Binding is used to set up a bidirectional communication channel responsible for triggering a redraw and notifying any change in data from the user input. The following are examples of major property wrappers used **@State**, **@ObservedObject**, **@Environment**, **@StateObject** etc. The developer write the code for the user interface which has the state property wrapper holding the data. The user interface will observe the state for an interaction, which triggers processing of the computational logic. The computation logic responds after processing and will trigger the UI refresh if there is any change. The computational logic and state is generally segregated as part of **ViewModel** class. The **ViewModel** interacts with the further layer of Swift code connecting to downstream system or device framework powering the features of the mobile application.

Testing support

In the iOS ecosystem XCTest is the framework for UI automation and unit testing. Recently in the year 2024 a new Swift testing framework was introduced for unit testing. The Swift Testing framework is compatible and can coexist with the XCTest.

The underlying principle behind the working of UI automation is to locate the UI element with a predefined identifier or pattern and trigger action/event. The trigger is sent through a proxy created by the UI testing framework. The test scripts are written in the XCUITest suite within the project using the API exposed by the testing framework.

In most programming languages unit test is executed by compiling only system under test and dependency. However, unit testing in iOS using XCTest differs from this model and does not work in isolation. In the XCTest, a test bundle is created compiling the entire application codebase linked to the unit test suite. The application code imported into the unit test suite exposes the functionality that is to be tested. The test suite bundle them and runs along with the mobile application code. The unit test code validates the assertion inside the XCTest runtime. Both the unit testing and UI automation requires the iOS code base compiled entirely to run the test.

A code walkthrough of test for a function adding two integers and returning the result will give insights in to the unit testing mechanism. The following code depicts the implementation for system under test:

```
//Calculator.swift
class Calculator {
 func add(_ a: Int, _ b: Int) -> Int {
  return a + b
 }
}
```

Swift testing syntax

The section focuses on unit test written with the Swift testing framework for **calculator** class. The Swift testing supports recent version of Swift with version 6.0 and above:

```
//CaculatorTest.swift
import Testing
@testable import <your app module name in this case HelloSwiftUIApp>
@Suite
struct CalculatorTests{
  @Test(arguments: [
    (2, 3, 5),
    (-1, 1, 0),
    (0, 0, 0),
    (-5, -7, -12)
  ])
  func testAddition(_ a: Int, _ b: Int, _ expected: Int) {
    let calculator = Calculator()
    let result = calculator.add(a, b)
    #expect(result == expected)
  }
}
```

The statement **import Testing** provided by iOS ecosystem will expose the relevant Swift Testing API available in the scope of file. The app module **HelloSwiftUIApp** is also exposed by the further import. The usage of the **@Test** swift macro with the parameter which gives the test inputs to validate the **add** function. The value in the **@Test** macro should match the function signature of the **testAddition** function. The assertion is written with the **#expect** macro as written inside the body of the unit test function. The **@Test** macro takes a parameterized argument list that resolves as the signature of the **testAddition** function for each item in the list. The testing framework will execute unit tests for each item in the argument list. Swift macros are compiler features to build reusable compiler understandable templates. These can be used to add shorthand versions for boilerplate code. The **Testing** framework implements this macro. The same pattern repeats and could be followed along with additional API provided to write advanced test cases.

XCTest testing syntax

This section focuses on the alternative test framework available in the Apple ecosystem. This was the long standing and traditional way in which the test was written for the Apple ecosystem. The unit test with the XCTest **Testing** framework for the **Calculator.swift** implementation is depicted in the following code:

```
// CalculatorTests.swift
import XCTest
@testable import HelloSwiftUI
class CalculatorTests: XCTestCase {
 let testCases: [(Int, Int)] = [
  (2, 5),
```

```
    (3, 6),
    (10, 9),
  ]
  func testAddition() {
    for testCase in testCases {
      let calculator = Calculator()
      let result = calculator.add(testCase.0, testCase.1)
      XCTAssertEqual(result, testCase.0 + testCase.1)
    }
  }
}
```

The **`import XCTest`** in the file is the framework exposing the relevant API to write the test. The import of the module **`HelloSwiftUI`** exposes the system under test. The XCTest test can be seen as an imperative style of unit testing mechanism where the intent should be explicit. The Swift testing on the other hand leverages Swift macros to simplify the code into a declarative style.

Toy Super App overview

In an imaginary world like ours, there existed an organization that wanted to build a mobile app providing a variety of services. The organization wanted to be an aggregator of different products. The mechanism to connect to the downstream system serving the data was already available. The task has been to build the mobile application targeted for iOS. The team came to know about the Super App concept and wanted to try to build the same. This narrative is the journey of the **minimum viable product** (**MVP**) developed by the organization building a Super App. The MVP aimed to build the three components of the Super App, setup the registering mechanism for a product and having the essential reusable library ready. The essential foundation for setting up a Super App is what the reader would get from the chapter.

> Note: **Explaining any code via narration may be counterintuitive and may pose to be a challenge to calibrate the understanding to one's psyche. This narrative has attempted to preempt the same. In the context of book the narrative is carefully crafted, to get most of the Toy Super App. It is recommended to have the codebase shared along the book to be ready alongside running on a machine. If the reader feels the connection between classes are not relatable, do not hesitate to pause and play around with the codebase. Ensure to add the break point and do exploratory tinkering with the code before reading further. This could give a boost to the read. The project is built to support Xcode version 16.0+.**

Figure 12.6 depicts the final output screens landing page for app and home page for two products **Wallet** and the **Movie**:

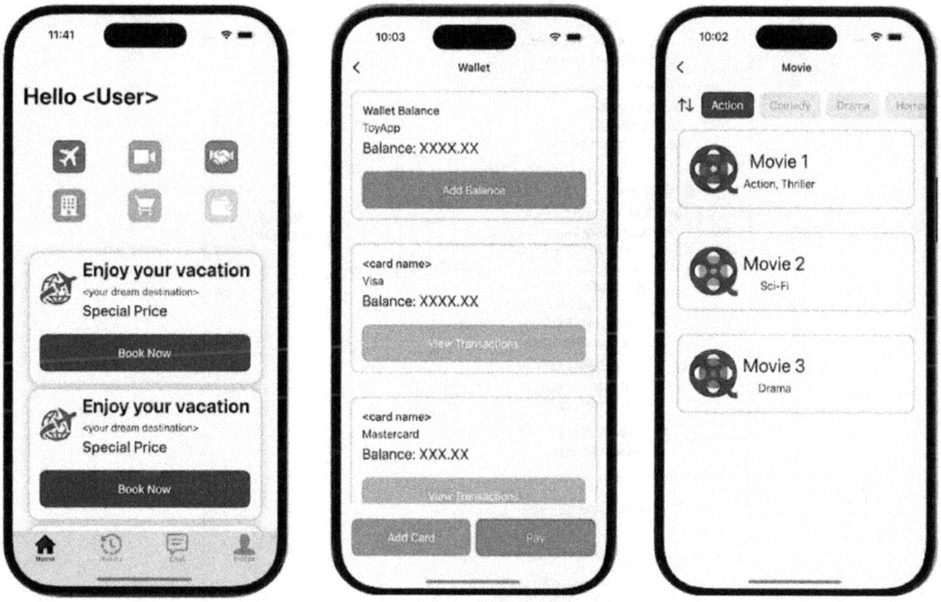

Container Product (Wallet) Product (Movie)

***Figure 12.6:** Wireframe main app and products home screen*

Project folder overview

The structure of the project anatomy of the Toy Super App is depicted in the *Figure 12.7*. The key component of the Super App is demarcated with boxes. The folder structure depicted in *Figure 12.7* is the simplest form of grouping done within a single Xcode project. In the *Figure 12.7* one can see the folder separates different components in the project. The entire code will be versioned in a single repository. As the codebase grows, the team can decide to move these folders to separate swift packages. Later in the chapter the concept of mono repo and multi repo is discussed. One will get the idea of along with organizing the components as separate packages leveraging **Swift Package Manager** (**SPM**). *Figure 12.7* depicts the folder structure overview along with the key design philosophy used to separate and modularize the components of the Super App:

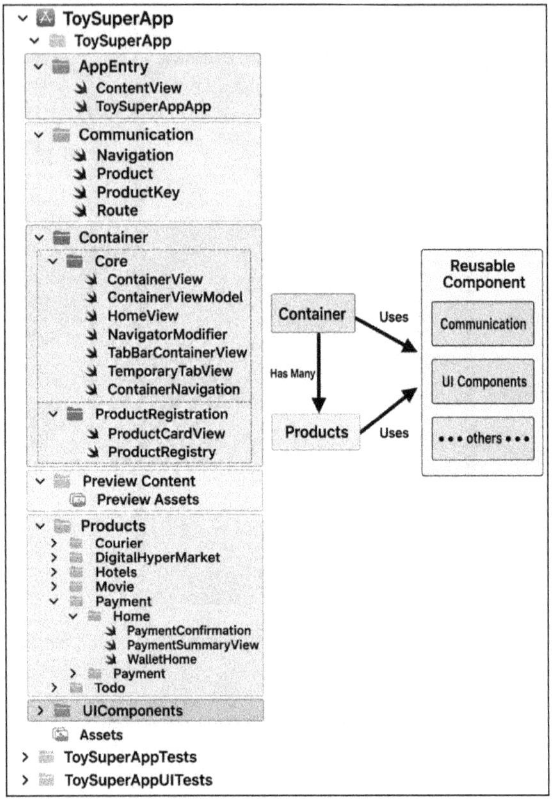

***Figure 12.7:** Project folder structure overview*

The chapter in the start introduced three components product, container and reusable module. *Figure 12.7* depicts the boundary of these groups marking the folders involved. Additional to these three components there is folder named **Communication**. **Communication** folders have files that defines the abstract interfaces and common classes used by product and the container. Later in section the responsibility fulfilled by each of the files within **Communication** folder are explored.

AppEntry folder group the files to setup the application's entry point. The entry point to SwiftUI view class is like what was explained in the `HelloSwiftUIApp`.

Container core

The Toy Super App is a simple app with tab bar having Home (icon) as default selected tab. The **Home** tab has a list of products and few cards. Refer to the landing screen in the preceding *Figure 12.6*. On clicking on the product, the respective product home page will be loaded. The responsibility of container component can be grouped into classes defined in two folders - core and the product registration. In the Toy Super App, the files inside the code folder deals with the container functionality. The tab view parent, navigation stack, view model supporting the views, the container views each the tabs etc., are the examples of the files. The decision of what should be in the code depends on the feature. In the Toy Super App all the tabs are wrapped inside the container. One can see the core section hosting the implementation of the Super App container features or entry point for call to action to a product or rendering landing page of a product.

One of the main responsibilities fulfilled by the container core is owning the skeleton of navigation. The container hosts for the navigation structure for the entire application. The Toy Super App follows a stack-based navigation where the SwiftUI parent defines the tab view, as the root view. The product pages are loaded onto the root on need basis when the user selects the product. Based on the call to action, the stack operation of push and pop is performed giving the user the functional experience expected from the app.

Consider the example scenario where a user opens the application, selects the wallet product from home and selects the pay functionality. *Figure 12.8* depicts the structure of the navigation in this scenario:

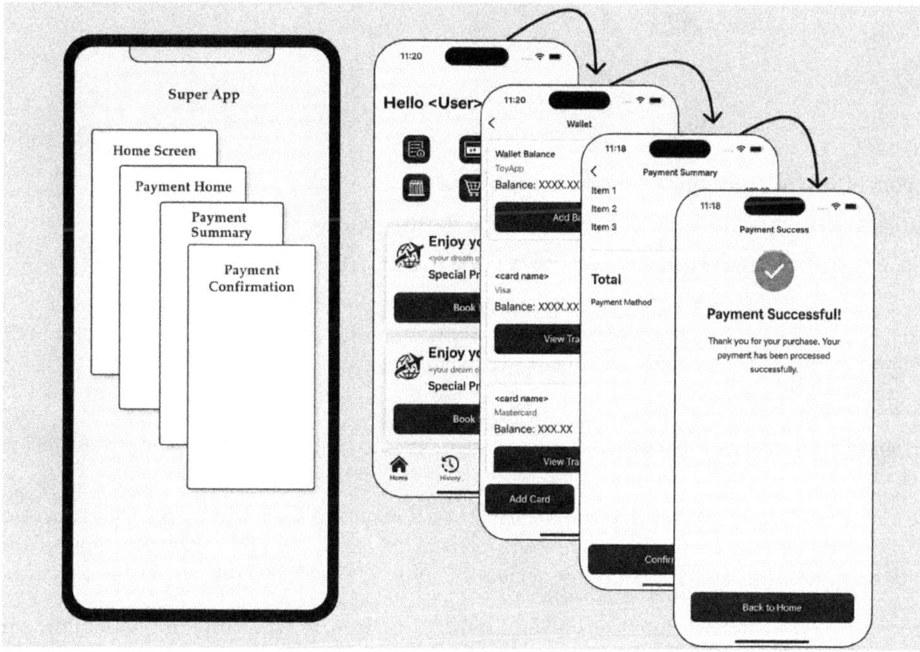

Figure 12.8: *Navigation stack snapshot for a simple payment flow*

After successful payment, the stack should have option to return the payment home. On the call to action to return from the payment summary or the pay success the pop action from the stack will take the user to previous screens. The navigation stack is UI component within SwiftUI framework. The Toy Super App has configured this navigation stack in the user interface layer of the core component. The following code is the **`ContainerView`** that represents the **`Container`** entry point and the navigation layer:

```
// ContainerView.swift
struct ContainerView: View {
 @StateObject private var viewModel = ContainerViewModel()
 @State private var routes: [Route] = [] // To manage the navigation path
 var body: some View {
  NavigationStack(path: $routes) {
   TabBarContainerView()
     .navigationDestination(for: Route.self) { route in
      route
        .productKey
        .home()
     }
  }
  .setNavigator(value: ContainerNavigation(popCall: { popRoute() }, push-
Call: { pushRoute($0) }))
```

```
 }
 func pushRoute(_ route: Route) {
  routes.append(route)
 }
 func popRoute() {
  if !routes.isEmpty {
   routes.removeLast()
  }
 }
}
```

The key components in the preceding codebase are as follows:

- **NavigationStack** is the SwiftUI view providing the capability of the stack.
- **TabBarContainerView** is the custom view written to host each tab view.
- The array variable **route** is the backing data structure to hold the data object associated with each view which is added to the navigation stack. Push and pop method on the route data structure will trigger the navigation calls. This happens as the **route** variable is bound with the **NavigationStack** view.
- Route is a custom class defined.
- The **pushRoute** and the **popRoute** will trigger the mobile to initiate the screen redraw as the top item in the stack changes.
- The modifier **navigationDestination** is the method that gets called when the **pushRoute** action is triggered and the code written inside the closure will present the view onto the navigation stack. A modifier is a SwiftUI capability and is an example of declarative syntax. Modifiers enhance the SwiftUI view properties.

Note: **Understanding the SwiftUI constructs is important. Therefore, to efficiently implement the same do read the other books from BPB that go in depth about SwiftUI.**

Communication

The **Communication** folder was briefly introduced earlier. It was explained to take the responsibility to host the files that are the abstractions used by both product and the container. In the context of Toy Super App MVP there are three classes: **Navigation**, **Route** and **Product**.

The following is the codebase depicting the **Navigation.swift**:

```
// Navigation.swift
import Foundation
import SwiftUI
protocol Navigation {
 func pop()
 func push(route: Route)
}
// Define an environment key
struct ContainerNavigationEnvironmentKey: EnvironmentKey {
 static var defaultValue: Navigation? = nil
}
extension EnvironmentValues {
 var navigator: Navigation? {
  get { self[ContainerNavigationEnvironmentKey.self] }
```

```
    set { self[ContainerNavigationEnvironmentKey.self] = newValue }
  }
}
```

The protocol **`Navigation`** and the environment key **`ContainerNavigationEnvironmentKey`** is responsible for abstracting out the responsibility enabling navigation. Such an abstraction encapsulates the navigation details from the product. A product will not know how navigation happens. Instead, the abstraction defines the contract which is used to invoke the navigation action. In the runtime the dependency is resolved to the action written in the container. The navigation protocol is injected as dependency to SwiftUI environment accessible in the view hierarchy leveraging the **`ContainerNavigationEnvironmentKey struct`**. The dependency is retrieved from the context by defining the **`@EnvironmentObject`** property for any SwiftUI view coming inside the view hierarchy. As seen in the SwiftUI sample app the code is written in a box model with nested container, peers and children in a hierarchy. The **`@EnvironmentObject/@Environment`** is the property wrapper mechanisms provided in the frameworks to retrieve a Swift object/struct injected in the parent. The binding of navigation object to the environment key happens inside the **`ContainerView`**. This is the first step to register the navigation mechanism. A product or even a view in the container can use **`Navigation`** protocol. What happens within Container is not an external concern and can be kept obscured. The capabilities exposed via **`Navigation`** protocol is best understood exploring the codebase associated with the chapter available along with the book in the repository. In the later section the code for using the **`Navigation`** protocol is depicted.

Product protocol

The product is the mini application which is hosted inside the Super App. The container needs to know only the essential details to operate. The implementation details of product are encapsulated from the Container component. The capability to communicate is achieved via the product protocol. Every product created should have a class that implements the product protocol. The registration of this class to container will establish the connection between product and container. The following code represents the implementation details of the **`Product`** protocol:

```
//Product.swift
import SwiftUI
protocol Product {
 var name: String { get }
 init()
 var productIcon: ImageType { get }
 func productHome() -> ProductHomeView
}
struct ProductHomeView: View {
 let view: any View
 init(view: some View) {
  self.view = view
 }
 var body: some View {
  AnyView(view) // The passed view will be displayed here
 }
}
```

There is a **`ProductHomeView`** alongside the protocol that serves as the container for the product home page.

Route

Route is the class that holds the data contract to invoke the navigation. The following code for depicts the same:

```
protocol IRoute: Hashable {
 var value: String { get set }
```

```
    var intVal: Int { get set }
}
struct Route: IRoute {
    var productKey: ProductKey
    var value: String
    var intVal: Int
}
```

ProductKey

ProductKey enumeration uniquely identifies a product in the application. A new case should be added to the **enum** for every new product being introduced to the Super App. This **enum** serves as a unique key that identifies a product within Super App. This should be defined by the team. The following code depicts the **enum** having the products listed in the Toy Super App:

```
enum ProductKey: CaseIterable {
    case todo
    case movie
    case courier
    case hotels
    case digitalHyperMarket
    case wallet
}
```

Products

This folder is where the different products in the Super App are organized. For each product, there is a separate subfolder as depicted in *Figure 12.7*. Every product should have a class/struct that extends the product protocol. Defining the class/struct for product is important to establish the main connection with the container of Super App. The establishing of the connection by setting up the dependency for the product is the registration. Any communication and dependency to be injected will be via this class in the container module. The dependency setup is handled in addition to the SwiftUI **@EnvironmentObject/@Environment** property wrappers. The usage of property wrappers which natively provides the capability to inject dependency in the UI hierarchy via the SwiftUI context. However, if the classes other than UI require the dependency from the container must be supplied via registration mechanism. The following code depicts the implementation for the **Payment** product. The pattern is repeated to configure every other product:

```
import Foundation
import SwiftUICore
struct Payment: Product {

    var name: String = "Wallet"
    var productIcon: ImageType = .name("wallet")
    func productHome() -> ProductHomeView {
        return ProductHomeView(view: AnyView(WalletHomeView()))
    }
}
```

Note: **As part of the Toy Super App, the payment product implements a wallet for MVP as a mechanism for payment.**

Product registration

This section of the Toy Super App has two Swift files: **ProductRegistry** and the **ProductCardView**. **ProductCardView** is the UI card that has the grid view for various products. The icon and the relevant details for the grid view come from the respective product as shown in the following code:

```
// ProductCardView.swift
import SwiftUI
struct ProductCardView: View {
 @Environment(\.navigator) var navigator
 private var products: [ProductKey] = ProductRegistry().products()
 var body: some View {
  LazyVGrid(columns: [GridItem(.adaptive(minimum: 80))]) {
   ForEach(products, id: \.self) { key in
    ZStack {
     IconCard(icon: key.icon())
      .padding(8)
     Button {
      navigator?.push(route: Route(productKey: key, value: "test", intVal: 1))
     } label: {
      HStack {
       Spacer()
      }.frame(maxWidth: .infinity, maxHeight: .infinity)
     }.background(Color.clear)
    }
   }
  }
  .padding()
 }
}
```

The **@Environment** property wrapper is used to access the **navigator** that has been injected to the container. Based on the grid selected, the entry page of the selected **Product** will be loaded. The entry point is defined as a part of the implementation of **func productHome()** for each product which implements the **Product** protocol.

ProductRegistry file has the following Swift code which has two parts: an extension for the **ProductKey** and the **ProductRegistry** class. The list of **ProductKey** is returned as part of the **ProductRegistry** class. The **ProductKey** extension binds the product class type with the different case. The methods to access the product home and icons is also implemented in the extension:

```
// ProductRegistry.swift
import Foundation
import SwiftUICore
class ProductRegistry {
 func products() -> [ProductKey] {
  return ProductKey.allCases
 }
}
extension ProductKey {
 func product() -> any Product.Type {
  switch self {
```

```
case .todo:
  return Todo.self
case .movie:
  return Movie.self
case .courier:
  return Courier.self
case .hotels:
  return Hotels.self
case .digitalHyperMarket:
  return DigitalHyperMarket.self
case .wallet:
  return Wallet.self
}
}
func home() -> some View {
 let product: Product = product().init()
 return product.productHome().navigationTitle(product.name)
}
func icon() -> ImageType {
 return product().init().productIcon
}
}
```

The **ProductRegistry** class thus fulfils the responsibility of consolidating the different products in the Super App. The **enum ProductKey**, which is part of the communication layer, is extended to bring in a creational design pattern. The product selected is initialized and returned by this extension and used inside the container to display the selected product.

Consolidating learning from Toy Super App

Now that we have looked at the individual class level detail, it would be ideal to summarize how all these fits into one coherent unit. The Toy Super App is a smaller scale version of a magnum opus. The three components build in the section only have the maturity of the initial foundational structure. This structure can be expanded further. The product is segregated with a clear separation of concern and a team focused only on a particular product will have to worry only about the files within the product folder. The one-time registration with the container is the only code that will ever be written outside the logical boundary of product code, connecting the product to container. The common reusable modules will be leveraged by both the container and the products.

The container orchestrates the navigation within the Super App. The container has the skeleton to which the product can be plugged in. The product will supply the entry point which gets injected to the viewport within the skeleton inside container. When a product tries to exit or navigate to another product, the request to transition within the application should go via the container module.

The communication folder is where all the abstractions are organized. The separate folder structure ensures that the common swift protocol and implementation are available for both container and product without complicating the dependency graph. This separation prevents any cyclic relation between products and container that brings tight coupling. *Figure 12.9* depicts the anti-pattern for having the communication with the container and the means to mitigate the same:

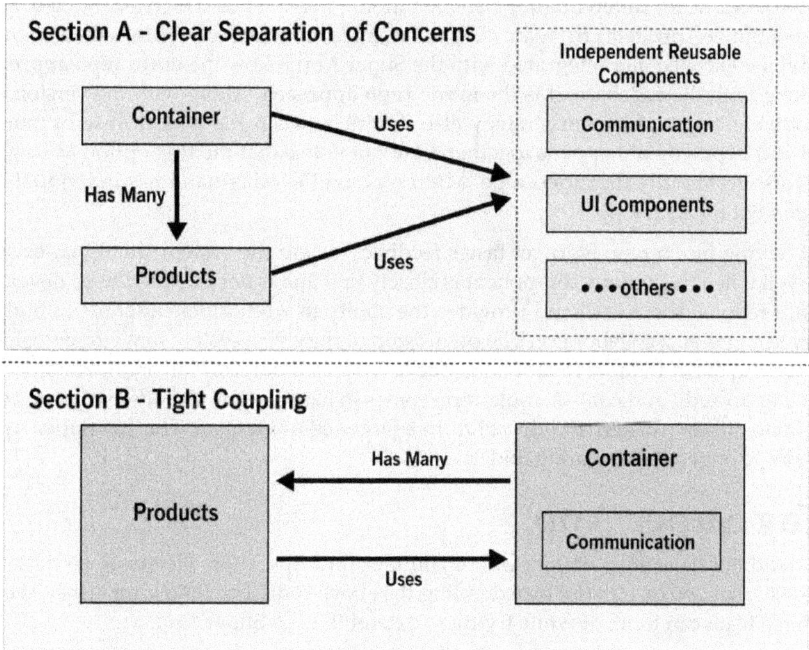

Figure 12.9: Tight coupling and means to avoid

The tight coupling of the code can be seen in the example in the above figure (*Section B*) where the communication is kept as part of the container. The product and the container use the communication layer. There forms a cyclic dependency. The communication as reusable component promotes clear separation of concern will help to avoid the cyclic dependency. The *Section A* in the *Figure 12.9* depicts the modified communication layer architecture which mitigates the cyclic dependency. The common layers used by the product and container should be separate and independent. The cyclic dependency will be an issue when all these folders are separate packages/libraries.

Note: **The folder organization is a choice to be decided based on the context of the Toy Super App. As the application grows, the necessity to have a separate library or other equivalent mechanism would be needed. The project team should keep check and prevent complex dependency graph between the different components in such a situation. The communication layer hops and the mechanism to reduce the transitive dependency to optimize the build time is also a factor to be kept in mind for the Super App architecture design.**

Mono repo and multi repo

Let us start with the question, *how can one organize any mobile code base?* The answer will be one of the following options:

- A single project with appropriate group or folder managed under one version control.
- A single project that uses the libraries and dependency managed from another team or opensource maintained outside in a separate repository.
- A single project aggregating for different libraries and dependency along with its own functionality maintained together under one repository. These libraries are part of the same versioned repository of the parent codebase in this case. At any point the libraries can be extracted independently outside to a separate repository and can be linked to the parent project without disturbing the working of functionality.

These options are the baseline for differentiating between mono/multi repos. The reason to talk about mono/multi repos in the context of Super App stems from the need to organize the codebase. A project where the components are independently version controlled and integrated with the Super App follow the **multi repo approach**. If the version control happens along with the codebase, it is the **mono repo approach**. Along with the version control difference between the two options, the deployment strategy also differs between the two. In case of mono repo since it is centrally managed and deployment happens together. One can notice that the first option as single project without any dependency is also technically the mono-repo. Multi repo on the other hand has individual deployment cycle and version management for each repo.

The philosophy of having mono repo is to get faster feedback where the system should co-exist near each other. Mono repo works well when the various component is closely knit and is not intended to be developed or versioned independently. Multi repo on the other hand provides the ability to work independently. In multi repo, each repo becomes a provider rather than a collaborator. The ownership of the entire system may not percolate in case of multi repo to each team owning the individual repo. This is due to the siloed nature. If an organization needs to handle this a process is required to do audit and control. multi repo comes in handy when the different teams evolve at different rates and the requirements are isolated and do not fit in a larger common goal. The Toy Super App MVP follows a mono repo with a single project as a separate folder.

Beyond Toy Super App

The Toy Super App did not have any network call or complex data operation. However, all these could be the next phase for development that one can try out by extending the above code. The following is the list of few possibilities and the nuances that a team can think of while trying to extend the Toy Super App:

- The decision of multi repo or mono repo should be debated. Irrespective of the outcome of decision in both mono and multi repo giving a level of autonomy for product will help in increasing the development pace. For example, enabling the autonomy for each product would mean to have a mini host application to run the product independently without the main codebase and other product. The lightweight host could possibly mimic the key feature of the main and enable a specific team to run the individual product in isolation without running the entire application.
- The downstream layers should also be seamlessly designed to integrate with each other. This is important to ensure good experience to end user. For example, consider a situation where the user login to the application and each time the user navigates to a different product the login flow re-triggers. In the normal sense, this is not a great user experience. The backend should be capable of abstracting this from the mobile layer. There should be one time login to authorize user and can access every product without separately signing in.
- Communication layer should not ideally contain responsibility specific about the product or container. Ideally as the time progresses the communication layer should have minimal change. This becomes important as the change affect all the consumer layer increasing the build time for the modularized Super App codebase.
- `ProductKey` in Toy Super App is a tech debt that violates the criteria of the communication layer having product information. The communication layer contains a specific enumeration of product names, violating the principle (stated earlier) that the communication layer should contain only common information. This ideally should be refactored to fulfill the criteria.

Try-it-yourself activity: Try to extend the MVP by adding a transaction history page. The transaction history page displays the list of payment made via the wallet for the different product or service within the Super App. The payment is not required for every product. The transaction history page is the place where the aggregation for transactions done by the user will be available on mobile app. This feature is a common feature for different product. In the activity the expectation is to reason about the implementation of a transaction history page on top of the Toy Super App MVP codebase.

Author's take on try yourself activity

The team can build the transaction history feature as a single page that consolidates all the transaction history details into one. In this case, the backend should either provide a single API, or the mobile should invoke the transaction history of the respective product to be aggregated into the common page. Doing the latter in the mobile layer is an anti-pattern as the non-determinism is high. The mobile will have to tackle the failure and retry for multiple permutations of individual product transaction history fetch. An alternative implementation is a case where the transaction history page will be separately included in each product. The team must analyze user experience data to conclude whether the transaction history should be on one page or as part of an independent product. The Super App is still a single app in the lens of the mobile user and in most cases, having a backend service is preferred that collates the common feature. This example depicts a pattern that the team can emulate and repeat for similar features. This example also gives a hint on the necessity of backend orchestration layer for cross cutting feature across products in a Super App.

Modularized Toy Super App

The section is code walkthrough on an extended version of the Toy Super App codebase. In this version the components maintained as folder are extracted as separate swift package. *Figure 12.10* depicts the transition from the simple version to the modularized version using the Swift Packages Manager for the Toy Super App:

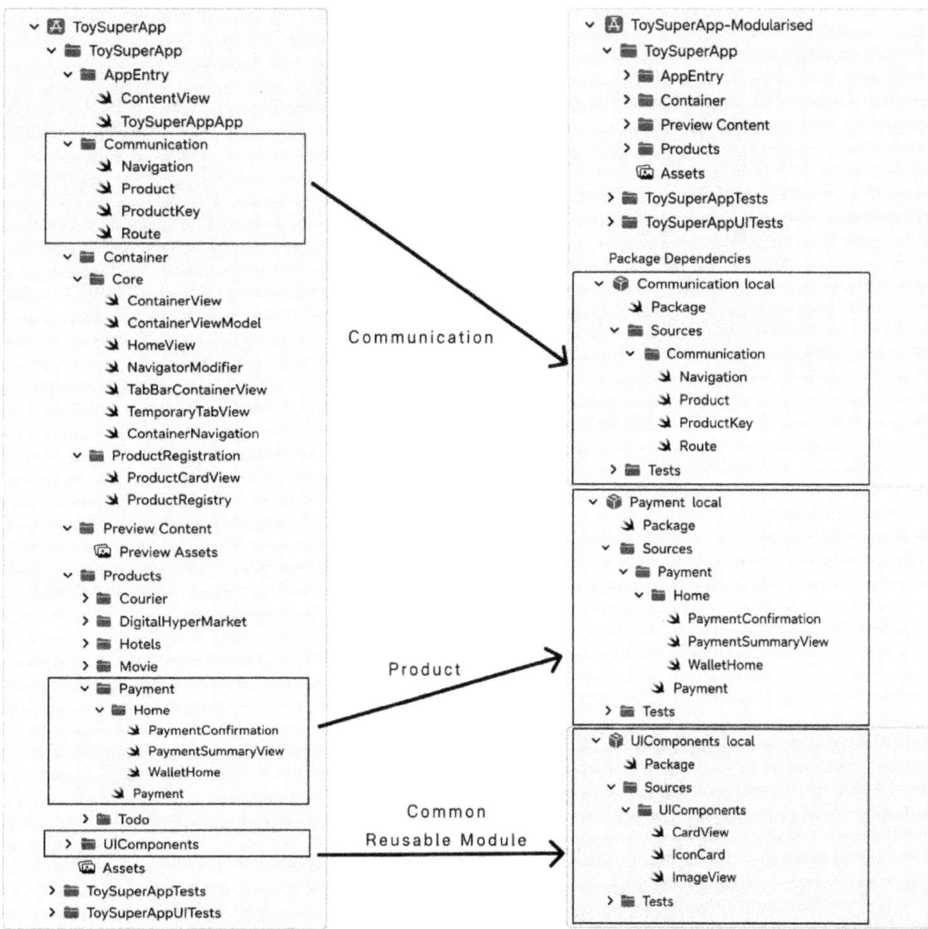

Figure 12.10*: Folder structure simple versus modularized with SPM*

The clear difference visible in the *Figure 12.10* is the folder migration and the change to Swift packages. The **Payment** product, **Communication** folder and the **UI Component** is migrated to Swift packages. The other products and common reusable modules which are logically separable can follow a similar strategy. The ownership and the team dynamics may differ for each organization for managing and owning the Swift packages. The key is that this structure for a Super App could provide an isolation for building independent modules coexisting in the same ecosystem preventing silos. The preceding codebase has multiple swift packages maintained in the same repository, implying a mono repo strategy. However, the Swift packages in the above case will be independent and hinting at effortless migration to multi repo if the team needs to change the strategy.

Note: **The keyword independent module and functional silos are the contrasting traits that ensure substance and scalability of the larger ecosystem. The team working on individual module will collaborate, however the independent nature of module is essential to ensure parallel development of multiple products in mobile application is achieved faster.**

The migrated version code is also available along with repository hosting code bundle associated with the book. The difference is the creation of Swift package and linking to the main app. The appropriate access modifier and changes are part of the same codebase ensuring the classes are exposed outside the Swift packages. Import of Swift package to appropriate files in the container, using the public entry points to register and connecting the SPM code is the structural change between the two versions.

Conclusion

The objective of the chapter was to introduce the reader to the world of Super App and the nuances around it. The initial setup for how to build a Super App is now covered and what one has experienced while reading the chapter is a flavor providing the proper foundation for any Super App. Building a Super App is a mindset shift in three lens operation, product and technology. An individual can follow the theme along practices and principles advocated in the other chapters of this book to build a robust Super App. The chapter thus provides a strong foundation necessary for majority of consumer class mobile applications.

The focus of the next chapter is on the creation of a logical map of a few architectures and patterns. This is done by carving out the responsibilities of components involved. The objective of the chapter is not to decide what is best. The idea will be to gather insights for the use cases where the architecture has worked out well.

Takeaway and reflections

Now that we have reached the end of the chapter, the reader shall be equipped with a familiarity and thought process to get started on building or being a part of a Super App ecosystem:

- Having worked through the Toy Super App, the reader will now appreciate the comprehension involved in technology side of Super App development. The reader would understand the implication of the term as an application that brings multiple businesses under one umbrella. It also gets the name as it is an all-encompassing self-contained service or product offering from an organization.
- Product, container and reusable are three components of Super App. There is a special reusable component called communication which is responsible to reduce the tight coupling between the container and product. This module will have abstract interface and classes which will be used by both product and container. The responsibility of these will be to enable the communication between the product with container or vice versa.
- Platform team is essential for the success, scale and sustenance of a Super App team.
- The platform team can be formed either by collective contribution from each squad building the feature or having a dedicated group. The decision is operational and contextual to project, depending on the need, budget and the availability of people.

- The Toy Super App built in SwiftUI has introduced a practical implementation of the various components of a Super App.
- In the Toy Super App, the navigation is based on a route or path using an abstract protocol navigation. Any navigation outside of the product should leverage this protocol. Similarly for a container the same protocol can be used for triggering navigation. Such a design is achieved by having a central method intercepting the route related call and brings the appropriate UI onto the screen.
- This route-based approach is an example that shows the architectural eloquence that enable a clear separation of concern. The product module which is designed is loosely coupled with each other.
- The container is the key feature hosting Toy Super App.
- The same structure with the necessary syntactical changes could be replicated for Android (using Kotlin and Jetpack Compose) or a cross-platform framework (such as Flutter).

CHAPTER 13
Introduction to Mobile Architecture

Introduction

Any developer will look for recurring patterns when trying to understand and read an existing code base. The ideal state for any codebase would be to follow an architecture. The architecture gives a structure to the codebase. Following an architecture implies having a recurring pattern that helps any new individuals to onboard to the ecosystem easily. The individual shall be able to navigate the codebase and start contributing with ease. For a software codebase, it becomes essential to incorporate relevant patterns to improve readability and maintainability of the codebase. This will help increase the productivity of the development team. Architecture discussed in this chapter sets the guidelines and structure for equipping the team to operate with the mindset required to establish a scalable codebase.

There are patterns that slow the team. These are termed as anti-patterns. Anti-patterns are the result of ignoring the required guidelines to be followed in the codebase. Avoiding introducing any new anti-patterns and clearing up the debt of anti-pattern is essential to maintain the sanity of an evolving codebase. Anti-patterns learned from the collective wisdom from experience in the industry could become a source for learning and being proactive to prevent these anti-patterns from recurring. The team with the knowledge shall move forward without repeating the same mistakes.

As a developer, one should invest in understanding these architectures, patterns and anti-patterns. The goal would be to acquire the skill to effectively leverage all three in project execution.

Structure

This chapter covers the following topics:

- Patterns and architecture
- Mobile architecture
- Factors influencing architecture
- Reactive programming paradigm
- Architectures
- Mechanism complementing architecture

Objectives

The purpose of the chapter is to look at the prevalent means to architect a mobile codebase. The chapter explores the prevalent themes in the development community and dissects them to be accessible to developers. The chapter also has the ambitious goal to break the notion that it is hard to think in terms of pattern and architecture for an individual with limited industry experience. The chapter will look at various independent themes that fall under the larger umbrella of architecture. A historical evaluation of the popular architectures in the context of mobile development is a theme explored in the chapter.

Patterns and architecture

One can deduce that progress is faster not by reinventing but by improving, innovating, and solving challenges. This idea resonates with the software industry as well. The software industry has been emerging in the technology landscape. Pursuing the continuous progress and individual's nature to keep track and catalog the learning has been the catalyst for the growth. The curation of the recurrently occurring category of problem statement and their solution will act as the baseline to model a similar software system. From the mid-20th century, there have been many catalogues that collated sourcing the information from the problem statement and their solution. These catalogues evolved along with the evolution of programming languages. The industry at the early stages was majorly concentrated with system software and later in the timeline, object oriented programming emerged. As the focus shifted to consumer-grade enterprise software, the popularity of a particular catalog, **Gang of Four** (**GoF**), flourished. The popularity was amongst the practitioners building such consumer applications, a group that includes the mobile development community. Demystifying the terms pattern and architecture is the focus of the section.

Note: **Understanding the different catalogues is intellectually stimulating. In the context of the mobile application development, the GoF catalogue is the one which a mobile developer will most likely encounter in the day-to-day development.**

Patterns literally mean a recognizable repetition or regularity in something. In the context of the codebase, the major constituent is the design pattern, also known as the code pattern. The design pattern can either be enforced by the framework or defined by a developer within any project. Patterns are used to address a specific localized problem statement within the code written for the software. A typical software will have interaction within the codebase, other external systems or third-party components. The software which is monstrously sized can be modeled to be a combination of logical components. These components collectively function together to attain the common goal.

Architecture is a set of decisions that define the structure of a project's components and their relationship. The architecture definition could include the patterns used, roles, and responsibilities of components used within a project. For individuals, understanding the architecture will give the confidence to be effective in navigating the code. This understanding gives an idea of how the code is organized and provides a clear direction when trying to modify the codebase. From the point of view of a software developer, architecture defines how the code is organized and structured. For a simple software, an architecture definition will have minimal components and details of external interaction. This granularity can differ and for a complex system the architecture defined could be multiple layers. Each layer will be subsystem interacting with one another. The subsystem will behave as a smaller independent unit with respective components and details of interaction within itself. For a complex application it is ideal to split into such smaller units.

Chapter 12, Use Case of Developing a Super App has the mobile application which is complex in nature. In the chapter one can see that the Super App is architected to operate at scale by dividing into smaller subsystem depicting a modular architecture. The Super App will have independent modules coexisting with clear boundaries functioning together inside a single app. These smaller units or subsystems are flexible to have separate architecture with own structures while recommendation will be to have a uniform style across.

An external interaction is another component that influences the architecture. In a mobile application the external interaction will be the connection to any downstream system, third-party library or device feature. There are a variety of patterns and architectures followed across the industry. Based on the context and the kind of problem statement being solved, the pattern and architecture leveraged would be different. Taking mastery of every item is impractical and not ergonomically sound. One should aim to decipher and understand the fundamental building blocks of each of these patterns and architectures and revisit the catalogue. The knowledge accumulates over a period. By garnering expertise in the fundamentals and as the time progresses, the possibility gets opened for mixing and matching the approaches. This could even lead to discovering new patterns and architecture.

Mobile architecture

The question arises as to why focus on mobile architecture. For an organization, the end-to-end architecture shall cover mobile and other front-end architecture definition. The end-to-end architecture gives the topology of the software system involved in the enterprise. A developer who wants to understand a particular sub-component/software within the enterprise should have a zoomed in view of the respective component architecture. The zoomed in view is very much required for a team to have focused direction to make progression. The mobile will also have the zoomed in view of architecture which encourages the team to build a scalable and sustainable mobile application codebase.

Chapter 8, Scalability in Mobile Development: Part 2 briefly touched upon the layers of architecture while exploring the folder structure and naming conventions in the mobile development codebase. The presentation, domain, and data form the separate logical components of the architecture. The logical boundaries of these three layers are decided based on the responsibility and purpose of the components. As part of this chapter the idea is to further explore each layer in context of architecture.

> Note: **Architecture is a guideline that evolves. Operating with these guidelines along with being creative and innovating to optimize the problem domain is a key skill to aim. Rote-learning hundreds of architectures may not help in an intellectual journey or effective utilization of skill on the ground.**

Presentation layer

The presentation layer has the responsibility of handling the code related to the user interface in a mobile application. The main responsibilities fulfilled by the presentation layer are styling, handling user action, responding to input actions from the end user, and managing the state. A state for the mobile application represents the current condition portrayed on the screen for the mobile device. The data backing a user interface which when changes trigger the transition is the responsibility of the presentation layer. Managing this data and deciding when and how the transition is triggered is termed as the state management. The mobile application operates by providing a means for the user to interact with the hardware. The presentation layer plays a pivotal role that handles the user-related behavior of the application. Managing the state thus becomes a key focus area for a developer to ensure functional accuracy of the user experience provided in the application. A robust state management strategy is part of the presentation layer and is the component that influences the architecture. User interfaces are another component of presentation layer. User interfaces are driven by the input from the end user. These inputs are encoded to state, which specifies the current data or condition of the application. In some cases, it also triggers an action. Both state encoding and triggering action can occur simultaneously. When an action occurs, the computation begins and the domain rules transform the input. The response to action after transformation is relayed back to the end users via the transformed state. The lifecycle that the user interfaces go through encompasses the responsibility taken up by the presentation layer which majorly involves the state management and transformation.

For a mobile application, the information handled varies from a simple static data to complex dynamic data presented via the user interface. In the codebase the state management deals with managing and maintaining both static and dynamic data. The source of the data could be a downstream system, file storage, value hardcode in code etc. For most mobile applications, the user interface corresponds to a major portion of the codebase. The user interface forms the means to reach consumers. The presentation layer thus becomes a critical piece of the codebase. Due to the critical nature the state-management strategy becomes a major pattern recurring in the codebase. The recurring nature thus led the team to use the state management strategy as the primary label by which mobile architecture is identified. Some of the examples of state management strategies are BLoC in Flutter, MVVM in native iOS/Android, and reactive programming approaches and these forms the label to represent the architecture followed in mobile application.

Domain layer

A domain layer hosts the code that defines the behaviors and nature of a mobile application. A domain layer is a logical layer that acts as the processing unit for the functionality/feature supported by the mobile application.

The data which the mobile application deals with when interacting with the downstream system passes through the domain layer to reach the presentation layer. The transformation logic, orchestration logic etc., are the responsibility of the domain layer. The domain layer forms the conduit that connects the data layer and the presentation layer. The presentation does not define or know about how the data is fetched or what happens with the data collected from the end user. The domain layer interacts with the presentation layer using the models/data representation. The domain layer has these data/models defined. The model is essentially a data type or a structured representation of the information. Depending on the complexity of the use case the data to handle could be a simple or complex collating information from multiple sources. A domain thus will have transformation logic involved to handle raw data. The raw data thus will get transformed to meaningful domain model which can be consumed by the downstream.

The domain layer is responsible for processing and responding to the user inputs or triggers from the presentation layer. The domain layer provides the response, with which the state management related logic will be triggered in the presentation layer. The domain layer does the data processing for both input from the user and the response from the downstream system. Field validation or transformation of date strings are examples of some of the input handling logic written in the domain layer. Another responsibility of domain layer is to orchestrate the different sources from which the mobile fetches the data and combine or transform results. When there is only single source for the downstream then the domain layer acts as a simple pass-through layer if the downstream gives the data in the format expected by client. The transformation may not be required in this case. The request and response in such case do not require much processing, making the domain layer logic thin.

For the data fetched from downstream systems, the data layer is the connector to this system. The data layer explained next forms the wrappers or abstraction which the domain layer will use. Any change in underlying downstream system does not affect the domain layer with this design choice.

Data layer

The third layer, the data layer acts as the abstraction over downstream systems and the hardware capabilities accessed by the mobile application.

The responsibility of the data layer is to be the central and single source of truth to connect with the data source. The domain layer passes the input and fetches the data from the downstream system using the data layer. The data layer does not deal with the functional logic exposed to the end user. The domain layer gets the response in the raw form and takes the role of transforming the data. The transformed data is channeled back to the presentation layer.

The presentation, domain and data form the major three layers in the codebase. The responsibility of the three layers is the guiding principle to organize the mobile codebase. While it is not mandatory to have all three layers for the mobile application codebase, it is the team who can decide based on the use case and define these responsibilities within the codebase. The three layers when followed will pave the way to achieve scalability, testability, maintainability, reusability, and flexibility. The downside that an individual would feel with the increase in the logical layer is the cognitive overload, boilerplate, and debugging overhead across layers. The benefit of the layering outweighs the complexity and challenges faced by a large team. It is recommended to enable the team to get equipped with the structure. This would bring long-term gains to the ecosystem.

Writing abstraction for all the hardware capabilities in data layer is not always possible in the strict sense. There is dependency on the development framework. For example, accessing the camera has a user interface action such as a shutter button, zoom slider, flash toggle, etc. These cases are example where the development SDK enforces a tightly coupled nature of the user interface with hardware capabilities. Going by the principle of data layer the code snippet for such feature will break responsibility advocated by data layer. Any deviation in the responsibilities of the layers is not a great design. In such cases the standard practice or recommendation is to keep the hardware related code snippet near to the layer which is closer to the responsibility fulfilled. In the example since the features are related to user interface, the code snippet is better placed in the presentation layer.

Architecture in practice

The possibility to structure the codebase as an amalgamation of multiple state management strategies and architecture patterns is always open. The architecture is a guideline and principle. Mixing and matching these patterns and deciding what adds convenience to the problem at hand is contextual. These choices should be finalized by the team. Consider the case of building an application. This application requires server driven UI with offline-first data sync as the capability. The application codebase will have the three logical layers. Additionally, the offline-first and data sync capability would be a separate problem statement altogether. In such a situation additional pattern to solve the data sync and offline-first could be modeled as a separate layer.

Note: **Trying to reinvent pattern without a clear goal is not a great use of time. For an already solved problem statement the enterprises can explore the possibility to adopt other product without reinventing the wheel. Leveraging a support of a third-party package or product is recommended strategy in the initial stage of growth or when the feature being built is not the primary business. The availability of a robust product in the market solving a problem statement the business aims to incorporate in their own product will ensure a faster time to market than custom building the same capability from scratch.**

Thought experiment

Architecting login feature: The section will leverage the details shared till now to think through a use case and apply the learning. Consider a simple login feature, which has two input fields and a button. The button is a call to action invoking the login API. The implementation for the feature will have the user interface related code written in the presentation layer. The login screen and the call to action invoking the domain layer is the major functionality implemented at the presentation layer. The responsibility of the code written in domain layer will be the input validations and the invocation to the downstream system. A developer designing the domain layer and beyond is presented with two options, one is with a data layer and the other without data layer.

The million-dollar question would arise when presented with the two option as to why a separate layer required to just call the login API. *Can the responsibility for login API invocation be part of the same domain layer?* The data layer in this case is just providing the abstraction of the downstream system. The data layer which is a hop could be avoided. The logic could be implemented at the domain layer without having this abstraction.

The thought experiment prompts the reader to reason about the previously-described use case and evaluate the necessity of the data layer. Additionally, the reader should expand further on the use case by designing the implementation of the sign-up feature with an auto login capability. The influence of this feature addition on the architecture layers will be an interesting use-case to reason with and will help to expand readers intellectual horizon on architecture layer.

Author's take on the thought experiment

The separation of concerns and responsibility of classes in each layer is the differentiating factor from the two choices of with or without the data layer.

Consider the case where the team is ambitious to maintain a strong test strategy for the codebase. The login feature discussed thus, would have to maintain proper **dependency injection** (**DI**) mechanism that would be necessary for writing scalable unit test for the classes written at different layers. The purpose of such separation of concern while writing unit test is to control and minimize the non-deterministic behavior and to contain the scope of unit testing. A class (user defined data type) can either use a dependency or can implement the logic within itself. The controlling of scope for testing is required when the class (user defined data type) has external dependency. A unit test focus will be to test the self-contained behavior. The accuracy of dependency is not the parent problem. Therefore, a mechanism is required to optimize the scope of testing while writing unit test. For example, while writing a test for user defined type in the domain layer there will be a method that has external dependency that communicates with the downstream system. The behavior of the external system is not in control of the mobile codebase. The unit test written around this functionality will be non-deterministic. The recommendation here is to trust that the external system works perfectly and to isolate it via mocking. The responsibility to test the external system does not lie with the consumer mobile code snippet. In such a case the domain layer would require a means to control the behaviors of the response from the network client by mocking the dependency. The unit test at the domain layer will be validating the business rules and transformation logic applied to the login API response (both success and failure). In each of the unit test the focus should be only to test the logic written in the domain layer. By having a *has-a* relationship with the data layer the domain can be tested independently without worrying about the data layer.

Note: **In object-oriented design there are different kinds of relationships between data types such as has-a, is-a, one-to-one, one-to-many, etc.**

The capability to control the behaviors of the APIs will thus ensure the tests written are deterministic and do not depend on the external entities. Introducing the sign-up page shall also follow the same ideology.

In an alternate case where there is no separate data layer in the architecture the probability that the team will face challenges in scaling is high. The entire code that connects to the downstream will be in the domain if there is no data layer. In the use case explored the login network call will be written in the domain layer. Adding the autologin feature post sign up will require the login related code snippet duplicated in the domain layer for sign up feature. If the data layer is written, the possibility of reusability across login and sign-up becomes an option. Consider a situation where further features such as social login, biometric authentication, etc., are added. In these cases, if the choice is to go with no data layer, adding more functionality to the login page would mean the class in the domain layer getting bloated and will have the responsibility of handling multiple cases. A bloated class is not a good ingredient for a scalable and sustainable codebase. Unit testing will also become harder in such code structure.

Factors influencing architecture

A mobile application architecture can be influenced by various factors such as the platform, technology, features being built, the team's history, etc. All these factors contribute to the key decision made by the team.

The section intends to explore a few use cases of a few mobile applications. The use cases explore the factors that contributed to the key decision in architecture.

Use case 1: Tax filing mobile app

The premise of the use case 1 is a mobile application project to develop a tax filing application. The team already had the portal on the web which was used by the end consumer. The organization decided to provide the tax filing service via mobile application. The team planned to build both iOS and Android version of the application. The following options were in consideration for the choice of technology stack:

- Native Android and iOS application
- React Native application
- Compose multi-platform - KMM supporting iOS and Android

The first problem statement was to finalize the technology choice. After that in the technology choice there were different options for architectural patterns. These architectural patterns include the popular opinion and recommendation from communities of the respective technology stack chosen. For an organization, it would be ideal and implicit to choose a style that is not too far off from the community recommendation. One may debate the need for the choice to be closer to the community recommendation. The choice for the architecture closer to the community recommendation reduces time required for bootstrapping and onboarding a team. Any individual hired to the team will have higher probability of being familiar with these choices. The choice of a style that differs from the popular opinion would add the effort to onboard and would have risk of failure if team cannot pick up. Getting acquainted with the style depends on various factor. The organization will have to invest with the hope of getting a potential result.

The choice of an architecture for the first time every historically brings a chicken-and-egg problem. If the first group that chose the technology did not invest in experimenting and figuring out the right pattern and architecture, no community path would have formed for those who follow and adopt the technology. In this use case the tax consulting organization did not have the technology acumen or budget to take the route of experimentation; rather, the focus was on bootstrapping and early time to market the product.

The use case does not deal with the architecture choice directly. However, if looked closely the use case presents the factor that influences the architecture.

Note: **The key takeaway from the use case is the influence of choice of technology, the community around the technology and the risk appetite of the organization.**

Table 13.1 lists examples of architecture pattern that can be used in the different development frameworks. This table depicts the influence of choice of technology on architecture:

Platform/Framework	**Architecture options**
Native iOS	MVC, MVVM, VIPER, clean architecture
Native Android	MVVM, MVI, MVP, clean architecture
React Native	MVVM, Redux, Flux, clean architecture
KMM	MVVM (commonly), MVI, clean architecture, shared business logic with platform-specific UI

Table 13.1*: Architecture options in various platforms*

Use case 2: Banking app modernization

A pattern can be seen in the industry that an organization outsources the development to an external team. In some instances when the organization decides to change the outsourced team, a transition period would be imminent. The organization decision to change could be motivated by many reasons. For the new team the existing architecture of the codebase is an important element that affects the progress and the decisions. The worst-case scenario would be the new team left with code patterns that does not follow any best practice or architecture. A code in such a state would be highly rigid towards refactoring. For the team taking over such a codebase would be challenging. The difficulty will prevail to fitting in any new architecture or patterns.

The team will either rewrite the entire functionality or nitpick the relevant code and rewrite it partially. For the rewrite scenario where the existing code is decommissioned, the choice of architecture depends totally on the new team. When the existing code is reused the team may have to choose the patterns that are compatible with legacy. The legacy code thus becomes one of the considerations that affects the architecture in the use case.

Note: **The key takeaway from the use case is the influence of the existing codebase affecting the decision of the architecture choice in the modernization or revamp of a legacy mobile application when an existing code is reused.**

Use case 3: News feed iOS application

An organization that publishes the news about sports has gained popularity amongst the masses. The organization took a web-first approach for the news feed service along with an Android version of the application. Given the popularity and traction received, the team decides to expand service to cater the audience using the iPhone as well. The organization assembled a team to develop the news feed iOS application. The organization required only a smaller team at most two developers for iOS development. The complexity and sophistication of the application were very minimal. The possibility of scaling beyond the newsfeed was also not in the roadmap. The key goal was to reach maximum consumers. The team looked at popular opinions in the community and came to know there are a variety of architectures to choose from. The **View, Interactor, Presenter, Entity, Router** (**VIPER**) architecture caught their attention. The era of this use case was when UIKit was the native framework to develop iOS applications. The two-member team decided to evaluate the choice.

The team came up with the following summary for the VIPER:

- Expansion for the acronym is the components each alphabet represents, such as view, interactor, presenter, entity, and router.
- The view is a user interface layer that manages the components.
- Interactors contain the business rules and logic for a screen. They communicate with the external data sources (APIs, databases, etc.) via a separate class and thus shielding presenter from any knowledge of how data is fetched or persisted.
- Presenter is the layer that tells the view on what needs to be displayed and is a relay between the interactor, which will channel the input and output.
- Entity is the data model.
- The router is responsible for coordinating the navigation between screens.

All these components of VIPER were required for every screen. In case there is reusable logic, the idea is to extract it into a separate class. The concept of VIPER is to have a clear separation of concerns with more straightforward classes that promote stability and scalability.

The two iOS developers were fascinated with the nomenclature and the structure. The news feed application planned had only a list view for feeds, a details page, bookmark capability, and a basic login capability. The mobile application approximately had 20-30 screens for the entire flow. The healthy debate on whether it is worth adding the boilerplate required for the VIPER got triggered. The debate focused on the need to absorb the complexity and overhead of the boilerplate for such a small use case. The two developers, with careful deliberation, decided not to go with VIPER. The law of parsimony, explained later in the chapter, asserts that the simplest form of designing things will be more economically viable. These factors, the minimal app complexity, the boilerplate overhead and the principle of parsimony, played a part in influencing the decision-making in this use case.

Note: **The key takeaway from the use case is that the complexity of the operating context and the specific need of the mobile application under development can influence decision-making in choosing the architecture.**

Use case 4: Car dealership app

An automotive dealership decided to build a digital ecosystem to complement their services with a vehicle booking mechanism. The dealership had the choice of a mobile application and website. The team decided to go mobile-first. The mobile application targeted two personas in the ecosystem—the employee working at the dealership and the consumer of the car. The user journey that surrounded these two personae was different. What the user could do on the mobile app depended on the privileges defined by the role and the access. The team decided to go with the then-recent player in the market as the technology partner for building mobile applications. The technology partner was also new to the automobile domain and did not have any promising data on the best practices or patterns to be used by competitors. The choices in the market presented a variety of options for the technology strategy. The team had to run experiments with a prospective technology choice and the pattern. The experiment was validating the possibility of the expected features in the automobile sector. The team created **proof of concepts** (**POC**) to verify the experiment. These POCs were designed with the possibility to leverage them later in the actual implementation of the product. Past knowledge of building mobile applications was helpful for working hands-on with the various technologies. The use case is an example where the development team has the potential to become a contributor to community knowledge when exploring new technology.

Note: **The key takeaway from the use case is that the unavailability of context will cause the team to do experiments where observation can influence decision-making in choosing the technology and architecture.**

The four use cases explored in the section look at some of the major and most probable factors a team will have to encounter while defining the architecture.

Reactive programming paradigm

Reactive programming is a paradigm based on the observer pattern to develop software applications. It is majorly beneficial for use cases which are event-driven. In the recent advancement in mobile ecosystem the frameworks took a declarative approach towards designing presentation layer development. The declarative approach can be seen in **Combine framework** on the iOS ecosystem and Kotlin Coroutines **Flow** in Kotlin. All these fundamentally follow the reactive paradigm approach. A similar pattern is seen in cross-platform development frameworks as well.

One should not assume that the reactive paradigm is only applicable for writing code in presentation layer. The paradigm can be seen in multiple layers of a mobile application codebase. Any use case that falls into the bucket of event-driven nature will work well with the reactive programming paradigm.

Reactive paradigm follows a structure where there are two prominent roles: an observer/subscriber and a publisher/subject. The publisher responds to a trigger by delegating the operation to be processed by a processing unit. The processing unit coordinates to give back the result to the publisher. Every publisher can be seen as hub for the event handling. Each publisher will have distinctive properties, purpose, and lifecycle. A trigger is an occurrence of some event that activates publisher to process and respond or broadcast the results to the subscribers. A publisher is observed by a structure identified as a subscriber/observer.

A subscriber registers with the publisher to listen to the values emitted by the publisher. The values emitted by the publisher are identified as an event observed by the subscriber. A series of publishers, along with the respective subscribers combined will function to achieve a larger computational goal. *Figure 13.1* represents the roles, responsibility and the interaction of the publisher-subscriber duo:

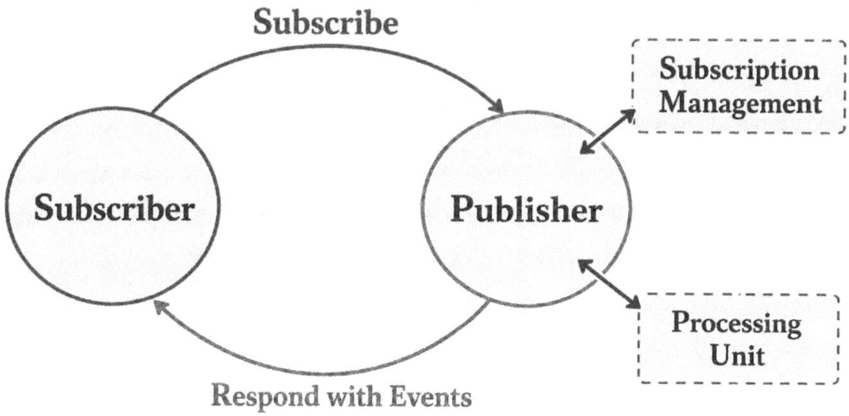

***Figure 13.1**: Components in reactive paradigm*

The publisher-subscriber duo is configured to do logically independent task. Multiple duos are combined and collaborate to form a chain of events and transformation to achieve features that constitute the mobile application. This strategy of combining multiple publisher-subscriber duo is a divide and conquer approach for solving complex problems. Each publisher subscriber duo will have an independent responsibility to be fulfilled. Such a design complemented with clear separation of responsibilities of the independent tasks will be required to scale any software.

A publisher can have more than one subscriber. The relationship between a publisher and subscriber can be seen as an interested party (subscriber) listening to an entity (publisher) broadcasting data. The capability or behavior exposed by the publisher defines what kind of subscription is possible. The publisher will have the subscription management as one of its capabilities. Subscription management takes care of the lifecycle of the subscriber interacting with the publisher. The capability of the publisher is not limited to subscription management; it also defines how the data/event is notified to subscribers.

Figure 13.2 depicts examples of three different publisher exposing capabilities:

Figure 13.2: *Example of publishers with different capability*

A subscriber consuming a publisher will thus be getting the values based on the kind of capability exposed by the publisher. The subscriber listening to the publisher P1 (Example: weather updates publisher) depicted in *Figure 13.2* receives continuous events until the subscription is explicitly cancelled by the subscriber. The publisher P2 (Example: file download publisher) on the other hand is like P1, however after certain period the event complete and stop after notifying to subscriber. P3 (Example: network call publisher) is a publisher with exactly one event. All these publishers can have other capabilities as well. The preceding example showcases one of the capabilities. *Figure 13.2* depicts a consumer-centric view of a publisher. The figure shows how capabilities of a publisher are perceived by the subscriber is portrayed. Publisher retaining the past events data, publisher acting as a broadcaster, asynchronous event handling, error handling or exception handling are examples of other capabilities a publisher can have.

The earlier *Figure 13.1* on the other hand depicts a provider-centric view showcasing the internals of a provider. In that *Figure 13.1* the provider has two components: subscription management and the processing unit. The subscription management manages the subscribers. The processing unit is where the handoff to the logical computation happens. The computation which the publisher is responsible to handle starts with a trigger and the input data. The processing unit is responsible for channeling these inputs when the respective trigger is received. What and how a provider should do the processing is solely dependent on what is programmatically configured on to the publisher.

The reactive framework influences the different kinds of publishers and subscribers available. The most prevalent use cases found in the industry are typically made available within the reactive library in the development framework. The capabilities of these predefined publisher is already built, and the team's role will be to use these publishers. The team then shall write the business logic, trigger to activate and configure subscriber for listening a publisher. The framework can support creating customized publishers and subscribers. In such cases the developer can customize the capabilities of the publisher from scratch. The capabilities unavailable inherently in the framework could be built separately with a custom publisher.

There are special classifications of publishers that act as upstream transformer. These publishers play the role of transforming the event from one publisher and re-publishing them according to their own configured capability, effectively wrapping the source publisher. The transformation inside the publisher thus changes the behavior seen by the subscriber. Publisher emitting the weather data every minute and subscriber has the requirement to increase the interval to 5 minutes is an example of the situation which require such transformation. The weather data will be coming from a backend server at a frequency of 1 minute. This data is consumed by the mobile application. In such a case, unnecessarily throttling the data from the backend is not scalable as the weather data will be used by multiple clients with different frequency requirement. Also, it is not intuitive as well to consume all the data from a resource utilization perspective. The solution will be to throttle the frequency at the client side. Alternatively, throttling the emitted value may seem too simple to write a new publisher to customize the frequency. Writing a new publisher for the frequency might be a strategy one can opt for. Such a publisher should take on multiple responsibilities both for managing the weather data and controlling the frequency logic. For a publisher responsible to get the data from the backend throttling a frequency is not a concern to be worried about. This should be ideally the responsibility of the layer that consumes the emitted data. Such a design brings a clear separation of responsibility. This design is possible with a mechanism that takes the existing publisher and transforms the publisher with expected frequency. The transformed version via publisher thus has a clear segregation of responsibility with reusability of the base functionality. The transformation follows the **decorator pattern** and ensures the base functionality is unchanged. In this case the transformer will throttle the publisher to emit the data every 5 minutes instead of 1 minute for the weather data. The reactive mechanism in reactive programming is known by multiple labels, predominantly called as **operators** or **transformers**. The examples of these are **`filter`** (only allow items that match a condition), **`debounce`** (suppress items emitted too quickly), **`flatMap`** (flatten nested streams), **`distinctUntilChanged`** (skip duplicate consecutive items), **`take`** (take the first n items), etc. The decorator pattern applied on a publisher is prevalent in the reactive paradigm. The frameworks provide the capability to chain multiple transformers as well. This capability thus enables building an ecosystem of reusable **operators**.

Figure 13.3 depicts the conceptual model of how the operators are connected to a publisher along with the journey of event transformed for subscriber to consume:

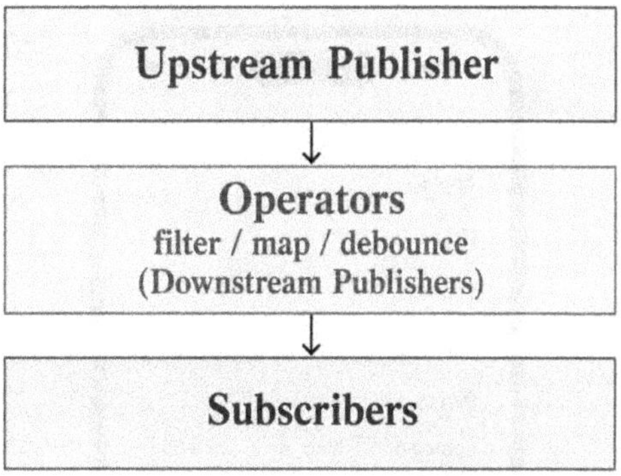

***Figure 13.3:** Role of operators in reactive paradigm*

Until now the section focused on the abstract concepts. Next let us investigate through the examples of the reactive library prevalent in industry. Combine is a library that is part of the iOS native development toolkit. One who explores the developer documentation will find the classes **`CurrentValueSubject`** and the **`PassThroughSubject`**. These are two classes which are examples of the publishers in the Combine framework. The Apple Developer documentation explains the capability of the **`CurrentValueSubject`** is to hold the last received value and notify the subscriber whenever the value changes. One can see the **`CurrentValueSubject`** as a publisher that remembers the last state. The **`PassThroughSubject,`** on the other hand, is a publisher that just sends the value to the subscriber and does not retain any value. Similar structures are available in other frameworks as well, for example, the RxDart, which is a library that implements the reactive paradigm in Dart. RxDart is used in Flutter. The **`PublishSubject`**(equivalent of **`PassThroughSubject`**) and **`BehaviorSubject`** (equivalent of **`CurrentValueSubject`**) are the publishers in the library.

Looking through some of the case studies would help demystify the reactive paradigm, further.

Case study 1: Search application

In this section the idea is to explore the use case of a mobile application functioning as a search engine. The application codebase has the responsibility to process the search query input and fetch the result from the downstream. The user entering the search query is also presented with probable query suggestion. This suggestion which is displayed to the user is fetched from a separate API. This fetching of suggestion via API is triggered when the characters are keyed in by the end user. The result which returns response to the search query is displayed on the screen to the user. This narrative represents a search engine behavior in the simplest form. The application can benefit from using reactive patterns. The search and suggestion features can be modeled as an action, processing unit and a result observing unit. For example, action is the search query input action, the processing unit is the API fetching mechanism and the user interface observing the result as the observing unit.

The user enters the values into the search input field letter by letter. For each letter the suggestion API shall be invoked continuously. The result is returned from suggestion API and is immediately updated to the screen. The user can select from the suggestion list and by doing so the search session concludes. A search engine with a larger active user base requires higher server compute. Higher compute can be achieved by scaling the systems. The design will add to the cost. In search engine application the experience that the end user gets where the search result is delivered faster is a critical expectation. The team will have to design the systems balancing cost and ensuring the experience is not tarnished. There are request triggers for every character being typed. For a user who is continuously typing the character does not ideally expect a suggestion. The result returned may not meet the original intention of the end user as well. When there is a delay in typing, a character could be potential trigger to provide suggestion and potential search result. By defining the code such that the search and suggestion are triggered only when typing is paused, unnecessary backend server calls can be avoided and optimized. Such a design of feature will reduce the cost to the organization and provide value to the end user. This also ensure the mobile power usage and performance are optimized.

Figure 13.4 depicts the search screen of the mobile with the user keying in the query:

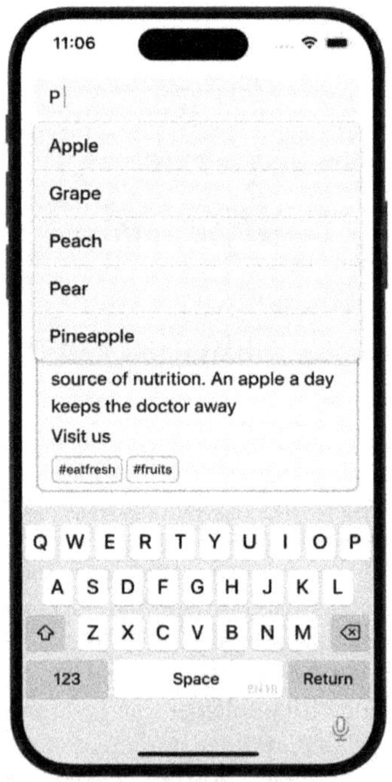

Figure 13.4: *Search engine home page*

Figure 13.4 depicts that the result returned by the server for the search query and the suggestions are displayed on the screen. This search result will be invalidated as soon as the user changes the search query, as the backend server will respond to the new results.

As the user key in search query, the suggestion appears in the list. The suggestion apple, grape etc., can be seen listed in *Figure 13.4*. The potential result is also loaded in screen beneath. When the user continues to enter the query the suggestion and the result will get additional context. The additional contexts will re-trigger suggestion and search results API to return the updated response that gets reloaded on screen. The new data will be much closer to what user is searching for due to the additional context. The problem specified earlier on the redundancy is evident in the use case. If the search query is large, then a backend request will happen for every keystroke. The result for each may not be relevant for the end user. The suggestion list may be important however since the user actively typing it is reasonable to consider they already know what they are looking for. A mechanism for the mobile application to throttle API calls until the user pauses the typing could be a strategy to reduce the redundant calls.

Note: **Studies on keystroke dynamics and typing speed show that the delay between typing words is typically in the 200–500ms range (Link to further read for the observed latency threshold in Appendix Reference) The reactive paradigm has a mechanism to optimize the delay to avoid the redundant call by using the debounce operator.**

The insights discussed till now has offered the view where search use case is the right candidate for an event-driven approach. A search mobile app thus can be architected with three layered architecture. The reactive component shall support each layer dividing and coordinating the various responsibilities. Invoking the backend API for both search and suggestion will be the data processing to be done on the mobile application. For every change in the value entered in text field, these APIs should be triggered. The API for search and suggestion has the potential to be the publisher that gets the input query text as the trigger. The trigger will activate the publisher to do the processing. The publisher takes the responsibility to establish the connection to the downstream and returning the result. The user interface screen subscribes to this publisher and listens to the result from downstream. The user interface layer then displays the query suggestion list and search result list.

The preceding explanation is a very high-level functioning; however, on the ground, there will be much more than just a single publisher and subscriber combinations. Before diving to search let us explore a generic three tier architecture in mobile with reactive components as depicted in *Figure 13.5*:

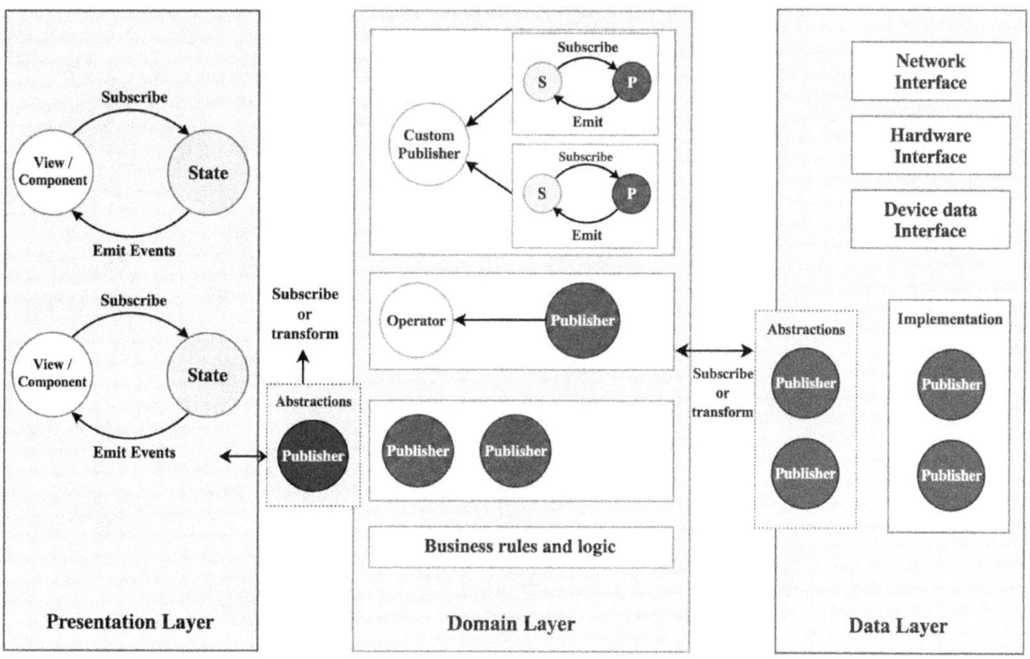

***Figure 13.5**: Mobile codebase slice for reactive paradigm*

Figure 13.5 depicts a thin slice of a single feature. The feature leverages the reactive paradigm in various layers, such as data, domain, and presentation. The data layer and the domain layer have the reactive paradigm used to address two responsibilities: one where the events are observed within the layers and the other where the publisher is exposed to a further layer. For example, the presentation layer will rely on the publisher exposed by the domain layer. Presentation layer subscribes the data from the downstream API published and on receiving the response it displays on to the screen. The necessary mapping to the user interface to display the screen state is maintained at the presentation layer on the subscribed side which get update with the response received. *Figure 13.5* depicts the view and component subscribing to the state. View/component is the user interface, and the state represent the information that changes and is displayed to end user. The state change occurs when the backend API returns error or result. The result or the error is implemented in the lower layer and a publisher exposed by the domain layer will act as the source for propagating the result or error to the subscriber at the presentation layer. The state change gets propagated directly or as a transformed version of the publisher from the domain layer via abstraction.

While implementing a publisher that connects one layer to another, the publisher object will either be a pass by reference or pass by value. If there is transformation (using operator or logic), there will be altogether different underlying type for the publisher which goes to the upstream layer.

Figure 13.6 contextualizes the reactive paradigm to search feature implementation described in this section. It shall resonate with the thin slice represented in *Figure 13.5* and maps the respective code structure of the search feature.

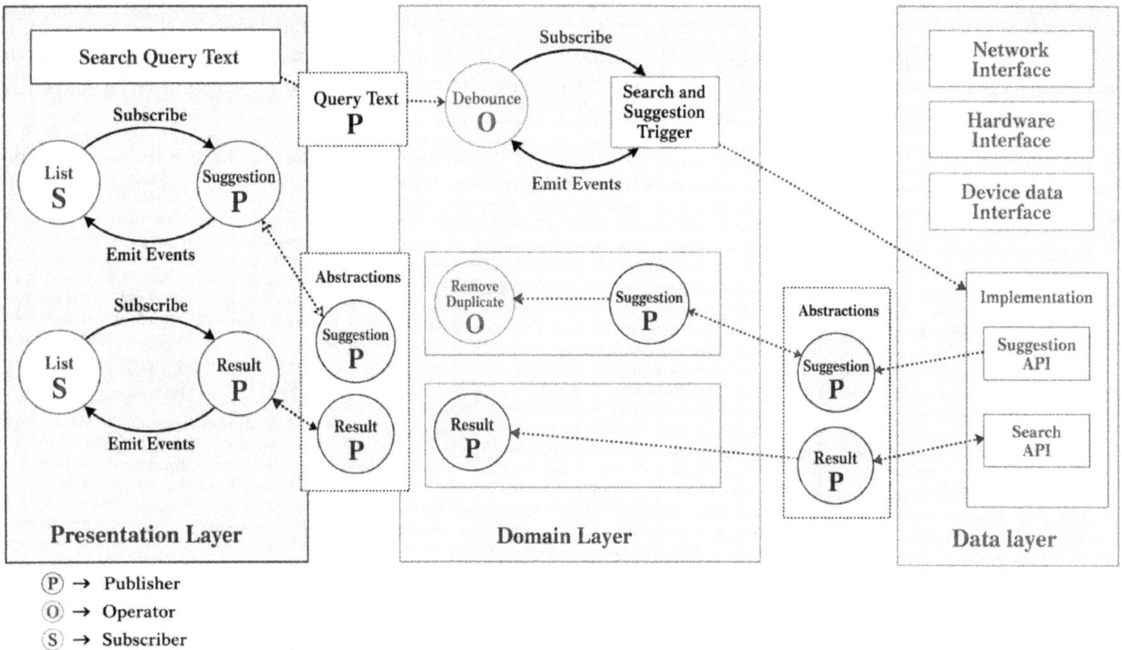

***Figure 13.6:** Search feature architecture topology*

The user entering the query is the trigger to kick start the search and suggestion API invocation. The trigger is channeled to the domain layer. *Figure 13.6* uses arrow depicting the direction in which a publisher is subscribed to receive the data. Query text entered by the user is another publisher at the presentation layer. The query text change is observed by the domain layer. The classes at the domain layer have the subscriber listening to the text published by the query-text publisher. The text change event gets cascaded to the publisher at the other layer. This text change event is the source that activates a chain of publisher subscriber interaction ultimately leading to invoke the API call in the data layer. The situation portrays a case where different publisher-subscriber collaborate to send input from user interface to the data layer. The publisher at the presentation layer is observed and when the event occurs, sends a message to the consuming layer, in this case the domain layer. The query-text publisher is throttled to control the number of text change events been triggered that activate the API invocation. The throttle is done by inducing a delay using the debounce operator. This ensures API is called only when the user pauses and not between every keystrokes. The publisher in the domain layer that gets trigger is responsible for responding with result and propagating the trigger further to the data layer. As the downstream system responds the data is propagated back from the data layer to presentation via the publisher exposed. The direction of the flow of the response data is opposite to the query text change flow. The data layer exposes the publishers for API which the domain layer can listen to for receiving the results. The domain in this case takes the responsibility of either just being a passthrough or do light weight transformation of the result. The optimization that can be done at the domain layer is to prevent and filter the duplicate by checking the difference with the result already sent. The domain layer exposes the publishers which the presentation layer can subscribe to and update both suggestion and search-result on the respective user interface. Both lists will redraw the user interface to display to the end user as and when update data is received.

The publishers at the data and domain layer send the data in the direction depicted by the arrow in *Figure 13.6*. This use case demonstrates how a publisher-subscriber pair coordinates and handles a larger task by divide and conquer to smaller logical activities. This smaller task collectively achieves goal defined by the larger task.

The next focus is to look at the pseudocode for presentation and domain layers. The implementation details of each of these will strengthen the conceptual understanding for the reader.

Pseudocode for the presentation layer

The following is the pseudocode for the **SearchView** and **SearchViewModel** classes in the presentation layer:

Note: The usage label Component in the pseudocode is to denote a cohesive unit of functionality that could be a class or struct as per the programming language.

```
Component: SearchView
- UI Elements:
        - InputField: searchTextField
        - ListView: suggestionOverlayList
        - ListView: searchResultList

Component: SearchViewModel
- State:
        - Observable<String> queryText
        - Observable<List<SearchResult>> searchResults
        - Observable<List<Suggestion>> suggestions
- Method: setupSubscriptions()
        Action 1:
 Subscribe: queryText with debounce
 Trigger: search()
 Update: searchResults
        Action 2:
 Subscribe: queryText with debounce
 Trigger: fetchSuggestions()
 Update: suggestions
- Method: search()
        Input: current queryText
        Action:
        - Invoke: SearchDomain.search(query)
        - Return: Observable<List<SearchResult>>

- Method: fetchSuggestions()
        Input: current queryText
        Action:
        - Invoke: SearchDomain.getSuggestions(query)
        - Return: Observable<List<Suggestion>>
```

The two components of the pseudocode are the UI screen (**SearchView**) and the **ViewModel**. The **ViewModel** has three publishers:

- Publisher which holds the query
- Publisher that emits suggestion data
- Publisher that emits the search result

As explained in *Figure 13.6*, the sequence of execution starting from the presentation layer can be deciphered, starting with a query change publisher triggering the invocation to get the suggestion and search result. The response received at the data layer from the API is propagated via the respective publisher for suggestion and search result. These publishers can be observed to receive the emitted data. The response is transformed to map to the user interface by the domain layer. The presentation layer subscribes to the publisher exposed by the **SearchDomain** class from the domain layer to receive the search or suggestion data.

Sending multiple requests is not a great software design as it consumes unnecessary resources. The **debounce** operator is used to transform the publisher throttling the request.

Pseudocode for the domain layer

Following is the pseudocode for the **SearchDomain** class in the domain layer:

```
Component: SearchDomain
- Method: getSuggestions(query)
     Input: query
     Action:
       - Invoke: SearchDataLayer.getSuggestion(query)
       - Return: Observable<List<SuggestionData>>
- Method: search(query)
     Input: query
     Action:
       - Invoke: SearchDataLayer.search(query)
       - Return: Observable<List<SearchResultData>>
```

The domain layer has the **SearchDomain** component, which has the implementation to get the suggestion and search data. The **SearchDomain** invokes the method from the data layer. As discussed earlier, the query-change publisher subscribed by the domain layer triggers the backend API call and gets back the results. The logic to link query-change publisher subscription with **SearchDomain** is in the **setupSubscription** method written in **SearchViewModel** pseudocode.

In both the case of the domain and presentation layer, the publisher is a single event publisher. The publisher emits zero (on error) or one item (response) and then completes. The response is forwarded to the respective subscribers. The publisher at the data layer gets the trigger, sent from the query change. Query change will be observed by the domain layer to send the trigger. The query change publisher has the direction of flow towards the data layer while the publisher handling the API in the data layer carries the response back towards the presentation layer.

The data layer can also be designed by following the reactive pattern using publisher and subscriber. Alternatively, the data layer could be just a standard asynchronous API call with a callback or promise. The data layer typically contains additional information that the upstream layer may not require; therefore, the domain layer takes care of transforming the response to a meaningful representation of data for the upper layers. The use case is thus a great starting point that explores the different dimensions of the reactive paradigm.

Case study 2: Live sports data

Building an application that provides the score for a live match is a use case that requires an event-driven mechanism. The score for the game is fetched or notified from the backend, and for every update, the user interface reloads the update value. The data layer will establish the connection to the score feed and expose it to the domain layer. The connection to feed, the request and response handling is done at data layer. A feed for live data is implemented on top of a Socket API. This would require establishing of connection, sending the request for feeds and later when the feeds are not required pausing or stopping the connection explicitly. The domain layer abstracts these connect, disconnect and request data methods, along with the publisher that emits the score. The presentation layer uses the exposed methods to get the feeds. The domain layer additionally may handle the operator logic to filter any duplicates and transform them to a user-representable format. The flow explained here is a simplified version, with the domain layer acting as a simple passthrough layer. The domain layer takes the responsibility to enable communication between the presentation layer and the downstream system via the data layer.

Case study 3: Weather station

The publisher, is an abstract construct. The context in which the publisher is used, the roles and responsibilities fulfilled adds more meaning and purpose to publisher. Publisher with right capability should be used to meet the requirement of the context. The lifecycle of a publisher is mapped to the purpose it serves. An application that requires continuous data would require a publisher with capability to emit the data whenever an event occurs. The weather data is continuous in nature, and the publisher should never stop until explicitly asked. For the weather station as the sensor measuring the data detects changes, the backend system will get notified. The mobile application listens to the change establishing a connection to backend. A mobile app codebase can either polls or establishes a callback connection to get notified on weather data. The data received is updated to the user interface. The lifecycle of the publisher is dependent on the scope that the publisher is declaring. In the case of a weather app, it will be live until the application is live in the memory of the mobile phone. When the application is killed, the publisher in the mobile is also destroyed from memory. When exposing the publisher for the connection to the top layers, the team should design a mechanism to pause and resume the data being published. When the application is not active and later returns to the foreground this method could be used to optimize the compute. This use case presents another scenario where reactive programming mechanism is leveraged.

With the last use case and the details shared in the reactive paradigm section the fundamentals are covered. These details have given a strong foundation which can be extended to explore the implementation nuances and orchestrating the mechanism in different technology framework. The team will have to focus on understanding the labels given to the reactive components in the respective mobile development frameworks while implementing the reactive patterns.

Architectures in practice

There are a variety of architectures out there in the market. The architecture is influenced by the platform and technology for the mobile application codebase. As part of the section, the idea is to look at some of these architectures in use by various mobile application frameworks. The section also explores the responsibilities of the component in the architecture.

> Note: **For most consumer-facing mobile applications, the user interface is one of the key and core components when talking about architecture. In the community, the state management technique is regarded as the architecture for mobile application. As the application grows and more classes and components are introduced, the relevance of classes beyond the presentation layer, such as those for state management will grow. The logical separation to make the code scalable will become essential beyond the presentation layer. The layers explained earlier in the chapter, the data, domain, and presentation, will thus become necessary to structure the codebase.**

The intent of the various architectures explored in this section is not to compare them to one another and find which is better. The section will not do an exhaustive analysis of the architecture. The idea is to give a benchmark to the various possibilities in the ecosystem. At the end the reader shall be equipped with the ammunition to tackle any other architecture or pattern with ease. Each of these architectures has solved a particular class of problems at some point in timeline. As the technology and context evolved over time, new problems and challenges appeared. The contextual need triggered the emergence of other kinds of architecture.

Model View Controller

In the UIKit era of the iOS ecosystem, most projects started with the **Model View Controller** (**MVC**). It was prescribed in the official documents as well. The models in the MVC were responsible for the data. The computation around the data and logic to change for the user interface is at the controller. The controller plays the mediator to update the view with the data as well. The controller was the center of architecture. The responsibility for handling the interaction and communication with the downstream system and mobile capabilities was also mediated via controller.

At some point in time, the controller started becoming bloated, and the team started addressing the controller as being challenging to read and maintain. This problem where controller was bloated was popularly known as **Massive View Controller**. The massive view controller led to a search for different architecture possibilities to organize codebase.

Massive View Controller is a problem that affects the aesthetics of the code. If the team segregated the massive view controller to separate smaller components logically, then the likelihood of having better and readable code is high. This led to a drift toward other forms of architecture.

Note: **The Massive View Controller became a consequence of two separate aspects. One is the development framework enforced the convention of having a class inherited from the special class `UIViewController`. The other is the `UIViewController` was tightly coupled with the view related code. This created the inherent inertia for developers preventing creation of separate classes instead of bloating controllers. `SwiftUI` has removed the dependency of the `UIViewController` to a certain extent when using the latest approach for development.**

Beyond MVC

The alternatives to solve the Massive View Controller problem came in other forms of MV* architecture, such as **Model View Presenter** (**MVP**), **Model View ViewModel** (**MVVM**) or **Model View Intent** (**MVI**). The MVP, MVVM, and MVI are followed in both Android and iOS projects. The MV component in the architectures MVP, MVVM and MVI have a similar responsibility as that of the model and view explained earlier.

Model View ViewModel

In the MVVM, the **`ViewModel`** classes mediate the communication between the model and the view. The **`ViewModel`** holds data (the model) class to be displayed on UI. **`ViewModel`** is responsible for being the epicenter of business logic. The recommendation is to use the three-layer approach along with MVVM so that **`ViewModel`** does not connect to the downstream system directly. Without the three-layer architecture the ViewModel will have to handle network and downstream system logic. This is a common anti-pattern that bloats the class and affects the scalability of the codebase. Instead, the **`ViewModel`** will deal with abstraction representing the specific domain related class for the feature being built. If the segregation is ignored the view model class shall bloat when the application feature becomes large. MVVM scales with the three layers by segregating responsibility to domain and data layer. MVVM is prevalent architecture style used in industry for mobile codebase. MVVM serves as the state management strategy for the presentation layer.

MVVM on Android (Jetpack Compose and XML based layout) and SwiftUI have a binding mechanism. With the binding where the underlying framework shall propagate the data changes to redraw the user interface implicitly. The developer does not need to worry about explicitly triggering the method to update user interface. As per the official documentation, the data binding in the XML based layout mechanism in Android only came into effect in Android Studio 1.3 (July 2015). If the data binding mechanism is not there it becomes the developer's responsibility to explicitly invoke the redraw function managed at the ViewModel.

When comparing MVVM in iOS with MVC one may think that the controller in MVC is renamed to **`ViewModel`** in MVVM. The architecture evolution from MVC to MVVM could, in such an argument, be seen as just a label transition. Such a perception is incorrect. At the deeper level, there are fundamental differences in the responsibility and the intent of a view model when compared to controllers. The data binding capability makes it possible to have a loosely coupled `ViewModel` from the view, ensuring independent unit testing for the `ViewModel` and amplifies the benefit of having the `ViewModel` separate. The `ViewModel` can be unit tested independently to cover logic and the state which get displayed on UI. Testing the view will be execution intensive and would require setup. The view being the constantly changing part of the mobile codebase would increase the development cost. Therefore, maximizing the unit test as the gate keeping mechanism and validating the rendering accuracy of view to meet the UI/UX could be easily possible by separating the logic from the view to `ViewModel`.

In a case where there is no binding, the reference to the view will be required to update the user interface. This additional method will be there as part of the `ViewModel`. MVC was prevalent in the iOS ecosystem when UIKit was heavily used in earlier days. MVC is no longer a hot topic and the community barely uses MVC. The shift toward MVVM from MVC signaled the segregation of responsibilities in code. The user interface-related logic was maintained at the controller. The responsibilities such as handling business logic, getting data from downstream systems, and transforming data were managed by the `ViewModel` layer. The `ViewModel` then uses a binding mechanism provided by the framework to update the view. UIKit related projects is an example where data binding was not there by default. In this case explicit setting of the value to the user interface was required. The code written in MVVM was not very intuitive from a readability point of view and clear separation of concerns.

Note: **Data binding is the case where the data change with the value/state variable associated for the UI rendering is implicitly handled by the development framework.**

A similar challenge existed in Android as well when data binding was not there. The `ViewModel` in this case had to be aware of the user interface which became a bottleneck to mock and test the logic easily.

Figure 13.7 (a) depicts the architecture diagram for MVVM, and *Figure 13.7 (b)* illustrates the class diagram for a product list feature implementation with MVVM. *Figure 13.7 (a)* shown without a data layer is for clarity and simplicity to understand the responsibility of ViewModel. The recommended implementation inserts an abstraction in form of a repository or data layer between the ViewModel and the downstream system connectors.

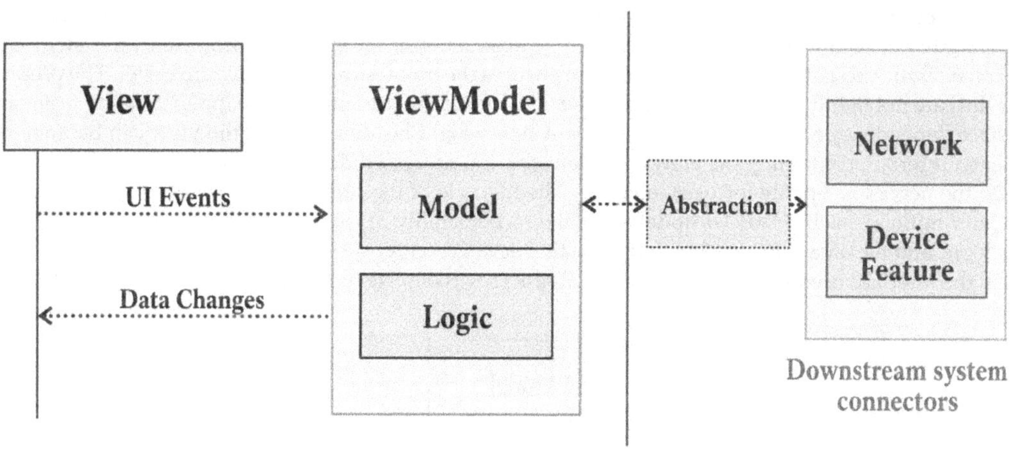

Figure 13.7 (a): *MVVM generic block diagram for iOS and Android*

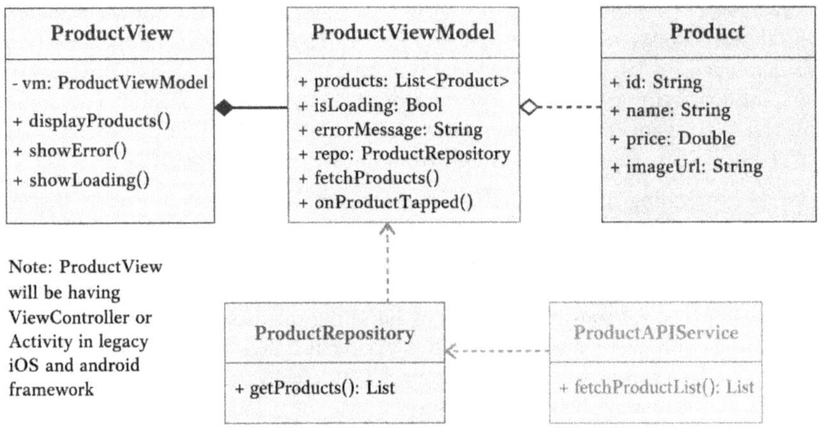

Figure 13.7 (b): *Product list feature class diagram with MVVM*

Figure 13.7 (b) depicts the case where the view model is not massive, and the API fetch is implemented in a separate class. The same approach can be followed for other features in the application.

Model View Presenter

MVP was popular when data binding was not innately available in the development framework. MVP was a pattern that scaled well when the view update had to be explicitly triggered, to render the state changes to screen. The MVP pattern is based on separating the responsibility of updating the UI to an injected dependency. The MVP defines the interface for presenter and view. The implementation of the presenter holds the reference to the view via the interface. Such a mechanism ensures only necessary detail of the view is exposed to presenter. The view holds the reference to presenter. Having the bidirectional relation via interface to send messages each other help to communicate between view and the presenter. The abstraction is an interface (protocol in the Swift language) implemented by the presenter class. The abstraction ensures the unit testing for classes are easier. The presenter and the view thus are not tightly coupled with each other. For testing the presenter can be independently tested mocking the interface dependency for presenter in the view. A lightweight headless test for the view can be done mocking the presenter interface connecting the view. The view gets the processed data from the presenter. The view uses the data to do the necessary update for user interface. The lifecycle of the presenter starts with the view instantiating the presenter in the view. In MVP, UI updates are the responsibility of the view and the presenter will handle the business logic, and the data is forwarded to update the view. Presenter should not have any reference to UI element other than the interface used to send data to view. *Figure 13.8(a)* depicts the architecture diagram for MVP:

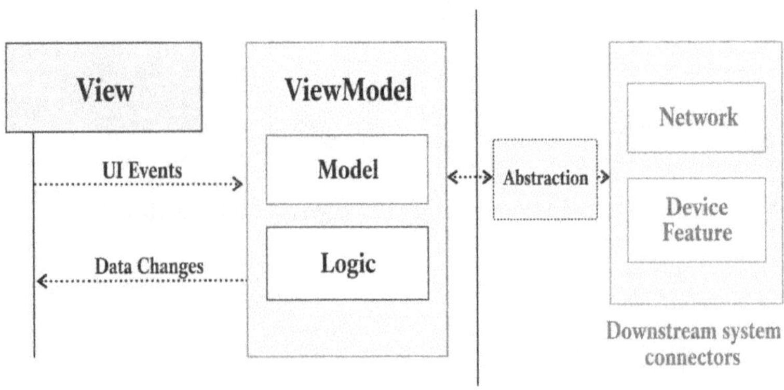

Figure 13.8 (a): *MVP generic block diagram for iOS and Android*

Figure 13.8 (b) depicts the class diagram for the product list feature implementation following the MVP pattern:

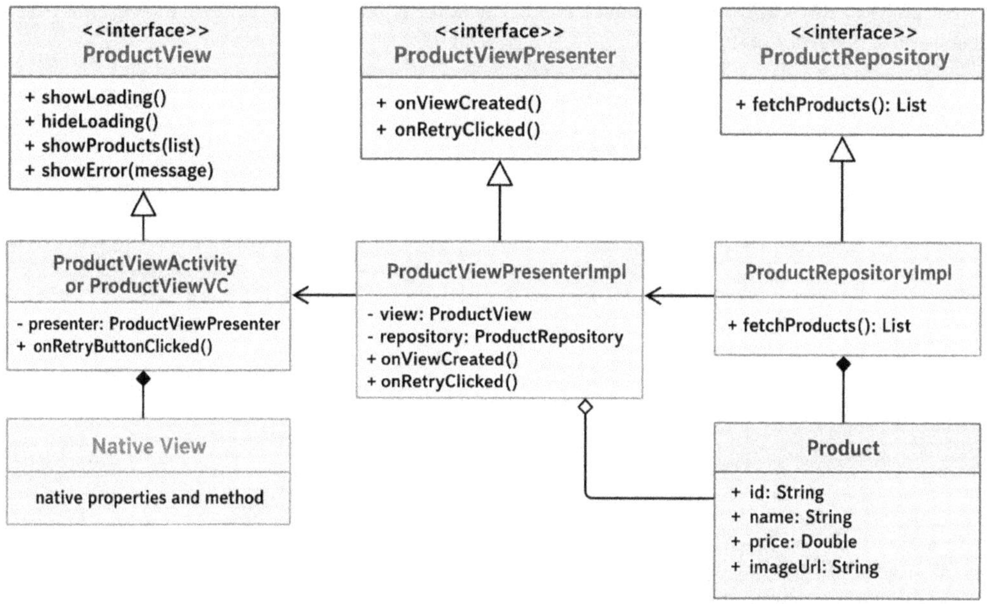

***Figure 13.8 (b)**: Product list feature class diagram with MVP*

The class diagram depicts the Activity/ViewController hosting the view implementing the **`ProductView`** interface. The Activity/ViewController is passed as a reference to the presenter. There exists a bidirectional communication between view and presenter. The interface which was explained earlier will ensure their responsibilities are separate and the communication is enabled. The Activity/ViewController calls the presenter for any user event. The presenter sends the data as response via the interface. The repository is the class with which the presenter connect to the downstream systems. The approach followed can be replicated for other features in the application.

Note: **While one can force-fit the MVP for the modern SwiftUI or Jetpack Compose based codebase, the pattern would not be appropriate and is not required. The data binding provided with the framework brings a clear separation of concern, separating UI from the logic.**

Model View Intent

In any architecture, data flow is a key parameter that could influence the readability of the codebase. In the case of MVVM, the data flow is bidirectional in nature. A UI receiving the user interaction would trigger an event in the view model. A change in logic inside the view model can trigger a state change that, through the binding mechanism, updates the UI. The bidirectional data flow in architecture component is error prone. The probability for the developer to introduce unintentional side effect is high in such cases. The developer may also find it difficult to debug. Consider a case where a functional issue has been analyzed on a mobile application. The issue could be a logical error either when user interface communicates to domain layer or vice versa when a user interface gets redraw on a response. Having the data flow bidirectional within the view model increases the cognitive load for a developer to debug the code. Multiple such occurrence will multiply the overhead. The effect of bidirectional data can be controlled by bringing a dedicated component responsible for mediating the communication. This component is called the **`Intent`**. Any user interaction will be sent as action from view to ViewModel via **`Intent`**. The state change from the business logic and computation in the ViewModel is sent back to view layer via the **`Intent`**. The **`Intent`** is the central theme of MVI pattern. Intent is the object responsible for any state change to the user interface or action to be sent to the ViewModel. Any developer now has dedicated class to look at which is the source for any data changes.

Note: The MVI state management strategy will sound like the Redux explored later in the chapter. The difference is that MVI deals at the feature level, while the latter is best suited for state management at a global app level spanning different features.

Figure 13.9 depicts the architecture diagram for MVI:

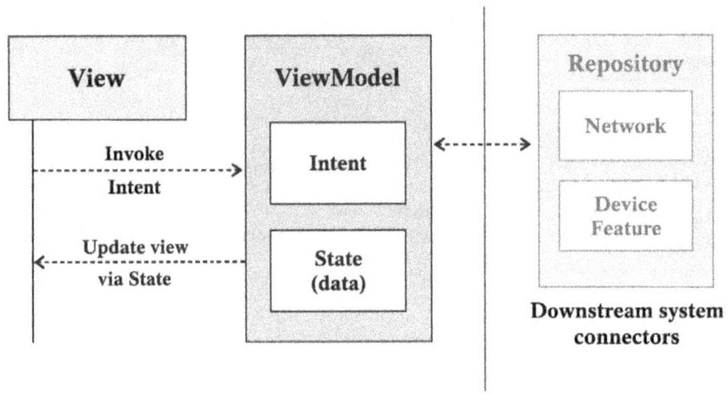

***Figure 13.9**: MVI generic block diagram for iOS and Android*

In the MVI the **`ViewModel`** still exists and holds responsibility to handle the business logic and connecting to other layers. In principle the capability where code snippet can update or get the latest state is only via the Intent. The **`ViewModel`** receives an action via **`Intent`** from the view. The **`ViewModel`** responds to an action after the processing by emitting the state changes back to the view. The modified state will trigger the redraw of the user interface. The processing done by **`ViewModel`** will be a business logic executed or a request to the downstream system for data fetch. Once the response is received data is sent via the **`Intent`** to update the state. For other architecture pattern the difference is that any component can modify the state causing side effect. However, in case of MVI the **Intent** is the only component that has access to the state to update and retrieve. This MVI prevents the side effect caused by accidental change of the state. The MVI enforces any state change to be intentional and via **`Intent`**. The state cannot be modified or created by any other components.

Business Logic Components

The Flutter cross-platform framework recommends the **Business Logic Components** (**BLoC**) as state management strategies. The BLoC advocates separating the processing at the presentation layer to user interface, action and emitted state. In Flutter the UI element is called a widget. The business logic component leverages the input and output streams to handle action and emitted state. The action and events are the processing related components. These components manage the business logic and hold the processed data which should be presented to the user. The fundamental theme followed in this architecture pattern is having the business logic as an independent component separated from widget. Streams are reactive elements in the Flutter ecosystem which act as a publisher. Streams emit a continuous value to an observer. The input stream connect the presentation layer to send action and trigger the BLoC class. The BLoC listens to the action which can be thought as an input stream. The processing happens for action once it is received by the BLoC Flutter class. Once the processing is completed, the output stream responds with the feedback, which the widget (presentation layer) listens and renders appropriately. If looked at carefully, one may be able to see a reactive style of programming in the BLoC, where the BLoC uses a stream that is equivalent to the publisher. The difference in BLoC is the label specific to Flutter state management strategy. The BLoC is a subset of the reactive paradigm which is the larger umbrella defining data flow and propagation of changes in any event-driven ecosystem. *Figure 13.10* is the BLoC architecture for a typical Flutter project:

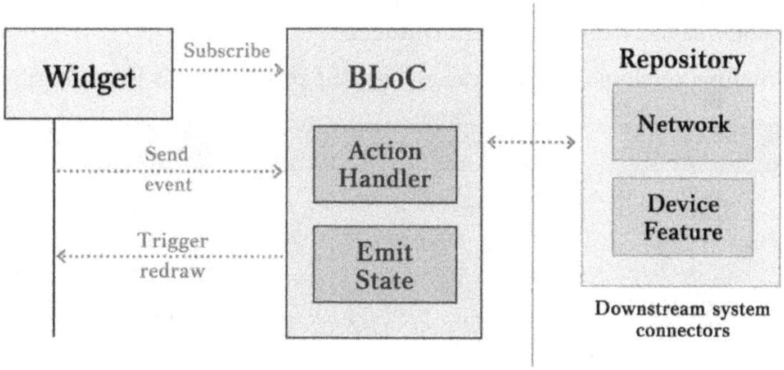

***Figure 13.10:** BLoC for Flutter*

Figure 13.10 depicts a widget dispatching the action trigger and listening to the emitted state to redraw. These actions are sent to BLoC. Within the BLoC the action handler delegates to either a downstream handler or logic written within. Once the action is processed, the BLoC responds by emitting the state. The logic thus is maintained separately from the presentation and following the software design principles of composing smaller units of functionality. The BLoC class can be designed to use dependency externalizing the logic to other classes. This approach helps to keep the BLoC focused on its core responsibilities. The responsibilities fulfilled by BLoC will be to ensure the action is delegated and state is emitted back.

BLoC ensures the state management and business logic remain separated from the user interface. The BLoC component can be unit tested easily. Let us take the counter-narrative where there was no architecture pattern in the Flutter project. In such a case, the worst possible situation is the case where a developer writing the business logic within the widget. The widget will become massive and will not be readable, maintainable, and testable. With the usage of BLoC or similar pattern, the aforementioned problems shall be mitigated.

Redux

A mobile application depends on the correct state management strategy to project accurate information to the user. The state management being incorrect will confuse the end user and lead to a frustrating experience. The state could be at a screen level or an application level. Typically, for most mobile application, the backend system would be the source of truth that gives a unified experience across multiple screens within the product. For optimal computational efficacy, reducing the calls to the backend systems would be a software design choice. This decision could pave the way for mobile application to depend on persisted state management. Similar is the case for other use cases of offline-first applications. In offline-first mobile application the expectation will be to function without network access. In this the mobile cannot rely only on the backend as the source of truth. A consistent state management becomes even more critical for offline-first app with sync capability with backend. The development team shall encounter the need to prevent any data discrepancy. Data discrepancy could be due to incorrect code logic causing unintentional save, overwrites, or inconsistent presented data. Managing the side effects caused by any change in code is an important criterion to be considered. The team should ensure the side effect caused is accurate and intentional for the feature. Deviating from this would lead the mobile application to be error prone, bringing a catastrophic experience for the end users.

The use case of a mobile application for an agent (an intermediary for a financial institution) is an example to look at to understand an offline-first application. The business of the financial institution is to provide loans, insurance, and a few other products. Being offline-first the application should ideally operate seamlessly, even when there is no network. The data shall be synced later with the server for processing the product offering from the financial institution. The data entered will go through the approval process as well. Such a mobile application can have multiple forms, which are dynamically driven and configured by the rules. The dynamic nature of the forms could depend on the input data and product type. In such mobile application there will be standard data forms that can be reused. Such reusable data should ideally be persisted once and cross-referenced in multiple forms. The possibility of displaying the same data in multiple contexts is high for data such as profile details of a user applying the product.

The agent will be able to sell multiple products for the same user. Entering the profile details every time is not a great use of time, having the details saved will be a better experience

Figure 13.11 depicts a miniature version of the use case where the profile details is used within the various forms:

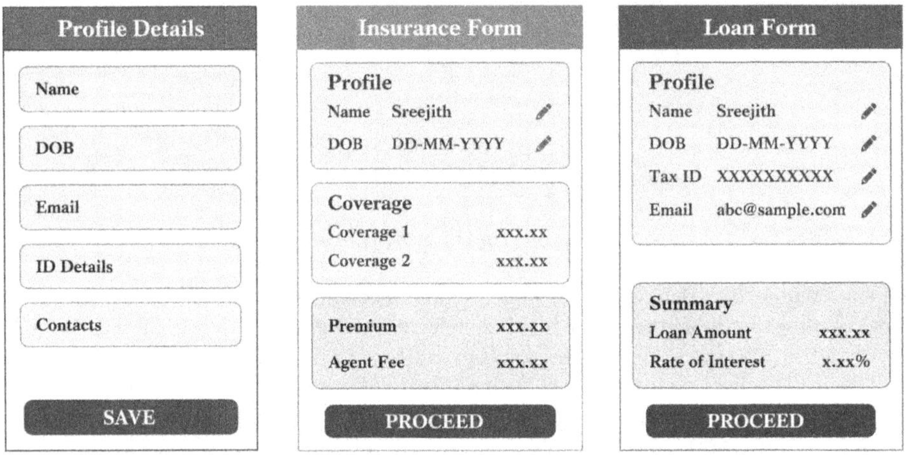

***Figure 13.11**: Wireframe for profile detail feature*

Figure 13.11 depicts separate subset details profile details used in two forms: the insurance form and loan form. A situation may arise where the code implementation incorrectly introduces an error causing a value different from what was originally entered in the profile details showing in the other forms. The underlying reason could be due to the insurance form is not fetched from the right source and gets an old, cached value. Similarly, there could be a case when the user saves the value from the insurance form not updating the original source. The new value does not get saved to the profile details. The occurrence of both these is not the accurate functioning of the feature. The profile data should be unique for an individual. The agent using the mobile application should have a feature to enter the details of prospective customers and edit the data from any pages and the data should be consistent.

Following the Redux pattern for such a use case could create a structure that ensures data consistency. The philosophy advocated by Redux is that a single source of truth exists for state, and only a designated action defined in the code can modify the state. The state modification shall not happen by any means other than sending this action. Thus, a programmer can only modify the state intentionally. Such a situation will ensure that unknown side effects of state modification are not there. The data store should not mutate or alter by any other means, other than the action, ensuring there is no side effects.

Figure 13.12 depicts the platform-agnostic version of the Redux pattern applicable for iOS or Android:

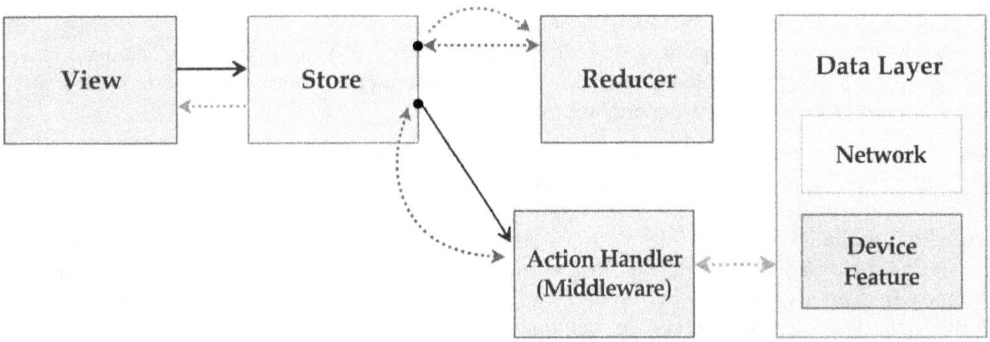

***Figure 13.12**: Redux architecture for iOS or Android*

Note: A Reducer is a pure function, a function that does not introduce side effect and for same input give the same output. In the context of Redux the Reducer for a given state and dispatched action returns a new state without mutating the original. This pattern ensures Redux state is predictable for debugging and a bug can be traced to a specific state change or action.

Figure 13.12 highlights the association of `View` with the `Store`. `Store` mediates the dispatch of an event to update and give back the state information to redraw the user interface. The reducer and the action handler are the two components that the `Store` interacts with. The reducer deals with managing the state, and the action handler or middleware deals with the logic or getting data from the downstream. The middleware, once receiving the data, will pass the response to store via a reducer. If there is a state change the user interface is notified. In short, any update to store can only be done via a reducer. The solid line in *Figure 13.12* depicts a stronger association of the components in the Redux style. The state for the screen is managed within the store object. The store object can be localized for feature and will be responsible to change a particular information within the state encapsulated in it. An example to quote from use case explained earlier in the wireframe is the form to save profile details. The component in the profile details will have only the responsibility to send action to modify profile details. The team ideally in the context of profile details should not use reducer which have the capability to change any other details.

Commonality of architectural styles

In all the architectures mentioned in the section, one can notice the central theme revolves around two constructs: the direction of data flow and the responsibility segregation in the various layers. The domain or the data layer is fulfilling an equivalent responsibility in all cases. The presentation layer is where differences are prevalent. For an architecture evolution the need to minimize the side effects became the central goal. Any side effect in the ecosystem had to be intentional and deterministic. In the programming world, there are different libraries that enhance and accelerate the responsibility fulfilled by the components in the architecture. There will be choices in these libraries that would make a particular architecture pattern stand out over others solving a particular class of problem. Irrespective of these, an architectural decision taken up within a team should be purpose driven and solution driven. It should never lead to make the code look fancy and sophisticated.

Note: A side effect can be seen as an impact caused by a code change on the surrounding code other than the primary expectation of the code snippet.

The overlap of problem domain may lead a team mixing of architectural styles. While there are no hard and fast rules on what needs to be done for architecture, the team should ideally try to follow a typical pattern recommendation from community with a mindset to evolve based on context. For any new member joining the team the learning curve and onboarding effort could increase if the code structure does not follow themes prevalent in the community. The new member may have to rely on documentation, or an individual with the context will become important.

Mechanism complementing architecture

An architecture is at its best when the purpose is met, and the codebase can scale. The architecture provides the structure to reduce the possibility of unintentional side effects. When there are blind spots for an architecture the team should introduce mechanisms to support architecture to prevent risk associated with the blind spots. These mechanisms should ideally help to make the best ecosystem complementing the current architecture. The parameters to look at will be aspects such as for testability, maintainability and readability of a codebase. The key trait of an exemplary architecture is enabling the developer to write code with proper separation of concerns between the classes. The developer being able to write tests that are not brittle and having a high confidence to change the codebase increases the architecture's adoptability. This section looks at some of the top items relevant to the mobile application codebase that complements the architecture.

Sustainability

The code written should have a long-term life. The code shall be key to sustaining the software for long running business. Rewriting the code is a huge cost. Ensuring sustainability thus would be essential. Sustainability should be complemented by the confidence to make changes and build features with optimal effort. The team should be able to make the progress without causing any unintentional side effects. This trait is the measure that defines sustainability.

The strategic decision-making ability and an evolving architecture will contribute to the goal of sustainability. The team should leverage knowledge from the industry. The standards, best practices, patterns, and anti-patterns in the framework should be adhered to ensure the code written shall sustain. An example is the case of the folder structure and convention that the team need to be aware of mentioned in *Chapter 8, Scalability in Mobile Development: Part 2*. Folder structure is one of the key decisions which has an influence on the architecture and vice versa that ensure sustainability.

For a team formed with a diverse set of individuals, there could be the influence of past conditioning in each of their decision-making. The amalgamation of ideas, debate and reasoning of the individuals could bring the best of options.

The type of mobile application and the objective of the organization will influence the team size. A faster time to market requirement would mean the team to run parallel streams. All these factors can only be efficient if the mobile application codebase is structured to cater to operate at scale.

Sustainability and scalability are two sides of the same coin. The reader may treat these to be same in most cases. Both these are very much closely related and have influence on each other. The subtle difference is that the sustainability focuses on the life of the codebase while the scalability focuses on the ability to handle growth efficiently.

There are some key themes that bubble up in most of the discussions of architecture and organizing the code. A short run-down on the same was inevitable; without it, the context of architecture would have been left incomplete.

Law of parsimony

The **Keep It Simple, Stupid** (**KISS**) and **You Ain't Gonna Need It** (**YAGNI**) are the principles that resonate with the law of parsimony, which would be a guiding light for the team members while writing the code.

> Note: **In philosophy, Occam's razor is the problem solving principle that recommends searching for explanations constructed with the smallest possible set of elements. It is also known as the principle of parsimony or the law of parsimony.**

For the reader practical application of this law is applicable when presented with competing ideas. Consider the situation where competing ideas have logically equal explanatory power to be the solution for a problem statement. The choice that has the minimum assumption would be economically viable. Law of parsimony can be understood better from a situation. Consider a debate or conversation on the choice of solution. If the solution has given importance to a probable situation occurring in future, the discussion may drift on developing for future compatibility. The team at the stage of discussion may not be even sure if the day will come when this will be implemented. The implementation based on such an assumption should be deferred, leaving a provision to incorporate or extend the capability later when the need arises.

Don't Repeat Yourself

Don't Repeat Yourself (**DRY**) is a key principle one should consider, as this reduces the cost and overall complexity of maintenance. The key theme is that there should not be any duplication within the system. The team should apply this principle in the development. The team should advocate and enforce the principle whereby the choice of the right architecture and the team alignment could help the codebase scale. The side effect could affect a reusable component when a variability is required only for a subset of features. An individual may unknowingly change the behavior of the component reused in multiple places leading to unintended outcomes. This should be watched and having test suite should help identify these issues earlier.

Cohesion

The measure of how each of the modules or classes is related to each other represents cohesion. The cohesion can vary from low to high, where a low cohesion means the module tries to do too many unrelated things. In principle, low cohesion is not great for readability and ease for individuals involved in maintaining the codebase. The difficulty comes when an individual is trying to make sense of a code with low cohesion. On the contrary, a high cohesion means a module does a single thing very well.

Coupling

Coupling is a measure that depicts how dependent a module, or a class, is on another. The coupling varies between the possibilities of being tightly coupled versus loosely coupled. A tightly coupled system is prone to cause side effects and bugs. The principle of composition over inheritance recommended in object-oriented design is an example for designing a loose coupled software system. Composition in codebase implies has-a relationship between two entities. The has-a relation can be via interface that abstracts concrete dependency from one another. This brings a loosely coupled nature between the entities.

Any software has both historic and evolutionary nature. The preceding list of items are not exhaustive. This list presents the major principles that may help to make the conversation simple and logical when discussing architecture. The recommendation is to look at similar facets that the team can incorporate in the development cycle to ensure sustainability.

Note: **The following are some examples for an individual to take forward in the context of the sustainability and scalability: SOLID principle, clean architecture, separation of concerns, GRASP, etc. The appendix of the book has quoted some of the additional readings for the same.**

Testability

Testability is a measure that gives a perspective of how the codebase is organized to write different forms of automated tests. *Chapter 5, Quality Assurance for Mobile Development* has narrated in detail the quality assurance for a mobile project. The relevance of unit testing and having an ideal test pyramid was also highlighted in the chapter. One should write code catering to write better tests. Writing better tests and structuring code to be testable is a critical parameter that goes hand in hand with quality assurance. The architecture of the code influences the ease of writing automated tests and the maintenance of test. Testability is best when the smallest logical unit can be tested. In the case of a mobile application codebase, the smallest unit could be the function. These smaller units integrate and work together to perform the larger goal of the application. Given that each of these are independently tested, collective functionality will only need the bare minimum integration tests.

Another challenge with poor patterns in test is the determinism of the test execution. Consider an example use case where the location API of the hardware is used to get the geo coordinates. The coordinates are passed to an API to get the list of nearby service centers in a retail application. The team implements the user interface for this feature. The location API uses hardware capability and fetching the service center list is via network client to backend system. Consider case when the team focus on writing unit tests for the presentation layer with two external dependency locations fetch and the backend service. The unit test case at the presentation layer will have scenarios listed as follows, which are externally dependent:

- User interface behavior when the location API permission is denied.
- User interface behavior when the location API permission is allowed, and the coordinate is fetched.
- User interface behavior when the store list API is successful.
- User interface behavior when the store list API fails.

All the scenarios listed require either a manual re or ias dependent on an external entity, which is not deterministic. Such a situation will not help the test case to be automated. In such a case, the presentation layer, which is the system under test, should be injected with a mock to control the behavior of the location API and backend API. This will help to simulate success and failure. The presentation layer thus can be tested independently without worrying about how the external API is implemented.

In the preceding scenario, the mechanism the team can use to achieve loose coupling is DI. A DI is to supply the instance for a type that has a *has-a* relationship with a class externally. There are different means of DI, such as constructor injection, method (setter) injection, service locator pattern, interface injection, or usage of third-party libraries. A constructor and method injection are similar in nature, where the instance is passed at a different lifetime of the parent object. A service locator is using a dictionary with a key and using the creator to instantiate objects when needed. The dictionary acts as a container for the dependency creation. Writing a DI container may be overhead. There are widely used DI libraries that can be reused from the community.

The previous explanation was DI at runtime. There is compile-time capability to inject dependencies as well. The underlying working of such a DI technique will be to leverage programming language feature exposed to customize compiler capabilities. For instance, the compiler precondition flags can be used to bifurcate and inject dependency at compile time based on the target (compiler argument or flag). Both the compile time and runtime fit well for a particular use case. *Table 13.2* compares the compile time and runtime DI:

Compile time DI	Runtime DI
Performance is better with minimal runtime overhead.	It will have relatively higher performance overhead than compile time due to dynamic resolution.
The type-safety is ensured for the dependency at compile time, and errors related to the dependency can be detected early.	The type-safety is not hundred percent fledged and will depend on the container implementation and language feature. The error detection in this will be at runtime.
Static dependencies cannot be modified at runtime, thus may bring less flexibility for the programmer.	The flexibility is more due runtime nature feature to modify a dependency based on logic dynamically.
Typically seen to have more boilerplate code (e.g., code generation or annotations). It is hard to change mock dependencies easily as these are tightly coupled.	The boiler plate code is minimal. The effort will be to register dependency. The dependency is loosely coupled between the different targets. For example, the dependency container for the unit test will be different from the release codebase.

***Table 13.2:** Compile time versus runtime DI*

In conclusion, one can see that strong gatekeeping mechanisms and testability of the codebase will, in turn, influence the architecture decision for a project. The evolution of architecture will happen with the exposure to problems faced in project grows. The wisdom in the larger community could be reused to solve many common occurring problems. Looking into the community will give a head start in the abyss of possibilities to solve different problem statements. The team can improve the existing solution to become the best version of itself along with meeting the expectations of the engineering needs.

GoF Design Patterns

GoF is a catalogue of a popular set of twenty-three patterns in a book titled *Design Patterns: Elements of Reusable Object-Oriented Software*, published in *1994*. The name GoF became popular in the community, and it was credited to the four authors involved.

GoF has three categories: structural, behavioral, and creational. The structural patterns are responsible for enabling the composing of objects to form larger structures, the behavioral pattern deals with the interaction of different objects with each other, and the creational pattern focuses on the creation of objects by influencing the lifecycle.

As part of this chapter the focus is not to cover exhaustive list of patterns. The idea instead is to introduce a few and highlight the necessity of the team to be aware of the Design Pattern. The team should be equipped to leverage the pattern when applicable for a use case. Following are some examples use cases for the patterns:

Example one

The mobile application in runtime has a singleton pattern leveraged for main application object. Throughout the lifecycle of the application, from start to exit, there will only be one instance of the application object in the memory. For iOS, it is the class **`UIApplication`**, and for Android, it is the class **`Application`**, which serves as the default application instance that is available in the respective development framework.

Example two

The reactive paradigm explained earlier is an example of the observer pattern where a class subscribes to a publisher and listens for the event being broadcast. Examples are **`ContentObserver`** or **`BroadcastReceiver`** in android and **`NotificationCenter`** or **Key-Value Observing** (**KVO**) in iOS.

Example three

The decorator pattern is best suited for use cases where multiple layers of decorators can be stacked. An example with slight variation of the decorator pattern can be seen in the data layer that leverages repository to abstract the details of the source for data fetch. The example portrays a case that uses an in-memory cache to reduce network calls. The API that returns same data all the time can use the decorator pattern. Invoking the network call continuously is not optimal usage of computational resources. The approach is to cache the data. The logic at the repository layer will return data from the cache if available or else the data will be fetched from API call to the backend. On success of the backend API call the data would be saved to cache. *Figure 13.13* is the class diagram for the implementation of the decorator pattern for the use case in two variations. The left side shows a decorator composed as explained, while the right shows a nested version for the same use case. The remote repository will decorate the local repository passed as dependency in the nested version.

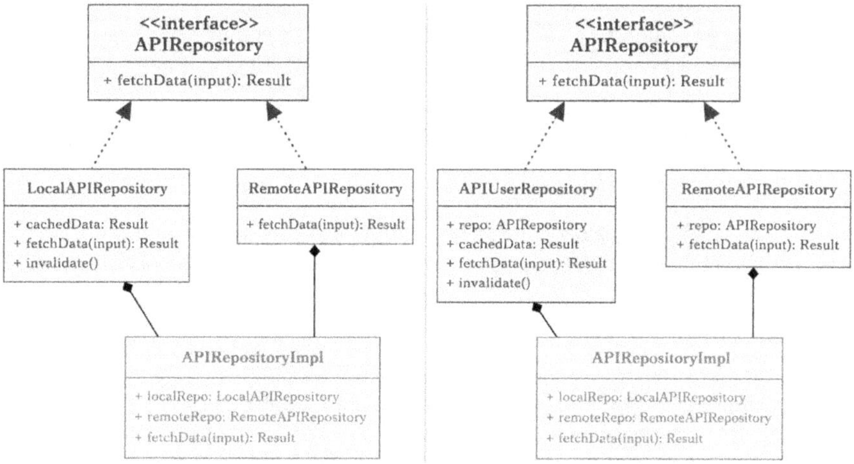

Figure 13.13: *Class diagram for decorator pattern*

Another example of the decorator pattern can be seen in the case where a **`TextField`** decorated with validation rule. The **`TextField`** will have different validation based on the feature. Capability to dynamically add validation or styling, variation of user interface or composability of the user interface elements can follow the decorator pattern.

Example four

Consider the use case for a retail application on the checkout page, the organization has provided multiple payment options. The implementation at the checkout page needs to know only payment method name and the response for the payment. The internal details of how payment processing is done are irrelevant for the checkout page. *Figure 13.14* represents the class diagram that uses the strategy pattern for the payment feature implementation:

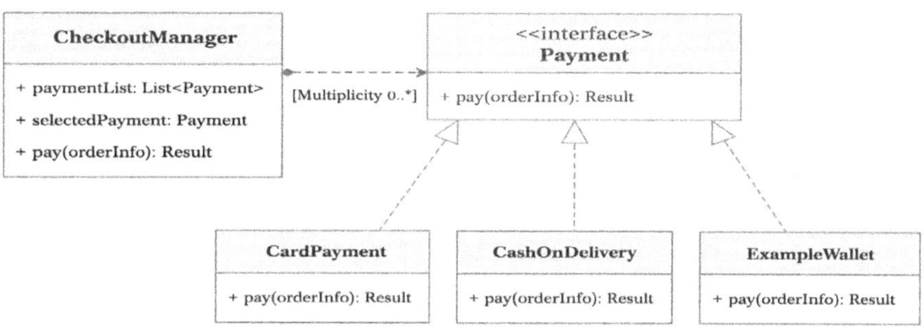

Figure 13.14: *Class diagram for strategy pattern*

The checkout manager in the example is the class which is not aware of the underlying implementation of the payment type. A new payment type addition is decoupled from the implementation of the checkout manager.

Conclusion

The purpose of exploring the means to architect a mobile codebase has reached a culmination. The reader after reading the chapter is equipped with the standard nomenclature and logical toolkit to structure any codebase. Like any other software, the mobile codebase is also influenced by various factors. Along with the technical aspect the stakeholder must calibrate the various factors such as operational factors and skill set to evaluate decisions for the architecture choices. An engagement that needs faster time to market and does not have time to experiment may follow a get-it-done-quick approach. This would require a simple and easy to modify structure for the code. The team may be in a firefighting mode to deliver the outcome faster, implying a lightweight architecture that enables the team to onboard faster. In contrast, the same architecture may become problematic for a larger project or one that scales beyond the initial release. Later in the development the time market and ease of development may not meet the expectation. One should understand that there is no one-size-fits-all kind of solution for architecture choices.

In short, the reader with the detail in the chapter shall understand the responsibility of a particular component. With this information one can debate the pros and cons and decide the architecture with the right fitment for the respective context. For the pattern, which is already solved within the community, learning from the use cases should be the baseline for calibrating any decision.

The next chapter is the final chapter of the book where the mobile application system thinking is explored by looking at the use cases and applying the learnings from other chapters to these to reach the probable solution.

Takeaways and reflections

The end of this chapter marks the entry into the world where the reader is now equipped with foundational context to understand mobile architecture and nuances. The reader will now be able to clearly spot patterns and areas with which a codebase can be structured to scale. The following are the takeaways of this chapter:

- Patterns are a recognizable repetition or regularity that form a part of architecture.
- Architecture is a set of decisions that defines the structure for a project with its constituents and relationships.
- Any mobile application project structure can be logically divided into presentation, domain, and data layers.
- Choice of technology, risk appetite of the organization, complexity faced by the team, and being oblivious to historic details of the product are some of the key themes influencing the architecture decision for mobile.
- Reactive extension introduced in the .NET framework popularized Rx libraries in other languages, thereby bringing an event-driven mechanism in development. The modern framework for mobile application development, such as SwiftUI, Compose Multiplatform, Flutter is heavily influenced by a reactive style.
- MV* architecture includes architecture patterns such as MVC, MVP, MVVM, and MVI.
- The presentation layer is the critical part of the mobile application. The usage of MV* is analogous to the project architecture even though in reality it talks about state management in the mobile codebase.
- Good architecture should ensure that code is readable, testable, maintainable, and sustainable in the long-term.

Chapter 14
System Thinking in Mobile Development

Introduction

A mobile developer mostly faces the question of elucidating different approaches and considerations required to develop a mobile application. Answering the question will be the job description for a mobile developer taking the consulting role of helping an enterprise. To acquire such thinking, one must either go through multiple development journeys or learn retrospectively by looking at case studies. The chapter will focus on three case studies. The three case studies shall look at the key parts in the journey of building such a mobile application. The readers shall be able to correlate these case studies with topics discussed in the previous chapters. The information shared in the chapter will give enough exposure to internalize these experiences.

Structure

This chapter covers the following topics:

- Event-driven mobile application
- Monitoring app via connected sensors
- Surveillance app

Objectives

The purpose of this chapter is to accelerate the reader's journey to think holistically in mobile development. The chapter discusses three case studies that will enable the reader to become familiar with practical insights to build a consumer-facing mobile application. The chapter focuses on conceptual system design for the three different use cases and the nuances surrounding these. The focus of this chapter will be to look at the scope, architecture, learning, and challenges faced in the three case studies. The downstream system to which the mobile application connects will be treated as a black box. The chapter also assumes that the downstream system is amenable to making the end-to-end functioning of the system better.

Event-driven mobile application

An event-driven mobile application encompasses a reactive application that requires a constant update on the UI. The information refreshed on the screen is the key data that the user is interested in. The criticality of data makes the precision required for the data displayed as a non-negotiable expectation. This description matches the class of applications that do live e-auction, trading, or a weather forecast application. In each of these cases, the frequency of data refresh is different. Consider the UI listing items on the home screen, which has a constant data refresh. On selecting the individual item, the user can be navigated to the details page of the selected item. The complexity of the details page may vary depending on the kind of domain being targeted. For example, for a trading system, it will be the fundamental and technical analysis information, whereas for the weather application, it will be the additional details of the weather conditions and a comparative data of the entire day. To make the explanation simpler, the case study anchors the idea to the hypothetical auction system. Other than the functional requirement, the foundational code design will be similar for any event-driven system, be it trading, weather forecast, etc.

Let us explore the functional details of the digital auction application. A digital auction mobile application can be seen as a user interface giving the user virtual rooms to participate in an auction. The end user may have multiple virtual rooms and can join one of these to take part in the auction. The digital auction provides the facility for the end user to participate simultaneously in multiple auctions. In the mobile application, this translates to the user joining multiple rooms listed on the main page and taking part in the auction on the details page. The details page gives the user historical data for a similar item auctioned. This data will help users to make an informed choice while bidding. The individual who is involved in the auction could be a buyer or a seller. The buyer will keep a watch on the live price change, and the seller is the one who will put the item up for bid. The application has other features, for example, payment, order tracking for physical items being auctioned, onboarding, support, etc. A buyer can mark their favorite rooms to see the price change, and similarly, the seller can get the price change for an active bid. The mobile application is common for buyers and sellers, and on the home screen, both buying- and selling-related features will be present. The price of the item will fluctuate when an active bid is happening. For the auction system, the bid happens in the designated auction window, and the price change will occur only during this time frame.

Understanding the downstream is important to make better decisions for ensuring better code design for a mobile application. The core backend systems for the auction will manage the price changes and the trends for the items as the bidding progresses. The system that the mobile application interacts with is equivalent to a publisher. A consumer can connect and request to observe the data from the downstream. The order management web service is also part of the core system, with the responsibility for the price change trigger, bid closure, and order confirmation. There are other downstream **application programming interfaces** (**API**) available, such as the search API for finding the product that is auctioned, the seller API to put an item up for auction, etc., which the mobile connects to. These backend systems together provide the capabilities to the end user to participate in an auction via the mobile application.

Note: **A trading system follows a similar structure. A trading system will have a regulated entity that controls the price. The volatility will be high depending on the popularity of the item being traded. The details page of the trading system is much more complex as there is other data similar to the price, which is constantly updated. This is in comparison with the auction, where only the past few bids are listed in the case study. The complexity of UI/UX presented to the end user is also comparatively less for the auction application.**

Figure 14.1 depicts the wireframe for the home and the detail page for the auction application:

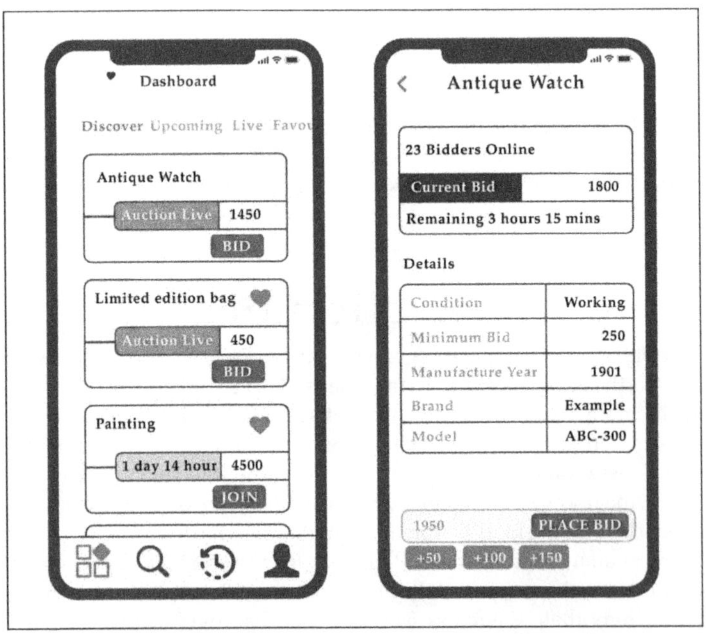

***Figure 14.1**: Wireframe for dashboard and product details*

In *Figure 14.1*, the list of items for which bids can be placed by a buyer is depicted. The seller will have a similar structure where there will be an option to sell. The update for the item listed by the seller when active in **BID** shall be available. The live auction will have the price change occurrence updated on the screen as soon as the new **BID** happens for the item. When selecting the item from the list, the user will be navigated to the **Details** page of the item. Additional details for the item, along with the option to quote a new price and place the bid, are presented to the user in the detail page as depicted in *Figure 14.1*. While the user navigates to the **Details** page, the information presented in the list screen is not in focus. The price changes in the list can be paused. The list is the home screen of the mobile application, and the application has other tabs for search, history, and profile screen as well. The behavior to pause the price change for the item listed is applicable when the user moves to other tabs as well. Additionally, the price change should trigger only if the auction is live and the item is on the active screen on the mobile screen for the end user.

Note: **The other feature of the mobile application works like any retail product purchase app. The details of the surrounding features are not discussed in depth. One can gain experience by exploring any retail mobile application that sells products.**

For developing an event-driven application, special design considerations are to be kept in mind. The following list gives insights into the same:

- **Optimize redraw**: The pages can have multiple items where there will be a continuous change of data. In such a screen, the developer should ensure that only the affected portion of the screen is redrawn. An anti-pattern that affects the performance will be for redrawing the entire page or other components that do not change. In the auction application, the price change is where the redraw gets triggered. In the user interface, only the text rendering price for the item should be redrawn. Any other user interface components on the screen should not be redrawn.
- **Optimize compute**: The team should handle the pausing of the price change subscription on an inactive screen to avoid unnecessary computation. The user can navigate and move across multiple screens in the application. This would mean that any screen that goes out of focus will be an inactive screen. When the screen displaying the price change becomes inactive, the price change can be paused. The price change shall resume when the page becomes active again. This pattern of pause and resume repeats for any item/list for which a price change is depicted. A typical mobile application uses a stacked navigation structure. The auction application will also follow the pattern. Consider the case when the user navigates to the **Details** page from the list screen or the search list. The **Details** page is the currently active screen and the one that needs to display the price change of the selected item. The home page, which was listing the other item when navigating to the details page, will become inactive and can now be paused. The mobile can instruct the backend to stop sending the price change for the items that are not actively displayed to the user. As the user navigates back from the detail to the home screen, the price change for the product list can be resumed to track active bids.

Now that the context of the mobile application has been established, the next section focuses on the system design thinking required for the mobile application.

System design

The system design would require an essential understanding of how things work end-to-end. This section will take the reader through the pathway that a mobile developer encounters when developing the auction application.

A standard mobile application displays data from a downstream system via a network call. In this use case, the data displayed is time-variant, and the changes are published as a stream of continuous events observed by the mobile application. The auction application has the price of the item changing very frequently, and the mobile needs to display the same to the end user as and when the event occurs. Unlike a standard network call, where there is a request and response, the price change behavior is different and is a special use case. The connection established to the backend will act as a channel to observe the price change, which is continuously sent. Typically, mobiles operate via a socket connection for such a use case. The mobile application also has other standard API calls where the data is fetched, transformed, and presented to the user to take the next action. These APIs are network calls with a single request and a corresponding response. The search, marking favorite, payment, order history, etc., are examples of features leveraging such APIs. These features form the regular capabilities equivalent to any other mobile application.

Figure 14.2 gives an overview of the components relevant to building the auction mobile application. The client application supports multiple channels through which the end user can access the service provided. These channels are browsers, tablets, and mobile devices. For the application development team, the MVP is on the mobile application explored in the section.

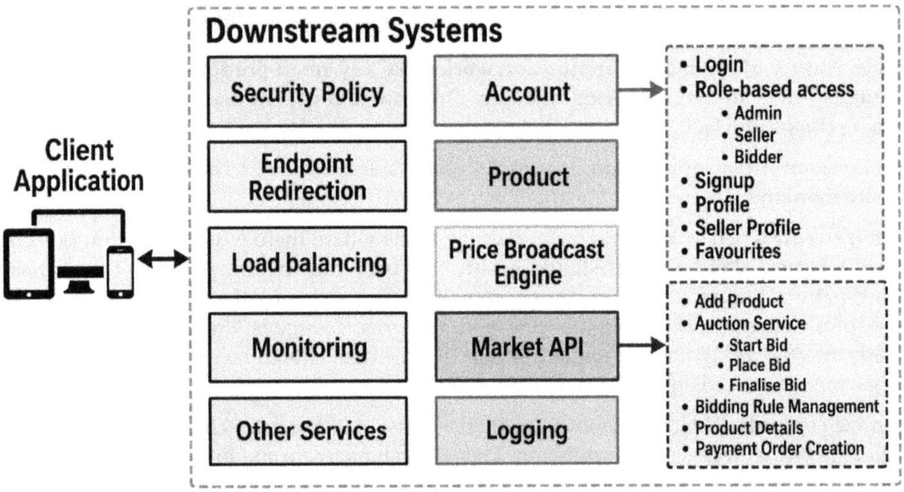

***Figure 14.2**: System overview*

The key differentiator in engineering required for this use case will be a broadcast management layer for handling the time-variant stream of data. The broadcast management layer is additional to the network abstractions. The various operations for the broadcast management layer include establishing the connection, pausing, resuming, requesting a payload, and disconnecting. Additionally, the broadcast management layer will also hold the responsibility to be a central hub to maintain the subscription management of multiple auction rooms subscribed together, which get displayed on the screen. The screen that displays the price changes leverages the broadcast management layer to request and get the value for all auction items. The broadcast management layer is expected to have the capability to handle multiple subscriptions for price movements without error or loss. This price change should be displayed simultaneously in the list screen. The backend server that emits the price change shall be a system that has a stream-enabled socket connection. The server system emits the price change as and when the new bid is placed in the auction. The event broadcast layer would be connected to the server and can subscribe to observe changes for particular items. The broadcast layer will thus get the price movement for multiple items for which the subscription is requested.

Figure 14.3 represents the sequence diagram for the price change event triggered in the backend:

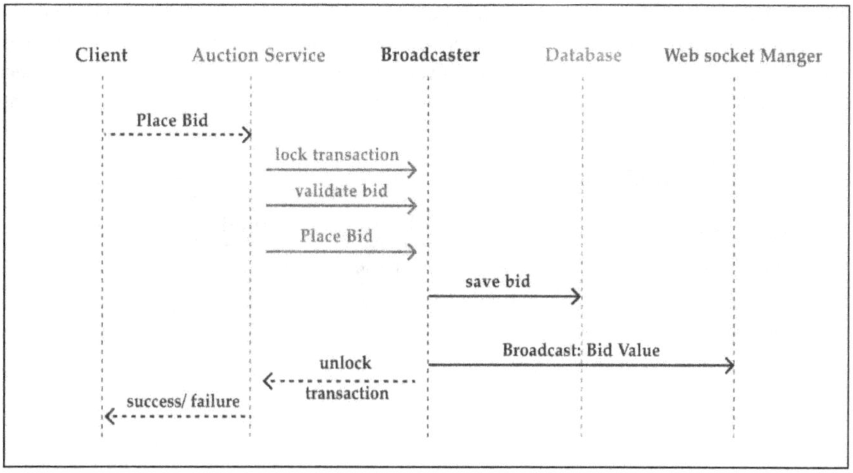

Figure 14.3: *Sequence diagram for place bid call*

The sequence diagram depicts the backend service, which handles the place bid request. The place bid from the client is processed in a sequential manner. The validation of the price to be higher than the current bid is handled by the end result of the place bid, ensuring the value is updated to the highest value. After processing, the request-response is broadcast to a WebSocket manager. The response can further be forwarded to all the clients that are observing the price change. Generally, a WebSocket, once the connection is established, works with commands and responses. *Table 14.1* represents a simple contract for the commands that a WebSocket server accepts to connect and subscribe to the auction price change:

Command	Payload

Connect	`payload => {`
	`"clientId": "xxxx",`
	`"authToken": "xyz.abc.123"`
	`}`

Disconnect	`payload => {`
	`"reason": "user_logout"`
	`}`

Send (command, payload)	`payload => {`
	`command : "subscribe" ,`
	`productID: 123456`
	`}`

	`payload => {`
	`command : "pause" ,`
	`productID: 123456`
	`}`

	`payload => {`
	`command : "resume",`
	`productID: 123456`
	`}`

	`payload => {`
	`command : "unsubscribe",`
	`productID: 123456`
	`}`

Table 14.1: *Command payload overview for broadcast web socket server*

Table 14.1 is a minimalist version of the contract for the WebSocket. The information can be the reference for a mobile engineer to devise the solution for designing a **`BroadcastManager`** layer. The contract details for the command, along with the socket API of the client, can be used to create a wrapper to manage the WebSocket connection. *Figure 14.4* depicts the class diagram for the **`ConnectionManager`** layer that abstracts the WebSocket client connection:

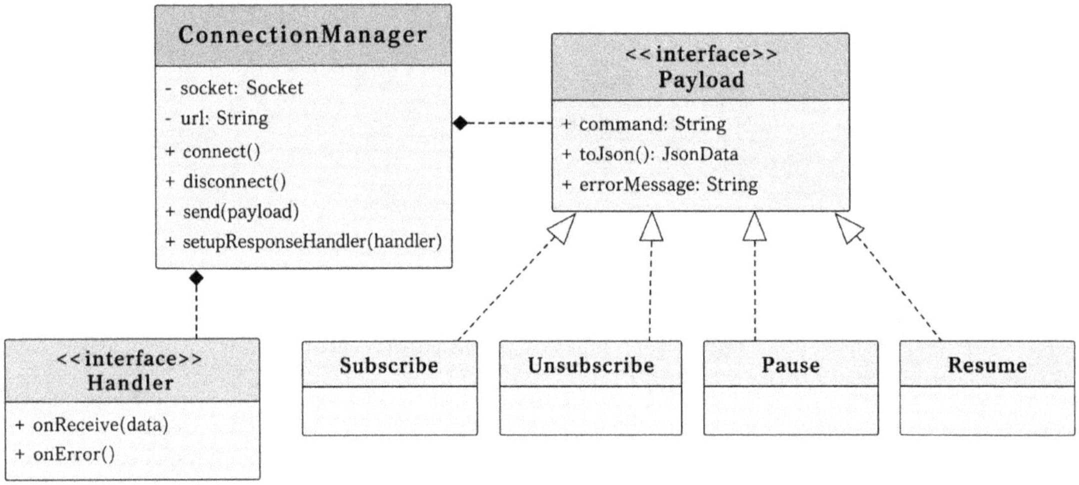

***Figure 14.4**: Class diagram for WebSocket ConnectionManager*

The construct defined in *Figure 14.4* forms the foundational layer to connect and communicate with WebSocket. An additional **`BroadcastManager`** layer above the connection manager is required, with the responsibility to serve as an abstraction to connect and manage the price change for the presentation layer. At this juncture, one may wonder if the team is duplicating the responsibility fulfilled by **`ConnectionManager`**. The answer is that the **`BroadcastManager`** layer is not a duplicate and has a greater purpose. The responsibility of the **`ConnectionManager`**, as discussed earlier, is to provide the abstraction for the WebSocket connection establishment and sending and receiving the request/response. The **`BroadcastManager`**, on the other hand, will manage thelifecycle of the price change subscription beyond the connection establishment and will be used by the presentation layer of the application. To understand the responsibility fulfilled by the **`BroadcastManager`**, consider the use case of the auction listing screen. As per the wireframe in *Figure 14.1*, there are different groups of auction lists (discover, upcoming, live, favorites, etc.). For each group, the auction items can be different. When the user navigates between these groups on the screen, the mobile application should display the price movement for each item in the list for which the auction is live. The **`BroadcastManager`** can be seen as the state machine managing the active and inactive price movement for auction items. The **`BroadcastManager`** acts by creating a mapping of the screen with a list of products, and based on the current active screen, will subscribe, pause, and resume the price movement. The **`BroadcastManager`** ideally would be the best candidate for the domain layer of the codebase.

Figure 14.5 depicts the class diagram for the **`BroadcastManager`**, along with how the **`BroadcastManager`** interacts with the user interface and connection manager:

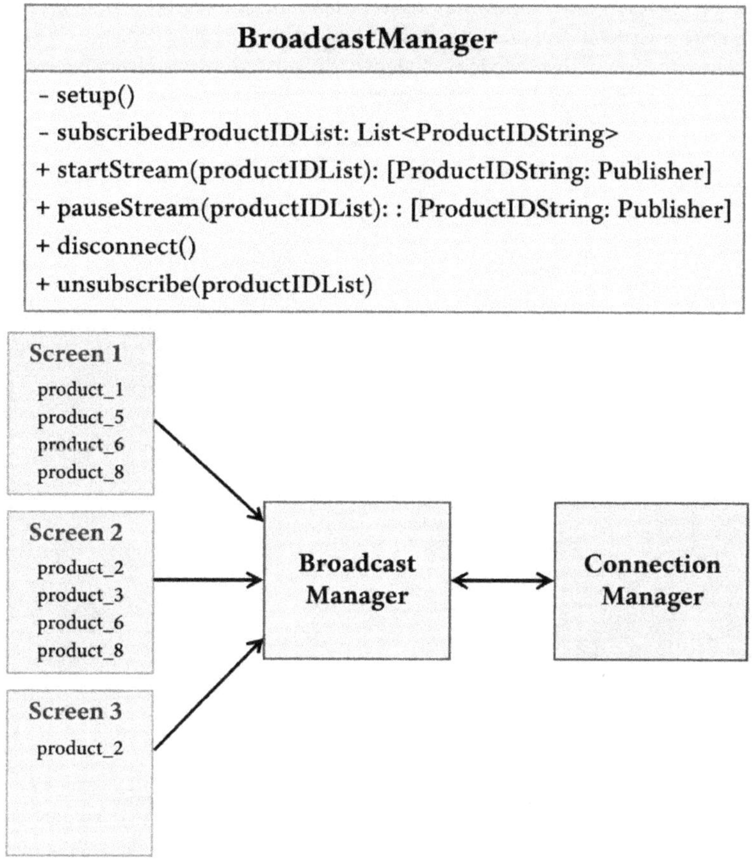

Figure 14.5: *BroadcastManager class diagram and interacting entities*

The **BroadcastManager** fulfils the responsibility to optimize the price movement at the page level. **BroadcastManager** achieves this by intercepting the subscription request from the different pages and leveraging the pause and resume to optimize the subscription.

A simple implementation of the **BroadcastManager** depicted in *Figure 14.5* can be described as a case where the **setupStream** and **pauseStream** methods take a list of product IDs as a parameter. These methods are the entry and exit functions for each screen to invoke while transitioning in and out of a screen. The **setupStream** and **pauseStream** return a map data structure with the **productID** key and the price change publishers value. The user interface for each item can now listen to the respective price change publisher, which is mapped to the auction item corresponding to the **productID**.

Consider the case where the user is transitioning from one page to another. Here, the **pauseStream** method will be invoked with a list of product IDs in the page that disappears. When the subsequent screen is loaded, the **setupStream** method will be invoked with the active product ID list. The **setupStream** has the logic to filter the **productID** which are already subscribed. The connection enablement or a separate subscription request is not required for these product IDs. Instead of calling the subscribe, resuming the price change will be enough to get the latest price change value. In a broadcast system, the subscribe method typically adds overhead such as network and initialization cost. The software should be designed to avoid these by reducing and optimizing the total number of subscription calls initiated from the client. Only for items that have not been subscribed a new request shall be sent. The code is written to send subscription requests only for the newly added **productID**. A successful subscription gets added to the list of products at the **BroadcastManager** layer. Pause and resume should be a capability that the backend managing the price change exposes for the mobile client.

The presentation layer must worry only about the product that is in the active screen, and it is the responsibility of the **BroadcastManager** to ensure all the other products stay paused for price change. *Figure 14.6* is the sequence diagram that shows the interaction of the **BroadcastManager** when transitioning from Screen A to Screen B:

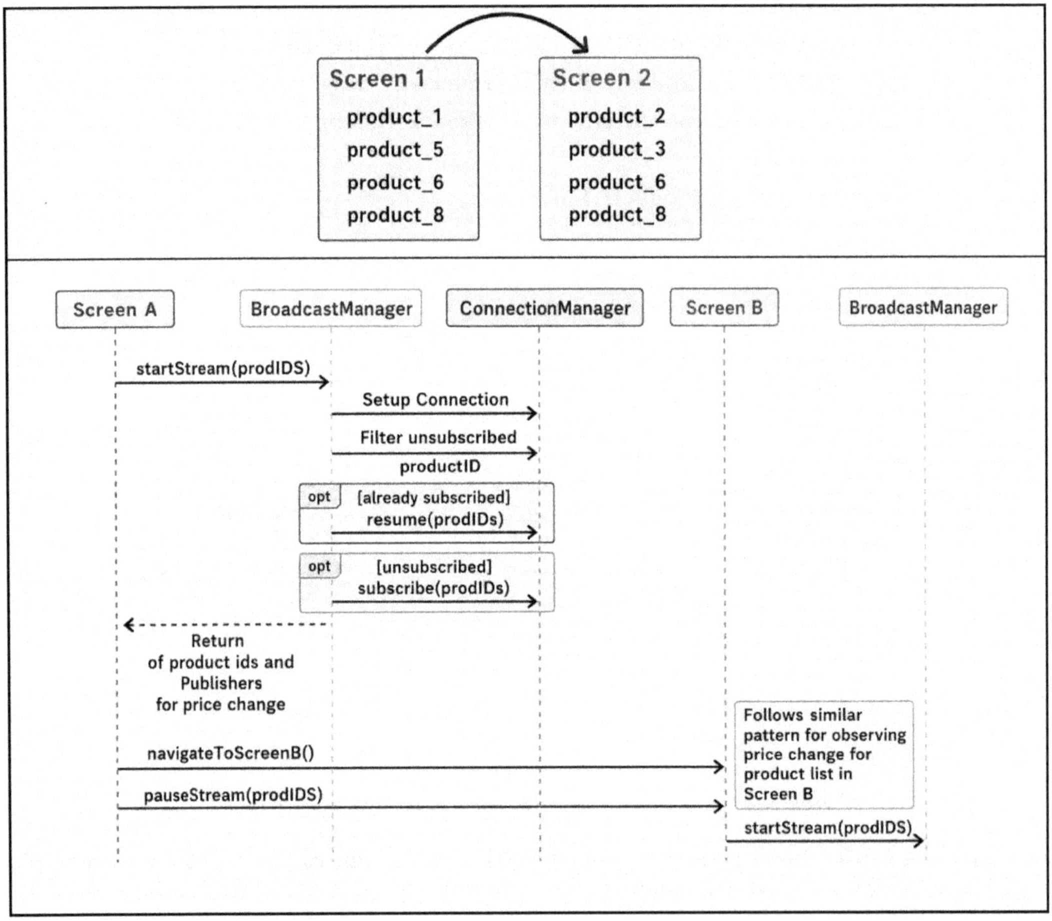

Figure 14.6: *Sequence diagram for transition between two screens*

In *Figure 14.6,* both Screen A and Screen B have different sets of product IDs. The simple implementation of the pause and resume is depicted in the sequence diagram. The **BroadcastManager** uses pause and resume logic as explained earlier to optimize the subscription call. The transition back to the previous can also be seen in a similar context for pause and resume, with the additional user interface-related navigation logic removing the view from the stack.

The narrative explores the event-driven mechanism within the Auction application, managing the price change. Other functional features exist, such as the login, sign-up, seller listing, transaction API, payment integration, support, and profile management. All these features have a backend API that the mobile application could consume to perform the operation. *Figure 14.7* is the high-level architecture diagram of the mobile code base for the auction application:

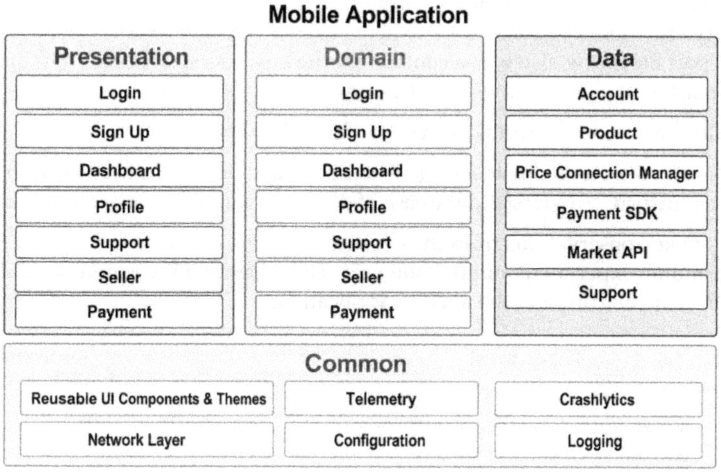

Figure 14.7: *Auction mobile app high-level architecture diagram*

Figure 14.7 follows the three-layer approach, segregated into presentation, domain, and data. The presentation and the domain share a similar module structure. Both these layers contain a module corresponding to each application feature. The presentation layer has the user interface with state management logic, and the business logic ideally is managed at the domain layer. The presentation layer will only be responsible for responding to the event on the screen. The computation or the logic is delegated to the domain layer. The domain layer depends on the data layer, which establishes the connection to the downstream layer, third-party service, and hardware feature. The camera, location, secure store, and biometrics are the hardware features leveraged in the auction application.

The names of modules in the data layer may differ from the presentation or domain layer. An example to quote is the account module in the data layer. The account module deals with the backend system that exposes login, signup, and profile API. Another example is the product module that deals with order management, product search, bidding process, etc. In both these cases, the API exposed via the respective backend system is modelled as is. The data layers mirror the external system or the hardware feature that the application leverages. The domain or presentation layer, on the other hand, will be segregated based on the feature exposed to the user for the mobile application use cases.

In summary, we can conclude the system design philosophy for the auction mobile application code base revolves around three themes: the three-layered code separation, event-driven mechanism, and the robust state management strategy. The state-management strategy is important to ensure the user interface redraws are optimal and hardware resources are optimally consumed. Reactive programming is a solved problem in mobile space. The libraries provided by the development framework are optimal for supporting a continuous stream of data for the user interface. Using these frameworks is the recommended strategy for the team.

Technology choice

For this use case, the team actively evaluated Flutter and found it to be the most suitable choice. The context that led to the decision is listed as follows:

- The team had limited time to market.
- The team looked at data on the target audience for the application. The market was dominated by users using an Android device. The iPhone users were less than 20% of the total target users.
- The branding team was following a design inspired mainly by the Material Design which was recommended in the Android ecosystem. This resonated with the technology choice, as Flutter supported Material Design.

- The stakeholder was also not sure of the market condition for hiring. The time leverage to invest to find the availability of two sets of technology expertise acted as a detractor for going native. The operational coordination post the hiring also was a concern for the business stakeholder. The stakeholder also wanted an MVP approach with optimal investment during the early stage of the engagement.
- The mobile application being built was an experimental investment.

The decision was not taken only on the business ask. The tech evaluation of Flutter was also done. The experiment evaluating the framework helped to understand the ease of doing the features relevant to this application with Flutter.

Table 14.2 summarizes the key observations from the evaluation. These experiments are summarized in the table as the feature, the corresponding experiment and the outcome. The experiment was done by creating a sample project in Flutter for some of the critical feature of the auction application.

Feature	Experiment	Outcome
Impact of screen performance on the continuous redraw because of price change	• The experiment is to implement a screen mimicking the price change equivalent of auction app. • The project should list the mock products. • The value of the price for the product changes in a mock socket backend. • Mock socket emits a random number value. • The number of items kept in the list was 50 mock products.	With the sample application, the experience was validated with the stakeholder, and the team was able to achieve a device refresh rate (60fps or 120fps) expected for screen rendering with Flutter. Thus, the Flutter was equipped to handle continuous redraw without performance drop.
Availability of library for socket connection	• Validate the availability of a library that enables socket connection in the community.	The team identified that the community had options that enabled the team to leverage and write socket connect, and the library did support the other platforms, apart from mobile. The stakeholder had a vision to take the product beyond mobile once the MVP is successful.
Payment provider support with Flutter	• Evaluate if the partner libraries for example payment provider has a setup and SDK that is compatible with the Flutter codebase.	The payment provider which the organization partnered with, did not have libraries compatible with the Flutter development kit. The team checked for the roadmap of the payment provider for the Flutter-compatible payment library. The timeline for the Flutter Payment SDK release matched the timeline for the auction application development. This de-risked the development in Flutter.
Hardware features	• Evaluate support for camera, location, secure store, and biometrics feature support in Flutter.	The Flutter ecosystem had enough libraries provided by the community that allowed access to the different hardware features. The feature expected in the application was readily available.
Open issues	• Evaluate open issues in the Flutter framework.	While there were open issues in the Flutter framework, the team did not see any issues that would impact the Auction mobile application.

Feature	Experiment	Outcome
Comparison with native	• Evaluate the pros and cons of native application development versus Flutter.	The possibilities of the user interface via the Flutter widget ecosystem and its adherence to the branding guidelines expected by the application turned out to be strong points favoring Flutter. Choosing native development would have added a bottleneck to bring components following Material Design on iOS, as this required separate effort for custom-implementation. The probability of the app requiring sophisticated hardware-intensive or platform-specific operation was nil. The team thus was able to conclude Flutter being advantageous than native.

Table 14.2: *Flutter framework evaluation summary*

The following summarizes the key takeaways for the reader from the first case study:

This case study was intended to bring the practical exposure to the reader for the most plausible use case that replicates a typical problem statement for event-driven and screen intensive consumer-facing mobile applications. While the first case study centered around the auction mechanism, if the structure is relabeled to other industries, the architecture and solution would work as is. The respective module may change to match the target functionality of the domain. The reader should always re-evaluate the technology choice, rather than defaulting to what was used in the case study. The business context which necessitated the mobile application should also be considered. For technology choice the key points narrated in *Chapter 3, Cross-platform Versus Native* will bring the reasoning ability to the reader to make the right decision.

Monitoring app via connected sensors

This case study explores an organization in the retail segment, maintaining storehouses for perishable products. Every storehouse is equipped with a set of devices with the following intent:

- Safety mechanism and device to detect any catastrophic event and react accordingly.
- Device for pest detection and control, and quality of the working environment.
- Temperature control hardware to regulate temperature.

The current setup for the organization was that each of the individual sensors needs to be verified and audited independently. The hardware modules should be independently tested and checked. The maintenance was becoming a time-consuming and human-intensive task. Given the nature of the business, keeping a regular check was mandatory. The team wanted to streamline the maintenance and proposed to consolidate the individual sensors connected to a centralized hardware module. The centralized hardware can now become the hub for maintenance personnel with a mobile application to get insights on the networked sensors.

The outcome of the modernization was aimed at allowing the team to avoid a lot of manual processes which previously required manual maintenance checks on these sensors. The individual device would be spread out across the building, and the data entry, which had to be manually transcribed for the device, can now be coordinated by the centralized hardware. The mobile application could connect to the hardware providing the ability for the maintenance person to get insight into the networked sensors. The design thinking required to develop the mobile application is the crux of the section. *Figure 14.8* gives an overview of the to-be architecture, including the downstream system to which the mobile connects:

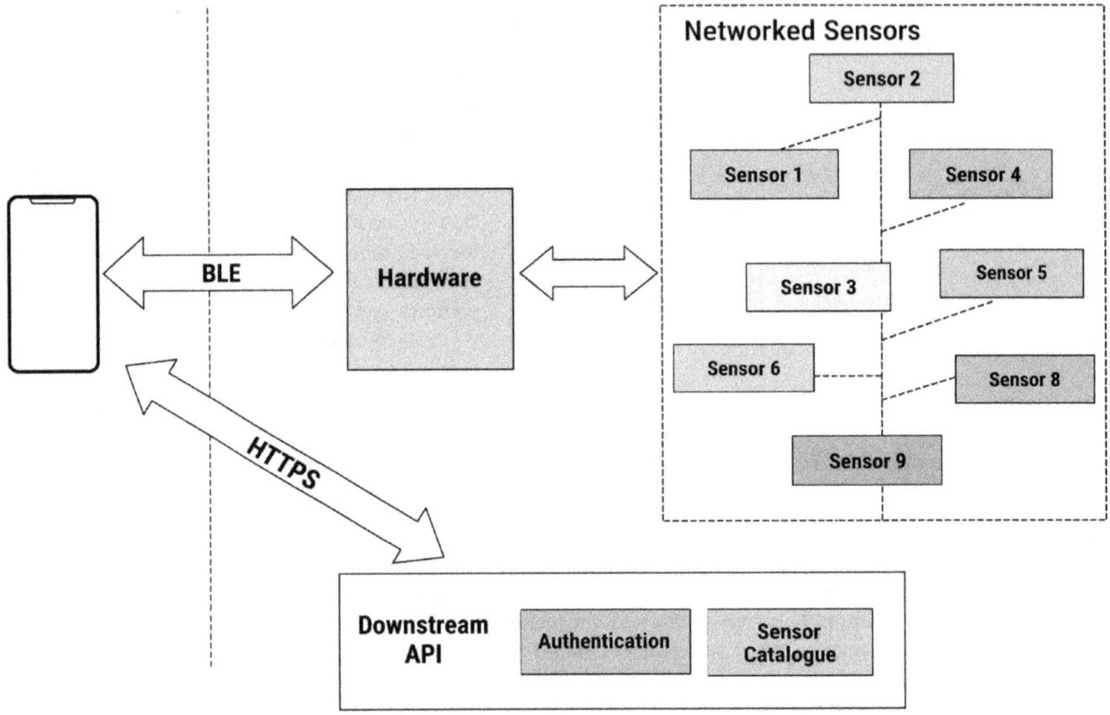

Figure 14.8: System overview

The hardware development and how these devices are provisioned is a black box and is not necessary for the mobile development team. The key insight required for the mobile is the contract and the mechanism with which the mobile can communicate with the hardware. The team had decided the hardware would be **Bluetooth Low Energy** (**BLE**) enabled for the initial phase. In the future, the addition of capabilities for other connectivity technologies was kept open. The hardware team had defined the contract and come up with a specification for the command to be sent to get the details of the sensor. This mobile application reduced the time required for the maintenance personnel to check for all the network sensors. The idea mobile-based hardware monitoring concept was an ambitious investment for the organization. The organization had heavy bets on the idea and was seen as a worthy investment bringing a lot of operational efficiency. This idea of the mobile application with hardware also had the potential to be automated from remote locations as a future enhancement.

Mobile application scope

The scope of the mobile application was to build the client layer connecting the hardware. With the mobile application the maintenance personnel could access the details from the hardware to do the check on the sensors. The mobile communicated via BLE, thus constraining the individual to be present near to the hardware installed to communicate. The mobile application will connect to the hardware listed on screen. The mode of communication had multiple layers of command to be executed and had custom protocol to be followed while transferring data. The data transfer (acted as command and response) was between the mobile and the hardware module via BLE. All these are internal working details and for the end user, it would be the selection of actions on the screen. There was a special requirement to stay away from the modern design. The special requirement came as the end users were not very familiar with the conventional mobile user interface. The organization has a predisposition that the modern design was not intuitive for the maintenance personnel. The stakeholder of the organization wanted a minimalistic design and focused action. The logic that backed this hypothesis was discovered by the organization after user research amongst the professionals who handled the maintenance. A corollary of the decision was the mobile interface having mechanism to support the end user in form of help text. The help and tooltips for end users became the high-priority requirement. For a normal mobile application having the help text everywhere in the application would seem to be counterintuitive as per the norm of the human interface guideline. The stakeholder sponsoring the engagement gave the ultimatum to override the human interface guideline considering the target audience. The application was not intended to be B2C and did not have the intent to upload to the app store. The plan was to distribute via a private enterprise app store. The platform restriction for following the guideline was not there when distributed via private store. The core capability of the entire mobile application was the BLE-enabled communication to the hardware.

The major components of the codebase are the presentation, the domain layer, and the connector to a third-party system. The third party includes the hardware and backend service. The networking module primarily deals with authenticating the user and fetching configuration for the hardware. The BLE component itself was grouped to host and abstract functionality that handles scanning of hardware, establishes a connection, and sends different commands to hardware. The commands will trigger controlling, monitoring, and maintenance of the networked devices via the hardware hub. The BLE component abstraction is implemented on top of the Bluetooth API exposed by the platform to scan and establish a connection. The communication layer was responsible to send and receive data. These data packets adhered to the contract specified by hardware team. The data byte format of the request sent should follow the respective command structure. The data byte received should be interpreted as per the specification. This layer is responsible for implementation of the specification defined by the hardware enabling communication.

Major features

The capabilities of the mobile application can be divided into two: hardware communication layer and the application features. The following are the major functionalities identified for the first phase for the hardware communication layer. The following list describes the capabilities exposed by the hardware that can be consumed via the BLE feature of a mobile device:

- Scanning hardware devices enabled by BLE.
- Connecting to the hardware module.
- Fetch the sensor devices connected to the hardware.
- Send command to do operations on individual devices. Example: get details, status, maintenance, etc.
- Authentication/Authorization to use the mobile application and the hardware.
- Trigger an update for the firmware for the hardware.

The application-related feature included the login feature, the user interface to communicate and display data from the hardware. The data from the hardware was reporting the details of the sensors connected in the network which the maintenance personnel can monitor. The journey of securely connecting to mobile applications and completing the maintenance activity of the networked devices was essential. This was part of the building safety procedure and thus got prioritized to be targeted for the first phase. The organization's larger goal was to build a product offering for other enterprises. Phase one was a check on the feasibility and market acceptance via the minimum viable product.

Sensor configuration

There were different kinds of sensors in the network. The status or command that needed to be sent, varied for each of these. The possibility of the sensor manufacturer changing the command after upgrade was also open. This essentially meant that there was a possibility for change in the contract of the request and response in the communication mechanism. The command and the response for each type of device were also different. The team developing the mobile application had to build the capability to handle the variations in the networked sensors. The different types of sensors and the command structure formed the configuration for respective sensors. A mobile application should know these in advance to send a command to fetch and display the information.

The organization in the MVP phase had the requirement to support 10 categories of devices. For each device, an average of three to five commands was there in the specification. It would have been a nightmare to maintain all these hardcoded on mobile codebase as the number of devices that the hardware had to support was more than fifty post MVP phase. The team took the design decision to delegate this responsibility to the backend service to handle the command as configuration fetched to mobile application. The heavy lifting of providing the configuration on the need basis was taken up by the backend. The mobile can now incrementally request command configuration of the required network sensor connected to the hardware. This design is more scalable than hardcoding the configuration for every sensor in the mobile codebase.

The code also has presentation layer and business layer as in other mobile application codebases. The difference is the user interface for this application is minimal. The business layer to handle the different device types is the unique problem statement to be addressed as part of the application.

Note: **One could alternatively think that sensor configurations can be sent via the BLE from the hardware, instead of a backend API call. Whilst this is theoretically possible, the computational overload that the hardware must own is not the appropriate design choice. The focus and goal of the hardware module was to be a control center, ensuring the networked sensors are efficient and effective.**

Overview of BLE

BLE is a wireless communication technology used for short-range and quick connections. The technology uses low power, and the data transfer happens as a small burst of data. For large-sized data, the data will have to be divided into chunks and transferred. The BLE device plays two roles: the device that scans and connects is called the central, and the device that acts as the broadcaster is called the peripheral. In this case study, the mobile plays the role of central, and the hardware plays the role of peripheral. The central device must scan, connect, and search for the **Generic Attribute Profile** (**GATT**). Once the GATT profile is identified, the devices can communicate with each other. The GATT profile has two components: service and characteristic. These two are the classifications in the BLE device to define how data is exposed to the external world. Any typical BLE device can have multiple services, and each service associated has characteristics. From the BLE device playing the role of central (via the mobile application), finding the appropriate characteristics to send and receive the data is the core functionality that the team should implement.

In this case, the data to be transferred or received is large. As said earlier, since the data transfer happens as a short burst of data, a large data may get divided as a multipart of smaller chunks. The mobile device will have to receive the response data and concatenate it based on certain protocol or contract agreed with the source. The sending of the data request will be handled by the BLE layer exposed by the framework of the mobile device. In this use case, the commands are smaller units, all below the maximum size allowed for a typical BLE device. The max data size that can be transferred for the communication depends on both, the central and peripheral. In general communication channel will take the lowest supported size from the central and peripheral. For example, when the central device supports 256 bytes and the peripheral supports 1024, communication between them will be limited to 256 bytes per transfer. When receiving 1024-size data, the mobile device will receive four callbacks. A common design for handling such data transfer involves sending a dedicated start byte sequence at the beginning and a terminating byte sequence at the end to identify and reconstruct the large data at the receiving side.

The development framework for iOS and Android has provided a built-in mechanism to connect and talk to BLE devices. The framework is used to scan BLE hardware and to establish a connection with the hardware of interest. After connecting to the hardware, the mobile can send the command by transferring the data to the hardware. The response for the command from the hardware module is handled in the data receiving callback. One key design consideration dictated by the hardware module was the data received at the mobile was multipart, and the mobile had to concatenate and ensure that the data was synchronized and that it was not corrupted. The data was then transformed into meaningful entities by the business layer to display to the end user.

The hardware team shared the definition for the contract. This contract defines the identifier for the BLE peripheral, the GATT profile, and the command request with respective response specification. The mobile development team had to implement these to communicate with the hardware. Given that there could be a malicious entity in the vicinity, the command was also there to establish some form of authorization and authentication between the peripheral and mobile device.

Architecture overview

The section looks at the key components that constitute the architecture of the mobile codebase. Starting from the presentation layer through the business layer connecting to the BLE module is explained in detail in this section. *Figure 14.9 (a)* depicts the high-level architecture for this mobile application:

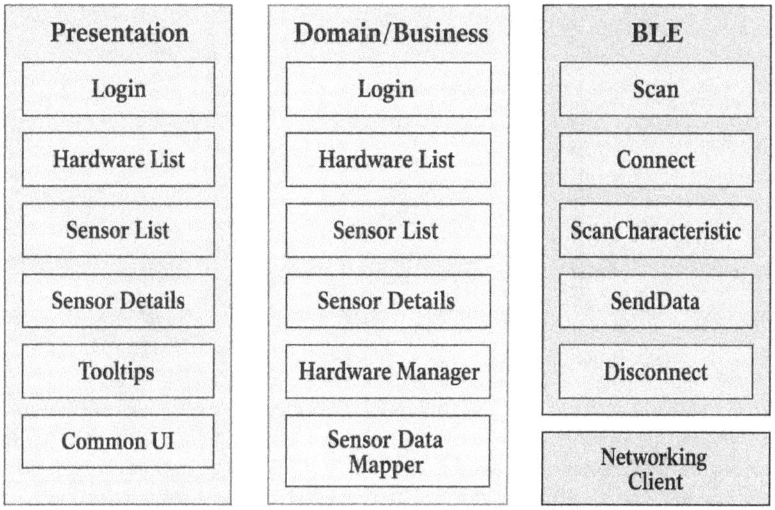

Figure 14.9 (a): *Mobile app codebase high-level architecture diagram*

In the *Figure 14.9 (a)* the components are depicted in individual blocks. Each block forms a cohesive unit. Following such an architecture helps to organize the codebase in a manageable format for the organization. The presentation layer has the block representing the features the user will see on the mobile. The computation required for these features is represented in the respective blocks in the business layer.

Figure 14.9 (b) depicts the wireframe of the **Hardware List**, **Sensor List** and **Sensor Details** screens:

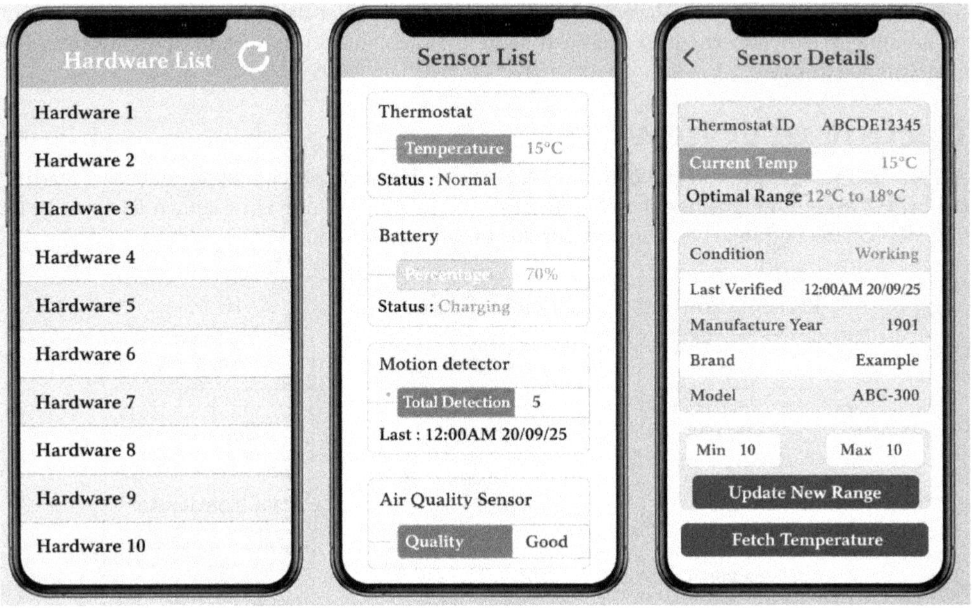

***Figure 14.9 (b)**: Wireframe for Hardware List and Sensor screens*

Unlike the first use case mentioned in the chapter, this mobile application only has a simple user interface to login, listing the BLE hardware, listing networked sensor and Sensor Details screen. A three-layer architecture was not chosen here. The team felt the additional data-layer abstraction would add unnecessary complexity for a simple user interface and this may not add value to the codebase. The presentation layer deals with the user interface and state management, whereas the business layer has the logic to support the presentation layer by invoking the backend API or the BLE abstraction layer. The business layer will fetch and pass the response in transformed format to screen. These two layers provide the necessary abstraction required for the application, where the business layer could be unit tested and will be scalable.

In the business layer, the Hardware List block in the architecture uses the BLE layer to scan and list the nearby hardware. To establish the connection, the connect method should be invoked. There will be a corresponding presentation layer responsible for displaying the list of device identified in the scan. The business layer for the Hardware List will keep track of the connection status of these hardware in the list. Once connected to the hardware the command could be sent to hardware. The first command will give the list of the sensors connected in the network. The hardware responds with the Sensor Details and can be displayed on the list. On selection of the sensor item, the further command to fetch the status and the command-related details for the particular sensor type is invoked and Sensor Details is shown. The details screen will have the option which maintenance personnel can choose to get additional details of the selected sensor. This will give the personnel ability to do the maintenance check on the respective individual sensor.

In the preceding section, it was discussed that sensor configuration will be fetched from the downstream system. This ensures the mobile application has the command and response resolution mechanism decoupled from the mobile codebase and delegated to external configuration. The external configuration is fetched from a webservice and the `HttpClient` in the Sensor Details page. The Sensor Details block in the business layer depicted in *Figure 14.9 (a)* handles the logic for the Sensor Details page.

Figure 14.10 depicts the flowchart for how the maintenance personnel interacts with the mobile application:

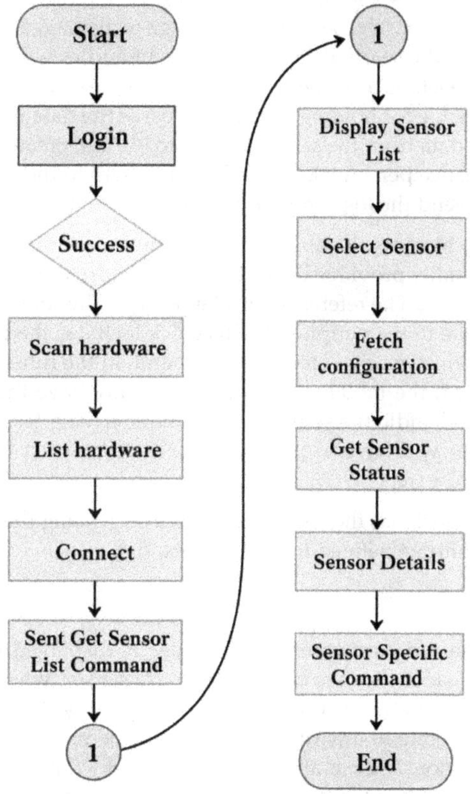

***Figure 14.10**: Flowchart for the application workflow*

Note: **The narrative has been kept technology agnostic. A reader can apply the same philosophy to any platform and can be mapped for either cross-platform or native technology.**

Next let us explore the responsibilities of the blocks depicted in *Figure 14.9 (a)* for the business layer:

- **Login**: Validation for inputs, invoking of the downstream API for login, and parsing data which can be consumed by the presentation layer (Login, Sensor Details, and Reporting) fulfilled by the code written under the Login block.
- **Hardware List**: The hardware is the main interface that the mobile connects with. Maintenance personnel, depending on the number of buildings to cover or the size of the building will have multiple hardware to connect for performing the maintenance related activities. The Hardware List block will get the data for the list view depicted in the *Figure 14.9 (b)*. The code abstraction to scan lists of nearby hardware, managing the BLE-related permission and managing the error state is handled by the Hardware List block. Another responsibility that the block manages is connecting to the hardware device selected by the end-user from the Hardware List. The block depends on the Hardware Manager layer that exposes the scan and connect related operations.
- **Sensor List**: Once the maintenance personnel connect to the hardware, the individual gets access to the sensor connected to the hardware. The mobile application presents the option to interact with these sensor and do the maintenance related activity from the mobile. This block corresponds to the second screen in the *Figure 14.9 (b)*. The block handles the fetching of the list of sensors by sending a command to the hardware. The command to fetch sensors is sent after establishing the successful connection. The response of the hardware for the command sent from mobile is also processed and transformed at this layer.

- **Sensor Details**: From the list of sensor displayed on the screen, the maintenance personnel can select the details page of individual sensor. The Sensor Details page is displayed to the end user. This Sensor Details block handles the details of the selected sensor. BLE command as well as API will be involved to get the Sensor Details. The Sensor Details received from the BLE command will be bytes of data. The **Sensor Data Mapper** module is responsible for holding the logic to parse the data into a meaningful representation for the respective sensor. The data from the sensor is used to log and create reports for the inspection done on the sensor by the maintenance personnel. The data is then sent to the downstream systems by the mobile application. The action to send the logs and the reports will also be part of the Sensor Details page.
- **Hardware Manager**: This block is the abstraction that manages the connected hardware. This block is responsible for the functionality provided by the BLE layer. The reference to the current connected hardware device is managed in the block. The reference thus helps to get the connection status and to send command via the BLE to communicate to the peripheral. This block includes the code responsible for the validation and conversion of the response received for BLE command. In the future when additional communication technologies are introduced, the mobile application will only have the lower layer changed. This layer will act as a single place to handle the switching of the underlying technology. The block thus acts as the adapter and business layer will have to pass configuration to select the connecting technology used to communicate with the hardware.
- **Sensor data mapper**: The block has the code that focuses on parsing the response for different commands. The module follows the contract defined for the sensors.

Sensor data mapper

A sensor responds to command via the hardware. The response is displayed to the maintenance personnel on the mobile screen. For example, consider the case of a temperature sensor, where the maintenance personnel will be interested in getting the live temperature status. Another case will be the maintenance personnel interested in changing the temperature. The mobile in any of these can send the respective command via the BLE module. These are examples of operation previously the maintenance personnel would have done manually going near each sensor. The manual process being automated and available in the mobile improves the speed and efficiency of the maintenance procedure. When the whole gamut of sensor is connected with the mobile and can communicate that is the value the application brings to the table. Examples of other sensors are humidity, air quality, etc.

When there are different kinds of sensor an interesting technical problem arises. For a mobile application codebase, there will be different commands applicable for the variety of the sensor type supported. The additional complexity where each device may have different response structure will have to be addressed by mobile application. The code has to handle the parsing mechanisms for the response for each sensor type. One of the major roles of the sensor data mapper module in the architecture is to handle this logic to resolve and parse the data for the different sensors.

Table 14.3 depicts example of different sensors sending different data, which need to be parsed by the business layer:

Sensor type	Response format

Temperature	`{`
	`"value": 22.8,`
	`"unit": "°C",`
	`"status": "normal"`
	`}`

Motion detection	`{`
	`"detected": true,`
	`"last_triggered": "2025-06-03T15:18:00Z"`
	`}`

Sensor type	Response format

Air quality	`{`
	`"co2_ppm": 480,`
	`"index": 1.2,`
	`"status": "good"`
	`}`

Battery percentage	`{`
	`"level_percent": 87,`
	`"status": "ok"`
	`}`

***Table 14.3:** Response data sample for different sensors*

The data from *Table 14.3* implies that the device-level data mapping should be maintained to know the respective data for each device. The table clearly shows the non-universal nature of the response. The sensor data mapper block depicted in the *Figure 14.9 (a)* will have class definitions for all these corresponding to these different responses. Once the BLE callback receives the data, the mobile device knows which command has been sent thus can use the mapping to parse and resolve the data using the respective logic for each sensor.

Components enabling BLE communication

The high-level architecture discussed has given a few insights about the layer where the BLE component was present. For the iOS devices, the framework called **`CoreBluetooth`** is used, and for Android, the SDK named **`android.bluetooth`** has all the APIs required to connect, scan, and send data to BLE device.

Note: **One should also understand that if the team ever wants to implement BLE with cross-platform, the libraries available will follow a similar structure BLE functionality exposed by cross-platform will internally have to use the native frameworks.**

Figure 14.11 depicts the class diagram with the entities involved in BLE component. These are abstractions over the native APIs exposed by the platform. The classes leverage the platform API underneath to connect and interact with BLE device.

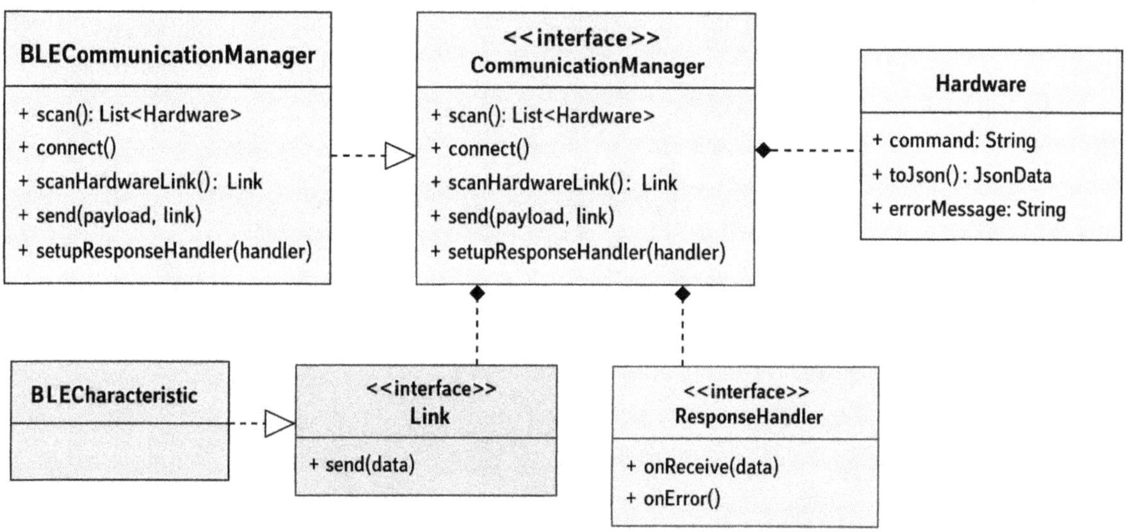

***Figure 14.11:** Class diagram for BLE component layer*

The additional abstraction may seem to be an overhead introduced in the codebase instead of directly using the framework provided API. The overhead introduced is in consideration with the long-term vision for the mobile application to support multiple communication mechanisms. The BLE was just one means to communicate with the hardware as part of the minimum viable product. As long as the hardware follows the same contract of commands and responses, the BLE component layer could be used as is by renaming the BLE-specific class names to technology-agnostic names and by adding support for the additional communication technology. The business and presentation layer thus will stay intact.

Let us look at the key takeaways from the second case study. This case study introduced the library thinking, where building the ConnectionManager focused on making the reader think beyond a typical mobile architecture. The use case has the usage of abstraction to build a layer that makes the entire mobile codebase extensible. The code in the use case is capable of scaling as the lower layer is loosely coupled. The application can customize the underlying technology used to communicate with hardware without changing the top layer. One should always cultivate such a thought process leading to design of loosely coupled layers in any mobile application development. Designing a system with clear separation of concern ensures codebase to be optimal. This thought process is essential theme that ensures the mobile codebase scales. The mindset for iterative improvement, the flexibility to change, and the ability to shed any bias could be an accelerator to bring in such thinking.

Surveillance app

An organization operating as a security system service provider had to build a mobile application that connects to the camera in a network to relay the live feeds. The organization was operating with a special set of cameras. These cameras had the capability to mechanically control rotary operation and the zoom feature from a mobile device. These cameras follow the **Open Network Video Interface Forum** (**ONVIF**) protocol, which allowed the operations to be triggered via command sent to the camera devices. The command to the camera was being sent via network. As per the ONVIF standard, not all cameras are mandated to support all the operations. The camera could support a subset of operation as well. The organization did not restrict the mobile application to only support the ONVIF camera; the mobile application supported other cameras used only for live feeds as well. As part of the mobile application, the organization aimed to build the capability to communicate with the networked camera device and display the live feed on the mobile application. The ability to pan, tilt, and zoom for ONVIF camera was provided as the option to the end user. Other than the camera related operation the mobile application also gave the capability to annotate, take screenshots, record the video feed, and save to the mobile device. *Figure 14.12* depicts the system overview for the mobile application and the interaction with the camera device connected in the network:

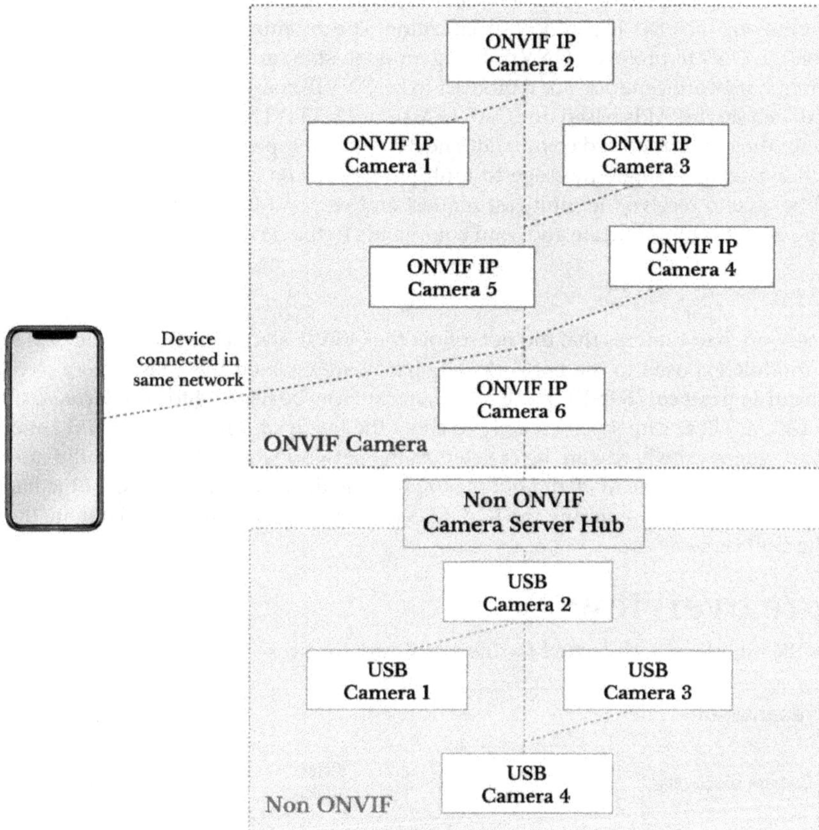

Figure 14.12: *System overview*

In comparison to other use cases explored in the chapter, this application has no separate downstream. The camera module works as a standalone unit connected to the intranet. For the mobile application to work it should be connected to the same intranet where the cameras are connected. The purpose of the application was to control and view the camera output in the local network. The camera itself can have authentication mechanism which when enabled should be adhered by the client mobile application. After the discovery the credentials should be configured otherwise the camera feed will not show up on the mobile application.

In summary, the scope for the mobile application was to build the following functionality identified for the first phase of the application development:

- Scanning the cameras connected in the network.
- Configure the authentication for the individual cameras.
- View camera thumbnail on successful configuration.
- Camera details page with live feed and additional control operations.
- Non-ONVIF camera support.
- Record, screenshot, and save.

ONVIF

ONVIF defines the specification for the common interface for the products that are IP-based. These devices are primarily in the physical security and surveillance domain. A hardware vendor shall create products based on these specifications and can release the product to the market. These products can be used, and a client can communicate with these devices following the ONVIF protocol specification. The organization had the vision to build a client-side application based on the ONVIF protocol. ONVIF, being an open standard, will allow interoperability of different cameras from different hardware vendors. For a product to be ONVIF compatible, these devices have to implement a set of standardized web service APIs based on SOAP/XML over HTTP. The client will make the API call to interact with the devices by sending the supported command. The discovery happens via the **user datagram protocol** (**UDP**) multicast. The multicast sends a single message to multiple devices on a network using a special IP range. The ONVIF device will be able to receive the multicast request and respond back to the client with the details. These details can further be used to communicate and send commands to the device in the network.

USB camera

The devices in the network had cameras that did not follow the ONVIF standard. These were USB interface cameras which a hardware module exposed to the network. The hardware enabled the USB camera feed to be broadcast using **real-time streaming protocol** (**RTSP**). The live stream can now be listened to and decoded by a media player on the mobile application. These cameras were only to show the live feed. The camera could annotate, record, and save a screenshot and videos. The hardware layer acted as the network abstraction which the mobile interacted to get the details of the USB camera. The MVP did not plan to include the discovery feature for the hardware. The USB camera was configured manually by entering the IP details for the hardware module to initiate the connection and configuration for the USB camera.

Architecture overview

Figure 14.13 depicts the high-level architecture for the mobile application:

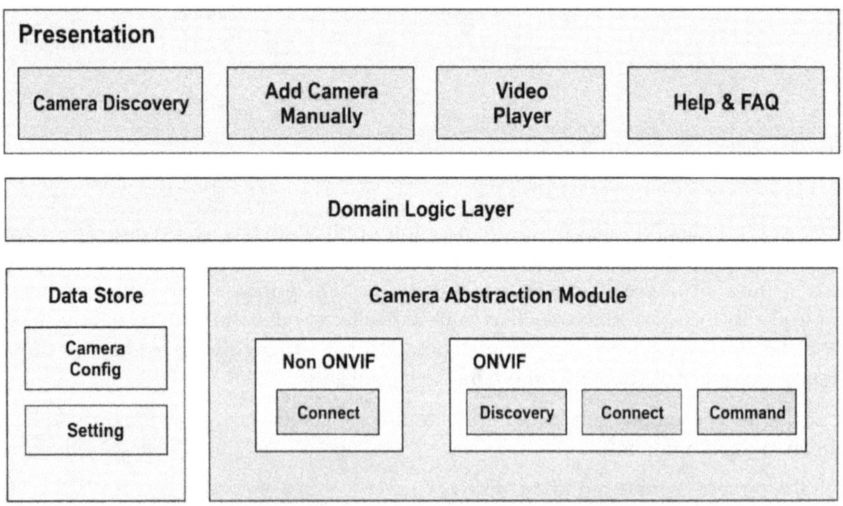

***Figure 14.13**: Mobile app codebase high-level architecture diagram*

The architecture diagram in the mobile application has fewer layers. One may find the major components such as the video player and the camera abstraction module, are external library integrations. Building both components in-house is not pragmatic. Developing these in-house will be a costly and time-consuming affair for the organization. A partnering approach would be ideal to address the technology expertise required to add the video player and ONVIF capability to the application. The remaining module is a user interface to show the video player and add camera configuration. The camera configuration includes the IP address, user name, password, and port. An ONVIF camera has discovery mechanism and post discovery there will be authentication challenge. The end-user should configure the user name and password necessary to connect and see the live feed.

The application allowed the configuration to be saved on the device. This software design enabled the mobile application to skip the discovery each time for the same set of camera. The action for pan, tilt, zoom, etc., was part of the ONVIF library. The **call to action** (**CTA**) on the video player for the operation was available to end user. The video player library also provided the screenshot, recording, and annotating options. The organization aimed at supporting multiple camera hardware vendors.

> Note: **The given narrative does not specify specific library or the development framework. Given the nature of the application, where core features such as video stream and on-device recording are used, the probability for native technology to stand out giving better performance is high.**

Let us look at the key takeaways from the third case study. This case study is an example of a mobile application that acts as an aggregator of services provided by a third party. The application was also not heavy on features. In this case, writing multiple layers was skipped by the team as compared to other case study. The case study presented the idea to be pragmatic and minimize reinventing an already existing solution in the market, if fully suits the operating context. Leveraging existing solution helps to reduce the time to market. It is an anti-pattern if an engineer wants to build everything from scratch and these are not the primary product of the organization. There will be cases where building from scratch is beneficial, however the choice should be followed by careful evaluation of the context. Asserting that one strategy fits for all may not be a great thinking.

Conclusion

The purpose of the chapter was to give the audience flavors of real-life case studies. The chapter helped to collate some of the key themes discussed in the other chapters. The first case study focused on the event-driven system. The system design explained for the first case study centered around two ideas: optimizing the screen redraw and choice of technology. The second case study introduced the design consideration for mobile application communicating with external BLE hardware. The second case study centered around the thinking required for an SDK first approach in mobile codebase. The third case study was an example of a mobile application that did not require sophistication in the implementation layer but instead became an aggregator for third-party products.

Join our Discord space

Join our Discord workspace for latest updates, offers, tech happenings around the world, new releases, and sessions with the authors:

https://discord.bpbonline.com

Appendix A
Mindset for AI Adoption in Mobile Development

Artificial intelligence is a vast subject in itself. Fear of missing out, unpredictability, and indecision could loom over all of us. The advent of GenAI and its adoption have shifted the paradigm of how software engineering is perceived. The advancement in GenAI brings two important facets highlighting the impact on software engineering:

- Trust in a GenAI-generated mobile application.
- Ownership of the failure affecting the end user of the GenAI-generated mobile application.

A probable future for software engineering is specifying intent in natural language to GenAI. The majority of the development of the software thus happens via GenAI. The GenAI is responsible for inferring, thinking, and constructing the outcome from the specified intent. A chat interface is the simplest mode of GenAI to specify intent and get the outcome. The individual can input natural language in the chat interface. From there, the tool will have the capability to make changes in the file or folder provided as context to the tool. The files and folders will contain the context of the software project under development. Given the access, the chat interface can act on behalf of the individual to handle installing the necessary tools as well. This represents the agentic mode of GenAI. The GenAI tools can connect and coordinate with tools or other systems (e.g., MCP). The GenAI tools then curate, process, think, and generate the code. Such a situation is predicted to become the new way of working. As of 2026, the impact and penetration of GenAI are empirically proven with the community publishing case studies for projects leveraging agentic mode. Beyond the simplest form of chat, the team can configure a workflow with agentic mode in GenAI where the code generation, code verification and fixing of any issues found in the verification stage happen as an automated loop. Effective AI adoption requires a holistic understanding of the mobile application landscape. The holistic understanding empowers the mobile developer in their day-to-day AI-assisted development. Reading the book ensures the reader is equipped with knowledge to ensure GenAI is producing the intended outcome that scales.

The first facet addresses how confident a consumer will feel when using AI-generated software. From the consumer's point of view, the mindset will be that any software product is attested by an organization for its quality. The consumer expects the software to meet the highest quality possible at any time and in any situation. An organization should have a fail-safe strategy and a meaningful message displayed on the screen to let the end consumer of the mobile application know about failure. The message should convey an alternative choice or reassurance that the issue will be resolved as early as possible. The first facet thus can be summarized with the understanding that the onus is on the organization or entity owning the software. The trust in the organization and products is retained as long as the quality is ensured.

The second facet puts forward the theme of responsibility and ownership for failure to meet the product's expected quality. Owning the responsibility has two dimensions, looking at the cause and acting to prevent similar occurrences in future. The other dimension would be accountability to solve it. The former is a proactive measure, and the team may get involved in identifying the cause and preventing recurrence. The latter is reactive, where accountability for resolving the failure when it occurs becomes the next step. In the latter, the focus will also be on the need to prioritize among multiple failures when there are a lot of observations to be addressed. Now, how will the GenAI tool know the current context, and on what basis will the priority be decided? The urgency in solving a particular issue may need to be altered due to external factors. Often, these details are not encoded as data accessible to the GenAI tools. GenAI does not hold the context or the collective intelligence of the team, which are observations from product usage. In both of these cases, it would require a human agent to encode the context. The best strategy in this case will be to have a combination of humans along with GenAI. GenAI thus augments the end-to-end development progress where there is a human in the loop to validate and orchestrate.

GenAI is non-deterministic in nature for the response it generates. This creates a predictability gap where the outcome can deviate from the intent. Taking preventive measures and following practices to ensure the outcome matches the expectation are the key. For a software engineering problem, there are a zillion possibilities and combinations that act as solutions. A human touch is needed to decide the optimal approach if there are subjective elements involved. The human touch will inevitably be required until an alternative technology revolution occurs, where the human mind is replicated or replaced by machines in such situations. GenAI accelerates the capacity to produce results that otherwise would have taken more time to see.

An additional understanding one should have is that the product developed should provide value to the end consumer. Products may be developed and overhyped without serving any real purpose. In such cases, there will be zero usage and adoption of the product. The GenAI now has commoditized the ability to develop purposeless software at speed. If the individual does this without putting thought into the problem being solved, it will lead to a situation creating AI-waste that is never used. The ability to decide the purpose served by a product is with a human agent. These decisions that are context-relevant and encoded in the tacit or tribal knowledge of the individuals involved will become the key for a purposeful product. Harnessing the tacit and tribal knowledge brings the unique value proposition of every product and dictates the shape of the product development.

In summary, responsibility and ownership naturally emerge as expectations for GenAI-generated outcomes. The risk appetite of the organization and the comprehensive nature of the gatekeeping mechanism for a product developed dictate how much development can be offloaded to GenAI where the non-determinism can be tolerated. To ensure quality, it becomes important to build a measure that provides a safety net that acts as checks and balances for product quality. This strategy, when powered by humans in the loop, ensures that the product deployed is proactively validated. This signifies the relevance of AI as an assisting mechanism to accelerate software engineering.

Appendix B

Learnings from AI Adoption in Mobile Development

This section further explores how AI adoption in mobile application development will be faster by leveraging the topics narrated in the book. The idea is to present three meta models that one should hold in the back of their thinking, which help one be rational and pragmatic in GenAI adoption. The following themes have emerged from experience gained while practicing AI-assisted software engineering on various industrial-strength mobile application projects and trials. The ideas discussed, combined with the expert knowledge from this book, empower the reader as a mobile engineer.

The first meta model to hold in the mind is the two facets of acceleration – the capability and the capacity in a product development lifecycle. Capability talks about intent fulfilled by the product and the problem it addresses, whereas capacity talks about the volume of effort required for the entire product development. AI-assisted software engineering accelerates the capacity and, to a certain extent, capability. However, the core theme and definition of what the product should do or what it is solving, etc., stays with the human (stakeholder or teams) driving the initiative. The degree to which AI-assisted programming accelerates outcomes will depend on what the team is trying to achieve.

The next meta model that one should understand is the nature in which an individual approaches a technology. When asked about AI's effect on software engineering, a wide spectrum of responses can be expected. The spectrum starts from a persona saying AI is just hype and cannot add value to software engineering, and on the opposite end of the spectrum, the response will be that AI can do everything. Being on either end is not a great choice. The recommendation is to be a skeptic with optimism. The mindset of a skeptic with optimism will help with faster adoption of AI. Such a persona is likely to adopt any new technology when it shows promise to enable and accelerate the current ways of working. A skeptic will look for evidence and proof, and a positive response to the search will lead to its adoption.

The third meta model is the knowledge hierarchy. An intellectual journey to seek knowledge on a particular topic can be seen as a transition across various levels. These knowledge levels can be categorized into a spectrum starting from the formal definition to the skill required to implement or manifest the effect of the formal definition on the ground. The various levels of knowledge can be mapped from top to bottom as follows:

- **Formal knowledge**: Knowledge level to define these systems in the form of mathematical and theoretical frameworks.
- **Abstract knowledge**: Ability to explain and articulate the system in the form of abstractions represented in higher-level concepts and paradigms derived from formal knowledge.
- **Schema knowledge**: Ability to explain and articulate the system with information that encode the meta details of the system without specifics of implementation or tool used.

- **System knowledge**: Ability to explain the specifics of the system and its interaction with other systems, understanding the responsibilities of each in an ecosystem.
- **Conceptual knowledge**: Ability to articulate the concept, not limited to the primary technology domain, thereby ensuring the verbal knowledge can be mapped to other technology domains and speculate about its applicability in those domains.
- **Verbal knowledge**: Ability to explain the specifics to a peer in the same technology domain.
- **Procedural knowledge**: The knowledge required to perform the skill required in the technology domain, for example, the details of the syntax and specifics of the framework that help to hand-code and write programs.

An individual or team who understands the formal knowledge and is able to traverse through various levels, translating this to the procedural knowledge for developing the product, possesses the ability to execute top-down. When leveraging AI, the procedural skill is taken up by the GenAI, and the team will have to define the intent at a higher knowledge level. The ideal expectation is that GenAI does the reasoning to generate a result closer to the intent specified. The context of the problem being solved, the details of the invariant, do's, don'ts, etc., specified as instructions, thus form the key activity performed by the developer. Once the instruction is provided to the LLM, the output is generated and verified. If there is any feedback, the loop repeats (starting from instructing the GenAI tool to correct the generated code to meet the specifications of the intended outcome). In the non-AI world, the dexterity required along with the ability to write code faster was the primary factors affecting the development time. However, AI-assisted programming shifts the key skill to the individual/team's ability to instruct AI to generate the code matching the intent specified as input in natural language. Writing optimal instructions with clear context will become one of the key skills. The procedural knowledge required will shift to detecting the unintended outputs from GenAI. In an extreme case where GenAI is not able to generate the proper code, the procedural knowledge would come in handy.

In the context of mobile application development, this book gives details up to and including the design of the various systems. The individual who gets accustomed to the details narrated in the book will be able to think at the schematic level for a mobile application project. Taking the learning journey beyond mobile applications will be the leap that would cultivate a holistic software engineering mindset for any kind of software. The formal knowledge is beyond the scope of the book. Acquiring formal knowledge would mean possessing mathematics and computer science foundations.

In conclusion, a skeptic who is optimistic about experimenting and looks for proof that GenAI brings value, thereby leading to adoption, is an ideal mindset one could cultivate. Such a persona should understand the difference between capacity and capability and should be able to traverse through various levels of knowledge, which the book will be a companion for.

Join our Discord space

APPENDIX C
References

The book has references to products and tools that are relevant to mobile application development. The usage of these references in this book is to bring parity in the understanding of the real-world industry usage of the concepts explained in the chapters. The author and publisher do not endorse these products, and the book is independent of and not affiliated with, endorsed by, authorized by, or sponsored by any of these. It is advised that the reader do due diligence to evaluate these with alternatives to choose the best for the context in which they are operating. The conceptual understanding will help the reader to make this journey of selecting from the various options smoother. The book has taken the liberty to reference historic events and facts that occurred in the evolution of the mobile application development ecosystem. The relevant links and citation that give additional context beyond the intended scope of this book are also added in the appendix, which help the interested reader to look back at the history.

Some of the links are relevant for multiple chapters, but the duplicate references are avoided after their first occurrence.

Chapter 1: Stepping into Mobile Development

1. Dynabook: **https://dl.acm.org/doi/epdf/10.1145/800193.1971922**
2. Newton Message Pad: **https://apple-history.com/nmp**
3. The usage of the following names is only for descriptive purposes to explain mobile development-related concepts:
    a. Apple and related products referenced are trademarks of Apple Inc. **https://www.apple.com**
    b. Google and related products referenced are trademarks of Google LLC. **https://www.google.com**
    c. Slack referenced is a trademark of Slack Technologies, Inc. **https://slack.com/intl/en-in**
    d. Samsung referenced is a trademark of Samsung Electronics Co., Ltd. **https://www.samsung.com**
    e. Oppo referenced is a trademark of OPPO Electronics Corp. **https://www.oppo.com**
    f. Amazon referenced is a trademark of Amazon.com, Inc. **https://www.amazon.com**
    g. New Relic referenced is a trademark of New Relic, Inc. **https://newrelic.com**
    h. Zeplin referenced is a trademark of Zeplin, Inc. **https://zeplin.io**
    i. IntelliJ referenced is a trademark of JetBrains s.r.o. **https://www.jetbrains.com/idea/**
    j. Facebook referenced is a trademark of Meta Platforms, Inc. **https://www.facebook.com**
    k. InVision referenced is a trademark of InVisionApp, Inc. **https://www.invisionapp.com**
    l. Figma referenced is a trademark of Figma Inc. **https://www.figma.com**
4. **Apple Push Notification service** (**APNs**): **https://developer.apple.com/documentation/usernotifications**
5. **Firebase Cloud Messaging** (**FCM**): **https://firebase.google.com/docs/cloud-messaging**

6. **Bring Your Own Device** (**BYOD**): **https://www.ibm.com/think/topics/byod**
7. SQLite: **https://www.sqlite.org/**
8. Room: **https://developer.android.com/training/data-storage/room**

Chapter 2: Planning Your Mobile App Project

1. Agile and Agile Manifesto: **https://agilemanifesto.org/**
2. Xamarin official support: **https://dotnet.microsoft.com/en-us/platform/support/policy/xamarin**
3. Scrum framework: **https://scrumguides.org/**
4. Kanban framework: **https://kanbanguides.org/the-kanban-guide/**
5. **Extreme Programming** (**XP**) framework: **http://www.extremeprogramming.org/**

Chapter 3: Cross-platform Versus Native

1. Android development is Kotlin first: **https://developer.android.com/kotlin/first**
2. MAUI reference: **https://dotnet.microsoft.com/en-us/apps/maui**
3. Cordova: **https://cordova.apache.org/**
4. Capacitor versus Cordova: **https://ionic.io/resources/articles/capacitor-vs-cordova-modern-hybrid-app-development**
5. Ionic official website: **https://ionic.io/**
6. The usage of the following names is only for descriptive purposes to explain mobile development-related concepts:
    a. Apple and related products referenced are trademarks of Apple Inc. **https://www.apple.com**
    b. Google and related products referenced are trademarks of Google LLC. **https://www.google.com**
7. Flutter GitHub repository: **https://github.com/flutter/flutter**
8. Flutter official website: **https://flutter.dev/**
9. React Native repository: **https://github.com/facebook/react-native**
10. React-native official website: **https://reactnative.dev/**
11. Low code reference: **https://www.kony.com/index.html**, **https://www.tagitmobile.com/**
12. Material Design : **https://m3.material.io/**
13. PhoneGap (Apache): **http://www.extremeprogramming.org/**
14. Android NDK: **https://developer.android.com/ndk/guides**
15. DEX file format: **https://source.android.com/docs/core/runtime**
16. Objective-C: **https://developer.apple.com/library/archive/documentation/Cocoa/Conceptual/ProgrammingWithObjectiveC/Introduction/Introduction.html**
17. TypeScript: **https://www.typescriptlang.org/**
18. **JavaScript Interface** (**JSI**): **https://reactnative.dev/docs/the-new-architecture/why**
19. Mono runtime: **https://github.com/mono/mono**
20. Visual Studio / Visual Studio for Mac: **https://visualstudio.microsoft.com/**
21. **Progressive Web App** (**PWA**): **https://developer.mozilla.org/en-US/docs/Web/Progressive_web_apps**
22. Capacitor official website: **https://capacitorjs.com/**

Chapter 4: Organizing a Mobile Development Team

1. Miller's Law in Cognitive Psychology: George A. Miller's original 1956 paper *The Magical Number Seven, Plus or Minus Two*
2. **Root cause analysis** (**RCA**): **https://asq.org/quality-resources/root-cause-analysis**
3. Mob programming: **https://www.agilealliance.org/resources/experience-reports/mob-programming-agile2014/**

Chapter 5: Quality Assurance for Mobile Development

1. ISO 9000 standards history: **https://www.iso.org/standards/popular/iso-9000-family**
2. **Test-driven development** (**TDD**): **https://agilealliance.org/glossary/tdd/**
3. Test pyramid (testing strategy model): **https://martinfowler.com/articles/practical-test-pyramid.html**

Chapter 6: Balancing Design and Engineering

1. Liquid Glass: **https://developer.apple.com/videos/play/wwdc2025/219/**
2. Design language or design vocabulary, Human interface guidelines: **https://developer.apple.com/design/human-interface-guidelines/**
3. Material Design guidelines: **https://m3.material.io/**
4. Conway's Law: **https://www.melconway.com/Home/Conways_Law.html**

Chapter 7: Scalability in Mobile Development: Part 1

1. Git (version control system): **https://git-scm.com/**
2. **Architecture Decision Record** (**ADR**): **https://adr.github.io/**
3. **Trunk-Based Development** (**TBD**): **https://trunkbaseddevelopment.com/**
4. Pair programming: **https://agilealliance.org/glossary/pair-programming/**
5. **Extreme Programming** (**XP**): **http://www.extremeprogramming.org/**
6. Sencha Touch: **https://docs.sencha.com/touch/2.4/**

Chapter 8: Scalability in Mobile Development: Part 2

1. GitHub Actions (**https://github.com/features/actions**), **GitLab** (**https://about.gitlab.com**), CircleCI (**https://circleci.com**), and Jenkins (**https://www.jenkins.io**) are referenced solely for instructional purposes and do not imply endorsement, sponsorship, or affiliation with any company, organization, or service provider.
2. Deploying iOS (consolidated version): **https://docs.flutter.dev/deployment/ios**
3. Deploying Android (consolidated version): **https://docs.flutter.dev/deployment/android**
4. TestFlight: **https://developer.apple.com/testflight/**
5. App Store Connect: **https://appstoreconnect.apple.com**
6. Google Play Console: **https://play.google.com/console**
7. Apple Developer Program: **https://developer.apple.com/programs/**
8. subosito/flutter-action: **https://github.com/subosito/flutter-action**
9. Semantic versioning specification: **https://semver.org**

Chapter 9: Mobile Application Development and Cross-cutting Themes

1. Apple App Store (descriptive use only): **https://www.apple.com/app-store/**
2. Google Play Store (descriptive use only): **https://play.google.com/store**
3. App thinning: **https://developer.apple.com/documentation/xcode/doing-basic-optimization-to-reduce-your-app-s-size**
4. iOS Universal Links: **https://developer.apple.com/ios/universal-links/**
5. Android App Links (Applinks): **https://developer.android.com/training/app-links**
6. **General Data Protection Regulation** (**GDPR**) (EU statutory mandate): **https://eur-lex.europa.eu/eli/reg/2016/679/oj/eng**
7. **Payment Services Directive 2** (**PSD2**) (EU statutory mandate): **https://eur-lex.europa.eu/eli/dir/2015/2366/oj/eng**
8. **Health Insurance Portability and Accountability Act** (**HIPAA**) (US statutory mandate): **https://www.hhs.gov/hipaa/index.html**
9. **Federal Communications Commission** (**FCC**) (US statutory body): **https://www.fcc.gov/**
10. **Securities and Exchange Board of India** (**SEBI**) (statutory body): **https://www.sebi.gov.in/**
11. **Reserve Bank of India** (**RBI**) (statutory body): **https://www.rbi.org.in/**
12. Dynamic analysis: **https://owasp.org/www-project-mobile-app-security/**
13. Mobile app sandbox iOS: **https://developer.apple.com/documentation/security/app-sandbox**
14. Mobile app sandbox Android : **https://source.android.com/docs/security/app-sandbox**
15. SSL pinning: **https://owasp.org/www-community/controls/Certificate_and_Public_Key_Pinning**
16. Spatial audio: **https://developer.apple.com/documentation/avfaudio/audio-engine**

Chapter 10: Introduction to Swift, Kotlin, and Dart

1. Swift language official website: **https://www.swift.org/**
2. Swift setup instruction: **https://www.swift.org/install/**
3. Dart language official website: **https://dart.dev/**
4. Dart setup instruction: **https://dart.dev/get-dart**
5. Online dart code editor and runner: **https://dartpad.dev/**
6. Kotlin language official website: **https://kotlinlang.org/**
7. Kotlin setup instruction: **https://kotlinlang.org/docs/command-line.html# compile-a-library**
8. Flutter official website: **https://flutter.dev/**
9. Flutter installation guide: **https://docs.flutter.dev/install**
10. Impeller rendering engine: **https://docs.flutter.dev/perf/impeller**
11. Skia rendering engine: **https://skia.org/**
12. State class in Flutter: **https://api.flutter.dev/flutter/widgets/State-class.html**
13. Flutter/Dart package repository (pub.dev): **https://pub.dev/**
14. Flutter test package documentation: **https://api.flutter.dev/flutter/flutter_test/flutter_test-library.html**

Chapter 11: Kotlin Multiplatform for Mobile Development

1. Kotlin evolution and adoption as official language for Android: **https://blog.jetbrains.com/kotlin/2017/05/kotlin-on-android-now-official/**
2. Compose Multiplatform: **https://www.jetbrains.com/compose-multiplatform/**
3. Android studio setup: **https://developer.android.com/studio/install**
4. Gradle overview: **https://developer.android.com/build/gradle-build-overview**
5. Kotlin Multiplatform Wizard: **https://kmp.jetbrains.com/**
6. Compose internal: **https://github.com/JetBrains/compose-multiplatform-core/blob/jb-main/compose/runtime/design/how-compose-works.md**
7. Add SVG to the Android project: **https://developer.android.com/studio/write/vector-asset-studio**
8. Jetpack Compose: **https://developer.android.com/compose**
9. **Low Level Virtual Machine** (**LLVM**): **https://llvm.org/**
10. **Java Virtual Machine** (**JVM**): **https://docs.oracle.com/javase/specs/jvms/se21/html/index.html**
11. Skiko (Skia for Kotlin): **https://github.com/JetBrains/skiko**
12. SwiftUI: **https://developer.apple.com/xcode/swiftui/**
13. kotlin.test: **https://kotlinlang.org/api/latest/kotlin.test/**

Chapter 12: Use Case of Developing a Super App

1. Super App Part 1 - The Fundamentals: **https://whitefalconpublishing.com/blockchain-certification/gnosis/?4sjcfbrp**
2. SwiftUI overview: **https://developer.apple.com/swiftui/**
3. iOS Development book titles to complement the empirical knowledge in this book: **https://bpbonline.com/**
4. Swift testing framework: **https://developer.apple.com/xcode/swift-testing/**
5. Create first project xcode: **https://developer.apple.com/documentation/xcode/creating-an-xcode-project-for-an-app**
6. Xcode: **https://developer.apple.com/xcode/**
7. Xcode setup: **https://developer.apple.com/documentation/safari-developer-tools/installing-xcode-and-simulators**
8. Micro frontend: **https://micro-frontends.org**
9. Microservices: **https://martinfowler.com/articles/microservices.html**
10. **Swift Package Manager** (**SPM**): **https://www.swift.org/documentation/package-manager/**
11. XCTest framework: **https://developer.apple.com/documentation/xctest**

Chapter 13: Introduction to Mobile Architecture

1. MVC writeup from Apple.com archives: **https://developer.apple.com/library/archive/documentation/General/Conceptual/DevPedia-CocoaCore/MVC.html**
2. Android official guide to app architecture: **https://developer.android.com/topic/architecture**
3. SOLID principles: Publicized by Robert C. Martin in the OOD talk and write ups
4. VIPER architecture: **https://www.objc.io/issues/13-architecture/viper/**

5. Redux pattern: **https://redux.js.org/**
6. Reactive programming, Reactive Extensions / Rx: **https://reactivex.io/**
7. Combine framework: **https://developer.apple.com/documentation/combine**
8. RxDart: **https://pub.dev/packages/rxdart**
9. UIKit: **https://developer.apple.com/documentation/uikit**
10. YAGNI principle: **https://martinfowler.com/bliki/Yagni.html**
11. Occam's Razor / Law of Parsimony: **https://plato.stanford.edu/entries/simplicity/**
12. DRY principle: **https://martinfowler.com/bliki/BeckDesignRules.html**
13. Jetpack Compose: **https://developer.android.com/compose**
14. Keystroke: https:**//dl.acm.org/doi/10.1145/3626705.3627784**

Chapter 14: System Thinking in Mobile Development

1. **Bluetooth Low Energy** (**BLE**) and GATT profile: **https://www.bluetooth.com/specifications/specs/**
2. Onvif: **https://www.onvif.org/**
3. RTSP: **https://www.rfc-editor.org/info/rfc7826**
4. WebSocket protocol: **https://datatracker.ietf.org/doc/rfc6455/**
5. CoreBluetooth framework: **https://developer.apple.com/documentation/corebluetooth**
6. android.bluetooth SDK: **https://developer.android.com/reference/android/bluetooth/package-summary**
7. **User Datagram Protocol** (**UDP**): **https://datatracker.ietf.org/doc/html/rfc768**

Index

www.ingramcontent.com/pod-product-compliance
Lightning Source LLC
Chambersburg PA
CBHW061352240926
51846CB00007B/1383